GENDER VIOLENCE

Gender Violence

Interdisciplinary Perspectives

THIRD EDITION

Edited by

Laura L. O'Toole,

Jessica R. Schiffman, *and*

Rosemary Sullivan

NEW YORK UNIVERSITY PRESS

New York

NEW YORK UNIVERSITY PRESS
New York
www.nyupress.org
© 2020 by New York University
All rights reserved

References to internet websites (URLs) were accurate at the time of writing. Neither the author nor New York University Press is responsible for URLs that may have expired or changed since the manuscript was prepared.

Library of Congress Cataloging-in-Publication Data
Names: O'Toole, Laura L., editor. | Schiffman, Jessica R., editor. | Sullivan, Rosemary, 1947–   editor.
Title: Gender violence : interdisciplinary perspectives / edited by Laura L. O'Toole, Jessica R. Schiffman, and Rosemary Sullivan.
Description: Third Edition. | New York : New York University Press, 2020. | Revised edition of Gender violence, c2007. | Includes bibliographical references and index.
Identifiers: LCCN 2019033758 | ISBN 9781479843923 (cloth) | ISBN 9781479820801 (paperback) | ISBN 9781479801794 (ebook) | ISBN 9781479801817 (ebook)
Subjects: LCSH: Women—Violence against. | Family violence. | Sex crimes. | Pornography—Social aspects. | Women—Violence against—United States. | Family violence—United States. | Sex crimes—United States. | Pornography—Social aspects—United States.
Classification: LCC HV6250.4.W65 G48 2020 | DDC 362.82/92—dc23
LC record available at https://lccn.loc.gov/2019033758

New York University Press books are printed on acid-free paper, and their binding materials are chosen for strength and durability. We strive to use environmentally responsible suppliers and materials to the greatest extent possible in publishing our books.

Manufactured in the United States of America

10 9 8 7 6 5 4 3 2 1

Also available as an ebook

DEDICATION

For Stephen Meade for your unflagging support, and to Christian Meade and Katie O'Brien for your steadfast feminism and commitment to social justice in these troubled times. And in memory of Kevin O'Toole, who lived a life of care and concern for all living things. You were the epitome of a gentleman. I miss you.

LOT

For Pat, who helped to shoulder the burden and kept me fed, with eternal thanks.

To Emma, Ethan, and Ronen, whose commitment to justice and compassion inspires and enlightens me, and to the joyful presence of Isaiah and Esther. You carry my hope and faith into the future.

JRS

To my wife, Ellen, who inspired me throughout this project through pep talks, gentle encouragement, and reminders about the big picture.

To my children, Rob, Gabe, and Alanna, for teaching me about a depth of love that I did not think was possible.

To my mother, Barbara, for role modeling resilience, compassion, and faith.

RMS

CONTENTS

PREFACE

Conceptualizing Gender Violence

LAURA L. O'TOOLE, JESSICA R. SCHIFFMAN,
AND ROSEMARY SULLIVAN

As we write this preface to our third edition, the ongoing struggle to eradicate gender violence, or at least lessen its pervasiveness, is as salient as ever. Gender violence is still integrally entwined in myriad world events and the experiences of individuals worldwide. Consider political strife and civil upheavals such as the genocidal attacks against the Rohingya people of Myanmar in which rape is a quotidian feature or the upswing of awareness about sexual harassment in workplaces including Hollywood, universities, restaurants, modeling agencies, factories, the arts, and seemingly everything in between. Acts of gender violence are ubiquitous throughout history. Rape has been a correlate of war for centuries. Working women experienced men's coercive sexual behaviors long before the term *sexual harassment* was coined.

While specifics of gender violence may change, the underlying causes cry out for attention. The pervasiveness and intricacies of gendered systems and relationships, as well as our greater understanding of the intersubjective experience of cisgender and transgender men and women in various cultural contexts, all demonstrate the extent to which problems of gender are in need of continued and rigorous study. Data indicates that support for egalitarian views among US eighteen- to twenty-five-year-olds has decreased significantly in the past two decades (Coontz 2017) contributing to a climate of power differentials that increase the likelihood of violence. In a sad commentary on the normalization of gender violence, the forty-fifth president of the US was caught on video claiming that he had grabbed women's genitals without consent, yet a sufficient number of people did not view his actions as a serious barrier to voting him into office. All paint a picture of the Sisyphean effort it requires to eliminate gender violence.

We continue to build on the stalwart efforts of generations past, while faced with new permutations that reflect increasing complexity within societies and global relationships. The urgency to address gender violence is evidenced by the many current events deemed newsworthy on an international scale given their political implications or the celebrity of perpetrators. Even so, these represent only a fraction of the violence against women, children, and the LGBTQ+ communities committed on a daily basis across the world. If you read your own local newspaper or scan televised newscasts or online news sources, you will find hundreds of similar events in any given month. These incidents, while often writ small, stand as clear testimony to the insidious problem of gender violence.

Framing the Concepts of Gender, Violence, and Gender Violence

Gender is the culturally specific constellation of personal attributes assigned to men and women and a central organizing principle among human groups. It is a primary characteristic that structures intimate relationships and provides guidelines for dividing labor, assigning social values, and granting privileges. In most contemporary societies, dualistic gender systems endure, with clearly demarcated boundaries between that which is considered masculine and that which is considered feminine—temperamentally, physically, sexually, and behaviorally—though restrictive binary categories are giving way to more fluid understandings of gender in some cultures, with implications for how we understand the topics we address in this book.

For example, Germany now requires that all public documents, including birth certificates, add either a third gender category or dispense with gender altogether. At present, eight countries recognize more than two genders on passports or national identity cards (Eddy and Bennett 2017). In the US, California, Oregon, and Washington allow a third option on birth certificates, and New York City enacted a law allowing "X" as a choice as of 2019 (Newman, 2018). These changes acknowledge that "[y]ou can't necessarily read from people's bodies what their gender means to them" (Appiah 2018).

Gender is simultaneously a deeply embedded aspect of individual personalities and structural social arrangements; yet, it is also contested social terrain. Gender relations are a complicated mix of congeniality and conflict; yet, in either case, they are almost always imbued with an asymmetrical distribution of power. They are the product of social and cultural dynamics, historical forces, political and economic imperatives, and interpersonal interactions. In many societies and for many individuals, however, it is the *conflicted* aspects of gender relations that are the most prominent.

Violence extends from individual relationships to the arrangement of power and authority in organizations to the relations among countries of the world. Broadly speaking, violence is a mainstay in the entertainment and news media, in national and international politics, in family dynamics, and in our social constructions of sexual desire. It simultaneously intrigues and repels us. Although most violence worldwide is male-on-male, the emergence of self-conscious women's political movements, greater global attention to universal human rights and human security, and academic inquiry begs closer scrutiny of the patterns of male violence against women and children, as well as against other men, both in intimate relationships and in public expressions. It is clear, for example, that societies differ in the amount of violence tolerated and types of violence that occur, making it possible to envision successful methods to reduce its prevalence.

We understand violence as the extreme application of social control, usually understood as the use of physical force. It can take psychological forms, when manifested through direct harassment or implied terroristic threats, or symbolic forms, through interactions and advice that shape how women internalize caution and fear (e.g., the home is safe) while simultaneously *increasing* fear (Morgan and Björkert 2006). Violence can also be structural, as when institutional forces such as governments or medical systems impinge on individuals' rights to bodily integrity or contribute to the deprivation of basic human needs. By our definition, gender violence is any interpersonal, organizational, or politically oriented violation perpetrated against people due to their sex, gender identity, sexual orientation, or location in the hierarchy of male-dominated social systems such as families, military organizations, or the labor force. Much of the violence in contemporary society serves to preserve asymmetrical gender systems of power. Salter (2012, 3) points to an insidious aspect of gender-based violence, what he terms "invalidation," whereby "the power to dismiss, trivialise or silence the perspective of another is not evenly distributed throughout society but [is] rather a specific dimension of masculine privilege . . ."

Compulsory aggression as a central component of masculinity serves to legitimate male-on-male violence; sexual harassment is a means of controlling women's public behavior and access to power; assaults on gay, lesbian, and transgender people serve as punishment for "gender transgressions"; and rape is a standard tool for domination in war, in prisons, and in too many intimate relationships. Clearly and consistently documented throughout human history, the forms that such violence assumes—rape, intimate partner violence, child abuse, and murder—constitute some of the most pressing and enduring social problems. Given the centrality of gender and the ubiquity of violence, it is no wonder that they are interwoven in our social systems. The systems in which they are embedded are complex; simplistic explanations or simple solutions will not suffice. Explicating the problem of gender violence demands a comprehensive, multifaceted framework.

The Structure of this Edition

This volume attempts to provide such an interdisciplinary framework. It is the outgrowth of our personal and collegial efforts to understand the phenomenon of gender violence to a fuller extent than discipline-specific analysis currently allows. Our own scholarly training includes degrees in clinical social work, education, and sociology. We see the value of our disciplines in explaining the significance of context in the study of gender violence. As participants in inter-disciplinary gender studies throughout our careers, we have been engaged by the important analysis of our colleagues in the social sciences and humanities that has enriched the study of gender relations, in many cases preceding our disciplines in uncovering significant social facts as well as the subdued and silenced voices of women, children, and marginalized men.

The poems and chapters in this book have contributed to our own understanding of the interpersonal and structural dynamics of gender violence, as well as both the historical evolution and the contemporary manifestations of gender relations. We share that understanding here, weaving together the voices of other scholars and artists with our own thoughts on how to best interpret the vast and ever-expanding literature on gender violence. We do this while acknowledging that the literature cannot completely represent the horrifying expanse of empirical evidence and personal experiences of physical and sexual assault, harassment, and murder.

Although documenting and exploring the violation of women has been a primary focus of research and activism among feminist and pro-feminist analysts, we have chosen to include a broader set of questions that spring from the study of gender and violence. In what ways are ideas about gender and sexual identity used to legitimate violence against individuals and groups, regardless of how one identifies with their gender assigned at birth? To what extent does the social construction of gender influence male-on-male violence? Can and should men and boys be acknowledged as indirect victims of violence against women, at least in some cases, such as those who witness intimate partner violence? By widening our analytical lens, we are able to incorporate important connections among violence against children, heterosexual women and men, and lesbians, gay men, and transgender people, and we suggest important questions about structural and interpersonal violence for future analysis.

There are some victories: women elected to high office in increasing numbers around the world, the #MeToo movement and its correlates, the Women's March on Washington and throughout the globe that continues to inspire local action to address specific problems from Austria to Nigeria, Kyrgyzstan, Japan, and many locales in between. These developments encourage us to persevere, to not lose hope in the face of the daunting effort required to create change despite grinding disappointments. We write this fully committed to reducing human suffering and in the belief that change is possible—indeed essential.

Gender Violence is organized into three parts. Part 1 contains a sociohistorical exploration of gender violence, focusing first on some foundational ideas and theoretical concepts about its construction, then more specifically on a template that allows us to analyze gender violence across the globe. Part 2 examines various forms of gendered violence. Part 3 presents inspiring insights and practices to help us transform gender relations and end gender violence. Each section of the book includes an introduction, suggested readings, and chapters that represent important contributions to the study of gender violence from a wide spectrum of academic and activist perspectives. Although many chapters address issues of gender violence in the US, we have integrated a sizeable number of international perspectives. We include research-based articles, theoretical and critical analyses, and essays.

The reader will notice that every section is prefaced by a poem. We have organized the book this way in part to set the tone for the more scholarly analysis that follows and in part to periodically break away from this analysis to hear voices unfettered by disciplinary jargon or academic theory. Understanding gender violence requires a merging of the analytical and experiential realms. Working toward a solution will ultimately require an understanding both of social dynamics and of the pain and tragedy that gender violence wreaks in the lives of women, men, and children around the world.

This volume is necessarily incomplete. There are many more insightful analyses, theoretical elaborations, and powerful voices than space permits us to include. Many have yet to speak, and our search for solutions is far from complete. We hope this book will contribute to the dialogue among students, activists, and scholars concerned about understanding and eradicating gender violence. We believe such a dialogue is crucial, and we have attempted to design the book in a way that is accessible to all these constituencies.

Many people have encouraged us to take on this project and provided helpful commentary along the way. Colleagues, friends, and family who have supported and inspired us in various, often indispensable ways include Cecile Andrews, Robin Brownstein, Carolyn Byerly, Cassandra Cupka, Jacque Ensign, Felicity Gray, Marie Laberge, Rachel Lodge, Kay McGraw, Steve Meade, Tom Menduni, James Mitchell, Kathleen O'Toole, Carol Post, Carol Rudisell, Rebecca Schachter, Carol Schouboe, Ellen Smith, Barbara Sullivan, and Pat Timmins. Ryan Cramton, Nicole Gostanian, Lily McCaughey, Deleesha Moore, and Dan Titus provided significant technical assistance in building crucial components of the manuscript. Ronen Elad, Christian Meade, Emma Timmins-Schiffman, and Ethan Timmins-Schiffman read chapter drafts and provided us with numerous helpful suggestions. We also sincerely appreciate the tenacity and courage of many current and former students at the University of Delaware, Guilford College, Roanoke College, Salve Regina University, and Westfield State University who confront the difficult questions we pose about gender and violence, often bearing the weight of great personal trauma. They have taught—and continue to teach—us a lot.

Our editor, Ilene Kalish, supported our desire to update this work. She particularly gave us great leeway to bring our vision to fruition. Assistant editor Sonia Tsuruoka was always available to answer our many questions; she helped us beyond expectations. We thank the contributors to this volume for their vision, with special gratitude to Elizabeth Erbaugh, William Gay, Ryan Harrod, Anastasia Hudgins, Chrysanthi Leon, Debra Martin, Melinda Mills, Susan Miller, Irene Comins Mingol, Jennifer Naccarelli, Bailey Poland, Janice Raymond, Corey Shdaimah, Carole Sheffield, Margaret Stetz, and Miriam Valdovinos whose original efforts immeasurably augment the value of this book. Finally, we mourn the loss of Harry Brod, whose untimely passing prevented the inclusion of his inimitable voice in this volume.

Editors' Note

As this book goes to press in April 2020, the world has been upended in unimaginable ways. Among its effects, the novel coronavirus that causes COVID-19 requires social distancing, relegating people across the globe to confined living spaces. This virtual imprisonment increases the risk of gender violence. Preliminary data from international NGOs indicates already spiraling rates of intimate partner violence and child abuse. In short, this pandemic within a pandemic is exposing the social, economic, and political fault lines that we address in this volume.

PART I

The Roots of Gendered Violence

The two sections included here explore the conditions that give rise to gendered violence, providing a framework for our subsequent analysis. Section 1 historicizes gender violence as interpersonal, community, and political-economic phenomena and spans early to contemporary settings. Section 2 takes a global perspective in analyzing the widespread cultural and historical trends that are associated with the seemingly intractable scourge of gender violence. Taken together, these sections show that understanding gender violence requires broad historical and theoretical knowledge, as well as smaller-scale case-study analysis to capture the culturally specific contours that gender violence assumes. Readings in part 1 encompass the disciplines of anthropology, bioarchaeology, economics, gender studies, history, political science, theological studies, and sociology.

Historicizing Gender Violence

The roots of gender violence run deep in human history, making attempts to trace them difficult. Male violence, specifically, is so widespread that biological determinism has often dominated debates about its origins. As such, gendered violence is often explained as a natural and universal consequence of the biological differences between men and women. Age-old theories posit that superior strength and a variety of hormonal stimuli predispose men toward violent, controlling behavior. Such an amalgam of traits juxtaposed against the purported natural passivity and compliance of the weaker female, it has been argued, will likely produce violence in men, against women, in certain situations. One form of this argument suggests that males' innate drive to reproduce stimulates behavioral responses that lead to what we now define as rape.

Despite the longevity of such explanations, other compelling theories exist. The influence of the contemporary feminist movement on academic inquiry contributes to the reframing of central questions about gender relations, challenging deeply embedded intellectual traditions. A social constructionist framework suggests that *patriarchy*—the system of male control over women—is a human invention, not the inevitable outcome of biological characteristics. In order to denaturalize gender violence, then, one must uncover the *social* roots of male dominance and other institutionalized systems of power to understand the extent to which power, control, and violation become valued attributes in human communities. This argument has important implications; if patriarchy is a social construction, then the violence that results from it becomes more problematic and less easy to dismiss as "human nature." More recently, intersectional approaches extend theories of patriarchy to situate gender violence within multiple sites of dominance and oppression including class, race, and sexuality systems. Through these analytical frames, gender violence in all of its manifestations becomes a social problem with a beginning and, ostensibly, an end, rather than a taken-for-granted aspect of the human condition. In order to bring about its demise, however, we must take on the difficult challenge of uncovering its origins.

The Contributions of Marx and Engels

Although the patriarchal family was not a central concern of Karl Marx's social theory, he did suggest that its modern form was a microcosm of class antagonisms that later developed on a grand scale in society (Marx 1978). This foreshadows recognition of the family as a site of social stratification and inequality. Applying the logic of Marxian economic theory more systematically to the condition of women, Friedrich Engels theorized the legal, monogamous family, in which women exchange sexual and domestic services for economic security and men retain sexual control of women in marriage, as the equivalent of slave ownership (see Smith, this volume).

Further, the emergence of the concept of private property and its appropriation by men, according to Engels (1884), are the central historical events from which the modern social order, and systematic gender violence, have emerged. In this model, women are economic dependents; eventually defined as the property of fathers or husbands, they are subject to the violence that accompanies the status of slaves.

The Marx-Engels theory was the first to attribute women's deteriorated status to a sociological, rather than biological, source. More than 130 years of social and economic analysis have not diminished the significance of theorizing economic arrangements in gender systems of power; however, economic determinism is no more satisfactory than biological determinism in explaining the origins of patriarchal domination. Given the complexity of human social life, any singular statement of cause and effect is doomed to fail. Anthropologists, political theorists, sociologists, and historians studying gender have built on the Marxian-Engelsian framework, though in different applications; each discipline contributes significant analyses to our project.

The Significance of Sex/Gender Systems

Anthropological research provides most of the early evidence supporting a social, rather than biological, theory of gender. Studies such as those that Margaret Mead (1935) conducted among peoples of New Guinea showed gendered behavior to be a relative concept: different cultures define masculinity and femininity according to their own social needs; indeed, cultures may have more than two gender categories. Men are not inherently aggressive, and women not inherently passive and subordinate. The gender-based division of labor, although apparently universal, takes many shapes and forms. Such findings have enabled social theorists to define sex (nature) and gender (culture) as mutually exclusive, though interrelated, phenomena.

Studies of kinship systems in tribal social life provide a foundation for understanding early cultural definitions of gender, since all early human social life was organized through these systems. The incest taboo is a particularly significant human invention, in that it allows for the exchange of women among men of different kin groups, which in turn facilitates trade and alliances. Eventually, however, it also contributes to the ascension of men into roles of social power

(Lévi-Strauss 1969). Some analysts suggest that the practice of exchanging women transforms them over time into tribal resources—commodities, rather than self-determined individuals.

Gayle Rubin's classic essay "The Traffic in Women: Notes on the Political Economy of Sex" (1976) called into question many of the key assumptions about kinship and gender that had dominated anthropology prior to the modern feminist movement. Rubin uses the works of Marx, Engels, and Lévi-Strauss in a fundamentally different frame of analysis: a feminist critique that reconceptualizes the essence of early kinship systems and links them to contemporary gender relations of power.

The crux of Rubin's argument is that the construction of sexual meaning, not the commodification of women per se, is the hallmark of early kinship structures. Given the elaborate differences among kinship systems historically and cross-culturally, Rubin replaces the notion of emergent patriarchy with the concept of sex/gender systems. All cultures have sex/gender systems in which a socially constructed set of relations that define and regulate sexuality, masculinity, and femininity emerge. These relations, though initially kin-centered, also serve as the framework for creating increasingly elaborate economic and political systems. In contemporary cultures, kinship exists within such a complex of institutional structures. What was crucial for early feminist scholarship is this: in the earliest human groups, the exchange (and oppression) of women did not exist for its own sake. It fulfilled central functions for group survival.

Contemporary sex/gender systems, still replete with oppressive sexual meaning and regulation, do not fulfill the same economic and political functions that kinship once did. Kinship has been stripped of all its early functions, save for reproduction and the socialization of individuals. Following this logic, according to Rubin, the contemporary sex/gender system seems to exist only to organize and reproduce itself (1976, 199) rather than all of human activity. Contemporary sex/gender systems, therefore, serve no clear functions other than reproducing oppressive and repressive gender relations. More recent analyses of binary gender systems and heteronormativity extend the critique by more fully fleshing out the social constructions of gender and sexuality. These power analyses shed ever more light on gendered violence, as this volume illustrates.

Patriarchy and Women's Agency

Until recently, scholarly writing viewed sex/gender systems as restrictions imposed on women by men. Given that patriarchy predates recorded history, of course, it is difficult to trace its origins to a single causal factor, such as physical force or economic exchange. What if its *origins* were relatively benign?

Historian Gerda Lerner (1986) developed a theory that uses a materialist conceptualization of history (in the tradition of Marx) as a starting point for understanding the origins of patriarchy. Combining her own exhaustive study of historical artifacts from the earliest human communities and a fresh interpretation of the academic literature from the mid-twentieth century, Lerner built a scenario that centralizes women's agency, and hence depicts them as cocreators of history. According to Lerner, patriarchy is initially the unintended consequence of human social organization, a process that most probably emerged out of the negotiated labor of males and females interested in mutual survival and the continuation of the species.

Human biological difference does not predict or determine male dominance, but it is certainly a major factor in the elaboration of a rudimentary division of labor. Given extremely short life spans and the vulnerability of human infants, women would probably choose to engage in labor that involves less risk in order to heighten the chances that their offspring would survive. The gathering and child-rearing work that was predominantly, although not exclusively, performed by women was highly valued and central to early cultural production. It is only through the lens of modern, predominantly male interpreters that such work is devalued relative to men's hunting.

According to Lerner (1986, 53), "Sometime during the agricultural revolution, relatively egalitarian societies with a sexual division of labor based on biological necessity gave way to more highly structured societies in which both private property and the exchange of women based on incest taboos and exogamy were common." In Lerner's formulation, women may have initially viewed their procreative abilities as tribal resources independent of coercion on the part of male kin. A complex combination of ecological, climatic, and demographic changes probably intervened to produce a scarcity of women in some kin groups that eventually gave rise to the idea and practice of exchange.

Although patriarchy was formally established by the beginning of recorded history, it probably took centuries for patriarchy to emerge as a concise system. By the time women became consciously aware of the emergent power relations that formed early patriarchal systems, they were hardly in position to do much about it. Once male control was identified, Lerner's research suggests, individual women chafed under its bonds and used various forms of resistance to secure status for themselves and their children. Although women may have been active agents in the creation of cultural arrangements that eventually limited their freedom, and may even be complicit in maintaining their personal power rather than pursuing collective rights for women, there is also a long historical record of active agents in proto feminist resistance to patriarchal control.

Violence and Male Power

The use of force to maintain privilege is the significant characteristic of male behavior in patriarchal societies. It contributes to the development of the elaborate systems of economic and social inequality within and across gender. A central fact acknowledged but generally underanalyzed by historians is that women were the first slaves (Lerner 1986). Slavery is a significant institution through which male violence against women is exercised and racial hierarchies are invented (see Brooten, this volume). In the quest for women, invading clans would kill adult males on the spot and enslave women and their children. Rape and other forms of physical and psychological violence were used to control women in their new communities. It was through mastering techniques of violent coercion on female captives that men eventually learned how to dominate and control other men without simply killing them. Martin and Harrod (see this volume) extend early theories about men's violence to include the complicity of women. Both violence toward women and the elaborate social structures that developed around such practices serve to appropriate key aspects of women's independence and institutionalize patriarchy. Over time, overt and covert forms of violence come to characterize "normal" gender relations, the enforcement of heteronormativity, and systems of racial control institutionally and interpersonally.

Male control of women in families, which has endured the "progress" of centuries, is certainly not the only manifestation of androcentric sex/gender systems. Just as the construction of gender differs cross-culturally, gender violence takes many cultural forms: ten centuries of foot binding in China; witch burning in sixteenth-century Europe; female genital cutting in Africa; female castration by physicians in the late nineteenth- and early twentieth-century US; and honor-based killings in the Middle East. Indeed, discrimination, which underlies gender violence, begins before birth where preference for boys, often due to the burdens of dowry expectations, leads to high rates of pregnancy terminations and infanticide, particularly in India, the Republic of Korea, China (Advocates for Youth 2012), and Eastern Europe. This has produced skewed populations of "missing" women—approximately 117 million fewer than estimates predict would have been born (United Nations Population Fund n.d.). Similarly, the long history of marginalization of, and violence against, LGBTQ+ individuals and communities is an outgrowth of binary gender systems and social relations of power.

As these examples illustrate, gender violence and physical security are not merely a feature of micro-level interactions among intimates but are deeply embedded at the levels of community and nation state (see Table P1.1 and Figure P1.1). So universal and widespread are the institutionalized forms of violence against women, for example, that Caputi and Russell (1990) developed the concept of *femicide* to describe the systematic and global destruction of women.

Although males are the primary perpetrators of violence against women, women are not only victims but are often collusive in the creation and preservation of violent or harmful traditions. Such is the case for genital cutting, carried

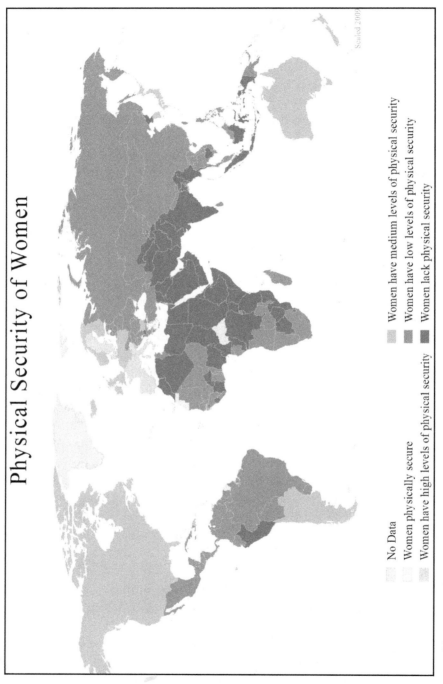

Physical Security of Women

No Data

Women physically secure

Women have high levels of physical security

Women have medium levels of physical security

Women have low levels of physical security

Women lack physical security

Scaled 2009

Figure P1.1. World Map. Only five of the six shaded areas in the key to the map are represented. There is no place designated as "Women physically secure" in the world.
Source: Valerie M. Hudson et al., *Sex & World Peace* (New York: Columbia University Press, 2012).

TABLE P1.1. Locus and Manifestations of Gender Violence

Locus and Agent	The Family	The "Community"	The State
Forms of Gender Violence	*Physical Aggression* Murder (dowry/other) Battering Genital mutilation Feticide Infanticide Deprivation of food Deprivation of medical care Reproductive coercion/ control	*Social Reference Group (cultural, religious, etc.)* *Violence directed toward women within or outside the group. Physical abuse* Battery Physical chastisement Reproductive coercion/ control Witch burning Sati Sexual assault* Rape	*Political Violence (policies, laws, etc.)* Illegitimate detention Forced sterilization Forced pregnancies Tolerating gender violence by nonstate agents
	Sexual Abuse Rape Incest	*Workplace* *Sexual Aggression* Harassment Intimidation *Commercialized Violence* Trafficking Forced prostitution	*Custodial Violence (military/police, etc.)* Rape Torture
	Emotional Abuse Confinement Forced marriage Threat of reprisals	*Media* Pornography Commercialization of women's bodies	

Source: Margaret Schuler, *Freedom from Violence: Women's Strategies from around the World* (New York: UNIFEM, 1992), 14.

out by older women; female relatives' protection of men involved in incestuous relationships; dowry deaths, which are sometimes facilitated by female relatives; the perpetuation of rape myths; and body-altering surgeries, diets, and fashions (think of the clear-cut damage of high heels). Far from *blaming* women for their complicity, it is important to understand how such actions provide some modicum of power within social systems where women are devalued. Similarly, men may also be victims of gender violence, in ways that we explore more fully throughout this volume.

The Social Reproduction of Gender Violence

Gender relations and expectations are situated in the various social structures of societies: labor markets, political systems, families, schools, health-care systems, and so on. We have thus far theorized gender as a set of social relationships, and sexuality as a social construction that is enforced by institutionalized sex/gender systems. But it is also important to underscore the centrality of gender and sexuality as deeply felt aspects of a person's identity. Our awareness of what constitutes appropriate behavior, the patterns of interaction in our families and peer groups, our selection and observation of reference groups, and the structure of opportunities available to us all contribute to our evolution as gendered and sexual beings. The extent to which violence becomes embedded in our repertoire of behaviors is, in part, related to our individual propensities to accept and internalize aspects of socially prescribed gender roles and relationships and whether or not we subscribe to the tenets of heteronormative cultures.

Connell (1987) developed the critical concepts of *hegemonic masculinity* and *emphasized femininity* to refer to the dominant, idealized notions of sexual character that exist in a society. These idealizations are accepted as "normal" by society, although they always exist in opposition to quite a range of "real" human personalities and behaviors. For example, the hegemonic—or controlling—form of masculinity in the early twenty-first-century US requires the ability to be powerful, aggressive, rational, and invulnerable, to control oneself and others in a variety of social situations. This usually implies athleticism, financial success, and the heterosexual domination of women, as well as a sufficient distance from characteristics deemed feminine by the culture. The extent to which men and boys in the US comply with this set of characteristics varies widely, but the manliness of most will be judged by their ability to measure up to this standard of masculinity.

For women, the ideal standard is clearly articulated but not as restrictive as the one prescribed for men. Emphasized femininity is constructed as a counterpoint to masculinity: emotional, nurturing, vulnerable, dependent, sexually desirable, and malleable, rather than controlling. There is a certain amount of ambivalence built into contemporary femininity, however, because these behaviors are idealized but at the same time are not highly valued by the culture. Women acting in stereotypically masculine ways have received a certain amount of social acceptance in some arenas (such as in corporate boardrooms, where the most successful women "act like men," or in sporting events such as women's boxing), but the drumbeat of popular culture continually presents the traditional roles of wife, mother, and sexual ornament as of primary importance.

At various points in human history, and particularly in the present, hegemonic masculinity becomes a breeding ground for gender violence. It is reproduced generally through the early socialization of boys in families and schools, through mass media images, and in male-dominated institutions such as the military, sports teams, politics, and science. Adherence to traditional femininity can be, quite literally, a health hazard for women, as socially prescribed acquiescence to male dominance may be an open invitation to male aggression. These constructions are further complicated when individuals and communities express gender and sexuality in nonbinary ways. The roots of male dominance and heteronormative cultures may be relatively simple, but the elaborate psychological and institutional systems that have evolved and sustained it over time are exceedingly complex.

SUGGESTIONS FOR FURTHER READING

Wendy Brown, *Undoing the Demos*, 2015

R. W. Connell, *Gender and Power: Society, The Person, and Sexual Politics*, 1987

Gerda Lerner, *The Creation of Patriarchy*, 1986

Valerie M. Hudson, Bonnie Ballif-Spanvill, Mary Caprioli, and Chad F. Emmett, *Sex & World Peace*, 2012

Steven Pinker, *The Better Angels of Our Nature: Why Violence Has Declined*, 2011

María de Jesús Mother of Weeping Rocks

Claudia Castro Luna

It starts early
before you learn to speak
even before
you leave the hospital
in your mother's arms
that your body is not your own
that women's paychecks are cut short
that women's wombs remain law controlled
you'd think after all these years
things would be different
the pink that casts your gender
a diaphanous cage
passing as rosy charm
a fine chainmail
to be worn at all times

1

Gendered Violence in Small-Scale Societies in the Past

DEBRA L. MARTIN AND RYAN P. HARROD

Rock art depicting decapitated heads (see Schaafsma 2007) or the actual act of cutting off the head painted on ceramic vessels (Brody 1983, 115) is hard to ignore. Such iconography is often used by archaeologists to identify the presence or absence of violence in small-scale societies of the past. Given issues of preservation, the relative scarcity of elaborately designed artwork, and the more mobile nature of small-scale societies, however, iconography is rarely available to identify violence in the past for most cultural groups. The presence of weapon-like tools (Blitz 1988; Taylor 2001) and structures that appear to be fortifications (Wilcox 1979) are also typically cited as an indication of the presence or threat of intergroup conflict. However, the cultural symbols and rhetoric around violence today in our own lives is indicative of how rapidly changing human behavior can be. While useful for framing the potential role for violence, violent imagery, fortified habitation areas, and weapons do not tell the whole story.

Bioarchaeology is the study of human skeletonized bodies from burials in the past. The skeletonized bodies of people provide an additional line of evidence about the ways that violence was used and who was most at risk for dying a violent death. While not all traumatic injuries are the result of violent conflict, there are often clear markers on the bone that are indicative of interpersonal violence (Brink 2009; Galloway 1999; Spencer 2012). Reconstruction of the mortuary context and the demographic structure, or the age and sex distribution of those who died, can also reveal patterns of violence in the past. For example, two sites in East Africa near the beginning of the Holocene are identified as some of the earliest evidence of violence among humans, based on the types of injuries on the bodies (Lahr et al. 2016; Wendorf 1968).

By adopting a bioarchaeological approach, we seek to explain human behavior within an evolutionary and biocultural framework. Studies that integrate human skeletal remains, archaeological context, landscape, and ethnohistoric information can fill in the gaps in our knowledge about ancient people and help us understand the history of violence. Many small-scale early societies did not leave written records and so reconstructing behavior from human remains is a very valuable source of information.

Bioarchaeological studies have the potential to situate modern-day problems within a larger temporal and spatial framework. Using these cross-cultural and temporal analyses, bioarchaeology contributes to understanding human variation within and across different cultures as well as non-Western ways of dealing with and adapting to challenges. Building on a prior publication (Martin and Harrod 2015) that assessed the evidence for violence in past societies, we focus specifically on the presence of violence against women in small-scale societies in North America with comparisons to extant small-scale societies in other parts of the world.

Gendered Violence

Violence, especially gender-specific violence, was highlighted on an international scale in 2017 with the #MeToo campaign and the #TimesUp legal fund. The goal of these two social movements in the US is to give a voice to women who are most at risk for sexual harassment and violence and to provide assistance to those who lack financial resources to speak out against their harassers and rapists. Beyond sexual harassment, these highly politicized actions help to remind us that women are at as high a risk of violence today (Garcia-Moreno et al. 2005; Garcia-Moreno et al. 2015) as they were in the past (Barr 2005; Martin et al. 2010; Tung 2012; Wilkinson 1997). Additionally, besides being at a higher risk, the prevalence of violence against women is underreported and overlooked because, in many ways, abuse of females has a long history of being illegal but almost universally promoted and sanctioned by those in power, who tend to be male.

As well, much of the violence discussed publicly tends to focus on culturally sanctioned forms of violence such as warfare and other patterns of male-centered violence. An example of how this works was presented in stark relief by the study conducted by Sylvia Walby and colleagues (2016). They found that violence against women increased in most of the United Kingdom based on the Crime Survey for England and Wales (CSEW) data for 1994 through 2014. Although public officials reported that the CSEW data indicated that overall violence was declining, they failed to mention that the larger population database indicated there was an increase in violence against women (Walby et al. 2016, 1227). Such statistical manipulations of data on violence can often mask gendered violence and violence against women.

Given the difficulty of accurately reporting violence that specifically targets women in contemporary times, revealing and uncovering gendered violence and violence against women in the past, when there are no written records, is challenging. Anthropologists are trained to assess social phenomena like violence in a broader context, applying a wider lens and considering not only violent encounters but also the cultural beliefs and social structures that underlie the evidence of these events. Applying evolutionary theory and a mix of cultural, temporal, and cross-cultural approaches, and informed by an integrative biocultural model, we can look beyond proximate and ultimate causes and identify how and why gendered violence changes.

Small-Scale Societies versus Socially Complex Societies

The majority of research on ancient violence is most often conducted on what anthropologists refer to as socially complex societies. These include the large, hierarchical city-states that emerged at different times in multiple places such as Egypt, Mesopotamia, and Mexico. From these kinds of large city-states there are written records in addition to a great deal of archaeological evidence on practices such as warfare, raiding, taking captives, and other forms of violence. However, the question we are trying to answer is, What can be known about violence in small-scale societies for which we have no written records? For North America, archaeologists have dominated the literature with a focus on the qualities we mentioned above, iconography, weaponry, and defensive architecture, which tends to focus on the roles of men and the evidence of warfare. Additionally, early ethnographic literature of indigenous groups living in the Americas historically focused on either the violence of the colonial experience in the 1500s or on oral tradition and ethnohistoric documents that detailed indigenous forms of warfare.

John Bodley (2015, 5–6) differentiates what he calls "small-scale autonomous societies" from "large-scale imperial societies" based on a number of factors, including political organization, economic activities, and how much surplus their subsistence strategy produces. Differences in these factors specifically influence the type and prevalence of violence in small-scale societies. For example, this would include closer relations among individuals within the group, the tendency of spaces to be occupied by multiple members of the community, and greater importance placed on avoiding social stigma and violations of normative behavior. This is crucial for determining the prevalence of different types of violence. Research has shown, for example, that domestic violence or intimate partner violence is higher in small-scale communities where women have lost social support structures or kinship ties (Leyaro et al. 2017; Sedziafa et al. 2016).

Small-scale societies in the past have unique and rich cultural patterns that provide some insight into thinking about the origins and pathways of violence as a behavior that is culturally learned and supported by ideology and social organizational structures. We know that violent behaviors are deeply embedded within the cultural matrix of societies, and to be able to imagine what gendered violence is in these early smaller societies provides insight into understanding what it means to be human. Our earliest ancestors started out in these kinds of small-scale societies, although there is no one cookie-cutter pattern for what they look like cross-culturally. In fact, it is focusing on the range of variability in violent practices that is most illuminative of how humans have used, and continue to use, violence in everyday life.

Violence from an Anthropological Perspective

Anthropologists have produced an enormous database on patterns in gendered violence both cross-culturally as well as going back to the Paleolithic and forward to today. Taking a broad view of anthropological studies on violence in human groups demonstrates that it is universally related to ideologies, inequality, sex/gender, and power. This is best illustrated by the online collection of anthropological studies focused on violence.[1] Even with this rich possibility of intersecting cultural factors, the question of violence as a human universal continues to be debated among scholars. Beginning with Hobbes ([1651] 2003) and Rousseau ([1762] 2008), the argument has been about whether or not violence is innate or learned. Early on, the debate was won by Rousseau and his "blank slate" followers, but beginning in the 1950s, there was a reemergence of scholars who were arguing for the propensity for violence being a human universal that is intimately tied to our biology (Ardrey 1961, 1966; Dart 1953; Lorenz 1966).

As a result of a long-standing tradition of nurture over nature in anthropology, this early work was often rejected. An international symposium was held in 1986 and a document called the Seville Statement (Adams 1989; Adams et al. 1990) was put forth. The intent was to state without reservation that there was no scientific support for a biological propensity for violence. The importance of this document is that it hindered research that explored the more nuanced and complex intersections of culture and biology as a component to understanding violence. Yet, while some say violence is a cultural construct, research studying chimpanzee behavior has offered scientific support for violence having a mix of biological underpinnings and behavioral and social conditioning (Crofoot and Wrangham 2009; Goodall 1979; Goodall 1986; Nishida et al. 1985; Watts et al. 2006; Wrangham and Peterson 1996).

It has been difficult to say exactly when forms of violence we associate with early humans (raiding, low-level warfare, captivity/enslavement, interpersonal fighting, and ambushes) take hold. Many of these activities are associated with male coalitions, not lone individuals. Early humans were foragers and hunters for millions of years before the adoption of agricultural practices that led to the domestication of plants and animals around ten thousand years ago. From three million years ago to the agricultural period, humans practiced big-game hunting, and that is less dangerous and most productive if done as a group. We assume that these early male coalitions that formed to hunt large game were the same kinds of arrangements that were used for raiding, ambushes, and small-scale warfare (Martin and Harrod 2015). If this is correct, then biology need not enter into the understanding of the proliferation of male behaviors related to the formation of coalitions that use weapons formerly used in subsistence activities to the use of weapons and the safety of numbers to attack other humans. Understanding the relative contributions of aggressive behaviors and cultural conditioning has not gotten us very far in understanding anything universal about violence.

The notion of forms of hunting underlying forms of conspecific (same species) violence is supported by the research findings of primatologists Nishida and colleagues (1985) and Goodall (1979) who observed and recorded chimpanzee violence. They showed that chimp violence is different from other mammals' practice of conspecific killings. Chimpanzee violence is organized and it is a cooperative venture that is carried out against premeditated victims. In fact, chimps are the only nonhuman primate species that form male coalitions to attack and kill individuals from other groups. These studies illustrate the evolutionary trajectory of violence in humans, showing that it is quite distinctive, that it grows out of male coalitions where there is safety in numbers, and that it was likely a fundamental aspect of early human behavior.

Violent encounters that result from cooperation strengthen in-group bonds while creating distrust and antagonism for those outside the group. Male chimps may compete within their group for access to females and this, too, is a behavior that favors aggressive action as an expedient way to solve a problem. However, male chimps still form coalitions that collaborate to keep out males from other groups even as they compete against each other for females within the group. Research shows that both conflict and cooperation are part of the lives of female chimpanzees too (Boesch et al. 2008; Muller 2007). For females who do not have to compete for access to males, they do often compete for access to food resources and they have been known to form coalitions (Goodall 1986; Nishida 1989). Unlike males, the female coalitions are often made up of mother-daughter dyads (Goodall 1979; Hiraiwa-Hasegawa 1988). Female-on-female violence, then, is much rarer and it is also less lethal than male violence. Thus, evolutionary forces that shape human behaviors have selected for both inter- and intragroup cooperation, competition, and conflict; however, it is a complex balance showing that cooperation and violence are not simply opposite expressions of the same behavior.

While chimp studies offer one perspective for how we might begin to imagine the origins and evolution of gendered violence in the last common ancestor, we must recognize that the human trajectory has been quite different from that of chimps. With at least four million years of independent behavioral evolution, the violence we study today is not the same as violence among chimpanzees. Yet, we gain some perspective by thinking about the uses of violence in our deep past and it opens up a path to imagine the role of gendered violence in that past.

Biocultural Approaches to Gendered Violence

Over the last few decades, a growing number of researchers have begun to look beyond particular violent events and to focus not only on social, political, and environmental factors but also on historic factors as well. One of the challenging aspects of studying violence is that it is difficult to define it specifically for ancient cultures. Also, cross-cultural comparisons are difficult because, as this volume demonstrates, violence plays out in very different ways dependent upon cultural ideologies and customs. Utilizing definitions that are shaped by world events in the present are problematic because they are influenced by current political and social events that may not have relevance for other times and places. Today violence is almost always defined as something aberrant and outside of the norms of the culture, but this may or may not hold true for some cultures. At best, studies focused on past small-scale societies that did not leave written records provide a historically situated snapshot for expanding how violence is understood in cross-cultural perspectives.

By the time we see the rise of *Homo erectus* and *Homo ergaster*, our ancestors had begun a journey that would move them away from being bound by biology alone. Marks (2015) argues that somewhere along this journey we moved beyond apelike ancestors to become "Ex-Apes." Goodman and Leatherman (1998) argue for a paradigm shift away from notions of the genetic basis for behavior to one where humans are seen as a product of the complex interaction between biology and culture. This is important for violence research because it means that neither an evolutionary perspective (Eibl-Eibesfeldt 1979; Liddle et al. 2012; Wilson and Daly 1995; Wrangham 1999) nor a purely cultural perspective can explain the full range of variability in violent behaviors that are documented for small-scale societies in the past. It cannot be captured by the nature versus nurture debate perpetuated by Hobbes and Rousseau several centuries ago or the typological and racist science that dominated prior to World War II. When we attempt to explain the human capacity, motivation, and allowance for violence, it is apparent that there is no single cause for the use of violence.

Pinker (2011) argues that we are now living in the most peaceful times in human history based on dramatic declines in homicide rates and war-related deaths. However, there are problems with this interpretation that times are better and violence is declining. As stated above with the example from the United Kingdom and the CSEW database, not all violence is declining, as the analysis shows there has been an increase in violence against women (Walby et al. 2016). While their study was looking at changes in the prevalence of violence over the last few decades, Pinker has tried to argue that it has declined over the last few centuries. The problem is that he compares data from populations that are not truly comparable. The assertion that the apparent trend is not a decline is based on an explosion in the world population and a focus on periodic episodes of lethal violence in small-scale societies (see Falk and Hildebolt 2017; Ferguson 2013).

A focus on these manifestations of violence is misleading, as it ignores a suite of other violent encounters that are higher among states compared to small-scale societies, including violence against women. Evaluating regional trends in violence in Tanzania using the country's 2010 Demographic and Health Survey (DHS), Vincent Leyaro and colleagues (2017) found that violence against women differed based on the involvement of women in subsistence and economic activities. Comparing agricultural activities and fishing based economies they came to the conclusion that "it is likely that regions and societies with cultures shaped by values related to a more visible and valuable role for women in the household will also exhibit fewer inequalities within the household in general, and less domestic violence in particular" (Leyaro et al. 2017, 25).

Violence against and among Women

Although males are by far more likely to die from violence, both in the past as well as today, female mortality from violence is an understudied area that can contribute to better understanding the complete picture of violence in human evolution. Female-directed violence within a group is typically inter-household (i.e., domestic abuse or intimate partner violence and child abuse). "Women should be more aggressive in situations in which their role performance requires control over others' behavior and they have relatively more power—namely, in the domestic sphere" (Campbell 1999, 224).

There is an extensive literature on the history of domestic abuse and intimate partner violence as it has developed in historic and contemporary times, but our goal is to examine skeletal remains to reveal possible patterns of violence against and among females living in ancient populations. As such, it is important to understand that females may not only be victims of violence but may also in some cases be active aggressors as well. These contexts include polygamous head wives who often beat younger wives, situations where females lord over household captives/slaves, and social settings where there are women in competition for resources (Burbank 1994; Harrod et al. 2012; Jankowiak et al. 2005; Rassam 1980). There may also be violence among various clans within matrilineal societies. These kinds of patterned behaviors offer a more nuanced and full accounting for violence in human groups in the past and demonstrate the complexity in the ways that violence is used.

Women as Captives and Slaves

For most Americans, the notion of slavery likely brings to mind Africans being exploited by plantation owners in the Southern States. They are often surprised to discover the role of the Spanish and slavery in the Americas and that slavery is not simply a product of colonial expansion but has been around for far longer and is found throughout the world (Brooks 2002; Gutiérrez 1991; Larsen 2001). In general, the most common type of enslavement in the past was of women and children who were abducted during an ambush during which the males of the community were murdered (Barr 2005; Brooks 2002; Cameron 2011; Marshall 2015; Patterson 1982). This is supported by research that indicates violence against females in the form of raiding and taking captives was a common practice that has been documented in many early prestate populations (see Cameron 2008; Carocci and Pratt 2012; Marshall 2015).

Several researchers have highlighted the presence of captive taking in North America (Cameron 2015; Carocci and Pratt 2012). For example, there are ethnographic accounts of slaves among the Northwest Coast cultures like the Tsimshian, Tlingit, Haida, and Kwakiutl or Kwakwaka'wakw (Ames 2001; Boxberger 1997; Donald 1997; Ruby and Brown 1993) or the Northern Iroquoian cultures like the Iroquois and Huron (Starna and Watkins 1991; Tooker 1991). People taken captive and held as slaves are an important trade resource found prior to contact, for example, along the Northwest Coast where they were an integral part of the potlatch exchange (Boas 1967; Ruby and Brown 1993). The majority of slaves appear to be female but despite this disparity, the society as a whole was egalitarian in terms of male/female status.

The capture of women (and often their children) in raids has been well documented by research from the Northeast and Southwest regions of North America. Wilkerson and his team (1997) provide a comprehensive analysis of nonlethal head wounds from adult males and females from the site of Riviere aux Vase in Michigan (c. 1000 CE). What these researchers convincingly demonstrate is that there are clear differences between male and female cranial and facial trauma with three times more injuries found on the women than the men. Additionally, the pattern of these wounds seemed to suggest that they related to efforts to dominate these women and to beat them into submission (Novak 2006). Ethnohistoric data from historic sources suggest that these early Iroquois-speaking people who today call themselves the Haudenosaunnee practiced forms of raiding and capture of women as part of an adaptive strategy to increase the productivity of individual households.

Similarly, at the site of La Plata in New Mexico, also dated to around 1000 CE, Martin (1997) found a high proportion of females with healed cranial and facial wounds. Furthermore, all of the women who had been beaten about the head eventually died in their 30s and were buried in abandoned pit structures with no grave offerings. This pattern of being beaten about the head, which causes disorientation, confusion, and submission, is documented by the patterned depression fractures seen on the tops and sides of the women's heads.

The work of both Wilkinson and Martin suggest that there is a long history of raiding and warfare that was endemic over many generations in these past societies. However, the type of violence against women is by no means universal. While the capture and abduction of women and children was likely accomplished through nonlethal domination and beatings in both of these contexts, the reason for capture and the subsequent treatment of captives was not necessarily similar. In the Riviere aux Vase site, if female captives assimilated and became hard working members of the Iroquois-speaking groups that held them hostage, they could, over time be adopted and socially accepted into the group. We know this because at the time of death, some of the women with healed head wounds were buried with high status grave items and other forms of social identification that tied them to the group. Thus, through a process of violence, captive women may have had longer and better lives and even higher status than they might have had prior to being taken captive. In this case, nonlethal violence was used to coerce females into accepting their fate as captives, and once they did so, some apparently were afforded the opportunity to become high status women. Nonlethal violence was used to coerce females into accepting their fate as captives, and once they did so, they were afforded the opportunity to become women with some means.

However, this was clearly not the case for captive women from the La Plata sites in New Mexico. The people living there were the ancestors of the Pueblo Indian groups living in the American Southwest today. The presence of captive women in this large aggregated agricultural community in 1000 CE was likely motivated by a need for additional labor. All of the women with trauma also had a number of pathologies indicative of habitual hard labor and repeated beatings. This was measured by the number of head and body fractures, the presence of inflammation and wear-and-tear on their arm and leg bones, and the fact that when they did die, they were haphazardly placed in pits without grave offerings. Females from this site who did not have any of the markers of beatings and hard labor were buried in prepared mortuary pits in a flexed position with many grave offerings. Unlike Riviere aux Vase, these women were not integrated into the society, and they were not afforded the same burial treatment as other members of the group. They came into the community as outsiders, and stayed that way until they died.

Several of the women with wounds on their bodies showed a pattern of repeated beatings. For example, one female demonstrated a severe but well healed depression fracture to the top of her head and she was suffering at the time of death from a dislocated and inflamed left hip. She was also placed in an abandoned pit structure. Another female had a large healed cranial depression fracture on the back of her head, as well as a more recent traumatic injury in her left hip. She also showed problems with her lower back. This pattern of repetitive or cumulative injuries, referred to by clinicians as injury recidivism, was an additional factor in assessing the impact of gendered forms of violence on women's daily lives. They clearly were at differential risk for injuries and pathologies. Others have documented this pattern in ancient societies from across the globe (Judd 2002; Martin and Tegtmeyer 2017; Redfern et al. 2016).

Controlling and capturing women is very well documented in the ancient world by using multiple lines of evidence such as patterned trauma on the human remains, archaeological reconstruction of the mortuary context, and ethnohistoric resources. However, the role of captive taking and slavery in the past is only one form of violence perpetrated against women. While rape and sexual assault may also have been part of women's daily lives, these are less likely to leave knowable traces on skeletons, so that aspect has been difficult to measure and demonstrate for past populations.

Violence among Women

Finally, like today, there are contexts where females may use nonlethal violence against other females. Looking at violence perpetrated by women, Underwood (2003) has suggested that violence is useful in women dominating other women, reaffirming social or household status, and establishing a hierarchical pecking order in communities especially among unrelated women. In a previous publication (Martin and Harrod 2015), we cited an example from Morocco where women who are "political" and "clever" can gain power if they have a "forceful personality" (Rassam 1980, 176). We also cited research conducted among a Turkana pastoral community in Kenya that revealed both domestic violence by husbands and violence between cowives in the polygamous marriages that were the norm.

There is one potential bioarchaeological example of violence between women. Walker (1989) and Lambert (1997) examined skeletal remains from the Channel Islands of Southern California (300 BCE–1500 CE). The distribution of nonlethal head wounds on males and females show an identical pattern. The fighting appears to be highly ritualized and performed by adult members of both sexes who may have been high-status leaders within the groups. Based on grave goods and location of the burials of these individuals, males and females with nonlethal wounds were treated at death as high-status individuals. Walker explains that this represented ritualized fighting among higher-status males.

Lambert (1997, 89) suggests that the violence among the women could also be the result of competition among higher-status females. Walker connects these head wounds to temporal trends in resource density and an increase in trauma is seen during periods of low environmental productivity such as droughts. The function of the violence was possibly a mechanism whereby high-status individuals could act out staged fights that were designed to be a performance. Fighting in this context was meant to subdue and knock out some individuals but not to kill them. In this case, nonlethal violence was used as a positive community event that included performances of violence by both males and females.

Understanding violence against women and violence perpetrated by women in early small-scale societies is challenging but suggests that there are often different and complex variables at work that are culturally sanctioned and part of everyday behaviors. At Riviere aux Vase, the violence was due to captivity and accommodation with eventual incorporation into the group. The Channel Island violence was more about ritualized battles performed collectively by higher-status male and female individuals. At La Plata, head wounds appear to be a pattern of violence used to capture and subdue females raided from other areas. Among the Turkana, we learned that the head wounds on males were related to male-on-male violence during warfare and raiding. Females sustained blows to the head from husbands and other cowives, offering definitive support for the notion that like males, females can be the victims of violence, but they also can be the aggressors.

Violence is an expedient response that often provides results quickly for the person who initiates it. While everyday patterns include collaborative and cooperative activities, violence can be used to quickly establish order or change behaviors that might otherwise go unchanged. Violence in the cases presented here can be seen as the "solution" to some "problem" at least as perceived by the initiator or perpetrator. Violence also underscores inequality and so is a handmaiden to power and the ability to enforce differential access to resources within community boundaries.

Conclusions

The origin and evolution of violence is linked to male violence along with female violence in complex ways and must be studied and understood together. It is a complex story that a biocultural perspective can elucidate as the cultural context must be understood in order to tease out the different motivations for violence and the expected outcomes. In all of the populations studied, nonlethal violence played multiple roles throughout a well-established social order. Nonlethal violence is often used to subdue and control individuals without killing them and is as important as lethal violence, if not more so, in understanding the existence and continuation of violence.

The importance of understanding violence through an evolutionary lens is that it can offer insight into why violence remains such a steady constant of human existence, but also why it is so wildly different as we look at it across different cultures and in different time periods in the past. Looking at domestic violence in our own culture illustrates just how pervasive gendered violence still is. There are as many as two to four million women a year victimized and it is the leading cause of bodily and cognitive injuries among women with about one-third of all emergency room admissions of women due to domestic violence (Stern 2004).

Understanding the origin and evolution of gendered violence must take both males and females into consideration using a biocultural perspective to provide necessary insight. Both biology and culture play important roles in understanding human behavior, and this is especially true for violence. In the archaeological case studies, lethal and nonlethal violence played multiple roles within well-established social contexts. Taking a broad evolutionary and anthropological perspective on gender violence alongside the other disciplinary approaches can add breadth and depth to understanding the ways that gender violence is entrenched within cultural systems.

NOTE

1 Virginia R. Dominguez, "Violence: Anthropologists Engaging Violence, 1980–2012." A Virtual Issue from *American Anthropologist*. American Anthropological Association. Retrieved from http://anthrosource.onlinelibrary.wiley.com

2

Overcoming the Religious and Sexual Legacies of Slavery

An Overview

BERNADETTE J. BROOTEN

I, too, live in the time of slavery, by which I mean I am living in the future created by it.
—Saidiya Hartman (2007, 133)

This chapter invites and enables readers to engage with the history of slavery over centuries and across continents—in particular, with its effects on enslaved women and girls and past religious complicity in it.[1] I hope that this new way of viewing slavery will motivate readers to create new strategies for overcoming the vestiges of slavery that continue to shape our daily lives in ways that are often difficult to see. Consider the following modern-day experiences:

"As a descendent of African slave women," writes Amina Wadud, a leading scholar of Islam who usually wears the Muslim headscarf in public, "I have carried the awareness that my ancestors were not given any choice to determine how much of their bodies would be exposed at the auction block or in their living conditions. So, I chose intentionally to cover my body as a means of reflecting my historical identity, personal dignity, and sexual integrity" (2006, 221).

When Doris Davis, an Orthodox Jewish leader from Long Island, sought a divorce, her husband refused to write her a bill of divorcement (Hebrew: *get*). Without a *get*, the Orthodox Jewish community would not recognize her divorce, and she would not be allowed to remarry within the community. In 2004, she sought the help of the Organization for the Resolution of Agunot, which staged rallies outside the husband's home and then posted his photo in synagogues in Brooklyn, where he lived. This community solidarity succeeded, and he eventually wrote her the *get*.[2]

In the summer of 2008, a group of young White women attended a bachelorette party on the West Coast. They hired a male stripper—blond, muscular, tattooed, dressed in a tight black swimsuit—and took turns playing with him, laughing at the raunchy fun. The stripper grabbed one woman by her hair, pushing her head down toward his groin. He grabbed another woman, pushed her down on all fours, and straddled her from behind as she laughed and he grinned at the camera. One of the women at the party, a devout Catholic who attends church with her adoring husband every Sunday, captured each moment of sexual play on her digital camera.

How do these contemporary situations relate to the history of slavery? Each of these women's stories began generations before they were born, when owning or dominating a human body was not only legal but morally permissible and codified by their religions. Slavery had a profound impact on Jewish, Christian, and Islamic thinking and laws about bodies, sex, and marriage, as well as property and ownership. As a result, many slaveholders forced enslaved persons into sex, compelled individual enslaved women and men to breed enslaved babies, and forcibly broke up intimate relationships between enslaved persons—debasing the humans they owned as well as corrupting sex, marriage, families, and themselves. Slavery therefore influenced how enslaved persons thought about their bodies, how they moved and used their bodies, and which choices were open to them. Enslaved persons, women and girls in particular, often succumbed to the terror of sexual violence, but they also resisted attempts at their dehumanization.

Although slavery technically has been outlawed around the world, its repercussions continue to ripple through modern society, influencing how women perceive themselves and are treated. The effects are both so entrenched in our culture and internalized by individuals that many people often do not see or think about them. With slavery so deeply ensconced in our history and having been so intimately connected with sex, it would be surprising if the imagery of slavery had simply disappeared from our consciousness and imagination. This chapter proposes ways to imagine and build relationships and communities that are not tainted by the lingering effects of past slavery.

The three stories of contemporary women above echo those of such women from the past as Essie Mae Washington-Williams, the daughter of onetime segregationist US Senator Strom Thurmond, who had impregnated her mother, a fifteen-year-old family servant. (Thurmond went on to become president of the Baptist Young People's Union.) Or of Callie House, who led three hundred thousand ex-slaves to petition the US government for reparations in the nineteenth and early twentieth centuries. Or of Sally Hemings, enslaved by Thomas Jefferson, who entered into a sexual relationship with Hemings when she was thirteen or fourteen and Jefferson was in his midforties. Or of Rosa, a fifteenth-century Russian slave woman who sued for her freedom in Valencia, in what is now Spain, on the grounds that her Christian owner, and father of her two children, had treated her more like a mistress than a slave (Blumenthal 2010). Or of Mariyya the Copt, given by the Christian military ruler of Alexandria, Egypt, to the Prophet Muhammad, who took her as a concubine and freed her after she bore him a child. Or of Monica, mother of early Christian theologian Augustine, who told her friends that in becoming wives, they have become slaves. Or of Hagar in Genesis, whom Sarah gave to her husband Abraham in the hope that Hagar would bear them a child; Abraham cast her out into the wilderness for acting uppity to Sarah, but Hagar managed to survive and raise her son Ishmael. Slavery shaped all of these women's lives, as well as those of the men and children connected to them.

In today's world, slavery's legacies for sexuality and marriage are myriad, as are women's responses to them. One woman covers her body to shield herself from the bold gaze of male onlookers, a freedom denied to enslaved women whose bodies were used for sex without their consent. Another woman struggles with a thin line between slavery and marriage that is enshrined in religious law: just as only an owner may free an enslaved person, so, too, may only a husband free his wife from the marriage bond. Yet other contemporary women enjoy the freedom to explore their sexuality, which can include domination and slavery imagery.

Slavery as a legal institution has existed for most of recorded history and was allowed by Jewish, Christian, and Islamic sacred texts, traditions, and religious law. The forms of slavery varied considerably but shared the underlying concept of owning a human body. That concept has had a profound impact on Jewish, Christian, and Islamic thinking about sexuality and about marriage between women and men. At the same time, these religions have within them the mercy and compassion necessary to overcome slavery and its long-term effects.

Legal slavery ended in the US [on December 6, 1865]. For that reason, many people think that slavery and its reverberations are a thing of the past. Sadly, slavery continues to exist; the International Labour Organization estimates that 12.3 million people live in conditions of forced labor or virtual slavery (Andrees and Belser 2009, 181). The goal of ending slavery once and for all is both urgent and possible.

Legal slavery has been part of the world's civilizations for so long, and absent so briefly, that the habit of mind that considers slavery normal continues. But people are beginning to ask: Under what conditions are our food and manufactured goods produced? Do persons from whose labor we benefit live in debt bondage from which they can never escape? Do our neighbors have domestic workers whom they do not pay, whose passports they have removed, and whom they physically abuse? What are the working conditions of sex workers, including those in the pornography industry; do their economic circumstances allow them to consent freely to sex work; are they unionized; what is their medical condition, and do they have health benefits? The answers to these questions can help us prevent worker exploitation and forced labor, and the physical and sexual violence that often accompany them.

Facing up to slavery can free people and society from its taint [and pose] the possibilities for creating joyous, healthy expressions of sexuality, starting today. . . . Communities can eroticize racial and gender equality by creating a healthy society and beneficial interactions among individuals and groups (NPR 2006). Men do not have to dominate women. Sexuality does not have to be racially charged. But that requires taking an earnest look at the persistent effects of slavery on social values, religious thought, and economic realities. Such is our task.

Reading Sacred Texts and Religious Law

Some readers may wonder whether it might not be better to ignore biblical, Talmudic, and Qur'anic texts about slavery and their connection to marriage and sexuality. After all, legal slavery has been abolished, rendering texts on slavery irrelevant. But the interpretation of sacred texts lies at the heart of Judaism, Christianity, and Islam because many followers of these religions seek to base their lives on the values expressed in these and other classical texts.

Slaveholding societies have left their mark not only on the wording of sacred texts but also on the ways in which religious people interpret them. For most of history, Jews, Christians, and Muslims read these texts through the lens of slavery: most religious leaders in the past considered slavery morally acceptable, and that belief colored their thinking on all aspects of social and personal interactions. Overcoming the legacy of slavery therefore requires reading scripture and religious law through the lens of freedom—all texts, not only those about slavery. This means reading sacred texts with compassion for enslaved persons and creating religious support for freedom for all persons. It is illogical, for instance, to separate the biblical texts on slavery from those on marriage, family, and sexuality by arguing that although the slavery passages no longer apply, the overall texts in which they are embedded should guide contemporary life.

Teachings on slavery in the Jewish and Christian Bibles, the Talmud, the Qur'an, and early Islamic jurisprudence affected enslaved women differently from enslaved men, and . . . toleration of slavery shaped religious teachings about marriage and sexuality. For example, enslaved women's sexual vulnerability and ability to give birth to children had a profound impact on their experience of slavery. . . . Although slavery and slavery-derived concepts are embedded in these texts, freedom and compassion are quintessentially biblical, Talmudic, and Qur'anic values. . . .

Religious claims raise the question of who deserves to be free, a question that resonates in public-policy choices in the US, both historical and contemporary. The answer is that every human deserves to be free. But Judaism, Christianity, and Islam did not always find this to be true. Whereas ancient Israelite (biblical) law closely regulated the enslavement of fellow Hebrews, it allowed Israelites to enslave foreigners forever. Early rabbinic (Talmudic) law granted enslaved foreigners some rights. For most of Christian history, enslaved Christians did not have an advantage over non-Christians. Islam did not allow the enslavement of fellow Muslims, but it did allow Muslims to enslave non-Muslims. The founders of the US saw no conflict between declaring liberty to be an inalienable right and distinguishing in the constitution between "free Persons," "Indians," and "all other Persons" (enslaved persons, who were each counted as three-fifths of a free person). In the eighteenth and nineteenth centuries, virtually all Christian supporters of slavery in the US drew on the Bible to make their case, and abolitionists did the same. The majority of people in the US at this time were Protestant Christians, most of whom shared the Protestant view that the meaning of the Bible was plain for all to see and that the Bible should form the basis of public policy. The country was riven over whether the Bible supported slavery or condemned it. This created a theological crisis that still echoes today, because some Christians still struggle over whether to interpret the Bible literally and whether it should play a role in public policy (Noll 2006).

* * *

Christians who believed in the justice of slavery were basing their belief upon centuries of religious thought. . . . The laws of ancient Israel allowed slavery; Abraham was a slaveholder, Jesus never prohibited slavery, and the New Testament commands enslaved persons to obey their owners in all things. But one can also mount a biblical case against slavery. African American abolitionist David Ruggles . . . defined slavery in the US as adulterous, pointing to the increase in mixed-race children born to enslaved women, to the fact that enslaved persons were not legally allowed to marry, and to the silence of slaveholders' wives in the face of their husbands' adultery. Ruggles (1971) unmasked slavery's contradiction of the Christian values of chastity, marriage, and family.

Jewish leaders and the American Jewish community were also drawn into the debate over slavery. In 1861, Rabbi Morris Raphall delivered a sermon in the B'nai Jeshurun Synagogue of New York, expressing surprise that anyone should doubt Scripture's support for slavery (Jewish-American History on the Web 2009). Raphall cited biblical laws on slavery from Exodus, Leviticus, and Deuteronomy to demonstrate the legitimacy of slavery. He also found justification for enslaving the "fetish-serving benighted African" in Genesis 9:25, where Noah cursed Ham's son Canaan, stating that Canaan should be the "meanest of slaves" to his brothers.[3]

In contrast, Rabbi David Einhorn of Baltimore argued that the Bible tolerates but does not promote slavery, just as it tolerates polygamy, which the members of his congregation would certainly oppose. In 1861, in the slaveholding state of Maryland, Einhorn, sharply criticizing Raphall, appealed to Jews to reject slavery: "*Such* are the Jews! Where they are oppressed, they boast of the humanity of their religion; but where they are free, their Rabbis declare slavery to have been sanctioned by God, even mentioning the holy act of the Revelation on Sinai in defense of it" (Jewish American History on the Web 2008). These debates show that everyone was reading their sacred texts and religious laws through the lens of their own experiences with slaveholding and the lens of their own vision of justice. Although some Christians and Jews insist that the meaning of the Bible is plain for all to see, its meaning has been contested since it came into existence, and the Bible contains differing policies on slavery.

The rise of modern racism created yet another lens through which to read the Bible's teachings on slavery. Unlike in ancient slavery, which was not based on race, modern racist theories undergirded the trans-Atlantic slave trade. These racist theories supported not only the enslavement of Africans but also racial apartheid in Africa and segregation in the US, including laws prohibiting interracial marriage (known as antimiscegenation statutes). Just as slavery supporters and antislavery advocates appealed to the Bible, judges in the US from the nineteenth through the twentieth centuries justified bans on interracial marriage with religious and biblical arguments; and public officials, including former President Harry S. Truman, viewed interracial marriage as contrary to biblical teaching (*New York Times* 1963) . . . Opponents of interracial marriage developed a theology of separate races that drew upon the story in Genesis 10–11 of the dispersion of the sons of Noah throughout the world. They claimed that the biblical account represented God's plan for the races to live separately from one another and not to intermarry (Botham 2010).

Johnson (2010) and Botham (2010), troubled by past Christian appeals to the Bible in support for slavery and by laws against interracial marriage, draw parallels to contemporary debates over sexual orientation. They argue that earlier generations' use of the Bible to support policies that most Americans now consider wrong warns us about the dangers of basing public policy on the Bible.

* * *

Nineteenth-century slavery supporters stressed that Jesus and his apostles, who saw slavery all around them, did not call for its abolition. Glancy (2010) finds that she has to agree. Although Jesus did challenge social hierarchies, he did not call upon his followers to refrain from slaveholding. And despite Paul's preaching a message of freedom, he did not speak out against the sexual use of enslaved women, even though that reality was known throughout the Roman world. Briggs (2010) points out that when Paul condemned prostitution, he focused on how going to a prostitute dishonored the male body, not on how prostitution exploited the female body, even though many prostitutes in the Roman world were enslaved and were therefore left without choice (1 Corinthians 6:13–18, New Revised Standard Version).

Jews in the rabbinic tradition, which includes most religious Jews today, do not interpret the Bible separately from ancient and medieval rabbinic commentary on it. Unlike Protestants, rabbinic Jews do not believe that one should go back to the Bible alone, ignoring later commentary. Although reading the Bible in conjunction with rabbinic commentary brings in a certain elasticity missing from Protestant literalist interpretation, Labovitz (2010) shows that rabbinic thinking about slavery and gender has its own problems. For example, one ancient rabbinic commentary interpreted the term "soul" in the biblical phrase "who purchases a soul" to include both a wife and a slave (the *Sifra* on Leviticus 22:11). Labovitz argues that Jews need to rethink the rabbinic metaphor of "acquisition" of a woman in marriage and to find ways of thinking about marriage that do not involve the ownership of property.

Many verses in the Qur'an refer to unfree persons. Although the Qur'an encourages believers to seek freedom, it also allows male slaveholders sexual access to "what their right hands possess," that is, to their enslaved women (Qur'an 4:3; 23:5–6; 70:29–30). Ali (2010) argues that verses containing broad principles of justice should take precedence over verses bound by the specific historical circumstances of the time, such as slavery. Ali thus presents a way to live and honor the precepts of the faith without perpetuating injustices grounded in historical behavior that we now consider abhorrent.

The Legacies of Slavery for Women and Girls

Religious Understandings of Marriage between Women and Men

Slavery as a legal category has had a powerful impact on religious marriage law and continues to influence ideas about relationships between husbands and wives. Ancient Israel and other cultures of the Ancient Near East, the Roman world that shaped early Christian and early rabbinic understandings of marriage, and the Arab society in which early Muslim communities developed Islamic marriage law were all slaveholding societies. These societies were hierarchical, granting the male head of the family power over his household; these men, if not slaveholders, probably aspired to be such. Although Jewish, Christian, and Muslim religious leaders have always recognized the difference between slavery and marriage between men and women, they have sometimes applied concepts from slavery to marriage.

The example of Monica, mother of fourth- and fifth-century church father Augustine, illustrates how deeply interconnected slavery and marriage were. As Briggs (2010) writes, Monica reminded her friends not to resist their husbands, even when their husbands beat them so severely that their faces were disfigured, because their marriage contract rendered them slaves. The long Christian toleration of wife beating and spousal rape is part of this history, as is the double standard regarding fidelity, which punishes a wife's extramarital sex more harshly than a husband's, or even dismisses a husband's sexual affairs (Basil of Caesarea, Canonical Letter 188, canon 9; Canonical Letter 199, canon 21). Christian leaders (nearly all male) knew that Roman law (made by men) did not prohibit male slaveholders from having sex with their slave girls or women, and that some did so. Even though Christian leaders considered sex with one's slave girl or woman to be fornication (if the man were unmarried) or adultery (if he were married), they did not make prevention or church punishment (such as temporary or permanent excommunication) a moral priority. Slavery and chastity have thus coexisted uneasily within Christian history. By promoting chastity while tolerating slavery, Christian leaders created an impossible situation for both free wives and enslaved girls and women. Free wives suffered their husbands' infidelities with enslaved women, while enslaved women were vulnerable both to male sexual advances and wives' jealous anger.

The interweaving of slavery and marriage, far from being incidental to Christian thought, reaches back into the New Testament, which commands wives to obey their husbands, children their parents, and slaves their masters (Colossians 3:18, 4:1; Ephesians 5:21–6:9; Titus 2; 1 Peter 2:13–3:7). These texts highlight the tension inherent in slavery. Enslaved wives may not have been able to obey their enslaved husbands if the master or mistress gave a contradictory command. Enslaved children may not have been able to obey their parents, if the slaveholder even allowed the children to live with their parents. And enslaved Christian women, told to obey their masters in everything, faced the dilemma of how to deal with the master who sought sexual relations with them. Enslaved women and men did not have the same freedom as did free women and men to pursue the Christian virtue of avoiding fornication. I highlight these tensions within the New Testament not to condone wifely obedience, children's obedience in all things, or problematic understandings of sexual transgression, but rather to illustrate how slavery can strike at the heart of the institution of the family and render enslaved persons sexually vulnerable even when they defiantly resist and seek to preserve family bonds not recognized by law and express their sexuality as they see morally fit.

Although church leaders no longer officially teach that slaves should obey their masters, the New Testament texts commanding wives to obey their husbands are often read at Christian wedding ceremonies. In this way, the structure of the slaveholding household continues to affect people's lives. And Christian children whose parents sexually or physically abuse them still have inadequate support to resist the command to "obey [their] parents in everything" (Colossians 3:2 NRSV). The New Testament also commands husbands to love their wives and never to treat them harshly, fathers not to provoke their children, and masters and mistresses to treat their slaves justly and fairly (Colossians 3:19, 4:1; cf. Ephesians 5:25, 6:4, 9, NRSV). But for most of history, Christian leaders did not see corporal punishment of wives, children, and enslaved persons as contrary to these commands.

Ancient rabbis, who also lived in slaveholding societies, developed the concepts of Jewish marriage law that remain foundational for many Jews today. Labovitz (2010) shows how these rabbis drew parallels between the acquisition of a free wife and the acquisition of a slave person. Metaphorically, they classified wives as ownable and marriage as the purchase of property. The Hebrew word for husband is *ba'al*, which one can also translate as "master" or "owner." The early rabbis also derived legal practices concerning betrothal and marriage from a father's biblical right to sell his daughter into slavery (Exodus 21:7–11, Jewish Publication Society, NRSV). Labovitz argues that the rabbinic concept of marriage as a man's acquisition of a wife underlies the rabbinic teaching that a man may divorce his wife, but a woman may not divorce her husband. This inequality in divorce remains a problem for Orthodox Jewish women today.

Ali (2010) demonstrates that the early Islamic jurists similarly thought of marriage between a man and woman as ownership. They employed the category of "dominion over" (Arabic: *milk*) for both slavery and marriage, and they drew analogies between divorcing a wife and freeing an enslaved laborer. Further, the Qur'an and classical Islamic jurisprudence draw an explicit parallel between a man's wife and his slave woman: a man is permitted to have sex with both. The concept of marriage as a man's dominion over a woman presents challenges for contemporary Muslims seeking to create religious marriages based on gender equality.

Slavery's Corruption of Sexuality

Slavery as an economic institution is not separate from marriage, sexuality, family, and childbirth. Centuries of accepting slavery as normal have left their mark on how the descendants of slaveholding societies think about moral issues. The concept of owning another human being's body led to the right of sexual access to that body . . . From the time of the ancient Israelites through to the spread of slavery in the New World, slavery included masters having sex with enslaved women and girls; jealous mistresses taking out their rage on enslaved persons who were unable to defend themselves against either master or mistress; and owners increasing their wealth by making sure that their enslaved laborers had as many children as possible. To be sure, slavery differed from culture to culture and by legal system. Slavery in the US (and the Americas as a whole) was much harsher than in many other times and places.

Slaveholders' control of the sexual and reproductive functions of enslaved girls and women was central to the institution of slavery. This feature of slavery is at least as old as ancient Israel. Wright (2010) argues that Exodus allows a father to sell his daughter into slavery in part because Israelite lawgivers saw female sexuality as inherently the property of a man, whether the father, the husband, or the slaveholder. The New Testament, which commands slaves to obey their owners in all things, never explicitly prohibits the sexual use of enslaved persons. Glancy (2010) raises a troubling question. Jesus taught his disciples not to imitate the hierarchies that they saw around them, not to be a lord or a tyrant, but instead to become a "slave to all" (Mark 10:44; cf. Matthew 20:26–27, 23:11; Mark

9:35; and Luke 22:26, NRSV). Although appreciating the radical character of this teaching, Glancy asks what it might have meant for women whose enslavement included sexual exploitation.

Chastity and slavery have rarely coexisted. Male slaveholders—Jewish, Christian and Muslim—considered sexual access to their enslaved women to be their right. As Glancy (2010) shows, Ambrose, an early Christian theologian and bishop, assumed that Christian men would continue to have sex with their enslaved women even though he preached against it . . . Ambrose warned Christian men that if they had sex with their enslaved women they should ensure that these women still submitted to their mistresses (Ambrose 2000, 14). Other early Christian theologians also warned men against sex with their enslaved women, and canon law (early Christian religious law) did not penalize Christian men who had done so (Basil of Caesarea, Canonical Letter 188, canon 9; Canonical Letter 199, canon 21). Similarly, the early rabbis, who also lived in a world in which slavery included sexual contact between owners and enslaved girls and women, did not explicitly prohibit it.

As Ali (2010) shows, the Qur'an and the early Islamic jurists explicitly allowed male slaveholders sexual access to their slave girls and women. In contrast to the Jewish and Christian leaders who preceded and were contemporaneous with them, the early Islamic jurists gave some rights to enslaved women who bore children fathered by their owner, if the owner acknowledged paternity. The children were born free, the owner was not allowed to sell the mother, and mother was to be freed upon the owner's death.

Slavery in the US differed markedly from other systems of slavery in that enslaved women had virtually no hope that they or the children they bore their masters might benefit from the connection to the master. This harshness affected both the slaveholders and the enslaved. Given what we know about Jefferson's sexual relationship with Hemings, his words in *Notes on the State of Virginia* strike a poignant note: "The whole commerce between master and slave is a perpetual exercise of the most boisterous passions . . . The man must be a prodigy who can retain his morals and manners undepraved by such circumstances" (Jefferson 2002, 195).

Far from being unique, Jefferson's sexual contact with his slave girl represents the logic of slavery documented throughout this chapter. Their sexual contact began when Jefferson was in his midforties and Hemings was thirteen or fourteen and living in Jefferson's Paris home as a maid. At the same time, Jefferson sought to live a moral life and to inspire the people of the US to do so as well. Jefferson found a moral guide in Jesus of Nazareth and set out to extract from the New Testament those sayings and actions of Jesus that he deemed historically authentic. Among these, Jefferson included this passage from the Gospel of Matthew 5:27–28: "Ye have heard that it was said by them of old time, Thou shalt not commit adultery: But I say unto you, That whosoever looketh on a woman to lust after her hath committed adultery with her already in his heart" (Jefferson 1989, 46). . . .

The problem of not being able to live up to one's morals runs deep in the history of slavery in the US. Responding to romantic notions about the sexual relationship between Jefferson and Hemings, Bay (2010) argues that asking whether Hemings consented to the relationship and whether she loved Jefferson are the wrong questions. Jefferson literally owned the bodies and the fecundity of his enslaved women. He wrote, "I consider a woman who brings in a child every two years more profitable than the best man on the farm," because the enslaved babies she produced were "capital" (Jefferson 1953, 45–6). Hemings, like other enslaved women, did not have any legal right to refuse to have sex with Jefferson. Jefferson, like other slaveholders of his time, could not have been prosecuted in the US for raping Hemings (Block 2006, 65).

Clinton (2010, 213) puts the relationship between Jefferson and Hemings in a broad historical context by narrating three hundred years of the history of European American men's sexual contact with enslaved and free (but subordinate) Black women. In doing so, Clinton highlights the hypocrisy of slavery, exposing "the contradictions within racial separatism and the American ideals of sexual purity and Christian virtue."

Racial-Sexual Stereotypes: Blaming the Victim

Because of the US history of slavery, assumptions about the sexuality of African American women in the US differ from those made about European American women.[4] Roberts (2010) analyzes the paradox between the media's display of scantily clad Black women in hypersexual poses and the deafening silence about Black women's sexual desires. Racial stereotypes rooted in the beliefs of the slavery era pervade US culture. These include the asexual Black Mammy who cares for White children but not for her own; the hypersexual, irresponsible Jezebel who tempts White men to sin; the Welfare Queen who cheats the taxpayers; and the domineering Black Matriarch who is to blame for her children's failures. The sexual stereotypes of enslaved women as licentious extends far back into history; modern racism extended it to all Black women and also used the myth of Black hypersexuality as a reason to enslave Black people. . . .

Two stories illustrate how slaveholders have blamed the enslaved victims for their sexual exploitation. The nineteenth-century US slave narrative written pseudonymously by Harriet A. Jacobs describes how her owner, "Dr. Flint," who had recently become a church member, told her to obey him by having sex with her. The fifteen-year-old "Linda" sensed Mrs. Flint's jealousy, even though "I had hitherto succeeded in eluding my master, though a razor was often held to my throat to force me to change this line of policy" (Jacobs 2001, 29). Dr. Flint, already the father of eleven slaves, threatened to sell her or to beat her if she did not give in, and said, "I would cherish you. I would make a lady of you. Now go, and think of all that I have promised you" (ibid., 32).

Centuries earlier, around the second century CE, the popular *Acts of Andrew* recounted the legend of Maximilla, a Christian woman who tried to lead a celibate life, much to the chagrin of her pagan husband, Aigeates (Prieur 1989). To avoid sex with her husband, Maximilla devised the remarkable successful plan of selecting her beautiful and "by nature extremely undisciplined" slave woman to act as her surrogate. The slave woman's character and euphemistic name "Euklia" (Greek for "of good reputation") seem to have predestined her for the task. Not being pure (because she was enslaved and thus by definition impure), she could not be corrupted. The whole plan went horribly wrong when Euklia, like Hagar in Genesis, took pride in sleeping with the master and even told others. In response, her master mutilated her body and cast her out into the street until she should die and the dogs consume her corpse. But the *Acts of Andrew* describes Maximilla as the "blessed one," not criticizing her with a single word.

The logic of slavery is to blame the enslaved for their plight. This connection of slavery, impurity, and criminality was also evident in the entertainments put on for the masses in Roman amphitheaters. The elaborate shows included nude, enslaved prostitutes and public execution of criminals (Briggs 2010).

Resilience and Resistance

Throughout history, enslaved women and girls, men and boys, have resisted the role of victim. Beginning with Genesis, in which Hagar fled her mistress Sarah's harsh treatment, fleeing slavery is an age-old form of resistance (Genesis 16, NRSV); flight from cruelty testifies to enslaved persons' rejection of their treatment as lesser beings or as property and challenges anyone today who believes that slavery may have been morally tolerable in the past. If slavery were morally acceptable to enslaved people, why do the most ancient of historical sources document their attempts to flee their owners?[5]

In some circumstances, enslaved women were able to take legal steps to challenge their position. Of the ninety-four lawsuits demanding freedom that were filed between 1425 and 1520 in Valencia, in what is now Spain, thirty-three were filed by enslaved women who claimed that their masters had fathered their children or that their own fathers were free men, and thus they were due their freedom under the law. They characterized themselves as virtuous or as devoted concubines to their masters. Of these thirty-three women, fifteen won (Blumenthal 2010).

Enslaved women in the US had no such right. Antebellum inheritance cases illustrate how little enslaved women in the US could hope to gain from a liaison with the master. In Louisiana, some masters freed their enslaved sexual partners in their wills. But heirs frequently contested these manumissions because under state law, a man was not allowed to bequeath more than 10 percent of his estate to a concubine. If the value of the concubine herself exceeded 10 percent of her master's estate, she remained enslaved (Schafer 1994, 185). In the "sexual economy" of slavery in the US, judges had to walk a fine line between recognizing men's right to control and dispose of their property as they wished, and preserving the racial hierarchy that kept wealth in the hands of Whites while keeping many African Americans enslaved (Davis 1999).

In spite of their precarious position, enslaved girls and women sometimes initiated sexual relationships with their masters or other free men. Sexual attractiveness and the ability to bear the master or his son a child could be an enslaved woman's best hope for a better life and could even entitle her to legal rights. In the Roman Empire, including among early Christians, most unmarried men could free an enslaved woman and then legally marry her. Similarly, a woman enslaved to a Muslim man who acknowledged paternity of her children gave birth to free children, could not be sold, and would be free upon the master's death. Contrast Hemings' situation as Jefferson's slave with that of Caenis, formerly enslaved concubine of first-century CE Roman Emperor Vespasian: "Even after he became emperor he treated her almost as a lawful wife" (Suetonius 1997).

Public Policy and Law

When the Civil War ended in 1865, the majority of religious people in both the North and the South who found biblical support for slavery did not turn to the book of Deuteronomy, which commanded slaveholders to give freed slaves what they needed to start a new life. They turned back to what they knew: slavery as a God-given right. De facto slavery persisted, particularly in the Southern states. A number of African American men were arrested on trumped-up charges such as loitering and forced into industrial slavery (Blackmon 2008). The Ku Klux Klan, a Protestant Christian terrorist organization, employed all means of violence against formerly enslaved people and their descendants. The Klan's reign of terror included sexual violence against women and men, practiced with impunity (Cardyn 2002).

[We must consider whether] the US criminal justice system still reflects the attitudes of the slavery era. This will seem implausible to some readers, especially decades after the Civil Rights Movement. In fact, the conceptual linkage between slavery and imprisonment in the US dates to at least the Thirteenth Amendment to the Constitution, which abolished slavery in 1865: "Neither slavery nor involuntary servitude, except as a punishment for crime whereof the party shall have been duly convicted, shall exist within the US, or any place subject to their jurisdiction." But the problem of how US society treats African Americans (and others) who break the law actually lies deeper, in the assumption that only the virtuous deserve freedom or citizenship. Nineteenth-century abolitionists understood this assumption, promoting narratives of formerly enslaved women and men who strove to attain Christian virtue (Grimes 1825).

Every society needs a criminal justice system to hold perpetrators accountable for their behavior. That justice system, if it is to retain its authority and effectiveness, must carefully determine guilt and innocence, and must treat convicted persons according to the highest moral standards. A moral society is one that treats all its members—even the weakest, most vulnerable, and most damaged—with equal respect for their rights as human beings. But as Barry (2010) documents, African Americans are incarcerated in numbers highly disproportionate to their percentage of the population, which means that prison policies disproportionately affect them. Certain prison practices echo the treatment of women enslaved in the US, including shackling while women are giving birth (a practice that in its brutality goes even beyond the treatment of most enslaved women in the US), the removal of newborns from their mothers, and using men to guard female prisoners.[6]

The attitudes of the slavery era also continued to shadow the US justice system's treatment of women who have been sexually assaulted. In the time of slavery, European Americans portrayed Black women as hypersexual, and enslaved women had no legal right to protection from rape (Roberts 2010; Townes 2010; Hopkins 2010; Bay 2010; Clinton 2010). After the Civil War, the Ku Klux Klan used sexual violence against African Americans with impunity. Today, Black women are less likely to report a rape, prosecutors are less willing to file charges, and juries are less prone to convict than if the rape complainant were White (Kennedy 2003; Nash 2009).

What Has Changed and Why?

Changing the Stories We Tell

People in the US are beginning to recognize the ways in which the stories they tell about themselves and each other reinforce the damage done by slavery. They are also starting to realize that it is possible to change those stories to reflect the society that they wish to create . . . Foster (2010) analyzes how stories about slavery can keep women whose ancestors were (or could have been) enslaved separated from those whose ancestors were (or could have been) slaveholders. The difficulty of sustaining interracial friendships between women hinders the struggle for racial and sexual equality, making it more difficult to promote the goals of feminist sexual ethics: sexual relationships based on meaningful consent (that is, consent without any form of pressure, whether economic, familial, social, or political) and the mutual respect and pleasure of each partner. . . . Foster argues that we can change our stories, because it has been done before. Nineteenth-century progressive African American women claimed the title "Mrs." (whether or not they were married) to counter the prevailing view that they lacked sexual virtue and family ties. Foster challenges us to create new stories that will unite rather than divide. This includes recognizing that many enslaved women were not raped, not all African Americans are descendants of slaves, and many enslaved women resisted victimhood.

*Religious Communities and Governments Face Up
to Past Support for Slavery*

In 1975, John Francis Maxwell, a Roman Catholic priest, introduced his collection of Catholic historical sources on slavery by arguing that it was not good enough to sweep evidence of the church's complicity under the rug. He proclaimed that an error of such gravity requires official correction, investigation of its causes, and attempts to ensure that it does not happen again (Maxwell 1975). This eminently reasonable proposal matches what we expect from government, business, and nonprofit organizations, but we rarely expect religious institutions to correct their mistakes.[7] Yet the church was complicit in slavery. Popes were slaveholders; canon law excommunicated those who persuaded an enslaved person to flee from their master; in the fifteenth century, the Vatican granted official approval to Portugal and Spain to engage in the slave trade in West Africa "to invade, conquer, crush, pacify, and subjugate any whomsoever Saracens, and pagans, and other enemies of Christ . . . and to reduce their persons to perpetual slavery" (Pope Nicholas V 1455); and the Vatican supported slavery as late as 1866 (Zanca 1994).

. . . [We must examine] why Roman Catholicism and other branches of Christianity, Judaism, and Islam accepted slavery for so many centuries, and consider how slavery shaped gender and sexual ethics in these three religious traditions. We can also consider how Jews, Christians, and Muslims draw upon the compassionate values of their traditions to overcome the lingering effects of slavery.

The Book of Leviticus prefaces its slave law with instructions on how to prevent slavery: "If any of your kin fall into difficulty and become dependent upon you, you shall support them; they shall live with you as though resident aliens." Leviticus also reminds the Israelites of their own past enslavement (Leviticus 25:35, NRSV). As in the time of Leviticus, society can create public policies that support the millions of persons worldwide at risk of enslavement.

Christian ethicist Townes (2010) proposes a way to think about public policy that is free of the racial-sexual stereotypes developed during and after the US system of slavery. She describes how the lingering perception of African American families as depraved has shaped contemporary welfare policy. She suggests that the stereotypes of the Welfare Queen and the Black Matriarch, for example, led lawmakers to focus on preventing teenage pregnancy rather than on resolving the deeper structural problems of bad schools and the lack of affordable day-care centers. Townes argues that the Protestant work ethic, combined with a focus on the individual in isolation from the community, has contributed to the injustice of social policy in the US. But Christian values can also help to create a more just society. . . .

Creating a sexual ethics untainted by slaveholding values requires first gaining a clear understanding of the religious belief that owning another person's body is morally permissible and then developing sexual ethics based on the premise that all human beings deserve freedom. . . . "Sexual ethics" means far more than individual decisions about whether to have sex, when, or with whom. . . . [It] includes a society's assumptions about the sexuality of an ethnic group; the ways in which young people's access to health care, safe neighborhoods, and a good education affect their sexual experiences and choices; how a criminal justice system treats an incarcerated woman while she takes a shower or gives birth; whether religious marriage grants equal rights and responsibilities to each party; whether religious and civil marriage are restricted to one man and one woman or include same-gender marriage; whether prosecutors and juries respond to all rape complaints based on the merits of the case rather than unbiased assumptions; and how families and communities respond to sexual abuse within a family.

* * *

We are witnessing unprecedented progress in facing up to the history of slavery. The Church of England has apologized for having sustained and benefited from slavery in the Caribbean in the eighteenth century. Archbishop of Canterbury Rowan Williams explained, "The Body of Christ is not just a body that exists at any one time; it exists across history and we therefore share the shame and the sinfulness of our predecessors, and part of what we can do, with them and for them in the Body of Christ, is prayerful acknowledgement of the failure that is part of us, not just of some distant 'them'" (Bates 2006).

In the US, both the House of Representatives and the Senate have apologized for slavery and for subsequent discriminatory laws[8] . . . Supporters [of actual reparations] include religious and civic organizations.[9] Some other religious denominations and groups have apologized for slavery but made no move toward reparations.[10]

* * *

[There are] many and diverse ways to address the long-term economic effects of slavery. Some may support governmental reparations to direct descendants of enslaved persons, or scholarships or health care targeting affected communities. Others may work toward the public disclosure of past relationships to slavery, such as the statutes enacted by some cities and states, which may expose past corporate relationships to slavery.[11] For example, in 2005 JP Morgan Chase apologized for its predecessor bank in Louisiana's ownership of slaves and acceptance of slaves as collateral, and it established a $5 million scholarship fund for Black students in Louisiana (Slawsky 2005).

Some . . . will reject the idea of reparations, instead working for racial and ethnic equality through other means. I hope that all readers of this chapter will see that moving beyond slavery urgently requires action of some type. . . . Everyone can contribute something to freedom each day, in memory of those who lived in slavery all the days of their lives and in compassion with those who are living in slavery now.

NOTES

1 This is not to deny how horrific slavery was for men or its long-term effects on them but rather to fill in an important gap in the public and religious understanding of slavery.

2 In Hebrew, *agunot* means "chained women" and designates wives whose husbands refuse to give them the bill of divorcement that would allow them to remarry.

3 Raphall notes that the English translation used by his congregants had "servant of servants" for *'eved 'avadim*, but he himself offered the rendering "meanest of slaves."

4 Assumptions about women of other ethnic backgrounds also exist, but they differ from those about women whose ancestors could have been enslaved or could have been slaveholders.

5 E.g., Laws of Hammurabi 16–20, Deuteronomy 23:15–16 (which commands that Israelites grant refuge to fugitives.)

6 Several states have banned shackling during labor and delivery. In a recent decision, a federal court of appeals held that the Eighth Amendment to the US Constitution protects pregnant women in prison from the unnecessary and unsafe practice of shackling during labor (see *Nelson v. Correctional Medical Services, et al.* F.3d, 2009 WL 3151208 8th Cir.).

7 Even the intense public scrutiny in the clergy sexual abuse scandal in the Catholic Church has not resulted in adequate institutional reflection on the moral priorities of the hierarchy, and the Vatican continues to resist giving laypeople oversight over personnel or financial decisions.

8 *Apologizing for the Enslavement and Racial Segregation of African-Americans*, HR 194, 110th Cong., 2nd sess., *Congressional Record* 154, n. 127, daily ed. (July 29, 2008) H 7224; *Apologizing for the Enslavement and Racial Segregation of African-Americans*, S. Con. Res. 26, 111th Cong., 1st sess. (June 11, 2009), *Congressional Record* 155 (June 18, 2009) S 6761.

9 Supporters include the NAACP, Southern Christian Leadership Conference, Nation of Islam, and the National Baptist Convention. In 2001 the United Church of Christ passed a resolution on reparations. Other denominations that have addressed reparations to some extent include the United Methodist Church, the Presbyterian Church (USA), and The General Assembly of the Episcopal Church.

10 These include the Southern Baptist Convention, sisters from three Roman Catholic orders, the Dominicans, the Lorettos, and the Sisters of Charity of Nazareth.

11 Among others, these include the cities of Chicago, Los Angeles, Detroit, San Francisco, and Philadelphia; and the states of Illinois, Iowa, California, and Maryland.

3

Theorizing Women's Oppression

SHARON SMITH

Classical Marxism provides a solid theoretical foundation for understanding the root of women's oppression. But no foundation can or should be viewed as a finished product; it must be built upon to realize its potential. Likewise, theory must be further developed and adjusted as necessary to reflect changes in material circumstances, while also correcting past errors that become clearer with the value of hindsight.

One of the central tenets of historical materialism is that social relations are not static but remain in a process of ongoing negotiation via class and social struggles, as workers and all those oppressed by the system fight for the betterment of their own conditions of life. The needs and wants of the capitalist class have never single-handedly determined the terms of social relations—including those of women.

More than 150 years have passed since Karl Marx and Frederick Engels penned *The Communist Manifesto*. And the world has changed significantly since then. Although they were often able to anticipate future sites of struggle, they were also constrained in other respects by the historical limits of the social relations of their time. Marx's and Engels's articulations of women's oppression often contain contradictory components—in some respects fundamentally challenging the gender status quo while in other respects merely reflecting it. Their most significant limitation was that they believed, along with their contemporaries, both that humans are innately heterosexual[1] and that women are biologically suited for their nurturing and childrearing role in the family.[2] Fundamental challenges to these naturalist assumptions did not materialize until the rise of the women's and gay liberation movements, amid a mass radicalization, in the late 1960s and early 1970s.

One of the most important theoretical achievements of second wave feminism involved a debate over the role of women's domestic labor, which resulted for some in what has become known as *social reproduction* theory—situating women's domestic labor as a crucial aspect of the social reproduction of the capitalist system as Marx conceived it. Marxist-feminist Lise Vogel, who played a key role in developing social reproduction theory, recalled the marginalization of the domestic labor debates: "Most feminists eventually rejected the domestic labor literature as a misguided effort to apply inappropriate Marxist categories. Most

Marxists simply disregarded the debate, neither following nor participating in it. Neither potential audience fully grasped the ways that socialist feminists were suggesting, implicitly or explicitly, that Marxist theory had to be revised."[3]

In this chapter, I will assess the key elements of Marx and Engels's theory, which connects women's second-class citizenship in society overall with their role inside the nuclear family—while identifying key theoretical questions that need further development or correction. I will also examine some (though not all, due to space considerations) of the theoretical advances of 1970s social reproduction theorists who specifically addressed the role of working-class women's unpaid domestic labor in the service of capital, and its connection to the oppression that affects women of all classes. Theirs was not an easy task, since Marx implied a theoretical framework for this understanding but did not pursue it himself.

Marx and Engels: The Role of the Nuclear Family in Women's Oppression

Marx and Engels were in many respects well in advance of their time in seeking to end women's oppression, while pursuing its relationship to class society and the role of the family. Even in their early writings, they recognized that women's oppression is endemic to capitalism, noting the subservient role of women in property-holding families. In *The Communist Manifesto*, written in 1848, they argue that ruling-class men oppress their wives in their own families and that communists intend to free women from this oppression, stating, "The bourgeois sees in his wife a mere instrument of production. . . . He has not even a suspicion that the real point aimed at [by communists] is to do away with the status of women as mere instruments of production."[4]

In *The Origin of the Family, Private Property and the State*, written shortly after Marx's death, Engels explores the historic rise of private property and its social ramifications.[5] As the title implies, Engels connects the rise of class society with the rise of individual family units (in the form of the classic "patriarchal" family[6]) as the means by which propertied classes possess and pass on private wealth, and also with the rise of the state, representing the interests of the ruling class in the day-to-day class struggle. Engels argues that the nuclear family developed first among property-owning families, but eventually, the nuclear family form became an economic unit of society as a whole.

Marx spent the final years of his life on intensive research on non-Western and precapitalist societies, focusing on kinship and gender relations in particular, resulting in an enormous compilation of what has become known as his "ethnological notebooks."[7] Engels used portions of Marx's ethnological notebooks in writing *The Origin*—primarily those discussing the anthropological data of nineteenth-century anthropologist Lewis Henry Morgan's 560-page volume *Ancient Society*, published in 1877.

Morgan's anthropological research was among the first materialist attempts to understand the evolution of human social organization. While much of Morgan's data is primitive and has since been discredited by advances in the field, a wealth of more recent anthropology has provided ample evidence to support a basic evolutionary progression of human society.[8]

Engels ties the rise of the nuclear family directly to the rise of women's oppression. As he argued, the "modern individual family is founded on the open or concealed domestic slavery of the wife, and modern society is a mass composed of these individual families as its molecules." By using the term "domestic slavery," Engels links women's subservient status to their unpaid domestic labor as two sides of the same coin.

In addition, Engels makes two insightful observations about the consequences of women's subservient status being intrinsic to their role in the patriarchal family. There is: (1) a sexual double standard that requires monogamy *for women only* and (2) the tolerance of domestic violence against women at the hands of their husbands. Engels argues that the monogamous family ideal is based upon fundamental hypocrisy. From its very beginning, to ensure that the patriarch's children were his own, the family was stamped "with its specific character of monogamy for the woman only, but not for the man." In the patriarchal families of Rome or Greece, women were legally restricted to monogamy while men were allowed to practice polygamy.

Even after polygamy was legally abolished in most societies, men continued to enjoy greater sexual freedom. Acts of infidelity on the part of women, which Victorian society condemned in Engels's time (and for which contemporary capitalist society still holds a sexual double standard), are "considered honorable in a man, or, at the worst, a slight moral blemish which he cheerfully bears." To this day, prevailing ideology assumes that men are "naturally" inclined to desire multiple sex partners while women's biology makes them more content with just one.

In addition, Engels observes that due to the ideal of the monogamous family, "adultery became an unavoidable social institution—denounced, severely penalized, but impossible to suppress."[9] Engels argues that the frequency of sex between married men and unmarried women became institutionalized over time. It "flourishes in the most varied forms throughout the whole period of civilization and develops more and more into open prostitution."[10]

Thus, side by side with the development of monogamous marriage grew the commodification of sex in the form of prostitution. "With the rise of the inequality of property," he argues, "wage labor appears . . . and at the same time, as its necessary correlate, the professional prostitution of free women side by side with the forced surrender of the slave."[11] As Engels writes, "monogamy and prostitution are indeed contradictions, but inseparable contradictions, poles of the same state of society."[12]

This observation by Engels is especially insightful since he could probably not have imagined, living in nineteenth-century Victorian England, the degree to which the sexual commodification of women would turn into a massive and highly profitable industry in the century that followed, or that sexual objectification would become such a central feature of the oppression of all women in modern capitalism.

Secondly, in *The Origin* Engels draws attention to the frequency with which women are on the receiving end of domestic violence within the nuclear family—long before the second wave of feminism emerged in the late 1960s and finally made these issues a centerpiece for theory and struggle. Engels describes the drastic decline of women's status as a consequence of the rise of the classic patriarchal family, and the brutality that accompanied it, arguing that the rise of this new family form brought with it a degradation of women that was unknown in preclass societies.

Describing male supremacy within the patriarchal family as "the world historical defeat of the female sex," Engels writes, "The man took command in the home also; the woman was degraded and reduced to servitude; she became the slave of his lust and a mere instrument for the production of children.[13] . . . In order to make certain of the wife's fidelity and therefore the paternity of his children, she is delivered over unconditionally into the power of the husband; if he kills her, he is only exercising his rights."[14]

While in this passage Engels describes the classic patriarchal family norm, domestic violence is not an archaic product of the Middle Ages, as is all too evident today. On the contrary, the right of husbands to beat their wives was legally established by law in early capitalism and continued far beyond that era. In colonial America, husbands were allowed to beat their wives—but not on Sundays or after 8 p.m., to avoid disturbing the peace. Not until 1911 did all US states (except Mississippi) outlaw wife beating. Until 1973, English law permitted husbands to restrain their wives if they attempted to leave. Fathers still "give away" their daughters to their new husbands in Christian marriage, and in some US states it is still impossible to prosecute husbands for raping their wives.[15]

At the same time that Engels offers these valuable insights, the process he describes above is highly unlikely to have taken place as a sudden and single "world historical defeat" of the female sex, resulting from the rise of the patriarchal family. Marx's ethnological notebooks also make clear that Marx, while sharing much of Engels's framework, held a more dialectical view of these historical processes than Engels.

While both Marx and Engels describe the patriarchal family as enormously oppressive to women, Marx's notes also focus on the earlier contradictions that eventually gave way to the rise of class society and a patriarchal family form. Marx describes a much lengthier process that began during the latter stages of primitive communism, establishing some forms of gender inequality well before the existence of large-scale agriculture and the patriarchal family. As Marx observes, "*Paternal authority* . . . began to appear as a feeble influence in the *syndyasmian* [pairing marriage but without exclusive living arrangements], and [it became] fully established under *monogamy* while it passed beyond *all* bounds of reason' in the patriarchal family of the Roman type."[16]

Marx also differs with Engels's view of the future prospects for the institution of monogamy. Despite Engels's scathing attack on enforced monogamy within the nuclear family described above, he nevertheless guesses that socialism will bring with it a flowering of *monogamy*, in the form of "individual sex love"— albeit in conditions of equality, in which men join women in their exclusive commitment to each other.[17]

Marx did not assume that the monogamous family would survive class society as Engels did. On the contrary, he writes in his notes (agreeing with Morgan), "As the *monogamanian* family has improved greatly since the commencement of capitalism, and very sensibly in modern times, it must be supposable that it is still capable of further improvement until the equality of the sexes is attained. Should the *monogamanian* family in the distant future fail to answer the requirements of society, assuming the continuous progress of civilization, it is impossible to predict the nature of its successor." As Brown, whose own research into Marx's notebooks is substantial, comments on this passage, "Marx emphasizes, through his use of underlining, the need and possibility for the 'equality of the sexes [to be] attained.'"[18]

The integration of some key conclusions found in Marx's ethnological notebooks has helped to advance our understanding of the historical processes involved in the rise of women's oppression. And Brown is undoubtedly correct in asserting "Engels remains within a relatively deterministic and unilinear framework, whereas Marx's formulation allows for greater variety in outcomes and for a much greater degree of human agency, especially for women."[19]

These necessary corrections do not diminish Engels's profound contribution. And taken together, Marx and Engels provide a broad theoretical framework that locates the source of women's overall oppression as stemming primarily from their reproductive role within the family and the family's role as an economic unit in class society.

Working-class families have been transformed in many ways since Marx's time, but they have not disappeared as a social institution by any means. The 1960s women's liberation movement successfully challenged the notion that marriage and childrearing should be the sum total of all women's life ambitions, which combined with women's increasing participation in paid labor has led to dramatic changes in traditional family structures.

Fewer women today take their husband's last name upon marriage. Likewise, thanks to the LGBTQ+ movement, more same-sex couples are raising children, challenging gender stereotypes inside families. The rise in divorce has produced many more single-parent households, typically headed by women and living in poverty. As more women have taken on jobs outside the home, many women are having fewer children and doing so later in life. The responsibilities of domestic labor have tended to decrease compared with decades past. While improved household technology is a contributing factor, less time is spent cooking and cleaning because standards of cleanliness are less rigid and home-cooked meals less frequent as a result of women's greater participation in paid labor.

Despite all these changes, however, the essential function of the working-class family for capital remains the same: reproducing labor power. The family's adults shoulder virtually the entire financial responsibility for maintaining its members, whether in a single parent or extended family household, employed or unemployed. The day-to-day responsibilities of family still center around feeding, clothing, cleaning, and otherwise caring for its members, and that responsibility still falls mainly on women. Understanding how and why this is the case will not only theoretically address the source of women's oppression, but also how it affects all women's status in society.

Social Reproduction and Domestic Labor

Since the 1970s, a growing number of married women—now including the majority of women with small children—hold jobs. Married women with children are more likely to work part-time to accommodate their family obligations, and more likely to move out of the workforce temporarily when they have children. But women are nevertheless today a permanent and large part of the workforce, even if individual women tend to move in and out of paid labor or work fewer hours compared with male workers. Capitalism has come to rely upon women as a permanent, low-wage sector of the labor force, located in overwhelmingly female occupations.

Over the last century, women's increasing participation in the workforce has been accompanied by a corresponding reduction in their time spent on domestic labor. As Vogel comments, "By the early 1900s, food preparation was less time-consuming, laundry was in some ways less onerous, and schools had taken over most of the task of teaching skills. More recently, frozen food, microwaves, laundromats, and the increased availability of day care, nursery, kindergarten, and after-school programs have decreased domestic labor even further."[20]

At the same time, it is the enduring role of women's domestic labor inside the working-class family that explains the oppression of women of all classes. "Lack of equality," Vogel argues, "represents a specific feature of women's (and other groups') oppression in capitalist societies. Only subordinate-class women perform domestic labor, . . . but all women suffer from lack of equality in capitalist societies."

Thus, the relations between working-class women and men are unequal inside the family, but so are those between all women and all men throughout society. As Vogel described, "On the one hand, subordinate-class women and men are differentially located with respect to important economic aspects of social reproduction. On the other, all women are denied equal rights. In actual societies, the dynamics of women's subordination respond to this dual positioning, among other factors."[21]

Sexism affects women in all classes of society—just as racism targets people of color of all classes and homophobia affects LGBTQ+ people of all classes. Special oppression is a cross-class phenomenon. This is the only way to explain why the upper echelons of business and government remain overwhelmingly White and male.

At the same time, women are also divided by class, as are all the oppressed. As Marxist-feminist Martha Gimenez comments, while women of all classes share certain experiences of oppression, women of different classes are also simultaneously locked into an antagonistic relationship. Thus, as she notes, crucial class differences between women reflect

> important class and socioeconomic status differences in women's experiences of biological reproduction as well as differences in the organization of social reproduction: the use of paid domestic workers not only by capitalist women but by women affluent enough to afford them highlights how oppression is not something that only men can inflict upon women. The real advances upper-middle-class professional and business women (those earning six-figure salaries) have made in the last 30 years presupposes the existence of a servant stratum, drawn from the less skilled layer of the working class, including a large proportion of women from racial and ethnic minorities, often undocumented immigrants.
>
> While the nature and number of divisions among women varies at the level of social formations, class divisions are common to all capitalist social formations and all social groups (e.g., immigrant populations, races, ethnicities, etc.) are themselves divided by class.[22]

How do Marxists reconcile this seeming contradiction: women of all classes are oppressed under capitalism, yet class differences also divide women? The answer is surprisingly simple, based on the extension of Marx's analysis provided by social reproduction theorists.

If the economic function of the working-class family, so crucial in reproducing labor power for the capitalist system—and at the same time forming the social root of all women's oppression—were to be eliminated, the material basis for women's liberation could be created. This outcome can only begin to materialize with the elimination of the capitalist system, replaced by a socialist society that socializes the domestic labor formerly assigned to women. While a socialist society does not automatically achieve women's liberation, it creates the material basis for doing so, with continued struggle.

Smith explicitly connects women's subordinate role in the family to other facets of women's oppression in society at large: "The oppression of women in class societies quite clearly cannot be reduced to any economic analysis. . . . But the social oppression of women makes no sense without a Marxist analysis of the family." Echoing Engels, she adds, "It is the family system which creates the virgin, the prostitute, pornography and the oppression of women."[23]

NOTES

1 Any analysis of LGBT oppression is entirely absent from both Marx's and Engels's analysis, even though more recent Marxist scholarship has pinpointed the roots of gay oppression, like women's, in the rise of the nuclear family. See, for example, Sherry Wolf, *Sexuality and Socialism: History, Politics and Theory of LGBT Liberation* (Chicago: Haymarket Books, 2009).

2 Neither did their feminist contemporaries challenge certain Victorian assumptions about women's roles. Elizabeth Cady Stanton, a key figure in the radical suffrage movement, delivered a speech at Seneca Falls, New York, in 1892, listing four points regarding the rights of women. The last point stated, "Fourthly, it is only the incidentals of life, such as mother, wife, sister, daughter, that may involve some special duties and training."

3 Lise Vogel, "Domestic Labor Revisited," *Science & Society* (New York: Guilford Press), Vol. 64, number 2, Summer 2000, 165.

4 Karl Marx and Frederick Engels, *The Communist Manifesto* (New York: International Publishers, 1948), 27.

5 Engels, *The Origin of the Family, Private Property and the State* (New York: International Publishers, 1972).

6 The classic patriarchal family is a specific family form that existed among ancient Greeks and Romans, of absolute rule by the male head of the household over its male and female dependent members.

7 Chapter 3 of the 1972 edition of the *Ethnographical Notebooks of Karl Marx* is available at the Marxist Internet Archive: "Marx Engels Selected Works," Marxists Internet Archive. Retrieved from https://www.marxists.org.

8 As Marxist historian Hal Draper agues in "Marx and Engels on Women's Liberation," in *International Socialism* 44 (July/August 1970): "There is a myth, widely accepted among the half-informed, that Morgan's anthropological work is now simply 'outmoded,' like Ptolemaic astronomy, and is rejected by 'modern anthropologists'. . . . [I]n this respect Darwin and Newton are outmoded as well."

9 Engels, *Origin*, 131.

10 Ibid., 129.

11 Ibid., 130.

12 Ibid., 139.

13 Ibid., 120–21.

14 Ibid., 122.

15 "The Power to Make a Difference," *OPDV Bulletin*, the biannual newsletter of the New York State Office for the Prevention of Domestic Violence, Spring 2000.

16 Quoted in Heather A. Brown, *Marx on Gender and the Family* (Leiden, Netherlands: Brill, 2012), 157–58.

17 Engels's concept of "individual sex love" is discussed at length in Draper, "Marx and Engels on Women's Liberation."

18 Heather A. Brown, *Marx on Gender and the Family* (Leiden, Netherlands: Brill 2012), 154.

19 Ibid., 175.

20 Vogel, "Domestic Labor Revisited," 165.

21 Ibid., 165.

22 Martha Gimenez, "Capitalism and the Oppression of Women: Marx Revisited," *Science & Society*, Vol. 69, no. 1, January 2005, 28.

23 Joan Smith, "Women and the Family, Part 2," *International Socialism* 104, January 1978, 13.

4

Sexual Coercion in American Life

EDWIN M. SCHUR

There are, indeed, many good reasons for expecting to find a close link between sex and coercion in modern American society. Coercive sexuality is a predictable corollary of American outlooks on sex. In particular, sexist attitudes and habits, a misguidedly mechanistic approach to the question of what sex is, and the commercializing instinct encouraged under modern capitalism combine to shape our sexual thinking and sexual goals. All these tendencies (and the general cultural values that they reflect) push us in the direction of sexual indifference and insensibility. When one adds the pervasive socioeconomic inequality that depresses and diminishes the lives of so many Americans, the stage is well set for sexual coercion to be widespread.

Under the general conditions of modern life, Toffler and other critics warned, people become disposable. Our distorted thinking about sexuality and the tenacious hold on us of sexist outlooks only serve to exacerbate this broad tendency. Virtually all the aspects of social and sexual relations are conducive to sexual intimidation and victimization. In an era of secondary relations (to recall Kingsley Davis's term), the other person tends to be seen as a means of achieving our own purposes. He or she is not valued intrinsically. Even in the context of supposedly intimate relationships, using the other person may become the actual norm. The prospect of that happening in other situations, then, must be extremely high.

How is this general tendency affected by our more specific ideas regarding sex? The modernization of sex has contributed to an objectified and scientized conception of sexual acts. Sex came to be seen largely as the production of orgasms and the satisfaction of biological needs. It was studied primarily as a matter of physiological capacity and measurable results. From that standpoint, the way in which sexual needs were satisfied was not deemed terribly important. Nor was there much emphasis, really (despite the usual humanistic call for it), on mutuality in sexual relations. Rather, the focus was on sex as something the individual got, or gave. In addition, the positive valuation of sexuality as natural led the biologically oriented sexual modernizers to develop a quantitative theme. They seemed to imply that as regards sexuality (and as Americans tended to assert in so many areas), more is better. High total sexual outlet, it seemed, was good, and a low total outlet bad.

When applied in a context of mutual "pleasuring," and as an antidote to longstanding sexual repression, these new ideas had considerable value. But . . . they produced distortion as well. There has been relatively little discussion of their possible bearing on sexual coercion and violence. It seems clear, however, that thinking of sex in this way—particularly when social relations of all kinds tend to be depersonalized anyway—might facilitate sexual abuse. The individual is encouraged to view sex not only as a need that must be satisfied but also as a "thing" that should be sought and obtained. If it cannot be gotten in more acceptable ways, then perhaps it should be taken—by force, if necessary.

Such a conception of one's sexuality meshes well with the contemporary decline in ability to really see the other person. This ability is impaired by the widespread dissemination of unreal sexual imagery, as well as by the general depersonalization in American life. When such imagery triggers abstracted sexual response, there is a sense in which the actual person on the receiving end of that response isn't really there at all. In addition, the fact that many people in our society are routinely selling their sexual services must also contribute to a dulling of sexual sensitivity. When sexuality can be bought and sold so readily, and treated as a mere service, how much attention must be paid to the person with whom one "has" sex?

That these types of response may make it easier to abuse people sexually should be obvious. A psychological distancing from the other person enables the abuser to disregard the latter's wishes and feelings. (This same basic point has been made regarding the relative ease of killing people through high-altitude bombing and other even more detached techniques of modern warfare.) Such distanced others are more readily conceived of as being there to be used. They can do things for us, or we can with seeming impunity do things to them.

Let me reiterate that, while coerced sex is totally unlike lovemaking, the abuser may nonetheless think that what he (or she) is "getting" is "sex." (Indeed, it is the modernized conception of sexuality just commented on that makes such a belief possible. Only with an orgasm-preoccupied view of sex could coerced sex acts be held to produce "satisfaction.") Based on their interviews with over a hundred convicted rapists, two researchers insist on "the part that sex plays in the crime. The data clearly indicate that from the rapists' point of view rape is in part sexually motivated." They go on to describe rape as "a means of sexual access," and to comment that, "when a woman is unwilling or seems unavailable for sex, the rapist can seize what isn't volunteered."[1] In a similar vein, another writer—who interviewed a general sampling of men regarding their attitudes toward rape—states: "In the conception of sex as a commodity, sex is something a man can buy, sell, get for free, or steal (rape)."[2]

Disposable Women

Sexual indifference within our society provides a general impetus for the use of coercion. Distribution of the results, however, is highly skewed. At least with respect to adults (and it might also be true of child abuse, though at present we cannot be sure) most sexual victimizers are male and most of the victims are female. This is not just due to average disparities in physical strength. As writers on rape and sexual harassment—and on the situation of women more generally—have frequently noted, it reflects the overall social dominance of males and subordination of females. The power that is involved in this patterning of coercion is not just physical. It is social, psychological, economic, and—in the broadest sense—political.

Sexual objectification exhibits this skewed distribution. In our society, it is primarily women who are presented as sex objects. They are presented in that way for—and (the idea lingers) they exist for—the sexual pleasure of men. (In that not-yet-dispelled conception, they also exist to service men in other ways— primarily as housekeepers and childrearers.) When the general status of females is limited (in large measure) to their sexuality, men are likely to see every specific woman primarily as a potential source of sexual satisfaction. The object-like status of women, furthermore, is closely tied up with ideas of sexual property.

Equating women with their sexuality (the process Firestone called "sex privatization") and restricting them in other spheres are two sides of the same (sexist) coin. This extreme sexualization implies limiting women's access to, and not taking them seriously in, nonsexual roles. If they are to be kept in their place, women's freedom of choice must be restricted and their economic dependence on men preserved. Social stigmatization of women, whenever and wherever they step out of line, helps to sustain these limitations.[3]

Much like the alleged pedestal, which in fact helps keep women down, thinking of women as "the sex" helps to ensure their control by men. In this conception their primary use is sexual, and they are all too easily seen as being sexually usable. Presumably, one can conceive of a situation in which men were socially and economically dominant and yet not sexually coercive. However, the trivialization and sexualization of women are highly conducive to such coercion—at least in a society such as ours in which a general pattern of sexual indifference prevails. Furthermore, forced sex is in a way the ultimate indicator, and preserver, of male dominance. Its occurrence and even the perception that it may at any time occur reassure males of their power and help to keep women subordinate.

These conceptions of their dominance, and of woman's secondary (and largely sexual) status, are—as feminists have been insisting—heavily built into the basic socialization of males in our society. Men have learned to respond to women—at least initially, and sometimes more lastingly—not as individuals but in category terms. And, to a large extent, it is a woman's sexual presence that overwhelms other bases for response. In addition, the socialization of most males has strongly endorsed the idea that it is normal for males to be sexually aggressive. This fact lay behind Susan Griffin's claim, in an already-classic discussion of "Rape: The All-American Crime," that "in our society, it is rape itself that is learned."[4]

It should be emphasized here how very closely male conceptions of sexual satisfaction have been tied to images of conquest. Most American men, it is reasonable to believe, still tend to think in terms of "making out" and "scoring." Add the counterpart term for anticipated female acquiescence, "putting out," and one has a capsule summary of culturally approved male outlooks on sex. The crucial point, of course, is that men are *supposed* to try to coerce women into sexual activity.

To the extent this scenario embodied the traditional double standard, "good" women were supposed to say no (however much they desired sexual relations) and to put up resistance by fending off advances. In general, the socialization counterpart of male sexual aggression was female sexual passivity. Citing this theme, feminists depicted women as having been socialized to be victims. In some ways, both sexes were learning their roles in the rape scenario. And this basic learning, we can be fairly certain, continues to be reinforced through pornographic depictions of rape—in which, characteristically, both persons are portrayed as (eventually) enjoying the action.

The most insidious aspect of these learned conceptions is that they are so closely linked to our general ideas concerning masculinity and femininity. As Diana Russell has aptly suggested, a "virility mystique" inclines men to associate sex with coercion and violence. Real men are supposed "to be able to separate their sexual responsiveness from their needs for love, respect, and affection." They are expected to respond not to specific female persons but to the presence or depiction of any sexy woman. They are supposed to be able to perform sexually in each and every such instance. Russell concludes, I think sensibly, that "if men were not taught to separate sexual feelings from feelings of warmth and caring, rape would be unthinkable, and fewer men would impose their sexuality on unwilling women in other less extreme ways too."[5]

The other side of this equation has been the female's induced submissiveness and absorption in fantasies of romance. Germaine Greer argued, in *The Female Eunuch*, that the masculine-feminine distinction in modern society rests on a "castration" of women: "Men have commandeered all the energy and streamlined it into an aggressive conquistadorial power, reducing all heterosexual contact to a sadomasochistic pattern."[6] Sexual autonomy and assertiveness are not, in this pattern, open to women. As a recent analysis of mass-marketed romances brought out, these popular depictions reinforce the belief that "pleasure for women is men."[7] Attracting them, arousing their lust, and perhaps being overwhelmed by them is what women are for.

By no means do I wish to imply that giving women equal opportunity with respect to sexual coercion would be a good thing. Free choice to formulate one's own sexual desires, and the ability to pursue them actively, ought to be maximized. But this must be done without encouraging victimization. The equalizing of a sexual distortion cannot be viewed as a social gain. My comments here are intended only to underscore the key role our prevailing gender system plays in perpetuating and shaping coercive sexuality. There is little doubt that that role is substantial. The individual (male as well as female) becomes "disposable" under conditions of social modernity. But for women this situation has long obtained—not just as a vague threat—as a recurring feature of their daily lives.

Inequality and Violence

Modern American society is characterized by high levels of socioeconomic inequality and interpersonal violence. These conditions, separately and in combination, help to determine present-day patterns of sexual victimization. The reference to combined (or additive) effects is important, for most experts are agreed that a great deal of the violence in our society is due to the inequality. One of the major theories about the occurrence of large-scale violence attributes it to "relative deprivation." As the term relative deprivation indicates, you don't have to be in absolutely dire straits to feel deprived—and, as a consequence, frustrated, resentful, and hostile. This helps to explain how there can be such high levels of violence in a society that many think of as being extremely affluent.

* * *

In our media-saturated society, the constant depiction of affluent lifestyles—to which almost all Americans are exposed—can only increase a poor person's feelings of frustration and resentment. Author Charles Silberman has aptly noted that "the poor may be invisible to the rest of us, but we are not invisible to them; their television sets thrust them inside our homes every day of the week. For members of the lower class, consequently, life is a desperate struggle to maintain a sense of self in a world that offers little to nourish, and much to destroy it."[8] To the extent feelings of relative deprivation lie behind some acts of sexual coercion, these media presentations may have special significance.

The playboy mentality, much routine advertising, and perhaps even the basic conception of women as objects to be appropriated and displayed convey the message that sexuality is linked to affluence. As I mentioned earlier, the poor person therefore feels doubly deprived. Among males, there must be a nagging realization that one is not going to be able to get either the affluence or the women who are depicted as most desirable. (And, though its influence on sexual coercion is not as great, poor women must have a sense that achieving the pinnacle of sexual desirability is probably beyond them.)

For the man especially—given our culture's definition of masculinity—taking sex through force or violence may be one kind of response. It may represent an eruption of general and pent-up frustration and hostility. Yet it may also sometimes be seen as a "solution" of sorts to the perceived sexual deprivation. (In this regard, I would stress once more that our mechanistic conception of sexuality allows the belief that what one is getting to such acts is "sex.") We know, of course, that not all poor people commit acts of sexual coercion. And, if we had complete information about those incidents of coercive sexuality that are not currently recorded, we might well find that middle-class rates exceed those of the lower classes.

However, that is no reason to doubt that poverty and the attitudes it engenders help to determine the extent of sexual coercion in our society. Researchers often want to test formal theories quantitatively, to determine the main cause of rape, or child abuse, or harassment. Given our tendency to individualize, especially, it is understandable that "cause" might be thought of in terms of supposed differences between offenders and nonoffenders. The question "Why do some persons do this, while others do not?" is certainly a legitimate one to pursue. On the other hand, when a behavior pattern becomes endemic to the entire society, the very issue of widespread prevalence becomes at least as important as that of individual differentiation.

From that standpoint, statistical comparison studies of individuals tend to be inadequate. A less rigorous but more far-reaching examination of multiple factors that may contribute to the overall situation may be appropriate. I think that is true in this case. Some instances of sexual coercion may be traceable primarily to poverty and its frustrations, others primarily to the depersonalizing and sexist outlooks that affect all of us. Often, some combination of these influences maybe involved. Statistical tabulations and correlations are not going to enable us to isolate a single primary cause of a pattern that is this pervasive. Depersonalization, sexism, and inequality all help to shape it.

So, too, does the violence that suffuses American life. Since the 1960s, several national commission reports (on crime, civil disorders, and violence) have documented and publicized the prevalence of interpersonal violence in our society. It has come to be recognized that violence has had a central place in our history,[9] and hence cannot be viewed as some contemporary aberration. Criminologists frequently note that violent crimes comprise only a small proportion of all criminal offenses. Yet it is generally agreed that the US exhibits extremely high rates of crimes of violence. . . .

Crime rates do fluctuate over time, for a number of reasons. For example, the age structure of the population (proportion in the most crime-prone categories), the extent to which people are concentrated in urban settings, and (as regards officially recorded statistics) the level of police resources and activity can all affect crime rates. However, nobody disputes that there is a great deal of violent crime in America today. Nor that fear of being a victim of such violence is widespread.[10] Even though, statistically, the probability of such victimization is lower than that of being killed or injured accidentally, such fear is understandable and its personal impact all too real.

If Americans are highly fearful of violence, they may nonetheless become inured to it. The greatest danger from television depictions of violence, I believe, comes through an indirect and long-term impact of that sort. There is much less likelihood of specific crimes being caused by direct imitation of fictional enactments of violence than of the audience developing a general sense that violent behavior is now routine. If and when such a feeling does develop, then people—in all kinds of situations—may be more likely to resort to violence than they would have been otherwise. The daily litany of local killings reported on the evening news may, in that sense, be at least as consequential as more lurid, but fictional, portrayals of crime and violence.

For our purposes here, media (and pornographic) depictions of sexuality are, obviously, of special relevance. Wide exposure to depictions that link sex and violence can—again, more probably through subtle attitudinal change then by direct example—lead people increasingly to associate the two. As I mentioned earlier, the likelihood is not great that an individual will immediately go out and commit a rape following a specific exposure to pornography. But if Americans are fed a steady diet of such depictions, it could, more generally, erode those sensibilities that should help to deter sexual coercion. Extensive use of sadomasochistic imagery in the highly popular rock music videos is one sign that this diet is growing. Violent pornography readily and inexpensively available . . . is another.

If we go beyond sheer physical violence to consider the more general question of coercion, we again find ample supporting "tradition" in our culture. Americans place a high value on results, and have not always been too scrupulous regarding the means used to achieve them. Notwithstanding our alleged disposition to support the underdog, we are quick to exploit personal advantage. Our culture's approval, or at the very least acceptance, of "cutthroat competition"—whether in business, athletics, or elsewhere—enables Americans to disregard the costs to others of their efforts to get ahead. And, similarly, pressuring other people to do things they might not want to do is in the vaunted tradition of American salesmanship.

I have suggested four general factors that may contribute to the prevalence of sexual coercion: depersonalization, leading to sexual indifference; the persisting devaluation (and sexualization) of women; pervasive socioeconomic inequality; and culturally induced habituation to force and violence. My emphasis, in these comments, has been on features of our culture and social system that are conducive to people's committing acts of sexual victimization. But the same sociocultural factors produce victims as well as offenders. Inequality, especially, contributes to both sides of the victimization process but in an interestingly unbalanced way.

Given the current feminization of poverty (in which females represent a large proportion of those below the official poverty line),[11] we would expect many women, too, to develop feelings of relative deprivation that could lead to violent behavior. Presumably some instances of maternal child abuse reflect such a situation. Generally speaking, however, felt deprivation does not drive women into becoming sexual victimizers. Here we see the combination of inequality and basic socialization coming into play. It is men whose status has rested on demonstrating (along with financial success) their aggressiveness through sexual conquest and control. Women have been socialized to be relatively passive, and to play the sexual object role. Sexual aggressiveness, at least until very recently, has been deemed inappropriate—indeed unfeminine—behavior.

When women have experienced feelings of sexual deprivation, they have tended to internalize them rather than to try by aggressive means to assuage them. And by the same token the frustrations of economic deprivation have pushed women in different directions from those characteristically taken by men. The latter are much more likely to become sexually coercive in such situations. And when they adopt illicit means of alleviating their financial plight, men will tend toward methods we define as masculine—for example, armed robbery, which women as well would be perfectly capable of in physical terms. Women will deal with this situation in ways more consistent with approved female roles. Thus, their major cash-producing deviance will involve selling their sexuality. (Among men, but on a considerably smaller scale, homosexual prostitution represents a similar adaptation to economic insufficiency.)

The Balance of Power

As regards situations of direct sexual coercion, economic dependency may, again, contribute to women's victimization. Power, we must remind ourselves, is central to the entire phenomenon of coercive sexuality. Equality and coercion are mutually exclusive concepts; one can only be coerced by someone who has greater power. This power is not only physical, though physical power may indeed sometimes be involved. (Thus, depending on their strength relative to that of a male attacker, some women may be at a physical disadvantage when assaulted sexually. Weak and unaggressive males in prison may be especially vulnerable to "homosexual" rape—usually carried out, in fact, by heterosexuals. The vulnerability to abuse by adults of young children of either sex also is, in part, physical.)

But more significant, overall, are disparities in social (perhaps also psychological) and economic power. As I have noted, the widespread subjection of women to sexual victimization is part and parcel of their general subordination and devaluation in our society. That women's claims of victimization are not often enough taken seriously, nor the offenders severely punished, are further indicators of women's relatively low social power. This general condition is regularly seen in the high vulnerability to coercion of specific women—especially in certain key situations.

Marriage is one of these, and employment another. (A third area—less significant because of its more limited social class distribution and because the woman's financial independence is likely to be greater—is psychotherapy. Recent disclosures of sexual abuse of female patients by male therapists have highlighted the power disparity and authority-dependency aspects of this relationship.)[12] In both of these crucial life situations, financial and social dependency frequently mean that a woman has extremely limited freedom of action. She cannot easily walk away from the situation, if equally secure alternatives are not available to her. This helps to explain the high vulnerability of women to abuse by their husbands. It also highlights the predicament of women workers who are being subjected to sexual harassment.

Reducing Sexual Coercion

America did not invent sexual coercion. But its current cultural priorities and system of social stratification certainly encourage its prevalence. No doubt some amount of forced sex has existed in most societies. Yet ours seems unusually coercion-prone. It is important to recognize this as a general state of affairs. We are not going to alter the situation very much by doing something to (or "for") individual rapists, harassers, and child abusers. For coercion to be significantly reduced, our cultural priorities and approved behavior patterns—as well as the distribution of income and opportunity—are going to have to change.

Actually, in this area more than on other sexual issues, law enforcement does have a role to play. These situations are very different from the victimless crime ones. As regards some potential rapists, for example—especially the more affluent ones (who have more to lose by being caught and punished)—stringent laws may have some real deterrent effect. Then, too, these offenses are so horrendous that a strong symbolic statement (through law) condemning them seems warranted. Even so, and however just we may find it to punish the violators, we need to recognize that the effects of such measures can only be limited ones.

Ultimately, the root conditions themselves will have to be confronted. This means an all-out attack on sexism and depersonalization. But it also means that we must reduce the inequities and priorities that our form of capitalism sustains. Based in part on data drawn from anthropology, Julia and Herman Schwendinger assert that a society's "mode of production" is the most basic determinant of the prevalence of rape. They state further that "the exploitative modes of production that have culminated in the formation of class societies have either produced or intensified sexual inequality and violence."[13]

The problem in applying this to modern societies is that virtually all of them (socialist societies included) are class societies of some sort. Modern capitalism has no monopoly on exploitation or violence, nor on sexism. On the other hand, our particular no-holds-barred version of capitalism does seem to provide special encouragement of coercion. Whether uniquely or not, it does, I believe, promote the "amoral individualism" and "callous and instrumental indifference to suffering"[14] that the Schwendingers cite as major factors in our rape situation. Whatever one thinks, overall, about the relative merits of socialism and capitalism, the fact remains that rape (and other sexual coercion) will not be significantly reduced if the present systemic inequality is allowed to persist. As the Schwendingers note, such a reduction requires addressing the economic underpinnings of violence and violent crime in general.[15] On this point, at the very least, their argument seems unassailable.

NOTES

1 Diana Scully and Joseph Marolla, "Riding the Bull at Gilley's: Convicted Rapists Describe the Rewards of Rape," *Social Problems* 32 (February 1985), 257.
2 Timothy Beneke, *Men on Rape* (New York: St. Martin's Press, 1982), 26.
3 See Schur, Labeling Women Deviant, on the reproduction of gender in everyday interaction. See also Nancy Henley and Jo Freeman, "The Sexual Politics of Interpersonal Behavior," in Jo Freeman (ed.), *Women: A Feminist Perspective*, 2nd ed. (Palo Alto, CA: Mayfield, 1979).
4 Susan Griffin, "Rape: The All-American Crime," *Ramparts* (September 1971), as reprinted in Chappell, Geis, and Geis (eds.), *Forcible Rape*, 50.
5 Diana E. H. Russell, *The Politics of Rape* (New York: Stein and Day, 1975), 263–64.
6 Germaine Greer, *The Female Eunuch* (New York: Bantam, 1972), 7.
7 Ann Barr Snitow, "Mass Market Romance: Pornography for Women is Different," in *Powers of Desire*, eds. Ann Snitow, Christine Stansell, and Sharon Thompson (New York: Monthly Review Press, 1983), 253.
8 Joseph Julian and William Kornblum, Social Problems, 5th ed. (Englewood Cliffs, NJ: Prentice-Hall, 1986), 201–2.
9 Hugh Davis Graham and Ted Robert Gurr, *The History of Violence in America* (New York: Bantam, 1969).
10 See the discussion in Silberman, *Criminal Violence, Criminal Justice*, 3–20; see also John E. Conklin, *The Impact of Crime* (New York: Macmillan, 1975).
11 For a concise discussion, see Barbara Ehrenreich, *The Hearts of Men* (Garden City, NY: Doubleday Anchor Books, 1983), 172–82.
12 See Joanna Bunker Rohrbaugh, *Women: Psychology's Puzzle* (New York: Basic Books, 1979), 393–95; and Phyllis Chesler, *Women and Madness* (New York: Avon, 1972).
13 Julia R. Schwendinger and Herman Schwendinger, *Rape and Inequality* (Beverly Hills, CA: Sage, 1983), 179.
14 Ibid., 204.
15 Ibid., 220.

Global Gender Violence

A Template for Exploration

Scholars and activists around the globe continue to investigate occurrences of gender violence and provide explanations that illuminate its causes. Given the tremendous incidence of abuse and the varieties of contexts in which it occurs, it is not possible to give a full range of examples and responses in this text. Instead, we offer essays that we hope will provide a foundation for thinking broadly about the subject including patterns of abuse and some encouraging responses. Use this material as a lens to view your own culture and a platform from which to consider others.

Examples taken from news headlines abound. The US government begins attempts to bar victims of intimate partner violence from applying for asylum (Nazario 2019). The Australian Prime Minister, responding to an in-depth report on decades of institutionalized sexual abuse against children, issues an apology to thousands of victims (Baidawi 2018). In India, a combination of social status, ingrained beliefs about women's lesser worth, and a dramatic imbalance of men to women caused by sex-selective abortions in favor of boys may have led to a crisis of sexual assaults (Khan 2016).

These examples are points on a large map: they are neither representative nor exhaustive, yet they provide a window into how gender violence is both global and specific. People everywhere experience violence through the practice of gendered beliefs and behaviors that reflect both the particularities of the locale and the pervasive presence of gender imbalance. All societies struggle with systemic beliefs that sustain patterns of abuse and support perpetrator impunity. Whether the subject is sexual harassment on the job, laws that diminish culpability for men who are violent toward women, sexual exploitation of refugees and migrants, or the removal of genitalia in an effort to control sexual desire, these actions develop and are supported within a framework of gendered violence. In every society social relations have been influenced by the cultural, political, and economic conditions within which they emerged. Gender, as a central organizing principle, mediates the distribution of power, and power facilitates violence.

Anthropologists view all normative, sanctioned social traditions as cultural, raising questions about outsider response to practices deemed repugnant. Yet, international women's rights groups generally agree on a number of customs as violent including early and forced marriages, genital cutting, female feticide or sex selection, "honor killings," widow burning, foot binding, widow humiliation or required sex, young girls consecrated to temples as sex workers or handmaidens, caste-based discrimination and violence, and body-altering practices such as eating disorders and plastic surgery in order to conform to an ideal of beauty (Merry 2009, 127). Responses to these issues require reflection about one's own culture's culpability in gender violence and sensitivity to historical and current power dynamics between cultures.

Cultural Bias

What any one of us may find a repulsive or violent practice depends on what our own culture dictates. Okin (1999) argues that when a culture's beliefs regarding treatment of women are determined and articulated by men (who hold more power), women's interests and safety may not be considered. In her view we must pay special attention to inequalities within groups in order to evaluate whose interests are served by cultural practices. Expanding on Okin, Merry (2009), claims that "certain human rights are universal, fundamental, and inalienable and thus cannot and should not be overridden by cultural and religious traditions" (84). These perspectives illustrate the tension between traditional anthropology's insistence on cultural relativism and a growing feminist human rights viewpoint.

A narrow focus on harmful practices to women in non-Western societies masks damaging traditions that exist in every culture. The danger for those of us in the West is that we may focus on the "othered" nature of phenomena such as genital cutting and honor-based killings and avoid thinking about how our own practices and social institutions support gender violence. Acknowledging the horrors that people experience in other cultures does not diminish the experiences in our own backyards. For example, concerns about honor may be a motivating factor for Western perpetrators of intimate partner violence.

The Role of Political Power and Women's Representation

One measurement of power is political presence. Of the 191 countries that report data on women in parliamentary and presidential systems of government, there are four without a single woman and twenty-eight with fewer than 10 percent representation of women. Only Rwanda, Cuba, and Bolivia have more than 50 percent of representation by women (Inter-Parliamentary Union 2018). Even in countries that have adopted quota systems to increase the participation of women, progress has been slow (Londoño 2017). Of the 146 nations in a World Economic Forum survey, seventy have had women leaders (Geiger and Kent 2017). In the US, where political leadership is associated with tremendous power, sexism and stereotypes continue to interfere with the capacity for a woman to be elected to the office of the president (Friedman 2016).

While the lack of political representation and the prevalence of gender violence may not be directly connected, and it is certain that women are not monolithic in their political beliefs, it is likely that many social conditions that disproportionately affect them would get more attention if women's voices were included in the political arena (see Devlin and Elgie 2008 and Sawer 2000). There is strong evidence that when women are in positions to affect policy and legislation women's rights are advanced (Tripp, 2015). A study of seventy countries found that the single most important indicator of policy change affecting violence against women was feminist mobilization (Htun and Weldon 2012). Evaluation of effective methods is particularly important at a moment when "current trends of increased conservatism, militarism, and reliance on religion as a sole source of legislation are becoming global. . . . [and if] unchecked, the risks to women are increasingly coupled with devastating manifestations of violence in the private and public spheres" (Women's Learning Partnership 2012).

States and Failed States

States play a central role in constructing gender violence and sanctioning (in both meanings of the word) its practices. Certainly, the stability of states plays a role—where the rule of law is weak, vulnerable populations suffer from lack of a responsive or functioning authority. At the same time, strong states, particularly if they lack women's representation and feminist organizing, may not develop legislation to address gender violence, may overlook gender violence in political agendas, and may even create laws and policies to undercut means to address it. Where political systems collapse and new forms of organization develop, progress on gender violence can be lost. Weakened political systems may have little energy to expend on expanding progressive agendas and then may rely on or turn a blind eye toward familiar traditional practices that disadvantage women.

The Effect of Armed Conflict

Armed conflict creates tremendous social instability. The United Nations (UN) defines "conflict-related sexual violence" to include "rape, sexual slavery, forced prostitution, forced pregnancy, forced abortion, enforced sterilization, forced marriage and any other form of sexual violence of comparable gravity perpetrated against women, men, girls or boys that is directly or indirectly linked . . . to a conflict" (United Nations Security Council 2016, 1). In many cases the victims of conflict-related sexual violence are persecuted minorities (ibid.) and estimates indicate that only one in ten or twenty cases is documented (ibid., 3).

In the past, most conflicts occurred between recognized states. We are in a new era in which conflicts are increasingly fomented by nonstate actors, making it extremely difficult to negotiate resolutions. Terrorists target women and girls as a "premeditated, systematic and strategic" effort to both create chaos and drive people out of their homes and villages and to serve as a lure for recruiting new members (ibid., 8). Simons (2018) reports that the jihadist chief of police in Timbuktu, Mali, forced young women to marry fighters sometimes only for days or weeks to justify forcing them to have sex with the men. Another horrifying example of harm is the reported use of hormonal treatments of young girls by the self-styled Islamic State in order to hasten their physical maturity to increase their value for "sale and sexual exploitation" (United Nations Security Council 2016, 8). Since the perpetrators in these cases are nonstate actors there are no established paths through which organizations can pressure them to alter their abusive policies.

At the writing of this volume, there are twenty-five active wars and armed conflicts (Council on Foreign Relations 2018). Though women are increasingly represented as combatants in some conflicts, they are still by far the minority of aggressors (Buchowska 2016). Though all people suffer the immense horrors of war, women are particularly vulnerable as they may be targeted as spoils of war and are frequently subjected to rape by combatants, sometimes as a precise tactic of war (ibid.). Women suffer very specific, and often disproportionate, consequences of collateral damage (Hynes 2004), though the term itself is problematic since many of the effects that women suffer are intentionally inflicted.

In some areas of conflict, men may become habituated to violence and sexual violence may become normalized. Due to post-conflict disorder and weakened institutions, basic resources may be lacking, making people more vulnerable to abuse. Patriarchal control often intensifies during periods of chaos and crisis (Cosgrove 2016) thus constricting women within the home or encouraging early marriage, sometimes to combatants, to provide protection. Although rape as an aspect of war has been acknowledged throughout human history, it took the establishment of the international criminal tribunals for Rwanda and the former Yugoslavia for sex crimes to be expressly prohibited under international law (Pocar 2012, iv).

In 2016, the UN released a report on conflict-related sexual violence that highlights areas of particular concern. It found, for example, that male victims of sexual violence lack any legal protection in 62 countries (United Nations Security Council 2016, 4) and that in some conflict areas women are required to accept marriage to their rapist (ibid., 5, 15). While it is evident that conflict opens a space for sexual assault, rape is not universally present in conflict zones. Alcoff points out that "in an extensive study of 48 armed conflicts in Africa, 64% . . . were found *not* to involve any form of sexual violence" (2018, 25).

Without diminishing the destructive forces of war, scholars offer some examples that illustrate that gender equality has advanced following conflicts. Women in France gained the vote in part due to their contributions to the Resistance during World War II (Offen 2000), and Tripp (2015) finds that, following conflict in several African countries, women's political representation increased as they were pushed into hitherto masculine roles by historical forces.

Gendered norms may impoverish men's experiences in the world through expectations that they suppress the gentler aspects of themselves and thus deny their own humanity. When this leads, in extreme cases, to committing interpersonal violence toward others, or to encouraging men to take up arms in conflict, the detrimental effects on the violent male can be considered a form of gender violence. The frequently debilitating results of warfare on the warriors provides an example.

International Concerns and Western Hegemony

In a highly connected world, where information is at our fingertips, people are increasingly aware of events in distant places. The knowledge gained provides us with the opportunity to develop opinions and to respond through action. Though international concern about gender violence often highlights very specific manifestations, caution is required. Do our responses reflect an imposition of our own culturally situated values? How can we respond with sensitivity and respect?

Although it is beyond the capacity of this volume to create a comprehensive list of incidence or prevalence of gender violence worldwide, we will address some specific examples that have gained prominence in the imagination of the public. Genital cutting (the term preferred by African activists, often called Female Genital Mutilation, or FGM in the West) and what is referred to as "honor killings" are among the most discussed and most sensitive illustrations. In addition, the recent surge in migration in many parts of the world has created openings for various forms of gender violence in vulnerable populations.

In the parts of Africa where genital cutting (the removal of all or part of a woman's genitalia) is most practiced, it is sometimes embraced as a symbol of post-colonial national solidarity against attempts of the West to impose a form of cultural hegemony (Merry 2009, 135). However, there are active efforts to stem its occurrence in countries where local women's groups object to the practice and base their responses on culturally sensitive efforts (Duggar 2011, Shell-Duncan et al. 2011). Senegal, Guinea, and Burkina Faso, all in the region of West Africa where genital cutting is widely practiced, have seen thousands of villages abandon the practice through community-led education focused on health and human rights (Advocates for Youth 2008).

Honor-based killings, defined as efforts to maintain or regain a sense of family honor threatened by actual or perceived actions of the victim, take place within a larger context of honor-based value systems. Though these structures are prevalent within cultures where women are subordinate to men (Gill 2014), it is important to recognize that women are subordinate in many ways across many (if not all) cultures. If we view honor killings as a reflection of "culturally constituted ways of 'being a man' that link masculinity with authorized acts of aggression" (ibid., 3), we must also ask how any culture reflects masculinity with authorized, or at least tolerated, aggressive acts against women.

The legal situation for perpetrators of honor crimes is undergoing change. Honor crimes may be prosecuted (if at all) under separate legal statutes that allow perceived impugned honor as a mitigating circumstance to reduce punishment. However, some countries have recently altered their legal codes to increase criminalization for such crimes (United Nations Office on Drugs and Crime 2014).

Migration, whether due to economic need such as crop failure, famine, and lack of jobs or due to a desire for safety and stability, increases vulnerability to gender violence. This problem has reached crisis proportions as many people find that life in their countries of origin offers no safe haven from war or poverty, and droughts that lead to starvation increase along with global warming. The UN estimates that 70.8 million people are forced from their homes, a mass of humanity hard to comprehend (Dargas 2019). Migrants lack legal standing and are often unprotected. For example, sex may be demanded in exchange for passage across a border or through a territory, and minor refugees are exploited for trafficking, prostitution, and sexual slavery with people perceived to be LGBTQ+ targeted for torture (United Nations Security Council 2016).

National and International Efforts to Address Gender Violence

The World Health Organization (WHO) (2013) estimates that more than one-third of the world's population of women is affected by intimate partner violence and nonpartner sexual assault. Though the WHO report reflects an astounding number of victims, the total would be much higher if it included other forms of gender violence. However, as the report asserts, the variance in prevalence both within and between countries is a hopeful indicator that such violence is not inevitable.

Despite women's lack of political power in governance, people all across the globe work to address gender violence. Their attempts take many forms, reflecting the analysis, needs, and resources available in the societies themselves. Local and international women's rights efforts to analyze and address gender violence increased in scope and activity starting in the late 1960s, originally in the West, inspiring movements in countries around the world. Since the 1990s international bodies have often stepped into the lacuna where states have failed to act. Both the 1993 World Conference on Human Rights in Vienna and the 1995

Fourth World Conference on Women in Beijing helped to more prominently situate concerns about many forms of gender violence around the world. The UN, nongovernmental organizations, and a tremendous variety of feminist organizations, often led by women, have contributed immeasurably to the progress that has been made to highlight areas of concern and to find solutions for gender violence (see Sanford, Stefatos, and Salvi 2016).

In recent decades, international actors have increased their vigilance about and response to gender violence. The UN contains an Office of the Special Representative on Sexual Violence in Conflict that works to "[engage] in high-level advocacy to generate national ownership, leadership and responsibility" where civil society has eroded (United Nations Security Council 2014, 2). The UN also deploys Women Protection Advisors to ensure that gender analysis is included in peacekeeping and special political missions to help prevent conflict-related sexual violence (ibid.).

One interestingly hopeful path to reduce gender violence is through "the autonomous mobilization of feminists in domestic and transnational contexts" (Htun and Weldon 2012, 548). Indeed, it is the adoption of feminist ideas that has affected the success of policies to address violence against women. Civil action, rooted in feminist principles, appears to be effective (ibid.).

Still, vigilance is mandatory. On the same day that the *New York Times* reported that the French government enacted a slate of measures to combat intimate partner violence (Breeden 2019), they also reported that the newly elected conservative government of Spain declared the intention to repeal an existing law that is intended to stop violence against women. Both actions took place on International Day for the Elimination of Violence Against Women (Minder 2019).

This introduction provides a brief overview of cultural and historical conditions that affect how gender violence is articulated in local contexts. It is only a sketch. There are many additional case studies available to illustrate the fluidity of cultural definitions and practices about gender, sexuality, and violence. Indeed, culturally specific social conditions provide the basis for the great variation that still exists in gender relations worldwide. The chapters in this section include a broad range of disciplines and perspectives that provide a starting point to understand both the similarities and differences in gender violence across cultures and contribute to a macro-level analysis that is so often lost in public discussions.

SUGGESTIONS FOR FURTHER READING

Aili Mari Tripp, Myra Marx Ferree, and Christina Ewig, *Gender, Violence, and Human Security: Critical Feminist Perspectives*, 2013

Maria Eriksson Baaz and Maria Stern, *Sexual Violence as a Weapon of War?: Perceptions, Prescriptions, Problems in the Congo and Beyond*, 2013

Cynthia Enloe, *The Big Push: Exposing and Challenging the Persistence of Patriarchy*, 2017

Aisha K. Gill, Carolyn Strange, and Karl Roberts (eds.), *'Honour' Killing and Violence: Theory, Policy and Practice*, 2014

Sally Engle Merry, *Gender Violence: A Cultural Perspective*, 2009

Anatomy Lesson

Cherríe Moraga

A black woman and a small beige one talk about their bodies.
About putting a piece of their anatomy in their pockets
upon entering any given room.

When entering a room full of soldiers who fear hearts,
you put your heart in your back pocket,
the black woman explains. It is important, not to intimidate.
The soldiers wear guns, *not* in their back pockets.

You let the heart fester there. You let the heart seethe.
You let the impatience of the heart build and build
until the power of the heart hidden begins to be felt in the room.
Until the absence of the heart begins to take on the shape
of a presence.
Until the soldiers look at you and begin to beg you
to open up your heart to them, so anxious are they to see
what it is they fear they fear.

Do not be seduced.

Do not forget for a minute that the soldiers wear guns.
Hang onto your heart.
Ask them first what they'll give up to see it.
Tell them that they can begin with their arms.
Only then will *you* begin to negotiate.

5

The Socio-Cultural Context of Rape

A Cross-Cultural Study

PEGGY REEVES SANDAY

In her comprehensive and important analysis of rape, Susan Brownmiller says that "when men discovered that they could rape, they proceeded to do it" and that "from prehistoric times to the present rape has played a critical function" (1975, 14–15). The critical function to which Brownmiller refers has been "to keep all women in a constant state of intimidation, forever conscious of the knowledge that the biological tool must be held in awe for it may turn to weapon with sudden swiftness borne of harmful intent" (1975, 209).

Brownmiller's attribution of violence to males and victimization to females strums a common theme in Western social commentary on the nature of human nature. Most of the popularizers of this theme present what amounts to a sociobiological view of human behavior which traces war, violence, and now rape to the violent landscape of our primitive ancestors, where, early on, the male tendency in these directions became genetically programmed in the fight for survival of the fittest. Human (viz. male) nature is conceived as an ever-present struggle to overcome baser impulses bequeathed by "apish" ancestors. (For examples of this general theme, see Ardrey 1966; Lorenz 1966; Tiger 1969.)

The research described in the present chapter departs from the familiar assumption that male nature is programmed for rape, and begins with another familiar, albeit less popular, assumption that human sexual behavior, though based in a biological need "is rather a sociological and cultural force than a mere bodily relation of two individuals" (Malinowski 1929, xxiii). With this assumption in mind, what follows is an examination of the socio-cultural context of sexual assault and an attempt to interpret its meaning. By understanding the meaning of rape, we can then make conjectures as to its function. Is it, as Susan Brownmiller suggests, an act that keeps all women in a constant state of intimidation, or is it an act that illuminates a larger social scenario?

This chapter examines the incidence, meaning, and function of rape in tribal societies. Two general hypotheses guided the research: first, the incidence of rape varies cross-culturally; second, a high incidence of rape is embedded in a distinguishably different cultural configuration than a low incidence of rape. Using a standard cross-cultural sample of 156 tribal societies, the general objectives of the chapter are:

1. to provide a descriptive profile of "rape prone" and "rape free" societies;
2. to present an analysis of the attitudes, motivations, and socio-cultural factors related to the incidence of rape.

Description of the Evidence

In most societies for which information on rape was available, rape is an act in which a male or a group of males sexually assaulted a woman. In a few cases, descriptions of women sexually assaulting a male or homosexual rape are reported. This study, however, was oriented exclusively to the analysis of rape committed by males against women.

The standard cross-cultural sample published by Murdock and White (1969) formed the basis for this research. This sample offers to scholars a representative sample of the world's known and well-described societies. The complete sample consists of 186 societies, each "pinpointed" to an identifiable sub-group of the society in question at a specific point in time. The time period for the sample societies ranges from 1750 BCE (Babylonians) to the late 1960s. The societies included in the standard sample are distributed relatively equally among the following six major regions of the world: Sub-Saharan Africa, Circum-Mediterranean, East Eurasia, Insular Pacific, North America, South and Central America.

This analysis of rape was part of a larger study on the origins of sexual inequality (see Sanday 1981). Due to the amount of missing information on the variables included in this larger study, thirty of the standard sample societies were excluded, reducing the final sample size to 156. Since many of the variables included in the larger study were pertinent to the analysis of the socio-cultural context of rape, the same sample was employed here.

The information for coding the variables came from codes published in the journal *Ethnology*; library materials; and the Human Relations Area Files. The data obtained from the latter two sources were coded by graduate students in anthropology at the University of Pennsylvania using codes developed by me on one-third of the standard sample societies. When the coding was completed, a random sample of societies was selected for checking. The percentage of items on which coders and checkers agreed averaged 88 percent of the twenty-one variables checked for each society. Disagreements were resolved either by myself or still another coder after rechecking the material.

There was a significant discrepancy between the number of societies for which information was obtained on rape for this study and that obtained by other authors employing the same sample. Broude and Greene (1976) were able

TABLE 5.1. Comparison of Two Codes for Rape

Society No.[a]	Society Name	Sanday Code[b]		Broude & Greene Code[b]
		Rape Code	Type of Rape[c]	
11	Kikuyu	3	Ceremonial rape	No information
19	Ashanti	1	Rape is rare or absent	No information
13	Mbuti	1	Rape is rare or absent	Agrees with Sanday Code
14	Mongo	1	Rape is rare or absent	Agrees with Sanday Code
28	Azande	3	Rape of enemy women	Disagrees (rape rare)
			Rape cases reported	
41	Tuareg	1	Rape is rare or absent	No information
60	Gond	1	Rape is rare or absent	No information
66	Mongols	1	Rape is rare or absent	No information
70	Lakher	1	Rape is rare or absent	Agrees with Sanday Code
91	Arunta	3	Ceremonial rape	No information
108	Marshallese	3	Gang rape is accepted	Agrees with Sanday Code
127	Saulteaux	3	Rape used as threat	No information
143	Omaha	3	Rape used as punishment	Disagrees (rape absent)
158	Cuna	1	Rape is rare or absent	Agrees with Sanday Code
163	Yanomamo	3	Rape of enemy women	Agrees with Sanday Code
166	Mundurucu	3	Rape used as punishment	Agrees with Sanday Code
169	Jivaro	1	Rape is rare or absent	No information
179	Shavante	3	Rape used as punishment	No information

[a] Refers to standard sample number listed by Murdock and White (1969).
[b] See Table 5.2 for the two rape codes.
[c] For each of the societies listed, the ethnographic descriptions of the incidence of rape are presented later in this chapter.

to find information on the frequency of rape in only thirty-four of the standard sample societies, whereas for this study information was obtained for ninety-five of these societies. This discrepancy raises questions about the operational definitions of rape employed in the coding.

Although the codes used in the two studies were similar, my definition of "rape prone" included cases in which men rape enemy women, rape is a ceremonial act, and rape may be more a threat used by men to control women in certain ways than an actuality. Broude and Greene appear to have excluded such incidents from their coding and to have focused only on the intra-societal incidence of uncontrolled rape. The differences in these operational definitions are apparent from the information presented in Table 5.1.

A sub-sample of societies are listed in Table 5.1 along with the codes used in this study and the code given by Broude and Greene (1976). Broude and Greene report no information in nine societies where information on the incidence of rape was recorded in this study. The two codes agree in seven out of

TABLE 5.2. Cross-Cultural Incidence of Rape

Sanday Code	No. and % of Societies		Broude & Greene Code (1976, 417)	No. and % of Societies	
Incidence of Rape (RA4)—	N	%	Frequency of Rape	N	%
1. *Rape Free.* Rape is reported as rare or absent	45	47%	1. Absent	8	24%
2. Rape is reported as present; no report of frequency or suggestion that rape is not atypical.	33	35%	2. Rare: isolated cases	12	35%
3. *Rape Prone.* Rape is accepted practice used to punish women, as part of a ceremony, or is *clearly* an act of moderate to high frequency carried out against own women or women of other societies.	17	18%	3. Common: not atypical	14	41%
Total	95	100%		34	100%

the remaining nine and disagree in two cases. Broude and Greene report that among the Azande rape is a rare occurrence, while in this study the Azande were classified as rape prone due to the practice of raiding for wives. Broude and Greene report that rape is absent among the Omaha, whereas I found evidence from several sources that rape is present. The ethnographic descriptions that led to my rape codes for the eighteen societies listed in Table 5.1 can be found in the following sections profiling "rape prone" and "rape free" societies.

Broude and Greene (1976) find that rape is absent or rare in 59 percent of the thirty-four societies for which they found information on the frequency of rape (see Table 5.2). They say that rape is "common, not atypical" in the remaining 41 percent. In this study, 47 percent of the societies were classified as "rape free"; 35 percent were classified in an intermediate category; and 18 percent were classified as "rape prone" (see Table 5.2). Thus both studies support the first general hypothesis of this study: sexual assault is not a universal characteristic of tribal societies. The incidence of rape varies cross-culturally.

Profiles of "Rape Prone" Societies

In this study a "rape prone" society was defined as one in which the incidence of rape is high, rape is a ceremonial act, or rape is an act by which men punish or threaten women.

An example of a "rape prone" society is offered by Robert LeVine's (1959) description of sexual offenses among the Gusii of southwestern Kenya. In the

European legal system which administers justice in the district where the Gusii live, a heterosexual assault is classified as rape when a medical examination indicates that the hymen of the alleged victim was recently penetrated by the use of painful force. When medical evidence is unobtainable, the case is classified as "indecent assault." Most cases are of the latter kind. The Gusii do not distinguish between rape and indecent assault. They use the following expressions to refer to heterosexual assault: "to fight" (a girl or woman); "to stamp on" (a girl or woman); "to spoil" (a girl or woman); "to engage in illicit intercourse." All of these acts are considered illicit by the Gusii. LeVine uses the term *rape* "to mean the culturally disvalued use of coercion by a male to achieve the submission of a female to sexual intercourse" (1959, 965).

Based on court records for 1955 and 1956 LeVine estimates that the annual rate of rape is 47.2 per 100,000 population. LeVine believes that this figure grossly underestimates the Gusii rape rate. During the same period the annual rape rate in urban areas of the US was 13.85 per 100,000 (13.1 for rural areas). Thus, the rate of Gusii rape is extraordinarily high.

Normal heterosexual intercourse between Gusii males and females is conceived as an act in which a man overcomes the resistance of a woman and causes her pain. When a bride is unable to walk after her wedding night, the groom is considered by his friends "a real man" and he is able to boast of his exploits, particularly if he has been able to make her cry. Older women contribute to the groom's desire to hurt his new wife. These women insult the groom, saying:

> "You are not strong, you can't do anything to our daughter. When you slept with her you didn't do it like a man. You have a small penis which can do nothing. You should grab our daughter and she should be hurt and scream—then you're a man." (LeVine 1959, 969)

The groom answers boastfully:

> "I am a man! If you were to see my penis you would run away. When I grabbed her she screamed. I am not a man to be joked with. Didn't she tell you? She cried—ask her!" (LeVine 1959, 969)

Thus, as LeVine says (1959, 971), "legitimate heterosexual encounters among the Gusii are aggressive contests, involving force and pain-inflicting behavior." Under circumstances that are not legitimate, heterosexual encounters are classified as rape when the girl chooses to report the act.

LeVine estimates that the typical Gusii rape is committed by an unmarried young man on an unmarried female of a different clan. He distinguishes between three types of rape: rape resulting from seduction, premeditated sexual assault, and abduction (1959).

Given the hostile nature of Gusii sexuality, seduction classifies as rape when a Gusii female chooses to bring the act to the attention of the public. Premarital sex is forbidden, but this does not stop Gusii boys from trying to entice girls to intercourse. The standard pose of the Gusii girl is reluctance, which means that it is difficult for the boy to interpret her attitude as being either willing or unwilling. Misunderstandings between girl and boy can be due to the eagerness of the boy and his inability to perceive the girl's cues of genuine rejection, or to the girl's failure to make the signs of refusal in unequivocal fashion. The boy may discover the girl's unwillingness only after he has forced himself on her.

Fear of discovery may turn a willing girl into one who cries rape. If a couple engaging in intercourse out of doors is discovered, the girl may decide to save her reputation by crying out that she was being raped. Rape may also occur in cases when a girl has encouraged a young man to present her with gifts but then denies him sexual intercourse. If the girl happens to be married, she rejects the boy's advances because she is afraid of supernatural sanctions against adultery. Out of frustration, the boy (who may not know that the girl is married) may resort to rape, and she reports the deed. In some cases, one or more boys may attack a single girl in premeditated sexual assault. The boys may beat the girl badly and tear her clothing. Sometimes the girl is dragged off to the hut of one of them and forced into coitus. After being held for a couple of days the girl is freed. In these cases, rupture of the hymen and other signs of attack are usually present.

The third type of rape occurs in the context of wife abduction. When a Gusii man is unable to present the bridewealth necessary for a normal marriage and cannot persuade a girl to elope, he may abduct a girl from a different clan. The man's friends will be enlisted to carry out the abduction. The young men are frequently rough on the girl, beating her and tearing her clothes. When she arrives at the home of the would-be lover, he attempts to persuade her to remain with him until bridewealth can be raised. Her refusal is ignored and the wedding-night sexual contest is performed with the clansmen helping in overcoming her resistance.

Of these three types of rape, the first and third are unlawful versions of legitimate patterns. Seduction is accepted when kept within the bounds of discretion. Abduction is an imitation of traditional wedding procedures. Abduction lacks only the legitimizing bridewealth and the consent of the bride and her parents. In both of these cases LeVine says, "there is a close parallel between the criminal act and the law-abiding culture pattern to which it is related." Seduction and abduction classify as rape when the girl chooses to report the incident.

Data collected from the standard cross-cultural sample allows us to place the hostility characterizing Gusii heterosexual behavior in cross-cultural perspective. Broude and Greene (1976), who published codes for twenty sexual practices, find that male sexual advances are occasionally or typically hostile in one-quarter (26 percent) of the societies for which information was available. They found that males were typically forward in verbal (not physical) sexual overtures in 40 percent of the societies, that females solicited or desired physical aggression in male sexual overtures in 11 percent of the societies, and that males did not make sexual overtures or were diffident or shy in 23 percent of the societies.

Examination of a variety of "rape prone" societies shows that the Gusii pattern of rape is found elsewhere but that it is by no means the only pattern that can be observed. For example, in several societies the act of rape occurs to signal readiness for marriage and is a ceremonial act. Since this act signifies male domination of female genitals, its occurrence was treated as a diagnostic criterion for classification as "rape prone."

Among the Kikuyu of East Africa it is reported that in former times, as part of initiation, every boy was expected to perform the act of ceremonial rape called *Kuihaka muunya* (to smear oneself with salt earth) in order to prove his manhood. It was thought that until a boy had performed the act of rape he could not have lawful intercourse with a Kikuyu woman and hence could not marry. During the initiation period boys would wander the countryside in bands of up to one hundred in number. The object of each band was to find a woman on whom to commit the rape. The ideal woman was one from an enemy tribe who was married. In practice it appears that the ceremonial rape consisted of nothing more than masturbatory ejaculation on the woman's body or in her presence. Immediately after the act the boy was able to throw away the paraphernalia which marked him with the status of neophyte (Lambert 1956).

Rape marks a girl as marriageable among the Arunta of Australia. At age fourteen or fifteen the Arunta girl is taken out into the bush by a group of men for the vulva-cutting ceremony. A designated man cuts the girl's vulva, after which she is gang-raped by a group of men which does not include her future husband. When the ceremony is concluded the girl is taken to her husband and from then on no one else has the right of access to her (Spencer and Gillen 1927).

In other rape-prone societies, rape is explicitly linked to the control of women and to male dominance. Among the Northern Saulteaux the assumption of male dominance is clearly expressed in the expectation that a man's potential sexual rights over the woman he chooses must be respected. A woman who turns a man down too abruptly insults him and invites aggression. There is a Northern Saulteaux tale about a girl who was considered too proud because she refused to marry. Accordingly, a group of medicine men lured her out into the bush, where she was raped by each in turn (Hallowell 1955). Such tales provide women with a fairly good idea of how they should behave in relation to men.

The attitude that women are "open" for sexual assault is frequently found in the societies of the Insular Pacific. For example, in the Marshall Islands one finds the belief that "every woman is like a passage." Just as every canoe is permitted to sail from the open sea into the lagoon through the passage, so every man is permitted to have intercourse with every woman (except those who are excluded on account of blood kinship). A trader, well acquainted with the language and customs of one group of Marshall Islanders, reported the following incident. One day while standing at the trading post he saw twenty young men enter the bushes, one after another. Following the same path, he discovered a young girl stretched out on the ground, rigid and unconscious. When he accused the young men of cruel treatment they replied: "It is customary here for every young man to have intercourse with every girl" (Erdland 1914, 98–99).

In tropical-forest societies of South America and in Highland New Guinea it is fairly frequent to find the threat of rape used to keep women from the men's houses or from viewing male sacred objects. For example, Shavante women were strictly forbidden to observe male sacred ceremonies. Women caught peeking are threatened with manhandling, rape, and disfigurement (Maybury-Lewis 1967).

Perhaps the best-known example of rape used to keep women away from male ritual objects is found in the description of the Mundurucu, a society well known to anthropologists due to the work of Robert and Yolanda Murphy. The Mundurucu believe that there was a time when women ruled and sex roles were reversed, with the exception that women could not hunt. During that time, it is said, women were the sexual aggressors and men were sexually submissive and did women's work. Women controlled the "sacred trumpets" (the symbols of power) and the men's houses. The trumpets are believed to contain the spirits of the ancestors, who demand ritual offering of meat. Since women did not hunt and could not make these offerings, men were able to take the trumpets from them, thereby establishing male dominance. The trumpets are secured in special chambers within the men's houses, and no woman can see them under penalty of gang rape. Such a threat is necessary because men believe that women will attempt to seize from the men the power they once had. Gang rape is also the means by which men punish sexually "wanton" women (Murphy and Murphy 1974).

Another expression of male sexual aggressiveness, which is classified as rape in this study, is the practice of sexually assaulting enemy women during warfare. The Yanomamo, described by Napoleon Chagnon and Marvin Harris, are infamous for their brutality toward women. The Yanomamo, according to Harris (1977), "practice an especially brutal form of male supremacy involving polygyny, frequent wife beating, and gang rape of captured enemy women." The Yanomamo, Harris says, "regard fights over women as the primary causes of their wars" (1977, 69). Groups raid each other for wives in an area where marriageable women are in short supply due to the practice of female infanticide. The number of marriageable women is also affected by the desire on the part of successful warriors to have several wives to mark their superior status as "fierce men." A shortage of women for wives also motivates Azande (Africa) warfare. Enemy women were taken by Azande soldiers as wives. Evans-Pritchard calls these women "slaves of war" and says that they were "not regarded very differently from ordinary wives, their main disability being that they had no family or close kin to turn to in times of trouble" (1971, 251). The absence of close kin, of course, made these women more subservient and dependent on their husbands.

Another source on the Azande discusses how the act of rape when committed against an Azande woman is treated. If the woman is not married, this source reports, the act is not treated as seriously. If the woman is married, the rapist can be put to death by the husband. If the rapist is allowed to live, he may be judged guilty of adultery and asked to pay the chief twenty knives (the commonly used currency in marriage exchanges) and deliver a wife to the wronged husband. This source indicates that the rape of a woman is not permitted, but the punishments are established, suggesting that rape is a frequent occurrence (Lagae 1926).

Among some American Indian buffalo hunters, it is not uncommon to read that rape is used as a means to punish adultery. There is a practice among the Cheyenne of the Great Plains known as "to put a woman on the prairie." This means that the outraged husband of an adulterous woman invites all the unmarried members of his military society to feast on the prairie where they each rape the woman (Hoebel 1960). Among the Omaha, a woman with no immediate kin who commits adultery may be gang-raped and abandoned by her husband (Dorsey 1884). Mead reports that the Omaha considered a "bad woman" fair game for any man. No discipline, no set of standards, other than to be cautious of an avenging father or brother and to observe the rule of exogamy, Mead says, kept young men from regarding rape as a great adventure. Young Omaha men, members of the Antler society, would prey upon divorced women or women considered loose (Mead 1932).

Summarizing, a rape-prone society, as defined here, is one in which sexual assault by men of women is either culturally allowable or largely overlooked. Several themes interlink the above descriptions. In all, men are posed as a social group against women. Entry into the adult male or female group is marked in some cases by rituals that include rape. In other cases, rape preserves the ceremonial integrity of the male group and signifies its status vis-à-vis women. The theme of women as property is suggested when the aggrieved husband is compensated for the rape of his wife by another man, or when an adulterous woman is gang-raped by her husband and his unmarried compatriots. In these latter cases, the theme of the dominant male group is joined with a system of economic exchange in which men act as exchange agents and women comprise the medium of exchange. This is not to say that rape exists in all societies in which there is ceremonial induction into manhood, male secret societies, or compensation for adultery. For further illumination of the socio-cultural context of rape we can turn to an examination of rape-free societies.

Profiles of "Rape Free" Societies

Rape-free societies are defined as those where the act of rape is either infrequent or does not occur. Forty-seven percent of the societies for which information on the incidence or presence of rape was available (see Table 5.2) were classified in the rape-free category. Societies were classified in this category on the basis of the following kinds of statements found in the sources used for the sample societies.

Among the Taureg of the Sahara, for example, it is said that "rape does not exist, and when a woman refuses a man, he never insists nor will he show himself jealous of a more successful comrade" (Blanguernon 1955, 134). Among the Pygmies of the Ituri forest in Africa, while a boy may rip off a girl's outer bark cloth, if he can catch her, he may never have intercourse with her without her permission. Turnbull (1965), an anthropologist who lived for some time among the Pygmies and became closely identified with them, reports that he knew of no cases of rape. Among the Jivaro of South America rape is not recognized as such, and informants could recall no case of a woman violently resisting sexual intercourse. They say that a man would never commit such an act if the woman resisted, because she would tell her family and they would punish him. Among the Nkundo Mongo of Africa it is said that rape in the true sense of the word— that is, the abuse of a woman by the use of violence—is most unusual. If a woman does not consent, the angry seducer leaves her, often insulting her to the best of his ability. Rape is also unheard of among the Lakhers, and in several villages the anthropologist was told that there had never been a case of rape.

Other examples of statements leading to the classification of rape free are listed as follows:

Cuna (South America), "Homosexuality is rare, as is rape. Both . . . are regarded as sins, punishable by God." (Stout 1947, 39)

Khalka Mongols (Outer Mongolia), "I put this question to several well-informed Mongols:—what punishment is here imposed for rape? . . . one well-educated lama said frankly: 'We have no crimes of this nature here. Our women never resist.'" (Maiskii 1921, 98)

Gond (India), "It is considered very wrong to force a girl to act against her will. Such cases of ghotul-rape are not common . . . If then a boy forces a girl against her will, and the others hear of it, he is fined." (Elwin 1947, 656)

The above quotes may obscure the actual incidence of rape. Such quotes, leading to the classification of societies as "rape free," achieve greater validity when placed within the context of other information describing heterosexual interaction.

There is considerable difference in the character of heterosexual interaction in societies classified as "rape prone" when compared with those classified as "rape free." In "rape free" societies women are treated with considerable respect, and prestige is attached to female reproductive and productive roles. Interpersonal violence is minimized, and a people's attitude regarding the natural environment is one of reverence rather than one of exploitation. Turnbull's description of the Mbuti Pygmies, of the Ituri forest in Africa, provides a prototypical profile of a "rape free" society (1965).

Violence between the sexes, or between anybody, is virtually absent among the net-hunting Mbuti Pygmies when they are in their forest environment. The Mbuti attitude toward the forest is reflective of their attitude toward each other. The forest is addressed as "father," "mother," "lover," and "friend." The Mbuti say that the forest is everything—the provider of food, shelter, warmth, clothing, and affection. Each person and animal is endowed with some spiritual power which "derives from a single source whose physical manifestation is the forest itself." The ease of the Mbuti relationship to their environment is reflected in the relationship between the sexes. There is little division of labor by sex. The hunt is frequently a joint effort. A man is not ashamed to pick mushrooms and nuts if he finds them, or to wash and clean a baby. In general, leadership is minimal and there is no attempt to control, or to dominate, either the geographical or human environment. Decision making is by common consent; men and women have equal say because hunting and gathering are both important to the economy. The forest is the only recognized authority of last resort. In decision making, diversity of opinion may be expressed, but prolonged disagreement is considered to be "noise" and offensive to the forest. If husband and wife disagree, the whole camp may act to mute their antagonism, lest the disagreement become too disruptive to the social unit (see Turnbull 1965).

The essential details of Turnbull's idyllic description of the Mbuti are repeated in other "rape free" societies. The one outstanding feature of these societies is the ceremonial importance of women and the respect accorded the contribution women make to social continuity, a respect that places men and women in relatively balanced power spheres. This respect is clearly present among the Mbuti and in more complex "rape free" societies.

In the West African kingdom of Ashanti, for example, it is believed that only women can contribute to future generations. Ashanti women say:

> I am the mother of the man. . . . I alone can transmit the blood to a king. . . . If my sex die in the clan then that very clan becomes extinct, for be there one, or one thousand male members left, not one can transmit the blood, and the life of the clan becomes measured on this earth by the span of a man's life. (Rattray 1923, 79)

The importance of the feminine attributes of growth and reproduction are found in Ashanti religion and ritual. Priestesses participate with priests in all major rituals. The Ashanti creation story emphasizes the complementarity and inseparability of male and female. The main female deity, the Earth Goddess, is believed to be the receptacle of past and future generations as well as the source of food and water (Rattray 1923, 1927). The sacred linkage of earth-female-blood makes the act of rape incongruous in Ashanti culture. Only one incident of rape is reported by the main ethnographer of the Ashanti. In this case the man involved was condemned to death (Rattray 1927, 211).

In sum, rape-free societies are characterized by sexual equality and the notion that the sexes are complementary. Though the sexes may not perform the same duties or have the same rights or privileges, each is indispensable to the activities of the other (see Sanday 1981 for examples of sexual equality). The key to understanding the relative absence of rape in rape-free as opposed to rape-prone societies is the importance, which in some cases is sacred, attached to the contribution women make to social continuity. As might be expected, and as will be demonstrated below, interpersonal violence is uncommon in rape-free societies. It is not that men are necessarily prone to rape; rather, where interpersonal violence is a way of life, violence frequently achieves sexual expression.

Approaches to the Etiology of Rape

Three general approaches characterize studies of the etiology of rape. One approach focuses on the broader socio-cultural milieu; another turns to individual characteristics. The first looks at how rapists act out the broader social script; the second emphasizes variables like the character of parent-child interaction. A third approach, which may focus on either individual or social factors, is distinguishable by the assumption that male sexual repression will inevitably erupt in the form of sexual violence. These approaches, reviewed briefly in this section, guided the empirical analysis of the socio-cultural context of rape in tribal societies.

Based on his study of the Gusii, LeVine (1959) hypothesizes that four factors will be associated with the incidence of rape cross-culturally:

1. severe formal restrictions on the nonmarital sexual relations of females;
2. moderately strong sexual inhibitions on the part of females;
3. economic or other barriers to marriage that prolong the bachelorhood of some males into their late twenties;
4. the absence of physical segregation of the sexes.

The implicit assumption here is that males who are denied sexual access to women will obtain access by force unless men are separated from women.

Such an assumption depicts men as creatures who cannot control their sexual impulses, and women as the unfortunate victims.

LeVine's profile of the Gusii suggests that broader social characteristics are related to the incidence of rape. For example, there is the fact that marriage among the Gusii occurs almost always between feuding clans. The Gusii have a proverb that states, "Those whom we marry are those whom we fight" (1959, 966). The close correspondence between the Gusii heterosexual relationship and intergroup hostilities suggests the hypothesis that the nature of intergroup relations is correlated with the nature of the heterosexual relationship and the incidence of rape.

The broader approach to the etiology of rape is contained in Susan Brownmiller's contention that rape is the means by which men keep women in a state of fear. This contention is certainly justified in societies where men use rape as a threat to keep women from viewing their sacred objects (the symbol of power) or rape is used to punish women. In societies like the Mudurucu, the ideology of male dominance is upheld by threatening women with rape. Just as the quality of intergroup relations among the Gusii is reflected in heterosexual relations, one could suggest that the quality of interpersonal relations is reflected in the incidence of rape. In societies where males are trained to be dominant and interpersonal relations are marked by outbreaks of violence, one can predict that females may become the victims in the playing out of the male ideology of power and control.

A broader socio-cultural approach is also found in the work of Wolfgang and Ferracuti (1967) and Amir (1971). Wolfgang and Ferracuti present the concept of the subculture of violence that is formed of those from the lower classes and the disenfranchised. The prime value is the use of physical aggression as a demonstration of masculinity and toughness. In his study of rape, Amir placed the rapist "squarely within the subculture of violence" (Brownmiller 1975, 181). Rape statistics in Philadelphia showed that in 43 percent of the cases examined, rapists operated in pairs or groups. The rapists tended to be in the fifteen to nineteen age bracket, the majority were not married, and 90 percent belonged to the lower socio-economic class and lived in inner-city neighborhoods where there was also a high degree of crime against the person. In addition, 71 percent of the rapes were planned. In general, the profile presented by Amir is reminiscent of the pattern of rape found among the Kikuyu, where a band of boys belonging to a guild roamed the countryside in search of a woman to gang-rape as a means of proving their manhood and as a prelude to marriage. Brownmiller (1975, 181) summarizes Amir's study with the following observations:

> Like assault, rape is an act of physical damage to another person, and like robbery it is also an act of acquiring property: the intent is to "have" the female body in

the acquisitory meaning of the term. A woman is perceived by the rapist both as hated person and desired property. Hostility against her and possession of her may be simultaneous motivations, and the hatred for her is expressed in the same act that is the attempt to "take" her against her will. In one violent crime, rape is an act against person and property.

The importance of the work of Wolfgang and Ferracuti, Amir, and Brownmiller's observations lies in demonstrating that rape is linked with an overall pattern of violence and that part of this pattern includes the concept of woman as property. From the short descriptions of rape in some of the societies presented above, it is clear rape is likely to occur in what I would call, to borrow from Wolfgang, cultures of violence. Rape-prone societies, as noted, are likely to include payment to the wronged husband, indicating that the concept of women as property also exists. This concept is not new to anthropology. It has been heavily stressed in the work of Levi-Strauss, who perceives tribal women as objects in an elaborate exchange system between men.

The second type of approach to the understanding of rape focuses on the socialization process and psychoanalytic variables. This approach is reflected in the following quote from the conclusions of David Abrahamsen, who conducted a Rorschach study on the wives of eight convicted rapists in 1954. Abrahamsen (1960, 165) says:

> The conclusions reached were that the wives of the sex offenders on the surface behaved toward men in a submissive and masochistic way but latently denied their femininity and showed an aggressive masculine orientation; they unconsciously invited sexual aggression, only to respond to it with coolness and rejection. They stimulated their husbands into attempts to prove themselves, attempts which necessarily ended in frustration and increased their husbands' own doubts about their masculinity. In doing so, the wives unknowingly continued the type of relationship the offender had had with his mother. There can be no doubt that the sexual frustration which the wives caused is one of the factors motivating rape, which might be tentatively described as a displaced attempt to force a seductive but rejecting mother into submission.

Brownmiller (1975, 179) includes this quote in her analysis of police-blotter rapists, and her reaction to it is rather interesting. She rejects Abrahamsen's conclusions because they place the burden of guilt not on the rapist but on his mother and wife. The fact of the matter is that dominance cannot exist without passivity, as sadism cannot exist without masochism. What makes men sadistic and women masochistic, or men dominant and women passive, must be studied as part of an overall syndrome. Abrahamsen's conclusions certainly apply to Gusii males and females. With respect to the way in which Gusii wives invite sexual aggression from their husbands consider the following description of various aspects of Gusii nuptials:

> ... the groom in his finery returns to the bride's family where he is stopped by a crowd of women who deprecate his physical appearance. Once he is in the house of the bride's mother and a sacrifice has been performed by the marriage priest, the women begin again, accusing the groom of impotence on the wedding night and claiming that his penis is too small to be effective. ... When the reluctant bride arrives at the groom's house, the matter of first importance is the wedding night sexual performance. ... The bride is determined to put her new husband's sexual competence to the most severe test possible. She may take magical measures which are believed to result in his failure in intercourse. ... The bride usually refuses to get onto the bed: if she did not resist the groom's advances she would be thought sexually promiscuous. At this point some of the young men may forcibly disrobe her and put her on the bed. ... As he proceeds toward sexual intercourse she continues to resist and he must force her into position. Ordinarily she performs the practice known as *ogotega*, allowing him between her thighs but keeping the vaginal muscles so tense that penetration is impossible. ... Brides are said to take pride in the length of time they can hold off their mates. (LeVine 1959, 967–69)

The relations between parents and children among the Gusii also fit Abrahamsen's conclusions concerning the etiology of rape. The son has a close and dependent relationship with his mother. The father is aloof from all his children but especially his daughters. The father's main function is to punish, which means that for the Gusii girl, her early connection with men is one of avoidance and fear. On the other hand, the relationship of the Gusii boy with his mother is characterized by dependence and seduction.

Studies of the etiology of rape suggest several hypotheses that can be tested cross-culturally. These hypotheses are not opposed; they are stated at different explanatory levels. One set phrases the explanation in socio-cultural terms, the other in psycho-cultural terms. Still another, only touched on above, suggests that male sexuality is inherently explosive unless it achieves heterosexual outlet. This latter assumption, implicit in LeVine's hypotheses mentioned above, also draws on the notion most recently expressed in the work of Stoller (1979) that sexual excitement is generated by the desire, overt or hidden, to harm another. If the latter were the case, we would be led to believe that rape would exist in all societies. The argument presented here, however, suggests that rape is an enactment not of human nature but of socio-cultural forces.

Thus, the prevalence of rape should be associated with the expressions of these forces. Some of these expressions and their correlation with the incidence of rape are examined in the next section.

Socio-Cultural Correlates of Rape

Four general hypotheses are suggested by the work of LeVine, Brownmiller, Abrahamsen, Wolfgang, and Amir. These hypotheses are:

1. sexual repression is related to the incidence of rape;
2. intergroup and interpersonal violence is enacted in male sexual violence;
3. the character of parent-child relations is enacted in male sexual violence;
4. rape is an expression of a social ideology of male dominance.

These hypotheses were tested by collecting data on: variables relating to child rearing; behavior indicating sexual repression; interpersonal and intergroup violence; sexual separation; glorification of the male role and an undervaluation of the female role.

All but the first of the general hypotheses listed above were supported. There is no significant correlation between variables measuring sexual repression and the incidence of rape. Admittedly, however, sexual repression is very difficult to measure. The variables may not, in fact, be related to sexual abstinence. These variables are: length of the post-partum sex taboo (a variable that indicates how long the mother abstains from sexual intercourse after the birth of a child); attitude toward premarital sex (a variable that ranges between the disapproval and approval of premarital sex); age at marriage for males; and the number of taboos reflecting male avoidance of female sexuality.

The correlations support the hypothesis that intergroup and interpersonal violence is enacted in sexual violence against females. Raiding other groups for wives is significantly associated with the incidence of rape. The intensity of interpersonal violence in a society is also positively correlated with the incidence of rape, as is the presence of an ideology that encourages men to be tough and aggressive. Finally, when warfare is reported as being frequent or endemic (as opposed to absent or occasional) rape is more likely to be present.

The character of relations between parents and children is not strongly associated with the incidence of rape. When the character of the father-daughter relationship is primarily indifferent, aloof, cold, and stern, rape is more likely to be present. The same is true when fathers are distant from the care of infants. However, there is no relationship between the nature of the mother-son tie (as measured in this study) and the incidence of rape.

There is considerable evidence supporting the notion that rape is an expression of a social ideology of male dominance. Female power and authority is lower in rape-prone societies. Women do not participate in public decision making in these societies, and males express contempt for women as decision makers. In addition, there is greater sexual separation in rape-prone societies, as indicated by the presence of structures or places where the sexes congregate in single-sex groups.

The correlates of rape strongly suggest that rape is the playing out of a socio-cultural script in which the expression of personhood for males is directed by, among other things, interpersonal violence and an ideology of toughness. If we see the sexual act as the ultimate emotional expression of the self, then it comes as no surprise that male sexuality is phrased in physically aggressive terms when other expressions of self are phrased in these terms. This explanation does not rule out the importance of the relationship between parents and children, husbands and wives. Raising a violent son requires certain behavior patterns in parents, behaviors that husbands may subsequently act out as adult males. Sexual repression does not explain the correlations. Rape is not an instinct triggered by celibacy, enforced for whatever reason. Contrary to what some social scientists assume, men are not animals whose sexual behavior is programmed by instinct. Men are human beings whose sexuality is biologically based and culturally encoded.

Conclusion

Rape in tribal societies is part of a cultural configuration that includes interpersonal violence, male dominance, and sexual separation. In such societies, as the Murphys (1974, 197) say about the Mundurucu: "men . . . use the penis to dominate their women." The question remains as to what motivates the rape-prone cultural configuration. Considerable evidence (see Sanday 1981) suggests that this configuration evolves in societies faced with depleting food resources, migration, or other factors contributing to a dependence on male destructive capacities as opposed to female fertility.

In tribal societies women are often equated with fertility and growth, men with aggression and destruction. More often than not, the characteristics associated with maleness and femaleness are equally valued. When people perceive an imbalance between the food supply and population needs, or when populations are in competition for diminishing resources, the male role is accorded greater prestige. Females are perceived as objects to be controlled as men struggle to retain or to gain control of their environment. Behaviors and attitudes prevail that separate the sexes and force men into a posture of proving their manhood. Sexual violence is one of the ways in which men remind themselves that they are superior. As such, rape is part of a broader struggle for control in the face of difficult circumstances. Where men are in harmony with their environment, rape is usually absent.

The insights garnered from the cross-cultural study of rape in tribal societies bear on the understanding and treatment of rape in our own. Ours is a heterogeneous society in which more men than we like to think feel that they do not have mastery over their destiny and who learn from the script provided by nightly television that violence is a way of achieving the material rewards that all Americans expect. It is important to understand that violence is socially and not biologically programmed. Rape is not an integral part of male nature but the means by which men programmed for violence express their sexual selves. Men who are conditioned to respect the female virtues of growth and the sacredness of life do not violate women. It is significant that in societies where nature is held sacred, rape occurs only rarely. The incidence of rape in our society will be reduced to the extent that boys grow to respect women and the qualities so often associated with femaleness in other societies—namely, nurturance, growth, and nature. Women can contribute to the socialization of boys by making these respected qualities in their struggle for equal rights.

6

Sexual Violence as a Weapon during the Guatemalan Genocide

VICTORIA SANFORD, SOFÍA DUYOS ÁLVAREZ-ARENAS,
AND KATHLEEN DILL

Judge Yassmin Barrios and her tribunal made world history on May 10, 2013, when they found former Guatemalan dictator José Efraín Ríos Montt guilty of crimes against humanity and genocide—the first time ever that a head of state had been convicted of these crimes in a national court. The eighty-year prison sentence was the just conclusion of a court process that was nearly derailed by threats to witnesses, presidential declarations denouncing the trial, and over one hundred appeals by the defense team. Perseverance, courage, and a commitment to the rule of law on the part of the survivors, prosecutors, and tribunal judges repeatedly pushed the case back on track. Although ten days later a corrupt constitutional court annulled the verdict on technical grounds,[1] the genocide sentence was an unforgettable moment in the historic struggle for justice in Guatemala. It was also the first time a Guatemalan court recognized the systematic rape and torture to which Maya women were subjected during Ríos Montt's reign of terror.

Beginning on March 19, 2013, the court heard 102 witnesses (94 for the prosecution and 8 presented by the defense) and 68 expert testimonies. The tribunal also reviewed hundreds of documents. The nine lawyers for the defense used every stalling tactic possible to avoid reaching the verdict—filing more than one hundred separate appeals. As the trial wore on, Guatemalans read about it in newspapers, watched news coverage on television, and listened to it live on national radio and on the internet. This brought the testimonies of survivors into the homes of any Guatemalans willing to learn how criminal state violence destroyed hundreds of thousands of individual lives and families, and in hundreds of cases annihilated entire Maya communities.[2]

Like the genocide itself, the organized use of sexual violence by the state was a public secret. Though it was not the central focus of the court case, the information had long been available from human rights reports, survivor testimonies, and truth commission reports. Reports from both the Commission for Historical Clarification (CEH 1999) and the Catholic Church's Nunca Más project (REMHI 1998) documented the fact that the army systematically deployed sexual violence as a counterinsurgency weapon. Sexual violence was ordered by the high command and enshrouded with impunity by official denial. During the war, army soldiers and other security officers were responsible for 94.3 percent of all sexual violence against women (CEH 1999; Rompiendo el Silencio 2006, 32).[3] Of the 1,465 cases of rape reported (CEH 1999, 23), fully one-third of the victims were minor girls (CEH 1999 23).[4] Women who survived bore the physical and psychological consequences, including pregnancy and sexually transmitted diseases, as well as the social stigma attached to victims of rape (REMHI 1998, 210).

While female witnesses recounted in detail how they were gang-raped by army soldiers, indigenous women observing the trial covered their heads with their shawls in solidarity. Witness Elena de Paz Santiago told the court what Guatemalan soldiers did to her at the army base when she was a child: "I was 12 when I was taken to the army base with other women. The soldiers tied my feet and hands. . . . They put a rag in the mouth . . . and started raping me . . . I do not even know how many soldiers had a turn. . . . I lost consciousness and blood ran from my body. When I came to, I was unable to stand" (Sentencia por genocidio 2014, 514). The fact that the prosecution called Ms. de Paz Santiago and other women as witnesses, and that their testimonies support claims that sexual violence was systematically used as a genocide strategy, signals a relatively new development in the practice of international law.

Sexual violence has long been explained as an unfortunate outcome of war in which men are placed in extraordinary circumstances that provoke aberrant behavior. This is no longer a tenable theory. The work of the International Criminal Court, the United Nations Special Rapporteur on Violence against Women, feminist scholars, and human rights advocates has done much to reframe the issue. This conceptual shift was clearly expressed by the United Nations Special Rapporteur on Violence against Women, who reported in 2009 that studies of wartime rape "conclusively demonstrate that sexual violence is not an outcome of war, but that women's bodies are an important site of war which makes sexual violence an integral part of wartime strategy" (Ertürk 2009).

Planning a Genocide

When oral arguments in the 2013 genocide trial came to a close, eighty-six-year-old Ríos Montt demanded to speak, breaking the silence he had held since the trial began. Far from displaying any remorse for the genocide committed during his regime, he stated: "I never authorized, I never proposed, I never ordered acts against any ethnic or religious group" (Burt 2013). He also denied that he commanded army troops, despite leading the junta that came to power through a military coup in March 1982. He then asserted that his role was purely administrative. As the Adolf Eichmann trial proved, pushing papers does not excuse responsibility (Arendt 2006). Yet Ríos Montt was much more than an administrator; he had command responsibility of a vertical military organization (Sanford 2014). As the de facto president of Guatemala, Ríos Montt initiated genocide, beginning with propaganda against the indigenous Maya and any other Guatemalan who dared to question oppression, inequality, and poverty.

Following the US-sponsored overthrow of democratically elected President Jacobo Árbenz in 1954, successive military governments in Guatemala fought against "the enemy within" as defined by the United States' Cold War–era anti-communist National Security Doctrine. The Guatemalan government applied the doctrine to justify eliminating any person who challenged the regime by working to bring sociopolitical change to the nation—it was not necessary to carry a gun to be a target. According to the Guatemalan truth commission (CEH 1999): "The broad concept of enemy wielded by the State was re-launched with particular violence and intensity in the eighties, and included not only those actively seeking to change the established order, but all who might potentially decide to support the struggle at some point in the future."[5] Victims of the doctrine included men, women, and children from all strata: workers, professionals, religious leaders and lay workers, politicians, peasants, students and academics; in ethnic terms the vast majority of victims were Maya.[6] Once the security forces had destroyed the social bases of dissent in the city and assassinated rural community leaders, the war machine focused its full attention on Maya communities.

Anticommunism fused with patriarchal structures and centuries-old prejudices against the majority Maya population produced a climate ripe for the dehumanization of a targeted population. The conflation of Maya identity with guerrilla insurgency was exaggerated by the dictatorship with the intent to deploy this alleged widespread Maya/guerrilla affinity to justify the elimination of present and future members of the Maya population. Genocide ideologues implicitly acknowledged the poverty and exploitation of Maya life as they argued that if the Maya were to join the guerrillas in their demands for social justice, the army would lose the war.[7]

When a *population* is classified as an enemy, as opposed to specific elements within a group, women become primary targets for sexual violence rather than collateral damage. Women are recognized as "reproducers" in both the biological and socioeconomic senses of the term (Meyer 2003, 126). Although women's work is undervalued by general populations, analysts understand that it is essential, especially during times of crisis (Sen and Grown 1987). Because sexual violence harms women's ability to perform their roles, military analysts know that when the goal is to destabilize or destroy a population, targeting women will help them reach that goal.[8]

There is another compelling reason why when a population is the target, sexual violence against women is considered militarily advantageous. Despite the fact that the crime is committed against the actual victims, men experience their inability to protect women as a demoralizing humiliation and perceive it as an attack on their own power and dignity. Sexual violence against women committed by an invading army is a potent symbol clearly intended to demonstrate victory over the opposition. As Radhika Coomaraswamy states: "It is a battle among men fought over the bodies of women" (Ertürk 2009, 15).

Thus, the Guatemalan state launched a campaign designed not only to crush communities suspected of resistance but also to debase the reproductive bodies and degrade the sociocultural status of Maya women. Leaked (and authenticated) army documents refer to Ixil women as "cockroaches" and Ixil children as "chocolates" (Dada 2014). Within this idiom, forced displacement; the organized rape of women and girls; systematic slaughter of unarmed men, women, and children; and the burning of hundreds of villages was reduced to a simple order: "Kill the cockroaches and leave no chocolates" (Dada 2014).

Training Soldiers to Rape

Cynthia Enloe reminds us that historically rape has provided cost-free recompense for soldiers and collaborators, converting captive young women into the "spoils of war" (Enloe 2000; see also Moradi 2016). However, when rape is used as a weapon of genocide, more is involved than the forfeiture of women to conquering forces. Under the direction of Ríos Montt, the military simultaneously identified the Maya population as the enemy and stipulated that soldiers have sexual contact with women. Psychological operations for the troops included "recreation zones designed to maintain the soldier's fighting spirit," which featured "contact with the female sex."[9] Military plans included sexual contact as part of the soldier's "rest and recreation" because the normalization of rape was utilized to maintain control over the troops.

According to testimonies gathered by the CEH, the women used by the army to accustom soldiers to the practice of rape were prostitutes: "The Army took prostitutes to the soldiers who went to the lieutenant before being passed on to the rest of the soldiers." The CEH documents that women identified as "prostitutes or whores were passed from the lieutenant to all the soldiers during one week." Then, the CEH reports that "some [soldiers] passed up to 10 times." It is also noted that the army "changed" the women every three months (CEH 1999, 27).

In its replication of this lexicon, the CEH is shockingly passive and vague in its reporting of sexual violence, utilizing the term "pass" instead of rape. It fails to identify the absolute impunity under which the military operated and, in so doing, the full magnitude of sexual violence against women. Under what conditions would a woman, even if she was a prostitute, willingly go to a military base to be "passed" among dozens of soldiers on a daily basis for three months? The CEH fails to specify the sexual violence to which these women were subjected, despite knowing that the army brought a new group every three months, which suggests the level of physical and psychological battery experienced by these women. Perhaps one of the legacies of genocide is that even those seeking to chronicle the truth of the unimaginable can fall victim to its doublespeak, a phenomenon Marguerite Feitlowitz refers to as "a lexicon of terror" in her magisterial work by the same title (Feitlowitz 1999). What is certain is that this "training" produced the expected outcome.

Maya women survivors interviewed by the authors in four departments of Guatemala reported that they were selected by army officers to provide the service of delivering tortillas to the soldiers each day. It was understood that they would be gang-raped when they made their delivery to the army base, but the women went hoping to protect their daughters from the same fate. In Rabinal, women were forced into rotations at the local military base. Gilberta Iboy[10] described being part of a captive group: "There was so much fear, but by necessity we had to go to the plaza [in Rabinal] because they would not give the men permission to leave the village. In Rabinal, the soldiers captured us and took us to the outpost. We were assaulted. . . . They kept us there for a week and then they let us go" (Dill 2004).

Tomasa Toj[11] was still unable to talk about what happened to her: "They kept us in the military outpost for twenty-five days. We were there with other young women from various villages. The soldiers raped the women and some ended up pregnant . . . [The interview ended there because the woman could not continue]" (Dill 2004). Given the fact that, along with other village women, Ms. Iboy was held for a week and Ms. Toj for twenty-five days, their testimonies strongly suggest that the women previously identified by the CEH as "prostitutes" were also kidnapped and held on army bases as sex slaves.

A former G-2 (army intelligence) officer recounted rapes to REMHI investigators, making clear the way in which superior officers organized massive sexual violence:

> Some of the guys came and said, "Come on, don't you want to go grab some ass?" I thought to myself, "Wow, just like that?" One said to me, "There are some girls, and we are grabbing them." I responded, "We'll see." There were only two girls. They were prisoners. The guys said they were guerrillas, right? And, they were massively raping them. When I got there, I remember there was a line of 35 or so soldiers waiting their turn. They were surrounding them and raping them. One got up and another *passed* [authors' emphasis] on. Then he got off and another passed on. I calculate that those poor women were raped by 300 soldiers or maybe even more. Sergeant Soto García grabbed them. He was a bad man. He wanted whatever woman we found and he liked to rape them because he knew that we were going to kill them anyway. (REMHI, 212–13)

The G-2 officer went on to explain how gang rape was planned to reduce the spread of sexually transmitted diseases among the troops. On another occasion, some seventy men had raped a woman and some of them had raped her two or three times: "There were some soldiers who were sick with gonorrhea and syphilis, so the lieutenant ordered them to wait to *pass* [authors' emphasis] last after the rest of us were done" (REMHI, 213–14).

Guatemalan soldiers were trained to think of gang rape as a bonding exercise among the troops as well as an effective weapon for the extermination of the civilian enemy. Because the troops were not being directed to engage an armed insurgency, but rather to annihilate villages and terrorize civilian communities, the army needed to dehumanize the soldiers as well as their intended victims. *The Counterinsurgency War Manual (Manual de Guerra Contrainsurgente)* states: "The soldier normally has great aversion toward police-type operations and repressive measures against women, children, and sick civilians, unless he is extremely well indoctrinated in the necessity of these operations."[12] One survivor testified to the truth commission: "There were always rapes inside the army bases . . . sometimes by [soldier's] choice, other times by order [from superiors]. They would say: 'We have to break the asses of these whores' or even worse things."[13]

The army prepared its soldiers by subjecting them to brutality, torture, and psychological manipulation. Once their resistance was extinguished and a blood lust established, soldiers were taught that entire communities were "breeding grounds" for subversives. This process would ensure that the fully indoctrinated would carry out abhorrent attacks on women, children, elderly and disabled persons, oftentimes in front of their families—while those who remained appalled by the violence were too afraid to disobey orders.

As the vessels from which new "subversives" would emerge, women's bodies were transformed into primary targets. Jean Franco recounts some of the most horrific CEH testimonies of rape in Guatemala: "Women were mutilated, their breast or bellies cut, and if they were pregnant, fetuses were torn from their bodies. In one case, a woman's breasts were cut off after the rape and her eyes were pulled out. Her body was left hanging on a pole with a stick in her vagina" (Franco 2007, 39). Franco rightly concludes: "Such ferocity can only be explained on the grounds that women represented a significant threat" (ibid., 27).

Modern-Day Conquistadors

The prosecutors of the Ríos Montt trial focused on the evidence of state violence against the Ixil Maya; however, the army's genocidal campaign was not limited to that region or that ethnolinguistic group. Rape survivors and witnesses have confirmed that it was common knowledge in Maya villages across the country that the army was committing massacres and that soldiers were raping women. That means that systemic rape was a "public secret" shared by the residents of a village and the army that occupied it. But within the context of military impunity, even if remaining silent might not save your life, speaking out would certainly end it. This further underscores the power and authority with which sexual assaults were deployed by the army.

Power in Guatemala is a racialized phenomenon and the symbolic superiority of White and Ladino men over the Maya was a catalyst for genocidal violence. In the same way that racism is a key to understanding the fury with which Ríos Montt's military plans were carried out against hundreds of Maya communities throughout the country, the patriarchal ideology resulted in a misogynist spiral of violence against women. Within this rubric of racist patriarchy, Maya women were objectified as enemy "property" deserving cruel destruction. Thus, the Guatemalan army raped and tortured women with the same ferocity with which they torched fields of sacred maize, burned houses, and slaughtered animals, leaving these signs of destruction to further terrorize any survivors (Sanford 2003).

The state achieved several goals by recreating and affirming the historic relations in which indigenous women were the property of, and thus subordinate to, masculine European and Ladino power. In 1999, the CEH concluded that "massacres, scorched earth operations, forced disappearances and executions of Maya authorities, leaders and spiritual guides, were meant not only to destroy the social base of the guerrillas, but above all were meant to disintegrate cultural values that ensured cohesion and collective action of communities."[14]

Michelle Leiby uses data gathered by truth commission reports to compare the army's use of sexual violence in Guatemala and Peru (Leiby 2009). She points out that in the case of Guatemala, there exists a direct relationship between the perceived threat to the state and the number of rapes committed by soldiers. Although the war continued through December 1996, only 11 percent of sexual violence occurred after 1984, when it was clear that the Unidad Revolucionaria Nacional Guatemalteca (URNG) had been effectively defeated (ibid., 460). Leiby cites testimonies of Guatemalan soldiers that demonstrate that rape and in particular gang rape was as integral to the army's strategy as was the spectacularly violent killing of "subversives": "The commander has his group of killers, and he tells them how they have to kill. Today they are going to behead or hang them; today they are going to rape all the women. Many times, orders are given to the soldiers before they go out. . . . They were also ordered to do the 'percha' . . . where 20 or 30 soldiers would rape a single woman" (ibid., 459).

Other army sources asserted that if soldiers hesitated to rape they were berated by their superiors, and those who refused to rape were punished (ibid., 459). Based on her analysis of the data, Leiby concludes that while the military in Peru targeted actual or suspected guerrillas or other opponents of the state, "sexual violence in Guatemala was an explicit tool of repression, employed indiscriminately against the indigenous peasantry." Victims were not punished for joining the insurgency. Victims were not interrogated for information. Instead, sexual violence was used to spread fear and terror through entire "communities of interest" (ibid., 466).

Thus, to be a Maya woman—the heart of a community of interest—was to be at the mercy of a merciless army. Juana Sis[15] described what happened when the army surrounded her settlement near the village of Chichupac, Rabinal: "soldiers captured us and they tied us up. They marched us to Chichupac and they assaulted us. They threatened us and accused us of being guerrillas and they raped women. It was the same in the Xesiguan community. They raped women in the community and they ordered some to go to the outpost [in Rabinal] and they raped them there. The soldiers respect no one" (Dill 2004).

At the same time, the army manipulated and indoctrinated Maya collaborators so they participated in this attack against their own communities. Dorotea Chen[16] of Buena Vista, Rabinal, was raped by Maya men from the neighboring village. The rapists were members of the local militia instituted by the military and referred to as the Civil Patrols (PACs). The state forcibly recruited Maya men into PACs in order to extend its reach into every indigenous municipality in the country. Like enlisted soldiers, PAC members were brutalized and threatened with death if they did not follow orders. Some indigenous men fled into the mountains to avoid having to serve in the PACs. Some stayed behind and were horrified by what they were forced to do, while still others were eager to take advantage of their newfound power and impunity: "The PAC from Xococ arrived here and dragged young women out of their houses and they took them to Xococ where they raped them. Afterwards, they would send them back home but they always returned [for more] every so often. A great many of the women here have been raped" (Dill 2004).

Almost all cases of mass and organized rape operationalized by the army and their proxies took place in rural Mayan communities, especially during the height of the violence between 1980 and 1983 (CEH 1999). The Guatemalan army's deployment of systematic sexual violence during the genocide devastated individual victims as well as the indigenous groups to which they belonged. Of the twenty-one ethnolinguistic Maya groups in Guatemala, K'iche, K'anjob'al, Mam, Kekchi, Ixil, Kaqchikel, and Chuj communities were either most often the victims of massive rape or were more recorded by human rights observers. As researchers who have worked with K'anjob'al, K'iche, Kaqchikel, Akateco, Achi, Mam, Ixil, and Tz'ujil communities, we have found that the rape of Maya women was intended to terrorize, subjugate, debilitate, and demoralize entire populations. We have not encountered a department in Guatemala where women were not raped.

The Political Economy of Rape

In addition to the demoralizing spectacle of power and impunity that the "public secret" of mass rapes provided, by aiding, abetting, and promoting rape as a military strategy, the Guatemalan state also achieved some economic goals.

Drawing from research conducted in Rwanda and Mozambique, Meredeth Tur-shen argues: "In civil wars, armies use rape systematically to strip women of their economic and political assets. Women's assets reside in the first instance in their productive and reproductive labour power and in the second instance in their possessions and their access to valuable assets such as land and livestock" (Turshen 2001, 56).

In Rabinal, families that lived in the Chixoy River basin were especially targeted for violence because the state wanted their land for a World Bank–funded hydroelectric dam (Johnston 2010). It is not surprising, then, to learn that the first cases of mass rape in that municipality occurred in the villages located on the banks or on the approach to the river. Hermenegildo Cuxum,[17] a man from Canchún, Rabinal recalls:

> In March 1980, soldiers assassinated three men from Canchún who were visiting in the nearby community of Río Negro. One man was shot in the hand, but was able to escape and return to the village. Later, more army troops came. Three hundred soldiers entered Canchún, demanded information about the guerrillas and threatened the community. This time, the soldiers raped five women and five young girls before they left. We knew that we had to escape into the mountains to save our lives, but two elderly women were unable to come with us. One woman's body trembled too much to travel and the other woman was blind [so we had to leave them behind]. When we returned to the village, we discovered that in a savage and incomprehensible act, the soldiers had killed them. (Dill 2004)

Across the indigenous highlands of Guatemala, women were raped wherever the army displaced Maya communities, during massacres as they razed villages, in public buildings and churches converted into army detention centers, in military bases, and in so-called model villages where the army forcibly concentrated massacre survivors.[18] For many Maya women, rape and the ensuing loss of their way of life defined how they experienced the war.

Concluding Remarks

Genocide is an all-consuming type of violence. As researchers, it is impossible to convey the measure of human suffering experienced by its victims. We are often reduced to making lists. All told, we know that the Guatemalan genocide took the lives of some 200,000 civilians, 50,000 people were disappeared, 626 villages were annihilated, 1.5 million people were displaced, and 150,000 people fled to refuge in Mexico (CEH 1999). But we do not know how many women and girls were raped, how many were abducted by the military and forced into sexual slavery, how many gave birth to children who were the product of sexual assault, or how many suffered from the venereal diseases transmitted during the rape(s). Despite real advances in international law, there has been little progress in prosecuting these crimes.

In this chapter, we have touched upon a number of ways in which the Guatemalan genocide operationalized rape: to terrorize the Maya population, destabilize the reproductive role of women, demoralize the enemy, provide soldiers with the spoils of war, and train them to commit hyperviolent acts, usurp land, and to reaffirm historic relations of power between the Euro-American elite and the Maya. Jelke Boesten detangles the various types and intents of sexual violence during war by carefully analyzing what she calls "rape regimes" (Boesten 2014). Because her study focuses on Peru, which like Guatemala is a country with a large indigenous population, Boesten also recognizes that sexual violence can be used to reinscribe racialized socioeconomic hierarchies present during peacetime. During the Ríos Montt regime, the systemized rape of Maya women was a weapon of genocide used to accomplish multiple ends, all of which supported the singular operational goal—breaking emergent Maya communities.

On May 10, 2013, José Efraín Ríos Montt was sentenced to the maximum penalty of fifty years' imprisonment for genocide and thirty years for crimes against humanity. The tribunal found that racism played a key role in the execution of acts of barbarism and ordered the development of concrete measures to provide dignified reparation to the victims. One of the measures ordered was for then president of Guatemala Otto Pérez Molina (who is also implicated in the Ixil genocide)[19] and several ministers to ask forgiveness from the Ixil people and especially Ixil women for the acts of genocide and sexual violence suffered. The verdict offered a modicum of justice for the survivors and opened the possibility that Guatemalan society might reconcile itself with its own history of racist exclusion and genocide.

However, Guatemala's elite quickly seized back control. On May 20, 2013, the Constitutional Court overturned the verdict on the pretext of procedural irregularities. In February 2014, the same court ruled that Ms. Claudia Paz y Paz, the attorney general who indicted Ríos Montt, was to be removed from her post six months early. Then in April 2014, the College of Lawyers in Guatemala suspended Judge Yassmin Barrios. She was able to defend herself and has resumed practice, but these blatantly corrupt maneuvers lend a Kafkaesque quality to the state of governance in Guatemala and remind everyone that the rule of law has yet to be established. Nonetheless, justice continues to move forward under the leadership of Attorney General Thelma Aldana. In January 2016, eighteen former high-ranking army officers were arrested for various war crimes . . . The historic Sepur Zarco sexual slavery case is being tried in Guatemala City, marking the first time a domestic court has heard charges of sexual slavery during armed conflict as an international crime (Burt 2016).

NOTES

1 Ten days later, the Constitutional Court vacated the guilty verdict and ordered that the trial restart from the point reached on April 19, 2013, the day a lower court called for the suspension of the trial due to unresolved appeals by the defense. See Kate Doyle, "Guatemala's Genocide on Trial," *Nation*, May 22, 2013. On January 11, 2016, the defense team successfully delayed the start of the retrial. See Anna-Catherine Brigida, "Retrial of Ex-Dictator Ríos Montt: Will a Changed Guatemala Shine Through?" *Christian Science Monitor*, January 11, 2016.

2 The CEH documented 626 army massacres in Maya villages.

3 CEH 1999, 32.

4 Based on our field experience and conversations with colleagues, we assume sexual violence against men and women was underreported. See Theidon, 2016.

5 CEH 1999, vol. 21 chap. 2, p. 3811 epigraph 1947.

6 CEH 1999, vol. 51 chap. 4, vol. 51 chap. 41 pp. 24–25i epigraph 15.

7 CEH 1999, vol. 51 chap. 4, p. 291 epigraph 31.

8 Conversely, when the goal is to eliminate individual targets without destabilizing and alienating the community; military leaders have an incentive to prevent their troops from perpetrating sexual violence.

9 Ejercito de Guatemala (1982), Plan Victoria 82, appendix B, 39.

10 Pseudonym.

11 Pseudonym.

12 Ejercito de Guatemala, Manual de Guerra Contrasubversiva (resumen) (1965), Anexo A, p. 10.

13 CEH 1999, Testigo CEH (T. C. 53).

14 CEH 1999, Capitulo Cuarto, p. 29, epigraph 32.

15 Pseudonym.

16 Pseudonym.

17 Pseudonym.

18 CEH 1999, Testigo CEH (T. C. 53).

19 Ex-president Otto Pérez Molina was arrested on September 2, 2015, and charged with corruption. He is accused of directing a customs fraud scheme, which eliminated government import taxes in exchange for payoffs. He is awaiting trial in a military prison. See Jan Martínez Ahrens (translation by Martin Delfin), "Guatemala's Jailed Ex-Leader: 'I Didn't Want Any Deaths Just to Save My Skin,'" *El País*, December 15, 2015. In October 2015, Jimmy Morales, a television comedian backed by right-wing military and elite business interests, won the presidential election with the slogan "Not Corrupt, nor a Thief." See Elizabeth Malkin and Nic Wiritz, *New York Times*, "Jimmy Morales Is Elected New President of Guatemala," October 25, 2015.

7

Situating "Toxic" Masculine Subcultures

Toward Disrupting Gendered Violence

LAURA L. O'TOOLE AND JESSICA R. SCHIFFMAN

An all-male network of more than thirty thousand marines builds and exchanges folders with nude photographs and personal information about female colleagues—information that is used to harass and stalk them online (Phillips 2017). Universities enthusiastically support and recruit new prospects through men's fraternities and athletic teams—two of the most frequently implicated sites of sexual assault (Martin 2016). Proclamations from the emergent #MeToo movement recount women's (and some young men's) forced sexual encounters with powerful male entertainment, technology sector, and political elites.

This chapter attests to our continued efforts to understand the structural conditions and social relationships that underlie gender violence in light of rapidly changing political-economic agendas and technological advances. Specifically, we sharpen our focus on institutionalized sites where toxic enactments of masculinity predicated on dominance, control, and the obliteration of weakness typically associated with the feminine thrive. In such sites, institutional norms and "nondisclosure codes" protect perpetrators of violence and replicate structural inequalities rooted in gendered ideologies.

In prior editions of this book, O'Toole (2007) offered a revision of rape subculture theories. She suggested that, as used in the past, rape subculture theories are problematic in multiple ways. First, they apply a predominately gender-neutral frame of reference, unaltered, to sexual violence, when violence itself was recognized in the literature on men and masculinities as a gendered phenomenon (Messerschmidt 1993; Kaufman 2007; Kimmel 2009). Classic deviant subculture theory focused primarily on lower-class, urban males, often men of color. Yet in applying this theory to rape, it was the class and ethnicity—not the maleness—of the perpetrators that was put forward as the predominant explanatory framework. Explaining rape prevalence data, or the complexity of who rapes and why, is not as simple as conceptualizing race and class as categorical variables and/or collapsing them into "communities." Years of scholarly exploration of rape indicate that conduct variables—such as previous criminal record and, frequently, perpetrators' group affiliations—are much more salient for our efforts to understand such phenomena.

Rape subcultures are construed in the literature as *deviant*, although only certain violent subcultures were under the deviance microscope, despite what is suggested by the ubiquity of gender violence in many institutional contexts. Other particularly hypermasculine groups linked to sexual violation were normalized, rendered invisible by dint of the relative privilege of participants or, as Herman suggests, by the fact that sexual violence toward women and girls is so widespread that it is a veritable rite of passage (2015). Finally, subcultural explanations were theorized for rape in particular; the literature was virtually silent on the question of intimate partner violence, sexual harassment, bullying, and other forms of gender violence that also reflect specific institutional conditions and relationships, including misogynistic occupational subcultures.

In revisiting subculture theory as a gendered concept, O'Toole (2007) noted that there are clusters of group-identified individuals whose rhetoric and frequently ritualistic behaviors cohere with the sociological definition of subculture, although the prior literature stopped short of defining them as such. Masculinist subcultures may cut across race and class but share the characteristics of toxic masculinity, including the legitimation of coercive sexuality. Nestled within the sex/gender system of the larger culture and specific patriarchal institutions such as athletics[1], the military, and some types of fraternal organizations, masculinist subcultures appeared to flourish, even as the feminist movement, human rights agencies, governmental institutions, and educational and criminal justice administrators articulated strategies to prevent gender violence in them.

In the twenty-plus years that we have published on this subject, a rising phenomenon has deepened our concern about how gender violence is re-created and supported—a virtual reordering of *social reality itself*. This chapter, therefore, adds to our previous thinking about subculture theory by situating it within an analysis of how neoliberalism shapes gender relations and pushes concepts of fairness and equality out of the mainstream to be replaced by the authority of capitalist markets in all facets of life, including those that create and support gender violence.

Analyzing gender violence within the framework of the neoliberal project, and situating toxic masculinist subcultures within these political and economic conditions, can shed light on how hegemonic gender systems are reinforced and the way violence is deployed to maintain them. We further suggest that the neoliberal corporate state supports and exploits divisions in class, gender, and sexuality and thus we also make a claim for the omnirelevance of intersectionality to the study of neoliberalism in relation to gender violence.

To be clear, hegemonic systems of gender and the structure of gender relationships operate on multiple levels: they are societal, organizational, and familial, as well as internalized and acted upon by individuals. Gender violence is perpetrated in and through all of them. Indeed, a spate of recent academic and journalistic analyses link masculinity to both social and self-harm among men (see, for example Dastagier 2018 for a review). The contemporary notion of "toxicity" in regard to the outcomes of hegemonic masculine ideologies and practices has emerged in response to these observations.

Although not specifically labeled as such, Kaufman's (2007) model of the triad of men's violence against women, other men, and the self, as well as his explication of the fragility of masculinity in a world that promises no guarantees of universal male privilege, presages the notion of toxic masculinity. We suggest this model is increasingly helpful as it explains how men and women are held accountable to an atavistic gender binary in the context of twenty-first-century globalized neoliberalism. Our purpose here, however, is to focus on specific institutional sites where patterned gender violence occurs and to explore the structural conditions and relationships that produce and reproduce them.

Intersectionality, Social Structures, and Inequality

The concept of intersectionality is a significant component of contemporary analyses of structural inequality, formed largely as a critique of white solipsism[2] by feminist scholars of color (Collins 1986; Crenshaw 1989, 1991) in the late twentieth century. The concept has become a linchpin to understanding the institutionalization of racism, classism, sexism, and heteronormativity at all levels of human experience, with a particular focus on contextualizing individual and group experiences within various axes of domination. It is an important transdisciplinary heuristic for both academic inquiry and political work around identity politics. Using the lens of intersectionality illuminates the complexity of inequalities and the social divisions that often impede social change, while simultaneously providing the basis for disruptive praxis (Collins and Bilge 2016).

Crenshaw used the framework of structural intersectionality to map the marginalization of women of color in analysis and political responses to gender violence, through "the ways in which the location of women of color at the intersection of race and gender makes our actual experience of domestic violence, rape, and remedial reform qualitatively different than that of white women" (1991, 1245). Erbaugh, Jenness and Fenstermaker, Valdovinos, and Mills (this volume) extend the analysis to the ways in which an intersectional lens makes visible some of the unique and devastating problems of some of the most marginalized victims of violence, such as women of color, LGBTQ+ individuals, undocumented immigrants, and transgender women incarcerated in the US prison industrial complex.

Abrams (2016) reminds us as well that a myth of *universal* male privilege frequently underlies feminist critiques and obscures intersectionality *among* men, and that "masculine violence, in particular, operates on multiple systematic levels, many of which are not adequately contemplated" (311). For example, Schur (this volume) recognized in the mid-1980s that relative deprivation experienced by some men in a culture that valorizes power over others, financial and (hetero)sexual success, and male entitlement—hegemonic Western ideal masculinity—may be expressed in violent forms. Thirty years later, Abrams concurs that "perceived masculine inadequacy can lead to hypermasculine expressions of violence, such as domestic violence and sexual assault" (2016, 312), and we would add mass shootings to the litany as well. The misogynistic rhetoric and violent murderous outbursts of members of the online "incel" subculture, which we will explore in detail later, are current cases in point. Clarified through the lens of intersectionality, all of these manifestations of gender violence, and data about its perpetrators and victims, are also linked to the insidious encroachment of neoliberalism. The neoliberal project comes into focus as a pivotal structure that supports and *relies on* classism, racism, anti-LGBTQ+ discrimination, and sexism to thrive. In this view, intersectionality is reified through neoliberalism.

If we look at individuals or groups of individuals in order to assess who is more likely to commit gender violence (or the extent and scope of victimization among various demographics), we often lose sight of the superstructure that comprises the supporting framework. Therefore, we suggest using the metaphor of Google Earth—positioning and analyzing the vast problem of gender violence subcultures at a macro level *and then zooming in*—proceeding from structural and political intersectionality and the effects of global neoliberalism as the substrate for violence. The links that connect marginalized class, racial/ethnic groups, LGBTQ+ communities, women, and men who enact subordinated masculinities to greater disparities and increasing vulnerability come more clearly into focus from this more encompassing vantage point.

"Positioning" Neoliberalism

We choose to define neoliberalism as it is most widely used, knowing that it has a long history and has been differently theorized by scholars and across disciplines. As we choose to describe it, "neoliberalism" refers to the application and effects of ideas that Friedrich Hayek and Ludwig von Mises developed in the 1930s. The former advanced a concept that the market is a disinterested "mind," greater than the sum of its parts and greater than the knowledge of the individuals who contribute to it (1944). The latter supported a policy of unrestricted markets as the only viable system for human advancement (1949). The unregulated market, they believed, was a hedge against totalitarianism. These refugees from totalitarian Europe feared that government growth would suppress individualism and that a lighter government footprint led to healthier societies (See Judt, 2010).

Certainly, the lesson of Nazi Germany could make anyone fearful of governmental power, though many others believed, following theories developed by John Maynard Keynes, that government had an important role to play in managing economies, lifting up individuals left out or behind during periods of market fluctuation. Though economists continue to argue about Keynes's support for welfare states as they have been organized, it is clear that his theories provided the rationale for a post-WWII movement toward government support for boosting living standards and concurrent reduction in inequality (see Quadagno 1987). There is, however, absolute clarity about Keynes's support for issues affecting women that still resonate—birth control, laws about marriage, women's wage earning and economic status, and perhaps most germaine to this text, how to deal with sex offenses (Keynes 1925). In Brown's view, neoliberalism is a *"reaction against Keynesianism and democratic socialism"* (2015, 21; emphasis ours).

Probably the most significant turn toward the present incarnation of neoliberalism took place during the 1980s, an era during which the stars aligned for supporters of unregulated markets when both Margaret Thatcher in the United Kingdom and Ronald Reagan in the US wielded tremendous influence. These two world leaders relied on the theories developed by Hayek and von Mises to develop a new model of postwar conservatism in which government is viewed as the problem and the individual, not society, is the unit that requires governmental protection. In their view, "[t]he task of the politician is to ascertain what is best for the individual, and then afford him [or her] the conditions in which to pursue it with minimal interference" (Judt, 2010, 97).

Under the Thatcher and Reagan administrations, the state shifted from seeing itself as "a provider of public welfare to a promoter of markets and competition . . ." (Birch 2017). This shift away from a generalized support of institutions that ideally serve all citizens followed a concerted and successful effort to undermine trust in public institutions and to protect those with means from the will of the populace (see MacLean 2017). As Centano and Cohen (2011) assert: "First, it is imperative to recognize the cultural or ideational element in economic governance. Second, it is equally important to recognize that economic policies do not exclusively involve the search for universal principles, but rather also involve political choices about who wins and who loses" (25).

The influence of neoliberal ideas on governmental policy has been astounding. Whereas, until recently, policies in many parts of the world were promoted in order to ameliorate economic and social disparities, it has become common for governments to withdraw from those goals to allow free markets to determine the lives and well-being of citizens. Metcalf (2017) points to the deregulation of economies, the pressure to open national markets, and the privatization of governments as the nexus around which has arisen "a sickening . . . inequality" (n.p.). Alvaredo et al. find that "income inequality has increased in nearly all world regions . . . [marking] the end of a postwar egalitarian regime" (2018, 5). The report states that "very large transfers of public to private wealth occurred in nearly all countries, whether rich or emerging" (ibid., 10), creating limits on the potential for governments to address problems of inequality. Indeed, that may be the point of the entire neoliberal project.

As many critics have demonstrated, neoliberalism has had a devastating effect on those for whom the struggle for equality is ongoing: marginalized racial/ethnic groups, LGBTQ+ communities, and women among them. For example, Salter (2012) reports that where structural inequality affecting girls and women is greatest, rates of gender-based violence is highest. In its fundamental tenets, neoliberalism values only the pursuit of economic interests. Such thinking creates an absolute dividing line between haves and have-nots—defined by ownership of capital. Value resides only in monetary assets and wealth accumulation. As Judt points out, this leaves myriad other measures of well-being out of consideration as values:

> If you can sell it or buy it, then it is quantifiable and we can assess its contribution to (quantitative) measures of collective well-being. But what of those goods which humans have always valued but which do not lend themselves to quantification? . . . What of well-being? What of fairness or equity (in its original sense)? What of exclusion, opportunity? . . . What if we decided to "quantify" the harm done when people are shamed by their fellow citizens as a condition of receiving the mere necessities of life? (2010, 169)

Early feminist efforts to address violence against women identified the state's neglect to recognize the seriousness of gender violence as stemming from patriarchal structures that oppressed women and denied their security as citizens. Efforts to reform laws and policies were adopted as key measures in promoting women's well-being. As endeavors were underway in the US for the state to develop more supportive responses to gender violence, the neoliberal ethic of the marketplace was increasing its influence. "The call for state responsibility for preventing and treating victims was in direct contrast to the new ethics that was the cornerstone of the neoliberal agenda" (Bumiller 2008, 5).

All of this led to more regulation of the poor and minorities whose compromised opportunities were seen as cause rather than effect. Gender, race, and class divisions increasingly divided public opinion (Chancer 2005, 252). Reduction of costs, increased scrutiny of recipients of assistance, elimination of what was termed "waste," (but was in practice often a lifeline for victims of gender violence), and an increasing reliance on criminalization twisted original good intentions, all under the banner of market efficiency (Bumiller 2008). As regulations on the economy loosen, social disparities increase. Fear of social unrest (fed by growing wealth disparities) has led to increased criminalization and racialization of crime, including the creation of a privatized, corporate, carceral model for addressing gender violence (Bumiller 2008; see also Whittier, this volume).

These trends increase in the early twenty-first century, notwithstanding the evidence that dealing with structural inequities through legal and judicial avenues had opened pathways for some historically marginalized groups and individuals by the end of the twentieth century.[3] Ironically, though adherents to a neoliberal agenda desire a reduced state footprint, their policies increased the capacity of the state as a regulatory function and expanded oversight to governmental, quasi-governmental, and private entities. The prison-industrial complex, with all its internal and often gendered violence, is a case in point.

Connell theorizes neoliberalism as "an important case of indirect gender politics" (2011, 19) given its presumption that *homo economicus* is not gendered and that the market, and thus market mechanisms, is gender-neutral. Indeed, the myth of meritocracy drives the complicity of both proponents and victims of neoliberalism. But "neoliberalism can function as a form of masculinity politics largely because of the role of the state in the gender order" (ibid., 20) and the ever-increasing function of the market as a primary global governing structure. Moreover, the continued existence of a dual labor market, hiring bias, and sexual harassment at work—including hostile work environments—lend support to Wendy Brown's observation that "human capital may be built [on] gender-specific attributes" (2015, 100).

According to Fraser (2013), even feminism has inadvertently become "capitalism's handmaiden." Neoliberalism does its work on gender relations by virtue of its specific guiding principles, co-opting liberal feminist principles of individual achievement, choice, and meritocratic advancement (ibid.).

What the recent literature suggests, then, is that "gender subordination is both intensified and fundamentally altered" by neoliberalism (Brown 2015, 105). This is clearly the case for some women given that progressive changes ushered in by political feminism and the professionalization of feminist advances in social institutions over the last forty years have been challenged anew by a current aggressive antifeminist backlash (Messner, this volume) and rollbacks of important laws and regulations after the US national elections of 2016. Many men, especially those in working class occupations decimated by the decline of living wages as neoliberalism advances, experience downward mobility as an outcome of the Civil Rights advances for people of color and feminism's gains for women (ibid.). Others are less challenged by income inequality than by perceptions of the loss of access to women's bodies for sex given the social and legal advances of women's right to bodily control (Talentino 2018; Salter and Blodgett 2017). Some, including "angry White men" in the current political-economic climate, feel ravaged by a loss of entitlement to those things promised to men in traditional gender ideologies: economic and political power, access to women, and privilege in racial and global status hierarchies (Kimmel 2013; Ging 2017; Messner, this volume).

Many virulently misogynistic groups and subcultures on social media platforms (Ging 2017; Salter and Blodgett 2017) embrace a conservative political agenda that promises to "make America great again" (and to "Lock her up!" in reference to Hillary Clinton). Some are proponents of the new white national-ism; all of these vocal contingents feature misogynist- and antifeminist-tinged rhetoric. Comprehending the new gender order is complicated, however, by the ways in which the rhetoric and practices of various constituencies of aggrieved men show that traditional hegemonic masculinity is simultaneously embraced or rejected in depictions of male victimization (Ging 2017). For all, it seems, vio-lation of and vengeance against enemies—in theory and practice—is a primary weapon in the new race and gender wars.

Situating Masculinist Subcultures

Neoliberalism is significant in shaping contemporary sociopolitical structures. We now zoom in to several of the contexts most frequently associated with dis-proportionately high rates of gender violence. Several clear patterns emerge from the literature on sexual assault: the majority of victims know their assailant and although some men are more likely than others to rape, "some *social contexts* also are more amenable to rapes" (Martin 2016, 31; emphasis hers) than oth-ers. Martin theorizes that the organizational dynamics of military units; street, drug, and motorcycle gangs; elite schools; college fraternities; and men's athletic programs "make them more probable sites for sexual assaults, irrespective of individual men's attitudes or beliefs" (2016, 31).

Two high-profile incidents from the institutional context of contemporary universities, which Martin (2016) labels "rape-prone cultures," are cases in point. In 2011, Penn State University football coach icon Joe Paterno was fired, as sub-sequently were three other administrators, after covering up the sexual abuse of boys on campus by assistant coach Jerry Sandusky. This and the recent expo-sure of the decades of abuse of women gymnasts by Dr. Larry Nassar, protected by athletic and university administrators at Michigan State University, illustrate the extent to which the priorities of profitability, national rankings, and other indicators of neoliberal orientation dominate decision-making in these contexts. Martin problematizes this market orientation that undergirds universities' com-plicity with alumni and donors to protect the violent masculinity of fraternity and sports organizations. Sandusky and Nassar are both serving extended prison sentences for their sexual abuse; lower profile cases abound.

Fraternity Subcultures

The likelihood of committing sexual assault increases among residents of some all-male housing units; early research on assailants suggested that fraternity members in particular are highly implicated in campus rape (Koss, cited in Bohmer and Parrot 1993, 21–22). Two early in-depth studies of fraternity involve-ment in individually perpetrated rapes and ritual rapes by multiple perpetrators provide significant qualitative accounts for understanding these patterns. Martin and Hummer (1989) formulate an organizational perspective for understanding rape in fraternities, within which the social construction of brotherhood involves value for traditional masculinity and a normative structure that promotes loyalty, secrecy, and group protection.

During the pledge process, fraternities require recruits to participate in a variety of ritual practices, not unlike those used in military boot camps that valorize traditional masculinity and require subordination of self to the group. Pledges are also evaluated on their social ability with women, and sexual access to women is an advertised benefit of group membership in the recruitment process (Martin and Hummer 1989, 468). Secret rituals, hand-shakes, and mottoes function to maintain group boundaries and exemplify the expectation of loyalty among brothers (ibid., 464). Norms defining women as servers and sexual prey become translated into sexual aggression when fused with those prescribing the use of alcohol, violent behavior, and competition. Such in-group norms may be expressed in a variety of ways, including through revenge porn. One recent case exposes a fraternity member sharing recorded sexual encounters, some made without his then-girlfriend's knowledge, in a fraternity meeting and on a dedicated Facebook page entitled "Dog Pound" (Victor 2018b).

Studies of multiple offender rapes also implicate some fraternities as likely contexts (Harkin and Dixon 2009). Peggy Reeves Sanday's (1990) definitive study characterizes group rape as a ritual bonding activity for men in fraternities. The purpose of the activity is less about achieving sexual gratification than it is to affirm the shared masculinity and brotherhood of members.

Men in Sanday's study considered "pulling train" or the "express," in which brothers line up to take their turn having sex with a (usually) intoxicated woman, a routine aspect of their "little sister" program (1990, 7). The multiple-perpetrator[4] rape is a collective phenomenon, made possible by the loss of individual identity during initiation rituals. Pledges are routinely ridiculed as sexually inadequate until admitted as members. They are treated as "despised women" and referred to in terms demeaning them as "homosexuals." Many initiation rituals are designed to cleanse these supposed inadequacies; thus, Sanday argues that the successful pledge is stamped with two collective images: the purified body accepted into brotherhood and the despised and dirty feminine (1990, 155–56).

Recent research continues to validate earlier findings of empirical relationships between fraternity membership and rape behavior, implicating factors such as peer support, the internal culture and party orientation of the fraternity, and acceptance of rape myths (Franklin et al. 2012; Harkin and Dixon 2009; Schwartz and Dekeseredy 1997). But not all fraternities, or fraternity members, should be implicated because of the malevolence of some. According to Harkins and Dixon, "individuals may come into a group setting or situation with these beliefs common to a rape culture already entrenched. Alternatively, individuals may come into the setting and adopt the beliefs of that rape culture if group processes are at work. Either way, a sociocultural context is created in which the individuals of the group normalize rape myths, increasing the likelihood that multiple perpetrator sex offenses will be accepted and carried out by the group" (2009, 93).

Other recent research has shown that the orientations of fraternities—service versus party cultures, for example—are more salient than the mere fact of being male-only institutions (Humphrey and Kahn 2000). And levels of self-control, consumption of intoxicants, and resistance to peer pressure (Franklin et al. 2012) are relevant to which brothers are more likely to involve themselves in individual or group assaults. Clearly, then, the toxicity level and integration of members into the hypermasculine culture matters, as well as the extent to which the larger university's culture and governing actors will prioritize profit over ethics and the protection of vulnerable students and campus visitors.

Athletics, Sport, and Violent Spillover

With respect to campus rapes, early research suggests the second most implicated category of assailants is college athletes (Bohmer and Parrot 1993). In a study of locker-room discourse among members of two "big time" college sport teams, Curry (1991) identified a pattern of fraternal bonding not unlike that characterizing the fraternities described above. A similar preoccupation with masculinity, defined rigidly through physical prowess and heterosexual performance, results in locker-room talk that dehumanizes women and promotes rape. Warshaw similarly finds athletic teams to be breeding grounds for rape: "They are organizations which pride themselves on the physical aggressiveness of their members and which demand group loyalty and reinforce it through promoting the superiority of their members over outsiders" (1988, 112).

As with some fraternities, multiple perpetrator rape is conceptualized as "group sex" among athletes, in effect a homoerotic bonding of members to each other where the woman involved is no more than an instrument through which the ritual activity is enabled (Warshaw 1988). But the research also suggests that not all fraternities and athletic teams are breeding grounds for sexual assault (Humphrey and Kahn 2000). Those that emerge in the literature as "high risk" organizations, however, exhibit characteristics of toxic masculinity. Humphrey and Kahn found that high-risk teams exhibit "higher levels of sexual aggression toward women, hostility toward women, and peer support of sexual assault against women than perceived low-risk groups" (2000, 1320).

Higher education institutions are not the only contexts within which male sport subcultures emerge. Examples abound from high school through professional sports. Pappas and his colleagues' (2004) qualitative study of professional hockey players found that socialization into a culture of masculinity, in conjunction with objectification of women and alcohol use outside of the arena, combined to create a pack mentality that often resulted in violence against women. These same factors also "resulted in strong bonds of allegiance and loyalty" (308). Zirin, in analyzing recent high-profile cases such as the brutal rapes of teen girls in Missouri and Steubenville, Ohio that were chronicled on social media concludes that "jock culture supports rape culture" (2013).

Sports both reinforce masculinity and construct it within the ever-evolving gender order that is also constructed through neoliberalism more broadly. Messner notes that sports are contemporary sites of patriotism, militarism, and meritocracy and that gender is also an organizing theme in the construction of meanings around sports violence (1990b, 213). Indeed, Connell identifies sport as one of the most "gender-divided areas of culture in the global metropole." In the current neoliberal climate, she theorizes sport as "a highly commercial competitive enterprise," colonized by the market and characterized by "sharp gender divisions" (2011, 52–53). In many cases, whether high school, college, or professional athletes are involved in abusive situations, there are often few consequences for the most valuable perpetrators (Withers 2015). Moreover, protection for violent athletes often spills over from within the administrative structure of the sport itself to communities and fans whose loyalties are tied more closely to athletic victory than to victims of athletes' violence.

A theory of relative deprivation in masculinities may provide a link between athletics and misogynistic violence. In Conaway's view, it consists of four discourses of masculinity that posit impossible standards for most athletes to attain—misogynistic and homophobic bonding; obsession with physical performance; discouragement of emotion and empathy; and emphasis on sexual conquest. Perceived failure to adhere to or attain these standards causes a sense of inadequacy that is mitigated through performative gender violence (n.d.). The very value of the self is attached to (misplaced) aspirational goals that, when not reached, devalue the person in the context of a ranking system endemic to the neoliberal project. Shur (this volume) developed an early analysis that links relative deprivation—perceived or real—to the dangerous normalization of sexual coercion in US society.

Women's participation in sports, especially at the collegiate level, has increased precipitously since the passage of Title IX of the federal civil rights law in 1972. But at the same time, neoliberalism's push toward presumably meritocratic gender neutrality in markets masks the lack of genuine equity, the ubiquity of violence against women, and the unresolved hegemony of hypermasculine culture in many athletic spaces. The "project of commodification" in sports under neoliberalism, Connell observes, "reinstates gender division and gender hierarchy in highly divisive ways" (2011, 55).

Militarized Subcultures

One of the most enduring bastions of hypermasculinity is the military—and militarized occupations and subcultures such as police and vigilante/white supremacist groups. Theidon defines militarized masculinity as "that fusion of certain practices and images of maleness with the use of weapons, the exercise of violence, and the performance of aggressive and frequently misogynistic masculinity" (2009, 5). Although military and police agencies in the US and elsewhere have bent somewhat under the pressure of civil rights legislation and internal actors advancing a feminist agenda since the late twentieth century, the high incidence of discrimination and sexual assaults has endured. "Feminist strategies have achieved formal integration, but not cultural or substantive equality" in the US military (Abrams 2016, 307).

Indeed, representation without culture change has likely contributed to the failure of US military elites' widely articulated goals to eradicate rape and sexual assault. Women continue to be the primary victims of violence within militarized subcultures; for example, a 2018 report issued by the Pentagon stated that more than 6,700 incidents of sexual assault in the military had been reported in 2017—10 percent higher than the previous year and the highest count on record since such incidents have been tracked (Gibbons-Neff 2018). Research also suggests high incidence of intimate partner violence among families of active duty and military families (Tasso et al. 2016). Military culture is not only fiercely hypermasculine, but heteronormative as well; thus rape and assault of effeminate men, lesbians, and transgender individuals are also prevalent (Rich, Schutten, and Rogers 2012).

Benedict finds that the Department of Defense has failed to address a misogynist culture that puts its own female members at risk, seemingly more concerned with protecting male members from scandal than with protecting female members from rape (2008a). She reports that routine language used by drill instructors is rife with misogyny. "[I]ntructors still routinely denigrate recruits by calling them 'pussy,' 'girl,' 'bitch,' 'lady' and 'dyke.'" Quoting Army Spc. Mickiela Montoya, who served in Iraq, Benedict writes: "There are only three things the guys let you be if you're a girl in the military: a bitch, a ho, or a dyke. One guy. . . . told me in Vietnam they had prostitutes, but they don't have those in Iraq, so they have women soldiers instead" (2008b n.p.). Additionally, Abrams suggests that unless military culture is evaluated through a masculinities lens, one that "reveals how male power and status are constructed and how the quest to attain idealized masculinities is sustained," (2016, 305) systems that support the conditions for "violence as a tool to reclaim a sense of masculine entitlement and power" (ibid., 330) will continue to be replicated.

Toxic "Tech" Masculinity

One of the male-dominated occupational areas implicated in prevalent harass-ment and discrimination against women is the technology sector, a vast enterprise comprised of companies that are involved in computing—design, development, and applications—and/or the use of highly innovative and advanced technologies in the provision of goods and services. In computer operations alone (information technology, or IT work), the number of people employed increased from 450,000 in 1970 to 4.6 million in 2014 (Beckhusen 2016). The US Census Bureau reports that as the proportion of women in all occupations has slowly increased, however, the IT sector has bucked the trend. Here, the proportion of women has actually declined from 31.0 percent in 1990 to 25.0 percent in 2014 (Beckhusen 2016, 9). This decline quantifies the "leaky pipeline" thesis that women leave STEM fields to avoid the often hostile climate, although recent research suggests that many women are filtered out by complex layers of gender exclusionary practices in academia and science and technology work organizations (Blickenstaff 2005). And this shift appears simultaneous to the incorporation of a "gender neutrality" framework and a revitalized myth of meritocracy with the advance of neoliberalism.

The technology sector is one characterized by a highly masculinized culture where women are not only outnumbered but also subjected to harassment, dis-crimination, and hostile work environments as well as expected to be involved in highly sexualized activities outside of work. In the spring of 2018, for example, a biopharmaceutical conference in Boston featured topless dancers, with pasties and bikini bottoms and corporate logos painted on their bodies. A female execu-tive who witnessed the display called out conference organizers by updating an open letter written by two female biotech leaders to report similar problematic activities at a previous event two years prior (Leung 2018). Such incidents led to Chang's labeling of the tech sector as "Brotopia" (2018).

The tech industry also contains one of the great ironies identified in the study of contemporary masculine subcultures: highly confident and dominant mascu-line individuals and groups coexist with those created and inhabited by men who feel relatively deprived of the spoils of traditional masculinity, particularly with regard to access to women's bodies (Gismondi 2018). Chang (2018), for example, suggests that one of the primary reasons the tech industry is so lopsided with regard to the gender demography of its workforce is because it has sought to exclude women using the essentialist pretext that antisocial people are better suited to the work, and that women are less likely to be antisocial than men.

Many tech workers are self-described "geeks"—a term that originated as a pejorative applied by outsiders, now the basis for a subculture that revolves around a cultural archetype: "socially awkward, glasses-wearing white men"

(Salter and Blodgett 2017). The subculture includes both tech-sector laborers and tech users, such as gamers who often view themselves as devalued by the larger society (Salter 2017, 4). "Geek masculinity" is often characterized as toxic given its misogynistic ideology, articulated in online spaces by men who use technology as a medium and harassment as a mechanism to reassert male supremacy.[5] Ging cites Connell and Messerschmidt (2005) whose analysis of the complex enactments of contemporary masculinity suggest that geek masculinity "both repudiates and reifies elements of hegemonic masculinity" (2017, 5). That these concerns are creeping into the mainstream is exemplified by data from a survey that found more than a quarter of men between the ages of fourteen and twenty-four "felt women's gains had come at the expense of men" (Coontz 2017).

People who identify themselves as involuntarily celibate, or *incels*, are a particularly virulent subset of disgruntled and frequently white-supremacist tech users. According to Gismondi, the term was originally coined by a woman in Toronto but "has been co-opted by an online misogynistic subculture of men who blame women for their sexual frustration." These men "claim that the sexual revolution has led to a consequence-free life of pleasure for young women [clearly an arguable position—editor's note], while awkward or unattractive men are left behind" (Kelly 2018). Another current phenomenon consists of men attracted to such platforms as Infowars who internalize beliefs in the omnipresence of a malevolent government and powerful institutions that require them to "become more virile, and better-armed, to survive" (Williamson and Steel 2018, A1). They are eager consumers of products such as "Super Male Vitality," promising to improve virility (ibid., A12). Early research that points to decreasing sperm counts over a generation adds fuel to claims by some men's rights groups of an emasculinization of men in modern culture. "'Beta's make no sperm,' according to one blogger" (Bowles 2018, 1).

Some of these frustrated and angry men revere Elliot Rodger who went on a killing rampage in 2014, after writing a 141-page manifesto that attributed his virginity to women who had rejected him. Others have called for mass violence targeted at women, including rape and acid attacks, as part of the "Incel Revolution" (Gismondi 2018). Several more recent terrorist-style mass killings have been attributed to incels since Rodger's rampage, with one posting a Facebook message minutes before a rampage that killed ten people, eight of them women, saying "The Incel Rebellion has already begun! . . . All hail the Supreme Gentleman Elliot Rodger!" (Gismondi 2018). But Rodger is not the only source of incel ruminations. For at least the last twenty-five years, a French writer, Michel Houellebecq, has published numerous novels in which he expounds on a proto-incel philosophy of "misanthropic men who, precisely because they cannot achieve romantic or sexual satisfaction, believe that sex is the most important thing in life. . . . representing sex as something women owe men" and who contemplate violence as a response to rejection (Kirsch 2018).

Tolentino suggests that despite the rhetoric of sexual deprivation, closer inspection uncovers a masculinist subculture that desires "absolute male supremacy" (2018). Ging's analysis of multiple platforms in the "manosphere"—an online network of blogs and websites dedicated to masculinity and men's interest communities—finds clear evidence of antifeminist hostility over the "destabilization of white, male privilege" and perceptions of female encroachment in the labor force as responsible for the downward mobility of men (2017, 16). These aggrieved "alphas, betas, and incels"[6] sometimes join forces, creating hybrid masculinities to achieve their goals for the defeat of feminism. They also project their collective hostility onto other perceived beneficiaries of ascendant identity politics: the LGBTQ+ community and people of color.

Clearly, both the lens of intersectionality applied to men, and a focus on the displaced anger of those who feel they have lost their advantage in the contemporary market expose the toxicity of this loosely aligned "tech" legion. Once exposed it becomes clear that maintaining patterns of stratification *among men* ultimately serves neoliberalism and polarizes potential alliances organized around the principle of equality for all. Linking toxic masculinity, then, to an understanding of the influence of the neoliberal project and the current hegemony of capitalist elites is necessary in formulating responses to it.

Toward Disrupting Gender Violence

What are the mechanisms that can alter what Connell calls the "linked pattern of [masculine] toxicity" (2011, 13) so evident in these subcultures? By what means can we hope to alter the structural conditions and social relationships that underlie gender violence? We have witnessed tremendous changes in the legal and policy spheres over the past decades, many of them moving in the direction of increased protections and rights for women and other marginalized groups. Though political will to address these issues is crucial, and heretofore not constant, the pendulum continues to swing. Political movements on the right have gained traction in recent times and threaten those gains, but so have efforts to resist and organize on the left. Addressing the need for rights and protections for women is crucially important. Doing so without paying close attention to how these changes may affect the perceptions of some men and women who subscribe to a zero-sum theory of power and resource distribution and simultaneously embrace traditional gender ideologies, is clearly problematic.

The neoliberal project continues to promote individual choice and achievement as the only valid paths toward change, obscuring the need for structural change, and thereby overlooking those for whom existing structures are *barriers* to individual choice. Similarly, more traditional legalistic solutions to "gender problems" clearly provide only temporary solutions if cultural and structural conditions are not simultaneously addressed. If we are to disrupt gender violence, we must acknowledge and alter the institutionalized structures that create and uphold it and then develop alternatives that allow the individuals within such structures to carve new paths. Lewis, Marine, and Kenney (2016), for example, offer the vision of universities as potential progressive sites for significant change despite their complicity in supporting masculinist subcultures. In their study, they found that many young women on campuses use intersectional understandings of feminism to develop a politics of resistance to neoliberalism, through networks and community, to confront sexism and its masculinist manifestations.

We have shown here how prototypical sites of male power heighten violence against women—and we have also outlined how those sites disadvantage men *even while apparently providing them advantages*. Decades of research implicating them have led to some positive changes, such as the proliferation of "bystander intervention" programs to raise awareness among young men of factors that may signal potential gendered violence situations—and to encourage disruption of them. Or the concerted effort by the National Collegiate Athletic Association (NCAA) to develop and fund violence prevention programs (www. ncaa.org). Neither of these efforts are panaceas and, in fact, Messner's (2016) research suggests that bystander intervention efforts, situated within a medicalized and marketized violence prevention edifice, risk depoliticizing rape and sexual assault while reindividualizing the social construction of "the rapist."

For years, social scientists have theorized that addressing socioeconomic inequalities is an important step toward diminishing violence, including its gendered manifestations (see, for example, Shur, this volume). Thus, if men are also the targets of exploitation within the power structures that provide them with advantages (Connell 2011, 13), and there is much evidence to suggest this is the case, efforts must be made to pull back the curtain that obscures how these complex linkages are forged in order to build the alliances necessary for change. Current sociopolitical conditions outlined by Messner (this volume) suggest that we are in a moment of historic gender formation, given the convergence of neoliberalism and the institutionalization and professionalization of feminist practice. Certainly the sort of antifeminist backlash expressed in the vitriol and latent violence of incels is one possible outcome; there is also evidence that suggests potential for forging profeminist male alliances in antiviolence work. It is in that possibility we invest our hope for disrupting toxic masculine subcultures and lifting up currently subordinated masculinities in allyships that promote equity and social justice for all.

NOTES

1 While the question of the connection between violence and sports is unresolved, there is ample evidence of some relationship. In a review of the literature, Lopiano et al. (2016) found strong evidence of social support for violence against women among college athletes. Woods (2007) found that cultural upbringing may lead males to choose a violent sport in order to assert their manhood and that the violence of the sport may spill over into other

facets of their lives. Passero (2015) reviewed existing literature and found the level of violence of the sport is associated with the level of violence in athletes' lives off the field. Safraoui (2014) found that athletes in contact sports displayed higher levels of aggression than those in noncontact sports. Lemieux, McKelvie, and Stout (2002) linked off-field aggression to physical size rather than type of sport; although one is left to surmise that size is strongly associated with several sports. Issues regarding the level of competitiveness of the sport, the amount and type of bodily contact in games, the social status of the athletes in their communities, and other variables require further investigation. As more women enter sports at higher levels of competition and gain more social recognition, comparative studies of violence among male and female athletes could be instructive.

2   The poet and feminist Adrienne Rich suggests the solipsism of White feminists is "not the consciously held belief that one race is inherently superior to all others, but a tunnel-vision which simply does not see nonwhite experience or existence as precious or significant, unless in spasmodic, impotent guilt-reflexes, which have little or no long-term continuing momentum or political usefulness."

3   Significant advances that specifically addressed the legal condition of women included the passage of the Violence Against Women Act (VAWA) and the successes of Ruth Bader Ginsburg's legal advocacy, both before and after her appointment to the Supreme Court, offering examples of twentieth-century legal and judicial progress on behalf of women. Congress passed VAWA in 1994 to improve criminal justice and community responses to domestic violence, sexual assault, and stalking. It was the first federal law to address gender-based violence as such and to provide funding and services for a wide spectrum of remedies. Initiated by then Senator (later Vice President) Joe Biden, the act has had tremendous effect. VAWA was expanded in 2000 and 2005 (see "History of VAWA," The Women's Legal Defense and Education Fund, retrieved from www.legalmomentum.org). VAWA expired during the government shutdown of 2018, was temporarily reauthorized when the government reopened in January 2019, but faces an uncertain future.

First through her advocacy for women in her work with the American Civil Liberties Union and later from her position as the second woman appointed to the Supreme Court, Ruth Bader Ginsburg has created a legacy of opinions that have affected law and policy for gender equity. She has argued successfully against gender-based requirements for social security benefits, for equal application of protection requirements of the Due Process Clause of the Fifth Amendment, and against the prohibition to accept women to the Virginia Military Institute, a public institution of higher education, thereby disrupting an anachronistic all-male bastion. (See "Tribute: The Legacy of Ruth Bader Ginsburg and WRP Staff," ACLU. Retrieved from www.aclu.org.)

4   "Gang rape" was the term initially used to describe rapes by multiple perpetrators. Harkins and Dixon (2010) argue that "multiple perpetrator rape" is the preferred term for rapes by more than one offender but who are not necessarily affiliated with each other. "Gang rape" more accurately describes rapes by members of a group with shared allegiance, such as street gangs. Since affiliation is the key that distinguishes the two, it can be argued that multiple perpetrator rape by fraternity members could qualify as gang rape.

5   There are overlaps and fissures among women and men on the far right. Though not apparently active in the male-dominated digital space, a small contingent of self-styled "trad-wives" (traditional wives), philosophically associated with men who view feminism as the root of their problems, view sexual liberation as dangerous for women. Supportive of aggrieved men, these women embrace extreme conservatism and white supremacy but are not associated with incel culture (see Kelly 2018). Recent examples of political calls to reject immigration are often aimed at such concerns—associating people of color with danger to

(White) women's security and suggesting that men embrace a traditional role as protectors of women's sexual safety.

6 According to the Manosphere Glossary (n.d.), alpha males are at the top of the ladder of sexual action, betas are unable to "get enough" sex, and incels experience chronic sexual rejection. Hierarchy and status concerns are endemic to these descriptors, yet whatever differences are perceived in their composition, these "groups" will form alliances in order to create opposition to women, and feminist women in particular.

PART II

Manifestations of Sexual Coercion and Violence

Part 2 consists of five sections; each explores particular manifestations of gendered violence. Every section includes a historical sketch of the phenomena studied, as well as a discussion of suggested remedies for addressing the violence. We examine multiple causes and consequences of various forms of gender violence and draw attention to the similarities that exist among them.

Section 1 analyzes harassment and bullying, widely experienced forms of gender violence that are only recently receiving serious public attention. In section 2, we explore sexual violations in multiple contexts. Section 3 offers theoretical and policy analyses of intimate partner abuse. The effects of gender violence on children, as both victims and observers, forms the subject in section 4. In section 5, we consider the conundrum of commodified bodies within an overarching framework of neoliberalism and feminist practice.

These distinctions do not represent mutually exclusive categories. These types of violence are often treated as such in legal and policy arenas and even in how people identify their own victimization. In addition to articles that represent history and the social sciences, part 2 includes contributions from criminal justice, law, health education, nursing, social work, policy makers, and community activists.

Harassment and Bullying

Forty years after naming sexual harassment, a condition experienced by multitudes of working women (Farley 1978; 2017), a groundswell of testimonials unleashed by the international #MeToo movement occupied news headlines, social media campaigns, and courtrooms. *Time Magazine*'s Person of the Year for 2017 was "The Silence Breakers," women from across the occupational hierarchy who came forward, each emboldened by others before them, to name men who sexually harassed and/or assaulted them and suffered no repercussions. Many of those named were celebrities; most were serial offenders. The collective energy released by violated women and their male allies has since been responsible for toppling many powerful men in entertainment and the arts, politics, and from the very pinnacles of corporate hierarchies. It has generated new analyses of a gendered violence phenomenon so normalized, and often corporately managed, that it had been effectively depoliticized (Martin 2016; Farley 2017).

For many, the breaking point was the election of Donald Trump as president of the US, after numerous women accused him of sexual harassment and his own words implicated him in this regard. Working women in myriad occupational settings, young girls and boys in their schools, LGBTQ+ youth and adults at work and at leisure, and gamers and social media users online are all vulnerable to bullying, harassment, and assault that is frequently gendered and sexual in nature, and they often endure harmful consequences for years. Class, race, and nationality complicate their vulnerability. On many levels, the US election of 2016 seemed to legitimize incivility and abuse. In a study of workplace bullying, for example, a sizeable minority of participants (46 percent) agreed that "the brutish campaigns leading to the 2016 election negatively impacted the workplace" (Namie 2017).

Harassment, bullying, and other forms of physical and emotional abuse occur in the daily lives of many people marginalized by their locations in what Acker has described as *inequality regimes*, the "local, ongoing practical activities of organizing work that, at the same time, reproduce complex inequalities" (2006, 442). In this section, we extend Acker's intersectional approach to analyze complex power relations in "work" more broadly construed. Inequality regimes organized along race, class, gender, and sexuality hierarchies shape instrumental and emotional labor and social relationships. We can apply the concept to students in classrooms, teams, and peer groups; the paid and unpaid work of women and men in multiple sites; and the complex cultural labor that is required to negotiate social practices on the streets and in cyber spheres of activity. And as Hearn and Parkin suggest, "sexual harassment, bullying, and physical violence do not 'just happen'" (2001, 47). They coexist with complex formal and informal norms, and political-economic practices that reproduce historical hegemonic power relations, creating tensions between the political struggle to recognize these violences and the fact that they are frequently taken for granted.

Some definition is in order to distinguish between these related concepts. Harassment is, for legal and analytical purposes, generally separated into the related concepts of sex-based or gender harassment and sexual harassment (McLaughlin et al. 2012). The former encompasses gender-based discrimination of a nonsexual nature, such as "experiences of disparaging conduct *not intended* to elicit sexual cooperation; rather, these are crude, verbal, physical, and symbolic behaviors that convey hostile and offensive attitudes about members of one sex—typically women" (Lim and Cortina 2005, 483; emphasis ours). Sexual harassment involves sexualized behaviors that are unwanted and perceived to be coercive and that may involve touching, embarrassing gestures, sexual advances, physical and verbal assault, including threatening, obscene or derogatory statements or mediated with offensive or pornographic materials (Hearn and Parkin 2001, 5; Lim and Cortina 2005).

Bullying has long been viewed as a problem among young people, especially in schools—and as a gendered phenomenon as well (Hearn and Parkin 2001; Espelage et al. 2015). More recently it has been recognized a problem that adults encounter in the workplace, and analyzed as such (Hearn and Parkin 2001; Tattum and Lane 1994). Workplace bullying typically involves unwanted and persistent behaviors that a recipient perceives to be humiliating, intimidating, or otherwise offensive and can include a range of differential treatments, including isolation, excessive criticism, being shouted at, unjustified written warnings, denial of leave, or forced resignations (Hearn and Parkin 2001).

In 2017 alone, the Equal Employment Opportunity Commission (EEOC) reported 12,438 sex-based harassment complaints, of which 6,696 were specifically sexual in nature. Of these claims, men brought 16.5 percent. These numbers were relatively consistent for eight years prior (EEOC 2018). Although research methods vary considerably across studies and contexts, estimates indicate that 40 to 75 percent of women and 13 to 31 percent of men in the US workforce have experienced workplace sexual harassment (Willness et al. 2007; McDonald 2012). Extensive meta-analyses in Europe and Australia find similarly high rates (McDonald 2012). Women are largely victims and perpetrators are overwhelmingly men. And despite more opportunities for legal redress and heightened awareness through workplace trainings and highly visible court cases, most researchers believe that victims who perceive harassment report fewer than half of these incidents, especially if they lack social support or fear retaliation.

Research on workplace violence in the global south is typically subsumed under the concept of bullying (Willness et al. 2007).

Based upon extensive survey evidence, the Workplace Bullying Institute estimates that thirty million workers in the US experience bullying and another thirty million witness it, claiming that a majority of workers are affected by bullying at work (Namie 2017). There is also considerable evidence that bullying and sexual harassment *overlap* in workplaces (Hearn and Parkin 2001) and in schools (Espelage et al. 2015). A recent study of schoolchildren's experiences of bullying and sexual harassment, for example, suggests that approximately 28 percent of twelve- to eighteen-year-olds experienced bullying and nearly half of students in grades seven through twelve experienced some form of sexual harassment (ibid., 2542). Moreover, bullying is empirically correlated with the use of homophobic name-calling; under close scrutiny it appears to be a link in the *bully-to-harassment pathway*, an observable pattern identified by school-based researchers. Middle school bullies who incorporate homophobic slurs in their early perpetrations are more likely to become agents of sexual harassment before they enter high school.

Discovering Sexual Harassment

In 1980, the US government specified sexual harassment in the *Code of Federal Regulations* (No. 1604.11, 925) under provision of Title VII of the Civil Rights Act of 1964. The EEOC adopted a broad-ranging definition that includes quid pro quo forms of harassment (requests for sexual favor where submission is linked to conditions of employment), unwanted sexual advances, and the existence of hostile work environments. Both gender studies scholars and legal decisions have further expanded the range of contexts and experiences that constitute the phenomenon of sexual harassment. Especially significant have been the recognition of same-sex harassment in 1998 through the landmark US Supreme Court ruling in *Oncale v. Sundowner Offshore Services, Inc.*, the recognition of racialized harassment in the lives of women and men of color (Buchanan and Ormerod 2002; Kent 2007), and the hostility toward LGBTQ+ individuals in heteronormative settings (Hill 2009; Willis 2012).

The fact that sexual harassment was not legally defined until 1980 made gathering official data on the problem difficult until the last decades of the twentieth century. Social science research indicates it is far more widespread than government data actually document. That sexual harassment was only so recently defined is also very likely the consequence of two significant sociological phenomena: the social construction of sexuality and the organization of human activities into public and private spheres. The latter has its roots in early sex-based divisions of labor but is a fairly recent phenomenon along the arc of human history, solidified during the spread of industrial capitalism in the nineteenth century.

Modernizing societies dichotomized the public domain of production and the private sphere of home and family, thus relegating sexuality to the realm of the personal and private. Despite this legacy, the fact remains that a great deal of what we understand about sexuality is constructed in the public sphere of labor, law, entertainment, and media. And increasingly more sexual interaction is enacted in public spaces (Hearn and Parkin 1987), including online. Until quite recently, however, our intellectual frame of reference assumed that bureaucratic rules in workplaces and schools neutralize sexuality, thus veiling the extent to which sexualities pervade and are organized through activities and structures that constitute the public sphere.

Contemporary feminism provided a context within which sexual harassment could be named. One of the first large-scale surveys of working women found that 70 percent of respondents had experienced some form of harassment at work (Farley 1978). MacKinnon (1979) stretched the definitional boundaries by introducing the notion of sexualized environments—workplaces in which the "background noise" includes sexual discourse and innuendo. The anxiety and discomfort these settings produce for many women ultimately affects their capacity to work productively. And as feminist theory and research has become more intersectional over the last several decades, the literature has reflected deeper understandings of how the confluence of gender, race, class, and sexuality play out in the harassment experiences of individuals negotiating the inequality regimes in which they live and work.

Explaining Harassment at Work

Early activists and scholars focused explanations for sexual harassment at work on the sexual harassment of women by men. Conventional wisdom favors the natural/biological model that explains sexual harassment as an outgrowth of presumed natural attractions between men and women playing out in public contexts. Early feminist theory, however, generally rejected biological premises, adopting a structural approach that focused on the distribution of power and the division of labor in organizations. Feminists stressed the hierarchical nature of modern organizations and developed frameworks that problematized women's location in organizational structures relative to men (Kanter 1977) and the feminization of women's work (Gutek and Morasch 1982).

Eventually theorists have come to understand organizational contexts themselves as "sexualized" (Hearn and Parkin 1987; Tancred-Sheriff 1989) and gendered (Acker 1990). These organizational perspectives derived strength from the gender demography of modern organizations in which the majority of women workers are segregated into low-wage, sex-typed jobs with less access to organizational power than work performed by most men. Indeed, a significant number of women who experience harassment are victimized by superiors or other powerful men in their schools or workplaces and women in traditionally male occupations and work settings are particularly vulnerable (Willness et al. 2007; McDonald 2012; Van de Griend and Messias, this volume).

Lack of access to organizational power is not the only dynamic that enables harassment in organizations. Research has also established the existence of *contrapower harassment* by working peers, subordinates, and even clients to show how work roles and occupations of women are significant per se, regardless of the distribution of organizational power (Gutek and Morasch 1982; Gutek 1985; Willness et al. 2007; McLaughlin et al. 2012). Moreover, as Acker reminds us, gender does not operate apart from other systems of organizational stratification. "All organizations have inequality regimes, defined as loosely interrelated practices, processes, actions, and meanings that result in and maintain class, gender, and racial inequalities within particular organizations. (Acker 2006, 443)."

"Sex-role spillover" was an early explanatory model that captured dynamics that occur in workplaces when women at work are expected to be nurturers, mediators, and/or sexually available in accordance with the "natural" roles associated with the private sphere (Gutek and Morasch 1982). Women in traditionally female occupations such as clerical work, domestic service, and other caring occupations most typically experience this scenario since the association of job to gender expectations is strong.

Women in nontraditional occupations also experience sexual harassment. In fact, research suggests that women in male-dominated professions and/or male-dominated institutions suffer higher rates of victimization than women in more socially sanctioned female occupations (Mansfield et al. 1991; McLaughlin et al. 2012). Women who step beyond the boundaries of women's work into male-dominated occupations such as supervisory work (McLaughlin et al. 2012) or join masculinist institutions such as police, military, the trades, and athletic organizations also face hostility, intimidation, and harassment (Gregory and Lees 1999; Hearn and Parkin 2001; Willness et al. 2007; McDonald 2009).

Women of color in both the trades and professional occupations face racial and sexual harassment in their jobs (Buchanan and Ormerod 2002), often simultaneously as racialized sexual harassment, demonstrating the confluence of race and gender in women's lives (Kent 2007; Woods et al. 2009). Women's intrusion into male-dominated institutions may threaten both the solidarity and social privilege of the traditional occupants (Yoder 1991). McLaughlin et al. (2012) find that performing supervisory roles, even when legitimated by employers, actually increases the likelihood that women will experience gender-based and sexual harassment.

Most work organizations have ostensibly suppressed sexuality; their goals are, on the face of it, explicitly nonsexual. Though sexuality may appear suppressed, however, many of these organizations may tacitly encourage oppressive male sexuality among employees through exploitative ad campaigns, company events such as employee picnics and holiday parties, or through the frequent use of sexual metaphor in communicative processes. Some organizations have explicit sexual goals and sexualized cultures (Hearn and Parkin 1987), such as pornographic bookstores, "gentlemen's clubs," and establishments that specialize in intimate apparel and sex toys.

Williams (2007) explored the situations of women working in highly sexualized environments and found that demeaning and often degrading work expectations are frequently perceived to be job requirements, rather than experienced as harassment. She suggests that the notion of perpetrator be reframed to include organizations and not just individuals. More recently, research shows that the reindividualizing of work in the neoliberal economy has functioned to *minimize* organizational culpability for gender-based and sexual harassment, particularly in situations where personal care services and bodywork are involved. Brunner and Dever (2014) show that the blurring of lines between traditional workplaces and more flexible service delivery in a variety of settings complicates workers' perceptions of which behaviors are "organizational" and which are personal. This research demonstrates the importance of analyzing the transformation of work—and peoples' experience of it—in new service economies characterized by high levels of deregulation and insecurity (ibid., 461).

Many organizational cultures tend to be both heteronormatively organized and sexually charged, specifically around heterosexuality. For example, recent research on tech industry workers shows that employees are increasingly expected to endure (hetero)sexualized activities outside of the workplace as conditions of acceptance within it (O'Toole and Schiffman, this volume). The behavior of sexist and homophobic individuals is either not recognized, or worse, excused in these settings, and frequently contributes to the harassment and intimidation of LGBTQ+ employees; research on their work experiences shows sizeable self-reports of harassment and discrimination. According to Hill (2009), for example, Lambda Legal's 2005 Workplace Fairness Survey showed that nearly two of every five LGBTQ+ workers reported some form of discrimination based on sexual orientation.

Although more workplaces are perceived to be LGBTQ+ friendly since the turn of the twenty-first century, some gay and lesbian workers still report experiencing inequalities such as harassment, stereotyping, and gender discrimination (Giuffre et al, 2008) even in these more welcoming contexts. Hill's review of the research shows considerable backlash against corporate inclusion programs, documenting the resistance to full corporate membership for sexual minorities (2009, 38). Taken together, this workplace research shows that organizational structures, cultures, and work roles are not mutually exclusive and that harassment is a persistent and multifaceted organizational problem.

Harassment and Bullying outside of the Workplace

Most harassment research has focused on work and occupations, yet, sociocultural theories provide an important link between sexual harassment at work and that which occurs in other public and private contexts. Research on young people's experiences in schools, for example, confirms that bullying and harassment are common experiences. These behaviors begin in early childhood and affect heterosexual as well as gay, lesbian, and bisexual students and are so frequent that many students come to experience them as normal (Hlavka 2014; Van de Griend and Messias, this volume). Robinson's (2005) research on the relationships between masculinity and the harassment of girls in secondary schools shows how male students perform hegemonic masculinity through both sexist and sexual harassment of girls.

Efforts to effectively deal with the problem of harassment of children by their peers are often muddied by the fact that some teachers and parents may still tacitly accept behaviors that are frequently antecedent to it: teasing and bullying (Stein 1995). Hlavka's (2014) qualitative analysis of young girls' accounts of harassment and abuse experiences uncovered that respondents had "few available safe spaces; girls were harassed and assaulted at parties, in school, on playgrounds, on buses, and in cars" (ibid., 344). Her findings emphasize the extent to which sexual violence is normalized in their lives, as well as their acceptance of essentialist ideas about gender that construct compulsory heterosexuality. Girls describe boys and men as natural sexual aggressors and shared accounts of their deference and self-blame for violence they endure.

Studies of street harassment (Bernard and Schlaffer 1983; Gardner 1995) show that harassment is not only a vehicle through which individual men exercise power over women, but that it also often functions as a ritual of male bonding for participants. Public harassments are simultaneously expressions of male solidarity and bravado, and mechanisms for the social control and intimidation of females; racialized street harassment of women of color is often invisible (Mills, this volume). LGBTQ+ individuals are frequently targeted in public places. The antigay/lesbian violence that is often meted out based on the mere "appearance" of being gay—a perception of "gender betrayal" that threatens homophobic individuals and groups—can ultimately affect not only gays and lesbians but also "heterosexuals unwilling to be bound by their assigned gender identity" (Vazsquez 1992, 161).

As technology has become ever more sophisticated, so have the methods of perpetrating sexist and sexual harassment. Siegle cites a 2009 AP-MTV poll in which more than 17 percent of fourteen- to twenty-four-year-olds agreed that digital abuse is a serious problem for their age group and 47 percent had experienced cyberbullying (2010). She also reports that "24 percent of 14- to 17-year-olds report having been involved in some type of naked sexting," frequently under pressure (ibid., 15). Social media platforms, by virtue of their capabilities to facilitate both in-time conversations and invasive communications, are now recognized as a locus of harassment and gender violence, as Poland explicates later in this section.

The Politics of Sexual Harassment

Because feminists in the US were the first to name sexual harassment, there is a longer history of sexual harassment politics here than in other parts of the world. Countries in the European Union have more recently adopted nation-based and collective policies as a result of high-profile harassment claims in the US and their own societies. Comparative research, however, shows distinctly different conceptualizations, reflecting variations in culture, political institutions, and transnational politics (Saguy 2003; Zippel 2006).

Zippel suggests that in the US, there is a *politics of fear* wherein male employees are instructed to fear women's lawsuits, whereas in Germany, there is a *politics as usual* that allows men to ignore harassment and the laws that regulate it (2006, 5). For example, a reactionary chorus of #HimToo emerged in relation to a contentious confirmation process for US Supreme Court justice Brett Kavanaugh, who was accused of sexual assault by several women after his nomination was announced. The US president proclaimed that this is a "scary time for young men in America . . ." (North 2017). France has a more laissez-faire attitude toward workplace sexuality, where touching and sexual banter are still common. Many French consider US workplaces to be intolerant; yet more extreme forms of harassment are socially constructed as violence against women in the French cultural context (Saguy 2003, 4–5).

During the 1990s in the European Union, in keeping with a long tradition of protecting worker and human rights, all forms of harassment were legally conceptualized as violations of worker dignity (Zippel 2006). The differences in the trajectories and approaches in the US and Europe are fairly striking. In the US, sexual harassment policy has primarily evolved since the 1970s through the legal-regulatory process of using the courts to shape law. Having been originally regulated under the Civil Rights Act of 1964 as a form of workplace *discrimination* (not violence), the primary effect has been to penalize the differential treatment of women (and eventually men) based on their sex.

In Europe, sexual harassment regulations have been handled through creating laws in parliaments and the primary focus is on the experience of harm rather than discrimination (Saguy 2003; Zippel 2006). In both the US and the countries of the European Union, there is consensus that women should not be coerced to exchange sex for any work-related benefit (Zippel 2006). Contradictions notwithstanding, sexual harassment in all its forms has been found to have deleterious effects on its victims.

The Effects of Sexual Harassment

Sexual harassment is not just perpetrated by powerful and/or threatened individuals, it is a manifestation of the intractability of inequality regimes in organizations and in the extant sociopolitical system. Victims are affected economically, socially, and psychologically, given the ubiquity of sexual harassment and its aftereffects (Willness 2007; McDonald 2012; Van De Griend and Messias, this volume). Research has shown that Black women perceive cross-sex harassment by White men to be more upsetting, threatening, and embarrassing than harassment by Black men, which contributes to the likelihood and severity of their post-traumatic stress disorder experiences (Woods et al. 2009, 71–73).

Gender scholars have theorized that male sexual aggression is not a natural attribute but part of a social script that boys and men are socialized to accept and that girls and women are taught to expect. Men are socially rewarded for enacting sexual and occupational dominance, which serves both collective and self-interests. Situating these analyses within a structural framework helps to underscore the complexity of bullying and harassment.

Together with the more general social and political turn toward incivility and violence in our world, it is easy to comprehend the emergence of the new social movements cited earlier. They hold perpetrators and their organizational and political apologists accountable for the monumental harm they create in the lives of victims, their coworkers, and their larger social networks. The chapters in this section both conceptualize and explain a range of sexual harassment experiences, extending current understandings of the sites of harassment and the sublimation of political efforts to eradicate it. They point to the importance of both scholarship and activism as critical components of social change efforts.

SUGGESTIONS FOR FURTHER READING

Jeff Hearn and Wendy Parkin, *Gender, Sexuality, and Violence in Organizations*, 2001

Louise O'Neill, *Asking For It*, 2016

Michele A. Paludi, Jennifer L. Martin, James E. Gruber, and Susan Fineran, editors; *Sexual Harassment in Education and Work Settings: Current Research and Best Practices for Prevention*, 2015

Bailey Poland, *Haters: Harassment, Abuse, and Violence Online*, 2016

Ian Rivers and Neil Duncan, *Bullying: Experiences and Discourses of Sexuality and Gender*, 2013

Agoraphobia

Natasha Sajé

Without even trying I can think of a half-dozen women
afraid to drive, including my mother.
Oh, maybe not afraid, period, but afraid of:
highways, the big city, cross country, the beltway,
the high-speed merge, the GW bridge, the circles in D.C.
I always knew it as something to be feared and fought
because it crawls up on you like an ant,
then imbeds itself like a tick that you have to burn out,
pluck by the pincers and shake loose.
But the trick is finding it, figuring out
where it comes from and how it starts: the illness
that keeps you inside for a few weeks,
burgeoning traffic or even some small incident
barely worth mentioning or hardly noticed:
a flat tire, a misplaced key.
I remember my hands trembling on the steering wheel
of my first car, driving around the block,
a new license securely in my purse,
and realizing it was no good, that square of paper.
As I grew older I became conscious of it
in other women, and saw that it wasn't just driving,
that driving was only one facet of this stone:
the friend who stayed in after the birth of her second baby
as if suddenly the door had been locked from the inside,
and she and her daughter were drenched in gasoline
and the world were a burning match.
London shrank to the size of her house.
After a year she made her way to the doctor, the supermarket,
but she'd never really seen the city, and
after a week I knew it better than she
and became her guide. In busses she chattered,
not looking where she was going.
Is the fear more common in beautiful places?
To know that always beyond one's reach is the Place des Vosges
or the Pantheon, to be savored in tandem if at all.
Some women never get over it.

Their worlds shrink to the size of their bodies
and then still smaller, as when they feel their stomachs
wrench at the sound of steps on the street.
This madness carries itself sanely through the hours
as one learns to compensate: having groceries delivered,
living through the telephone.
Like Marlene Dietrich at the end of her life
in a Paris apartment, the feathered boas and smoking jackets
sold discreetly piece by piece to pay for rent.
Fear of the marketplace. Fear of buying and selling
and of oneself being sold,
for when all the clothes and memorabilia were gone,
Dietrich knew that her body—
the legs once insured by Lloyds,
the gravelly voice,
the arched eyebrows—
would be next to go.

8

Expanding the Conceptualization of Workplace Violence

Implications for Research, Policy, and Practice

KRISTIN M. VAN DE GRIEND AND DEANNE K. HILFINGER MESSIAS

Interpersonal violence that occurs within the context of the formal, paid workplace affects women (and men, to a lesser degree) across the globe, resulting in a wide range of health, economic, and social problems (Krug et al. 2002; Pina and Gannon 2012; Waters et al. 2005). In this chapter we argue the case for reconsidering the current conceptual definitions of workplace, coworkers, and workplace violence set forth by scholars, policy makers, and practitioners, with the aim of promoting a more holistic understanding of the complex relationships between women's diverse workplaces and their health and well-being. We contend that a broader conceptualization of workplace—including intersectional, transdisciplinary, and transnational approaches and analyses—in research, policy, and practice will enhance the understanding of women's experiences of violence in the context of the performance of their multiple work roles. As noted by Messias and colleagues (1997), women perform various types and forms of work across the span of their lives, only a portion of which occurs within the context of a formal, paid workplace. For example, women commonly engage in domestic work, home and family work, and care work in both formal workplaces and informal workplaces, such as their own homes or other people's homes. Although women of all ages engage in community work, volunteer work, and schoolwork, the locations where these activities occur are often not recognized as workplaces because the work is not for pay (Messias et al. 1997, 2005). A restrictive definition of workplace violence means that interpersonal violence and aggression occurring within the context of women's work outside the formal, paid workplace could be invisible to or unaccounted for by researchers, policy-makers, and practitioners. Furthermore, the perpetration of workplace violence is not limited to coworkers but may involve patients, patrons, clients, family members, students, faculty members, peers, and individuals not directly associated with the workplace, such as a person committing an assault or robbery (Huerta et al. 2006; Jackson et al. 2002; LeBlanc and Kelloway 2002; Matchen and DeSouza 2000; Timmerman 2003).

By challenging the androcentric definition of work as paid employment we advocate for more inclusive conceptualizations of women's workplaces, types of work, and the individuals who perpetrate aggression and violence. Expanding the conceptualization and measurement would broaden the scope and dimensions of research, policies, and practices related to workplace violence. In making our case for an expanded conceptualization of workplace violence, we begin with an overview of the global extent of the phenomenon and the contextual factors frequently associated with workplace violence. We base our argument that workplace violence occurs not only within the context of women's paid employment in a formal workplace but also within the contexts of other types of work in which women of all ages engage (Messias et al. 1997), on research conducted in Australia, Belgium, Brazil, Canada, Ethiopia, Finland, France, Germany, Indonesia, Italy, the Netherlands, Norway, Poland, Slovakia, Sweden, Taiwan, Turkey, United Kingdom, and the United States. We begin with an examination of the impact of workplace violence on women's health, well-being, and work, and then present our argument for expanding the concept and measurement of workplace violence. In the final sections, we discuss the research, policy, and practice implications of an expanded conceptualization of workplace violence that incorporates multiple dimensions of the phenomenon in terms of work settings, gender, sexual orientation, age, and geography.

The Global Contexts of Workplace Violence

Workplace violence is a global women's health issue that encompasses multiple forms of interpersonal aggression, impacts people across the lifespan, occurs in communities across the globe regardless of level of economic and social development, and transcends national borders (Krug et al. 2002; Messing and Östlin 2006). The negative health, economic, and social impacts of workplace violence are evidenced in research and scholarship conducted across the globe, from Australia (Hegney et al. 2006) to Taiwan (Wei and Chen 2012), Ethiopia (Marsh et al. 2009), Brazil (DeSouza and Cerqueira 2009), and the United States (Krieger et al. 2008). Although men and boys are subjected to violence within the contexts of their formal and informal work, working women are at higher risk for more frequent and severe sexual harassment (Berdahl and Moore 2006; IPEU et al. 2004; Nielsen et al. 2010; Pina and Gannon 2012; Sears et al. 2011; Street et al. 2007; Stock and Tissot 2012). A meta-analysis of seventy-one studies conducted in a wide range of US academic, private, government, and military organizations indicated high rates of employed women reporting nonsexual harassment (58 percent) and sexual harassment (24 percent) (Ilies et al. 2003).

Workplace violence affects women of all ages, social status, and power, although women who are younger, employed in low-status jobs, and those with lower social power are at higher risk for workplace violence (Pina and Gannon 2012). A survey of female faculty and staff in Ethiopian colleges indicated 86.3 percent of the participants experienced both abuse and sexual harassment in the workplace, including being yelled and sworn at, treated as an inferior, exposed to unwanted physical contact or sexual suggestions, and mistreated because of their gender (Marsh et al. 2009). Employment exposes young women to the risk of violence. Among a sample of employed female adolescents in the US, 52 percent reported workplace sexual harassment (Fineran and Gruber 2009). Yet young women also engage in the (unpaid) work of learning, spending a considerable amount of their time in school, where they also face risks of sexual harassment, bullying, or other forms of intimidation (Wei and Chen 2012). For example, research conducted in Taiwan with students between the seventh and ninth grades found 20 percent of the girls had been subjected to unwanted sexual remarks or jokes and 5 percent had been inappropriately touched at school (Wei and Chen 2012). In the US, undocumented immigrant women working in agriculture and food processing industries are at especially high risk of persistent sexual harassment and other abuses (Bauer and Ramírez 2010). Older women providing home-based care to others, as paid employees, volunteers, or family caregivers, are another group at risk for exposure to workplace violence (Choi et al. 2007).

Women with low social status and those working in nontraditional workplaces such as domestic workers (who work and sometimes live in their employers' homes) are at high risk for workplace aggression and sexual harassment. Domestic workers' exposure to workplace violence has been documented in research conducted in Canada (Aronson and Neysmith 1996; Hutchinson and Wexler 2007), Indonesia (Silvey 2006), Sweden (Elwér et al. 2010), and the United States (Allen and Ciambrone 2003). To assess domestic workers' experiences of sexual harassment, DeSouza and Cerqueira (2009) surveyed domestic workers in a large metropolis in southern Brazil, using a Portuguese language version of the Sexual Experiences Questionnaire (SEQ; Stark et al. 2002). More than a quarter of the participants reported having experienced some form of sexual harassment at work within the previous 12 months. The investigators also inquired if the women were familiar with Brazil's legal definition of sexual harassment, to which 92 percent responded in the affirmative. The majority (61 percent) considered domestic work rendered them more vulnerable to sexual harassment than other types of work. Interestingly, researchers in Canada reported similar findings from a survey of professional women who worked in other people's homes, in nursing, social work, child management, and behavior management (Barling et al. 2001). Respondents reported having heard sexual comments (28.9 percent), received sexual compliments (28.3 percent), having been subjected to sexist remarks (18.3 percent), sexually propositioned (15.1 percent), or been touched in an unwanted way (19.9 percent). These professional women working in others' homes also experienced nonsexual workplace aggression, which included being the target of verbal aggression (32.8 percent), being yelled or sworn at (17.4 percent), threatened by a knife (11.9 percent), or hit (6.1 percent). The researchers reported a high correlation (r = 0.92) between sexual harassment and workplace aggression, which supports the notion that these forms of violence co-occur and that they may be measured together (Barling et al. 2001).

The Gendered Dimensions of Workplace Violence

Across the lifespan, gender is a critical dimension of workplace violence. Sexual harassment and bullying begin during childhood and impact heterosexual boys and girls, as well as lesbian, gay, and bisexual students in the US (Gruber and Fineran 2008; Patrick et al. 2013). Among a sample of mostly White middle and high school students in the northeastern US, Gruber and Fineran (2008) found differences in rates of sexual harassment and bullying at school, with lesbian, gay, and bisexual students reporting more bullying than their heterosexual peers. Although heterosexual students reported being bullied more often than they were sexually harassed, lesbian, gay, and bisexual students reported more incidents of sexual harassment than bullying. The researchers measured the association of health outcomes with experiences of sexual harassment and bullying in school and found poorer health outcomes among girls when compared to boys and among lesbian, gay, and bisexual students when compared to heterosexual students. There is evidence that these forms of violence perpetrated in US schools persist into adulthood and occur in various other contexts among women and sexual minorities (Hill and Silva 2005; IOM 2011; Sears et al. 2011).

Women in highly gendered professions, such as nursing, teaching, domestic work, sex work, and other service professions, are frequently targets of workplace violence, as evidenced by research conducted in Canada (Croft and Cash 2012; Wang et al. 2008), Brazil (DeSouza and Cerqueira 2009) and other countries (Krug et al. 2002). Rates of reported workplace violence among nurses ranged from 16.2 percent in Italy (Camerino et al. 2008) to nearly 60 percent in Australian elder care settings (Hegney et al. 2006) and 62 percent among Taiwanese hospital nurses (Lin and Liu 2005). Across these various settings, nurses identified patients and their family members as the most frequent perpetrators of verbal abuse and harassment (Hegney et al. 2006; Lin and Liu 2005). Camerino and colleagues (2008) surveyed nurses in eight European countries (i.e., Belgium, Germany, Finland, France, Italy, the Netherlands, Poland, and Slovakia). Their findings indicated nurses experienced harassment and discrimination related to their national, sexual, racial, religious, or political characteristics, which was perpetrated by both colleagues and supervisors. Similarly, women working in the service industry in the US reported harassment by clients and customers (Gettman and Gelfand 2007).

Organizational Factors and Workplace Violence

Beyond the gender and sexual orientation of workers, certain workplace settings and organizational factors are associated with greater risks of sexual, physical, social, and economic violence. A recent review of the international literature by Pina and Gannon (2012) indicated organizations with both a higher ratio of men to women and more male-oriented jobs had higher rates of sexual harassment incidents than other types of organizations. In the US, other workplace and organizational characteristics associated with higher rates of workplace violence include role conflict, ambiguity, work overload (Bowling and Beehr 2006), and greater power differentials among levels within the organizational structure (Ilies et al. 2003). Internationally, communication technology has not only changed traditional workplaces and practices but also created new, virtual work spaces, where women employed as professional journalists and bloggers—and those who conduct other paid or unpaid work on the internet—are increasingly exposed to cyberbullying, sexual harassment, stalking, threats, and other forms of interpersonal violence (Citron 2009a; Hess 2014).

Employers who do not follow policies and procedures to keep employees safe from harassment contribute to the proliferation of hegemonic processes and structures that create hostile work environments and a culture of violence (Hertzog et al. 2008; Jackson et al. 2002; Pina and Gannon 2012). Earlier research conducted in the US indicated women who believed their organization was tolerant of sexual harassment tended to experience higher levels of workplace harassment than those employed in organizations that took complaints seriously and disciplined people who engaged in sexual harassment (Fitzgerald et al. 1997). The negative impact of sexual harassment in the workplace extends beyond the targeted individual. For example, a misogynistic work environment may also lead to increased withdrawal among others in the organization (Miner-Rubino and Cortina 2007). These findings support our argument that an expanded conceptualization of workplace violence must take into consideration diverse workplace contexts and the wide range of potential perpetrators.

Impact of Workplace Violence on Women's Health, Well-Being, and Work

Documented health effects of workplace violence range from mild to severe and include emotional, mental, and physical distress, lower overall health satisfaction, and death (Chan et al. 2008; Dehue et al. 2012; Gunnarsdottir et al. 2006; Krug et al. 2002; O'Donnell et al. 2010; Wasti et al. 2000). Bowling and Beehr (2006) conducted a meta-analysis of antecedents and consequences of workplace violence using ninety sources (e.g., scholarly articles, books and chapters, dissertations, theses, unpublished studies from 1987 through 2005).

They identified role conflict, ambiguity, and overload as the primary antecedents of workplace harassment. Consequences of workplace harassment included
strains, anxiety, depression, burnout, lower self-esteem, and lower life satisfaction (Bowling and Beehr 2006). In another meta-analysis of forty-one published
and unpublished studies, Willness and colleagues (2007) found similar problems
related to workplace sexual harassment, such as low physical and mental health
and post-traumatic stress symptoms. Other research conducted in Brazil with
female domestic workers (DeSouza and Cerqueira 2009) found low self-esteem,
anxiety, and depression among participants who were sexually harassed. Sexual
harassment was associated with neck pain among a weighted sample of working women in Quebec, Canada (Stock and Tissot 2012). Women employed at a
university in the US reported injury, illness, and assault as the result of sexual
harassment occurring within the previous twelve months (Rospenda et al. 2005).

Experiences of workplace violence may also impact women's economic,
career, and academic status. A recent Canadian study of 467 employed women
indicated workplace sexual harassment was more strongly associated with work
withdrawal and negative psychological health indicators, than were other forms
of workplace aggression (Dionisi et al. 2012). Lower job satisfaction and organizational commitment (Bowling and Beehr 2006; Chan et al. 2008; Willness et
al. 2007), higher job stress (Chan et al. 2008), and withdrawal (Chan et al. 2008;
Willness et al. 2007) were reported in crosscountry meta-analyses. A survey conducted in the Netherlands indicated employees who had experienced workplace
bullying had more work absences than those who did not report being subjected
to bullying behaviors (Dehue et al. 2012). In a survey of female adolescents at a
suburban US high school, Fineran and Gruber (2009) used a modified version
of the SEQ (Fitzgerald et al. 1995). They found the majority (58 percent) were
employed outside of school, primarily in food service and retail jobs. Girls who
experienced sexual harassment at work had rates of work stress, low job satisfaction, academic withdrawal, and school absences that were significantly higher
than other employed adolescents. The researchers also noted that the frequency
of sexual harassment (52 percent) reported by this sample of employed adolescents was much higher than rates reported in the published research using the
same instrument among adult women.

The widespread incidence of sexual harassment and workplace bullying
means millions of women face difficult, complex, and multifaceted decisions
related to how to respond to the violence and maintain their personal safety,
health, and well-being (O'Donnell et al. 2010; Pina and Gannon 2012). Common
responses include remaining silent, seeking to ignore the perpetrator, or submitting to the violence. When they felt it was safe and worth the risk, some Canadian women took direct actions to counter the aggression (Pina and Gannon
2012). The discrepancy between how women would like to respond to and how
they actually respond may be associated with the perceived risks of responding,

other social concerns of constraints, perceived social norms, or individual personality characteristics. Brinkman and colleagues (2011) reported women in the US who chose not to actively respond to workplace violence had lower levels of distress than women who responded confrontationally, which suggests that in some cases, direct action may result in further stress and health risks.

A cross-cultural study of employed female workers with prior personal experiences of workplace violence in Turkey and the US indicated responses varied across different cultural groups (Cortina and Wasti 2005). Among women who reported avoiding the situation and attempting to negotiate with the aggressor, more than two-thirds were Turkish and Hispanic Americans. In contrast, Anglo-American women tended to cope by detaching themselves from the stressor. Regardless of culture or class, the majority of women employed a variety of personal coping methods without filing a formal complaint.

One possible response to workplace violence is the decision to not participate in or not be present for certain work-related tasks (O'Donnell et al. 2010; Pina and Gannon 2012; Willness et al. 2007). If socially and economically feasible, some women may change jobs or quit work altogether. Although not definitive solutions to avoiding harassment, other strategies include being absent or taking sick leave in order to begin the healing process. In exploring the lived experience of sickness absence through in-depth interviews with Canadian women, O'Donnell and colleagues (2010) found some women eventually were able to make sense of the connection between a problematic work environment and their health. The researchers also reported cases of women dealing with the ongoing personal dilemma of whether or not to return to work, given the realization that absence from work, in and of itself, would not resolve the situation. Throughout the process, these Canadian women evaluated their various priorities related to work and health and sought to move forward with plans to seek health-related services, return to work, quit, retire, or go on long-term disability. In the global context, the ability to make such choices would of course depend on local labor policies and availability of legal and social resources.

Labor and social policies may impact women's decisions and responses to workplace violence, particularly regarding whether or not to report the incidents to authorities through informal or formal processes. While some victims of workplace violence may feel comfortable confiding in friends, coworkers or relatives (Cortina and Wasti 2005; Pina and Gannon 2012), formal reporting is not always feasible, safe, or in women's perceived best interests. As a result, women rarely file formal reports or complaints (Pina and Gannon 2012). Data from the 2002 US National Organization Survey (a national probability survey of workplaces) indicated only 29 percent of the companies with a sexual harassment policy in place had received a complaint of sexual harassment (Hertzog et al. 2008). The organizational environment may not only foster or inhibit workplace violence but may also moderate the rate at which women report incidents

(Vijayasiri 2008). Registering a report of harassment or aggression in the workplace can result in retaliation, lower job satisfaction, and increased psychological distress for victims (Bergman et al. 2002). As discussed above, there is substantial evidence of the detrimental economic, health, and relationship impacts of workplace violence in women's physical and mental health, work lives, and personal lives.

Expanding the Concept and Measurement of Workplace Violence

Most current definitions of workplace violence include physical or psychological violence by coworkers, manifest in sexual harassment, aggression, bullying, intimidation, assault, or other forms of discrimination or oppression (Jackson et al. 2002, Krug et al. 2002; Waters et al. 2005). Some definitions of workplace violence distinguish between sexual and nonsexual forms of interpersonal violence (Rospenda et al. 2005). While sexual harassment can rise to a legal violation (EEOC 2009), bullying and other forms of workplace incivility often do not violate the law in the US (Lim and Cortina 2005; EEOC 2009). Sexual harassment usually refers to some combination of unwelcome sexual advances, requests for sexual favors, or other types of unwanted sexual conduct that creates a hostile or offensive work environment (IEUP et al. 2004; EEOC 2009). Although not always explicit, an underlying assumption in these definitions is that the interpersonal violence occurs within the context of paid employment (Rospenda et al. 2005).

Other terms used to refer to nonsexual workplace harassment include workplace bullying, lateral violence (Croft and Cash 2012), workplace harassment, workplace abuse (Krieger et al. 2008), and horizontal or lateral violence (Vessey et al. 2010). Gender, sexual orientation, race, class, language, or other power differentials between perpetrator and victim often play a part in nonsexual workplace violence (Sue 2010). Within the nursing profession, where both perpetrators and victims tend to be women but differentials related to years of professional experience or age often exist, lateral or horizontal nonsexual violence is a widely recognized phenomenon (Croft and Cash 2012).

Measurement challenges include the co-occurrence of aggressions, especially the relationship between workplace incivility and sexual harassment (Barling et al. 2001; Dionisi et al. 2012; Lim and Cortina 2005). In Canada, Dionisi and colleagues (2012) noted that more women reported experiencing both sexual harassment and other forms of aggression at work than women who reported just one form of workplace violence. Furthermore, there are wide variations among specific measures of workplace violence. Worker's Compensation Claims data, surveys, and secondary incident reports are common sources of information used in calculating the incidence and prevalence of workplace violence (Wang et al. 2008). Yet definitions and measures of workplace violence vary widely. In a survey conducted in Iceland, investigators asked participants if they had ever experienced sexual harassment, bullying, physical violence, or threats at work (Gunnarsdottir et al. 2006). In contrast, a survey of Canadian women inquired about experiences of physical violence, workplace intimidation, or unwanted sexual attention (Stock and Tissot 2012). Researchers often inquire about negative interactions with people in the workplace, persistent psychological or physical abuse in the workplace, and work environments that are perceived as offensive, hostile, or intimidating (O'Donnell et al. 2010; Rospenda et al. 2005; Saunders et al. 2007).

The methodological variations and wide range of worker and workplace contexts add to the complexity of comparing rates of workplace violence across studies, time, and regions (Ilies et al. 2003; Nielsen et al. 2010; Wang et al. 2008; Waters et al. 2005). There is evidence to suggest that the definition of workplace violence, the survey methods used, and the sampling procedures all may impact women's responses to survey questions (Ilies et al. 2003). Analysis of responses to a random-sample survey of Norwegian employees indicated fewer participants responded in the affirmative when asked directly if they had experienced sexual harassment than when asked a range of questions about behavioral experiences in the workplace (Nielsen et al. 2010). In a study comparing experiences of US and Brazilian college students, the Brazilians were more likely than Americans to rate a scenario of heterosexual woman-to-woman harassment as sexual harassment that should be investigated (DeSouza et al. 2007). These findings suggest that individuals construct, define, and interpret experiences of workplace violence in different ways.

Although not all negative workplace interactions should be labeled workplace violence, it is important to recognize that workplace violence is not only limited to overt acts of aggression but also includes ongoing incidents of microaggression. Microaggression is a form of interpersonal violence manifest in subtle verbal insults or behavioral slights that occur repeatedly over time and are often directed at women and persons of racial, ethnic, class, gender, or other minorities (Sue 2010). The effects of multiple, seemingly nebulous acts of aggression are cumulative and can result in significant harm (Sue 2010).

Redefining Workplace Violence: Implications for Research, Policy, and Practice

Because most current workplace violence research, policies, and practices focus primarily on the formal, paid labor force (Gettman and Gelfand 2007), there are major knowledge gaps regarding workplace violence occurring within other work contexts and types (e.g., domestic, caring, volunteer, school, community, online work). Our proposed expanded conceptualization of workplace encompasses the multiple dimensions of women's work throughout the lifespan and across settings. Beyond the formal, paid workplace, women may be subjected to violence, aggression, and discrimination in the context of unpaid or volunteer work, domestic work, childcare, community work, schoolwork or education, work at home, work outside of the home, and work in both formal and informal workplaces (Messias et al. 1997). Confining the definition of workplace violence to the context of formal employment ignores women's involvement in multiple forms of work throughout their lifespan, work that occurs in various settings. By expanding the concept of workplace violence, researchers may be able to better identify commonalities and differences across diverse contexts and propose more appropriate and tailored interventions.

To more fully understand the scope and characteristics of workplace violence, future research should incorporate an expanded conceptualization that better reflects the diverse realities of women's work and workplaces, as well as women's multiple identities within those contexts (Messias et al. 1997). An expanded conceptualization would encourage more in-depth explorations of interpersonal violence in a wider range of workplaces and types of work, as well as critical examinations of the various dimensions of diversity that may be targeted through workplace oppressions. To both prevent and effectively intervene in cases of workplace violence, there is a need for more critical examinations of the multiple dimensions of difference (e.g., gender, race, class, language, age) that may be involved in workplace aggression. An expanded conceptualization would broaden the examination of workplace violence beyond gender-based aggression to include discrimination, bullying, sexual harassment, and assault related to race, ethnicity, class, nationality, sexuality, or other dimensions of unequal social status, position, and power.

The incorporation of an expanded conceptualization of workplace violence into research, policy, and practice will foster the consideration of harassment tied not only to gender but also to race, sexuality, nationality, language, religion, and other dimensions of difference, as well as diverse cultural meanings and personal constructions of work, work environments, and interpersonal relationships (Wasti et al. 2000). There is increasing consensus among feminist scholars that the intersectional nature of women's oppression, in which gender, race, ethnicity, class, sexuality, language, national origin, ability, and other dimensions of difference interact and are interwoven complex ways (Crenshaw 2008; hooks 1984; Spelman 2008; Weber 2010).

There is a need for further research on how various dimensions of power differentials potentially mediate or moderate the effects of workplace violence. Intersectional identities need not be controlled for one another but should be considered inextricable (Crenshaw 2008; hooks 1984; Spelman 2008). For example, perpetrators of microaggression often target women's various identities (Sue 2010). A study with African American women illustrated how critical it is to examine the multiple forms of harassment that women face because the co-occurrence of racial and sexual harassment impact occupational and psychological outcomes (Buchanan and Fitzgerald 2008). Research with Black, Asian, and minority ethnic women in the United Kingdom indicated these women believed race and culture were important factors in their experiences of workplace violence (Fielden et al. 2010). Many women ascribed to the premise that they would not have been sexually harassed if they were White or from a different culture. Similarly, a survey of men and women from five organizations located in a North American city indicated women experienced sexual harassment more often than men; minority workers more than White workers; and minority women more than any other race and gender combination (Berdahl and Moore 2006). Women in the US with low incomes, members of the working class, and multiracial/multiethnic women experience high rates of sexual harassment, which is significantly associated with poor health outcomes (Krieger et al. 2008). Unpacking the ways in which women's multiple identities are targeted in the various forms of sexual and nonsexual harassment and violence may lead to better understanding of the interconnectedness among these oppressions in women's formal and informal work lives and personal lives. Filling gaps in the literature regarding the effects of discrimination based not only on gender but also on the intersections of various dimensions of difference and power differentials is critical to understanding and effectively addressing workplace violence and preventing future occurrences.

Because sexual and nonsexual harassment are interpreted differently in various cultures, it is also important to consider these differences when defining terms and choosing measurement questions. Using both emic and etic constructs and measurements will help researchers understand the contextual nature when examining sexual and nonsexual harassment of working women. Historically, bullying and sexual harassment developed through separate disciplines (Gruber and Fineran 2008) and were studied as separate issues (Lim and Cortina 2005). Bullying was concentrated in the field of psychology and sexual harassment or sex discrimination in the field of feminism and women's studies (Gruber and Fineran 2008). These forms of violence, among others, are now studied across various disciplines (Gruber and Fineran 2008). Because women may experience harassment, bullying, aggression, violence, and microaggression in a variety of different contexts and at the same time, these phenomena should be studied together in transdisciplinary ways.

Expansion of transdisciplinary and transnational research on workplace violence is another area that warrants attention. Examples include collaborations between professionals in gender studies, economics, workforce, medicine, sociology, psychology, and public health. Using an expanded, more inclusive definition of workplace violence will enhance researchers' abilities to test and validate comprehensive measures that are more comparable across studies, disciplines, organizations, regions, cultures, and time. This will allow scholars to draw more reliable conclusions about the incidence of workplace violence, moderating factors associated with workplace violence, and importantly, prevention measures.

A model for transnational, transdisciplinary research on workplace violence is a multicountry collaborative study of domestic violence supported by the World Health Organization (García-Moreno et al. 2005). The research protocol for this ten-country study allowed for country-specific minor adaptations, such as additional questions or modified response options, without jeopardizing comparability. With the aim of enhancing understanding of the global prevalence of violence against women, health outcomes, risk factors, and service-seeking, the research team collected data from more than 24,000 women, using similar questionnaires in each country. The study was culturally relevant, yet comparable across countries (García-Moreno et al. 2005). To examine workplace violence transnationally, behavior-specific questions could be developed and examined across a wide range of work environments.

The conceptual definitions and measures researchers use in studies of workplace violence influence how human resources specialists, practitioners, and policy makers understand the connected nature of women's work, sexual harassment, and bullying within the context of women's health. Policy makers and human resource specialists should continue to refine relevant safety guidelines to protect employees from workplace violence and improve reporting processes and procedures. These legislative interventions and policies should recognize and incorporate women's multiple and interwoven identities. Furthermore, studies of the cultural aspects of workplace violence should include both emic and etic constructs and measurements. This may offer scholars more insight into the experiences of women within the context of women's cultures (Wasti et al. 2000).

We also recommend the broader application of tailored, theory-based workplace violence prevention and education interventions. Researchers in Hong Kong implemented a successful school-based sexual harassment intervention based on the Theory of Planned Behavior (Ajzen 1991). The aim was to encourage girls (ages 13 to 17) to protect themselves from sexual harassment by peers (Li et al. 2010). Tailored programs are needed for adolescent and adult women, as well as lesbian, gay, bisexual, and transgender people working and studying in formal and informal workplaces, schools, and communities. With a better understanding of the magnitude and effect of the problem, targeted and appropriate intervention strategies can be instituted in a variety of contexts to address issues from primary prevention to post-aggression support in communities across the globe (Krug et al. 2002).

Conclusions

Globally, workplace violence occurs in a wide range of work contexts (Dionisi et al. 2012; Rospenda et al. 2005; Wasti et al. 2000). It involves multiple types of interpersonal aggression perpetrated by individuals in diverse relationships with victims (Huerta et al. 2006; Jackson et al. 2002; LeBlanc and Kelloway 2002; Matchen and DeSouza 2000; Timmerman 2003). Going beyond conventional definitions that limit workplace violence to interpersonal violence occurring in conjunction with paid employment in the formal sector, we propose an expanded conceptualization of workplaces where women of all ages and other vulnerable individuals may be exposed to interpersonal violence. These workplaces include paid and unpaid work in the informal sector and in other contexts, including community service, family care giving, schooling and education (Dionisi et al. 2012; Rospenda et al. 2005; Wasti et al. 2000). This broader conceptualization reflects women's lived experiences of personal and work lives as interwoven and seamless rather than as distinct dichotomies (Messias et al. 1997).

Application of an expanded conceptualization must involve the acknowledgment and incorporation of various workplace contexts (e.g., formal, informal, community, educational institutions), diverse forms of work (e.g., paid, unpaid, volunteer service) and multiple types of interpersonal aggression into research, policy, and practice. Current definitions of workplace violence acknowledge the diverse types of aggression (e.g., sexual, physical, emotional, racial), but these are often studied separately (Lim and Cortina 2005). The incorporation of more interdisciplinary research into the field will enhance understanding of the dynamics of multifaceted workplace aggression.

Increasing awareness of workplace violence using a broader, more contextual definition could contribute to more effective policies, interventions, and programs. A better understanding of the broad scope and multiple dimensions of workplace violence should guide prevention and education programs tailored to women employed in wage work in formal and informal workplaces, as well as those engaged in unpaid work in homes, schools, and communities. Targeted and appropriate intervention strategies can be instituted in a variety of contexts to address issues from primary prevention to post-aggression support in communities across the globe (Krug et al. 2002).

We argue that employing an expanded conceptualization of women's workplaces will help to fill knowledge gaps (Marsh et al. 2009; Miner-Rubino and Cortina 2007), and contribute to more thorough descriptions of the global extent (Ilies et al. 2003), nature (Hertzog et al. 2008), and cost (Waters et al. 2005) of gender-based violence. This, in turn, may improve transnational comparisons of the incidence, contexts, policies, and practices, enabling policy makers and employers to develop more applicable regulations to prevent workplace violence, facilitate reporting, and improve follow-up procedures. In practice, a broader conceptual framework of workplace violence should foster the implementation of more effective screening and more comprehensive assessments of risks and exposure to physical, sexual, and emotional aggression in paid and unpaid workplaces (e.g., schools, homes, on farms, in brothels, in the community) among women across the lifespan. Enhancing public awareness of the extent and nature of the many forms and contexts of workplace violence is an important first step and one that will enhance prevention efforts (Krug et al. 2002).

Incorporation of intersectional, transnational, and transdisciplinary perspectives into research, policy, and practice will expand understandings and interpretations of women's experiences of workplace violence across their lifespan and within their own multifaceted cultural contexts and racial, ethnic, gender, and class identities, facilitating transnational and cross-cultural comparisons (Crenshaw 2008; hooks 1984; Spelman 2008; Weber 2010). The intent of an expanded conceptualization of workplace violence is not to erase or minimize distinctions and differences across the types and contexts of violence against women and other vulnerable individuals. Rather, the aim is to heighten awareness, expand research, facilitate transnational and cross-cultural comparisons, enhance policy initiatives, and improve education and prevention interventions and treatment options.

9

Everything from "Beautiful" to "Bitch"

Black Women and Street Harassment

MELINDA MILLS

Street harassment remains a problem "hidden in plain sight." The acts that constitute harassment are veiled from public recognition. Just as these actions are
unrecognized, so, too, are some of the targets, or victims, of this everyday form
of violence (Jones 2008). That is, at a distance, street harassment may appear
to be a casual or friendly conversation between strangers in public spaces, but
upon closer inspection, it becomes something much more ambiguous and nefar-
ious. Targets of street harassment can appear to be willing participants in these
social interactions, but often they feel coerced into conversations. Victims fear
the potential and actual repercussions from men who harass. Black women are
seldom depicted as the typical targets of street harassment, yet they experience
this and other forms of violence at disproportionate rates in comparison to the
national population (US Department of Justice 2006; Nash 2005; Wilson 2005;
Tjaden and Thoennes 2000a).

In this chapter, I center the experiences of Black women to bring the problem
of street harassment as they experience it into full view. I do so in part to interrogate the ways in which Black women are viewed. I discuss how the dominant
view of Black women obscures their experiences with harassment by constructing them through a set of controlling images that deny their vulnerability and
victimization. This construction conceals the extent to which they face everyday
violence in public spaces.

What Is Street Harassment?

Researchers have defined this social problem accordingly: "Street harassment
occurs when one or more strange men accost one or more women . . . in a public place which is not the woman's/women's worksite. Through looks, words, or
gestures the man asserts his right to intrude on the woman's attention, defining
her as a sexual object, and forcing her to interact with him" (di Leonardo 1981,
51–52). This definition underscores the extent to which the interactions that happen between strangers are largely unexpected and probably unwelcomed by the
targets of harassers' undesired attention.

Just as street harassment largely remains hidden in plain sight, so, too, are Black women as victims obscured from view. While national coverage of sexual assault and harassment of women has grown, negligible attention to intersectionality has resulted in a myopic understanding of the scope of harassment that victims face every day. The result has been a deflection of attention away from harassment, and a perpetuation of racism, sexism, and classism (see hooks 1984; Davis 1994). That is, despite increased media coverage, the faces of survivors of sexual assault and harassment have primarily been depicted as those of White women, and the sites of the assaults have been increasingly identified as their places of employment.

Very little attention has been paid to women of color, Black women in particular, as victims of violence in a variety of settings. The level of violence women of color face is disproportionate to the national population (see Lee et al. 2002). The omission of Black women from such public discourses is a lacuna in the existing literature. This lacuna occurs even as members of this group face higher rates of sexual harassment and assault (see US Department of Justice 2006; Tjaden and Thoennes 2000a). That Black women experience this violence and fail to see their experiences accurately, publicly represented, or taken seriously, speaks to both the negation of Black women as sufferers and survivors of violence and their erasure in society (Rankine 2014).

In this chapter, I draw attention to Black women's social position in what bell hooks (1984) calls a "white supremacist, capitalist, patriarchy" and consider how their experiences confronting street harassment serve as evidence of their oppression in US society. Following hooks, I focus on the particular ways in which Black women have been marginalized, if not made invisible, their experiences distorted and discounted, as they remain targets of various forms of violence. I take as a starting point this sobering reality that violence visited upon Black bodies, and Black women's bodies in particular, is both a historical and a contemporary phenomenon (Rankine 2014). Within this historical context, violence occurs in part through the everyday expression of street harassment, yet little attention has been paid to places where sexual harassment happens with great frequency and regularity for many women, and that such violence is unregulated in public spaces.

What Is the Scope of the Problem?

According to a national survey conducted by Holly Kearl (2014), the founder of the nonprofit organization Stop Street Harassment, a majority of the women respondents and some of the men (mostly those who identify as gay, bisexual, or transgender) reported experiencing street harassment. Kearl also found that, among the sample of one thousand women and one thousand men, those who had encountered street harassment had repeatedly been targets, experiencing street harassment more than once in a lifetime, up to several times a day. That is, respondents experienced street harassment as a regular occurrence, not an isolated incident.

The majority of the two thousand respondents interviewed in Kearl's study identified men as the perpetrators of street harassment. That so many respondents most commonly identified men as their harasser(s) points to a particular problem of patriarchy, that of men's aggression toward their targets. This pattern suggests that men are encouraged to participate or engage in such harassing behavior and that they are frequently rewarded for acting in aggressive ways. Sociologists Michael Kaufmann (2007) and Michael Kimmel (2009) make this point in their work, respectively pointing to the triad of violence that encourages men's violence toward other men, women, and themselves and citing toxic masculinity for its promotion of aggression.

These forms of aggression affect their targets and are not without consequence to men themselves. In this way, street harassment must also be understood as having public health implications, seen as a part of a set of other forces that compromise quality of life and wellness (Gardner 1995; Kearl 2014; Sheffield 2007). This is particularly the case for Black women, who arguably face heightened and expansive threats of violence in various spaces, and who are at greater risk for compromised health as a result of gendered racism (see Essed 1991; Wingfield 2007; Roberts 1998).

A Historical Look at Street Harassment of Black Women

The topic of Black women's experiences with street harassment remains an important, if understudied, area of social research. As historian Danielle McGuire (2010) discusses in her book *At the Dark End of the Street*, issues of gender and racial violence and public harassment ignited the Civil Rights Movement. Black women riding on public buses suffered great indignities and risked real and imagined threats from White male bus drivers and passengers. Many of these Black women risked bodily harm and injury from White men attempting to discipline and punish them (Foucault 1977). This discipline operates, then and now, as a mechanism of social control, a means of making sure that Black women know their place in society and in relation to others, particularly within the racial hierarchy (Bonilla Silva 2017). Black women's presence in public was often registered as resistance to their subordination, their bodies a provocation but certainly not an apology (Taylor 2018).

In retelling the story of Recy Taylor, a Black woman sexually assaulted by six White men in 1944, McGuire (2010) recuperates a narrative of strength and courage in Taylor's refusal to be silent after enduring being "kidnapped, blindfolded and raped at gunpoint by six white men" (see McDonald 2017, 1).[1] Taylor, who died on December 28, 2017, was returning home from church when she was attacked and then forced to beg for her life so she could return to her husband and new baby (see Chan 2017). Taylor relinquished her initial promise to remain quiet about her rape and being left for dead on the side of the road by her attackers. In an interview about the recently released documentary *The Rape of Recy Taylor*, McDonald (2017) noted that once Taylor spoke her truth and Rosa Parks came to Abbeville seeking justice for her, both women were threatened, as was Taylor's home.

Black women who offered testimonials, or spoke truth to power, faced these risks, but they "used their voices as weapons against white supremacy [. . .] Taylor's refusal to remain silent helped expose a ritual of rape in existence since slavery, inspired a nationwide campaign to defend Black womanhood, and gave hope to thousands suffering through similar abuses" (McGuire 2010, 47; see also Brooten, this volume). Black women resisted the image of themselves as threatening or ostensibly deserving of discipline; they refused to be silent because they were threatened by White men who "targeted Black women for mistreatment, calling them 'bitches' and 'coons'" (McGuire 2010, 12). Generalized efforts to keep African Americans in their place operated as a form of social control of Blacks, particularly those who increasingly were succeeding in life in spite of persistent oppression in the forms of structural and individual racism (Bonilla-Silva 2001).

Black women tried to walk with pride and dignity, despite the constant threats of sexual and racial violence and the "continuous campaign of terror that was just as much a threat to women as lynching was to Black men" (McDonald 2017, 1). These threats of "bodily injury or death" (McGuire 2010, 11) existed in a particular historical moment, yet persist past the mid-twentieth century. In particular, in the Jim Crow South, the fear of white violence continued, curtailing Black people's movement in general, and Black women's movements in particular. This is why one can view public harassment or street harassment as a mechanism of social control.

The harassment that attempted to circumscribe Black women's lives through the looming threat of violence is what sociologists Ruth Thompson-Miller and Joe Feagin (2014) call "Jim Crow's Legacy," or a kind of racial residue of segregation. Thompson-Miller and Feagin illustrate how this fear of violence worked to shrink the lives of Black people in the South at that time, and, I would argue, functions much the same to this day. In fact, Feagin (1991) documents this legacy of history, noting that Black people continue to experience discrimination and differential treatment in public, including public spaces such as sidewalks where power asymmetries get negotiated and often contested. One question that emerges in considering power asymmetries at the intersections of race and gender is this: How long will Black women suffer what McGuire (2010) calls the "silent injustices" of public harassment?

Taylor's case is important to include in discussions of Black women's experiences with street harassment since racialized and sexualized violence have been used to maintain the systemic oppression of Black women and uphold the notion that they deserve to be disciplined for being "out of place" or acting "out of line" (see Epstein 1997). This violence worked as a cautionary tale for others who witnessed and vicariously felt victimized. Where the logic of patriarchy meets white supremacy, violence gets expressed, and Black women often fail to be protected by men. Ostensibly "not-women" based on racist ideology, Black women are often denied their femininity, as well as the typical "protection of women" that traditional gender ideology of patriarchy expects of men. As writer Roxane Gay (2017) notes in her memoir, *Hunger*, Black women are often seen as masculine by default, by virtue of, ironically enough, their Black womanhood.

Many men, as the idealized embodiment of patriarchy, not only failed to protect all women but also expressly, actively, and intentionally violated that protection through their sexually assaultive behavior toward Black women. These double standards also function to stigmatize and shame Black women victims of gendered violence. While Whites worked to craft their own misleading and untruthful narratives and discourses about rape, Black women victims of rape were considered "whores." As "discredited victims" who were "smeared as prostitutes" (McGuire 2010, 33), Black women rape victims confronted and contested their devaluation and objectification in society and the reality that "their bodies were not their own" (McGuire 2010, 39). Much the same can be said about Black women who experience street harassment. Public discourses suggest that they, as "always already public texts," putatively hypersexual, aggressive, and emasculating, "deserve" whatever punitive reactions their transgressive bodies conjure up (Holloway 2011). But where do such notions of Black women come from?

Constructing Black Womanhood in "The Crooked Room": On Controlling Imagery and "Misogynoir"

Black feminist political scientist Melissa Harris-Perry notes in *Sister Citizen* that Black women often confront others' "limiting, often soul-crushing expectation" of them (2012, 34). This, in part, results from representations of Black women that are distortions of reality, damaging in their depiction of Black women as undesirable objects rather than empowered subjects. Harris-Perry posits, "When they confront race and gender stereotypes, Black women are standing in a crooked room, and they have to figure out which way is up. Bombarded with warped images of their humanity, some Black women tilt and bend themselves to fit the distortion" (2012, 34).

Harris-Perry urges us to consider Black women's behavior through a sociopolitical lens, rather than read Black women's behavior solely as an (in)accurate reflection of individual action. She writes, "To understand why Black women's public actions and political strategies sometimes seem tilted in ways that accommodate the degrading stereotypes about them, it is important to appreciate the structural constraints that influence their behavior. It can be hard to stand up in a crooked room" (2012, 34). But what explains the unsavory and distorted images of Black women? Black queer feminist, activist, and scholar, Moya Bailey, picks up this question in a 2010 post on the Crunk Feminist Collective website. Bailey shares with readers the term "misogynoir," a word she created to "describe the particular brand of hatred directed at Black women in American visual and popular culture" (2010). I argue, where misogyny (hatred of women) and patriarchy (male domination) meet racism (white superiority), misogynoir emerges.

Examples of "misogynoiristic" or negative portrayals of Black women abound in the media and society, where Black women are characterized as any number of racial and gender stereotypes, or what Collins calls "controlling images." Constructed as punitive mechanisms meant to oppress and assault Black women, four common controlling images popularized by and circulated in the media include "mammies," "matriarchs," "welfare recipients," and "hot mommas" (see Collins 1991). Following Collins, Stephens and Phillips (2003) argue that instead of disappearing or dissipating over time, controlling images of Black women persist. These images continue to be recycled and reproduced, growing more sexualized over time, as evidenced through the "freak" and "gold digger." These updated but still slanted images tend to perpetuate the myth of Black women's hypersexuality. Now perpetuated and internalized by various social groups, these images—which cast Black women as unsavory and undesirable—work to control Black women's bodies, deny them bodily autonomy, and adversely affect Black women's psychological health and wellness.

Finally, Cooper (2017) offers her own observations on the misogynoiristic evidence that circulates in American society. Cooper contends that "respectability politics," a term coined by Evelyn Brooks Higginbotham (1993), does little to save Black women from the various assaults directed at them (see also Houston 2015). Because being "respectable" is debatable and contestable, confining and restrictive, and it fails, like silence, to protect people (see Lorde 2017), respectability politics polices Black women, while accommodating the mistreatment and abuse of them. Cooper argues that Black women still bear the burden of racism and sexism, positing: "In this world, Black women have moved from 'fly girls to bitches and hoes' and back again . . . A world in which bitch trumps beautiful, ho trumps human, and gold-digger trumps golden. #EveryDamnTime" (2017, 248).

Cooper's comments speak to the way that Black women's bodies and sexualities are seen as unruly and unworthy, and that these tropes about Black women are particularly problematic. These narratives, or "socializing stories," attach to the body and socially shape how identities, rather than persons, interact in public spaces (Holloway 2011). Since Black women are seen as "always and already public" (texts), their bodies not their own but up for public consumption, inspection, and criticism, Black women then have experiences shaped by these mythologies of their accessibility and availability, and are largely denied privacy, even in public (see Holloway 2011, 17).

How do narratives about Black women shape their experiences of street harassment in the public sphere? What are the stories that Black women might tell about their own experiences? For answers to these questions, I conducted twenty face-to-face, open-ended, in-depth qualitative interviews with women who reported experiences of street harassment. I also spent two years in the field, conducting an ethnographic and autoethnographic study of an urban space in the Southeast US (see Richardson 2001, 1993). Conducting qualitative interviews with young women allowed me to ask them for their definitions of street harassment. By inviting them to tell their stories I was providing an invitation to them to tell the truth about their experiences not only with everyday violence on the street but also in various other spaces where they had such encounters (see Latina Feminist Group 2001). I transcribed each interview (which lasted on average about 60 to 90 minutes), and later analyzed the data using Grounded Theory Method (see Glaser and Strauss 1967; Strauss and Corbin 1998). From this analysis, themes emerged to indicate a pattern of behavior the women in my sample faced: everyday violence from men who harass. Next, I summarize some of the common themes from my interview conversations with Black women, and that emerged in my analysis of the data.

From "Beautiful" to "Bitch": On the Objectification, Sexualization, and Dehumanization of Black Women

In her book *Citizen*, poet Claudia Rankine (2014) offers a path into thinking about the way Black women are addressed as public texts in public spaces. In reflecting on a conversation Judith Butler had about hurtful language, Rankine recalls that Butler opined that "our very being exposes us to the address of another. . . . We suffer from the condition of being addressable. Our emotional openness, she adds, is carried by our addressability. Language navigates this" (2013, 43–44). As Black women navigate public spaces, they come to understand how men who harass them see them, how they are addressable to men. In my research, some respondents discovered that harassment begins with men occasionally offering compliments, by commenting on the attractiveness of their women targets. A few respondents felt that male strangers saying, "Hey, beautiful," "You look good," or "You're very pretty" was complimentary.

Many respondents faced less pleasant, more assaultive interactions with men in public spaces. Vanessa described the experience of being called a "bitch," and encountering men's verbal aggression:

> I mean I've had situations where guys will say, you know, "Fuck you, bitch," and obviously showing anger, but it's just like, how can I respond to them because it

may cause—I already don't want to be in this situation, but it may cause something else to get out of hand. "Well, fuck you," [the male harasser might say]. "Well, fuck you, too." But other than that, I just try to stay calm and free of drama. [Vanessa thought to herself]: "You wanna make remarks; that's fine." It is kind of irritating to me just to see, because you can feel when someone is staring at you, but I like to watch men watching women walk down the street and the women don't know it because their backs are turned, because I think what they do is disrespectful.

The threat of more harassment, escalated antagonism, and/or additional forms of violence loomed in these sorts of verbally aggressive encounters, as evidenced in Vanessa's comments. The unpredictability of the social interaction, of "excitable speech," and any consequent actions by men who harass made women targets feel particularly precarious (see Butler 2006, 1997). What Vanessa describes above also speaks to the vicarious victimization that women feel in moments when they become indirect targets of everyday violence, as witnesses who watch or observe other women being harassed, and implicitly wonder if/when they will be harassed as well.

A few respondents discussed the dilemmas of being called "beautiful" and a "bitch" (sometimes in the same moment, by the same perpetrator), while others recalled isolated examples of both. What explains this pattern of events, and the "double jeopardy" that being a Black woman presents in the face of gendered racism, of misogynoir? (see Beal 1969). One respondent, Rebecca, noted that she has heard "all this different stuff . . . Sometimes, I actually [think] it's really nice and can be flattering. It doesn't flatter me, but it can be. 'Oh, you're beautiful,' or 'Wow, you have such a nice smile,' and stuff like that. I don't know what the worst thing could be." Then, Rebecca recalled the consequences she paid for opting not to respond to a man who was harassing her: "When I didn't speak, once I was called a bitch." Rebecca's recollection illustrates the double-edged sword of words and of street harassment, a theme that other respondents discussed.

For instance, Olivia shared examples of men doting on her, admiring her looks, and telling her that they found her attractive. The same men who initially flirted with her and made bids for her attention eventually ended up verbally assaulting her; when she respectfully rejected their advances, they peppered her with unsavory names. She recalled:

This guy was trying to pick me up, I guess, and he was saying that—he saw me walking down the street, and he said something about, something that implied sex; it was a slang, but I didn't know it, because I'm not very good at slang and I was like, "Excuse me. What did you say?" And he was like, "Let me get in those skins," or something like that, more than I would know. And I was like, "Excuse you." And I started all on this whole thing about, "What would make you think that I would want to sleep with you just because you approach me on the street? Nowhere in what you see implies that I am looking for five dollars for two minutes of your time. Therefore . . ." And then he was like, "Bitch!" . . . As soon as he said, 'Bitch,'—I was in the military at the time—all my friends were guys, and they were like, "Who you calling a 'bitch'?" And the guy would be like, "Oh, is that your girl?" And they'd be like, "Oh, that's not my girl; that's my baby sister. So what are you doing? Why are you calling her a bitch?" And then he started on him [the harasser] and in the end, the guy just walked off.

The above excerpt illustrates the injurious impact of words, the way that words wound and that harassers attempt to impugn the character of Black women (see Delgado 1993; Matsuda 1993). Olivia's experience typifies social interactions of the Black women in my study, as many described similar sorts of objectification and dehumanization. They found themselves in social exchanges with men who appeared benevolent at first, but quickly became aggravated and verbally antagonistic when the Black women expressed *any* indifference to them.

Quick-tempered men who harass express their sense of entitlement to women, their actions suggesting that saying no to them is simply not an option. That Olivia and other Black women consciously chose to *politely* reject the advances of men suggest a generosity, a gesture of civility that is ironically denied to these very women. In addition, the irony of going from "beautiful" to "bitch" in the same moment was not lost on my respondents but was clearly lost on men who harass them in this way. That Black women face the fear of real and imagined threats when asserting their agency and their own rights to say no, to politely reject men, demonstrates the dangers of street harassment: that they often encounter heightened risks to their safety and to their lives in managing their mobility and bodily autonomy points to the problems of patriarchy. In public spaces, men who harass attempt to get women's attention, whether through flattery or the fire of racist and sexist epithets. Olivia's comments confront this view of Black women as sexually available, a topic I turn to next.

On Stereotypes and Sexual Innuendo: Gendered Racism in Street Harassment

Because many studies on street harassment have neglected to consider the unique experiences of Black women using an intersectional approach, any particular experiences that Black women have get categorically collapsed by gender and/or race (see Crenshaw 1991). Increasingly, people are attending to the intersections of race and gender, to understand how gendered racism affects Black women in public spaces. In a recent *Huffington Post* article, Jessica Prois and Carolina Moreno (2018) discuss some of the differential treatment that women of color often confront (in comparison to their White counterparts) during street harassment. Women of color hear evaluative remarks about their physical appearance (see Gardner 1995) and, according to Prois and Moreno (2018), experience verbal assaults that "involve fetishization, objectification based on race or ethnicity, and a host of other issues White women might not face, even as the victims are less likely to be believed."

Much the same holds true for the Black women respondents in my study. During our interview conversation, Rebecca provided an example of this, noting the range of "rude comments" that men who harass make, including men "speaking to you in a way that you know would be sexual, not just a polite, 'Hello. How you doing?' More like a, '*Hello*, and how are *you*?!'" (emphasis hers). Rebecca's comments underscore the reality that Black women are more likely to be dehumanized and sexualized (see also Collins 2004), while also being expected to graciously accommodate the verbally (and sometimes physically) assaultive behavior of street harassers. She shared her annoyance with being the object of men's desires, as she felt them staring at her: "Most of the times, men stare at my butt, when I walk away [. . .] And I can feel it, like when I'm walking, even if I don't turn around. Nine times out of ten, I know that they're watching me, and that's gross." That Rebecca reported feeling annoyed speaks to some of the emotional labor that women perform as a result of facing street harassment.

In instances of more intensified objectification, where respondents felt threatened or deeply discomfited by the male gaze and men's evaluative comments of their bodies and their physical appearance, women reported feeling displeasure and vulnerability (see Mulvey 1975). These women lamented and tried to avoid inviting the male gaze upon themselves. Men who harass reportedly made comments that highlighted but also fragmented women's bodies, drawing attention to particular body parts by saying, as one respondent put it (while laughing nervously), "very graphic stuff, you know, about 'I like your butt.' Or whatever. You know? Things like that, that I would not find that appealing in any circumstance."

Consider the experience of Tabitha, who recalled being sexualized by a male harasser. She recalled:

> I was younger then, and I was wearing a t-shirt and some pants or jeans, or something, and walking down the street. And there was a guy who was working in a shop, but he was kinda standing in the doorway, and his job, I think, was to sort of get people to come in off the street, and you know . . . and the t-shirt that I had on said, 'Hakuna Matata,' on the front of it, (she laughs), and that means, 'No Problems,' so he made a comment . . . but he said, not 'Hakuna Matata,' which means there's no problem, but 'Kuna Matiti.' And 'matiti' is breasts, so he was like, 'No problems, but you've got big breasts.' Basically, and so, I think that was, I was just really, really embarrassed . . . Yeah, it was just very blatant and graphic, and I just ducked into a store, again!

Shocked, embarrassed, and afraid, Tabitha sought refuge from the unwanted attention of this stranger. During our interview, she conveyed the dismay and discomfort she felt in having her body fragmented and fetishized, evaluated by a male stranger whose intentions remained unknown to her. Another distressing dynamic of the above experience for Tabitha stems from her inhabiting public spaces and being victimized in the middle of the day in a populated area. This point underscores the extent to which women are deemed "out of place" in public and "put back in line" through harassment (see Uggen et al. 2004).

Seeing Black women as always already sexually available, "unrapable," or wanting men's (unsolicited) attention encourages the kind of harassing behavior that poses a danger or threat to women. Vanessa recalled an incident where a man refused her rejection of him: "I was walking to my house and people pull over, and they're trying to give me a ride. And I was harassed by some man for *five blocks*; he would not leave me alone. He was like, 'Ma'am, please just take my phone number, please just call me anytime.' I'm like, 'I don't want your number,' and he'll say, 'Please, take it.' So he waited and I walked 2 more blocks and he came and found me again and gave me his phone number."

Despite often sounding dismissive of such interactions ("It's not really that serious"), Vanessa admitted that the unpredictability of street harassment worried her: "It's uncomfortable kind of, just because you never know how far this person may take it, even though I've never experienced anything like that, you still have to be cautious [. . .] It's kind of scary because you never know what might happen." Vanessa's concerns and experiences also speak to (the normalization of) the "continuum of violence" that Black women face, including street harassment, stalking, and physical and/or verbal aggression from men (see Smith et al. 2011). Unfortunately, Vanessa's experience is common and reflective of the many injustices and forms of everyday violence that Black women endure.

Vanessa's narrative also illustrates the powerful impact that witnessing has on her when she observes men who harass: "Yeah, street harassment is a problem, because sometimes it may be that they're not disrespecting me but the next woman that comes by they may say, 'Forget you, you ho,' and blah, blah, blah, you know? There's no need for you to be disrespectful because somebody is not interested in you." Here, Vanessa identifies one of the root problems of street harassment: a lack of respect of women. Her comments also hint at how harassers recycle the controlling image of the "freak" or the "whore" to normalize, justify, or excuse their actions, instead of taking responsibility (see Collins 2004). In the next section, I provide an example of a Black woman respondent forced to deal with misperception of herself as a "public woman."

From Being Out in Public to "Public Women"

Examples abound of respondents reportedly feeling seen primarily through a lens of sexual seduction, with male harassers viewing them as "always already sexual" beings. In returning for a moment to the research of Stephens and

Phillips (2003), one can better understand the story that one respondent, Flora, shared with me about being seen as a "public woman." Once when she was out walking at night, Flora recalled, a harasser pointedly asked her, "Are you working?" It is instructive that Flora is seen as a sex worker simply for showing up in public. Flora felt neither compelled to denigrate sex work or workers, nor to take offense at being mistaken for one. She was annoyed mostly at the harasser's perpetuation of the mandates of compulsory heterosexuality (Rich 1980) (as Flora identifies as a queer Black woman), and his inability to be civil and respectful to her.

As a darker-skinned woman, Flora is viewed as always already available, or a "public text"—a consumable body, visually and intimately (see Holloway 2011). Because Black women in public have historically been viewed as "public women" or prostitutes, they are regarded as "consumable subjects" or worse, objects "out of place" (see Kowaleski-Wallace 1997). Like many other Black women, Flora is seen as out of place simply for being out in public. By leaving the ostensible safety of the home, and entering the arguably dangerous space of the public sphere, Flora, too, becomes public. Men who harass her engage her accordingly. Flora is seen (or unseen as a person, perhaps more to the point) as hypersexual, presumed to be a sex worker who engages in public sex. Following Holloway, Flora becomes a public text when she moves her private body into public spaces. As Holloway (2011) argues, Black women's bodies have historically always already been on display, have suffered particular indignities and vulnerabilities through visuality, the spectacularity of their Blackness framing the way their femininity and womanhood are viewed, consumed, mis/used, and mis/understood.

As spectacular bodies, Black women are denied their subjectivity during street harassment, often rendered speechless by discourses informed by respectability politics that create a trap for Black women who talk back to men, or to the troublesome tropes about Black womanhood. As noted earlier, the deployment and circulation of controlling images works to define Black women, their bodies, actions, movements, and more, to reinforce "respectability politics." Respectability politics can be both potentially protective of and repressive for Black women: protective on the basis of "good girls" needing and/or deserving protection of men, and repressive, if one feels trapped or confined by social norms and the disparaging narrative about Black womanhood (see Cooper 2017; Holloway 2011; Rankine 2014). By all accounts, the Black women in my study are "respectable" women, yet this respectability failed to protect them from harm. Their experiences demonstrate the dangers that Black women face, in confronting the dangerous discourses that cast Black women in unsavory ways, and the dangerous discursive practices of men who harass, in part by relying upon and recycling controlling images of Black women.

Finally, Flora's experience with street harassment, like that of so many other Black women, reinforces the notion of public spaces being unsafe for women, especially when some men who harass women view women in public as "public women." This view demonstrates the dangers of gender codes of masculinity that condone, if not encourage, such behavior from men. Experiences like those Flora and other Black women describe suggest that women are safer in the home. Such a view not only supports traditional gender ideologies but also ignores Jana Leo's (2010) point: "The home is a high-risk situation." If anything, my research on street harassment suggests that Black women not only face the injustice of street harassment on a regular basis, but that they are also contending with other forms of violence, including that created by controlling images of their "unruly," "unworthy" selves.

Conclusions

Focusing on Black women provides an understanding of the particular ways Black women experience harassment. As I show above, and in support of the extant literature, Black women confront many controlling images during street harassment with men. In some ways, street harassment makes visible the persistence and prevalence of controlling images of Black women, the individual and institutional efforts to control Black women's bodies, and the extent to which people get trapped in discourses that attempt to define (or deny) their humanity. If Black women are denied their femininity and the attendant protection women and femininity "requires" from men generally in US society, it follows that Black women would also be denied their humanity and dignity during these hostile interactions. Street harassment leaves little room for women to talk back to or contest such images and the harassment that reifies these images.

Rather than remain silent or quiet about the injustices they experience (although many do for reasons too numerous to elaborate upon here), many Black women speak out against the unsavory stereotypes and problematic perceptions upon which many encounters with street harassers are clearly based. Speaking up may prove inevitably futile, however, given the tenacity of some harassers and the reality that street harassment connects to other forms of injustice on the continuum of violence. Nevertheless, Black women do challenge these problematic constructions of themselves, just as they challenge men who harass them. They devise strategies to navigate public spaces to buffer themselves from the injuries of unjust words and the injustice of street harassment.

NOTE

1 On Sunday, January 7, 2018, Oprah Winfrey made reference to the recently deceased Recy Taylor, thereby introducing her name and story of courage and heroism to mass audiences.

10

Gendered Harassment, Abuse, and Violence Online

BAILEY POLAND

Gendered online harassment and abuse have become increasingly noticeable sub-jects of academic study and public consciousness in recent years. Any number of high-profile examples come to mind, from abuses on Facebook and Twitter to Gamergate and beyond. Many of Donald Trump's tweets, sent both before and during his time as president of the US, serve as stark examples of the ways in which sexism, racism, xenophobia, and violence have become normalized parts of online discourse. Despite the damage caused by newsworthy attacks, however, online harassment and abuse are not limited to extreme examples: instead, gendered harassment is deeply ingrained in the experience of everyday life on the internet.

While this chapter looks at gendered online harassment and abuse, there are other forms of digitally mediated abuse in dire need of attention. The chapter attempts to include intersections of gender, race, sexuality, disability, and other facets of identity and marginalization, but an approach with gender as its analyti-cal lens will obscure or ignore as much as it reveals. Work that analyzes harass-ment and abuse through additional lenses is critically important. Keeping that limitation in mind, this chapter explores what gendered online harassment is, some of the main types of online harassment and abuse, Gamergate, faulty advice given to women experiencing harassment online, the effects of online abuse, and strategies for combating and resisting abuse.

Gendered Harassment, Online and Off

To understand online harassment and abuse, it is crucial to have a working defi-nition of key concepts that straddle online and offline spaces, including sexism and privilege, and the relationship of offline beliefs to online harassment.

Sexism is prejudice based on gender, combined with the privilege and power that enable people and systems to use that prejudice to cause harm. In other words, because men as a group hold the majority of social privileges, their preju-dices against women as a group are more likely to hurt women. Privilege can be understood as a set of social advantages associated with particular axes of identity. Privilege is associated with those forms of identity (and the associated benefits) that are presented as default and are overrepresented in positions of power and in the media and other spaces.

While privilege is used to describe broad social attitudes and modes of access that affect power, safety, and representation, sexism is understood solely as prejudice against someone on the basis of their sex. However, the ability to cause harm to a group (e.g., women) while conferring benefits on another group (e.g., men) is a core part of how sexism and privilege intertwine. Sexism as it affects online life is the major focus of this chapter, with the key caveat that online harassment and abuse are rarely—if ever—linked to gender alone.

When considering such links, it is also important to note that online harassment is rooted in offline beliefs, and that offline beliefs are supported and reinforced by the prevalence of sexist behaviors online. Attitudes do not develop in a vacuum, nor do they exist only online. Sexism and other biases offline were transferred into online spaces from the earliest days of the internet itself. White supremacist websites, according to research by Jesse Daniels, were among the earliest consistently maintained websites, and continue to be organizing centers for white supremacist activity online and off (Daniels 2009).

While it is tempting to believe that hostile online behaviors developed in an internet vacuum, the attitudes that shaped how people act online were brought to the internet from what they already believed, and given new audiences and new ways to spread. People may be more comfortable expressing extreme views online than they would in person, but such expressions still reflect their beliefs. In many ways, the activities aimed at building and reinforcing sexist dominance online are conducted to recreate offline patterns of domination. Offline, sexism may involve financial and political control, violence, and a number of seemingly invisible factors, such as policing how women talk.

As a result, we can think about gendered harassment, abuse, and violence online as expressions of sexism and privilege that use technology as a medium. Gendered harassment helps create, enforce, and normalize sexist dominance online. While harassment is a global problem, norms established in the early years of the internet tend to reflect Western patterns of use and abuse.

There is a distinct lack of neutrality in internet spaces, which is the lingering result of the internet's creation and history, and which allows men to frame women as interlopers in what are perceived as male-only online spaces. When women do participate on anything close to equal footing with men, it "threatens the asymmetrical, dominant position that some men apparently assume is theirs" (Herring 2002, 156). Women who expect to be able to take up as much space online as their male counterparts quickly find that men do not agree with that expectation. Through gendered harassment and abuse, men attempt to recreate offline conversational patterns. Sexist harassment and abuse in these situations are intended to silence women entirely or force them to conform to men's chosen norms.

In *The Internet of Garbage*, Sarah Jeong describes online abuse through two frameworks: harassing content versus harassing behavior. "When looking at harassment as content . . . the debate ends up revolving around civil rights versus free speech," Jeong writes (2015). She does not regard this characterization as helpful, as it sets up a spectrum on either end of which might be violent threats or minor annoyances. Instead, "behavior is a better, more useful lens through which to look at harassment" (ibid.). The framework Jeong proposes allows us to determine a response to the behavior itself, avoiding the "free speech" arguments discussed later in the chapter. When considering types of harassment, keeping behavior in mind (rather than the details of the content) can be helpful.

Types of Gendered Harassment, Abuse, and Violence

Digitally mediated sexist hostility exists on a spectrum from annoying to severe and even deadly. That some behaviors seem like "mere" annoyances should not disguise the fact that they are part of a pattern that silences and harms women. Some of the behaviors described in this section are not solely gendered and represent abuses enabled by digital technologies and tools—when those abuses are committed because the target is a woman, they become gendered.

Derailing and Mansplaining

Derailing and mansplaining are everywhere. Although individual instances might be little more than annoying, these behaviors create barriers to women's participation that men don't experience. Derailing occurs when a man interrupts and attempts to redirect conversations. An individual might ask questions or make accusations only tangentially related to the original topic. Derailing may involve asking questions that a Google search could answer, or asserting "not all men" when the conversation is about systemic issues. Derailing allows men to demand free education from women, repeatedly interrupt women, and try to refocus women's attention.

"Mansplaining," a term emerging from responses to an essay by Rebecca Solnit, is a condescending version of derailing (Solnit 2012). The term refers to a man who explains something to women, whether or not the man knows anything about the subject and regardless of the women's expertise (even, perhaps especially, when the women have greater experience or expertise). Mansplaining lets everyone know men think their own opinions and ideas should be more carefully considered than women's.

Sexual Harassment and Gender Stereotypes

Sexual harassment and gender stereotypes are dominance tactics that aim to restore control of online conversations to men by painting women as inferior to men and demanding women's silence. Harassers use "sexual objectification and gender stereotyping to make women feel unwelcome, subordinated, or altogether excluded" (Franks 2012, 658). Harassment frequently begins with sexual objectification, the deployment of gender stereotypes about women in the face of resistance, and an escalation of aggression until women acquiesce or fall silent. These interactions sometimes culminate in violent threats.

Escalating from sexual harassment to gender stereotypes and threats is a common tactic—similar to a street harasser insulting or attacking a woman who doesn't respond favorably. These acts are conversational strategies used to give men control of a space while reinforcing stereotypes about women as shallow, vapid, or valuable only insofar as they are sexually appealing. The threat of physical and sexual violence is deployed when sexual harassment and gender stereotypes fail to silence women.

Free Speech Claims and Gender Essentialism

Free speech and gender essentialism are frequently invoked to silence women (and are commonly used by cisgender women against transgender women, as well). Reshaping an argument to make it seem as though a woman said something damaging to free speech is a quick way to gain support for harassing her. Such claims argue that free speech includes freedom from criticism or social repercussions. Gendered stereotypes, such as describing women as hysterical, unintelligent, and vindictive, are also deployed. The imagined deficiencies of the targeted woman are then applied to all women.

The tactic of reframing criticism of sexism as an attempt to limit free speech redirects focus from the speech itself onto women's reactions, framing responses to sexism as the problem. Positioning women as hysterical creates a positive contrast for men—framing men as reasonable, calm, and authoritative. The implication is that women cannot participate in conversations without becoming overly emotional, while men can. Men's opinions, then, should be taken seriously, while women can be dismissed. Gender essentialist and free speech arguments are a useful strategy for avoiding addressing a woman's argument.

Double Standards and Tone Policing

Another common tactic is to create a situation in which how women speak becomes grounds for disagreement while the content is ignored. Men position themselves as discursive arbiters and implicitly validate their own conversational choices. This creates a double standard, policing women's speech patterns while exempting men from criticism (or, again, framing criticism by women as an attack on free speech). Men can participate respectfully or aggressively without comment; women get no latitude, particularly if they express anger or annoyance.

The derailing strategy of focusing on how women speak is sometimes called tone policing. While anyone can engage in tone policing, it is frequently aimed at women to prevent them from participating in discussion. When an online disagreement focuses on how a man feels about what a woman said, there is no longer a conversation but an attempt to establish dominance.

Threats of Violence

Many violent threats contain ultimatums: if a woman doesn't silence herself, she will be violently punished. One threat I received read, for example, "How about I shove my dick in your mouth and you shut the fuck up?" Threats like this recreate offline patterns of violence online. Women receive a significant number of threats, which tend to be linked to gender, race, and sexuality. Rape threats are the most obviously gendered threat, and play on offline rates of sexual assault to create an environment of intimidation and fear.

Abusers deny the seriousness of threats, call threats jokes, or accuse women of sending fake threats to themselves. The impact of a threat is therefore not necessarily in whether it will be carried out. While a threat is frightening, another purpose is reminding women that violence is a perpetual possibility, that gender stereotypes will be used against them, and that there are few consequences for threatening women.

Doxxing and SWATting

Doxxing involves gathering, centralizing, and distributing a target's personal information. Email addresses, home addresses, workplaces, phone numbers, Social Security numbers, credit card information, medical details, and more can be exposed. Abusers then have immediate access to material that can be used to wreak havoc. *Wired* writes that the term comes from "'dropping dox,' an old-school revenge tactic" (Honan 2014). Doxxing is designed to make anonymity impossible or to make a public target feel unsafe.

Doxxing enables SWATting. The FBI defines SWATting as "a hoax call to 9-1-1 to draw a response from law enforcement" (FBI 2013). SWATting is typically done under the guise of a prank or for revenge. SWATting calls typically reference a hostage situation, potential suicide, or life-threatening event requiring a police response in the hopes of subsequent injury or death for the target. For example, in December 2017, a man in Kansas was killed by police after a SWAT call was placed over the video game *Call of Duty*, with which he was not even involved (Statt 2017).

Gamergate

Gamergate is a chilling example of how online harassment and abuse spiral out of control. Although the roots of the violence are deep, Gamergate began with "the Zoë post," a continuation of domestic violence that became the springboard abusers used to enact violence on as many marginalized people as possible. The patterns established before Gamergate and perfected during it have continued to be employed by misogynists and white supremacists since Gamergate declined.

The Zoë post was an inflammatory piece about award-winning video game developer Zoë Quinn by her ex-boyfriend Eron Gjoni, filled with a mix of hyperbolic accusations and outright lies. Gjoni posted the screed in various websites' comments sections, and then on 4chan. 4chan, and 4chan's /b/ and /pol/ boards, have long been a repository for online harassment, and Gjoni found a credulous, angry audience. Gjoni asserted, among other false claims, that Quinn had multiple affairs during their relationship. He spent the next several months coaching the mob and feeding harassers information. While Gjoni was eventually placed under a restraining order, much of the damage was already done.

Gamergate was named by actor Adam Baldwin. On Twitter, Baldwin included the hashtag #Gamergate when linking to a video that repeated Gjoni's accusations. The mob was looking for ways to hide their abuse beneath a veneer of legitimacy, and seized on the hashtag and Gjoni's suggestion that Quinn had slept with a games journalist who was reviewing Quinn's award-winning game *Depression Quest*. They said Gamergate was "actually about ethics in games journalism," because the accusation pointed to a breach of journalistic ethics: Quinn was sleeping with people for good reviews!

This accusation is not uncommon, given the popular belief that women who get ahead slept their way to the top. The story also provided reason to deny *Depression Quest* legitimacy, a long-cherished goal of the harassers. Critically, however, the accusation is false. While Quinn and Nathan Grayson had a relationship, Grayson never reviewed *Depression Quest* (Quinn 2017). This information proved irrelevant to Gamergaters, because their narrative was all that mattered. The lie continues circulating despite all available facts: Gamergate's adherents call the facts indications of collusion, rather than evidence they might be wrong.

Another favorite Gamergate target was Anita Sarkeesian, creator of Feminist Frequency and the Kickstarter *Tropes vs. Women in Video Games*, a feminist analysis of video games. Sarkeesian's presence was another outlet for Gamergate's ire. At the height of Gamergate, in October 2014, Sarkeesian canceled a speaking engagement at Utah State University after the university received a threat of "the deadliest school shooting in American history" if she appeared (McDonald 2014). When the school refused to put additional security in place or prohibit weapons from being brought to the lecture, Sarkeesian felt she had no option but to cancel her appearance.

For the next several months Gamergate targeted not only Quinn and Sarkeesian but also women, queer people, men of color, and anyone who so much as hinted that Gamergate might be more about abusing people than about ethics.

The harassment escalated from gendered harassment to threats, doxxing, SWAT calls, and stalking. Gamergate's targets were those they described as "social justice warriors" (SJW). An SJW analyzes society, media, or pop culture or is a person who cares about justice and diversity. One of Gamergate's goals was maintaining a status quo in which appealing to cisgender straight White men should be the primary goal of anything video game related. The push for gaming to become more diverse was perceived not as an attempt to help the industry grow but as an effort to oppress gamers.

The major figures of Gamergate were not limited to its targets; people also saw Gamergate as an opportunity to build brands on hatred. Milo Yiannopoulos pivoted from mocking gamers to becoming their advocate against "feminist bullies," increasing his profile in the US and launching a sponsored speaking tour (Yiannopoulos 2014). A nearly identical pattern occurred with lawyer Mike Cernovich. Early on, Cernovich wished men would "put down the fucking video games" but soon recognized that Gamergate was not about games journalism (Cernovich 2014). Cernovich and Yiannopoulos did not see just an audience—they saw a market.

Cernovich's tactics were among the most dangerous. He hired private investigators to dog Quinn, and began working with Gjoni after the restraining order was put in place. Cernovich and Gamergate regarded this restraining order as an attack on Gjoni's free speech—a common tactic, as noted previously. However, the litigation Cernovich threatened never materialized; instead, he harassed and intimidated victims, relying on Gamergate as personal attack dogs—and as a customer base. Cernovich's ongoing strategy, even after Gamergate itself died down, has been to promote conspiracy theories, provide dubious legal advice, and offer a constantly rotating platter of targets.

Cernovich and Yiannopoulos continue to use their platforms to cause harm, although Yiannopoulos's Twitter account was banned when he coordinated attacks on actress Leslie Jones (Isaac 2016). While both men were responsible for inciting harassment, Gamergate also developed its own outlets for coordination. After being banned from even discussing Gamergate on 4chan, its members moved to 8chan, a website built on the same principles as 4chan but without the rules 4chan moderators have tried to enforce. Gamergate was responsible for multiple SWAT calls, most of which were planned on 8chan; at least one resulted in a SWAT team being sent to the wrong location (Robertson 2015).

While Gamergate's actions spread into every facet of its targets' lives, urged on by Cernovich and Yiannopoulos and planned on 8chan, Twitter was an abuse epicenter. Gamergaters could easily create multiple accounts—if one was suspended, another account took its place. This ensured Gamergate looked much larger than it was. During a period studied by Women, Action & the Media (WAM!), 12 percent of the reports of harassment, threats, and violence were linked to Gamergate (Matias et al. 2015). Globally, more than 1.2 billion people play games, yet at an outside estimate only seventeen thousand people posted to the Gamergate hashtag, whether in support or opposition (Balo 2014). Despite its small numbers, Gamergaters accounted for more than 10 percent of Twitter harassment. Twitter continues to have issues with the harassment and abuse of marginalized groups, and abusers continue using Gamergate's tactics against their perceived enemies.

Inescapable Bad Advice about Gendered Online Harassment

Don't Feed the Trolls

"Don't feed the trolls" dates back to early online communities, where "trolling" referred to attempts to disrupt conversations. In that context, ignoring a troll could work: if you don't let a troll take over, they are powerless. Now, however, invoking "don't feed the trolls" most often tells women to stop talking about abuse.

"Don't feed the trolls" isolates a target by demanding her silence rather than the silence of abusers, suggests abuse is a status quo, and tells women they should not expect abusers to face consequences. Abusers may want attention, but beyond that, they want to harass and abuse without censure. Current discussions of "trolling" rely on a definition that no longer fits the present context (Phillips 2013). If gendered abuse was a mild inconvenience—which is what "trolling" implies—then there would be no need for discussion. However, gendered harassment and abuse negatively affect women's ability to work, socialize, and interact online. Ignoring it is not an option.

Everyone Gets Harassed

When women discuss online abuse, a common response is that everyone gets harassed. Claiming "everyone gets harassed" erases specific experiences, intersections, and volumes of abuse. Although a Pew Research Center study about online harassment found roughly equivalent levels of offensive name-calling aimed at both men and women, cyberstalking and sexual harassment were far more severe for women—especially women between the ages of eighteen and twenty-four (Duggan 2014). Pew also found that men and women are almost equally likely to be called offensive names, purposefully embarrassed, threatened, or to endure sustained harassment.

The Pew study never addresses the frequency or volume of that harassment, however. An earlier study found women received more than twenty-five times as many sexually explicit or harassing messages than men (Meyer and Cukier 2006). Other reports show women of color experience "harassment more than any other group" (Citron 2014, 14). "Everyone gets harassed" is, therefore, misleading—and even if everyone does get harassed, it doesn't follow that we should simply accept it.

It's Just the Internet

Claiming abuse happens because "it's just the internet" dismisses women's concerns as trivial. This argument rests on an idealized internet where everyone has equal access to resources, and suffers equally—which is not the case. A common formulation of the argument is, "You're upset about mean words online while other women are really oppressed." The argument is that online abuse doesn't matter, and that true oppression only exists elsewhere. "It's just the internet" attempts to decontextualize women's online experiences.

As has been the case for far too many victims, however, abuse occurs online and off, and "it's just the internet" treats online behavior as if it occurs in a vacuum. Online and offline behaviors and beliefs affect, inform, and reinforce each other. Talking about online abuse as though it is inevitable also kills conversations about solutions. The internet is what we make it, and an environment where abuse is tolerated can no longer be acceptable.

Just Block Them

"Just block them" is ostensibly a good idea, as it removes harassment from the target's sight. However, blocking abusers does not prevent abuse. Creating a new account to continue engaging in harassment takes mere seconds. In the case of a mob, blocking can become a full-time activity. "Just block them" doesn't prevent a target from having to see the initial abuse that occurred, either. All blocking does is remove harassing content from a target's sight—and no one else's. Advising women to block their harassers puts women in a permanently reactive stance and offers no strategy for ending harassment.

"Just block me" is also used by harassers challenging their target to respond in some way. The statement indicates to the target that the abuser is deliberately overstepping a boundary and, if blocked, abusers go on to say they've been censored. "Just block me" demonstrates an obvious problem: the burden of dealing with harassment is too often placed on its target's shoulders.

It's a Public Forum

Saying the internet is a "public forum" typically goes hand in hand with treating blocking as a form of censorship, and arguing that free expression involves the right to speak to anyone at any time—but not the right to determine one's boundaries for conversations. The public forum argument insists that women be receptive and passive in the face of harassment, and treats harassment as an acceptable part of public discourse.

The argument also leads to silencing: "the internet is a public forum, so maybe you shouldn't have said anything to draw such negative responses." Sending an offensive or threatening response is made unquestionable, while women's speech itself is again problematized. Calling the internet a public forum invokes a conceptualization of the internet in which abusive comments are suitable behavior, and vilifies attempts to make online spaces safer. However, if the only way for women to avoid abuse is not to talk, whose free speech has been affected?

Turn Off Your Computer

Telling women to leave online spaces seems logical: after all, if there are no women to abuse, that solves the problem. However, abusers are not held responsible for their own behavior. End to Cyber Bullying responds strongly to telling targets to shut off their computers: "Why should a victim be required to interrupt an online experience because of someone else's maliciousness?" (Prevention for Teens 2014). Walking away also doesn't mean the abuse stops. Everyone else can see and participate in the abuse or have their opinion shaped by it.

Leaving the internet means lost personal connections, destroyed livelihoods, and isolation. If the targets are no longer online to counter abusive narratives, that absence can have long-lasting effects on job searches, personal connections, and more. "Just turn off your computer" tells women their options are to put up with abuse or not to be online at all. These options are not acceptable—women live, work, and play in online spaces and deserve to do so in safety. It is time we hold abusers accountable.

The Effects of Gendered Online Harassment and Abuse

Gendered harassment online, especially sustained abuse experienced across time, has a variety of negative effects. Targeted women report personal, professional, and psychological harms as a result of harassment.

Personal Harms

Women experience a number of personal limitations online, such as reducing activities to avoid harassment. Limiting online hobbies might include refraining from blogging on certain topics, commenting on specific websites, or visiting particular forums. Women might turn down connections with other people for fear of exposing themselves to harassment and abuse, or they might limit all online interactions by heightening security features to reduce the likelihood of being targeted.

Online safeguards continue to be a concern for women, who want to reduce how much of their personally identifiable information is available. Women are more likely to be concerned about location-based tracking than men (Rainie et al. 2013). Women, who are at a greater risk of stalking, have good reason to be worried about online tools that display location-based information. Online dating can also be a fraught experience for women. Women of color and transgender women in particular are subjected to fetishistic interactions. When rebuffed, men sometimes resort to overtly sexist, racist, and transphobic attacks. Few online dating platforms have adequate safety measures in place for women who are repeatedly harassed or stalked.

Further, so-called "revenge porn" is the act of taking once-consensual nude photographs of a woman—often an ex—and posting them online. "Revenge porn" as a term lends itself both to the stigma associated with consensual pornography, as well as to blaming the victims of these invasions of privacy. A damaged personal image is not the worst that has happened due to the nonconsensual sharing of these images: a number of young women have committed suicide after having nude photos or videos circulated online, and nearly half of women who have private photographs circulated on "revenge porn" websites or throughout their communities report considering suicide (Laws 2013).

Professional Harms

Nearly 100 percent of professional recruiters have connected with candidates on the networking site LinkedIn, found their blog, or looked them up on social media (Jobvite Resources 2015). Imagine a recruiter conducting a Google search and coming across post after post that defame a candidate or accuse her of causing problems in professional spaces. They might even see altered photos that make an otherwise-stellar candidate seem like too much trouble to hire. After all, a single individual's reputation can affect how an organization is perceived by customers.

While this scenario might seem far-fetched, business research shows that companies frequently use social media posts to reject job candidates. It is also not uncommon for women to be driven out of a specific profession or position due to gendered harassment, as seen in the narratives of women and some men in the #MeToo movement started by Tarana Burke and popularized by discussions of abuse in Hollywood and elsewhere (Garcia 2017). While prominent in heavily male-dominated industries, sexism has the ability to ruin women's careers in any field.

Small business owners are also disproportionately affected by gendered attacks and harassment. Coordinated attacks by groups of people that leave fake negative reviews on websites such as Yelp can result in an immediate loss of business, and online hacking and other attacks can take down a small business website, causing lost ranking in search engines and customer dissatisfaction. Women whose careers depend on online exposure and connections are at a significant risk for losing their livelihoods over gendered harassment. Women who start online businesses are also much less likely to receive funding to start a new company, which means women begin their online careers at a disadvantage; gendered harassment can be the final nail in the coffin for a woman's online business or her entire career.

Psychological Harms

Gendered harassment is intended to wear women down, erode their confidence, and make the psychological cost of online visibility too high a price to pay. The consequences of dealing with harassment and threats varies between individuals. However, some patterns have emerged in the research. One study found that "misogynist comments were seen as more harassing online than in traditional settings" (Biber et al. 2002, 33). The study found that people tend to apply slightly more stringent standards to how we interact with each other on the internet versus face-to-face situations.

Other reactions occur subconsciously—women do not choose to be offended but inescapably respond to harassment and abuse. During one study, participants were asked to record gender-biased incidents and their reactions to them; researchers found that sexist interactions "affected women's psychological well-being by decreasing their comfort, increasing their feelings of anger and depression, and decreasing their state of self-esteem" (Swim et al. 2001, 31). Women react to sexism by adjusting how they speak, walk, take up space, and interact with the world.

Sexist comments contribute to women's awareness of their surroundings and have an underlying effect on how women act and feel in that space. As with offline harassment, "sexual harassment . . . has been shown to have long-lasting and severe effects on its victims no matter where it occurs" (Franks 2012, 673). Women cannot simply choose to ignore harassment and abuse, or its effects, and tend to experience feelings of undermined personal agency (Citron 2009b). Women who are subjected to online harassment are at risk of experiencing a number of adverse psychological outcomes, including anxiety, fear, shame, depression, reduced personal and professional goals, significantly higher rates of suicidal ideations and attempts, and more (Staude-Müller et al. 2012). The psychological effects of gendered online harassment are serious, and sometimes deadly.

Dealing with Gendered Harassment and Abuse

There is no one right way to deal with online harassment and abuse. Women, in light of an ongoing lack of institutional support, have cobbled together ways of making the internet survivable. However, each strategy has its own limitations and shortfalls.

Blocking, Muting, Reporting

Blocking, muting, and reporting tend to be reactive, and typically mean someone has been exposed to abusive content before they take action. Blocking harassers is one of the few tools women have to stop one-to-one harassment, however briefly. Most blocking mechanisms are still easily circumvented, which means a block is typically a stopgap measure. Many women opt to mute or hide harassers as well. Muting allows harassers to see and interact with their target, but the target no longer sees notifications, and someone who has been muted may not realize it and thus not go looking for ways to circumvent that feature.

Reporting abuse is rarely an effective strategy, even though it results in consequences for abusers on occasion. While report-filing procedures are important, reporting places a disproportionate burden on the targets. Reporting abuse is time-consuming, requires women to relive the harassment, and generally does not provide efficient or effective results. Sending in an abuse report can require a woman to provide links to or screenshots of the abuse, which means ongoing exposure to the abuse. Many reporting functions themselves are also ineffectively automated, or place a burden on underpaid human teams.

Privacy Settings

Many women use privacy settings to reduce exposure to harassers. As cyberstalking is now included in one of four reported stalking cases, controlling who has access to one's online profiles is a matter of vital importance (Dreßing et al. 2014). Women may use privacy settings to avoid everyday harassment and keep stalkers at bay. A study on Facebook users showed women are more concerned than men about the utility of privacy controls (Kuo et al. 2013). The researchers suggest that social media networks should avoid one-size-fits-all solutions for privacy. Different demographic groups have varying desires and needs for privacy settings, highlighting the importance of having diversity among development and design teams.

The goal of adjusting privacy settings is to control access to posts and information, and still, privacy options tend to be opaque and inconsistently applied. Further, women are presented with the choice of not engaging in open conversations or becoming the target of harassment campaigns, and are blamed for any negative outcomes regardless of which method they chose. Privacy settings act simultaneously as walls that keep out some abusers and that keep women from fully experiencing online life. The decision to shut oneself in is a trade-off that too many women have to make.

Moderation

Moderation occurs in a few ways—women can moderate comments on their own sites, websites can assign moderators and set rules for leaving comments, or outsource moderation entirely. Content filters can flag key words and mark comments for further review. Many women close their comment sections, a strategy adopted by major platforms including NPR, The Pacific Standard, and others.

Websites with multiple writers usually have visible commenting policies. These rules are useful for setting rules of engagement, but moderation still requires someone to read comments. In one article, *New Inquiry* reported that moderator roles tend to be disproportionately held by underpaid, undersupported young women (Wilson 2014). That there are so few resources in place to support moderators is a serious concern. Comment moderation, like all forms of defense against harassment, is a double-edged sword. While filters help, websites can be deluged with hatred that is impossible to contain. As with all solutions to online harassment and abuse, individual women are left largely to their own devices, to choose between a free and open online experience and constraining access to cut down on abuse.

Whisper Networks

Private discussions between women, what we might call whisper networks, are an essential part of dealing with abuse. Such discussions are not solutions but function as coping mechanisms. Women use formal and informal networks to share information about opportunities, education, activism, and predators. Many men who are revealed to be serial abusers had long been identified in whisper networks, as the late 2017 news cycle demonstrated (Garcia 2017).

Women's private networks might consist of email chains, Slack channels, Facebook groups, or other messages sent outside the public eye. Discussions among women have been used as a form of self-defense both online and off; study after study shows that such networks have immense benefits for women fleeing domestic violence (Krenkel et al. 2015). Women's networks are self-created and developed in the face of technological beliefs that run counter to women's needs and outright hostility to women's desire for such networks. Women's networks, whether public, private, or both, fill a number of necessary roles in online and offline spaces. Through these discussions, women learn about one another, connect to other women with similar interests, promote each other's work, engage in activism, and more.

Men's Role

Many men want to help but don't know how. The most obvious way to combat gendered harassment is not to engage in it. Criticism, for example, can be valuable, but gender stereotypes are something to watch for. Men are taught that it is acceptable for them to offer their evaluation of women's work, appearance, and thoughts in gendered ways and without being asked, which reinforces stereotypes and makes women feel unwelcome.

Leigh Alexander, a journalist and author, has written about how men can best respond to harassment and abuse: stop asking women what to do, expecting women to educate them, trying to explain harassment, and telling women how to respond (Alexander 2014). Although men mean well when they ask for advice on what to do or offer suggestions, these statements end up being more unwanted input. Alexander describes what men can do in lieu of these behaviors: express support for women, consider how responses will affect targets, support a woman's work rather than noting how she is being victimized, and even distract the harassers (without keeping the original target involved) (Alexander 2014). All of these actions offer opportunities for men to engage in genuine, supportive behaviors in the face of abuse.

Fighting Back

As we work on solutions to gendered online harassment, abuse, and violence, looking at cyberfeminist theories—and the work that's being done now—can give us a roadmap to a better future.

Challenging Gender Stereotypes

One of the challenges cyberfeminism faced was showing that the presumed link between technology and masculinity is not due to biological differences—a stereotype that persists despite all evidence to the contrary (Wajcman 2010). Persistent biases against women, along with deeply ingrained racism, remain prevalent in tech. The connection between technological prowess and stereotypical masculinity is due in part to the deliberate disassociation of technological activities from women's work (ibid.). Women were driven out of the computer industry and have yet to make significant inroads back into the field.

Cyberfeminists sought to overturn preconceptions about women and technology and to highlight how the internet might be used to eliminate oppression. The Old Boys Network, formed by a small group of women, led conferences and workshops that included everything from basic to high-level instruction in technology and internet use to lectures, presentations, and dinner parties (Wilding 1998). The goal of such organizing was to connect women with an interest in technology, provide a place to learn and explore, and explode the stereotype of the tech wizard as a White male nerd.

Organizations like Girls Who Code, founded by Reshma Saujani; Black Girls Code, founded by Kimberly Bryant; and Dames Who Game continue that tradition. Girls Who Code is described as an "organization working to close the gender gap in the technology and engineering sectors" (Who We Are 2015). Black Girls Code notes that "there's still a dearth of African American women in [STEM] professions, an absence that cannot be explained by, say, a lack of interest in those fields" (Bryant 2014). Dames Who Game is explicitly inclusive of "all people of any gender, sex, sexual orientation, gender expression, gender identity, race, religion, disability, nationality, socioeconomic status and immigrant status as members and community participants" and is designed to be welcoming and safe (Dames 2015). Each group emphasizes the need for such spaces to challenge stereotypes and enable marginalized groups to work with technology.

Diversity in Development

Design and development groups lacking in diversity, whether for websites or products, have a tendency to miss glaring issues that affect end users. A core tenet of cyberfeminist analysis is that all technology is developed in nonneutral settings by nonneutral actors. As Faith Wilding wrote, the internet exists in "a social framework that is already established in its practices and embedded in economic, political, and cultural environments that are still deeply sexist and racist" (Wilding 1998, 9). Even when racism and sexism are expressed without deliberate intention, as in the design of technology that unintentionally excludes certain end users, technology "is already socially inscribed with regard to bodies, sex, age, economics, social class, and race" (ibid., 9).

A lack of diversity in the development stage can have unforeseen but potentially disastrous effects on the end product. As a result, harassment and abuse flourish in online spaces in large part because websites and networks are not designed with violence prevention in mind, and abuse is seen as an environmental norm rather than a problem that can be dealt with. If people designing networks do not deal with sexist, racist, or other forms of harassment offline, they may not consider how such behaviors could be enacted online. A revisited cyberfeminist analysis of the historical, cultural, and social attitudes that influenced the formation of online spaces is an essential part of understanding how to look for and create solutions.

Organizations

The landscape of the internet changes rapidly, and new organizations devoted to combating gendered harassment online emerge regularly. A number of organizations currently attempting to educate people about sexism (online and off) and assisting people who have been targeted for harassment, abuse, or violence online are listed below[1]. While this list is only partial, each group brings important topics to the discussion of online harassment:

- Crash Override Network, founded by Zoë Quinn and Alex Lifschitz
- Everyday Sexism, founded by Laura Bates
- Feminist Frequency, founded by Anita Sarkeesian
- Heartmob, founded by Jae Cameron, Jill Dimond, Emily May, Debjani Roy, and Courtney Young
- Working to Halt Online Abuse (WHOA), founded by Jayne Hitchcock

A Call to Action

Gendered online harassment, abuse, and violence are among the most serious problems facing the internet today. A pervasive culture of abuse, the websites and social media architectures that enable it, and enduring hateful attitudes have created online spaces where abuse is rampant. Women feel alienated and unsafe in an environment that increasingly shapes media, politics, business, and everyday life. It is past time for a serious reckoning with the scope of the problem represented by gendered online harassment, the motivations behind it, the impact it has, and what strategies are effective in reducing its prevalence.

Further, most research that does exist relies on gender as its sole variable. While that factor is important for demonstrating that much online harassment is sexist in nature, the refusal to consider other variables leads to the erasure and elision of many issues that cannot be addressed by looking at gender alone. The intersections of identity provide a focal point for harassment, with racism, sexism, and other forms of hatred so deeply intertwined as to be indistinguishable. Research that is sensitive to these nuances of abuse must be conducted in order for us to see the full picture of online harassment and develop solutions that will actually work. Solving online abuse will require giving voice to the women who are ignored, as well as relying on their experiences and expertise as guideposts to a better and safer online environment.

Those of us with the power to do research, educate others, enforce consequences, and build safer spaces have a responsibility to do so. The internet is our home, but it was not built with all of us in mind. It's time for some serious remodeling.

NOTE

1 Although outside the scope of the work of this chapter, combating the internet-based grooming of children by predators is also a significant focus for numerous legal and civic organizations. The use of social media and other types of websites to prey on children or exchange illegal photographs is an area of particular focus for many scholars and activists. The overlap between gender-based harassment and predation aimed at children is also worth addressing; during Gamergate, for example, 8chan, which was developed as an organizational hub for coordinating harassment, also became a significant site for the exchange of child pornography, as O'Neill reported.

11

#MeToo Has Done What the Law Could Not

CATHARINE A. MACKINNON

Democratic House members dressed in black on Tuesday in a show of solidarity against sexual assault.

The #MeToo movement is accomplishing what sexual harassment law to date has not.

This mass mobilization against sexual abuse, through an unprecedented wave of speaking out in conventional and social media, is eroding the two biggest barriers to ending sexual harassment in law and in life: the disbelief and trivializing dehumanization of its victims.

Sexual harassment law—the first law to conceive sexual violation in inequality terms—created the preconditions for this moment. Yet denial by abusers and devaluing of accusers could still be reasonably counted on by perpetrators to shield their actions.

Many survivors realistically judged reporting pointless. Complaints were routinely passed off with some version of "she wasn't credible" or "she wanted it." I kept track of this in cases of campus sexual abuse over decades; it typically took three to four women testifying that they had been violated by the same man in the same way to even begin to make a dent in his denial. That made a woman, for credibility purposes, one-fourth of a person.

Even when she was believed, nothing he did to her mattered as much as what would be done to him if his actions against her were taken seriously. His value outweighed her sexualized worthlessness. His career, reputation, mental and emotional serenity, and assets counted. Hers didn't. In some ways, it was even worse to be believed and not have what he did matter. It meant she didn't matter.

These dynamics of inequality have preserved the system in which the more power a man has, the more sexual access he can get away with compelling.

It is widely thought that when something is legally prohibited, it more or less stops. This may be true for exceptional acts, but it is not true for pervasive practices like sexual harassment, including rape, that are built into structural social hierarchies. Equal pay has been the law for decades and still does not exist. Racial discrimination is nominally illegal in many forms but is still widely practiced against people of color. If the same cultural inequalities are permitted to operate in law as in the behavior the law prohibits, equalizing attempts—such as sexual harassment law—will be systemically resisted.

This logjam, which has long paralyzed effective legal recourse for sexual harassment, is finally being broken. Structural misogyny, along with sexualized racism and class inequalities, is being publicly and pervasively challenged by women's voices. The difference is, power is paying attention.

Powerful individuals and entities are taking sexual abuse seriously for once and acting against it as never before. No longer liars, no longer worthless, today's survivors are initiating consequences none of them could have gotten through any lawsuit—in part because the laws do not permit relief against individual perpetrators, but more because they are being believed and valued as the law seldom has. Women have been saying these things forever. It is the response to them that has changed.

Revulsion against harassing behavior—in this case, men with power refusing to be associated with it—could change workplaces and schools. It could restrain repeat predators as well as the occasional and casual exploiters that the law so far has not. Shunning perpetrators as sex bigots who take advantage of the vulnerabilities of inequality could transform society. It could change rape culture.

Sexual harassment law can grow with #MeToo. Taking #MeToo's changing norms into the law could—and predictably will—transform the law as well. Some practical steps could help capture this moment. Institutional or statutory changes could include prohibitions or limits on various forms of secrecy and nontransparency that hide the extent of sexual abuse and enforce survivor isolation, such as forced arbitration, silencing nondisclosure agreements even in cases of physical attacks and multiple perpetration, and confidential settlements. A realistic statute of limitations for all forms of discrimination, including sexual harassment, is essential. Being able to sue individual perpetrators and their enablers, jointly with institutions, could shift perceived incentives for this behavior. The only legal change that matches the scale of this moment is an Equal Rights Amendment, expanding the congressional power to legislate against sexual abuse and judicial interpretations of existing law, guaranteeing equality under the Constitution for all.

But it is #MeToo, this uprising of the formerly disregarded, that has made untenable the assumption that the one who reports sexual abuse is a lying slut, and that is changing everything already. Sexual harassment law prepared the ground, but it is today's movement that is shifting gender hierarchy's tectonic plates.

Rape and Sexual Violations

We live in a world where sexual violations are common. For 6.5 percent of women in the US, their first sexual experience is rape (Hawkes et al. 2019). Although there is general agreement that rape, the most extreme form of sexual violence, is morally indefensible, there are numerous points of conflict about interpretation and definition. Validating the voices of those who claim to have been sexually assaulted is complicated by cultural and personal beliefs about sexual behavior and gender. The difficulty of coming to widespread accord on events so steeped in conflicting values and opinions illustrates the polarities inherent in our social understandings of sex, power, autonomy, and the body.

Despite decades of extensive research on rape that has produced massive policy changes in some parts of the world, the problem persists. There are regions of the globe where significant changes in cultural understanding, law, or policy are slow in coming. This is despite the irrefutable evidence that rape and coercive sexual experiences occur frequently and are a common experience for women and a more common experience for men than is generally understood.

Frequency of Occurrence

In a study of several sites in Asia and the Pacific, 24 percent of men surveyed indicated they had committed at least one rape (Jewkes et al. 2013). In the US, an estimated 19.3 percent of women report that they have been raped during their lifetime. The figure for men is 1.7 percent. When other forms of sexual violence are considered, the estimate for women's victimization rises to 43.9 percent and 23.4 percent for men. Compared to women of all ages, those between the ages of sixteen and twenty-four appear to be victims of rape at much higher rates (Humphrey and Kahn 2000). Perpetrators against both men and women are overwhelmingly male (Breiding et al. 2014).

In one study, among all women who were found to have experienced rape or sexual assault, only 23 percent reported to police (Morgan and Kena 2018). Significantly, women who accept rape myths are less likely to recognize experiences as rape (LeMaire, Oswald, and Russell 2016). If so few women who experience events that meet the legal definition of rape recognize the experience as rape, they will not seek help and the offenders will not be held to account. Given that the social consequences of reporting sexual assaults can be devastating, staying silent may seem preferable. However, recent prominent cases of victims receiving public support for their accusations, though uneven, may be encouraging even more women to come forward when they see that "some powerful men no longer have defenders" (Vedantam 2018).

Scholars continue to debate how to collect the most accurate data so that we know how many people are affected and how best to respond to rape and sexual assault violations. For example, randomized phone calls are often used to collect information. However, there are limits to the methodological accuracy that illustrate a perennial problem. People may be unwilling to divulge something of a painful or shameful nature to a stranger over the phone, or they may speak languages that prevent them from responding, or they may be too young to be included. Surveys using various methods provide different results, but all are affected by the limits of the chosen method of data collection.

What Is Rape?

In this chapter the term "rape" indicates penetration of the vagina, anus, or mouth by a sex organ, other part of the body, or foreign object that is forced, coerced, or committed against someone who does not or cannot give consent. "Sexual assault," used here, references other unwanted sexual contact such as attempted rape, fondling, and exposure. All of these fall within the overarching concept of sexual violation. However, it is important to note that legal definitions differ across jurisdictions and may also differ according to the sex of the victim (Tracy et al. 2013).

However we define it, what constitutes rape differs markedly over time and across societies. It is only relatively recently that forced sex between married people is categorized as rape in some legal codes. In another example, in Pakistan a woman who is sexually attacked is considered culpable since the law does not distinguish rape from fornication and adultery (Mehdi 1997). At present, France is grappling with a legal code that does not view coerced sexual activity with a child as rape and assigns it lower penalties (Rubin and Peltier 2018). Swedish law now says that without explicit consent, sex is rape (Anderson 2018). These cases illustrate that a variety of circumstances including sex, gender, coercion, threat, impairment, age, consent, and level of violence are mitigating factors that may affect how rape is defined.

Theorizing Rape

Early feminist theorists of rape forged an understanding of sexual assault that started from women's experiences and attempted to counter the prevailing perception that rape was rare and usually the fault of the woman. Susan Brownmiller (1975), in one of the first feminist texts to develop a theory of rape, posits rape as inevitable and rooted in the physical capacities of the body; men rape, and women are raped. This assertion suggests that the body shapes society and social forces do not shape rape. Andrea Dworkin (1993) theorized that rape is an expression of male supremacy, whereby men rape because they can. Her perspective implicates social structures that privilege men rather than the physiological capacity of the male body alone. These foundational works provide the background to our evolving understanding of a complex problem.

Theorists continue to clarify the multilayered experiences of women as physical and social beings who are all harmed by rape but who perceive each occurrence of rape according to their embodied experiences as female, raced, sexed, classed, and aged beings. Cahill believes that "rape needs to be rethought as a pervasive, sustained, and repetitive, but not ultimately defining, element of the development of women's experience; as something that is taken up and experienced differently by different women but also holds some common aspects; as a factor that marks women as different from men; as an experience that perhaps begins with the body but whose significance does not end there" (2001, 4–5). Mardorossian cautions us that rape is viewed differently in the West, "where sex has come to be defined as key to one's identity [as opposed to some Eastern cultures where] . . . rape is marked as the defiling of the family's and village's honor rather than the victims' right to self-determination" (2002, 763). Helliwell (2000) alerts us to the danger of assuming that rape is universal. She suggests that, in the West, rape reproduces and marks a sexual polarity that is not shared by all cultures. Her study in Indonesia found that, to the Gerai people, rape is unthinkable. In that culture, sex and reproduction are shaped by a belief in the bodily sameness of men and women and an identity *between* men and women as opposed to the construct of *difference* that we assume in the West. She asks us to consider "relinquish[ing] some of our most ingrained presumptions concerning the difference between men and women and, particularly, concerning men's genitalia and sexuality as inherently brutalizing and penetrative and women's genitalia and sexuality as inherently vulnerable and subject to brutalization."

Pascoe and Hollander introduce the concept of "mobilizing rape" to point out that male dominance over other men is as salient as men's dominance over women in maintaining hierarchies of gender inequality. At a historical moment when rape has become increasingly unacceptable, men can claim their masculine bona fides through "the rape of (other men's) women, by the rape, real or symbolic, of other men themselves—and . . . by claims of *not* raping" (2016, 69). The latter provides the mantle of "good guys," although the basic framework of masculinity as dominant is not challenged, thereby leaving intact the support structure that encourages rape.

These theories hold promise for developing understandings of rape that encompass both what is held common in the experience and what is experienced differently among those affected by it. It is possible that "we will be able to understand rape only ever in a purely localized sense, in the context of the local discourses and practices that are both constitutive of and constituted by it" (Helliwell 2000, 798).

Rape and the Law

Most rapes are not reported to law enforcement officials. A global survey found overall low rates of reporting in most countries; fewer than 40 percent of women raped sought help from anyone and fewer than 10 percent out of those seeking help reported the event to police (United Nations Statistics Division 2015). It is estimated that fewer than half of rape victims define the experience as rape (Wilson and Miller 2016).

Using legal structures, where they exist, to find justice or resolution has often proven illusory. Historically, punishment for rape had little to do with acknowledgment of the harm to the raped person with the most severe penalties meted out in response to a perception of damage to male property. Ancient Judaic law, for example, specified punitive fees to be paid to fathers or husbands for the loss of virginity or exclusive sexual access to a raped woman (Porter 1986). Today, civil trials brought by survivors are common in the US, offering monetary compensation to the victim for physical and psychological damages. A recent case returned a $1 billion award (Victor 2018a). Still, the legal system has proven wildly unreliable for sexual assault victims.

Race and Rape

Sexual violations reflect the race bias of the social structure where they take place. During the time of slavery in the US, the racial double standard ensured that the sexual abuse of enslaved African women was not legally classified as rape (see Brooten, this volume). This history continues to influence rape cases today in the disparate attention to and outcomes for cases dependent on the race of the victim and defendant (Austen 2012). Indigenous women in the US and Canada have organized to resist high rates of sexual assault, often complicated by tribal and territorial jurisdictional issues that are vestiges of European colonial conquest (see Smith 2005).

Among the most heinous examples of socially stratified responses were the numerous death sentences and lynchings of Black men who were accused of raping White women from Reconstruction through the early half of the twentieth century in the American South (Davis 1983; Pleck 1990). There is convincing evidence that many of the rape charges leveled against Black men were politically motivated (Collins 2004). During the same time period, White men who forced sexual encounters with Black women acted with impunity (Edwards n.d.). Multiple scholars find racial disparity in news coverage of sexual assaults, with more attention given to White victims (Byerly 2012, Meyers 1997, Benedict 1992).

Law and Tradition

Even today, women who bring rape charges in Dubai can be jailed (Nordland 2017) while in Pakistan they can be executed as "adulterers" if they cannot produce four male eyewitnesses (Noor 2010). Vendetta rapes have been ordered by village councils against women as retribution for suspected sexual assaults attributed to their male relatives, thereby multiplying the number of victims. As traditional forms of Islamic law have gained traction in several countries, some Islamic legal scholars are actively working to redefine how rape is interpreted to allow women more options for justice (KARAMAH n.d.; Noor 2010), though resistance is strong (Tønnessen 2014). There is a glimmer of light from the Pakistani government that has attempted to rein in local councils through arrests, thanks in large part to efforts by local women's rights groups (Masood 2017).

Changing Laws

One of the most tangible effects of the feminist movement's attention to rape in the West has been an unprecedented rewriting of rape laws. The intention of the reforms has been to remove the barriers to "legal protection to female victims who failed to adhere to conventional standards of propriety, for disregarding women's experience of sexual violation, and for inflicting emotional distress on rape victims who report and prosecute rape charges" (Goldberg-Ambrose 1992, 173). Some reforms have focused on altering the legal definition of who can make a legitimate claim as a victim. In Mexico, for instance, prior to 1991, "the law stated that women had to be 'chaste and honest' to qualify as rape victims" (de la luz Lima 1992, 19). Since laws redefining rape were revised in Brazil in 2009, there has been a 150 percent increase in reports (Romero and Barnes 2013).

While there are improvements in legal approaches to rape, progress is not uniform. A recent narrowing of the definition of sexual assault by the US Justice Department to focus on physical harm will make it more difficult to prosecute (Oppenheim 2019). Efforts to enable married women to bring rape charges against abusive husbands have been another focus of reform. However, out of 189 countries reporting data, thirty-four do not explicitly criminalize marital rape (World Bank n.d.). In twelve countries perpetrators can avoid charges by marrying their victim (ibid.).

Gender-neutral laws were widely adopted in the US, redefining rape so that the sex of the victim and offender is immaterial. Critics point out that such laws may negate a focus on male abuse against women as the most salient characteristic of sexual assault, while others point to the need to address overlooked patterns of female-offending as well as same-sex rape (Rumney 2007). Although legal changes have enabled male victims of male rape to come forward, few have, due in part to social stigma. Female perpetrators of rape appear to be rare compared to men, though given local social constructions of male and female sexual agency, murky definitions of sexual assault, and a meager number of studies, there is much still to be explored (see Oliver 2007).

Other reforms have attempted to change rules of evidence in order to reflect evolving attitudes about rape. One such effort has been the institution of "rape shield" laws, which prohibit the introduction of a victim's past sexual history in court except under specific conditions. Lawmakers have also targeted date-rape drugs, such as Rohypnol, Ketamine, and GHB, used to incapacitate potential victims (Saum, Mott, and Dietz 2001). DNA evidence in rape cases circumvents the traditional "he said, she said" character of certain rape trials. As genetic analysis has become more accepted, men convicted of rape years ago have sometimes been exonerated (Dewan 2005).

Although efforts to change laws have been, for the most part, well intentioned, results have been imperfect. For example, gender-neutral laws focus on a "universal, hence necessarily non-bodily, understanding of rape" (Cahill 2001, 118). These changes may be necessary to erase the different values socially ascribed to the experiences of men and women. However, the outcome of treating women as not sexed "invokes an illusory generic that is implicitly sexed male [so that] the meanings that are specific to women's lives are rendered invisible" (ibid., 123) and such a "strategy which explicitly seeks a universal and all-encompassing definition of rape . . . should inspire suspicion as to its ability to describe a phenomenon that is so profoundly gendered as well as raced" (ibid., 112).

Some scholars argue that the reliance on the legal system has expanded state power and reinforced class and race disparities as well as contributed to high rates of incarceration (see Corrigan 2013, 5). There is ongoing debate within the antirape movement about whether dependence on the legal system supports feminist antirape goals or inadvertently co-opts them (ibid., 31).

Victims' continued lack of power is still evidenced by the difficulty of obtaining justice in cases of rape, a claim supported by the rarity of convictions. In a study of US lawyers and judges, Martin, Reynolds, and Keith found that "gender bias is an aspect of social interaction in legal contexts" (2002, 689) that appears to have implications for how they perceive rape. Studies from Europe and North America report mishandling of rape victims by the criminal justice system (Temkin 1986), and reports from Asia (Bucha 2005; Kristof 2005) and Africa (Aborisade 2014, Wood 2004) indicate how difficult it is for women in many parts of the world to socially, and even physically, survive bringing rape charges.

Social norms often lag far behind legal changes. Despite reforms, the police, the courts, and the public in general often blame victims for their victimization, an attitude even more pronounced for male victims. Reports of rape continue to be discounted by police and prosecutors, and convictions are rare. Of those rape trials that do result in the conviction of an offender for rape, almost all represent approximations of the stereotypical heterosexual stranger rape (Estrich 1987). If the victim and offender are acquainted, others are less likely to judge the event to be a legitimate rape (Bourque 1989).

In practice, married women and those involved in sex work have abridged rights to sexual self-determination. Likewise, in what appears to be an almost universal silence on the issue, male rape victims rarely make reports (Pelka 1997). Public awareness is limited to a casual acceptance of the brutality of prison rape exemplified by President Trump, who is reported to have suggested that journalists suspected of publishing leaked information should "spend a couple of days in jail, make a new friend, and they are ready to talk" (Deb 2018). Rape of men by other men outside of prisons is barely acknowledged.

Rape Response in Colleges and Universities

We are in the midst of an ongoing debate about whether universities do enough to safeguard students, or whether campus rape is an overinflated concern and the accused treated unfairly. Data reveals that rape occurs at the same rate for students as among the noncollege population (Baum and Klaus 2005). The dilemma is about how universities respond. Some argue that they have promoted excessively protective policies and standards that reduce women to fragile victims and men to monsters (Kipnis 2017; Saul 2017a). At the same time, many believe that universities do not do enough to protect students from repeat offenders (Saul 2017b) or adequately punish sexual misconduct complaints (Kaminer 2013).

Sexual Violations among Acquaintances

The frequency of rape among intimates is astounding. Among sexually victimized college women, fully nine out of ten knew their assailants (Fisher, Cullen, and Turner 2000). One study conducted among women who experienced other forms of partner violence concluded that 14 percent to 20 percent were also raped (McFarlane and Malecha 2005). There are also some hopeful signs that cultural changes and awareness of the problem may be having an effect. A recent study of high school students found that the number experiencing sexual dating violence had decreased from 10 to 7 percent between 2013 and 2017 (Hoffman 2018).

In considering acquaintance rape, Stewart (2014) points out that responses to claims of rape between people who know each other reflect how embedded our preconceptions are about men, women, and sex. She points to the complexity of the interaction itself and how it alternates between the routine sexualized play that is a feature of male-female interaction and violence and violation. It is the muddy character of the interaction that inspires the foundation for her proposal of a new legal concept, the *situated reasonable woman standard*, positioning women's socialized reactions as central to how cases should be evaluated.

Effects of Sexual Aggression

For women, sexually coercive experiences are associated with high levels of anxiety, guilt about sexual activity, and poor social and familial adjustment (Rogers 1984); depression and hostility (Check, Elias, and Barton 1988); alienation (Williams 1984); suicide attempts (Weis and Borges 1973; Warshaw 1988; McFarlane and Malecha 2005); feelings of diminished self-worth, depressed expectations for the future, eating disorders, lack of concentration, and sleep disorders (Warshaw 1988); phobias and delayed traumatic response (Burgess and Holmstrom 1974); increased use of alcohol and illicit drugs (McFarlane and Malecha 2005); and circumscribed activity thereby affecting educational and work opportunities (Association of American Colleges 1978; Hall 1985).

Women who have been sexually assaulted by acquaintances may suffer more complicated effects and show a slower degree of recovery than women who are raped by strangers (Warshaw 1988). The threat of contracting HIV/AIDS and other sexually transmitted diseases as the result of rape has increased the psychological trauma as well as the very real physical risk for victims (Carillo 1992; McFarlane and Malecha 2005). Rape appears to be a life-altering event in which "the embodied being of the victim is going to be deeply, even fundamentally affected" (Cahill 2001, 9).

Information on how rape affects male victims is sparse. The tremendous stigma attached to the victim of male-on-male rape, redolent of homophobia, has contributed to an apparent lack of sufficient knowledge about the effects of rape victimization. The little information available indicates that, whether victimized in prison or out, male victims of rape often experience a diminishment of manhood (Pelka 1997). The recent development of #HimToo, claiming significant false allegations against men, "ignores the reality of male survivors," and thus the actual him toos (North 2018).

Still, it is the pervasive threat of sexual attack against women in most societies that shapes and constrains the lives even of those women who have not directly experienced sexual assault (see Sheffield, this volume). Although the risk of rape poisons the atmosphere in which women live, it is also becoming apparent that public attention to the issue may plant fears and therefore contribute to a sense of danger that is both real and cautionary. In fact, such concerns may lead to the rise in women's support for authoritarianism, reflecting a desire for a sense of safety, as illusory as that may be. If women focus on what they need to do to protect themselves from assault, when they actually experience it they may blame themselves as an unintended consequence. It is urgent that we find a balance between adequate information about the threat of rape to aid in both self-protection and identification of abusers as well as to recognize under what circumstances and where safety resides.

The Rapist

As myths about rape victims abound, so, too, do unsupported beliefs about rapists. For example, in the racialized culture of the US, the imagined rapist, at least to Whites, is often a man of color (see Collins 2004, and for a view of the racialization of antirape efforts see Black Women's Blueprint 2016). The vast majority of rapes are intraracial (O'Brien 1987). George and Martínez found that "longstanding racial stereotypes about rape [and race] persist and that these are neither dormant nor benign" (2002, 117).

Men who sexually assault women are more likely than other men to believe in defined boundaries between masculine and feminine behavior (Kanin 1969), to identify with a definition of masculinity associated with entitlement (Jewkes et. al 2013), and to hold hostile views toward women (White and Koss 1993). They are likely to believe rape-supportive attitudes, such as "(a) women enjoy sexual violence, (b) women are responsible for rape prevention, (c) sex rather than power is the primary motivation for rape, (d) rape happens only to certain kinds of women, (e) a woman is less desirable after she has been raped, (f) women falsely report many rape claims, and (g) rape is justified in some situations" (Lottes 2011, 515). Abbey has found that young offenders who regret their behavior are less likely to repeat it the next year than are those who blame their victim (Murphy 2017). According to Malamuth, these men may be more empathetic (ibid.). It may be that by punishing all offenders equally, we overlook the possibility of rehabilitation for some (see Leon, Burton, and Alvare 2011).

Data on multiple perpetrator offenses is scant, with estimates ranging from 33 to 50 percent of total rapes in South Africa, 11 percent in England, and 2 to 26 percent in the US (Harkins and Dixon 2010). Adolescents account for a significant number of sex offenses including multiple perpetrator offenses (ibid.). It is particularly troubling that "[f]or those [multiple perpetrator] offenses committed against adult victims it appears that . . . sex offending occurs as a corollary of group membership (i.e., male bonding; rape myths) rather than being driven by deviant sexual interest per se" (ibid., 97). Such a claim implies that rape, at least under these circumstances, forms part of male group identification. This assertion is borne out in studies of male group membership in fraternities (Sanday 2000), sports teams (Zirin 2013), and the military (see O'Toole and Schiffman, also Stetz, this volume).

It may be that offering insights to young men about sex and intimacy as a routine aspect of life lessons could serve as a countervailing force to their exposure to the skewed information gleaned from pornography and popular culture. If they are given encouragement to think about consent as "informed, enthusiastic, sober, ongoing and freely given," we may see a reduction in sexual violations (Anderson 2019).

Contributions to this section offer a variety of perspectives to help elucidate the many complexities of sexual violations and encourage a broader understanding of its causes and effects.

SUGGESTIONS FOR FURTHER READING

Rose Corrigan, *Up Against a Wall: Rape Reform and the Failure of Success*, 2013

Doug Meyer, *Violence Against Queer People: Race, Class, Gender and the Persistence of LGBT Discrimination*, 2015

Chanel Miller, *Know My Name: A Memoir*, 2019

T. Christian Miller and Ken Armstrong, *A False Report: A True Story of Rape in America*, 2018

Mary White Stewart, *Ordinary Violence: Everyday Assaults against Women Worldwide*, 2nd edition, 2014

Home

Warsan Shire

no one leaves home unless
home is the mouth of a shark
you only run for the border
when you see the whole city running as well

your neighbors running faster than you
breath bloody in their throats
the boy you went to school with
who kissed you dizzy behind the old tin factory
is holding a gun bigger than his body
you only leave home
when home won't let you stay.

No one leaves home unless home chases you
fire under feet
hot blood in your belly
it's not something you ever thought of doing
until the blade burnt threats into
your neck
and even then you carried the anthem under
your breath
only tearing up your passport in airport toilets
sobbing as each mouthful of paper
made it clear that you wouldn't be going back.

You have to understand,
that no one puts their children in a boat
unless the water is safer than the land
no one burns their palms
under trains
beneath carriages
no one spends days and nights in the stomach of a truck
feeding on newspaper unless the miles travelled
means something more than journey.
No one crawls under fences

no one wants to be beaten
Pitied

no one chooses refugee camps
or strip searches where your
body is left aching
or prison,
because prison is safer
than a city of fire
and one prison guard
in the night
is better than a truckload
of men who look like your father
no one could take it
no one could stomach it
no one skin would be tough enough

the
go home blacks
refugees
dirty immigrants
asylum seekers
sucking our country dry
niggers with their hands out
they smell strange
savage
messed up their country and now they want
to mess ours up
how do the words
the dirty looks
roll off your backs
maybe because the blow is softer
than a limb torn off

or the words are more tender
than fourteen men between
your legs
or the insults are easier
to swallow
than rubble
than bone
than your child body

in pieces.
i want to go home,
but home is the mouth of a shark
home is the barrel of the gun
and no one would leave home
unless home chased you to the shore
unless home told you
to quicken your legs
leave your clothes behind
crawl through the desert
wade through the oceans
drown
save
be hungry
beg
forget pride
your survival is more important

no one leaves home until home is a sweaty voice in your ear
saying—
leave,
run away from me now
i don't know what i've become
but i know that anywhere
is safer than here

12

Sexual Terrorism in the Twenty-First Century

CAROLE J. SHEFFIELD

No two of us think alike about it, and yet it is clear to me, that question underlies the whole movement, and our little skirmishing for better laws, and the
right to vote, will yet be swallowed up in the real question, viz: Has a woman
a right to herself? It is very little to me to have the right to vote, to own property,
etc., if I may not keep my body, and its uses, in my absolute right. Not one wife
in a thousand can do that now.
—Lucy Stone, in a letter to Antoinette Brown, July 11, 1855

"The real question"—"*Has a woman a right to herself?*"—is as urgent and relevant
today as it was when Lucy Stone penned those words more than 160 years ago. It
is as urgent and relevant today as it was when I first wrote about sexual terrorism
more than thirty years ago. A woman's right "to keep [her] body, and its uses, in
[her] absolute right" has not been fully realized in the twenty-first century and
the achievement of that right is as tentative and fragile as ever. The continued
urgency and relevance of Lucy Stone's question was made extraordinarily visible
by the millions of participants in the Women's March of January 21, 2017. The
marchers had various motivations for participating in this historic event, but
there was a clear, resounding fear that the newly elected president, whose campaign was rife with misogyny, along with the Republican majority in both houses
of Congress, signaled further erosions of women's rights to bodily integrity.

The potential appointments of antireproductive choice candidates to federal
judgeships and to the Supreme Court have enormous long-term consequences
for a woman's right to control her body. The Republican Party's commitment
to defunding Planned Parenthood jeopardizes vital health care access for many
women and girls. TRAP laws—Targeted Regulation of Abortion Providers—have
been implemented to force closures of abortion clinics by imposing impossible
and medically unnecessary requirements. Several states are already approaching
pre–Roe v. Wade conditions. Additionally, women's health issues are jeopardized
by various challenges to health care reform. We continue to witness open and
unapologetic displays of misogyny at all levels of society—legal, political, cultural, and institutional. Structural and individual supports for men's violences
against women and girls remain tenacious. Despite cultural shifts in understanding and confronting men's violences against women and girls, the system

of men's violences against females, what I call *sexual terrorism*, has proven to be remarkably adaptable and sustainable.

More than three decades ago, the concept of terrorism captured my attention in an "ordinary" event. One evening I went to a nearby laundromat located in a small shopping center on a very busy highway. It was just after 6:00 p.m. and dark; the other stores were closed; the laundromat was brightly lit; and my car was the only one in the lot. Anyone passing by could readily see that I was alone and isolated. Knowing that rape is often a crime of opportunity, I became terrified. I wanted to leave, but I felt I was being "silly," "paranoid." The feeling of terror persisted, so I sat in my car, windows up, and doors locked. When the wash was completed, I dashed in, threw the clothes into the dryer, and ran back out to my car. When the clothes were dry, I tossed them recklessly into the basket and hurriedly drove away to fold them in the security of my home.

Although I was not victimized in a direct, physical way or by objective or measurable standards, I felt victimized. It was, for me, a terrifying experience. I felt controlled by an invisible force. I was angry that something as commonplace as doing laundry after a day's work jeopardized my well-being. Mostly I was angry at being unfree: a hostage of a culture that, for the most part, encourages men's violences against females, instructs males in the methodologies of sexual violence, and provides them with ready justification for their violence. I was angry that I could be victimized by being "in the wrong place at the wrong time." The essence of terrorism is that one never knows when it's the wrong place or the wrong time.

Following my experience at the laundromat, I talked with my students about terrorization. Women students began to open up and reveal terrors that they had kept secret because of embarrassment: fears of jogging alone, dining, shopping, going to the movies alone, or even being home alone. One woman recalled feelings of terror in her adolescence when she provided childcare for extra money. Nothing had ever happened, but she had felt a vague terror when being driven home late at night by the man of the family.

The men listened incredulously and then demanded equal time. The harder they tried the more they realized how very different—qualitatively, quantitatively, and contextually—their fears were. They agreed that even if they occasionally experienced fear in a violent society, they did not experience terror; nor did they experience fear of rape or sexual assault. The men could be rather specific in describing when they were afraid—typically in places that have a reputation for violence. But they could either avoid these places or, if not, they felt capable of self-protective action. Occasionally, minoritized men expressed situational fears of other men's violence (based on their race or their actual or perceived sexual/gender identity). Nearly all the women admitted fear and anxiety when walking to their cars on campus, especially after an evening class or activity. None of the men experienced fear on campus at any time. Above all, male students said that they *never feared* being attacked simply because they were male and *never feared* being attacked by a female. They *never feared* going out alone. They *never* gave any thought that their choice of clothing might put them at risk for violence. Their daily activities were not characterized by a concern for their physical integrity.

The response patterns of students have not changed over the decades. Women still articulate the same ever-present fear of men's violences as the women did in the very first discussion and men still claim that they do not experience fear except in specific and limited contexts. The differences between men's and women's experiences of fear underscore the fact that women's lives are bounded by both the reality of the pervasive danger of men's violences and the fear that reality engenders. As Lisa Price notes, "men's violence is so pervasive that virtually none of us live free from it, even if we do not always consciously pay attention to it" (Price 2005, 11). In their classic study *Female Fear*, Margaret T. Gordon and Stephanie Riger found that one-third of women said they worry at least once a month about being raped and many said they worry about it daily. When they think about rape, they feel terrified and somewhat paralyzed. A third of women indicated that the fear of rape is "part of the background," of their lives, and "one of those things that's always there." Another third claimed they never worried about rape but reported taking precautions, "sometimes elaborate ones," to try to avoid being raped (Gordon and Riger 1989).

Under sexual terrorism females are advised to restrict their behaviors, lifestyles, even physical appearances in order to avoid being a victim (and if they don't, they are routinely blamed for their victimization), yet after a (politically recognized) terroristic event, politicians and others in authority repeatedly advise us *not* to change our lives to accommodate fear. "If you do, then they win" is a common refrain.

Before September 11, 2001, the word *terrorism* invoked images of furtive organizations of the far right or left, whose members blew up buildings and cars, hijacked airplanes, and murdered innocent people in some country other than ours. In post-9/11 US, we have come to understand that terrorism can happen here, but our understanding of it is constrained by the concept of a foreign enemy who commits aberrant and outrageous acts of murder. However, there is another kind of terrorism, one that so pervades our culture that we have learned to live with it as though it were the natural order of things. Its target is females—of all ages, races, and classes. I call it *sexual terrorism* because it is a system by which men and boys frighten and, by frightening, control and dominate women and girls.

Sexual terrorism is a complex system of social control. It includes a wide range of nonviolent sexual intimidation and threats of violence, as well as many forms of overt sexual violence. Sexual terrorism is, of course, as political as any other form of terrorism. As a system of violence, it is rooted in power relationships and power struggles. It is the presumed normality of men's violences against women, the acceptance of these violences as unalterable facts of life that renders sexual terrorism unarticulated and, therefore, not "political."

Types of Sexual Terrorism

The central project of the political movement to end violence against women and girls as well as that of the prolific scholarship in the past fifty-plus years, has been to articulate a conceptualization of violence that reflects women's experiences with men's violences. As the power to name, define, and thus encode in law always rests with the dominant group, the reality that is reflected is one-sided and draws entirely from concepts, definitions, and laws that reflect men's ideas about sexual violence. Unsurprisingly, the master narrative has left out much of women's and girls' experiences.

In Kelly's classic study of women's narratives of their own experiences, the respondents identified eleven specific forms of violence they had experienced: the threat of violence, sexual harassment, pressure to have sex, sexual assault, obscene phone calls, coercive sex, domestic violence, sexual abuse, flashing, rape, and incest (Kelly 1988). As the antiviolence movement progressed through the latter decades of the twentieth century and into the twenty-first century, more diverse voices were included, particularly from advocates, activists, survivors, and resistors, resulting in even more forms being identified: stalking, cyberstalking, slut-bashing and slut-shaming, sexual exploitation industries, sexual slavery, revenge porn, medical violence, forced sterilization, compulsory heterosexuality, gender-policing, forced marriage, and femicide.

A global analysis of men's violences against women revealed additional forms: dowry murders, purdah, female genital cutting, trafficking, bride-purchasing, sex tourism, webcam child sexual abuse, compulsory pregnancy, "honor" killings, and acid-burning. We now know that rape takes a variety of forms, including stranger rape (not only the stereotypical stranger who jumps out of the bushes but also internet-facilitated stranger rape), date rape, acquaintance rape, drug rape, party rape, gang rape, and marital rape. Intimate partner violence and childhood sexual abuse are umbrella terms for many different forms of physical, psychological, and sexual violence. Sexual harassment manifests itself in many forms and in many areas of daily life: workplaces, educational institutions, public spaces (streets, parks, transportation, gatherings such as parades, concerts, athletic events), and on the internet.

British scholar Jeff Hearn argues that the term "men's violences" is appropriate because it identifies the agents of the violence (men) and acknowledges the plurality of the forms of violence (Hearn 1998, 4). Naming men's actual and symbolic violences against women exposes both the "ordinary" and the "extraordinary" forms of sexual terrorism and the spectrum of men's violences that women experience in their lifetimes. Naming the types of men's violences is an essential ongoing project as sexual terrorism has demonstrated an ability to manifest itself in new forms as well as identifying new targets. One recent study of college students found that transgender students experience the highest odds of potential crimes of sexual victimization (Griner et al. 2017). As men's gendered violences are reinvented, new "sense-making" frameworks that justify, rationalize, and normalize those violences will also appear in the public discourse.

Components of Sexual Terrorism

Not all violence is terroristic violence and the literature on terrorism does not provide a singular, precise definition. Mine is taken from Hacker, who maintains that "terrorism aims to frighten, and by frightening, to dominate and control" (Hacker 1976, xi). Scholars on terrorism agree more readily on the components that are necessary to define a system of violence as terrorism. Those components are ideology, propaganda, indiscriminate, and amoral violence, and voluntary compliance. After studying terrorism, I added a fifth component: perceptions of the terrorist and the victim. Combined, these components provide a framework for the structural analysis of the system of sexual terrorism. The specific content of each component varies over time as patriarchy is challenged and as it adapts and changes.

Chalmers Johnson argues in "Perspectives on Terrorism" that terrorism must be "explicitly rationalized and justified by some philosophy, theory, or ideology—however crude" (Johnson 1978). An *ideology* (the first element of the theory of terrorism) is an integrated set of beliefs about the world that explains the way things "are"—not objectively how they are but according to how the ideology defines the way things are. An ideology also provides a vision of how things ought to be. Through these dual functions, ideologies seek to be self-fulfilling, to make themselves come true. Ideological belief systems also serve to justify our social and political world. They propagandize certain perspectives and marginalize others. As comprehensive and complex sense-making systems, ideologies help us process and evaluate information and events—that is, they guide our thinking in trying to understand and make sense of everyday life. Ideologies provide context and meaning to our thinking and behavior. This is a dynamic ongoing process. "[W]e are never without context," explains Lynn Phillips, "for our lives do not exist in a social vacuum . . . Whether or not we are consciously aware of their influence, social messages, practices, and power relations impact on who we are and how we move through our lives" (Phillips 2000, 16).

Patriarchy, meaning the "rule of the fathers," is the ideological foundation of sexism in our society. Historian Gerda Lerner expanded on the literal meaning of patriarchy to show its application beyond the family. She maintained that patriarchy is "the manifestation and institutionalization of male dominance over women and children in the family and the extension of male dominance in society in general" (Lerner 1986, 239). Moreover, patriarchy asserts the superiority of males and masculinity and the inferiority of females and femininity. It is the architecture of gender that prepares, normalizes, and legitimizes men's violences against women. Dominance, aggression, power, and agency are attributed to males and masculinity; passivity, emotionality, dependence, and subordination are gendered feminine.

Furthermore, male supremacy, established through patriarchy, defines females as having a basic "flaw"—a trait that distinguishes males and females and legitimizes female inferiority. This "flaw" is female sexuality itself: it is tempting and seductive, and therefore disruptive; capable of reproducing life itself, and therefore powerful (Sheffield 1987, 172). Over centuries, in theories and practices, ideas of the evils of female sexuality justified men's control of the female body—through definition (and redefinition), through socialization and propaganda, through public policy, and through threats, intimidation, and violence. The eighth century BCE poet Hesiod described Pandora, the first human woman created by the gods, as "the beautiful evil, who was given 'sly manners, and the morals of a bitch' and whose betrayal doomed men to labor, suffer and die" (Holland 2006, 13–14). The twenty-first-century sitcom character in *Family Guy* proclaimed that "[w]omen are not people. They are devices built by the Lord Jesus Christ for our entertainment" (Young 2000).

Throughout millennia, patriarchal ideology has reiterated in innumerable and profound ways its core tenet that girls and women are for men's uses and that females are inherently untrustworthy. Female bodies and female sexuality are objectified, propagandized, and commodified—providing real and symbolic reminders that while female sexuality is both desired and dangerous (for men) *living while female* is precarious as a direct consequence of her sex and sexuality.

It is this belief system that undergirds and sustains sexual terrorism. In sexual terrorism, the perpetrators are overwhelmingly males and the victims are overwhelmingly girls and women. This is not accidental; it is by design. According to R. W. Connell, "It is the dominant gender who hold and use the means of violence" (Connell 1995b, 83). Lundy Bancroft notes that "an abuser can be thought of not as a man who is 'deviant,' but rather as one who learned his society's lessons too well, swallowing them whole. He followed the signposts his culture put out for him marking the path to manhood—at least with respect to relationships with women" (Bancroft 2002, 330).

Propaganda, the second component of the theory of terrorism, is the methodical dissemination of information for the purpose of promoting a particular ideology. Propaganda, by definition, is biased or even false information. Its purpose is to present one point of view on a subject and to discredit opposing points of view. Propaganda is essential to the conduct of terrorism. According to Francis Watson in *Political Terrorism: The Threat and the Response*, "Terrorism must not be defined only in terms of violence, but also in terms of propaganda. The two are in operation together. The violence of terrorism is a coercive means for attempting to influence the thinking and actions of people. Propaganda is a persuasive means for doing the same thing" (Watson 1976, 15).

Nearly all expressions of popular culture encode symbolic male violence against females: misogynistic music and videos, movies and television, casual clothing, gaming and comic books (and their online communities), stand-up comedy, and fashion photography and advertising (from sexual objectification of the female body to representations of rape and gang rape) to name only a few. The plenitude of oral, visual, and aural forms of misogyny serve to remind females that the world is a dangerous place for them *because* they are female.

Recently, there has been a proliferation of casual clothing, mostly T-shirts, which endorse, trivialize, and legitimize rape. T-shirts with slogans such as "Eat Sleep Rape Repeat" (Lhooq 2015), "Keep Calm and Rape a Lot," "Keep Calm and Rape Them," and "It's not rape/It's a snuggle with a struggle" are marketed to men. Women can purchase and wear a T-shirt that translates the rape-supportive myth that women ask to be raped with the phrase "Keep Calm and Rape Me" (Taibi 2013).

A 2012 Belvedere Vodka ad used the slogan "Unlike some people, Belvedere always goes down smoothly" superimposed over an image of a frightened-looking woman trying to escape a man's clutches (Harding 2015, 11–12). Giovani Versace and Dolce and Gabbana produced ads depicting gang/drug rape. Cesare Paciotti used depictions of murdered or frightened women to advertise shoes. The Ford Motor Company portrayed bound and gagged women in the trunk of a car. These examples are, of course, only the tip of the iceberg.

And then there's music (and music videos). As with advertisements, there are too many to mention here—which is exactly the point: popular culture is saturated with images and messages that celebrate and endorse men's violences against women. Such messages have deep roots and are not unique to the twenty-first century. For example, in 1963, the Crystals sang "He Hit Me and It Felt Like a Kiss"; in 1976, a billboard (as well as an ad in *Rolling Stone* magazine) depicted a battered woman tied to a chair declaring "I'm Black and Blue from the Rolling Stones and I Love It"; in 1990, the Geto Boys rapped, "She's naked, and I'm a peeping Tom/Her body's beautiful so I'm thinking rape/Shouldn't have had her curtains open, so that's her fate" (Geto Boys 1992). Rape anthems proliferated in the twenty-first century. Robin Thicke declares in "Blurred Lines": "I know you want it . . . I'll give you something big enough to tear your ass in two" (Thicke 2013). Rick Ross bragged about drugging a woman and raping her unconscious body in the song "U.O.E.N.O.": "Put Molly all in her champagne, she ain't even know it. I took her home and I enjoyed that, she ain't even know it" (Rocko 2013).

The most pernicious form of the propaganda of sexual terrorism is pornography. The pornography industry is big business and it operates just like any other mega-corporation. It has deep and highly profitable relationships with other big businesses such as banks, hotel chains, internet providers and cable companies, software developers, and more. Furthermore, the pornography industry is inextricably linked to all of the sexual exploitation industries: prostitution, strip bars, "gentleman's clubs," phone-sex operations, massage parlors, and trafficking. The continuum of pornography to sexual exploitation industries generates billions of dollars annually.

The scope of the mass media pornography industry is mind-boggling and its reach into our cultural psyche is perhaps incalculable. The line between actual sexual assault and pornography has become blurred. One experienced internet researcher was shocked when he discovered a site "urging users to share what it called 'fantasy' videos of sexual attacks," reports Craig Timberg (2013). The researcher also found "dozens of similar sites offering disturbing variations—attacks on drunken women, on lesbians, on schoolgirls" and was uncertain whether they were all "fantasy" videos or videos of actual crimes (2013). Fraternity pledges have been required to present stories with pornographic images and preferred sexual positions (Southall 2015). According to researcher Gail Dines, "mainstream porn, the porn you see within 15 seconds of typing 'porn' into Google, is cruel, abusive, violent and free" (Dines 2015, 2).

As with all commercial enterprises, creating consumer demand and finding new markets is essential. In 2013, Dines and Levy conducted a Google Trends Analysis for the Department of Justice and found that searches for "Teen Porn" more than tripled between 2005 and 2013, and teen porn was the fastest-growing genre over this period (2013).

In her speech at the 2015 National Center on Sexual Exploitation Symposium, Dines reported that "porn is deeply and increasingly implicated in virtually all forms of sexual violence. We cannot speak about rape, child sexual abuse, commercial sexual exploitation, teen dating violence, domestic violence, sexual harassment, college sexual assault, sexting, or teen suicide following cyberbullying without understanding porn as a driving force behind the normalization and legitimization of violence against women and children" (Dines 2015, 2).

Propaganda is the mechanism that ideology uses to create and maintain dominant cultural storylines—narratives and messages—which, in turn, function to impose a cultural reality. People then draw their notions of reality from the culture they consume. In the documentary *Advertising and the End of the World*, media scholar and filmmaker Sut Jhally argues that "in a sense, commercial culture is inside our intimate relationships—inside our homes and heads and identities . . . Culture," he maintains, "is the place and space where a society tells stories about itself, where values are articulated and experienced, where notions of good and evil, of morality and value are defined" (1997). Jhally's core question—"What are the consistent stories . . . ?"—should be applied to the entire spectrum of the propaganda of sexual terrorism. Michael Kimmel challenges us to consider, "What does it mean that the portrayal of women not only in pornography but also in video games and music lyrics (and on TV, and on the radio, and on the internet, and in every single type of media that is geared toward young men) is not only sexist and denigrating but also often outright and unapologetically hateful, violent, and misogynist?" (Kimmel 2009). He maintains that "these are questions about how guys view *masculinity* [emphasis added], not questions about the 'effects' of some media on people" (Kimmel 2009, 153).

The third component, which is common to all forms of terrorism, consists of *indiscriminateness, unpredictability, arbitrariness, ruthless destructiveness, and amorality* (Wilkinson 1974, 17). Indiscriminate violence and amorality are also at the heart of sexual terrorism. Every female is always a potential target of violence—at any age, at any time, in any place. Despite public policy mandates to gather national data, estimating the extent of men's violences against women and children remains phenomenally difficult and complex. Definitional issues, methodological differences, assessment of different time periods, and substantial underreporting make it nearly impossible to know precisely the prevalence of such violence. However, copious research and data collection speaks to the continuing pattern of intolerably high levels of men's violences against females in the twenty-first century.

According to the National Coalition Against Domestic Violence, a woman is beaten every nine seconds in the US and they estimate that ten million women are victims of intimate partner violence each year (2015). Homicide, of course, is the most lethal form of intimate partner violence and women are more likely to be killed by their partners than by strangers. Homicides are committed against women of all ages, races and ethnicities, but young women of color are disproportionately affected (Petrosky et al. 2017). The National Network to End Domestic Violence reports that, on average, three women are killed every day by a current or former male partner (NNEDV 2006). Nearly twice as many women (11,776) were murdered by current or former male partners as the number of American troops killed in Afghanistan and Iraq (6,488) between 2001 and 2012 (Hope Rising n.d.).

The full scope of the phenomenon of childhood sexual victimization in the US is believed to be far greater than what the current research suggests. The National Survey of Children's Exposure to Violence found that one in twenty girls, aged fourteen to seventeen years old, had experienced sexual assault or abuse during the study period of August 2013 through April 2014; 11.5 percent experienced sexual harassment, and 8.5 percent were exposed to an unwanted internet sexual solicitation (Finkelhor et al. 2015). K–12 students report high levels of sexual assault. According to the Equal Rights Advice and Counseling Hotline, calls have increased by 400 percent over the past ten years, many of them reports of sexual harassment of young girls by peers and educators (Shaman 2017).

The 1994 Violence Against Women Act mandated that the federal government collect valid and reliable data on sexual violence, particularly rape and stalking. The three national sources most often cited are the FBI's Uniform Crime Reporting (UCR) Program, the National Crime Victimization Survey (NCVS) conducted by the Department of Justice, and the Centers for Disease Control's National Intimate Partner Violence and Sexual Violence Survey. The FBI UCR data is based on actual reporting so, inevitably, it significantly underrepresents the prevalence of rape. The other two paint very different pictures because, in part, the objectives of the surveys are different (the first uses a criminological lens, the second a public health perspective) in addition to survey design issues. Consider the data from these sources for 2010: the FBI's UCR Program documented 85,593 rapes, the National Crime Victimization Survey 188,380, and the National Intimate Partner Violence and Sexual Violence Survey found 1,270,000 rapes (House, Kalsbeek, and Kruttschnitt 2014, 17).

Despite good-faith efforts, accurate data remains elusive. A 2014 Bureau of Justice Statistics report concluded that "the NCVS is not an adequate vehicle for the goal of accurate measurement" (House et al. 2014, 22). Responding to the CDC report, Claire Groden notes that "While finding an indisputable number of rape victims seems to be a Holy Grail, the CDC report certainly reveals that the most widely accepted estimates aren't high enough" (Groden 2014).

Most importantly, the crime reports and surveys do not provide insight into the everyday reality of sexism, sexual aggression, and misogyny that women and girls experience. Such insights though have become abundant through a variety of internet platforms: On the "When Women Refuse" Tumblr page women post stories of violence they experienced when they have rejected sexual advances; the website Everyday Sexism compiles women's and girls' "ordinary" and routine experiences of sexism; the Project Unbreakable Tumblr page is a forum for survivors of sexual assault, domestic violence, and child abuse. In 2014, #YesAllWomen erupted with more than a million stories of personal examples of sexual terrorism after a twenty-two-year-old man arbitrarily killed six people before taking his own life. He had left behind a "manifesto" that, according to Sasha Weiss, showed that "he was influenced by a predominant cultural ethos that rewards sexual aggression, power, and wealth, and that reinforces traditional alpha masculinity and submissive femininity."

The importance of #YesAllWomen, Weiss maintains, is that it "offers a counter-testimony, demonstrating that [his] hate of women grew out of attitudes that are all around us" (Weiss 2014). In 2006, Tarana Burke initiated #MeToo. In the fall of 2017, when several actresses came forward with allegations of abuse by Harvey Weinstein, #MeToo exploded into a global social movement. It has generated millions of posts on Facebook, Instagram, and Twitter and has launched vitally important public as well as private conversations about abuse and victimization.

Amorality pervades all forms of violence against females. Child molesters, incestuous fathers and other relatives, abusive partners, and rapists often do not understand that they have done anything wrong. As Connell (1995b) points out, men who attack women are not likely to view themselves as deviant. "On the contrary, they usually feel they are entirely justified, that they are exercising a right. They are authorized by an ideology of supremacy" (83). Bancroft, who has counseled abusive men for over thirty years, maintains that "the true cause of his abusiveness is how he *thinks*," and that an abuser "almost never does anything that he himself considers morally unacceptable" (2002, 21, 35). Bancroft asserts that it is the abuser's value system that must be interrogated, not their psychology. The views of men who are violent against women and girls are also routinely shared by family, friends, community members, media, police officers, prosecutors, defense attorneys, jurors, and judges.

The fourth component of the theory of terrorism is *voluntary compliance*. The institutionalization of a system of terror requires the development of mechanisms other than sustained violence to achieve its goals. Violence must be employed to maintain terrorism, but strategies for ensuring a significant degree of compliance must be developed. Sexual terrorism is maintained to a great extent by an elaborate system of sex-gender socialization that, in effect, instructs men to be terrorists in the name of masculinity and women to be victims in the name of femininity and female sexuality. It is also maintained by cultural narratives that blame victims and excuse offenders. The desired result of voluntary compliance is that men's violences are explained in ways that allow us to believe "it can't have happened, we say; or it happens all the time, we say—it is too rare to be credible or too common to matter" (Dworkin 1992, 5). Denial, then, must be both individual and collective, personal and systemic.

Sexual and "political" terrorism differ significantly in the final component—*the perception of the terrorist and the victim*. In "political" terrorism we know who the terrorist and the victim are. We may condemn or condone the terrorist depending on our political views, but we usually sympathize with the victim. In sexual terrorism, however, we typically blame the victim and excuse the offender.

The Commonalities across Forms of Men's Violences

Men's violences against women and girls share several commonalities: perpetrators are from all socioeconomic classes; victims are least likely to report men's violences; when reported, they rarely result in convictions or meaningful punishment; responsibility and blame is mostly attributed to victims rather than perpetrators; and they are generally not taken seriously. These commonalities are shaped and driven by prevailing dominant narratives about masculinity and female sexuality and agency. It is important to note that women and girls do not experience sexual terrorism in identical ways. Girls' and women's fears and experiences of men's violences vary and are influenced by many variables—race, social class, age, disability status, immigration status, sexual orientation, gender identity, and previous victimizations.

Men's violences against females are a potent alchemy of sex, gender, entitlement, power, and misogyny. *Power* should be broadly construed. It incorporates elements of control, domination, and humiliation in physical, emotional, or sexual forms. For example, the popularity of social media has created a space for revenge porn, which, as the name makes clear, is about retaliation. It is also about humiliation, as is internet slut-bashing and slut-shaming. In the sexual exploitation industries, misogyny and the drive for profit merge into making violences against females sexy.

Men's motives are complex and multidimensional and do not align with victims' experiences. In her study of rapists' motives, Katharine Baker found that "All rapes are, in part, about sex and masculinity and domination. But some . . . are predominately about sex, some . . . are predominantly about masculinity, and some . . . are predominately about domination" (Baker 1997). Riley, a rape survivor, maintains that "[r]ape is not about sex at all. This isn't just bad sex . . . How could anyone think that? It isn't even sex. Sex is consensual and rape is not. This isn't sex. Is it sex for the rapist? I don't think rapists know sex as sex. This is using sex as a weapon. Sex is absolutely a weapon" (Raphael 2013, 73).

Michael Kimmel identified three "cultural dynamics"—the culture of entitlement, the culture of silence, and the culture of protection—that are particularly useful in analyzing the mechanisms by which the system of men's violences against women and girls is perpetuated and legitimized (Kimmel 2009). The commonalities that underscore men's violences against women and girls, as well as the three dynamics identified by Kimmel, are mutually reinforcing and form a vicious circle that functions to mask the reality of sexual terrorism and to reproduce the gendered system of power and authority.

The Men Who Commit Violence against Women and Girls

The question "Who is the *typical* rapist, wife abuser, sexual harasser, incest offender, et cetera?" is raised constantly. The answer is simple: men. In his TED Talk "Violence Against Women: It's a Men's Issue," antisexism educator and writer Jackson Katz (2012) points out that "[i]t's amazing how this works, in domestic and sexual violence—how men have largely been erased from so much of the conversation about a subject that is centrally about men."

The men who commit acts of sexual terrorism are of all ages, races, and religions; they come from all communities, income levels, and educational levels; they are married, single, separated, and divorced. The "typical" abusive male does not exist. Decades of research has affirmed that perpetrators are most often men and boys we know: family members, friends, neighbors, teachers, coaches, doctors, peers, fellow soldiers, coworkers, supervisors, and bosses. That the perpetrators are known to us is obviously the case in terms of "family terrorism"—a term Rhonda Hammer maintains is appropriate "to describe the context of male violence against women and the assault of children (especially sexual abuse and incest) as well as elderly abuse" (Hammer 2002, 133). According to the National Sexual Violence Resource Center, 80 percent of victims of sexual assault knew their attackers (NSVRC, n.d.).

Blaming Victims, Not Perpetrators

The persistence of sexual terrorism must be understood in the context of the multitude of sense-making frameworks developed and adapted over time by patriarchal ideology that result in victim-blaming as the individual and cultural default position. By navigating through a maze of intersecting and reinforcing discourses we are meant to deflect our attention from the agent of the violence, the perpetrator, and to determine the "flaw" in the victim—her sexuality and/ or her agency. These narratives function as structures of surveillance which provide the basis for gender policing (including self-policing). They encode for us the myriad ways to assign culpability to the victim and to normalize and excuse the behavior of perpetrators. Victim-blaming is complex and takes many forms but, essentially, it is scapegoating. Scapegoating is an ideological process in that it provides ready-made scripts to explain and justify sexual terrorism for the benefit of the dominant group: "She shouldn't have been . . . (drinking, jogging, walking alone)"; "She shouldn't have gone to [insert name of celebrity's or athlete's or friend's] room"; "She should not have . . ."; "she should *just*"; and on it goes. Whenever a justification or explanation starts with "she should" or "she should not" and doesn't focus on the perpetrator, it's scapegoating. Collectively, these constructs are known as "rape-supportive myths" or "rape-supportive narratives." Diana L. Payne, Kimberly A. Lonsway, and Louise Fitzgerald articulated seven core rape-supportive myths:

1. She asked for it.
2. It wasn't really rape.
3. He didn't mean to.
4. She wanted it.
5. She lied.
6. Rape is a trivial event.
7. Rape is a deviant event.
   (Payne et al. 1999)

Not all rape-supportive reasoning focuses solely on the victim. "He didn't mean to," or "An attractive guy like that doesn't need to rape anyone," or "Oh, no, it can't be him—he'd never do that," are rape-supportive narratives that shift the focus to the perpetrators (Harding 2015, 6). Rather than assign blame, however, they are designed to dismiss the acts of sexual terrorism and to excuse men's violences against females. Many of the myths that center on the men who commit violence against females are rooted in beliefs of the culture of (male) entitlement (Kimmel 2009).

Bancroft identified seventeen myths about why abusers commit violence toward their partners (Bancroft 2002, 23–24). The myths are largely unchallenged by the broader culture "since cultural approval for partner abuse is disturbingly high in our society" (164). According to Bancroft, "entitlement is the abuser's belief that he has a special status and that it provides him with exclusive rights and privileges that do not apply to his partner" (54). Abusers consider themselves entitled to physical, emotional, and sexual caretaking as well as deference from their partners and a general lack of accountability for their behavior (56). Reflecting on the broader notion of entitlement among men, Bancroft references a 1997 study of college men majoring in psychology. The study found that 10 percent of the respondents believed that it was acceptable to hit a female partner for refusing to have sex with him and 20 percent believed it was acceptable to hit a woman if he suspected her of cheating (59).

Blaming the victim and excusing the offender often occur simultaneously. In blaming reporter Lara Logan for her own gang rape while covering the Egyptian uprising in 2011, Dan Rottenberg wrote in the *Broad Street Review*:

The male animal craves the drama of sexually conquering a woman, a proclivity that is difficult to change: "Earth to liberated women: When you display legs, thighs, or cleavage, some liberated men will see it as a sign that you feel good about yourself and your sexuality. But most men will see it as a sign you want to get laid." (Rottenberg, 2011)

When the acts cannot be denied—as a result of incontrovertible evidence and convictions—family, friends, community members, law enforcement, institutions such as education, religion, military, and media (including participants in social media platforms) activate the third cultural dynamic, "the culture of protection," so that the perpetrators avoid as much as possible having to take (much or any) responsibility for their behavior.

While this dynamic is as ancient as patriarchy itself, it has been highly visible in recent years, particularly in the news media and on social media. In March 2011, a *New York Times* reporter expressed concern about the "ruined lives of the [eighteen] young men" who had been charged with a gang rape of an eleven-year-old girl in Cleveland, Texas, "but did not acknowledge the girl's distress" (Raphael 2013, 62). Of the two high school football players from Steubenville, Ohio, whose rape of an unconscious girl in 2013 was captured on cell phones and uploaded to a number of social media platforms (but not reported to the police, emblematic of both the culture of silence and the culture of protection), CNN claimed the boys were "promising students," NBC News expressed regret over the boys' "promising football careers," ABC News made excuses for the rapists, and *USA Today* focused on the fact that the victim was drunk (Phillips 2017, 56).

Family and friends, perhaps unsurprisingly, are active participants in the culture of protection. In 2015, former Stanford swimmer Brock Turner was found guilty of three counts of sexual assault, yet his father refused to say he committed a crime. In a letter to the judge, he pleaded for probation rather than prison for his son, arguing that "[h]is life will never be the one that he dreamed about and worked so hard to achieve . . . He will never be his happy go lucky self with that easy-going personality and welcoming smile . . . That is a steep price to pay for 20 minutes of action out of his 20 plus years of life" (Landsbaum 2016). A childhood friend of Turner's refused to accept his culpability because he's "such a sweetheart and a very smart kid" (Kohn 2016). Judge Aaron Persky closed the circle of protection around Turner by sentencing him to six months in jail and three years' probation because "a prison sentence would have a severe impact on him" (Martin 2016).

The most insidious form of victim-blaming occurs when narratives are internalized by victims themselves. Self-blame for acts of violence perpetrated against them supports the culture of silence and the underreporting of men's violences.

Men's Violences against Females Are Not Taken Seriously

A shared characteristic of men's violences against females, whether criminal or not, is that they are not taken seriously. "The gendered politics of seriousness is serious," argues Cynthia Enloe in *Seriously! Investigating Crashes and Crises as if Women Mattered* (2013, 18). "The unquestioned presumptions about what and who deserves to be rewarded with the accolade of "serious" is one of the pillars of modern patriarchy. That is, being taken seriously is a status that every day, in routine relationships, offers the chance for masculinity to be privileged and for anything associated with femininity to be ranked as lesser, as inconsequential, as dependent, or as beyond the pale" (10).

Denying individual acts of violence as well as the systemic reality of men's violences, denying the gravity of these acts, joking about them, not *seriously* punishing the perpetrators, and normalizing the violences are all ways we deny the seriousness of men's violences against women. Evidence of the lack of seriousness is substantial. It is found in the passive and active consumption of men's violences in movies, music, video games, blogs, television, and social media. It is in the objectification and degradation of women in all forms of popular culture. It is in the passive and active participants who support particular acts of men's violences (by recording it and uploading it for others to consume, for example).

It is in the everyday, casual use of derogatory and dehumanizing language to refer to females. It is found in the voters who dismissed as inconsequential the behavior of a presidential candidate who groped women and openly bragged about it. It is in the rationalizations of jurors and judges who align themselves more with the perpetrators than with victims. Raphael maintains, "That rape is seen as fit material for humor demonstrates the extent to which the effects of rape have been trivialized" (Raphael 2013, 50). When a woman in the audience voiced her objection to rape humor, comedian Daniel Tosh responded by asking the audience, "Wouldn't it be funny if that girl got raped by, like, five guys right now? Like right now?" (Holpuch 2012). Rape "jokes" litter the landscape of social media. It took a concerted effort to convince Facebook to shut down rape-humor pages and other pages celebrating sexual violence (Raphael 2013, 147). Four words capture the lack of seriousness about men's violences against females. Four words incorporate denial, trivialization, entitlement, and the culture of protection. "Boys will be boys."

Underreporting of Men's Violences against Women and Girls

Given the weight and authority of patriarchal ideology that is entrenched in blaming the victim and that fuels the cultural dynamics of entitlement, silence, and protection, is it any wonder that crimes of men's (and boys') violences against women are significantly underreported and have low prosecution, conviction, and punishment rates? Substantial research has documented the persistent underreporting of all forms of men's violences against females. The common responses to women reporting a rape to police are indifference, disbelief, or outright punishment (Raphael 2013, 139). Disbelief is deeply rooted in patriarchal ideology: the concept of women as natural liars can be found in the writings of Hesiod, Rousseau, Balzac, Schopenhauer, and Nietzsche to name only a few (Jordan 2004, 36–42).

The legacy of disbelief contributes to the significant undercounting or unfounding of rape and sexual assault cases by police. In the 2014 report *Estimating the Incidence of Rape and Sexual Assault*, researchers note that there is "[a]mple evidence that the crimes of rape and sexual assault are substantially undercounted through police reports" (House et al. 2014, 36). The backlog in DNA testing of many thousands of completed rape kits remains a widespread national problem. The National Institute of Justice found that between 2002 and 2007, state and local law enforcement agencies failed to send DNA evidence to labs in 18 percent of unsolved rapes. Nearly one-half of the responding police departments said they did not send evidence to the lab because a suspect had not been identified. According to Raphael, "This response betrayed ignorance of the now well-established Combined DNA Index System, a national DNA database that can help identify a perpetrator" (Raphael 2013, 141).

Police disbelief of women who report rape, argues Raphael, is based on assertions that the majority of rape claims are false or minimizing rape as "bad sex" (Raphael 2013, 148). While repeatedly disproven by vigorous research, the idea of false rape allegations continues to thrive in the criminal justice system (as well as in the broader culture). The percentage of false reports of rape is about the same (2 to 8 percent) as false reports of other crimes (109). Jan Jordan, in *Word of a Woman: Police, Rape and Belief*, notes that "Over the last few years, women's fear of rape seems to have slipped from public and media consciousness, to be largely replaced by men's fear of false accusations. While once it was women who constituted the 'at risk' group, now men are seen as being at risk. In a climate where 'stranger danger' has been replaced by 'woman danger', access to justice for rape victims is destined to remain elusive" (Jordan 2004, 246). Furthermore, Jordan asserts, "When women accuse men of wrongdoing, they are doubted; when they retract they are believed. If they allege abuse, their word is suspect; if they retract an abuse allegation, their word suddenly becomes credible. One is prompted to ask: Why is women's word to be trusted only when it excuses and absolves men of responsibility for their violence against women?" (243).

Women and girls reporting criminal violations against them are met not only with disbelief or having their reports trivialized, they also face the possibility of harsher treatment by the criminal justice system. Recently, several victims have been incarcerated in order to force them to testify against their rapists. In 2012 in Sacramento, a seventeen-year-old girl was put in juvenile detention to ensure that she testify against her rapist (Victor 2016). In New Orleans, several victims of sexual assault and domestic violence were arrested on material warrants in order to ensure their testimony. In one case, the victim was jailed for eight days (Sledge 2017). Police have arrested victims for crimes unrelated to the assault (such as underage drinking or theft).

Universities have threatened and punished students who reported sexual assaults. Candice E. Jackson, Secretary of Education Betsy DeVos's acting assistant secretary for civil rights, claimed in July 2017, that "90 percent" of campus rape cases involved "alcohol and *regretful* [emphasis added] female students" (Brown 2017). After sharp public criticism over her remarks, she apologized for being "flippant." Her remarks, however, were more than flippant; they were uninformed and prejudicial.

The common denominator in underreporting of sexual assault is fear—fear of not being believed, fear of being blamed, fear of retaliatory violence, and fear of being punished. Victims, offenders, bystanders, the police and other officials in authority, and the media all participate in this "culture of silence" on men's violences against females. An early and consistent theme of the movement against men's violences against females was "breaking silence." In 1971, feminists organized the first national speak-out on rape. Across the country, *Take Back the Night* Marches have become annual events where women and allies take to the streets protesting men's violences and end with women speaking out—many for the very first time—about their victimizations. "Breaking silence" was a call to action heard and responded to by women who were abused by their husbands or partners, women who were sexually abused in childhood (and later, men who recalled being sexually abused in childhood), and girls and women hurt by the sexual exploitation industries. In 1991, Anita Hill's testimony before the Senate Judiciary Committee about her experience of sexual harassment by a nominee for the Supreme Court launched a long overdue but short-lived national conversation about sexual harassment. The conversation was reignited and reenergized again in 2017, gaining momentum as a result of women using social media effectively to share their experiences. Remarkably, *Time* magazine named "The Silence Breakers" as their Person of the Year in 2017.

Victims' needs to tell their truth has always been in opposition to the dominant culture's desire to silence victims as well as its need to conceal the issue of men's violences against females. Patriarchy employs many weapons in its arsenal to mitigate any successes of victims' efforts to subvert the culture of silence. Many victims have pushed back in creative and meaningful ways. The twenty-first century saw the internet and various social media platforms play an increasingly pivotal role in both maintaining and challenging the culture of silence. Jaclyn Friedman notes that the internet serves as a vehicle for both the condemnation of and support for victims of sexual violence: "When you talk on the Internet about being a survivor of sexual violence, two things will invariably happen," [Friedman] said. "You will be surrounded by support and you will be called hateful names and hear abusive things" (Phillips 2017, 49).

The influence of the culture of silence remains daunting and powerfully effective. As Miller and Biele explain, "[I]t's in men's interest to disbelieve, and women disbelieve because the truth frightens and appalls them" (Miller and Biele 1993, 50). The victim's fear that she will not be believed and, as a consequence, that the offender will not be punished is realistic.

The Prosecution and Conviction of Men's Violences against Women

Since most of the violences that men commit against girls and women are unreported, it is obvious that the majority of perpetrators are not punished. It is difficult to assess the prosecution and conviction rates of reported violence because there is considerable variability in the reporting and collecting of prosecution and conviction data across the fifty states and the federal government. In their study of "The Justice Gap for Sexual Assault Cases," Lonsway and Archambault offer an upside-down pyramid that reflects a summary ratio of the data: of one hundred rapes committed, an estimated five to twenty are reported to the police; 0.4 to 5.4 are prosecuted; 0.2 to 5.2 result in a conviction; and 0.2 to 2.8 are incarcerated. "Conviction rates," they argue, "are meaningless if they are computed based on a starting point where most of the attrition has already taken place" (Lonsway and Archambault 2012, 155). Their investigation led them to conclude that there is a "consistently widening gap between the numbers of reports versus arrests for forcible rape, which differs markedly from the pattern seen with other violent crimes" (ibid., 149–50). While they offer several possible explanations for the "justice gap," one is particularly compelling: the majority of rapes and sexual assaults do not fit the dominant narrative of "real rape," that is, rape perpetrated by a stranger.

The Justice and Gender-Based Violence Research Initiative of the Wellesley Centers for Women notes that "only a small portion of the child sexual abuse cases that enter the justice system lead to prosecution while many other cases drop out of the system along the way—a phenomenon referred to as case attrition" (2017). In 2015, the EEOC investigated 6,822 sexual harassment allegations and dismissed 52 percent since it had "no reasonable cause to believe that discrimination occurred" (Chalabi 2016).

In the past two decades, several policy initiatives resulted from police mishandling of intimate partner violence. Policies such as mandatory arrest, pro-arrest, and no-drop policies have been implemented as correctives. Whether they have been successful is not clear since evidence is inconsistent and conflicting. In reporting on one high-profile Silicon Valley case, Melissa Jeltsen interviewed Maureen Curtis, vice president for Safe Horizon's criminal justice and court programs, who noted that "the criminal justice system is designed to respond to specific incidents of physical violence, not patterns of abusive behavior. The focus on eruptions of physical violence can miss the bigger picture of the terror present inside a home" (Jeltsen, 2017). Intimate partner abuse is characterized by "the concept of coercive control, a pattern of verbal and psychological maltreatment that abusers use to dominate their partners. According to Curtis, many elements of coercive control, such as isolating a victim, obsessive behavior, harassing or threatening, [and] threatening to take the children [are] often not criminal behavior in most, if not all states . . . It does the most damage, and is the most terrifying, to victims and children who live in those homes" (2017).

The victim in one high-profile case characterized the physical violence and emotional abuse she suffered for ten years as "terrorism." She told the court, "that's how I felt—terrorized and controlled, held hostage by the fear of pain, humiliation and assault on my being and my daughter's" (2017). Her abuser was sentenced to six months in county jail and three years' probation. Accounting for time served, he will probably spend thirteen days in jail (*Daily Beast* 2017).

It is clear that much more work needs to be done to close the justice gap for victims of men's violences. The criminal justice system is a complex network of sectors, offices, and actors. The work to strengthen criminal justice responses must be multidimensional, comprehensive, and sustained. The work must be guided by principles that recognize men's violences against females as manifestations of gender inequality. Moreover, as the criminal justice system does not operate in isolation from the dominant culture, we can't expect meaningful progress within that system unless similar efforts are made outside of it as well.

Conclusion

Sexual terrorism in the twenty-first century is both the same and different as it was when first conceptualized thirty-five years ago. As an analytical framework, the components of sexual terrorism have remained essential to conducting structural and systemic analyses of the system of men's violences against women and girls. The addition of the fifth component, the perception of the terrorist and the victim, helps further efforts to theorize and understand the phenomena.

The commonalities that buttress the forms of men's violences and that reify the perception of terrorist and victim—the lack of seriousness, underreporting, blaming the victim, low conviction and punishment rates—have also remained constant. These commonalities shape our understanding of the victims, perpetrators, and the acts of violence. What has changed—and will change in the decades ahead—are the ways in which each component and each commonality is manifested in the culture. The first and second decades of the twenty-first century witnessed a proliferation of the guises of sexual terrorism. The forms of propaganda of sexual terrorism are not only pervasive and inescapable; they are bold, unapologetically misogynistic, and even prideful in the depth and expression of woman-hating and male entitlement.

Rape and forced sex have been (and continue to be) reframed as the type of sex that men and boys desire. The term "nonconsensual sex" is being used as a substitute for rape, therefore rendering rape unnamed and invisible. The internet and smartphones have become weaponized in the war against women and girls as they facilitate the mainstreaming of misogyny. Women and children are trafficked on well-known, highly profitable websites. Pornography's reach is boundless. The ubiquity of smartphone technology to document acts of sexual violence and instantly upload them for others to consume was unimaginable thirty years ago. The internet and smartphone technology have transformed men's sexual aggression into both spectacle and spectator sport. These changes are testimony to patriarchy's strength and adaptability and the endurance of the contempt and hatred for females. Patriarchy, as Renee Heberle, reminds us, "is never finally successful in its project of dominance. It is constantly reinventing itself and reconstituting the terms of its legitimacy" (Heberle 1996, 65).

Sexual terrorism, however, is more than an explanatory and analytical framework. It is a descriptive concept that deepens our understanding of the lived lives of females, of the everyday reality of being female in patriarchy. Whether directly victimized or not, the system of sexual terrorism circumscribes the life of every female. The burdens that victims bear are extraordinary. In the last two decades, men's violences against females have been widely acknowledged as a significant public health issue. The CDC estimates that $4.1 billion is spent every year on direct medical and mental health care services (National Center for Injury Prevention and Control 2003, 2). Too many girls and women have attempted or committed suicide as a result of men's violences, disbelief by authorities and/or communities, or gender-policing. Violences experienced in childhood deeply affect one's long-term quality of life, including health and productivity. Debilitating and costly health issues such as addiction, sexually transmitted diseases, obesity, fractures, and chronic diseases such as diabetes and heart disease have been attributed to childhood victimization (Dolezal, McCollum, and Callahan 2009, 6).

In addition to the emotional and physical burden of victimization, the financial cost is staggering. The full cost of violence to victims throughout their lifetime is unknown, but it includes a wide range of variables—lost wages, employment and housing instability, health care, missed educational opportunities, and justice system costs. Intimate partner violence is estimated to cost $9.3 billion (McLean and Bocinski 2017, 4). A CDC study on the "Lifetime Economic Burden of Rape Among U.S. Adults" estimates that the lifetime cost per victim is $122,461 (Peterson, DeGue, Florence, and Lokey 2017). Workplace discrimination against employees based on race, gender or sexual orientation costs businesses an estimated $64 billion annually. In 2011, The Equal Employment Opportunity Commission received 11,300 sexual harassment complaints and settled about 1,400 of them for a total of $52 million (Braverman 2013). Dianna Bo (2013) studied the cost of sexual violence in the military and concluded that for 2012, the total estimated cost was $322.6 million (94). In addition to the victims, taxpayers, investors, businesses, and consumers also carry a significant economic burden for men's violences against women.

In this dreary landscape, there is good news. Enloe reminds us that "it takes persistent, undaunted, collective work to get a trivialized phenomenon converted into a serious public issue" (Enloe 2013, 181). Women, girls, and men who are allies are actively engaged in this work. Courageous victims continue to speak out and to seek meaningful justice; in doing so, they are speaking for all victims. Individual and collective activism has and continues to make inroads in challenging unjust legal decisions, in providing safe spaces for victims, and in organizing for gender justice and against men's violences. Organizations and social media platforms such as Project Unbreakable, #YesAllWomen, Everyday Sexism Project, Everyday Feminism, hollaback, #Believe Survivors, #itsonus, #MeToo, #TimesUp, and many others, have creatively used technology as an instrument of social change.

Sexual terrorism shapes the cultural imaginary in profound ways. Changing that imaginary to one that embraces the fundamental human rights of females requires constant vigilance and effort to expose and eliminate the sense-making frameworks that undergird and normalize men's violences against women and girls. Only then can we deconstruct the systemic reinforcements of sexual terrorism and develop public policy to operationalize a vision of equality.

13

Lessons Still Being Learned from the "Comfort Women" of World War II

MARGARET D. STETZ

> A few of the girls were able to run away from the abductors. . . . What they
> said is the same in all cases. When the men came . . . they told them they were
> soldiers. They told the girls . . . don't run, stay in one place. They gathered them
> in one place. Then they marched them out of the school gate. . . . There was a
> truck. . . . [The armed abductors] put the girls in the truck.
> —Habila 2016, 33–34

If the description above sounds familiar, it should. The pattern that it follows, in recounting how young girls were rounded up to become sex slaves for a group of male fighters, is one that has been outlined on many occasions. First, there is the targeting of a vulnerable female population and the involvement of armed men who look upon their captives as nothing more than supplies for the taking, then the sudden removal and permanent loss of freedom, the enforced trafficking, etc. In this particular case, the account comes from Nigeria and reflects the experience of the adolescents known as the "Chibok Girls," more than two hundred of whom were abducted in April 2014 in a raid on their secondary school by Boko Haram militants. What happened next to the Chibok victims also repeats the past. As one survivor who later escaped has reported, the men who imprisoned them "said we were not students, we were just prostitutes"—a label that gave the captors a sense of impunity, as well as entitlement to sex (Habila 2016, 107). Any schoolgirls who did not manage to get away were then treated as "prostitutes" and subjected repeatedly to rape.

Throughout this story, the details of other sets of experiences, from different times and from different parts of the globe echo hauntingly, for there have been reports like these before. In some instances, they have involved the actions of small bands of armed militias and seemingly spontaneous incidents—war crimes of opportunity, as it were—that have led nevertheless to the same horrific fate for those held captive to provide sex in warzones. But in other cases, such results have been a matter of highly organized planning at the highest levels of military and governmental authority and have involved the trafficking not of a few hundred sex slaves but hundreds of thousands. The most notorious example of the latter sort of exploitation was the "comfort system" developed and implemented during the Asia-Pacific War and the focus, since the early 1990s, of ongoing political rancor between Japan and its neighboring nations.

After nearly fifty years of bearing their psychic and physical scars in secret, the survivors of Japan's system of World War II military sexual slavery began to testify publicly about the war crimes that were committed against them. Starting in 1991 with Kim Hak Sun, a so-called "comfort woman" from the Republic of Korea, these courageous women recounted their histories from a half-century earlier: stories of forced confinement in brothels after abduction or coercion and of countless daily rapes, over periods of months and sometimes years, by soldiers of the Japanese Imperial Army. Ever since they came forward—from the Philippines, Indonesia, Taiwan, China, Myanmar, Malaysia, and especially from Korea, the home country of perhaps the largest number of the roughly two hundred thousand victims—the world has heard in explicit detail about their sexual abuse. This egregious sexual violence was authorized by governmental policies that reflected not only racism but also misogyny and contempt for members of the powerless socioeconomic classes from which many of the women sprang.

Those targeted for exploitation were, moreover, often vulnerable in another way, for many were not "comfort *women*" but—like the Boko Haram's later victims at Chibok—underage *girls*. Lacking legal standing as adults and thus unable either to give or withhold consent, they were, when shipped or trucked to battlefront military brothels, the objects of organized child sex-trafficking by Japan. Using these adolescent and also preadolescent girls for sex was a violation, as well, of the International Convention for the Suppression of White Slave Traffic, to which Japan had agreed decades earlier (Yoshimi 2000, 157). Nonetheless, since these crimes were first widely exposed, a variety of Japanese political figures and their supporters have continued to insist that these sex slaves (including the many girls who were legally minors)—taken from nations that Imperial Japan's military occupied and controlled with the proverbial iron fist—were all volunteers, who freely chose to serve soldiers as paid prostitutes.

In 2013, for instance, the mayor of Osaka, Japan, who is also a coleader of the rightwing Japan Restoration Party, went on record as stating that "there wasn't clear evidence that the Japanese military coerced" anyone into being confined in these wartime brothels which, he declared, were in any case "necessary at that time" to "maintain discipline in the military" by offering a "rest" for the soldiers (Foster 2013). Although these remarks directly contradicted what the survivors themselves had said about how they were forced into the "comfort stations" and detained there by violence, such continued denials in Japan are not surprising, for they conform to a longstanding and still active narrative in the West, as well, around the subject of sexual assault. As Joy Castro, an American feminist academic, reminds us, when "women publicly share their accounts of harm . . . their stories are routinely met with disbelief, disregard, or worse"; frequently, it is those who have brought the accusations who wind up being "put on trial, interrogated, and judged" harshly, rather than the men who have committed the crimes against them (Castro 2018, 8).

In light of nearly thirty years during which details about the experiences of the former military sex slaves of World War II have circulated around the globe, we can see quite clearly the effect that their testimony has had in some areas, as well as the absence of effect in others. The positive results of their having come forward are obvious. These include the narrow and specific—the identification of several surviving Japanese officials responsible for instituting and/or overseeing the "comfort system" and thus the December 1996 ban by the Department of Justice under President Bill Clinton on allowing these war criminals entry into the US (Lee 2001, 152–53). In 2007, the US Congress passed an important measure: House Resolution 121, authored by Rep. Michael Honda of California, that called upon Japan—albeit without any response from the Japanese government—formally to acknowledge and apologize for the system of sexual enslavement that it instituted across Asia before and during World War II (Honda 2015).

The further-reaching consequences include the momentous step taken for the first time in June 1996 by the International Criminal Court of The Hague to prosecute wartime rape as a crime against humanity (Stetz 2001, 95). Without the insistence of the survivors of the "comfort system" upon the need for a new view of the heinous nature of organized sexual violence, whether during war or during sorts of other military campaigns, the stories of more recent rape victims—such as, for instance, the 2017 claims by women and girls from the Rohingya Muslim minority population in Myanmar of mass rape by uniformed Burmese security forces (Wheeler 2017, 15)—might not have been treated as seriously by the international community.

At the same time, we must also reflect upon the widespread failure of governments in general and military institutions in particular to learn the lessons that the survivors have communicated so bravely, at such cost to themselves. These lessons include the need for governments to be accountable for the actions of their agents in authorizing, condoning, or committing rape and then to articulate and demonstrate their accountability to future generations. Perhaps most appalling has been the refusal of Japan to accept full legal responsibility and so to issue official governmental apologies, as well as to offer government-sponsored reparations, to the survivors in *all* of the nations from which girls and women were taken.

Many of us know about the repeated dismissals of the "comfort women's" lawsuits in a variety of Japanese courts (Stetz 2002, 28). Most of us are aware, too, of the continuing struggles to write into Japanese students' textbooks more complete and accurate accounts of the victimization of Asian women by the emperor's forces in the period preceding and then during World War II, along with the implacable resistance in Japan to this educational project. Some will also have heard of attempts in 2015 by representatives of the Japanese government, which has often opposed this truth-telling, to interfere with the dissemination of information about the "comfort system" even in textbooks published and distributed in the US by the firm of McGraw-Hill (Fackler 2015). But only at the end of 2017 did another egregious, less-publicized set of actions come to light: the determined efforts of the Japanese government to suppress the speech of South Korean officials. In secret talks with South Korean governmental representatives that resulted in an "agreement" intended to resolve historical tensions over the issue—at least between Japan and one of the numerous nations from which girls and women were taken—Japanese negotiators insisted that only the euphemistic term "comfort women" should appear in all official Korean statements, thus banning the phrase "sexual slavery" from public use (Jung 2017).

I would like, however, to focus on the failures of countries other than Japan to take to heart sufficiently the testimony of survivors of the "comfort system" and to learn from it. Rather than blaming Japan alone, we should turn our attention to nations in a different region, one that has been every bit as guilty of choosing not to render justice to the survivors and of ignoring the implications of their testimony about war, militarism, sexual abuse, and exploitation. I refer to the West. I am speaking not merely of the denials of claims filed by the survivors of the "comfort system" in Western courts, especially in the US, or of the opposition to those lawsuits by the US State Department under President George W. Bush (Stetz 2002, 26–28). I mean instead to point a finger at the ways in which institutions such as the US military, both at home and abroad, so far have failed to implement productively—indeed, have rarely even tried to learn—the important lessons taught by the "comfort women's" experiences. This is not a Western problem alone for, at the same time, international entities, such as the United Nations' peacekeeping forces, have also shown a shameful disregard of the truths evident from the "comfort women's" stories and have instead reenacted the patterns of sexual assault, exploitation, and trafficking of underage girls and women in combat areas (as was charged in the Central African Republic in 2017).

Why, we might ask first, have so many governmental and nongovernmental bodies alike felt free to shut their ears to the "comfort women's" teachings? It is not as though the survivors of World War II sexual slavery have been invisible since Kim Hak Sun came forward and talked about what was done to her at the age of seventeen. On the contrary, they have been the subject of innumerable journalistic profiles in newspapers and magazines; memoirs and oral histories published in books; television and cinematic documentaries; feature films; academic studies; stage plays; novels; photographic exhibitions; and even art installations.[1] To pay no heed to the significance of the stories that the former "comfort women" have repeated again and again has required a conscious effort. Fueling that effort, however, have been two potent ideologies—sexism and racism. In all parts of the world, women's voices, women's complaints, and women's sufferings matter less than those of men, especially when it comes to the making of policy. In the West, moreover, the concept of listening to Asian women (let alone poor and relatively uneducated Asian women) as sources of information, wisdom, and advice about military matters is utterly unknown. Most of what the former "comfort women" have had to say about what happens during wartime when men are given limitless power over female bodies and the authorization, whether explicit or tacit, to commit rape has gone unheeded.

If any single survivor's voice, however, did have the potential to break through Western indifference, it was that of Jan Ruff O'Herne. Almost uniquely among the perhaps two hundred thousand women in Asia who were kidnapped, coerced, or recruited through trickery and imprisoned in Japanese military brothels, Jan Ruff O'Herne was White, educated, from a privileged background, and an English-speaker. As a woman of Dutch extraction who grew up in what later became Indonesia and who lived after World War II in both England and Australia, she was a figure with great appeal to Western audiences. A strong believer in colonialism, she spoke in idyllic terms of life in Java before Indonesian independence and lent support to conservative currents of nostalgia for white Western rule.

At the same time, however, her history as a former "comfort woman" gave her a unique sense of solidarity with Asian women that made her views appealing to progressive, antiracist readers too. Her 1994 memoir, *50 Years of Silence*, was published in Sydney, Amsterdam, and New York and, therefore, reached audiences on three different continents. A documentary of the same name, based on her autobiography, enjoyed wide release and even played repeatedly across the US on television stations owned by the Corporation for Public Broadcasting. During the discussions in Washington, DC, that preceded the passage of House Resolution 121 in 2007, she also testified before the House of Representatives.

There were certainly important lessons for those in positions of power to absorb from the account of her experiences in the 1940s, had political or military officials in the West cared to receive them. Chief among them involved the reports of what happened to Ruff O'Herne after her Japanese military captors suddenly released her and several other White women from the Semarang military brothel, where she was raped daily for three months, and sent her, along with the others, to a regular prison camp. The war was nearing an end, and it was clear that the Japanese high command was concerned about the possibility of an Allied victory, and thus with the consequences of Allied troops finding White women being subjected to rape. What occurred next is of tremendous significance to the understanding of issues involving wartime sexual violence. As Ruff O'Herne tells her readers,

One of the Japanese guards entered the house of one of the women at night. At first he made out that he had come for a chat and to do some trading. Then, suddenly, he turned on her and tried to rape her. Obviously he knew where we had come from and must have thought we were an easy target. There followed a lot of screaming and shouting and uproar and the soldier disappeared into the night.

The incident of this attempted rape was immediately reported to the camp commandant. At morning roll call, one of the Japanese guards was called and ordered to stand in the centre of the compound. The commandant marched up to him and dressed him down severely in a language we could not understand. The guard stood there, terrified. The commandant then took out his revolver and handed it to the guard. The poor man was then forced to shoot himself through the mouth. (Ruff O'Herne 1994, 113–14)

Ruff O'Herne's account offers clear proof, first, that whether or not soldiers rape women and otherwise abuse prisoners during wartime is not merely a matter of individual desire, volition, or impulse; it is instead a reflection of military policy. So-called sex acts are, like all acts performed by soldiers who live under a chain of command, reflections of decisions made at a higher level. As Ruff O'Herne notes in commenting upon this incident, "A short while ago we had been raped by at least ten Japanese a day, with the approval of the Japanese emperor, Hirohito, the Kempeitai [Japanese military police], and the highest military authorities. Now this man was forced to shoot himself for trying to do exactly the same thing" (114). In other words, the sexual assault of women occurred when—and only when—it suited the purposes of the military authorities and of the government that backed those authorities.

The story that Ruff O'Herne told also gives lie to the defense often used by those who attempt to rationalize or excuse the existence of forced prostitution and/or rape as a necessary "outlet" for soldiers in times of combat. Having access to women's bodies, even though this may be against the will of the women themselves, is (as the misogynist argument goes) a morale booster; therefore, military authorities set up brothels, allow brothels to be established near bases, or turn a blind eye to instances of rape in general, because they supposedly are concerned above all with the morale of their troops. It is clear, however, that nothing could be more demoralizing for his comrades than to witness a soldier being forced to execute himself.

In Ruff O'Herne's anecdote, the commander of the prison camp was not in the least interested in protecting the other soldiers' morale; he was interested only in reminding them that, in the face of an impending Allied invasion and possible Japanese surrender, raping White women was against orders, and the price of disobeying any order was death. Matters of sexuality did not occupy a space apart from ordinary questions of discipline, obedience, and military or governmental policy. On the contrary, they were as much under scrutiny and control as any other questions of conduct.

The Imperial Japanese Army did indeed regulate rape. Apart from exceptional moments, such as the one that Jan Ruff O'Herne records, when they prohibited a specific rape, military authorities created the conditions under which sexual abuse was permitted, encouraged, and even required. They also determined who the victims would be, for the "comfort system," as it was called, was integrally tied to racist notions regarding the inferiority of all Asian populations other than the Japanese, and thus of the suitability of non-Japanese women and underage girls for sexual exploitation. Most of the roughly two hundred thousand Asian women used as military sex slaves belonged, therefore, to nations and ethnic groups that Japanese racial ideology defined as "lower." As Bonnie B. C. Oh explains, "racial hierarchy . . . was determined by the skin color and by the geographical proximity of their native land to Japan." Korean women ranked below Okinawans, "[t]hen came the Taiwanese, Chinese, the Filipinas, and so on" (Oh 2001, 10).

In her classic feminist polemic *Bananas, Beaches and Bases*, Cynthia Enloe reminded readers that, more often than not, what "passes for inevitable, inherent, 'traditional' or biological has in fact been *made*" [author's emphasis] (Enloe 1990, 3). This is certainly true of military sexual violence. When armed forces commit rape, there is nothing "natural" or biologically necessary about it. Military rape of women not only becomes inevitable, it is deliberately *made* inevitable, when the following conditions are in place: 1) when male soldiers feel that they have limitless power over girls and women (whether civilian women or, in fact, women in the military); 2) when they believe themselves racially, ethnically, religiously, or otherwise distinct from and superior to the girls and women under their control and/or believe that gender alone constitutes a hierarchical difference sufficient to excuse their abuse of the subordinate party; and 3) when they are convinced that they are acting with the approval of those higher up (whether in the military itself or within the government), even while they are violating international law. To allow these conditions to exist is not merely to invite sexual violence but to promote it.

These are some of the lessons that the West could have learned—indeed, should have learned—from the testimony offered, at great price, by the elderly and often infirm women who have come forward since the early 1990s. They have spoken out at hearings, unofficial tribunals, press conferences, marches, protest rallies, and other gatherings, all of which have been covered by a variety of media. Conclusions based on their experiences have also circulated in a report issued to the United Nations Commission on Human Rights in 1996 by Radhika Coomaraswamy, the UN's Special Rapporteur on Violence Against Women (Lee 2001, 156–57). Because officials around the globe, especially military officials, have refused to pay attention, we have seen new and increasingly horrific episodes of sexual victimization arising out of every combat situation in the past three decades. Whether we look to recent or current wars in the Middle

East and in Africa, each time another example of war-related sexual violence or sexual exploitation by military forces is exposed to public view, authorities throw up their hands and feign surprise, instead of admitting that they could have predicted and prevented these occurrences, given the understanding of history that the "comfort women's" stories provide.

The United Nations and the US alike turned their backs on the situation in Darfur where, from 2003 through 2005, there was mass rape of Black Sudanese women committed by non-Black Sudanese militia (known as the "Janjawid") with government backing. According to Lisa Alvy writing for the *National NOW Times*, using information supplied by Amnesty International, the crimes against women in Darfur included being "forced into sexual slavery" (Alvy 2004/2005, 13). In this new setting, the old sufferings of the "comfort women" of World War II repeated themselves, just as they would a decade later in Nigeria, with the "Chibok girls" as the victims of Boko Haram.

Meanwhile, in the war that raged throughout Congo for a decade from the mid-1990s onward, "Congolese women. . . . [were] victims of rape on a scale never seen before," as each of the "dozens of armed groups in this war has used rape" (Nolen 2005, 56). Perhaps more appalling, though quite predictable, were the developments in Congo following the implementation of a United Nations–backed peace accord among the warring factions. As revealed by the *Washington Post* in November 2004, "Sexual exploitation of women and girls by UN peacekeepers and bureaucrats in the UN mission in Congo . . . [was] 'significant, widespread and ongoing,' according to a confidential UN report that documents cases of pedophilia, prostitution and rape" (Lynch 2004, A27).

In Congo, the very soldiers who were put in place to bring a bloody conflict to a halt used their mission as an opportunity to abuse the civilian population in numerous ways, including sexually. Although the UN code of conduct expressly forbade such conduct, the UN did not enforce its own rules; the "home countries" from which the soldiers came were "responsible for punishing any of their military personnel who violate[d] the code while taking part in a United Nations peacekeeping mission," and they chose to ignore these violations (Lacey 2004, A8). Given unlimited power over destitute Black African women (as well as children) and an absence of oversight or accountability for their actions, the international peacekeeping forces in Congo, who came from fifty nations, felt free to commit rape with impunity.

Allegations of rape by those charged with establishing order have not been confined to the African continent. During the Iraq War (2003–2011), civilian Iraqi women accused US soldiers on a variety of occasions of sexual assault. Quoting reports published in the *Guardian* newspaper in Britain, the feminist journal *Off Our Backs* cited transcripts of US Army investigations into thirteen alleged rapes by American servicemen early in the war, none of which, however, resulted in any action being taken against those accused ("News" 2005, 7–8). Perhaps the most notorious case involved the gang rape in 2005 by five US soldiers of a fourteen-year-old Iraqi girl, whose family was murdered to facilitate the attack on her, and who was then shot to death after her assault (BBC 2007). So horrendous was this crime that prosecutions did follow eventually, along with convictions, but only after there had been an attempted cover-up, requiring a whistleblower to come forward to expose the perpetrators.

In terms of personal safety, the picture has scarcely been better for American servicewomen, a number of whom have been targets of rape by their male colleagues. As Ann Scott Tyson wrote in May 2005 in the *Washington Post*, "Reported sexual assaults have risen in the Central Command region, which includes the Middle East and Central Asia, from 24 in 2002 and 94 in 2003 to 123 in 2004, according to figures the Miles Foundation obtained from the Pentagon's Joint Task Force on Sexual Assault Prevention and Response" (Tyson 2005, A3). Although these figures included assaults by men upon other men, women made up the majority of victims. When statistics have been gathered, moreover, from all regions where American military women are stationed, the results have been shockingly grim.

In an article in the *Nation*, Karen Houppert cited the numbers for 2007 alone: "2,688 sexual assaults were reported globally against women serving in the Armed Forces" (Houppert 2008). Since then, instead of diminishing, the totals have increased dramatically. According to a 2017 NBC News story titled "Sexual Assault Reports in U.S. Military Reach Record High: Pentagon," in the year 2016 "[s]ervice members reported 6,172 cases of sexual assault," which represented "a sharp jump from 2012 when 3,604 cases were reported" (NBC News 2017). Worse yet, "[w]ithin the recent report was an anonymous survey, conducted every two years, which found that 14,900 service members experienced some kind of sexual assault in 2016, from rape to groping," while "58 percent of victims experienced reprisals or retaliation for reporting sexual assault" (NBC News 2017). As has been shown again and again, fear of retaliation keeps many victims from coming forward, so we can be sure that the number of unreported assaults on servicewomen also remains high.

To ignore the experiences of such women is to leave all women in warfare—indeed, all women everywhere—less secure. Sexual violence has never been confined to military forces, let alone to the US military, but within the latter institution gender itself is still a difference that equals inferiority of status. As the "comfort women's" stories suggested to any observer willing to learn from them, wherever women are perceived as inferior to and of less worth than military men, the conditions are in place for sexual assault. Being at war, moreover, increases the likelihood of male military violence against women, including the abuse of women married to soldiers, as Cynthia Enloe has suggested in her examination of US Defense Department records of domestic violence in military households (Enloe 2000, 189).

The distressing realities of sexual assault uncovered by the recent surveys of US service members were, therefore, easy to anticipate. That so little was done to prevent these crimes speaks forcefully to the need for further lessons to be absorbed—particularly about what happens when military men are allowed to maintain (and thus are tacitly encouraged to act upon) a sense of gender privilege, sexual entitlement, and impunity. For any improvement to occur, these lessons must also lead to action; change must be implemented from the top of the hierarchy downward, involving concerted efforts to reshape an environment where sexual violence in many forms still flourishes and often goes unpunished.

Through their bravery and selflessness in bringing to light the terrible war crimes committed against them during World War II, the aged survivors of Japan's "comfort system" have achieved immense success. Because of them, wartime rape, forced prostitution, and the trafficking of girl children in war zones are now subjects reported regularly in the world press, as well as documented and protested by large numbers of human rights organizations and feminist groups. Unfortunately, though, despite their best efforts, the former "comfort women" continue to have little or no effect on military culture, whether in the West or elsewhere, as this remains unaltered in its view of women's bodies (those of both civilian and military women) and of sexual access to those bodies as rightfully under the control of military men.

Against all odds, the Asian women who have testified publicly since the early 1990s have tried to create an important legacy of information and knowledge and thus to prevent future abuses. Given their advanced age, with the few who are still left alive now in their nineties, they soon will be unable to continue speaking out and passing on their wisdom. That they appear already to have been marginalized and swept aside by the military and governmental institutions who most need to pay heed to their words is more than merely a matter for regret; it is an incalculable loss for women's human rights and a threat to human security in general. More than ever, the lessons they have taught *must* be learned.

NOTE

1 A brief list of these would include special issues of academic journals, such as the 1997 issue of *Positions: East Asia Cultural Critique*; volumes of historical studies, such as George Hicks's *The Comfort Women* (1994), Yuki Tanaka's *Japan's Comfort Women* (2002), Peipei Qiu's *Chinese Comfort Women* (2013), Caroline Norma's *The Japanese Comfort Women and Sexual Slavery During the China and Pacific Wars* (2016), Maki Kimura's *Unfolding the 'Comfort Women' Debates* (2016), and M. Evelina Galang's *Lolas' House* (2017); volumes of survivors' testimonies, such as Keith Howard's *True Stories of the Korean Comfort Women* (1995), the edited collection produced by the Washington Coalition for Comfort Women Issues, Inc., called *Comfort Women Speak* (2000), and Maria Rosa Henson's autobiography, *Comfort Woman* (1999); documentary films, such as Christine Choy and Nancy Tong's *In the Name of the Emperor* (1998), Dai Sil Kim-Gibson's *Silence Broken* (1999), and Tiffany Hsiung's *The Apology* (2016); feature films, such as Cho Jung-Rae's *Spirits' Homecoming* (2016) and Lee Na-Jeong's *Snowy Road* (2017); novels, such as Nora Okja Keller's *Comfort*

Woman (1997), Therese Park's *A Gift of the Emperor* (1997), Chang-Rae Lee's *A Gesture Life* (1999), William Andrews's *Daughters of the Dragon* (2016), Mihee Eun's *Flutter, Flutter, Butterfly* (2017), and Roger Rudick's *Story of a Comfort Girl* (2017); Chungmi Kim's drama *Comfort Women*, which was performed at the Urban Stages Theatre in New York City (2004); visual works and installations by artists such as Tomiyama Taeko, Yoshiko Shimada, Miran Kim, Mona Higuchi, and Chang-Jin Lee; displays of photographs, such as those exhibited in Washington, DC, at Georgetown University's Leavey Center in 1996 and at the Cannon House Office Building of the US House of Representatives in 1998; and volumes of photographic portraits of Indonesian survivors, such as Jan Banning's *Comfort Women* (2010).

14

Forty Years after Brownmiller

Prisons for Men, Transgender Inmates, and the Rape of the Feminine

VALERIE JENNESS AND SARAH FENSTERMAKER

When Susan Brownmiller published *Against Our Will: Men, Women, and Rape* in 1975, few anticipated that it would become a feminist classic published in more than a dozen languages. Even fewer imagined that it would foreshadow a proliferation of public discourse on sexual assault in an array of institutions, including the family, the workplace, higher education, sports, the Church, and the US military. Entering the word "rape" in Ngram[1] reveals that over the twenty years following the publication of *Against Our Will*, rape rapidly proliferated as a topic in books. In the period from 1985 to 2005, so, too, did the topic of prisons. And further, during the latter part of that time period, the topic "transgender" began to gain momentum. In 2003, the passage of the landmark Prison Rape Elimination Act (PREA) defined prison rape as a national social problem worthy of federal intervention; it memorialized in public policy the intersection between rape and prisons, and brought historic attention to the rape of transgender people behind bars.[2]

It is in the confluence of these seemingly disparate concerns—decades of thinking about rape as a form of gendered violence, prisons as uniquely dangerous gendered environments, and transgender people as gendered beings—that the sexual assault of transgender women in prisons for men recently has received unprecedented attention in the media. On April 5, 2015, for example, the *New York Times* ran a front-page article, above the fold and with a series of photographs, with the headline "Transgender Woman Cites Attacks and Abuse in Men's Prisons" (Sontag 2015, 1). As reported in the article:

> Rome, Ga.—Before she fell on hard times and got into trouble with the law, Ashley Diamond had a wardrobe of wigs named after her favorite divas. "Darling, hand me Aretha" or Mariah or Madonna, she would say to her younger sister when they glammed up to go out on the town. Ms. Diamond, 36, had lived openly and outspokenly as a transgender woman since adolescence, much of that time defying the norms in the conservative Southern city. But on the day she arrived at a Georgia prison intake center in 2012, the deliberate defeminizing of Ms. Diamond began. Ordered to strip alongside male inmates, she froze but ultimately removed

her long hair and the Hannah Montana pajamas in which she had been taken into custody, she said. She hugged her rounded breasts protectively. Looking back, she said, it seemed an apt rite of initiation into what became three years of degrading and abusive treatment, starting with the state's denial of the hormones she says she had taken for 17 years. (Sontag 2015, 1)

According to the *New York Times*, since her arrival in prison Ms. Diamond has dealt with inmates exposing themselves and masturbating in front of her, faced relentless sexual harassment and coercion, and survived an attempted rape in a stairwell. As she explains in the article, "Every day I struggle with trying to stay alive and not wanting to die. Sometimes I think being a martyr would be better than having to live with all this." As her attorney explains, "I wish I could say this [sexual assault] is a problem only affecting Ashley. . . . But while Ashley is brilliant and unique, her situation is not" (Sontag 2015, 1).

In this essay, we draw on a growing body of research, including our own work recently published, to consider the social organization of prison rape as it relates to transgender women. Just as Brownmiller (1975) focused attention on rape as a male prerogative, a weapon of force against women, and an agent of fear, our central focus is on "the rape of the feminine" in the context of prisons for men and with an eye toward the intersection of the state and violence. In the next section, we inventory some alarming facts about the rape of transgender women in carceral environments built for men (and only men). Thereafter, we describe and theorize the unique space and social relations in which this type of rape emerges in relation to the social organization of gender in prison. We conclude with comments about the relationship between embodiment, gender, and the rape of the feminine in a carceral context.

The Rape of Transgender Women in Prison: Some Alarming Facts

Transgender women in jails, prisons, immigration detention facilities, and other types of lockup facilities built for men face unique challenges, including being vulnerable to rape and other forms of sexual assault. Research converges on the conclusion that especially transgender women of color and transgender women behind bars live at great risk (Grant et al. 2011; Sexton, Jenness, and Sumner 2010). Commissioned by the California Department of Corrections and Rehabilitation (CDCR)[3] shortly after the passage of the Prison Rape Elimination Act, Jenness and her colleagues found that sexual assault was thirteen times more prevalent among transgender women in prisons for men (Jenness et al. 2007; see also Jenness et al. 2010). Fifty-nine percent of transgender inmates in a large-scale study of sexual assault in California prisons reported being sexually assaulted while incarcerated, whereas slightly more than 4 percent of 322 randomly selected inmates in three California state prisons for men reported being sexually assaulted (Jenness et al. 2007). These surprising findings were corroborated by Jenness and her colleagues in a second large-scale study that found that the prevalence rate for sexual assault of transgender inmates was 58.5 percent during their incarceration history in California correctional facilities (Jenness, Sexton, and Sumner 2011). Official data collected by the Bureau of Justice Statistics confirms the differential vulnerability of transgender people on a national scale. As revealed in Table 14.1, transgender prisoners experience exceptionally high rates of victimization relative to other prisoners. Moreover, studies done outside the US corroborate this alarming pattern (Blight 2000).

Behind bars, "the girls among men" (to use their preferred terms) are uniquely situated as they endure and respond to what Gresham Sykes called "the pains of imprisonment."[4] Unofficial and official data from the US and abroad consistently reveal that transgender prisoners are not only starkly more vulnerable to sexual assault by other prisoners, they are also differentially vulnerable to undesirable sexual acts with other prisoners that, by their own account, are neither against their will nor desirable but were "chosen" in order to manage the perils of prison life (Table 14.2). Some transgender prisoners report engaging in prison prostitution or "protective pairing"—a practice that involves "willingly" engaging in

TABLE 14.1. Sexual Victimization of Inmates in Prisons and Jails, 2011–2012

Sexual Victimization	All Inmates	All Heterosexuals	All Nonheterosexuals	Nonheterosexual Males	Nonheterosexual Females	Transgender Inmates (SE)
Prison and jail, inmate-on-inmate				11.9%	9.4%	
Prison and jail, staff sexual misconduct				6.1%	3.0%	
Prison, all types	4.0%					39.9% (7.3)
Prison, inmate-on-inmate	2.0%	1.2%	12.2%			33.2% (5.2)
Prison, staff sexual misconduct	2.4%	2.1%	5.4%			15.2% (5.2)
Jail, all types	3.2%					26.8% (6.4)
Jail, inmate-on-inmate	1.6%	1.2%	8.5%			15.8% (4.4)
Jail, staff sexual misconduct	1.8%	1.7%	4.3%			18.3% (5.1)

Source: Bureau of Justice Statistics, National Inmate Survey, 2011–2012.
Note: Nonheterosexual data were combined when reported by gender because of the small number of respondents. Therefore, we cannot directly compare rates for nonheterosexuals by gender with rates for transgender respondents.
(SE) = standard error.

TABLE 14.2. Select Differences between Random and Transgender Samples of Prisoners in California (%)

Variable	Random Sample	Transgender Sample
Prevalence of sexual assault	4.4	59.0
Prevalence of undesirable sexual acts	1.3	48.3
Weapon used if involved	20.0	75.0
Officer aware of the incident	60.6	29.3
Provision of medical attention (if needed)	70.0	35.7
Racial composition (% of incidents interracial)	17.2	63.9
Relational distance	Evenly distributed	Skewed toward familiarity

Source: Jenness et al. 2007.

sexual exchanges with an inmate in an effort to avoid being harmed by other inmates (Oparah 2012).[5] In-prison prostitution and protective pairing aside, the sexual assault of transgender women by other inmates more often than not involves a weapon, and the assailant is someone with whom the victim is familiar. Often these assaults fail to come to the attention of corrections officials, and as a result victims do not receive the necessary medical attention for their injuries (Table 14.2). In other words, the prevalence and the nature of sexual assault for transgender women locked up with men are distinctive in both quantity and kind. (For a recent review of various studies of sexual assault of transgender prisoners, see Stohr 2015.)

The Rape of Transgender Women Prisoners: Social Space and Social Relations

In a recent article tellingly titled "The Hundred Years' War: The Etiology and Status of Assaults on Transgender Women in Men's Prisons," Stohr concluded, "The incarceration of transgender inmates, particularly transgender women in men's prisons, has been fraught with difficulties, missteps, ignorance, and abuse. Because of the historical rigidity around gender issues and a basic lack of concern for those on the societal margins because of their gender identity, transgender women and men have existed in what must at times seem like a war zone in which they are the perpetual target of scorn, harassment, and assault" (Stohr 2015, 127). The dangers associated with being a transgender woman in a prison, jail, and other types of detention facilities built for men are born of a complicated nexus between social space, social relations, and the gendered nature of both. This is evidenced at the structural, cultural, and interactional levels of analysis.

At the structural level, lock-up facilities are arguably the most sex-segregated institutions in the US, and as such they are organized around gender in many ways. As Britton (2003) explained, "Ideas about gender have shaped prisons, literally and figuratively, from their very first appearance as institutions of social control. Nineteenth-century reformers made women's presumed inherent difference from men the primary basis of their case for separate institutions for women, run exclusively by female staff. In a similar way, ideas about masculinity played a role in the architecture and styles of discipline advocated in early men's prisons" (Britton 2003, 3).

Although the composition of correctional personnel has shifted over time (Martin and Jurik 2007), it remains the case that *the* most basic underlying assumption of prison operations is that this sex/gender system presents two, and only two, types of people: males and females. As a result, carceral environments are built and operated "for men" *or* "for women." Thus, the very existence of incarcerated transgender women is anathema to the structure of carceral environments, precisely because it calls into question the gender binary upon which these institutions are founded.

"The girls among men" occupy a demeaned social status in carceral environments built for men, which in a hypermasculinized culture makes them ever-available targets of sustained derogation. In their recent study of correctional staff and prisoners in Pennsylvania, Sumner and Sexton (2015) report transgender prisoners occupy a marginalized position relative to other prisoners. They share stigmatized institutional space with other "social undesirables," such as "many types of sex offenders ('pedophiles,' 'molesters,' and 'rapists' among them), mentally ill prisoners, and snitches" (Sumner and Sexton 2015, 30). Often, transgender women are presumed to be homosexuals and held in contempt by their nontransgender counterparts and correctional staff alike (Donaldson 1993; Jenness 2010; Sumner and Sexton 2015).

Moreover, transgender women are spoken of in disparaging terms by fellow inmates. Sumner and Sexton (2015) report the following remarks by male prisoners in a focus group in response to the question, "How do you think transgender prisoners should be treated?" One person said, "Like somebody with a mental disease"; another said, "Personally, I think [we should] open a big old oven and burn them"; and another said, "That's between them and God. I got my own stuff to worry [about]" (Sumner and Sexton 2015, 30). Other prisoners reported wanting staff to "keep them away from us" and "expose them" so other prisoners can know who they are and act accordingly (Sumner and Sexton 2015, 32). In the same study, staff commented, "If you have a penis, *it's* some kind of homosexual." Such homophobic reactions were amplified in a prison environment (Sumner and Sexton 2015, 25). The cultural milieu in which transgender inmates live is not lost on them, either. As they acknowledged, they are "discriminated against—not only by the staff but by inmates who don't understand our lifestyle," "looked down upon," and "mistreated" (Sumner and Sexton 2015, 30).

Revisiting Agnes in Prison: Gender, Embodiment, and Institutional Context

As a kind of theoretical trope, we revisited the famous case of Agnes (Jenness and Fenstermaker 2014), first reported by Harold Garfinkel (1967) and later referenced by West and Zimmerman (1987), to fundamentally reframe sociology's understanding of how gender operates in social life. Agnes came to a University of California, Los Angeles (UCLA), neuropsychiatric clinic in the mid-1960s to seek approval as an intersex and a warrant for the surgical "correction" of the "mistake" that was her penis (Garfinkel 1967). Agnes sought to convince Garfinkel and the clinic doctors that despite her penis, she was a "normal, natural" woman deserving of surgical attention, and that her "inner" female was adequately reflected in her identity, outward appearance, and demeanor. For us, imagining Agnes in a prison context—referred to as a transsexual by UCLA experts in the 1960s and who would be designated a "transgender" by prison officials in the modern era—further illuminates the question of the relationship between gender and sex category under two crucial conditions: (1) that by virtue of their presence in a men's prison, all transgender women were understood to be biologically male, and (2) that gender had to be accomplished under the condition of what Connell (2012) calls "contradictory embodiment" (i.e., disparity between the gendered presentation of self and the known "facts" of sex category). Thus, we asked, how does gender accountability work under these circumstances?

The original Agnes's fundamental task was to convince the medical doctors and other experts at UCLA, including Garfinkel, to conclude from her presentation of self as a woman that she was indeed a female (Garfinkel 1967). When Agnes and her counterparts go to prison, however, the task is much more complicated. With only the very rare exception, transgender women's sex assigned at birth dictates that they serve time in prisons for men.[6] As they manage the apparent contradiction between sexed body and gendered intention, the argument that they are female is rendered extremely problematic. Drawing on an original data set, as described in detail in Jenness (2010), we examined what happens when "Agnes Goes to Prison" and, in particular, what this reveals about the daily workings of gender.

To understand the dynamics that undergird Agnes as "a girl among men" in a prison for men, we described how transgender women present a feminine self as they seek to secure the judgment of others as "natural" females. Specifically, they engage in a set of activities that together constitute what we refer to as a pursuit of gender authenticity, or what they call "the real deal." These activities begin with an orientation to sex category through an acknowledgment that inmates in prisons for men are institutionally and interactionally understood to be male. To use the terms of transgender women in prisons for men, they are "clocked" (i.e., immediately defined as males) while they themselves understand that they are not "biologics" (i.e., ciswomen).[7] Nonetheless, transgender women in men's prisons express a desire to secure standing as a "real girl" or "the best girl" possible in a men's prison. This desire translates into expressions of situated gendered practices that embrace male dominance, heteronormativity, classed and raced gender ideals, and a daily acceptance of inequality in the context of the constant pursuit of respect and affirmation as women. (For extended discussion, see Jenness and Fenstermaker 2014.)

The analysis presented in "Agnes Goes to Prison" illustrates that whatever femininity is embraced, undertaken, and presented by transgender women in prisons for men, it is accountability to a putative sex category that is sought; if through the accomplishment of gender in this setting one can appear to embody the imagined biologic "real deal," then one is close enough—and good enough—to be deserving of some privilege and respect. As we argued in the conclusion, "The prison environment sets the stage both for embodiment to be understood as unforgiving *and* eminently *deniable*. Through the pursuit of the "real deal," however, gender expectations remain and demand that the transgender prisoner's behavior reflect an inherent femininity—"*as if* one were really and truly female" (Jenness and Fenstermaker 2014, 18). This dynamic is key to understanding the exceptionally high rate of the rape of transgender women as part of the routine practice of "the rape of the feminine."

The Rape of the Feminine

"Fight or fuck" is a refrain expressed by transgender women prisoners. It serves as a short-hand acknowledgment of the difficult circumstances in which they find themselves. For them, to "fight or fuck" is easily seen as a "secondary adjustment" to prison life. The structure and operation of gender in prison life requires them to manage a uniquely predatory environment designed to deprive them of liberty and, as a collateral consequence, incite fear and rob them of safety.[8]

Understood this way, it is unfortunate how little we know about the ways in which "the men" orient to and engage with "the girls among men" in prisons for men. Future research should focus on these prisoners—"the real men"—as the inmate population from which prison rapists are drawn.[9] What we do know is that "the real men" in prisons for men have a complicated gendered relationship to transgender women inmates. In a particularly telling exchange, Jenness reports interviewing an inmate who said he was a forty-nine-year-old drug dealer from another state, a large, African American, bald, muscular man who kept calling her "Miss Val." he explained to her that he is not gay, that he is "100 percent real man. The real deal." When she asked him about transgender inmates in the prison in which he was confined, he said, "They are what they are. Some of them are taboo. You don't mess with them. Some of them are okay." Thereafter, the following exchange occurred:

JENNESS: Who is taboo?
PRISONER: The ones with AIDS. The ones who sleep around and spread diseases. Those are the ones you need to stay away from. They are dirty.

Jenness then asked him how transgender inmates were thought of by other inmates, and he said, "Some guys are weak. They can't hold their own in here. There's no women and it gets old using your hand to get off. Oh, I'm sorry; sorry about my language."

JENNESS: No, please, explain it to me in whatever language makes sense to you and will help me understand.
PRISONER: Okay, you're locked up, you have no women, you get tired of using your hand, so you dump in them. They are like a dumping ground. You just dump your load in them. But, we know they are men. You have to act like they are women, but we know they are men. C'mon, man, they have what men have. Still, you can dump your stuff in her.
JENNESS: Why would she let you do that?
PRISONER: Hey, I didn't say I do it! I'm not weak. But, they want what women want: security, protection, comfort, companionship, someone to be nice to them and take care of them. But, also, some just want the sex. Some really like it. Others just do it to get what women want. They are not all the same. Ask *them* why they do it.
JENNESS: Are they good for anything other than sex?
PRISONER: Yeah, some guys like to talk with them and use them to, you know, keep the cell clean, wash their clothes, iron, sew, cook, you know, all the shit women do. I've done that, too. I mean, I don't want to do that shit. And, like I said, some of them do it because they like it—it makes them feel like women. But, others do it just to get what women want: men, protection, comfort, companionship, someone to talk to, you know. I guess, really, it's like on the outside. But, like I said, we know they are men. We don't get fooled in that way. But, we've got to talk to her like a woman because that's what she wants. (quoted more fully in Fenstermaker and Jones 2011, 154–55)

This exchange speaks volumes about the dynamics underlying prison assault and rape: an environment of deprivation, a practice of disdain toward the feminine (as visibly embodied by transgender women prisoners), and a preoccupation with gendered behavior. Perhaps most pertinent for this essay, and as detailed in "Agnes Goes to Prison" (Jenness and Fenstermaker 2014), is the collective collusion within the prison to render transgender inmates as "intelligible," or accountably, female. This collusion is undertaken in the context described succinctly by Oparah (2012) in her law review article "Feminism and the (Trans) Gender Entrapment of Gender Non-Conforming Prisoners": "Transgender women are forcibly placed in a location where they are likely to experience horrific sexual violence precisely because of their male genitalia, and where they are victimized because their female characteristics do not match their sex assignment as male" (Oparah 2012, 269).

These observations are especially provocative in light of a surprising finding developed elsewhere: transgender women in prisons for men report perceiving themselves as *more* feminine after being incarcerated than before being incarcerated, despite not having access to many of the accoutrements of femininity while in prison (e.g., cosmetics, clothing, etc.) (Jenness 2015). This suggests that prisons for men provide an environment whereby, in seeking out expressions of femininity to be a "girl among men," they experience enhanced feelings of femininity (2015). They do so even though they describe situations in which they, unfortunately, had to "man up," "put on my shoes," and "put down my purse and fight," and they report an awareness that "the men" call them "cum buckets." As one transgender woman in prison explained after describing being routinely raped by her in-prison husband: "It was awful, but when he did it, I did feel like his wife." This quote is particularly telling in a context in which transgender women also report desiring the status of wife—a status that affirms their identity and behavior as women—and in which the relationship between transgender women in prison who survive sexual assault and their assailants skews toward familiarity (see Table 14.2). Sumner and Sexton (2015, 34) reported on their research in Pennsylvania: "Numerous transgender respondents recounted tales with their boyfriends or husbands that ended in physical violence. One particular respondent explained that 'when you tell someone no, there is violence.'"

Although gendered violence, including rape and other forms of sexual assault, in interpersonal relationships is certainly not new, we may be entering a new era of important reconsideration of how we treat those who are incarcerated, including transgender inmates, as they experience such violence. For example, in January 2015, Barack Obama was heralded as the first US president publicly to utter the word "transgender."[10] Shortly thereafter, in July 2015, he marshalled considerable press coverage for saying, simply, "We should not be tolerating rape in prison and we should not be making jokes about it in our popular culture,"[11] and for being the first US president to tour a prison to promote criminal justice reforms.[12]

Forty years ago, Susan Brownmiller referred to rapists as "the shock troops of the Patriarchy." Such an idea may seem too extreme in these days of multiple "feminisms," "grrrlpower," "ho's," and "bitches." We would argue otherwise; after all, the cultural practices she identified then are exhibited still, from prisons to prep schools. The environment of the men's prison—so obviously different from the world in which most men and women reside—can nevertheless teach us lessons about the cultures and climates that promote rape. The tyranny of the sex categorical binary—male or female—brings with it often rigid expectations of accountable femininity and masculinity, including a presumption of heteronormativity. Such expectations, and the consequences that violation brings, is an ever-present reminder of what constitutes "appropriate" behavior. Thus, as in the world outside the prison, and depending upon the situation, sexual assault and sexual coercion can be made intelligible to all concerned by reaffirming the feminine as weak, vulnerable, and deserving of being demeaned and overpowered. Likewise, the masculine demands distance from and derogation of the feminine and draws its power from such behavior.

Understanding rape and sexual violence in this way places us all in the same dynamic of accountability that the Agnesses confront: How does everyday behavior get seen not only as appropriately masculine or feminine but convincing "enough" to convey an inner and essential male or female, or, as Judith Butler (2004) referred to it, a "personhood"? The question we must continually pose is how we may free ourselves not from expressing our gendered selves but from the tyranny of the binary. Where can we find the liminal places where the binary is even temporarily destabilized, where the "essential" male *or* female is momentarily "queered"? However unlikely their unique embrace of the feminine—set loose from the constraints of "biologics"—our imagined Agnes and her incarcerated sisters, surprisingly, may point the way to a social world that while gendered, is less dangerous for women.

NOTES

1 The Google Ngram View charts the frequency with which any word or short sentence appears in published books in American English, British English, and six other languages.

2 Signed into law by President George W. Bush on September 4, 2003, the Prison Rape Elimination Act (PREA) has many objectives. Its overall purpose is "to provide for the analysis of the incidence and effects of prison rape in Federal, State, and local institutions and to provide information, resources, recommendations, and funding to protect individuals from prison rape" (Public Law 108–79, 117). In only two months, the PREA passed through both the House of Representatives and the Senate unanimously and with surprisingly little discussion and no contestation. (For more on the history, content, and consequences of the PREA, see Jenness and Smyth 2011.)

3 California is home to one of the largest correctional systems in the Western world (Petersilia 2008). Well over 90 percent of California state prisoners are housed in thirty prisons for adult men. Among these prisoners, there are more than three hundred transgender inmates in prisons for men (Jenness, Sexton, and Sumner 2011). Assuming Brown and McDuffie's (2009) estimate that there are approximately 750 transgender prisoners in the US is correct, California is home to nearly half of all transgender prisoners in the US.

4 For Sykes (1958) and decades of prison researchers following him, the pains of imprisonment are born of the deprivation of liberty, the deprivation of goods and services of choice, the imposition of a rule-bound regime, and other universal characteristics of carceral environments.

5   For a detailed description of protective pairing, see "Hooking Up: Protective Pairing for Punks," an open letter by Stephen Donaldson, a prison rape survivor and LGBT advocate (Stephen Donaldson, "Hooking Up: Protective Pairing for Punks," Just Detention International. Retrieved from www.justdetention.org).

6   As Sumner and Jenness (2014) explain in their assessment of transgender correctional policies, when processing people through the criminal justice system, the first determination—whether to send the person to a men's or a women's jail or prison—is made via a "genitalia-based" approach rather than an "identity-based" approach. Taken-for-granted housing assignments based on anatomy are often justified as a means to an end, with the end being safety and security.

7   Transgender women in prison often use the word "clocked" to indicate that their ability to pass as women is effectively denied in a prison built for and inhabited exclusively by males. The use of the word "biologic" acknowledges biological differences between themselves and other "real women."

8   Transgender prisoners inhabit an environment where they—just as with other prisoners—must often defend themselves. As a transgender woman explained it: "People do what they have to do to take care of themselves. The difference with us is, well, violence is ugly. We don't want to be violent. We want to be beautiful. We're on hormones, girl. But hit me or disrespect me and I'll knock you out. I will. You would knock someone out too. You'd be surprised what you would do if you had to; you just haven't had to—have you?"

9   Of course, sexual violence against transgender women in prisons is not limited to prisoner-on-prisoner assaults; it also includes staff-on-prisoner assaults.

10 See Katy Steinmetz, "Why It's a Big Deal That Obama Said 'Transgender,'" January 21, 2015, *Time Magazine*. Retrieved from http://time.com.

11 On July 14, 2015, President Obama said these words in Philadelphia, Pennsylvania, in a wide-ranging speech on criminal justice reform delivered before the National Association for the Advancement of Colored People.

12 On July 16, 2015, President Obama toured El Reno, a medium-security prison with a minimum-security satellite camp in Oklahoma to promote criminal justice reform. See David Jackson and Susan Davis, "Obama visits prison to promote criminal justice plans." July 16, 2015. *USA Today*. Retrieved from www.usatoday.com.

15

Consent

LINDA MARTÍN ALCOFF

Consent is the central concept employed by most legal systems today as a way to demarcate legitimate from illegitimate sex, and in this legal realm consent is given a technical definition. However, it is not simply a legal term but also the central concept used in ordinary language to identify rape, assault, and abuse. We need to consider the real-world utility and effects of using consent as the definitive criterion, though these may vary in different locations and contexts. But I am also interested in the ideas about sex and about sexual relationships that are contained in operative meanings of the term as it is used in courts as well as in everyday speech. What does the contemporary reliance on the concept of consent reveal about our understandings of sex and of sexual violation?

As Estelle Freedman (2013) recounts in her history of rape in the US, consent did not always play the central role. Rather, in the nineteenth and early twentieth centuries, the concept of "seduction" had primacy in establishing the right to legal redress, and it effectively set aside the question of consent. Seduction, which was applied generally only to White women, essentially meant breach of promise. Seduction laws were meant to address the problem of manipulation in such cases as when a man promised to marry in order to procure sex but then reneged. Women's consent in such cases was based on an "understanding," resulting from either explicit or implicit promises, that legal marriage would follow sex. Seduction could also be used in cases where a man drugged a woman's drink or otherwise engaged in a more physical coercion, so, in practice, seduction laws were used in cases that ran the gamut from deceit to force.

We may smugly imagine such Victorian ideas as seduction and breach of promise to be far inferior to our own enlightened age, and based simply on Christian antisex attitudes, but the reality is more complex. Seduction laws helped to redress the economic difficulties of women left pregnant by men who had abandoned them. During this period, pregnant women could be legally fired and discriminated against in the hiring process, so abandonment was generally catastrophic. Also interesting is the fact that the concern with seduction and breach of promise defined the problem in terms of male words and actions rather than female chasteness or virginity, effectively putting the onus on men to explain why marriage had not occurred after sexual relations. In effect, any sexual relations between unmarried partners placed men under threat of a possible charge of seduction, which factored into some men's agitation to overturn these laws (Freedman 2013, 45). Seduction laws were important checks on male power.

However, as Freedman argues, seduction laws also "bolstered patriarchal authority and retained the centrality of marriage as woman's vocation" (2013, 38). Men convicted under these laws could avoid going to prison or paying fines (often to be paid to fathers) by marrying their victims. Such coerced marriages did not guarantee support: some men married to avoid punishment and then still abandoned their pregnant wives. Hence, seduction laws did not always protect women, and feminists were able to gather wide support for their replacement. The feminist effort to switch to a focus on consent was a liberal reform that would recognize women's interest in sexual autonomy, and not simply in fair, economic transactions for the use of their body.

Seductions sometimes occurred in situations that involved the same sort of rape-avoidance strategies Gavey documents: women acquiesced to pressure simply in order to avoid a violent rape or a beating or to avoid losing their livelihood (Freedman 2013, 42–43). In these cases, establishing consent did not help to redress the gender norms of heterosexual coercion or to discern either her sexual desire or her will.

As Carole Pateman and others have argued, consent is a concept imported from a liberal contract model of social relations with problematic baggage when applied to the issue of sex (Pateman 1980; Baker 1997; Cahill 2001). Contracts involve transactions or promises: for example, the promise to deliver a service or goods. Contracts also have a temporal dimension, ranging over a time frame beyond the actual moment of communication. To consent to sex can then be understood as a commitment to perform an act or deliver a good, in this case a service, either now or at some future point. However, in relation to sex, I can commit to perform, but I cannot commit to sustain a desire or a mood. Commitments cannot promise desire. Contractual approaches to sex can thus involve a consent to alienation, an alienation from one's body, feelings, and preferences. Furthermore, as Cahill (2001) points out, this can confer on the person who receives the consent the dangerous idea that they are "owed" sex, and that they have been wronged if it was not "delivered." Such ideas have a long history; resonating with the sorts of transactional practices Balzac describes.

Former sex worker Rachel Moran (2013) also argues that consent ignores the constrained options within which choices are too often actually made. For Moran and many of the women she worked with over several years, the choice to do sex work was a forced choice between homelessness, being unable to support their children, perpetual familial or partner abuse, or "willingly" performing sex work. As Jeffrey Gauthier puts it, "when an oppressive system effectively defines the choice situation of the oppressed class," rarely can our choices result in liberation (1999, 85). Women are generally analogous to workers under conditions of capitalism, Gauthier argues; that is, they are generally forced to bargain within unfavorable conditions.

Moran cites a study of prostitutes in Dublin in which

> twenty-nine out of thirty prostituted women stated that they "would accept an alternative job with equal pay." The authors of this study noted that the single interviewee who did not agree with that statement appeared to be under the influence of some substance at the time of the interview. That sounds about right to me, given everything I've seen in prostitution. The survival strategies of defiance and denial were most commonly practised by those who were so injured by prostitution as to have to block out their reality with alcohol and other mindaltering drugs, and I certainly remember my younger self among them. (Moran 2013, 175)

Whether or not all sex workers would prefer another form of employment, the relevant point here is that a focus on consent conceals what should be the real issue of concern. Whether consent occurs in the context of limited economic options or emotional pressure, it is separable from desire and can be manipulated under all too common conditions of constraint. By maintaining a *singular* focus on consent, we can actually make it more difficult to discern sexual violations.

As both Pateman and Cahill discuss, normative heterosexual sex even outside of explicit transactional relations assumes men ask and women answer, giving or withholding their consent. "[I]n the relationship between the sexes, it is always women who are held to consent to men. The 'naturally' superior, active, and sexually aggressive male makes an initiative, or offers a contract, to which a 'naturally' subordinate, passive woman 'consents'" (Pateman 1980, 164; quoted in Cahill 2001, 174). If men are approvingly assumed to be the active parties, normative feminine comportment involves receptivity. Hence there continue to exist a litany of derogatory terms and pathologizing theories about women who resist or hold out or "tease," and this itself can pressure women who want to be viewed as accommodating to the needs of others, that is, as caring (Gavey 2005). I often recount in my feminist philosophy classes an incident at a nightclub when I was out with a couple of girlfriends years ago. A man asked us, one by one, to dance, and we each politely declined, with a smile, explaining that we were there just to hang out with our friends. Hours later when we left we found the same guy in the parking lot, watching us and shouting at the top of his voice "BitchCuntDyke!" as if this were one word. The intensity of the response took us quite by surprise; it seemed so totally inappropriate. Many of my female students have similar stories. A courteous decline is sometimes all that is necessary to lose one's status as a normative feminine subject.

In such contexts even an affirmative consent can become equivalent to the "oh, all right" response: a resignation motivated to avoid a hassle, unaccompanied by sexual desire or will. The concept of consent thus provides a low bar for sexual agency. For these sorts of reasons, Pateman holds that "An egalitarian sexual relationship cannot rest on this basis; it cannot be grounded in consent" (1980, 164). Cahill helpfully explains that this is "because consent is not itself ungendered" (2001, 175). Our ubiquitous reliance on *women's* consent as the dependable criterion of blameless sex is in fact a symptom of our problematic gender norms: the exclusive focus on whether the woman consented or not fails to challenge conventions in which males ask and females answer, and in this way helps to secure this scenario as normative.

Consent is also problematic because its contractual implications are phenomenologically unsuited to the domain of sexuality, for reasons I just gestured at above. As a contract or promise, consent ranges over a specified time frame, but a verbal consent cannot ensure that my state of arousal or desire will continue unabated over the contracted period. Sexual feelings are not subject to this degree of predictability, control, or constancy. This is why some colleges have followed what has come to be called the Antioch model, which has an ongoing affirmative (or stated) consent requirement for each micro-step of the encounter, a requirement readily lampooned by comedians (Culp-Ressler 2014).

The etymological origin of the word "consent," however, means a "feeling with" or a "feeling together." While asking repeatedly for consent in the midst of sex does suggest comedy, the requirement is attempting to ensure that the sex involves something like just this interactive, *intersubjective* engagement, in which each partner stays attuned to the emotional states and experiences of the other(s). In reality, this kind of intersubjective attunement is not that difficult to accomplish, especially in intimate encounters in which all five senses may be enlivened. Knowing something about the state of your partner does not actually necessitate verbal assurances, though perceptive attunement to others' emotional condition needs to be learned, and there are typical gender-related gaps in who develops this skill. Any person's judgment of their partner's emotional state may well be fallible, however, and thus mistaken, in the absence of verbal communication. The idea that "consent" aims for a "feeling with" gives quite a different connotation than the association of consent with contracts, and brings it closer to the concept of "mutuality" that legal theorist Martha Chamallas (1988) argues would be a better approach to norming sex than contractual consent.

Lois Pineau argues that the Antioch model of affirmative consent has a legitimate but restricted utility, since its real intent, she suggests, is to regulate the real and sometimes nonideal world of casual college sex in which partners do not know each other very well. Pineau suggests that lovers in more substantial relationships could be exempt from the step-by-step requirement. But she also develops a model of communicative sexual practice that would be "more ongoing, more tentative more reversible than the one-shot affair [of consent] envisioned on the forceful-seduction model of sexuality" (Pineau 1996, 68).

Despite decades of such debates and explorations into the complexities and deficiencies of consent, it has remained the familiar, ready-to-hand implement in the arena of rape legislation and standard definitions. The question is why. One reason is because Western societies have limited conceptual repertoires in dealing with structural and group-related injustice, and hence usually emphasize only those harms that involve individual rights and contractual obligations between specifiable parties. It would seem that every political demand, whether for healthcare or a fair wage, has to be formulated in these sorts of terms—as a right, and as a right of individuals—rather than as a redress to structural injustice or the endangerment of communal values such as reciprocity and cooperation. The pragmatic advantage of making use of familiar conceptual approaches is clear, but we also need to reach beyond the present and consider how to make some conceptual progress in how we understand the workings of injustice and oppression.

Consent certainly has utility as a familiar conceptual tool for liberal Western societies, which some may take as overriding its phenomenological inadequacy. Yet it is important to acknowledge the ways in which consent can work against victims by placing the burden of proof in their court, so to speak, as well as implicitly reinforcing retrograde gender norms. Where, as we saw, seduction put the onus on men, consent has come to put the onus on women, who are usually the hermeneutically weaker party, subject to skepticism about their truthfulness, capacity for objectivity, and rationality. And consent can create the illusion of an obligation on the part of the one who gives it and an unbridled license on the part of the one who receives it.

Most importantly, the exclusive reliance on consent diverts our attention from the background structural conditions that may overdetermine its appearance. So, it is far from a panacea. Thinking beyond consent will require pushing back against the presumed hegemony of the legal domain to be the exclusive or privileged sphere of justice. The law in this domain, as it is currently constructed, operates to establish individual culpability; for this, consent is useful, but it puts serious limits on how we construe the ultimate nature of the problem or its solutions. We need to go beyond what currently configured courts may be able to work with, or prevailing discourses may be able to make plausible, in order to understand and remedy the epidemic of sexual violence in our societies.

Certainly, the story of our reliance on consent is more than a holdover of liberal ideology. There is a kernel of truth in the focus on consent, as Freedman's history recounts, by moving away from the question of transactions—in which fathers or families may be identified as the injured party—to the question of the victimized, which is in most cases a question about a particular woman. How was she disposed toward the encounter? Was there a willing, a turning toward, an intention?

Intimate Partner Violence

The gendered system that values the violent and controlling behavior of men while devaluing its victims permeates our lives. Controlled violence is endemic in sports, and the worlds of business and politics are rife with examples of extreme power and authority. These characteristics, often held up as a paragon for emulation and admired in one circumstance, spill over into the routine interactions of men and women in the realm of their private lives. Of course, sometimes violence is not so controlled—as witnessed in the many accounts that have come to light from the #MeToo movement.

A Legacy of Abuse

Public concern and official response to intimate partner violence (IPV) have been muted for much of human history. Historically, women were subject to the authority of men, who had the explicit support of the Church to correct women's behavior through punishment (see Ross, this volume). The legacy of medieval law, which permitted the authorized abuse of women, continued through the eighteenth-century Napoleonic Code, which in turn influenced the law in much of Europe. Such laws assured that men had absolute family power, including the use of violence against family members up to the point of killing (Davidson 1978).

In the mid-1600s in colonial Massachusetts, the Puritans "enacted the first laws anywhere in the world against wife beating" (Pleck 1989, 20), based on the belief that family violence was a sin. Neighbors were expected to be watchful of each other's behavior and to interfere when necessary. There were, of course, limits to the Puritans' vigilance, and records from that era include numerous cases of severe violence against wives (Pleck 1987; Eldridge 1997).

Urbanization and its attendant close living quarters made acts of violence against wives widely visible in nineteenth-century England. Police records from that era indicate that wife abuse was very common, with insubordinate and nonsubmissive behavior frequently cited as cause by the abusers (Tomes 1978). In his 1869 essay "The Subjection of Women," John Stuart Mill addressed the plight of battered women in England. His concern for wives "against whom [a husband] can commit any atrocity except killing her, and, if tolerably cautious, can do that without much danger of the legal penalty" (Mill 1988, 57) helped to mobilize efforts to rewrite English law.

In the mid-1800s in the US, the "ideal of an anger-free family" developed in close association with industrialization (Stearns and Stearns 1986, 11). The new standards for family behavior focused on the family and home as a refuge from the outer world of work and strife. By that time it appears that men who abused their wives may have been "more restrained in their violence" (Pleck 1989, 100) and that fewer men were abusive. Perhaps this resulted from changing views of the paternalistic responsibilities of men toward women.

A Movement for Change

Motivated by the second wave of the women's movement, the first refuge for abused women, Chiswick Women's Aid, opened in England in 1972. Provided with an alternative to staying at home with a violent spouse, local women overwhelmed the facility. The first shelter for abused women in the US opened in Minnesota in 1974 (Dobash and Dobash 1992). Today such shelters exist in most communities in the US, and they are increasing worldwide.

Advocates working with victims of IPV soon realized that lasting change in social conditions would not occur without increased public education and legislative action. Beginning in the mid-1970s, legislation in Great Britain and the US provided legal remedies and program funding for abused women (Dobash and Dobash 1987). Although women have no doubt benefited from the increase in resources provided by such legislation, one troubling result of relying on governmental institutions for financial and legal resources is "the state's role in reproducing relations of dominance and subordination" (Shepard and Pence 1999, 8). These are the very same institutions that form the underpinnings of intimate violence and that maintain the social inequities that support abuse (ibid., 10). This can be seen in recent developments in the US. Under the Obama administration, the Department of Justice operated under a broad definition of intimate violence, one that included nonphysical behaviors such as stalking and coercive control. This definition was severely curtailed by Donald Trump to only include prosecutable criminal offenses.

By the beginning of the twenty-first century, activists and scholars recognized that not all women experience intimate violence the same way. Initial claims that intimate partner violence occurs among all demographic groups were intended to avoid harmful categorization of some people (generally racial and ethnic minorities) as naturally violent and others as passive victims. What "began as an attempt to avoid stereotyping and stigma" (Richie 2005, 53) has led to a "false sense of unity" (ibid., 52) that masks the raced and classed nature of gender violence as experienced by women of color and poor women. As we continue to grapple with the "complex association between demographic and cultural factors" (West 2005, 170) that contribute to intimate violence, we must "remain self-conscious" so as not to collude in silencing the voices of abused women of color (Knadler 2004, 2).

Spurred on primarily by activism and writing produced by women in marginalized positions, scholars of IPV have begun to understand that "every culture has tenets that disenfranchise women, as well as empower them" (Dasgupta 2005, 67). Ignoring the particularities of marginalized women's stories prevents our understanding of "marginalized men as simultaneously being victimized by the state AND victimizing women" (Lawrence 1996, 25, original emphasis).

Contemporary theorists rightly point out that IPV has changed from a problem situated in heterosexual relationships where roles are strictly cast as male perpetrator and female victims. Several authors (Yerke & Defeo 2016; Calton, Henry, Coston, and Perrin 2018) highlight the severity of IPV in the LGBTQ+ community, with special attention paid to the transgender community and the specific coercive behaviors experienced by nonbinary victims.

Addressing the Problem of Intimate Partner Violence

Legal reform has focused primarily on increasing the criminalization of intimate partner violence (Pleck 1989; Zimring 1989). Because family privacy serves as a rationale to avoid criminalizing intimate partner violence, the effort to expand criminal law to include responses to wife abuse is an uphill struggle against a history of a narrow jurisprudence that proposes to intervene in families only in cases of "the taking of life, parental incest, and the imminent threat to the life or health of a minor child" (Zimring 1989, 552).

Worldwide reports reveal that alone, legal responses to intimate partner violence are ineffective. In the US, many states have enacted mandatory arrest and prosecution policies, meaning that if a police officer responds to an incident and believes that probable cause exists to indicate a domestic assault, the officer must arrest the perpetrator. In most states, following arrest and adjudication, perpetrators are then court-ordered into psychoeducational groups that are not led by clinically trained facilitators. Without an effective combination of clinical intervention and public policies, offender treatment groups function for a bureaucratic purpose, not a clinical one, thus creating a revolving door for domestic violence perpetrators, without significant psychological or attitudinal changes of group members (Sullivan and Claes 2013).

Efforts to change police and court procedures undertaken in locales around the world have met with some success. Due to the tremendous mobilization of the Brazilian women's movement, for example, separate police stations staffed by women are dedicated to addressing crimes of violence against women (Thomas 1994). In 1991, Brazil's highest court of appeal overturned a lower court's acceptance of the traditional "honor defense," which permitted a man to kill his wife if she had committed adultery. In Egypt, pro-womanist groups successfully lobbied for changes in interpretations of shari'a to permit women to work in the criminal justice system (Ammar 2000).

Although three approaches have emerged to address violence within intimate relationships—legal, therapeutic, and restorative justice (see Miller and Iovanni 2007)—it is the legal system that predominates. Given the focus on the criminal justice approach, and its inherent problems, efforts to evaluate how it is used to address intimate violence must be a priority. As Stubbs points out, "social and cultural dimensions . . . give meaning to the violence" (2002, 44), and the criminal justice system provides an imperfect method for assessing that meaning and addressing it.

Intersectionality and Intimate Partner Violence

According to feminist analysts, patriarchal power relations produce gender ideologies and cultural conditions that create and sustain intimate partner violence in heterosexual relationships. Combined with the cultural advocacy of violence as an effective and desirable interpersonal dynamic, these power structures produce what Ewing refers to as the "civic advocacy of [male] violence" (1982, 5). Stubbs asserts that "intimate partner violence . . . arises through strategies that attempt to implement gender ideologies" (2002, 43, citing Ptacek 1999).

The abuse of female intimates is made possible by the structural support of systems that maintain and reproduce male dominance and female submission (Radford 1987). According to this theory, the state, through its treatment of victims, is complicit in reinforcing passive acquiescence and conformity to narrow gender roles (Edwards 1987). Beliefs in the sanctity of the idealized family, which protect it from public scrutiny, serve to permit the abuses of women by men to whom they are tied by familial relationships. Anderson and Umberson note that heterosexual male offenders "construct masculine identities through the practice of violence" and that "the practice of domestic violence helps men to accomplish gender" (2001, 359–60).

As the former codirector of Emerge, the first program specifically created for abusive men in the US, Bancroft (2002) studied the tactics and manipulations of violent male partners. His research dismantled the many myths that victims and professionals hold about IPV, and described interpersonally violent men as overwhelmingly entitled and in complete control of their behaviors, subverting the belief that they act out of "passion."

The social institutions to which women turn for assistance have often been insensitive, resistant, and hostile. For members of minority communities in the US, the responses of helping agencies are complicated by racism; thus, for abused women of color, the criminal approach to intimate partner violence presents a dilemma. Because police have not historically been perceived as the allies of minority communities, it is difficult for many women of color to depend on them for assistance (Miller 1993).

Campbell and Mannell (2016) explored the sociological and historical factors that exacerbate the plight of ethnic minority women, and the racial and cultural barriers to receiving assistance. In their research, they evaluate the concept of individual agency and IPV victimization. They discuss that many victims of IPV have informal networks of support available to them, and that the specifics of those supports are culturally and ethnically embedded. While cultural factors such as gender roles, experience of racism, language barriers, and immigration status may impede access to official services, other elements of ethnicity and culture may assist victims of IPV. Access to extended family, friendship patterns, religious communities, and intergenerational connections help victims as they make safety plans and evaluate possible actions to take.

In Native American communities, extreme poverty, joblessness, rural isolation, and alcohol abuse may contribute to high rates of intimate violence, especially when understood within the frame of cultural decimation (Bachman 1992; Campbell and Mannell 2016). Like African American men, violent Native American men may have internalized the "qualities ascribed to them for centuries by the society around them" (Gunn Allen 1986). In this context, IPV is influenced by colonization and the erasure of more egalitarian social structures that existed in some tribes in favor of the patriarchal hierarchy promoted by missionary colonists. In her study on a reservation, Matamonasa-Bennett supports the influence of colonization on social structures and highlights the role of alcohol in IPV. Traditionalist Native Americans see these factors as "[d]isease[s] of the outside people" (2015, 1). Matamonasa-Bennett's research supported earlier findings that IPV, addictions, and a host of other social problems were rare in precontact societies.

Asian women in the US, particularly recent immigrants, face tremendous barriers to legal remedies for IPV. Traditional values of family loyalty and honor combined with beliefs that women's status is secondary to men's may promote interpersonal violence and prevent women from seeking help. Problems of reporting to official institutions include language barriers, isolation, fear of deportation (compounded for those with illegal immigrant status), and the cultural insensitivity of some service providers (Lai 1986). Wang and Chang (2014), replicated these findings while adding that the level of acculturation to western culture can increase risk or provide protection. Wang and Chang noted the dearth of research on IPV in the Asian American community, and the role of Asian "myths" (e.g., high academic and professional achievement) as damaging to help-seeking. They also warn that, as is the case with other ethnic groups, collapsing multiple Asian ethnicities under one umbrella, runs the risk of obscuring a collection of unique and diverse cultures with a singular term like "Asian American."

Latina and Hispanic women represent a diverse group that encompasses a variety of ancestral lands, skin colors, religious beliefs, and socioeconomic classes. Valid statistical information on IPV in the Hispanic and Latinx communities is sparse due in large part to cultural barriers that prevent access to services. For example, sharing explicit information and the intrusive questioning of police and counselors may be experienced as highly inappropriate. All of these issues are complicated by a dearth of services for those who are not fully comfortable communicating in English and who fear accessing services because they are immigrants who do not have full legal status (see Hass, Dutton, and Orloff 2000; Campbell 2016). Valdovinos (this volume) offers an expanded discussion about the intersubjective experience of undocumented victims of intimate partner violence, situating her chapter to reflect the unique struggles of this population in the increasingly hostile immigration environment created after the 2016 election. Recent findings that show fewer Hispanic women report IPV are attributed to fears of deportation.

Lesbians and gay men who experience IPV also face issues of prejudice and a lack of appropriate services. Cannon and Buttell (2015) examine the negative effects of heteronormative assumptions by service providers on LGBTQ+ victims. Their findings indicate that shelters are often inappropriate for lesbians and virtually nonexistent for gay men and transgender people. Homophobia is so pervasive that many lesbians and gay men never attempt to bring their cases to the criminal justice system. Avoidance by LGBTQ+ victims creates an illusion of invisibility, when in reality, rates of IPV are alarmingly high. Two reports by the Centers for Disease Control (CDC) (2013) and the National Coalition of Anti-Violence Programs (2015) illustrate the severity of the problem. The CDC reported that 44 percent of lesbians reported rape, physical assaults and stalking by intimate partners, people of color comprised more than 50 percent of IPV victims, and 26 percent of gay men experienced rape, physical assaults and stalking by intimate partners. Forty-five percent of victims did not report their assaults to police.

Emerging Global Issues in Intimate Partner Violence

In 2012 the World Health Organization (WHO) released data from a comprehensive survey of IPV conducted in ten countries. In a wide-ranging international study WHO confirms that violence from intimate partners is a significant problem in every country studied.

International research also reveals that the forms IPV takes may be culture and society specific (Davies 1994). For example, in Papua New Guinea, men's violence "prevents or limits women's participation in development" (Bradley 1994, 16). Such programs, which are seen as threats to male authority, may expose women to more violence and may undermine traditional systems that have offered women some protection in the past. Lane's (2003) study of Bangladesh links the likelihood of marital violence to the relative conservatism of communities. In more conservative areas violence was associated with women's increased autonomy, but there is reduced risk for autonomous women in less conservative areas. Unlike the West, where intimate partner violence is hidden due to the silence of victims and the complicity of social institutions, in other parts of the world it is seen as inevitable (Ammar 2000) or "normal and therefore not a problem" (Bradley 1994, 20).

These findings serve as cautionary examples. The imbalance of global and economic power between wealthy and poor nations mirrors and, perhaps, enhances the disparity of power between intimate partners (see Erez and Laster 2000, 8–9). Although the "economic content in violent behavior" is often overlooked, it comes into sharp focus in cases of dowry violence in India where "wife abuse [is] a means of extracting transfers" of money from the wife's family to the husband's (Bloch and Rao 2002, 1029). In this era of massive human migration, we must also be aware that "the intersection of race, gender and international relations situates the immigrant . . . woman in such a way that she has limited prospects for resistance" (Erez and Laster 2000, 10; see Shalhoub-Kevorkian 2000). Although IPV is widespread, responses must acknowledge the specific concerns of the culture in which it takes place. It is also important to recognize that in all societies "social values are dynamic and challenged by the direct and indirect activism of individual women" at the local level (Ammar 2000, 40)—people can, and do, resist.

Gendered Patterns of Homicide

Political upheaval plays a significant role in the safety of women throughout the world. As regimes and democracies fall (or strengthen) and nationalism proliferates, violence directed toward women increases (Anderson-Nathe and Gharabaghi 2017). Even a stable government, however, is no guarantee of safety. Murder rates are highest in regions where there is greatest disparity in wealth. In the US, though considered quite stable relative to many parts of the world, cities that have the greatest gaps between rich and poor also have high murder rates—and they are climbing (United Nations Office on Drugs and Crime 2014).

Across the globe, a significant number of murders are committed against women by "people who are expected to care for them . . . [and] the majority of men are killed by people they may not even know" (United Nations Office on Drugs and Crime 2014, 14). We know that when women are the victims of murder it is often at the hand of intimate partners, however, many nonpartner homicides may also result from a broader understanding of gender violence. Under scrutiny a pattern emerges, consistent worldwide, of male violence against both men and women (ibid., 13). If the one constant worldwide is that most violent actors are male, it is possible that most, if not all, violence stems from gendered structures of power, dominance, and frequently the effects of disempowerment experienced by men of lower social status. Sadly, while homicide rates have declined in countries that report reliable data, intimate partner/family violence rates have remained constant (ibid.).

Effects of Intimate Partner Violence

Current understanding of the range of behaviors that constitute IPV includes slapping, biting, kicking, punching, throwing objects, confining, denying care (food or medication), abuse of pets and property destruction, sexual abuse, stabbing, shooting, choking, burning, threatening, insulting, and degrading (NCADV 2019). Despite greater understanding of the gendered intersectional experience of IPV, research still supports that women are much more likely to be victims of male perpetrated IPV (NCDAV 2019; CDC 2017). A woman is most at risk to kill or be killed when she attempts to report the abuse or leave an abusive relationship (Campbell, Webster & Glass 2009; Sabri, Stockman, Campbell, O'Brien, Campbell, Callwood, Bertrand, Sutton, Hart-Hyndman 2014), and risk of harm to her children increases with separation (Bancroft and Silverman 2002, Sabri et al. 2014). In many cases, violence increases during pregnancy and creates dangerous health problems for the mother and fetus. Pregnant victims of IPV suffer significantly higher medical complications than pregnant women who are not abused (CDC 2017).

Women aged eighteen to twenty-four experience partner violence at higher rates than any other age group (CDC 2017). Subject to tremendous pressure to conform, young women often feel that involvement in a dating relationship is necessary to fit in. Lack of experience negotiating affection and sexual behavior, along with typical adolescent rejection of adult assistance, further complicate the dynamics of abusive dating relationships. Adolescents who experience partner abuse are at increased risk of depression and anxiety. Teenagers who experience IPV are at nearly triple the risk of attempting suicide than nonabused peers (NCADV 2019).

The chapters that follow address societal and personal aspects of IPV. Read together, these works provide a foundation for comprehending the contemporary intransigence of IPV and facilitate a wider understanding of the problem.

SUGGESTIONS FOR FURTHER READING

Guadalupe-Diaz, Xavier. *Transgressed: Intimate Partner Violence in Transgender Lives*, 2019

Renzetti, Claire, Diane Follingstad, and Ann Coker (eds). *Preventing Intimate Partner Violence: Interdisciplinary Perspectives*, 2017

Goodmark, Leigh. *Decriminalizing Domestic Violence: A Balanced Policy Approach to Intimate Partner Violence*, 2018

Koppelman, Susan. *Women in the Trees: U.S. Women's Short Stories About Battering and Resistance, 1839–2000*, 2004

To Judge Faolain, Dead Long Enough

A Summons

Linda McCarriston

Your Honor, when my mother stood
before you, with her routine
domestic plea, after weeks
of waiting for speech to return
to her body, with her homemade
forties hairdo, her face purple still
under pancake, her jaw off just a little,
her *holy of holies* healing,
her breasts wrung, her heart
the bursting heart of someone
snagged among rocks deep
in a sharkpool—no, not "someone,"

but a woman there, snagged
with her babies, *by* them,
in one of hope's pedestrian
brutal turns—when, in the tones
of parlors overlooking the harbor,
you admonished that, for the sake
of the family, the wife
must take the husband back to her bed,
what you willed not to see before you
was a woman risen clean to the surface,
a woman who, with one arm flailing,
held up with the other her actual

burdens of flesh. When you clamped
to her leg the chain of *justice*,
you ferried us back down to *the law*,
the black ice eye, the maw, the mako
that circles the kitchen table nightly.
What did you make of the words
she told you, not to have heard her,
not to have seen her there? Almost-

forgiveable ignorance, you were not
the fist, the boot, or the blade,
but the jaded, corrective ear and eye
at the limits of her world. Now

I will you to see her as she was, to ride
your own words back into light: I call
your spirit home again, divesting you
of robe and bench, the fine white hand
and half-lit Irish eye. Tonight, put on
a body in the trailer down the road
where your father, when he can't
get it up, makes love to your mother
with a rifle. Let your name be
Eva-Mary. Let your hour of birth
be dawn. Let your life be long
and common, and your flesh endure.

16

Domestic Violence

The Intersection of Gender and Control

MICHAEL P. JOHNSON

Does a chapter on domestic violence even belong in a book on gender violence? After all, for over forty years there have been reputable social scientists who have been willing to argue that women are as violent in intimate relationships as are men and that domestic violence has nothing to do with gender. Suzanne Steinmetz's controversial paper on "the battered husband syndrome" started this line of argument with the following conclusion: "An examination of empirical data [from a 1975 general survey] on wives' use of physical violence on their husbands suggests that husband-beating constitutes a sizable proportion of marital violence" (Steinmetz 1977–78, 501). A paper published in December 2005 provides a contemporary example (among many) of the same argument: "[Our] considerations suggest the need for a broadening of perspective in the field of domestic violence away from the view that domestic violence is usually a gender issue involving male perpetrators and female victims" (Fergusson, Horwood, and Ridder 2005, 1116).

Actually, despite forty years of sometimes acrimonious debate, the research evidence does clearly indicate that what we typically think of as domestic violence is primarily male-perpetrated and most definitely a gender issue. However, this conclusion is clear only if one breaks out of the standard assumption that intimate partner violence (IPV) is a unitary phenomenon. Once one makes some basic distinctions among types of intimate partner violence, the confusion that characterizes this literature melts away (Johnson 2005).

The first section of this chapter will demonstrate how attention to distinctions among types of IPV makes sense of ostensibly contradictory data regarding men's and women's violence in intimate relationships. The second section describes the basic structure of the types of IPV that most people associate with the term *domestic violence*, violence that is associated with coercive control, that is, one partner's attempt to take general control over the other. The third section presents a theory of domestic violence that is focused on the relationship between gender and coercive control. The fourth section addresses the role of gender in the type of IPV that does not involve an attempt to take general control over one's partner. The final section of the chapter deals with some of the intervention and policy implications of what we know about these types of IPV and their relationship to gender.

Gender and the Perpetration of Different Types of Intimate Partner Violence

How is it that thirty years of social science research on domestic violence has not produced a definitive answer to the question of whether or not men and women are equally involved in IPV? The reason is that the field has been caught up in a debate about *the* nature of IPV—as if it were a unitary phenomenon. Those who had reason to believe that IPV was perpetrated equally by both men and women cited evidence from large-scale survey research that showed rough gender symmetry in IPV. Those who believed that IPV was perpetrated almost entirely by men against their female partners cited contrary evidence from studies carried out in hospital emergency rooms, police agencies, divorce courts, and women's shelters. And each group argued that the other's evidence was biased. However, *both* groups can be right if (a) there are multiple forms of IPV, (b) some of the types are gender-symmetric and some are not, and (c) general surveys are biased in favor of the gender-symmetric types and agency studies are biased in favor of the asymmetric types. There is considerable evidence that this is in fact the case. There are three major types of IPV they are not equally represented in the different types of samples studied by social scientists, and they differ dramatically in terms of gender asymmetry.

The most important distinctions among types of IPV have to do with the role of coercive control as a context for violence. Two of the three major types of IPV involve general power and control issues. *Intimate terrorism* is an attempt to take general control over one's partner; *violent resistance* is the use of violence in response to such an attempt. *Situational couple violence*, the third type of IPV does not involve an attempt to take general control on the part of either partner.[1]

Although there were always clues to be found in the domestic violence literature of the 1970s and 1980s that there was more than one type of IPV (Johnson 1995), researchers have only recently begun to do research specifically focused on these distinctions. In order to make these distinctions, researchers ask questions not only about the violence itself but also about nonviolent control tactics. They then use the answers to those questions to distinguish between violence that is embedded in a general pattern of power and control (intimate terrorism and violent resistance) and violence that is not (situational couple violence). The specific measures used have varied from study to study, but the findings have been quite consistent.

Studies in both the US and England have shown that the intimate partner violence in general surveys is heavily biased in favor of situational couple violence, whereas the intimate partner violence in agency samples is biased in favor of male intimate terrorism and female violent resistance (Graham-Kevan and

Archer 2003a, 2003b; Johnson 2001). For example, using data from a 1970s Pittsburgh survey, Johnson (2001) found that situational couple violence constituted 89 percent of the male violence in the general survey sample, 29 percent in a court sample, and only 19 percent in the shelter sample. Why is this? The bias in general surveys comes from two sources: (a) the reality that situational couple violence is much more common than intimate terrorism and violent resistance, and (b) the biasing effect of the fact that as many as 40 percent of individuals approached in general surveys refuse to participate (Johnson 1995). Potential respondents who are terrorizing their partners are unlikely to agree to participate in a survey about family life for fear they will be exposed. Their violently resisting partners are unlikely to agree out of fear of being "punished" by their intimate terrorist partner for participating in such a survey. Thus, general surveys include very little intimate terrorism or violent resistance. In contrast with general surveys, agency samples are biased because intimate terrorism is more likely than situational couple violence to involve the sort of frequent and severe violence that comes to the attention of shelters, hospitals, the courts, and the police. Thus, agency samples include mostly cases of intimate terrorism and violent resistance.

Data from these studies also clearly demonstrate a strong relationship between gender and the different types of IPV. For example, in the Pittsburgh study intimate terrorism is almost entirely male-perpetrated (97 percent), and violent resistance is therefore female-perpetrated (96 percent), whereas situational couple violence is roughly gender-symmetric (56 percent male, 44 percent female).

When one puts together these findings regarding gender, type of IPV, and sample biases, the history of dissension regarding the gender symmetry of IPV is explained. Family-violence theorists who have argued that domestic violence is gender-symmetric have relied largely on general surveys, which are biased heavily in favor of situational couple violence, and they have found rough gender symmetry in their research, leading them to the false conclusion that domestic violence is not about gender. Feminist researchers, in contrast, have relied largely on agency samples that are heavily biased in favor of intimate terrorism (and violent resistance), showing a heavily gendered pattern, with men as the primary perpetrators of intimate terrorism and women sometimes resisting with violence. I would argue that intimate terrorism is what most people mean when they use the term *domestic violence*, and it is indeed primarily perpetrated by men against their female partners.

Domestic Violence (Intimate Terrorism) as Gendered Violence

In intimate terrorism, violence is one control tactic in an array of tactics that are deployed in an attempt to take general control over one's partner. The control sought in intimate terrorism is general and long-term. Although each particular

Figure 16.1 Domestic violence/intimate terrorism (adapted from Pence and Paymar)

act of intimate violence may appear to have any number of short-term, specific goals, it is embedded in a larger pattern of power and control that permeates the relationship. It is this type of IPV that comes to mind for most people when they hear the term "domestic violence," and it is this type that receives the most media attention, in movies such as *Sleeping with the Enemy* and *Enough*, in television talk shows and documentaries that deal with IPV, and in newspaper and magazine articles that address the problem of domestic violence.

Figure 16.1 is a widely used graphical representation of such partner violence deployed in the service of general control (Pence and Paymar 1993). A brief tour of the wheel, starting with economic abuse and moving through the other forms of control, might help capture what Catherine Kirkwood calls a "web" of abuse (Kirkwood 1993).

It is not unusual for an intimate terrorist to deprive his[2] partner of control over economic resources. He controls all the money. She is allowed neither a bank account nor credit cards. If she works for wages, she has to turn over her paychecks to him. He keeps all the cash, and she has to ask him for money when she needs to buy groceries or clothes for herself or their children. He may require a precise accounting of every penny, demanding to see the grocery bill and making sure she returns every bit of the change.

This economic abuse may be justified through the next form of control, male privilege: "I am the man of the house, the head of the household, the king in my castle." Of course, this use of male privilege can cover everything. As the man of the house, his word is law. He doesn't have to explain. She is to do his bidding without question. And don't talk back. All of this holds even more rigidly in public, where he is not to be humiliated by back-talk from "his woman."

How does he use the children to support his control? First of all, they too know he is the boss. He makes it clear that he controls not only them but their mother as well. He may use them to back him up, to make her humiliation more complete by forcing them into the room to assist him as he confronts her, demanding their verbal support and generally requiring their collaboration with his actions. He may even have convinced them that he should be in charge, that he does know what is best (father knows best), and that she is incompetent, lazy, or immoral. In addition, he may use her attachment to the children as a means of control, by threatening to take them away from her or hurt them if she isn't a "good wife and mother." Of course, being a good wife and mother means doing as he says.

Then there is isolation. He keeps her away from everyone else. He makes himself her only source of information, of affection, of money, of everything. In a rural setting he might be able to literally isolate her, moving to a house trailer in the woods, with one car that he controls, no phone, keeping her there alone. In an urban setting, or if he needs her to go out to work, he can isolate her less literally, by driving away her friends and relatives and intimidating the people at work, so that she has no one to talk to about what's happening to her.

When she's completely isolated, what he tells her about herself is all she ever hears about herself; he can tell her over and over again that she's worthless—humiliating her, demeaning her, emotionally abusing her. She's ugly, stupid, a slut, a lousy wife, an incompetent mother. She only manages to survive because he takes care of her. She'd be helpless without him. And who else is there to tell her otherwise? Maybe he can even convince her that she can't live without him.

If she resists, he can intimidate her. Show her what might happen if she doesn't behave. Scream at her. Swear at her. Let her see his rage. Smash things. Or maybe a little cold viciousness will make his point. Kick her cat. Hang her dog. That ought to make her think twice before she decides not to do as he says. Or threaten her. Threaten to hit her or to beat her or to pull her hair out or to burn her. Or tell her he'll kill her, and maybe the kids too.

Pull all these means of control together, or even a few of them, and the abuser entraps and enslaves his partner in a web of control. If she manages to thwart one means of control, there are others at his disposal. Wherever she turns, there is another way he can control her. She is ensnared by multiple strands. She can't seem to escape—she is trapped. But with the addition of physical violence there is more to power and control than entrapment. There is terror.

For this reason, the diagram does not include the violence as just another means of control, another spoke in the wheel. The violence is depicted, rather, as the rim of the wheel, holding all the spokes together. When violence is added to such a pattern of power and control, the abuse becomes much more than the sum of its parts. The ostensibly nonviolent tactics that accompany that violence take on a new, powerful, and frightening meaning—controlling the victim not only through their own specific constraints but also through their association with the knowledge that her partner will do anything to maintain control of the relationship, even attack her physically. Most obviously, the threats and intimidation are clearly more than idle threats if he has beaten her before. But even his "request" to see the grocery receipts becomes a "warning" if he has put her into the hospital this year. His calling her a stupid slut may feel like the beginning of a vicious physical attack. As battered women often report, "All he had to do was look at me that way, and I'd jump." What is for most of us the safest place in our world—home—is for her a place of constant fear.

Violent resistance. What is a woman to do when she finds herself terrorized in her own home? At some point, most women in such relationships do fight back physically. For some, this is an instinctive reaction to being attacked, and it happens at the first blow—almost without thought. For others, it doesn't happen until it seems he is going to continue to assault her repeatedly if she doesn't do something to stop him. For most women, the size difference between them and their male partner ensures that violent resistance won't help, and may make things worse, so they turn to other means of coping. For a few, eventually it seems that the only way out is to kill their partner.

Violence in the face of intimate terrorism may arise from any of a variety of motives. She may (at least at first) believe that she can defend herself, that her violent resistance will keep him from attacking her further. That may mean that she thinks she can stop him right now, in the midst of an attack, or it may mean that she thinks that if she fights back often enough he will eventually decide to stop attacking her physically. Even if she doesn't think she can stop him, she may feel that he shouldn't be allowed to attack her without being hurt himself. This desire to hurt him in return even if it won't stop him can be a form of communication ("What you're doing isn't right, and I'm going to fight back as hard as I can"), or it may be a form of retaliation or payback, along the lines of "He's not going to do that without paying some price for it." In a few cases, she may be after serious retaliation, attacking him when he is least expecting it and doing her best to do serious damage, even killing him. But there is sometimes another motive for such premeditated attacks—escape. Sometimes, after years of abuse and entrapment, a victim of intimate terrorism may feel that the only way she can escape from this horror is to kill her tormenter (Walker 1989).

It is clear that most women who are faced with intimate terrorism do escape from it. For example, Campbell's research finds that within two and a half years, two-thirds of women facing intimate terrorism are no longer in violent relationships (J. Campbell et al. 1998). The evidence also indicates, however, that escaping safely from such relationships can take time. Intimate terrorists entrap their partners using the same tactics they use to control them. If a woman has been so psychologically abused that she believes that her partner really can take her children away from her, how can she leave and abandon them to him? If a woman has no access to money or a job, how can she feed and clothe herself and her children when they escape? If she is monitored relentlessly and isolated from others, how can she get away and where can she go? If her partner has threatened to kill her and the children if she tries to leave, how can she leave safely?

What women in such situations typically do is gradually gather the resources they need to escape safely, sometimes doing this on their own, more often seeking help from others. They hide away small amounts of money until they have enough to get a small start, and they start working or going to school to develop a viable source of income, and they make plans with friends or a shelter to hide them during the period immediately after their escape, and they involve the police and courts for protection, and they join support groups to help them with their transition to independence and the emotional trauma produced by the psychological abuse, and on and on. The process is not a simple one. Catherine Kirkwood (1993) describes it as a "spiral" in which women leave multiple times, only to return, but each time garnering information and resources that will eventually allow them to leave for good. The process is complicated not only by the intimate terrorist's commitment to keeping her but also by the gender structure of institutions that may make it more difficult to leave than it would be in a more equitable society.

A Gender Theory of Domestic Violence (Intimate Terrorism)

Let me begin with a reminder that the foregoing discussion indicates that in heterosexual relationships the strongest correlate of type of IPV is gender. In heterosexual relationships intimate terrorism is perpetrated almost entirely by men and, of course, the violent resistance to it is from their female partners. The gendering of situational couple violence is less clear and will be addressed in the next section.

To a sociologist, the tremendous gender imbalance in the perpetration of intimate terrorism suggests important social structural causes that go beyond simple differences between men and women. For over two decades now, feminist sociologists have argued that gender must be understood as an institution, not merely as an individual characteristic. Although some gender theorists have couched this argument in terms of rejecting gender as an individual characteristic in favor of focusing at the situational or institutional level of analysis (e.g., Ferree 1990), I prefer a version of gender theory that incorporates gender at all levels of social organization, from the individual level of sex differences in identities and attitudes, and even physical differences, through the situational enforcement of gender in social interaction to the gender structure of organizational and societal contexts (Ferree, Lorber, and Hess 2000; Risman 2004). The application of gender theory to intimate terrorism that follows will start with individual sex differences and work up to the gender structure of the economy, the family, and the criminal justice system.

Why is intimate terrorism in heterosexual relationships (and violent resistance to it) so clearly a matter of men abusing women? First, gender affects the use of violence to control one's partner in heterosexual relationships simply because of average sex differences in size and strength. The use of violence as one tactic in an attempt to exercise general control over one's partner requires more than the willingness to do violence. It requires a credible threat of a damaging violent response to noncompliance. Such a threat is, of course, more credible coming from a man than a woman simply because of the size difference in most heterosexual couples. Furthermore, still at the level of individual differences but focusing on gender socialization rather than physical differences, individual attitudes toward violence and experience with violence make such threats more likely and more credible from a man than from a woman. Put simply, the exercise of violence is more likely to be a part of boys' and men's experience than girls' and women's—in sports, fantasy play, and real-life conflict.

Second, individual misogyny and gender traditionalism are clearly implicated in intimate terrorism. Although critics of feminist theory often claim that there is no relationship between attitudes toward women and domestic violence (Felson 2002, 106), the research that has addressed this question in fact clearly supports the position that individual men's attitudes toward women affect the likelihood that they will be involved in intimate terrorism. One example is Holtzworth-Munroe's work, which shows that both of her two groups of intimate terrorists are more hostile toward women than are either nonviolent men or men involved in situational couple violence (e.g., Holtzworth-Munroe et al. 2000). More generally, Sugarman and Frankel (1996) conducted a thorough review of the research on this question, using a statistical technique that allowed them to combine the findings of all the studies that had been published up to that time. Whereas Holtzworth-Munroe demonstrated an effect of *hostility* toward women, Sugarman and Frankel focused on the effects of men's attitudes toward the role of women in social life and found that traditional men were more likely to be involved in attacks on their partners than were nontraditional men. The details of the Sugarman and Frankel review provide further support for the important role of attitudes toward women in intimate terrorism. They found that men's attitudes toward women were much more strongly related to violence in studies using samples that were dominated by intimate terrorism than in studies that were dominated by situational couple violence. Of course, this is exactly what a feminist theory of domestic violence would predict. It is intimate terrorism that involves the attempt to control one's partner, an undertaking supported by traditional or hostile attitudes toward women.

Third, at the level of social interaction rather than individual attitudes, our cultures of masculinity and femininity ensure that whatever the level of violence, its meaning will differ greatly depending on the gender of the perpetrator (Straus 1999). When a woman slaps her husband in the heat of an argument, it is unlikely to be interpreted by him as a serious attempt to do him physical harm. In fact, it is likely to be seen as a quaint form of feminine communication. Women's violence is taken less seriously, is less likely to produce fear, and is therefore less likely either to be intended as a control tactic or to be successful as one (Swan and Snow 2002).

Fourth, general social norms regarding intimate heterosexual partnerships, although certainly in the midst of considerable historical change, are heavily gendered and rooted in a patriarchal heterosexual model that validates men's power (Dobash and Dobash 1979, 1992; Yllö and Bograd 1988). These norms affect the internal functioning of all relationships, regardless of the individual attitudes of the partners, because couples' social networks are often involved in shaping the internal workings of personal relationships (Klein and Milardo 2000). When those networks support a male-dominant style of marriage or a view of marriage as a commitment "for better or worse," they can contribute to the entrapment of women in abusive relationships.

Finally, the gendering of the broader social context within which the relationship is embedded affects the resources the partners can draw on to shape the relationship and to cope with or escape from the violence. For example, the gender gap in wages can create an economic dependency that enhances men's control over women and contributes to women's entrapment in abusive relationships. The societal assignment of caregiving responsibilities primarily to women further contributes to this economic dependency, placing women in a subordinate position within the family and creating a context in which institutions such as the church that could be a source of support for abused women instead encourage them to stay in abusive relationships—for the sake of the children or for the sake of the marriage. Then there is the criminal justice system, heavily dominated by men and involving a culture of masculinity that has not always been responsive to the problems of women experiencing intimate terrorism, which was often treated as if it were situational couple violence (Buzawa and Buzawa 2003). On a more positive note, there have been major changes in all of these systems as a result of the women's movement in general and the battered women's movement in particular (Dobash and Dobash 1992). These changes are probably a major source of the recent dramatic decline in nonfatal IPV against women and fatal IPV against men in the US (Rennison 2003).[3]

What about Situational Couple Violence?

It is not surprising that the institution of gender, in which male domination is a central element, is implicated in the structure of intimate terrorism, which is about coercive control. In contrast, situational couple violence, which is the most common type of partner violence, does not involve an attempt on the part of one partner to gain general control over the other, and by some criteria it appears to be more gender-symmetric. The violence is situationally provoked, as the tensions or emotions of a particular encounter lead one or both of the partners to resort to violence. Intimate relationships inevitably involve conflicts, and in some relationships one or more of those conflicts turns into an argument that escalates into violence. The violence may be minor and singular, with one encounter at some point in the relationship escalating to the level that someone pushes or slaps the other, is immediately remorseful, apologizes, and never does it again. Or the violence could be a chronic problem, with one or both partners frequently resorting to violence, minor or severe, even homicidal. In general, there is considerable variability in the nature of situational couple violence, a variability that has not yet been explored adequately enough to allow us to make confident statements about its causes.

Nevertheless, some researchers *have* made confident statements about one aspect of situational couple violence—its gender symmetry, a symmetry that in my view is mythical. The myth of gender symmetry in situational couple violence has been supported by the widespread use of a particularly meaningless measure of symmetry—incidence. Respondents in a survey are presented with a list of violent behaviors ranging from a push or a slap to an attack with a weapon. They are then asked to report how often they have committed each violent act against their partner (or their partner against them) in the previous twelve months. "Incidence of partner violence" is then defined as the percentage of a group (e.g., men or women) who have committed the act (or some set of the acts, often identified as mild or severe violent acts) at least once in the previous twelve months. The much-touted gender symmetry of situational couple violence is gender symmetry only in this narrow sense. For example, in the 1975 National Survey of Family Violence that initiated the gender-symmetry debate, 13 percent of women and 11 percent of men had committed at least one of the acts listed in the Conflict Tactics Scales (Steinmetz 1977–78). However, by any sensible measure of the nature of the violence, such as the specific acts engaged in, the injuries produced, the frequency of the violence, or the production of fear in one's partner, IPV (even situational couple violence) is not gender symmetric (Archer 2000; Brush 1990; Hamberger and Guse 2002; Johnson 1999; Morse 1995; Tjaden and Thoennes 2000b).

Thus, although situational couple violence may not be as gendered as intimate terrorism and violent resistance, many of the gender factors discussed earlier are implicated in the patterning of situational couple violence. For example, in situational couple violence the likelihood of injury or fear is influenced by size differences. A slap from a woman is still perceived as an entirely different act than is one from a man. Most important, our cultures of masculinity and femininity contribute to the couple communication problems that are often associated with situational couple violence (Johnson 2006).

Policy and Intervention

Different problems require different solutions. The fact that there is more than one type of IPV means that to some extent we must tailor our policies and intervention strategies to the specific characteristics of each of the types. Although situational couple violence is much more common than intimate terrorism—surveys indicate that one out of every eight married couples in the US experiences some form of situational couple violence each year—most of our policies and interventions are designed to address intimate terrorism rather than situational couple violence. This focus on intimate terrorism has developed for a number of reasons: (a) the women's movement has been extremely effective in educating both the public and the criminal justice system about the nature of intimate terrorism, (b) intimate terrorism is more likely to come to the attention of agencies because it so often involves chronic and/or severe violence and because victims of intimate terrorism are more likely than victims of situational couple violence to need help in order to cope with the violence or to escape from it, and (c) the significant percentage of partner homicides that are a product of intimate terrorism emphasize the need for effective intervention in such situations.

Although conservative men's groups have decried this dominant focus on intimate terrorism because it ignores the violence of women (which they do not acknowledge is almost always either violent resistance or situational couple violence), the safest approach to intervention is to start with the assumption that every case of IPV involves intimate terrorism. The reason for this is that interventions for situational couple violence (such as couples counseling) are likely to put a victim of intimate terrorism at considerable risk. If we were to do as one recent article suggested and recommend counseling that would help couples to "work together to harmonize their relationships" (Fergusson, Horwood, and Ridder 2005), we would be asking women who are terrorized by their partners to go into a counseling situation that calls for honesty, encouraging victims to tell the truth to a partner who in many cases has beaten them severely in response to criticism and who might well murder them in response to their attempt to "harmonize" (Johnson 2005).

Thus, our understanding of the differences among these types of IPV suggests that the best strategy in individual cases is to assume intimate terrorism and to work closely with the victim only (not the couple) until it is absolutely clear that the violence is situational couple violence. In the shelter movement, which for the most part works on a feminist empowerment model, this means working with the victim on coping with the violence within the relationship, providing safe temporary shelter, involving the courts through arrest or protection from abuse orders, developing a safety plan for the immediate future, and—if the victim so wishes—developing the strategies and resources needed to escape from the relationship safely.

How can we as a society work to reduce the incidence of IPV? First, we need to send the message that violence against intimate partners will not be tolerated. Arrest and prosecution would send that message both to the general public and to the individuals who are arrested. Second, the educational programs about relationship violence that have been developed in the battered women's movement and presented in many school districts around the country could become a regular part of our school curricula, teaching children and adolescents about equality and respect in our personal relationships. Finally, we can work to increase support for programs in hospitals, shelters, and the courts that screen for IPV and help its victims either to stop the violence or to escape from it safely.

NOTES

1 There is a fourth type, *mutual violent control*, that involves two intimate terrorists vying for control of their relationship. This type appears in very small numbers in some samples and there is some debate about whether it is a true type or an artifact of the constraints of imperfect operationalization.

2 I am going to use gendered pronouns here because the vast majority of intimate terrorists are men terrorizing female partners. That does not mean that women are *never* intimate terrorists. There are a small number of women who do terrorize their male partners (Steinmetz 1977–78), and there are also women in same-sex relationships who terrorize their female partners (Renzetti and Miley 1996).

3 It is important to note that this discussion of gender is relevant only to heterosexual relationships. In same-sex relationships, some aspects of gender may still be important (e.g., gender differences in attitudes toward and experience with violence might produce more violence in gay men's relationships than in lesbian relationships), others will be largely irrelevant (e.g., gay and lesbian relationship norms are more egalitarian, and sex differences in size and strength will be less likely to be significant), and some will play themselves out in quite different ways (e.g., reactions of the criminal justice system may be affected by officers' attitudes toward gay men and lesbians). Although we know considerably less about same-sex relationships than we do about heterosexual relationships, there is a growing literature that is important not only in its own right but also because it sheds light on some of the inadequacies of theories rooted in research on heterosexual relationships (Renzetti 1992, 2002; Renzetti and Miley 1996).

17

Violence in Intimate Relationships

A Feminist Perspective

BELL HOOKS

We were on the freeway, going home from San Francisco. He was driving. We were arguing. He had told me repeatedly to shut up. I kept talking. He took his hand from the steering wheel and threw it back, hitting my mouth—my open mouth, blood gushed, and I felt an intense pain. I was no longer able to say any words, only to make whimpering, sobbing sounds as the blood dripped on my hands, on the handkerchief I held too tightly. He did not stop the car. He drove home. I watched him pack his suitcase. It was a holiday. He was going away to have fun. When he left I washed my mouth. My jaw was swollen and it was difficult for me to open it.

I called the dentist the next day and made an appointment. When the female voice asked what I needed to see the doctor about, I told her I had been hit in the mouth. Conscious of race, sex, and class issues, I wondered how I would be treated in this White doctor's office. My face was no longer swollen so there was nothing to identify me as a woman who had been hit, as a Black woman with a bruised and swollen jaw. When the dentist asked me what had happened to my mouth, I described it calmly and succinctly. He made little jokes about how "we can't have someone doing this to us now, can we?" I said nothing. The damage was repaired. Through it all, he talked to me as if I were a child, someone he had to handle gingerly or otherwise I might become hysterical.

This is one way women who are hit by men and seek medical care are seen. People within patriarchal society imagine that women are hit because we are hysterical, because we are beyond reason. It is most often the person who is hitting that is beyond reason, who is hysterical, who has lost complete control over responses and actions.

Growing up, I had always thought that I would never allow any man to hit me and live. I would kill him. I had seen my father hit my mother once and I wanted to kill him. My mother said to me then, "You are too young to know, too young to understand." Being a mother in a culture that supports and promotes domination, a patriarchal, white-supremacist culture, she did not discuss how she felt or what she meant. Perhaps it would have been too difficult for her to speak about the confusion of being hit by someone you are intimate with, someone you love. In my case, I was hit by my companion at a time in life when a number of forces in the world outside our home had already "hit" me, so to speak, made me painfully aware of my powerlessness, my marginality. It seemed then that I was confronting being Black and female and without money in the worst possible ways. My world was spinning. I had already lost a sense of grounding and security. The memory of this experience has stayed with me as I have grown as a feminist, as I have thought deeply and read much on male violence against women, on adult violence against children.

In this essay, I do not intend to concentrate attention solely on male physical abuse of females. It is crucial that feminists call attention to physical abuse in all its forms. In particular, I want to discuss being physically abused in singular incidents by someone you love. Few people who are hit once by someone they love respond in the way they might to a singular physical assault by a stranger. Many children raised in households where hitting has been a normal response by primary caretakers react ambivalently to physical assaults as adults, especially if they are being hit by someone who cares for them and whom they care for. Often female parents use physical abuse as a means of control. There is continued need for feminist research that examines such violence. Alice Miller has done insightful work on the impact of hitting even though she is at times antifeminist in her perspective. (Often in her work, mothers are blamed, as if their responsibility in parenting is greater than that of fathers.) Feminist discussions of violence against women should be expanded to include a recognition of the ways in which women use abusive physical force toward children not only to challenge the assumptions that women are likely to be nonviolent but also to add to our understanding of why children who were hit growing up are often hit as adults or hit others.

Recently, I began a conversation with a group of Black adults about hitting children. They all agreed that hitting was sometimes necessary. A professional Black male in a southern family setting with two children commented on the way he punished his daughters. Sitting them down, he would first interrogate them about the situation or circumstance for which they were being punished. He said with great pride, "I want them to be able to understand fully why they are being punished." I responded by saying that "they will likely become women whom a lover will attack using the same procedure you who have loved them so well used and they will not know how to respond." He resisted the idea that his behavior would have any impact on their responses to violence as adult women. I pointed to case after case of women in intimate relationships with men (and sometimes women) who are subjected to the same form of interrogation and punishment they experienced as children, who accept their lover assuming an abusive, authoritarian role. Children who are the victims of physical abuse— whether one beating or repeated beatings, one violent push or several—whose wounds are inflicted by a loved one, experience an extreme sense of dislocation.

The world one has most intimately known, in which one felt relatively safe and secure, has collapsed. Another world has come into being, one filled with terrors, where it is difficult to distinguish between a safe situation and a dangerous one, a gesture of love and a violent, uncaring gesture. There is a feeling of vulnerability, exposure, that never goes away, that lurks beneath the surface. I know. I was one of those children. Adults hit by loved ones usually experience similar sensations of dislocation, of loss, of newfound terrors.

Many children who are hit have never known what it feels like to be cared for, loved without physical aggression or abusive pain. Hitting is such a widespread practice that any of us are lucky if we can go through life without having this experience. One undiscussed aspect of the reality of children who are hit finding themselves as adults in similar circumstances is that we often share with friends and lovers the framework of our childhood pains, and this may determine how they respond to us in difficult situations. We share the ways we are wounded and expose vulnerable areas. Often, these revelations provide a detailed model for anyone who wishes to wound or hurt us. While the literature about physical abuse often points to the fact that children who are abused are likely to become abusers or be abused, there is no attention given to sharing woundedness in such a way that we let intimate others know exactly what can be done to hurt us, to make us feel as though we are caught in the destructive patterns we have struggled to break. When partners create scenarios of abuse similar, if not exactly the same, to those we have experienced in childhood, the wounded person is hurt not only by the physical pain but by the feeling of calculated betrayal. Betrayal. When we are physically hurt by loved ones, we feel betrayed. We can no longer trust that care can be sustained. We are wounded, damaged—hurt to our hearts.

Feminist work calling attention to male violence against women has helped create a climate where the issues of physical abuse by loved ones can be freely addressed, especially sexual abuse within families. Exploration of male violence against women by feminists and nonfeminists shows a connection between childhood experience of being hit by loved ones and the later occurrence of violence in adult relationships. While there is much material available discussing physical abuse of women by men, usually extreme physical abuse, there is not much discussion of the impact that one incident of hitting may have on a person in an intimate relationship, or how the person who is hit recovers from that experience. Increasingly, in discussion with women about physical abuse in relationships, irrespective of sexual preference, I find that most of us have had the experience of being violently hit at least once. There is little discussion of how we are damaged by such experiences (especially if we have been hit as children), of the ways we cope and recover from this wounding. This is an important area for feminist research precisely because many cases of extreme physical abuse begin with an isolated incident of hitting. Attention must be given to understanding and stopping these isolated incidents if we are to eliminate the possibility that women will be at risk in intimate relationships.

Critically thinking about issues of physical abuse has led me to question the way our culture, the way we as feminist advocates, focus on the issue of violence and physical abuse by loved ones. The focus has been on male violence against women and, in particular, male sexual abuse of children. Given the nature of patriarchy, it has been necessary for feminists to focus on extreme cases to make people confront the issue, and acknowledge it to be serious and relevant. Unfortunately, an exclusive focus on extreme cases can and does lead us to ignore the more frequent, more common, yet less extreme case of occasional hitting. Women are also less likely to acknowledge occasional hitting for fear that they will then be seen as someone who is in a bad relationship or someone whose life is out of control. Currently, the literature about male violence against women identifies the physically abused woman as a "battered woman." While it has been important to have an accessible terminology to draw attention to the issue of male violence against women, the terms used reflect biases because they call attention to only one type of violence in intimate relationships. The term "battered woman" is problematical. It is not a term that emerged from feminist work on male violence against women; it was already used by psychologists and sociologists in the literature on domestic violence. This label "battered woman" places primary emphasis on physical assaults that are continuous, repeated, and unrelenting. The focus is on extreme violence, with little effort to link these cases with the everyday acceptance within intimate relationships of physical abuse that is not extreme, that may not be repeated. Yet these lesser forms of physical abuse damage individuals psychologically and, if not properly addressed and recovered from, can set the stage for more extreme incidents.

Most importantly, the term "battered woman" is used as though it constitutes a separate and unique category of womanness, as though it is an identity, a mark that sets one apart rather than being simply a descriptive term. It is as though the experience of being repeatedly violently hit is the sole defining characteristic of a woman's identity and all other aspects of who she is and what her experience has been are submerged. When I was hit, I, too, used the popular phrases "batterer," "battered woman," "battering" even though I did not feel that these words adequately described being hit once. However, these were the terms that people would listen to, would see as important, significant (as if it is not really significant for an individual, and more importantly for a woman, to be hit once). My partner was angry to be labeled a batterer by me. He was reluctant to talk about the experience of hitting me precisely because he did not want to be labeled a batterer. I had hit him once (not as badly as he had hit me), and I did not think of myself as a batterer. For both of us, these terms were inadequate. Rather than enabling us to cope effectively and positively with a negative situation, they were part of all the mechanisms of denial; they made us want to avoid confronting what had happened. This is the case for many people who are hit and those who hit.

Women who are hit once by men in their lives and women who are hit repeatedly do not want to be placed in the category of "battered woman" because it is a label that appears to strip us of dignity, to deny that there has been any integrity in the relationships we are in. A person physically assaulted by a stranger or a casual friend with whom they are not intimate may be hit once or repeatedly, but they do not have to be placed into a category before doctors, lawyers, family, counselors, etc., take their problem seriously. Again, it must be stated that establishing categories and terminology has been part of the effort to draw public attention to the seriousness of male violence against women in intimate relationships. Even though the use of convenient labels and categories has made it easier to identify problems of physical abuse, it does not mean the terminology should not be critiqued from a feminist perspective and changed if necessary.

Recently, I had an experience assisting a woman who had been brutally attacked by her husband (she never commented on whether this was the first incident or not), which caused me to reflect anew on the use of the term "battered woman." This young woman was not engaged in feminist thinking or aware that "battered woman" was a category. Her husband had tried to choke her to death. She managed to escape from him with only the clothes she was wearing. After she recovered from the trauma, she considered going back to this relationship. As a church-going woman, she believed that her marriage vows were sacred and that she should try to make the relationship work. In an effort to share my feeling that this could place her at great risk, I brought her Lenore Walker's *The Battered Woman* because it seemed to me that there was much that she was not revealing, that she felt alone, and that the experiences she would read about in the book would give her a sense that other women had experienced what she was going through. I hoped reading the book would give her the courage to confront the reality of her situation. Yet I found it difficult to share because I could see that her self-esteem had already been greatly attacked, that she had lost a sense of her worth and value, and that possibly this categorizing of her identity would add to the feeling that she should just forget, be silent (and certainly returning to a situation where one is likely to be abused is one way to mask the severity of the problem). Still I had to try. When I first gave her the book, it disappeared. An unidentified family member had thrown it away. They felt that she would be making a serious mistake if she began to see herself as an absolute victim, which they felt the label "battered woman" implied. I stressed that she should ignore the labels and read the content. I believed the experience shared in this book helped give her the courage to be critical of her situation, to take constructive action.

Her response to the label "battered woman," as well as the responses of other women who have been victims of violence in intimate relationships, compelled me to critically explore further the use of this term. In conversation with many women, I found that it was seen as a stigmatizing label, one which victimized women seeking help felt themselves in no condition to critique. As in, "who cares what anybody is calling it—I just want to stop this pain." Within patriarchal society, women who are victimized by male violence have had to pay a price for breaking the silence and naming the problem. They have had to be seen as fallen women, who have failed in their "feminine" role to sensitize and civilize the beast in the man. A category like "battered woman" risks reinforcing this notion that the hurt woman, not only the rape victim, becomes a social pariah, set apart, marked forever by this experience.

A distinction must be made between having a terminology that enables women, and all victims of violent acts, to name the problem and categories of labeling that may inhibit that naming. When individuals are wounded, we are indeed often scarred, often damaged in ways that do set us apart from those who have not experienced a similar wounding, but an essential aspect of the recovery process is the healing of the wound, the removal of the scar. This is an empowering process that should not be diminished by labels that imply this wounding experience is the most significant aspect of identity.

As I have already stated, overemphasis on extreme cases of violent abuse may lead us to ignore the problem of occasional hitting, and it may make it difficult for women to talk about this problem. A critical issue that is not fully examined and written about in great detail by researchers who study and work with victims is the recovery process. There is a dearth of material discussing the recovery process of individuals who have been physically abused. In those cases where an individual is hit only once in an intimate relationship, however violently, there may be no recognition at all of the negative impact of this experience. There may be no conscious attempt by the victimized person to work at restoring her or his well-being, even if the person seeks therapeutic help, because the one incident may not be seen as serious or damaging. Alone and in isolation, the person who has been hit must struggle to regain broken trust—to forge some strategy of recovery. Individuals are often able to process an experience of being hit mentally that may not be processed emotionally. Many women I talked with felt that even after the incident was long forgotten, their bodies remain troubled. Instinctively, the person who has been hit may respond fearfully to any body movement on the part of a loved one that is similar to the posture used when pain was inflicted.

Being hit once by a partner can forever diminish sexual relationships if there has been no recovery process. Again, there is little written about ways folks recover physically in their sexualities as loved ones who continue to be sexual with those who have hurt them. In most cases, sexual relationships are dramatically altered when hitting has occurred. The sexual realm may be the one space where the person who has been hit experiences again the sense of vulnerability, which may also arouse fear. This can lead either to an attempt to avoid sex or to unacknowledged sexual withdrawal wherein the person participates but is passive. I talked with women who had been hit by lovers who described sex as an ordeal, the one space where they confront their inability to trust a partner who has broken trust. One woman emphasized that to her, being hit was a "violation of her body space" and that she felt from then on she had to protect that space. This response, though a survival strategy, does not lead to healthy recovery.

Often, women who are hit in intimate relationships with male or female lovers feel as though we have lost an innocence that cannot be regained. Yet this very notion of innocence is connected to passive acceptance of concepts of romantic love under patriarchy which have served to mask problematic realities in relationships. The process of recovery must include a critique of this notion of innocence which is often linked to an unrealistic and fantastic vision of love and romance. It is only in letting go of the perfect, no-work, happily-ever-after union idea that we can rid our psyches of the sense that we have failed in some way by not having such relationships. Those of us who never focused on the negative impact of being hit as children find it necessary to reexamine the past in a therapeutic manner as part of our recovery process. Strategies that helped us survive as children may be detrimental for us to use in adult relationships.

Talking about being hit by loved ones with other women, both as children and as adults, I found that many of us had never really thought very much about our own relationship to violence. Many of us took pride in never feeling violent, never hitting. We had not thought deeply about our relationship to inflicting physical pain. Some of us expressed terror and awe when confronted with physical strength on the part of others. For us, the healing process included the need to learn how to use physical force constructively, to remove the terror—the dread. Despite the research that suggests children who are hit may become adults who hit—women hitting children, men hitting women and children—most of the women I talked with not only did not hit but were compulsive about not using physical force.

Overall the process by which women recover from the experience of being hit by loved ones is a complicated and multifaceted one, an area where there must be much more feminist study and research. To many of us, feminists' calling attention to the reality of violence in intimate relationships has not in and of itself compelled most people to take the issue seriously, and such violence seems to be daily on the increase. In this essay, I have raised issues that are not commonly talked about, even among folks who are particularly concerned about violence against women. I hope it will serve as a catalyst for further thought, that it will strengthen our efforts as feminist activists to create a world where domination and coercive abuse are never aspects of intimate relationships.

18

Religion and Intimate Partner Violence

A Double-Edged Sword

LEE E. ROSS

This chapter examines hypothesized relations between Judeo-Christian religion and intimate partner violence. Given their complex and controversial nature, the following two questions are explored: (1) whether batterers selectively misinterpret scripture to justify or rationalize violence toward women, and (2) whether certain religious tenets around faith, the nature of marriage, the role of women and men, obedience, forgiveness, and salvation constrict and inevitably bind women to abusive relationships. An integrative literature review is employed to draw inferences among male patriarchy, religious scripture, and intimate partner violence. Overall, the findings are twofold: (1) elements of male patriarchy are included in much of Judeo-Christian scripture, and (2) some abusers rely on literal interpretations of select scripture to rationalize and defend violence toward their partners. The implications of these findings are discussed in terms that advocate and promote mutual submission in marriage.

The dark clouds of intimate partner violence (IPV, hereafter) are so widespread that they threaten the landscape of nearly all cultures, age groups, and social classes. Transcending gender, race/ethnicity, and religion, IPV remains one of the principal causes of female injury in almost every country in the world (Catalano 2012; Hajjar 2004; King 2009; Scott 2009; Thomas and Beasely 1993). In Morocco, for example, IPV is so pervasive that the most common reason women seek to end a marriage is to extricate themselves from situations of domestic violence (King 2009). Promoted by certain attitudes that espouse male dominance, IPV stands as a global phenomenon affecting scores of women daily. While acknowledging its global reach across cultures and religions, the scope and context of this chapter is confined to Western societies with a specific focus on Judeo-Christian religion within the US. Beyond matters of convenience, Judeo-Christianity was chosen because, at 78.4 percent, it is the leading religious affiliation within the US. Sometimes written as Judaeo-Christian, it is commonly used to describe a body of concepts and values thought to be held in common by Judaism and Christianity.

This chapter explores relations between Judeo-Christian religion and IPV, which is defined as abuse that occurs between two people in an intimate relationship (including spouses, former spouses, and partners). Existing along a continuum, IPV ranges from a single episode of violence to ongoing battering, including threats as well as physical abuse, sexual abuse, emotional abuse, and even spiritual abuse (Centers for Disease Control, 2006). As women attempt to escape abusive relationships, there are realistic concerns that pastors and members of some religious communities might undermine their efforts by encouraging continued patience and faith as a way to overcome the abuse.[1] Given their complex and controversial nature, the present study explores the following two questions: (1) Do abusers selectively misinterpret scripture to justify or rationalize their violence, and (2) do certain religious tenets regarding faith, the nature of marriage, the role of women and men, obedience, forgiveness, and salvation constrict and inevitably bind women to abusive relationships? This chapter uses an integrative literature review to draw inferences between male patriarchy, Christian scripture, and IPV. In the process, it explores the origins of the Bible, the role of male patriarchy, and the misuse of scripture to sustain violence in intimate relationships. In hopes of informing social practice, it encourages practitioners to explore how their client's particular spirituality and religious beliefs might affect their attitude toward the use of violence in relationships. Overall, it seeks to promote a more constructive dialogue among religious leaders and parishioners to help stem the rising tide of IPV.

Extent of the Problem

Data from both secular and Christian studies suggest that on any given Sunday a significant percentage of women sitting in church pews are victims of domestic violence (Castle 2002; Potter 2007). Studies have confirmed that church parishioners are indeed victims of domestic violence and related abuses, including verbal abuse, physical abuse, sexual abuse, and spiritual abuse, but some religious communities have tended to minimize or deny that IPV and brutality are prevalent within their congregations (Brinkerhoff, Grandin and Lupri 1992; Potter 2007; Scanzoni 1988).

While both women and men perpetrate—and are victimized—by IPV[2], most researchers and practitioners find women are far more likely to be victims of domestic violence than men. Women also sustain greater degrees of injury and are victimized by more severe forms of violence than men (Websdale 1998). Among married couples, rates of IPV are considerably lower in comparison to nonmarried couples (Bureau of Justice Statistics 2005). Nonetheless, it is estimated that nearly 30 percent of all US couples (whether married or not) will experience IPV at some point in their relationship. Within this population it is estimated that anywhere between 3 percent and 10 percent will experience severe forms of violence at the hands of an intimate partner (Straus and Gelles 1990).

In fact, Berry (1995) suggests that intimate partners were responsible for 30 to 50 percent of all women murdered.

In an effort to escape abusive relationships, women rely on a variety of social networks, including family and friends, battered women's shelters, domestic violence hotlines, social services, and justice systems. Some victims turn to religion and religious institutions in search of refuge, social support, and spiritual guidance to alleviate pain and suffering. The process of seeking spiritual support reveals an array of trials, tribulations, and circumstances that are unique to religious settings and worthy of further exploration. When men and women enter into intimate unions in a Christian context they are often subscribing to a whole set of religious tenets and beliefs around the nature of heterosexual relations, childbearing, childrearing, and obedience to authority (see Knickmeyer, Levitt, Horne, and Bayer 2003). Yet, subscribing to these expectations, while being battered, invites confusion and makes it difficult to withdraw from an abusive relationship. Further compounding matters is the uncertainty regarding the role of religion in assisting (or possibly hindering) women who are trapped in abusive relationships.

Historical Context

For much of American history, the institutions of marriage and religion have been closely related (Christiano 2000). To this day, religious attendance and beliefs are positively correlated with a host of variables, marital status, childbearing, marital quality, and marital stability in the US as a whole (Call and Heaton 1997). However, connections between religious practices and IPV are not as clear-cut, yielding conflicting results. For example, Ellison and Anderson (2002) analyzed data from the National Survey of Families and Households and found that those who attended services more often reported less spousal abuse. In looking at denominational differences in spouse abuse, Brinkerhoff et al. (1992) found no association between church attendance and spousal violence. Others suggest that certain religious ideologies (e.g., variants of conservative Protestantism) may legitimize, or at least fail to adequately condemn, the practice of partner violence (Ellison and Anderson 2002; Scanzoni 1988). Still others proclaim that the strength of pro-family rhetoric and ideology in these quarters may blind clergy and others to the magnitude of this problem within churches, and could restrict the options of women once they are abused (Ellison and Anderson 2002; Nason-Clark 1997). Furthermore, some evidence suggests that discrepancies in a partner's religious beliefs and congregational beliefs may lead to an increased risk of violence particularly among men holding more conservative beliefs about disobedient wives and authority of the Bible (Ellison, Bartkowski, and Anderson 1999; Gelles 1974). Moreover, Pevey et al. (1996) have found that many Baptist churches use predominantly male images of God, preach the doctrine of wifely submission, and exclude women from leadership roles. As these images convey notions of male superiority and authority, coupled with an expectation of female obedience and submission, it is important to understand and appreciate the rather nuanced—yet inseparable—relationship between religious scripture, male patriarchy, and IPV.

Historically, physical discipline in the context of a marriage was not recognized as violence at all. Instead, it was regarded simply as one of the religious duties of the husband (see Hart 1992). For instance, if threats of approbation against a wife did not work, men were encouraged to "pick up a stick and beat her soundly, for it is better to punish the body and correct the soul than to damage the soul and destroy the body" (Hart 1992, 3). Through time and evolving societal standards, the state has intervened with domestic violence specific statutes and related sanctions to punish and deter IPV. Still, some question the propriety of state intervention in marital affairs. Andrew Klein, the former chief probation officer of a model domestic violence court, stated that he has heard batterers defy his state's domestic violence laws claiming that "restraining orders are against God's will because the Bible says a man should control his wife" (see Buzawa and Buzawa 2003, 59).

Methodology: Integrative Literature Review

Recent examinations into the relationship between religion and IPV have increased the need for and the production of all types of reviews of the literature (including integrative, systematic, qualitative, and meta-analyses). The present study uses an integrative review method because these typically include diverse methodologies (for example, experimental and nonexperimental research) capable of exploring relations between religion and domestic violence. An integrative literature review also allows researchers to evaluate the strength of scientific evidence while identifying gaps in past and current research. According to Whittemore and Knafl, "Well-done integrative reviews present the state of the science, contribute to theory development, and have direct applicability to practice and policy" (2005, 546). In the process, it identifies the need for future research, central issues in an area, and whether theoretical or conceptual frameworks are utilized (Cooper 1998).

In the present study the accessible population included both electronic and library resources. The criteria for inclusion were publications between 1980 and 2012. The majority of the research resulted from online computer searches utilizing the following data bases: Criminal Justice Abstracts, JSTOR, Religious Studies, and the Association of Religious Data Archives. Advanced searches were conducted using the following terms: domestic violence, family violence, religion, Christianity, and United States. Developing a clear and concise system for data collection greatly improves the reviewer's capacity to ascertain reliable information from all information sources (Cooper 1998). Inter-rater reliability of selected literature was verified by the author and reanalyzed by a graduate research assistant. From this integrative review, three themes emerged: male patriarchy, proof-texting, and matters of faith. These themes are fully illustrated and described in the paragraphs below. In the process, we explore the origins of the Christian Bible, examine its patriarchal nature, and identify human propensities to take scripture out of context to one's purpose.

Biblical Origins, Patriarchal Passages, and Proof-Texting

Scholars agree that early Israel was an oral society of pastoralism and subsistence farming (Schniedewind and Rendsburg 2010; van der Toorn 2007; Schniedewind 2004). As such, some have questioned how and why such a pastoral-agrarian society came to write and give authority to the written word. William Schniedewind (2004) went a step further by asking: Why did the Bible become a book at all? This question recognizes that the first biblical accounts were conveyed only orally, given a lack of writing and literacy skills. Naturally, in order to have a sacred text, a culture must first have writing. For that text to be the central authority of a religion, literacy must be widespread. To that end, the invention of alphabetic writing (circa, 3150 BCE) was a pivotal development in the history of writing, and when the Bible became a book, the written word supplanted the living voice of the teacher (Schniedewind 2004).

The translation of the Bible from its original languages (Hebrew, Aramaic, and Greek), is a complex story that is beyond the scope of this chapter. However, prior to the King James translation, earlier versions and translations included Syrian, Coptic, Armenian, and Latin Vulgate. Christian translations, on the other hand, culminated with the works of William Tyndale (in 1506), William Coverdale (in 1535), and John Calvin (in 1560). The King James Version (circa, 1611) replaced both the Bishop's Bible and the Geneva Bible as the English translation. The purpose of this new translation was to have a Bible that could be read in church services and at home. When examining the issue of family violence, it is interesting to note that both the old and new testaments of the Christian Bible contain many patriarchal passages that pay homage to man's dominion over women and children. These passages and the degree to which they can be exploited and misinterpreted are explored fully in the following paragraphs.

Patriarchal Passages

Besides Christianity, all world religions appear connected by the seeds and common threads of male patriarchy: a hypothetical social system based upon the absolute authority of the father or an elderly male over the family group (Bartkowski 1997). The concept is often used, by extension (in anthropology and feminism, for example), to refer to the expectation that men take primary responsibility for the welfare of the community as a whole, acting as representatives of a male God via public office. According to Buzawa and Buzawa, Christianity, Judaism, and other patriarchal religions simply affirmed male-dominated family structures that were already in existence. From the earliest record, "most societies gave the patriarch of the family the right to use force against women and children under his control" (Buzawa and Buzawa 2003, 57). Roman law, for instance, gave legal guardianship of a wife to her husband. This concept, patria potestas, included the largely unfettered ability of the husband to legally beat his wife, who became, in legal effect, his "daughter" (2003). By extension, patriarchal beliefs reserved leadership roles to males—while limiting female involvement in rituals—in the belief that women were less connected to God (see Levitt and Ware 2006). Earlier research by Jeffords (1984) suggests that beliefs regarding sex/role expectations within society contribute to a patriarchal system that assigns women a subordinate role to men. This is especially evident within religious circles as men assume primary leadership roles within nearly all facets of organized religion. In the Catholic Church, for instance, the idea of women seeking ordination and positions of authority is generally discouraged.

Many seminal texts, including the Torah, the Bible, and the Koran all contain passages that, if literally read, seem to subordinate women, or emphasize family solidarity and preservation to the exclusion of concerns over the physical safety of the wife (Buzawa, Buzawa, and Stark 2011). In the case of Christianity, much of the rationale for suggesting a relationship between religiosity and IPV is predicated on the assumption that members of the more fundamentalist groups tend to be more patriarchal. After all, strong patriarchal beliefs are "founded on the conviction that in the beginning Eve was created from Adam's rib in order to serve him" (Scanzoni 1988, 136). Consequently, and in close alignment with feminist interpretations, patriarchy tends to influence the reading of scripture. Moreover, "male and female biblical scholars alike tend to 'read as men,' having internalized the norms of androcentric scholarship in which the male focus and patriarchal worldview of the biblical text is paralleled in the practice and history of biblical exegesis" (Reinhartz 2000, 44). Regarded by some as patriarchal, misogynistic, and biased in its interpretation, Schussler's (1985) views on the male reading of scripture is expressed accordingly:

> Not only is scripture interpreted by a long line of men and proclaimed in patriarchal churches, it is also authored by men, written in androcentric language, reflective of religious male experience, selected and transmitted by male religious leadership. Without question, the Bible is a male book. (ibid, 130)

The above passage acknowledges the undeniable singular influence of the male voice and value system in the composition, reading, and interpretation of scripture. Although beyond the scope of this chapter, a similar parallel and voice is evident in the legacy of slavery within the US as slave masters—many of whom were preachers—used biblical scriptures to justify and uphold the institution of slavery. In instances of disobedience, for example, the holy word was reinforced with the most heinous and severe forms of physical punishment known to man—yet conveniently referred to as discipline in the name of the Lord (Douglass 1845).

Over time, various religious bodies have begun to recognize and acknowledge the symbolic reality of patriarchal scripture, proof-texting, and the potential for IPV within this context. Indeed, many denominations have taken reasonable measures to eliminate IPV and the physical domination of women. Some denominations have sermons especially designed to acknowledge and raise awareness about this issue. Yet, the transition from male domination to equality has been neither swift nor smooth. Rather, some victims, seeking refuge in the wisdom and comfort of clergy, oftentimes received further unexpected condemnation instead of sympathy and compassion (see Alsdurf and Alsdurf 1988). For instance, some are reminded that marriage is God's holiest institution and encouraged to remain silent, persevere, and lean on His everlasting words. Moreover, they are reminded that "what therefore God hath joined together, let not man put asunder." Taken from the King James Version (Matthew 19:6), this injunction is often a part of the Christian marriage ceremony that reemphasizes God's authority over man, and by extension, man's authority over women.

Concepts originating from male patriarchy assume added dimensions when examining the often-heard expression "rule of thumb." This expression is thought to have derived from English common law that allowed a man to beat his wife with a stick, so long as it was no thicker than his thumb. In 1782, Judge Sir Francis Buller is reported as having made this legal ruling. However, while the judge was notoriously harsh in his punishments, there is no evidence that he ever made the ruling that he is infamously known for (Phrase Finder 2011). Edward Foss, in his authoritative work *Judges of England*, 1870, wrote that, despite a searching investigation, no substantial evidence exists to support this opinion. Despite the phrase being in common use since the eighteenth century and appearing many thousands of times in print, it was not associated with wife beating until the 1970s. Hoff Sommers (1994) suspects that the link between the phrase "rule of thumb" and wife beating is a feminist-inspired myth of recent vintage. In her book *Who Stole Feminism?* Hoff Sommers (1994) credits Canadian folklorist Philip Hiscock for clarifying the origin of this expression. Arguing that the phrase came into metaphorical use by the late eighteenth century, Hiscock alleges "[t]he real explanation of 'rule of thumb' is that it derives from woodworkers . . . who knew their trade so well they rarely or never fell back on the use of such things as rulers. Consequently, carpenters and other craftsmen would measure things simply by 'the length of their thumbs'" (Hoff Sommers 1994, 203).

Closely aligned to this is the more contemporary expression of a "beat down," which generally connotes some type of verbal or physical assault on another person.[3] Gaining in popularity, this expression has found its way into the lexicon of popular media where the apparent level of violence involved is minimized (and de-emphasized) as witnesses regard a "beat down" as a cool topic of conversation, similar to: "man, look at Hannah's face. She really got a beat down from that bum." The popularity of this expression has led to a growing line of commercial products, including coffee mugs, T-shirts, and magnets, and has realized a modest measure of commercial success. Clearly, this expression, however popular and innocent, conveys messages of using violence to resolve conflict. Therefore, it is not surprising that some people, immersed in a culture of violence, threaten to perpetrate a "beat down" on children, peers, loved ones, partners, and spouses alike.[4]

Proof-Texting

Fortune and Enger assert that the practice of "proof-texting (the selective use of scripture, usually out of context) is commonly used to justify one's actions" (2005, 2). Perhaps the clearest example can be seen with the practice of corporal punishment. Various Bible verses that appear to advocate the use of physical discipline on children are found in the book of Proverbs (on at least six separate occasions). Two verses in particular read: "He that spareth his rod hateth his son: but he that loveth him chasteneth him betimes" (Proverbs 13:24, KJV), and "Withhold not correction from a child: for if thou beatest him with the rod, he shall not die. Thou shalt beat him with the rod, and shalt deliver his soul from hell" (Proverbs 23:13–14, KJV).[5] Both conservative and liberal readings of these proverbs have yielded varied, yet noticeably different interpretations. As to their origins, religious conservatives generally believe that the book of Proverbs was assembled by King Solomon and that passages that dealt with spanking presumably reflected his parenting beliefs (Boadt 1984). Religious liberals, on the other hand, tend to believe King Solomon first introduced "ancient oriental 'wisdom' to Israel and . . . the actual authors of Proverbs were the successive generations of wisdom teachers (or 'wise men') who had charge of the moral and practical training of young men of the court and upper classes" (Dentan 1991, 304). As such, "sparing the rod" was literally interpreted as a parent's failure to discipline a child that could lead to immorality, disrespect, and disobedience. Conversely, an alternative interpretation suggests that parents should avoid using the rod (to facilitate corporal punishment), given its potential for physical—if not psychological abuse. Ostensibly, in both instances, biblical support for corporal punishment and the physical domination and discipline of children is dependent on one's biblical persuasion and remains a matter of interpretation.

As with children, there are similar and numerous accounts of male domination and control over women in the Bible. For some conservative Christians, the seeds of male domination over women were planted in the Garden of Eden where in the book of Genesis it reads: "And the rib, which the Lord God had taken from the man, made he a woman" (Genesis 2:22, KJV)[6]. Given the alleged transgressions of Eve, women have since been regarded by many as somewhat "one-step removed" from the image of God. Because women had already led to the fall of man, and the argument goes, "it was right that he whom woman led into wrongdoing would have her under his direction so that he might not fail a second time through female levity" (Roy 1977).

Deeply ingrained within the above passages are images of subservience, obedience, and submission of women unto men (i.e., wives unto husbands). The failure to adhere to these marital expectations creates conflict that originates as emotional abuse, escalates into forms of moderate chastisement, and culminates in more severe violence. This progression could result from a selective reading of the following passage (where female adultery intersects with male jealousy), which provides enough ammunition for some men to use violence. When a wife while under her husband's authority, goes astray and defiles herself or when a spirit of jealously comes on a man and he is jealous of his wife, then he shall set the woman before the Lord and the priest shall apply the entire law unto her (Numbers 5:29, NKJV).

Given the general tendencies of religious leaders to ignore or fail to acknowledge abuse within their congregations—even in instances of adultery—they might appear complicit in the eyes of many. Nonetheless, some men might insist on their right to control their wives and justify that claim by referencing the expressions of the Apostle Paul in his letter to the Ephesians. There, he wrote:

> Submit to your husband as to the Lord. For the husband is the head of the wife as Christ is the head of the church, His body, of which he is the Savior. Now as the church submits to Christ, so in addition, wives should submit to their husbands in everything. (Ephesians 5:22–24, ESV)

While this directive tends to perpetuate the control of wives by husbands, the larger problem is that some men do not acknowledge the verses that immediately follow, where husbands are instructed on how to treat their wives. It reads:

> Husbands, love your wives, just as Christ loved the church and gave himself up for her to make her holy, cleansing her by the washing with water through the word, and to present her to himself as a radiant church, without stain or wrinkle or any other blemish, but holy and blameless. In this same way, husbands ought to love their wives as their own bodies. He who loves his wife loves himself. (Ephesians 5:25–28, NIV)

The above scripture serves to remind Christians of an obligation to do unto others, as they would have others do unto them: to love their neighbors as they love God, and to love their wife as God loves the church. The book of Matthew (7:12) expresses these sentiments and reminds us that these are the laws of the prophets.

A Matter of Faith

Some researchers acknowledge the irony, ambivalence, and contradictory nature of a victim's dilemma where "religion and spirituality [can] serve either as mechanisms for achieving resilience in the face of domestic assault or as contributors to women's vulnerability" (Bell and Mattis 2000; Potter 2007). Ironically, Giesbrecht and Sevcik (2000) found that women viewed both their experiences and recovery from abuse as occurring within the context of their faith. As one would hope, certain religious beliefs should function as a protective factor against IPV. Some females, for example, who seek partners who have similar religious and spiritual values have been shown to experience less violence (Higginbotham, Ketring, Hibbert, Wright, and Guarino 2007). Of those who experienced IPV, however, serious questions tend to emerge. For instance, to what extent should victims (as believers) trust in the Lord that all things will work out? Should parishioners who are victims of IPV seek retribution for their pain and suffering? In the book of Romans (12:19) the Apostle Paul writes, "beloved, never avenge yourselves, but leave room for the wrath of God; for it is written, vengeance is mine, I will repay, says the Lord." While this scripture is comforting and reassuring to victims, a strict adherence and reliance on it does not necessarily remove victims from danger. Ostensibly, when faith and patience are pitted against one's natural temptation for retribution and human justice, the resulting dilemma is both vexing and painful.

Regrettably, some of the literature on battered (Christian) women tends to suggest that highly religious victims interpret their victimization as divinely ordained. In general, battered women who were strongly religious tended to interpret their experiences of abuse according to the Genesis stories and the creation of the fall (Tkacz 2006). Sermons that speak without nuance of the virtue of "submitting to the will of God," for example, or of the way in which "God sends us suffering to test our faith," may have critical or even fatal consequences when embraced by those who might consider leaving abusive partners (Tkacz 2006). Ironically, yet perhaps expected, men who batter also cite scripture to insist that their partners forgive them. For example, in the very midst of the Lord's prayer, believers, in beseeching forgiveness for their own sins, are reminded that they, too, must forgive others, regardless of circumstances (see Matthew 6:9–15).

Potter (2007) found that Christian women were obviously disappointed when some pastors made recommendations for the women to pray about the relationship and to make greater attempts at being a "good wife" (2007, 278). Regrettably, these suggestions and admonitions are rather peculiar in their stereotypical design and makeup and appear racialized to some extent. For instance, some Christian women suggested their pastors appeared to hold the stereotypical image of the Black woman as a strong woman (Collins 2000; hooks 2003; Sudarkasa 1996), who was capable of withstanding and contending with abuse by an intimate partner.

Exploring Solutions

The foregoing discussion has attempted to document and describe the dynamics and religious context of IPV. While this study is not without limitations,[7] the remaining discussion focuses on ways to address this troubling issue. To that end, some research suggests that religious communities can provide a safe haven and resource for the victims of abuse, particularly through the informal support networks of churchwomen (Cox 1989; Ellison and Anderson 2002; Nason-Clark 2004). At the same time, it is perhaps more difficult for some religious leaders than other service providers to acknowledge the realities of IPV, as they are called upon to uphold the values and beliefs of the church while responding practically to the needs of victims (Shannon-Lewy and Dull 2005). To handle these tensions, religious leaders must confront the theologically sensitive issues of sex-roles, marriage and divorce, the history of the church's treatment of women, the sanctity of personhood, and the practical realities of their own limitations as a counselor (Alsdurf and Alsdurf 1988). Research shows that many spiritual leaders are woefully unprepared to deal with IPV (Cwick 1996; Miles 2000). As a matter of fact, Miles (2000), in the book *Domestic Violence: What Every Pastor Needs to Know*, suggests that the theological training and beliefs given most clergy might actually contribute to increased violence and abuse of women.

For clergy who try to successfully intervene in domestic violence situations, the research findings are rather interesting. For instance, Ware, Levitt, and Bayer (2003) found that religious leaders who endorsed female submission tended to promote interventions that protected the marriage over those that provided the wife with the support to divorce or separate. Moreover, rather than emphasize a doctrine of mutual submission, religious leaders attempt to control perpetrators through penance, peer mentoring, and restrictions on their religious participation.

In addition to research exploring the effects of religious sanctions within the church, there has been a growing scholarly interest in the role of faith-based services for perpetrators of domestic violence outside of the church (see Nason-Clark 2004). Here, evidence suggests that clients in a faith-based batterer intervention program are more likely to complete the requirements than men enrolled in secular equivalents. Moreover, abusive men in the faith-based program who "were encouraged by their priests or pastors to attend had higher completion rates than those whose attendance was mandated by the courts" (Nason-Clark 2004, 307).

To complement and further promote secular interventions, some have suggested that the prospect of prohibiting and successfully punishing domestic violence depends, foremost, on the state's willingness and capacity to reform criminal and family laws. Yet, even here, some feel that the possibility of state-sponsored reforms is strongly affected by social beliefs and ideologies about gender and family relations (Hijjar 2004, 9). After all, most religious leaders place a high priority on maintaining the family unit.

Despite these advances, there are those who regard the physical discipline of women as no more egregious than the use of corporal punishment on children, as both fall within man's dominion. Whether we accept or reject these notions, perhaps the biggest obstacle to change is the deeply ingrained and cultural relationship between Judeo-Christian scripture and male patriarchy. Like Siamese twins conjoined at the torso, separating religious imperatives from sex-role expectations requires a very delicate procedure where the survival of one depends very much on the survival of the other. Separating IPV from patriarchal scripture is equally challenging as they appear to go hand-in-hand, like love and marriage, where hopes of a peaceful coexistence hinge on the confluence of compassion, understanding, and mutual submission. Still, it is important to question whether the New Testament supports male patriarchy. Moreover, we must treat the Old and New Testaments separately rather than conflating them as the Christian scripture.

There are indications that historical theologians are beginning to respond to this challenge. In-depth examinations of the theory and practice of the subordination of women and the recovery of women are appearing more and more frequently (West 2006). "Churches must also be accountable for the ways that scriptures, liturgies, icons, policies, and teachings uphold the subjugation of women" (West 2006, 244). In a similar vein, religious institutions and churches need to identify organizational structures and institutional practices that deny women an authoritative voice within the church. This includes explicit affirmations of the integrity and worth of a woman's body and sexuality, with direct references to the inclusion of everyone, regardless of their sexual orientation (West 2006).

Conclusion

Clearly, certain sections of the Christian Scripture and their patriarchal and church context are inherently problematic as they can contribute to cultural and individual interpretations that support violence against women. In the process, Bent-Godley and Fowler (2006) suggest that evoking guilt by stressing the need to forgive an abuser seems common. Moreover, understanding the myriad ways in which interpretations of the Bible are manipulated and how religious practice and spirituality are affected is critical for preventing the retraumatization of women by their faith-based communities (2006, 291).

Likewise, the same Christian scriptures and church context can also prevent or lessen violence against women. In the previous decade 95 percent of church-women reported they had never heard a specific message on abuse preached from the pulpit of their church (Nason-Clark 1997). Furthermore, some Christian women may endure various forms of abuse (whether physical, emotional, sexual, or spiritual) but may not regard it as abuse.

Recently, efforts to educate and promote public awareness about IPV within the religious community has gained momentum. Religious leaders are beginning to employ a number of strategies, including premarital counseling sessions, marriage enrichment classes, and singles groups designed to promote an awareness and constructive dialogue about the reality of IPV. Perhaps most important in resolving this matter is increased awareness of the egalitarian principle of mutual submission. For instance, biblical scholars contend that the Bible does not mandate wifely submission but rather "mutual submission" between wives and husbands (Follis 1981; Scanzoni and Hardesty 1992). According to some researchers, mutual submission is more authentically Christian because both spouses recognize that they must follow Jesus Christ's model of self-sacrifice and other-centeredness in family decision-making (Bartowski and Read 2003).

In terms of working with domestic violence offenders, it is important to underscore the positive aspects of religious involvement and its potential to enhance efforts toward offender rehabilitation. Moreover, some studies suggest that regular religious attendance is inversely related to abuse among both men and women (Ellison and Anderson 2002; O'Connor and Duncan 2011). Other studies, commissioned by the American Psychological Association, found that humanistic, spiritual, and religious pathways play an important part in the desistence process (see Bonta and Andrews 2001; O'Connor and Duncan 2011; Norcross and Wampold 2011). For example, within the Oregon prison system O'Connor and Duncan examined the religious involvement of those incarcerated (during the first year) and found a "diverse and widespread human, social, and spiritual capital that [was] naturally supportive" in reducing violence (2011, 608).

Findings of this nature are significant and especially important, given their potential to inform practice. Moreover, social workers, probation officers, and therapists who work with domestic violence offenders need to explore how their client's particular spirituality and religious beliefs might affect their attitude toward the use of violence in relationships. For those who are incarcerated and sincerely interested in finding spiritual pathways to turn their lives around, what better place to start than with the principle of mutual submission? Upon doing so, it is important to appreciate the complex nature of scripture while guarding against misinterpretations that could further promote intimate partner violence.

NOTES

1   Possible scriptural justification for such patience and faith can be found throughout the Bible. For example, the book of Mark (10:9 NIV) states that "what God has joined together, let no one separate." A similar version is expressed in the book of Matthew (19:6 KJV).

2   While intimate partner violence and domestic violence are overlapping yet distinct constructs, for purposes of this chapter, these are used interchangeably. Although it is beyond the scope of this chapter, the realities of male victimization and physical child abuse are also acknowledged, nonetheless.

3   In popular culture a beat down can be paraphrased in terms of either a verbal and/or physical assault. Literally, it is understood as the act of physically assaulting another person.

4   "The Devil is beating his wife" is an expression, often heard in the southern parts of the US that appears to support IPV. It is commonly associated with the appearance of a sun shower: an unusual meteorological phenomenon where rain is falling while the sun is shining. Before anyone readily accepts this notion, however, it is appropriate to question whether the devil (or anyone for that matter) would beat their wife. See Hendrickson (2000) for further reference.

5   The adage "spare the rod and spoil the child" is often attributed to the Christian Bible. However, it first appeared in a poem by Samuel Butler in 1664. For further reading, see Rossi, H. (n.d.).

6   Translations of Bible verses tend to vary by their source. Regarding the origin of Eve, we find at least three different translations of Genesis 2:22, beginning with the King James Version: "And the rib, which the LORD God had taken from man, made he a woman, and brought her unto the man." The New American Standard Bible (1995) reads slightly differently as: "The LORD God fashioned into a woman the rib, which He had taken from the man, and brought her to the man." God's Word Translation (1995) also differs slightly as: "Then the LORD God formed a woman from the rib that he had taken from the man. He brought her to the man." For purposes of this chapter, all translations reflect the King James Version (2011).

7   A potential limitation of this literature review is that the search was limited to articles and journals retrieved from only five databases, Criminal Justice Abstracts, JSTOR, PsyINFO, Religious Studies, and the Association of Religious Data Archives, which tend to increase the probability of inadequate sampling. The significance of utilizing multiple channels for obtaining research articles is essential for increasing validity of the integrative review (Cooper 1984). Undoubtedly, other articles exist but were excluded from review if they were not found on the aforementioned searches at the time of review.

19

Intimate Partner Violence Survivors

The Struggles of Undocumented Latina Immigrants

MIRIAM G. VALDOVINOS

During my time working in domestic violence shelters, I witnessed that housing and employment requirements were difficult or impossible for Latina undocumented immigrant survivors to meet while protecting their status. One example highlights how these effects can have deadly consequences.

Berta was a model shelter resident who followed the rules, but the pressure to get a job and housing within a short time-frame required her to move out with few supports in place. There were limitations to offer support as she transitioned back to her community as an undocumented immigrant and single parent of four daughters under the age of ten. She left the shelter with hope to restart her life; within eight months, she and three of her daughters were dead by her hand (Associated Press 2007). It is hard to imagine the desperation Berta felt to take her life and the lives of her daughters. This reality temporarily shattered my hope to imagine change for other undocumented immigrant women. It also fuels my purpose to find better ways to identify ongoing struggles for these women.

In subsequent sections of this chapter, I delineate informal and formal help-seeking behaviors along with ongoing struggles that Latina women face as they navigate the Intimate Partner Violence (IPV) help-seeking process. For context, I offer a brief overview of Latinx immigration in the US.

Gender violence is a critical social and public health issue with serious consequences not only for women but also for societies, communities, and families. I acknowledge there is a spectrum of types of gender violence. However, I will focus on the experiences of undocumented Latina immigrant survivors in heterosexual relationships who experience IPV, the most common type of gender violence. IPV is not an isolated event but rather an ongoing pattern of perpetrator behaviors, attitudes, and beliefs used against a survivor. I focus on IPV patterns that consist of a variety of abusive tactics including physical violence, sexual violence, stalking, psychological aggression, and coercive tactics, occurring in multiple episodes over the course of the relationship. My focus highlights a public health perspective (Breiding, Chen, and Black 2014) and simultaneously addresses the abusive behaviors by a current or former intimate partner (e.g., spouse, boyfriend, or dating partner) that may amplify effects of violence on survivors.

Physical violence includes but is not limited to the following: hitting, slapping, punching, pushing, choking, kicking, and confining. Sexual violence includes forced intercourse or any type of unwanted sexual touching, advances, and sexual coercion. Examples of coercive tactics, specific to immigrant women include exploitation of their vulnerabilities such as threatening deportation of the undocumented immigrant survivor or threats directed toward family left behind in the country of origin (Vidales 2010). Lastly, I underscore a feminist perspective in which maintaining *power and control* stems from unequal power relations between women and men (hooks 1984; Johnson 2008). I also incorporate a social work perspective that centers the experiences of marginalized communities. This helps us grapple with issues of access to services or assistance as it relates to social justice and human rights frameworks (Perilla 1999). I use the terms "undocumented Latina immigrants" to refer to a social condition rather than as a social identity. Classifying a person as undocumented signifies that there are systematic barriers that prohibit them from getting assistance. For example, the 1996 Personal Responsibility and Work Opportunity Reconciliation Act (PRWORA) restricts the limits of public benefits and social services for both documented (those with legal authorization to reside in the US) and undocumented immigrants (Massey, Durand, and Malone 2002). PRWORA expands the restrictions already in most federal and state assistance programs and adds a barrier for states that want to include immigrants in state-funded services. The struggles of Latina undocumented immigrant IPV survivors need to be further examined under this context particularly in light of anti-immigrant sentiment.

Immigration Context

Approximately 56.6 million people in the US identify as Latinos, constituting 17.6 percent of the total population (Krogstad 2016). Of the 20.5 million Latinos who are foreign born, close to eleven million are unauthorized; they represent 82 percent of undocumented residents but only make up 3.7 percent of the nation's populace (Passel and Cohn 2012). Ngai (2004) chronicles the origins of the "illegal alien" in American law as illegal immigration emerged as a twentieth-century issue, and continues into the twenty-first century in US immigration policy. Mexicans and Central Americans comprise the majority of undocumented immigrants (Passel and Cohn 2012). Thus, US immigration discussions foster a racialization of the "illegal immigrant" (DeGenova 2002) and occur in a polemical context where race and ethnicity are politically charged (Chavez 2008).

Immigration and Gender

Women comprise 46 percent of the estimated eleven million undocumented immigrants residing in the US, altering our assumptions that the typical immigrant is male (Ruiz, Zong, and Batalova 2015). Women often articulate economic rationales for migrating or reunifying with family (Hondagneu-Sotelo 1994; Malkin 2007). Typically, women migrate with the support of preestablished social networks (Segura and Zavella 2007). Once they arrive, female immigrants experience gendered and racialized interactions when they engage in employment, education, and social relationships. Menjivar's (2000) study delineates how women have fewer financial and material resources, placing them at a disadvantage. Nevertheless, women actively seek help from community organizations for their families' needs, which permits them to expand and establish networks independent from men. Their networks provide linkages to access resources and are key in disseminating information.

Intimate Partner Violence and IPV Help-Seeking

Researchers in the area of IPV have broadly studied the etiology, prevalence rates, incidence rates, health consequences, and potential interventions to address the violence. According to the National Intimate Partner and Sexual Violence Survey (NISVS) (Black et al. 2011), more than one-third of women in the US have experienced some form of IPV such as rape, physical violence, or stalking during their lifetimes. Among those women, more than one third have experienced multiple types of IPV. Recent estimates also demonstrate that more than a third (37.1 percent) of Hispanic/Latina women have experienced physical violence by an intimate partner in their lifetime (Breiding, Chen, and Black 2014). IPV rates of Latina women are comparable to other ethnic and racial groups of women in national surveys, findings that require us to go beyond a culture-deficit or culture-blaming approach to explain IPV occurrences in Latino families.

The degree of violence may be similar in immigrant and nonimmigrant communities, but the severity of IPV effects indicates variation (Sokoloff 2008). Edelson, Hokoda, and Ramos-Lira (2007) indicate that Latinas who had been victims of domestic violence have significantly greater trauma-related symptoms than non-Latinas. Latina immigrant women are affected by IPV in various ways: some are typical of all IPV survivors and others are related to their immigrant status including family isolation, a lack of access to dignified employment, limitations navigating new language skills, and sometimes concerns with their legal status (Menjivar and Salcido 2002). Further evidence suggests that as Latinas became more acculturated, i.e., less traditional, more independent, and more educated, their risks of experiencing IPV increase (Cuevas, Sabina, and Picard 2010; Denham, et al. 2007; Garcia, Hurwitz, and Kraus 2005; Harris, Firestone, and Vega 2005; Hazen and Soriano 2007). Therefore, as Dasgupta (2005) argues, immigrant IPV survivors' experiences need to be recognized within the social context of gender, race, class, and immigrant-status relations while also recognizing the effects of cultural continuity and change.

The IPV help-seeking process is often sequential: "IPV survivors progress from private attempts to deal with the violence (e.g., placating and resisting) to informal support (e.g., family and friends) and as the violence worsens, survivors engage in more public help-seeking (e.g., from legal system or community agencies)" (Liang et al. 2005, 77). Some studies demonstrate a link between the severity of the violence and the help-seeking tactics used (Coker et al. 2000; Goodman et al. 2003). The theoretical framework I use aligns with Gondolf and Fisher's (1988) survivor perspective, which views IPV victims as resilient, persistent, and strong rather than submissive and passive in response to the violence (Walker 1984). The survivorship perspective demonstrates women are survivors, acting assertively and logically in response to the violence. Moe (2007) indicates that women resist their victimization even when the help-seeking efforts are unsuccessful due to institutional failures. Help-seeking efforts may be mostly unmet, but women actively engage in help-seeking behaviors to address the violence.

Survivors of IPV encounter many barriers when they seek help. For undocumented Latina immigrants, there are additional barriers. Institutions that exist to address IPV may overlook women living in the shadows and may not be equipped to address the specific issues that immigrant women face (Reina and Lohman 2015). Previous research illustrates some of these limitations for immigrant IPV survivors in health care settings (Gibson 2013) and public assistance (i.e., welfare) programs (Kullgren 2003). Latina undocumented immigrant survivors rarely share IPV experiences with health practitioners because they are afraid of the impact of their disclosures on their immigration status (Kelly 2006).

Help-Seeking Experiences for Latina Immigrants

Research studies have investigated help-seeking differences between Latina IPV survivors and non-Latina IPV survivors. The National Alcohol and Family Violence Survey (Kantor, Jasinski, and Aldarondo 1994) queried a nationally representative sample that included an oversample of Latinos. They found that women are active help seekers; however, Latinas underutilize both informal and formal resources relative to White women. Low acculturation, measured by preference for the Spanish language, is the only significant cultural barrier for Latinas seeking help. West and colleagues (1998) elaborate on these findings by taking into account the total amount of help-seeking. Less than 50 percent of the Latina survivors in this sample seek one or more types of help, while 66 percent of White women did so. Conventional patterns of help-seeking are similar across ethnic groups, with friends and relatives being the most likely source of support, but Latinas seek less help from both informal and formal sources.

Lipsky et al. (2006) studied a sample from a hospital-based study of adult female patients seen at an urban emergency department (ED) in Dallas, Texas. This research examined the relationship between IPV and health and social services utilization, with a focus on racial and ethnic disparities. Specific help-seeking behaviors were significantly associated with race and ethnicity among IPV victims. Non-Hispanic White and Black women were more likely to use housing assistance and ED services and Black women were more likely to use police assistance compared to Hispanic/Latina women. It is important to mention that non-Hispanic White women were nine times more likely and non-Hispanic Black women were six times more likely than Hispanic/Latina women to use the ED in the previous twelve months. This low utilization emphasized that many undocumented immigrant women may not access emergency room assistance even when they experience IPV (Berk and Shur 2001; Gibson 2013).

Ingram's study (2007) on IPV prevalence and help-seeking showed a different pattern. Overall, this study concluded that Latino households reported seeking help for IPV victimization at a similar level to that of non-Latino households in the sample. Comparable help-seeking patterns are observed for Latinos and non-Latinos. Respondents reach out for help in this order: talking to a family member, a friend, a health care worker, the police, and a clergy person. This research also found that Latino immigrants were less likely than nonimmigrants to seek help from formal agencies. Latinos were less likely to know about community IPV resources compared to non-Latinos. The only significant difference between Latinos and non-Latinos in the types of services they seek was that non-Latinos are more likely than Latinos to seek access to shelters. It is important to mention that immigration status was only asked in regard to the length of time the person resided in the US, so undocumented status was not assessed.

Though there is paucity in the literature, some scholars articulate a need to investigate factors that may exacerbate the effects of IPV for Latina undocumented immigrants. These include linguistic and cultural barriers (Acevedo 2000; Bauer et al. 2000; Murdaugh et al. 2004); experiences of structural inequality, such as legal issues tied to immigration (Amar et al. 2005; Bui 2003); and oppressive practices by agencies that are not equipped to handle the complexities of Latina immigrants' lives (Dutton, Orloff, and Hass 2000). An example of an oppressive practice is the disregard shelter programs have for complex legal consequences that affect undocumented immigrant women. Employment or housing may require government-issued identification cards or work permits that are unavailable to this population.

One of the largest research endeavors organized by a nonprofit community agency that offers legal and social services focused on the characteristics of help seeking and available resources for Latina immigrant women survivors (Dutton, Orloff, and Hass 2000). Surveys were conducted with women seeking help who experienced physical and/or sexual abuse, experienced only psychological abuse, and a nonabused control group. Forty-four percent of the participants reported being undocumented, the majority from Mexico. This study details the various types of help that women most utilize. Latina IPV survivors most often speak to female friends or relatives (i.e., mothers and sisters) and religious leaders first rather than helping professionals. They report the informal support is helpful when their relatives or friends encourage them to leave the abuse and when they receive emotional support. Some women do not disclose because of the shame and fear of the perpetrator. Most women reach out for help from personal networks. Women ask for assistance from the criminal justice system only after they cannot secure help with relatives and/or friends.

Concerns of Isolation and Social Networks

The most common reason previously cited for IPV survivors not talking to someone from their social network relates to isolation (Fugate et al. 2005). The layers of isolation intensify if immigrant women are far away from family which Menjivar and Salcido's (2002) extensive research demonstrates is often the case for immigrant women permanently living in various industrialized immigrant-receiving countries. The women may want to discuss the IPV with someone, but they do not have anyone available. This is also the case for most of the undocumented immigrant women whom I interviewed in my study (Valdovinos 2016). Unfortunately, their circumstances include the legal limitation that if they return to their country of origin, they could not return to the US due to their undocumented status, thus further isolating them from support systems. They may also experience cultural isolation when they immigrate, as they become a minoritized group and lose social status, access to financial resources, and the support of family and friends left behind in their countries of origin.

Immigrants may hold traditional values of familial ties and support, but their immigrant circumstances make these resources less available to them compared to US-born survivors. For example, women in Acevedo's study (2000) report that they consider reaching out for assistance but recognize their social support systems are geographically and/or emotionally unavailable. Therefore, social isolation intensifies for immigrants because their extended family support systems may be in another country. The immigration process often leads to fragmentation of the extended family, which Latina women may have relied on in the past to resolve conflict (Ginorio et al. 1995; Yoshioka et al. 2003).

A lack of economic resources and nonexistent or limited support systems often cause immigrant women to depend financially and emotionally on their intimate partners. Thus, they stay in abusive relationships longer (Brabeck and Guzmán 2009). A combination of fewer educational attainment opportunities, inferior incomes, and lower acculturation create more vulnerable and isolated experiences for Latina immigrant survivors (West, Kantor, and Jasinski 1998).

Understanding IPV and Societal Realities for Immigrants

In her research, Zavella (2011) states that Latino immigrants' illegality affects their sociopolitical condition through immigration sweeps, detainment, deportation, or harassment, which pushes them into clandestine lives. This reality influences their help-seeking efforts. Nondisclosure of the IPV because of their undocumented immigrant status adds complexity to accessing formal services. It also limits how their social networks may respond when they disclose the violence. One possibility could be that family and friends discourage the survivors from seeking formal help because they worry that the survivors' undocumented status places them at risk of discrimination, or worse, at risk of deportation. Interestingly, the women want the help, as long as their needs are respected.

A second possibility could be that family and friends blame the survivor for any repercussions that the perpetrator may face after the IPV is public knowledge. Criminal and legal systems have often promoted IPV interventions that address public safety concerns (Horton and Johnson 1993) in order to protect IPV survivors. This means that certain IPV behaviors may be prosecuted as criminal offenses. For perpetrators that are undocumented immigrants or in the process of legalizing their immigration status, an arrest for an IPV crime may have detrimental effects that reverberate across the family members (Vidales 2010). In my study (Valdovinos 2016), several respondents shared stories of the multiple stressors their families raised after women decided to report the IPV to the police. Sometimes the accused abuser lost permission to legally reside in the US after receiving domestic violence charges. Other times, their partners were deported and it affected the home finances. Family may blame the survivors for this situation rather than support their decision. Regrettably, the violence continues to be a secret, so it is difficult to address the effects.

Formal Help-Seeking Patterns

The frequency of seeking formal help varies depending on Latina undocumented immigrants' IPV experiences, occurrences, and intensity. This assistance may include calling the police, accessing shelter, obtaining protection orders for the IPV, receiving mental health services, and pursuing legal immigration, housing, and health services. The informal help seeking discussed above reinforces that going outside of their social networks for help is rarely the first step for immigrant survivors (Reina, Lohman, and Maldonado 2014). Often, Latina immigrants share that formal help-seeking behaviors are relevant in severe conditions when they fear for their life or their children's lives (Valdovinos 2016). These responses are observed in studies that focus on the help-seeking process as well (Moe 2007).

A large-scale interview project with immigrant Latina survivors (Amar et al. 2005), finds that less than a third of women (27 percent) call the police. These study participants were mostly from Central America, and Mexican women were least likely to call the police. Of the women who called the police, most made fewer than three calls (74 percent). In a smaller ethnographic study (Acevedo 2000), the women who called the police had mixed opinions about the assistance they received. Two women stated their partners were quickly released from jail only escalating the violence further. Language barriers and victims being ignored by police officers are also obstacles that hinder efforts to call the police to obtain assistance for the IPV situations.

Women also reach out to counselors but domestic violence shelters are a choice of last resort (Acevedo 2000; Valdovinos 2016). This is mostly due to lack of information regarding shelters and reticence to disclose IPV. Dutton and colleagues (2000) suggest that awareness of the signs of abuse and cultural sensitivity need to be a part of the efforts used by law and health care professionals.

Other common formal services include immigration assistance, maternal and child health care, and health insurance (Dutton, Orloff, and Hass 2000). Very few Latina immigrants access government resources such as Medicaid, food stamps, cash assistance (TANF), and social security benefits (Vargas and Pirog 2016). Undocumented immigrants are ineligible for most federal and state assistance (Massey, Durand, and Malone 2002), but as parents of US citizen children, they are eligible to access these programs for their children. However, ongoing fears of deportation continue to deter these parents from accessing help for their US citizen children and it is having an impact on their children's health (Vargas and Ybarra 2017).

Unique Barriers to Access Formal Help

IPV research with immigrant women has demonstrated that immigrants are less likely to access formal social services than their US citizen counterparts due to social isolation, language barriers, discrimination, and fear of deportation (Acevedo 2000; Ammar et al. 2005; Bui 2003; Dutton, Orloff, and Hass 2000). More specifically, the barriers faced by US Latinas when seeking IPV help include lack of information about legal rights and availability of domestic violence services; fear that IPV reports will result in citizenship denial or deportation; and distrust of police and fear that they will respond inadequately to IPV disputes (Rios 2007). The respondents in Rios' study also identified negative experiences with assistance programs, which include long delays or failure to obtain a shelter bed, difficulty communicating because of the lack of bilingual staff, geographic inaccessibility, and transportation difficulties. The isolation the women experienced suggests that they have less access to people that could share information about formal services. For those women who do navigate the formal system, accessing services takes multiple attempts. Reina, Lohman, and Maldonado (2014) also demonstrate that immigration status and the inability to understand IPV within given cultural norms are barriers for Latina immigrant survivors to seek formal help.

Undocumented immigrant Latina IPV survivors did not always passively accept the violence, and they use various strategies within different levels of social constraints to navigate their safety and survival. Their help-seeking behaviors are complex, diverse, and shaped not only by their IPV experiences but also by structural, cultural, and situational forces that can both impede and facilitate their efforts to reach out for help. Few studies focus explicitly on the help-seeking behaviors of undocumented Latina immigrants. Thus, there is a need to recognize formal help navigation for undocumented IPV survivors especially if there is an assumption that they may not seek help because of their immigration status. As Dutton and colleagues remind us, "The immigrant battered Latina may easily fall between the cracks of available complex systems of help because the unique web of contextual layers reflected in the nested ecology of her life may necessitate more individualized, coordinated, and comprehensive responses" (2000, 12).

Practice Implications and Future Steps

Research with immigrant communities remains limited especially with respect to the help-seeking efforts that Latina immigrant women incorporate when they are undocumented immigrants in the US. The studies described in this chapter identify help-seeking struggles Latina undocumented immigrant IPV survivors experienced when accessing both informal (e.g., talking to a family member, friend, or faith leader) and formal (e.g., calling police, seeking shelter, talking to a counselor) assistance. This analysis reveals that an array of circumstances affect when and how women seek help.

Understanding these concerns for undocumented immigrant Latinas in the twenty-first century's social welfare context offers one iteration of a larger dialogue that is still materializing. When serving immigrants, practice implications challenge scholars and practitioners to find ways to balance existing limited resources (Kullgren 2003; Romero and Romero-Williams 2013). Recently there has been increasing attention on the role of social welfare systems that collaborate with immigration enforcement to regulate how immigrants access provisions (Wessler, 2011). The few studies that have examined how deportation fears influence participation in public assistance programs by immigrant families continue to see less participation from these families and deleterious effects of the families' well-being (Vargas and Pirog 2016; Aýon and Becerra 2013). Having a deeper understanding of Latina immigrants' help-seeking efforts and struggles can help us to further influence social service provisions offered to immigrant IPV survivors.

If we want to improve the safety and well-being of undocumented Latina immigrant survivors of IPV, it is critical to acknowledge that it is not simply about having practitioners available to respond to them, but rather it matters *how* providers in these support systems respond. The disclosure of their immigrant status and the IPV is influenced by fear, stigma, and a reasonable distrust of how these systems will meet their needs. We must consider all the barriers undocumented women will encounter from when they receive referral information until the help is rendered. Often, the women with the most needs do not follow through with obtaining service provisions even though they are eligible for the aid (Villalón 2010). Hence, service provision may require step-by-step assistance to improve interactions and program delivery for immigrant survivors. Given an increase in deportations for even minor infractions, it is unclear how current policy may augment fears and decrease help seeking behaviors thus further endangering the safety of undocumented immigrants who experience IPV.

Service provision efforts need to go beyond IPV-specific services and offer a space of interdisciplinary interventions. It is imperative to incorporate these types of service provisions particularly when it comes to mental health therapeutic services or prenatal/postnatal care. Building partnerships with health care settings or schools could reach a larger audience, especially for isolated immigrant survivors. Strategies under the auspices of child and maternal health can further reach groups that may not look for IPV-specific help. Nevertheless, for undocumented immigrant survivors, advocacy efforts need to be persistent to ensure that accessibility to law enforcement and hospital emergency rooms is culturally responsive.

Women report that their children are of primary concern. As parents, they are invested in understanding how their children will heal as adults from the IPV wounds that linger; yet, the services rendered do not always recognize this point. Interestingly, a paradox is articulated when centering their children's concern. The women share that their children are the reason for staying in an abusive relationship as well as deciding to leave an abusive partner. With their children's well-being in mind, they assess their situations and realize that the violent environment is more detrimental to their children than the negative financial conditions that could persist a long time after their abusive partner is no longer in the picture. This realization is complicated and it occurs within a context of IPV dynamics intersecting with undocumented immigration status, so this crux requires a deeper analysis for meaningful practice changes.

Also evident is the need to address labor involvement and job training options for undocumented survivors. If the expectation continues to be that IPV survivors need to leave the abusive partner to survive, there is a risk of further displacing undocumented immigrant IPV survivors. Because employment limitations are enmeshed with their undocumented immigrant status, it is extremely burdensome to find work that pays a living wage to be able to support their children as single parents. The women's long-term barriers illuminate that simply asking undocumented immigrant women to leave a violent relationship is not appropriately assessing for long-term financial barriers. Self-sufficiency seems impossible without a legal work permit, but it continues to be a goal for which undocumented IPV survivors yearn. Job training programs could potentially offer useful tools, but policy changes are also required to ensure this is a viable option within the constraints of the law.

For IPV survivors in general, there are obstacles related to financial disruptions to their livelihoods (Moe and Bell 2004; Renzetti 2009). Financial barriers are also concerning for undocumented immigrant women. Decreased employment options are the reality with increased use of employment verification programs to ensure a person is authorized to work legally in the US. The implications of these realities are profound as the women find themselves without employment during vulnerable moments. To leave an abusive partner often means losing the only household income—that of the partner. Access to child support is nonexistent if their ex-partners are also undocumented immigrants. Being undocumented affects securing employment, and as single parents with limited support, it situates them outside of formal membership and social legitimacy as Ngai (2004) argued.

Policy Implications

The women's intersectional experiences (Bograd 2005) demand that the policy implications for IPV and immigration laws are understood. The immigration-related decisions that are made (or not made) at a federal level will impact the state level social service response as well as the local efforts to find alternatives that privately fund IPV interventions via foundations. Policymakers need to be aware of the unintended consequences of the multiple systems (local, state, federal, international) interacting with one another. An IPV immigrant survivor may have access to employment authorization, but this process requires a long wait to know eligibility. In theory, women are expected to wait without financial support, but in life, they need money to survive. Undocumented immigrant IPV survivors are at risk of falling through the cracks without proper recognition of the complexities they encounter with multisystemic policies.

Policies need to be critically examined since there is an initial focus on criminal justice responses which leads to policies mandating criminal justice interventions (e.g. mandatory arrest, victimless prosecution, shelters requiring orders of protection) (Fugate et al. 2005). If undocumented parents are detained and/or deported, their children are at risk of being placed in child protective services custody (Wessler 2011). The terrible choices involved for women who must face the possibility of losing custody of their children if they seek assistance for IPV illustrates the importance of addressing overlapping policy systems. The consequences of these policies are creating havoc in the daily lives of the women. This requires that IPV advocates have up-to-date resources, and that they connect with policy makers to influence policy changes.

Future Research

Culturally responsive methodologies and theories to resist the marginalization of undocumented immigrant IPV survivors are crucial. Multifaceted approaches, macro (policy advocacy), meso (community support), and micro (awareness) are essential. Future research should focus on IPV health effects for undocumented immigrant survivors especially when we consider that most immigrant women never enter a hospital or health clinic to disclose the IPV.

Ideally, the myriad experiences of undocumented immigrant women within global migration flows need to be captured. The various modes of migration, the different immigration policies across the US and other countries, and the diverse arrival treatment of immigrants of color influence their experiences and should inform policy and the interventions of helping professionals. Future research needs to go beyond the lumping of "Latina/Hispanic survivor" into one unitary group. By not generalizing, we can explore how diverse immigration experiences, sociocultural factors, and sociopolitical factors affect their experiences. This could capture a deeper understanding of the barriers of their unique situations and the ways they have overcome the violence. Ongoing issues need to strengthen our culturally responsive practices and cultivate caring processes at the forefront of our efforts. The well-being of many communities, families, and individuals inspire us to continue this work.

Children and Gender Violence

"Big happiness, small happiness." In China, this colloquialism signifies the birth of a son and of a daughter, respectively. Although China is not the only country where a cultural preference for males persists, it has attracted international attention because it has the world's worst case of "missing" girls. Currently in China, there are 33.5 million more males than females, a very significant statistical imbalance (Kotese 2017). This is slightly better than previous years, where the "one child" policy produced the most skewed gender balance in the world. This disturbing trend is rooted in more than patriarchal cultural ideology. In societies where males are more highly rewarded for their labor than are women and adult daughters are expected to leave their families, but sons are responsible for caring for elderly parents, sons are a good investment, whereas daughters are a liability (Renzetti, Edleson, and Bergen 2001).

This situation was exacerbated in China, where an aggressive population control policy imposed heavy economic penalties on families that had more than one child. Put in place in 1979, and just recently lifted, this strategy enabled China to address overpopulation, but it inadvertently promoted female infanticide. The widespread availability of ultrasound technology facilitated the systematic removal of girls from the population through sex-selective abortion, despite laws against using the technology for prenatal sex determination.

In response to myriad social problems introduced by this family-planning strategy, China phased out the policy in 2015 and eliminated it in 2016. Sociologists and demographers estimate that four hundred million births were prevented, with enormous social and economic consequences (Gracie 2015). Although formal policy in China changed to a "two child" policy in 2015, it has not been enough to bring the gender balance back into alignment (Kotese 2017).

Recent data implicates several other countries in the problem of "missing girls" (Advocates for Youth 2012). The belief that sons are more valuable undergirds a significant social problem that results in devastating discrimination against girl children.

Children are linked to a gendered system of power through their historical social position as the personal property of fathers, as well as their location in sex-stratified political states. Their rights to self-determination about work, bodily integrity, basic care, and life itself have been contested over time. By the early 1950s, the notion of children's rights emerged as an international policy issue worthy of serious attention. The United Nations (UN) approved the Declaration on the Rights of the Child in 1959, establishing as fundamental the right to access health care, housing, and education, as well as to be free from abuse, neglect, and exploitation. Thirty years later, the UN adopted the Convention on the Rights of the Child, expanding protections to prohibit involvement in armed conflict, prostitution, and pornography. Alone among member nations of the UN, at this writing the US is the only country that has not ratified it. Sadly, the world continues to be precarious for children.

Children's Exposure to Violence

Children are also exposed to violence through witnessing attacks that occur in their homes and communities. Around the world, millions of children live through war-related violence, and in the US, children of color who live in impoverished urban neighborhoods are disproportionately exposed to community violence (Mohammed, Shapiro, and Wainright 2015; Finkelhor, Turner, Shattuck, and Hamby 2015; Halevi, Djalovski, Vengrober, and Feldman 2016). It is within their own families, however, that children are most likely to witness violent assaults; and research suggests that exposure to intimate partner violence (IPV) appears to produce the most trauma for children (Osofsky 2018).

Fantuzzo and Fusco (2007) found that children were present in 43 percent of the police-involved events analyzed in their study and that the majority of events involved witnessing serious injuries to their mothers. Whether children see it or hear it or witness only the aftermath, IPV is a terrifying experience that profoundly affects the way they understand their world. Girls tend to suffer from lowered self-esteem, and boys exhibit greater levels of hostility and aggression (Edleson 1999). Both boys and girls who witness violence exhibit symptoms associated with post-traumatic stress disorder (PTSD) including anxiety, depression, sleep disturbances, and somatic complaints, and problems often persist in adulthood (McNeal and Amato 1998).

These early findings are supported by a more recent study by Wamser-Nanney and Cherry (2018). They found that in addition to symptoms of PTSD and depression, young girls and boys exhibited differences in how they expressed the emotional damage they sustained as witnesses to family violence. Female children experienced more overall PTSD symptoms, especially dissociation and reexperiencing flashbacks, while male children were actively involved with attempting to protect a parent in the midst of an IPV incident. This led to higher rates of psychological hyperarousal and emotional dysregulation among boys.

Media and Technology

Web-based content is omnipresent, allowing for instant access to an endless reservoir of media. This torrent of information allows adults and children to immerse themselves in an online world full of possibilities ranging from academic and empowering, to debased and violent. Given that these many forms of media are replete with violent images, many of them gendered in nature, concern about the effects of mass media on youth is warranted, particularly because it is through the mass media that "the social constructions of violence and social control emerge for popular consumption and legitimation" (Barak 2003, 200).

In a study that traces images of female victimization over the past thirty-one years, Lynch, Tompkins, van Driel, and Fritz (2016) found trends of male-oriented aggression toward gaming characters and a disturbing binary regarding female images: they are represented as "victims or vixens." Although most research suggests that viewing these images has no significant direct effect on engaging in violent behavior, exposure to media violence seems to promote higher levels of aggression through a process of dehumanization; the goal of the experience is to hit targets and revel in blood and gore, as opposed to acknowledging the hurt caused to virtual people (Greitemeyer and McLatchie 2011). These findings are more relevant than ever, given the recent research regarding the amount of time children are consuming online content, primarily videos, gaming, and social media. While scientific studies cannot establish a predictive link (nor can it discount one), dehumanized violence, particularly along gendered lines, has powerful anecdotal significance as report after report of mass shootings at schools, workplaces, and public venues occur with sickening frequency.

The independent research group Childwise published a study documenting that children between the ages of six and sixteen are spending six hours per day on screens (Wakefield 2015). The amount of time spent online exposes children to additional threats: abuse via technology. The US Department of Justice compiled a disturbing set of facts that underscores the danger of unsupervised access to online media: the most common place for children to encounter a predator was an online chat room. Approximately 13 percent of youth internet users experienced unwanted solicitation and 27 percent of the solicitations asked for sexual pictures from the children (USDOJ 2018).

A particularly monstrous example of child exploitation and abuse involving online transmission and commerce was uncovered recently in Canada. Investigators from Toronto's Sex Crime Unit discovered over 350,000 graphic images and nine thousand videos of child sexual abuse in the home of a former schoolteacher who ran a $4 million business distributing the images to over fifty countries around the world. Among the more than three hundred others arrested in this international child pornography ring were people who worked closely with children, including "40 school teachers, nine doctors and nurses, six law enforcement personnel, nine pastors and priests and three foster parents," according to the inspector in charge of the three-year investigation (Silva 2019, n.p.). Investigators claim to have "rescued" nearly four hundred children who were exploited; of course, the long life of web-based images has the potential to trail and further torment these children throughout their lives (Keller and Dance 2019).

Sexual Abuse

Child sexual abuse has been recognized as a social problem since the late 1970s, when women began to speak out about sexual assaults they had suffered as children, often at the hands of family members or trusted members of their communities. These personal testimonies sparked scholars to take a new look at an issue that had been relegated to silence. With the publication of *The Best Kept Secret*, Florence Rush became one of the first people to place contemporary child sexual abuse in a historical and cultural context. Finding that early religious law supported the sexual use of children, she asserted, "the sexual abuse of children by adults has never been established as an irrefutable legal and moral violation and to this day remains a debatable polemic" (1980, 73).

In the US and around the world, children are still sexually exploited in a variety of ways, including pornography (as illustrated above), prostitution, sexual molestation, and rape by both family members and unrelated persons. It is very difficult to develop comprehensive statistics on the sexual victimization of children given the multiple forms, locations, and causes of the abuse. The difficulty in gathering reliable information is compounded by the nature of such abuse—children are not generally prepared to discuss sexual matters inside or outside the family, and children may be threatened with dire consequences if they divulge the secret. Some children do not seek assistance because they feel complicit in their victimization, especially when the abuser is a family member whom they love. This point is emphasized by Armstrong (2007) in her essay "Who Stole Incest?" which challenges us to frame incest as a social issue that demands political solutions. Armstrong, who was one of the first people to assert a feminist position on the sexual abuse of children (see *Kiss Daddy Goodnight* 1978), critiques the dominant cultural discourse that frames incest as an illness rather than as a crime of violence against children.

Legal definitions of sexual abuse in the contemporary US emphasize the notion of consent. Most states consider incest illegal in all circumstances, and every state has laws identifying the age at which a person is considered capable of consenting to sexual activity with an unrelated person (ranging from fourteen to eighteen). In 2017, however, Nicholas Kristof of the *New York Times* discovered an exception to the laws designed to protect girls from coercive sexual abuse: parental consent. Kristof reported that thousands of young girls, some as young as eleven, were married to their abusers at their families' behest. Shockingly, he reported that forty-nine states in the US allowed child marriage, with Delaware as the only exception (Kristof 2017). According to Rape, Abuse & Incest National Network (RAINN) from 2009–2013, Child Protective Services agencies substantiated or found strong evidence to indicate that 63,000 children a year were victims of sexual abuse, yet thousands more cases undoubtedly go unreported (RAINN 2018).

Government data reveal that children are sexually abused in 10 percent of documented child-maltreatment cases, with male close relatives as the perpetrators in 88 percent of the incidents (US Department of Health and Human Services 2014). Self-report surveys indicate that at least 20 percent of women and 5 percent of men were sexually victimized as children. Girls are more likely to be abused within the family than outside it, and most incestuous abuse is committed by fathers and stepfathers against daughters (ibid.). However, reports of boys being sexually abused, especially by male coaches and religious leaders, have been increasing (Kimmel 2005; Sullivan this volume).

In other parts of the world, boys are subject to abuses that are compounded by an almost complete lack of social support. After a recent report of at least 165 cases of rape by educators in three schools in Afghanistan, attention has again focused on the tradition of *bacha bazi* in which boys are forced to dress as girls and are then raped or prostituted. The police sexually assaulted several of the raped boys after they made reports. A heroic effort by a local child advocacy group uncovered the assaults, but an activist, Mohammad Musa, was then detained by the Afghani intelligence agency and was forced to retract the report. Meanwhile, several of the boys who reported rapes have been found dead, in some cases at the hand of their shamed families (Zucchino and Faizi 2019a; Zucchino and Faizi 2019b).

Child sexual assault is correlated with myriad emotional, cognitive, physical, psychological, and behavioral effects, most of which are mediated by the victim's age or developmental level and the relationship of the perpetrator to the victim. Survivors of childhood sexual abuse are four times more likely to develop PTSD, drug and alcohol addictions, and suffer from major depression in adulthood (US DHSS 2014). For adolescent girls, sexual victimization is also correlated with sexual acting out and running away, both of which place girls at high risk for revictimization, unplanned pregnancy, and sexually transmitted diseases (Barnett, Miller-Perrin, and Perrin 2005; Baynard, Williams, Siegel, and West 2002).

In addition to the economic changes that accompany globalization, international and civil wars in the Middle East and Africa spur a massive increase in refugees seeking asylum in Europe and the US. Kingsley, Rice-Oxley and Nardelli (2015) tracked statistics for European asylum requests from 220,000 in 2014 to 900,000 in 2015. The UN High Commissioner for Refugees estimates more than half of all refugees are children fleeing desperate circumstances in their home countries, many of whom must travel alone. Women and children attempting to escape violence in their own countries are at significant risk for trafficking and forced prostitution at many points along the journey.

The exploding refugee crisis, particularly in the Mediterranean, grabbed headlines around the world. Mainstream and social media erupted with disturbing images and videos of heartbreaking trauma and desperate attempts for families, many with young children, to find safety. The image of Alan Kurdi, the dead three-year-old boy whose corpse washed ashore along the beaches of Turkey, was a pivotal moment of global outrage. Pictures of his tiny body facedown in the sand horrified the world, and yet many thousands more have died since.

Violence in Schools and Communities

More than 215,000 children have been exposed to gun violence at school since the massacre at Columbine High School (Cox et al. 2018). If the carnage in Littleton, Colorado, serves as a macabre milestone, there have been 208 multiple casualty attacks in American schools since that day in 1999. Sadly, these events are happening with horrifying frequency, so that any statistic about events or victims is almost immediately obsolete. Similar to the information about adults who commit mass murder, juvenile school shooters are overwhelmingly White, male, and armed with multiple weapons. Fulton (2017) conservatively estimated that 50 percent of mass shootings are rooted in IPV, with that trend evident in the histories of teenagers who commit gun violence at school. And while school shootings create a storm of media coverage and generate yearly tallies, daily gun violence in communities is most often perpetrated by men and kills and injures thousands more children.

Lockhart (2018) and Lopez (2018) tracked statistics and trends from the Centers for Disease Control and other government agencies. They discovered that Black children are ten times more likely to die by gun violence than their White peers. Lopez links racial stereotyping to inaction on the issue: "The racial breakdown may help explain the lack of national attention to more typical gun violence. We know that racial biases make White Americans more likely to perceive Black people as less innocent and even as criminals, which may, in some people's minds, make these victims more deserving of the gun violence in their communities" (2018).

Sexual Harassment

Because of its frequency, the numbers of people affected by sexual harassment, and the widespread and damaging outcomes for victims is arguably one of the most virulent forms of gender violence experienced by children. Children may be introduced to sexual harassment as early as kindergarten, when girls are subjected to a barrage of verbal attacks on their abilities, their options, and their bodies, all intended to remind them that they are expected to limit their aspirations. Not only does the harassment make girls feel like second-class citizens, but it also has a chilling effect on their willingness to call attention to themselves by participating in class, which ultimately may cause their school performance to suffer.

Boys who do not meet standards of athleticism are insulted with homophobic taunts. Even children who do not directly experience such assaults are affected by the excessive pressure to meet cultural ideals of masculinity and femininity (Martino 2000). Youth who internalize rigid gender expectations may cope with feelings of anxiety, inferiority, and powerlessness by engaging in self-destructive behavior such as alcohol and drug use, early involvement in sexual activity, participation in high-risk ventures, and self-inflicted violence.

Sexual Orientation, Gender Identity, and Violence

The last fifteen years have seen steady but uneven progress in confronting homophobia and dismantling oppressive systems that targeted gay and lesbian people for discrimination. Achievement of marriage equality in several countries, the repeal of "Don't Ask, Don't Tell" in the US military and the "Defense of Marriage Act" by the US Supreme Court stand out as moments of celebration and progress. However, LGBTQ+ children still experience bullying, harassment, and social exclusion at much higher rates than their nonsexual-minority peers (Centers for Disease Control 2012, 2015).

Suicide is the second leading cause of death among young people between the ages of ten to twenty-four; LGBTQ+ children are five times more likely to contemplate suicide and five times more likely to attempt suicide than their heterosexual peers. Queer youth with highly rejecting families are eight times more likely to attempt suicide (Centers for Disease Control 2012, 2015).

Transgender and gender nonconforming children have become significantly more visible in the last ten years. A report by Grant, Motet, Tanis, Harrison, Herman, and Keeling is the largest study to date about the challenges faced by transgender and gender nonconforming children. The report, entitled "Injustice at Every Turn," described a harrowing existence from 6,500 participants. The report documented an exponentially higher risk of physical and sexual abuse, substance abuse, suicidality, and family rejection (Grant et al. 2011).

The report also identified that transgender people have significantly higher rates of poverty, and racial/ethnic minorities experienced more frequent and more severe violence from family members and from the community. Research by Olsen, Durwood, DeMeules, and McLaughlin (2016) studied seventy-three prepubescent transgender children and offered some crucial examples of hope and resilience. Their work showed that when children socially transition with support and acceptance from their parents, there is no elevation in rates of depression and only slightly increased rates of anxiety. The major findings of their study: psychopathology is not inevitable and changes to the social environment that increase compassion and inclusion drastically change lives and outcomes.

The readings in this section urge us to reconsider commonly held beliefs about why, how, and by whom children are victimized. These articles challenge assumptions about children and gender violence by arguing for a more complex, nuanced understanding of the problems associated with children and gender violence.

SUGGESTIONS FOR FURTHER READING

Eduardo Duran, *Healing the Soul Wound: Counseling with Native Americans and Other Native Peoples*, 2006

Nadine Burke Harris, *The Deepest Well: Healing the Long-Term Effects of Childhood Adversity*, 2018

Judith Lewis Herman, *Father-Daughter Incest*, 2000

Bruce Perry and Maia Szalavitz, *The Boy Who Was Raised as a Dog: And Other Stories from a Child Psychiatrist's Notebook—What Traumatized Children Can Teach Us about Loss, Love, and Healing*, 2017

The Second Photograph

Margaret Randall

I have found another portrait.
You have me on your lap
flanked by my two grandmothers
both looking congenitally worried
as well they should.

You, on the other hand, seem vaguely crazed
as you certainly were,
your lips and eyes focused on different planes.

I have looked long and hard
at the hands in this picture.
Both women hide theirs, differently.
Yours, Grandpa, are loosely circled
about my three-year-old body.
Your right covers my left, your left
comes round my party-dressed buttocks,
your fingers strangely held as if in secret sign.

I am reading this into the image.
I am reading it because now, half a century later,
I understand why my eyes in the picture
take the camera head on, demanding answers.

Albuquerque, Spring 1986

20

Men, Masculinity, and Child Sexual Abuse

A Sex and Gender Question

ANNIE COSSINS

Empirical evidence shows that child sexual abuse is overwhelmingly committed by men and male adolescents, irrespective of the sex of the children who are abused, indicating that, like all other crime categories, sex is the key predictor of involvement in this type of criminal activity (Collier 1998). The central question that has engaged many social scientists in relation to the sexual abuse of children is what motivates men to engage in sexual activities with children rather than with their adult peers. Implicit in this question is the belief that sex with adult peers is the norm, whereas sex with children is a deviation from that norm. Much of the psychological literature on the behavior of child sex offenders contains studies that emphasize the nonsexual motivations behind child sexual abuse, the abnormality of sexual desire for children, and the normality of sex with adult women (Cossins 2000). Because such studies *begin* with the value judgment that sexual behavior with children is abnormal, they have failed to consider its prevalence as a sexual practice, thus failing to distinguish between what is abnormal as opposed to what is socially unacceptable. As Liddle (1993, 105) has recognized, "even a brief perusal of the [psychological] literature suggests that 'masculine sexuality' is not widely regarded as having causal centrality in the genesis of child sexual abuse."

Given the prevalence of child sexual abuse reported in various studies,[1] arguably a distinction needs to be made between what is considered to be socially unacceptable sexual practices and sexual practices that may be relatively common within the general community. In other words, it cannot be assumed that because child sex offending is socially unacceptable behavior, it therefore occurs infrequently or is only committed by "deviant" men. Because of the prevalence and sex specificity of child sexual abuse, this chapter argues it is necessary to examine the role that sexual behavior with children plays in offenders' lives as *men*. In undertaking this task, however, this chapter is not intended to condone or justify child sexual abuse or to imply that child sex offending is something of which any man might be capable.

The approach in this chapter challenges the methodology of the disciplines of psychology and psychiatry, which have tended to reduce a historically widespread and tolerated cultural practice (sex with children) to the individual biological or psychological natures of the offender. A focus on the characteristics or "pathology" of an offender might tell us something about that man's individual "makeup" but nothing about the wider social context of which he is a part or about the fact that the majority of victims are female and the majority of offenders are male. In fact, such an approach obscures the historical background of child sexual abuse (see Cossins 2000), the structures of power in men's lives, the social context of an offender's life, his active engagement with that social context, and how we might understand child sexual abuse as part of that engagement.

The aim, then, is to propose an explanation that addresses the motivations of offenders from an entirely different perspective, one that considers the role that child sex offending plays as a particular gender practice. This will involve analyzing whether there is a link between an offender's sexual behavior with children, his social practices, and the effects of other men's social practices on him. I argue that child sex offending, rather than being a deviant sexual practice, is a practice that is related to normative masculine sexual practices. In doing so, it will be necessary to examine the role that masculine sexual practices play in men's lives, in order to understand how such practices construct relations of power between men. At the same time, I consider the social significance of sex, that is, the specific cultural values associated with the male body and how these values affect individual social and sexual practices; such an approach is not commonly used in attempting to understand the relationship between men and crime.

Sex, Gender, and Child Sexual Abuse

To begin this inquiry, it is necessary to recognize that much of the discourse about men and crime in the social sciences has failed to make a conceptual distinction between sex and gender. These terms are often used interchangeably, and yet, in talking about sex, gender, and crime, it is necessary to be clear about the meanings of these terms. A number of feminist theorists have criticized the concept of gender on the grounds that it assumes that the body has no cultural or social significance and is an immutable, biological pregiven upon which gender inscriptions are made (see Collier 1998, 21–22; Davies 1997, 25–46; Gatens 1996, 3–20). In fact, the term *gender* has often been used to refer to sex in the social sciences, so that "the distinction between sex and gender turns out to be no distinction at all" (Butler 1990, 7). Similarly, the concept of gender has been criticized as being "an empty tautology" on the grounds that if everything men do is masculine, then "gender collapses into sex" (Hood-Williams 2001, 45). This means that attempting to understand men's various criminal and sexual practices needs to begin with making a distinction between the concepts of sex and gender and to recognize the meanings that different sexes carry at a cultural level.

In particular, what meanings do men attach to their bodies, and how do these meanings influence sexual practices such as rape and child sexual abuse?

In this chapter, *sex* is used to describe the sexual and physical differences between the two categories of human referred to as male and female, whereas the term *sexed* refers to the cultural values associated with particular sexual characteristics. *Gender* describes the cultural differences that arise from performance (Hood-Williams 1996), that is, active social practices or recurring accomplishments to use the terminology of West and Zimmerman (1991), who coined the phrase "doing gender" to describe the active participation of individuals in the construction of social categories.

A number of feminist theorists (Butler 1990, 1993; Gatens 1996; Grosz 1990, 1994; Grosz and Probyn 1995) have analyzed the role of sexual difference in the construction of male and female subjectivities, with the term *sexing* meaning that male and female bodies acquire specific cultural meanings at both an individual and institutional level. The "sexed bodies approach" is concerned with discerning these cultural meanings and the individual experiences that derive from the cultural significance ascribed to sex.

Although gender is created through active social practices, individuals give very specific cultural meanings to their bodies through these practices so that sex and gender are not arbitrarily linked (Gatens 1996). The sexed bodies approach views the body as being "interwoven with and constitutive of systems of meaning, signification and representation" (Grosz 1990, 18), which means there can be no conception of the body that is independent of the cultural values ascribed to different sexual characteristics. Indeed, the many social practices that are described as masculine or feminine constitute shared expectations about male and female biologies (Gatens 1996) in that different cultural meanings are ascribed to different bodies even though they may exhibit the *same* practices, with these meanings being contingent on the *sex* of the body carrying out the practice. This is most clearly seen in relation to the different meanings ascribed to male and female bodies engaging in similar sexual behavior—it is implicit in the term *stud* that the body is sexed male, and it is implicit in the term *slut* that the body is sexed female.

It is important to recognize that the relationship between the body and gender is not arbitrary in terms of social/cultural expectations, yet the body does not *determine* the social—although the body is "inescapable" in the practice and construction of gender, "what is inescapable is not fixed" (Connell 1995a, 56). This is a mistake that sociobiologists frequently make when trying to explain different male and female sexual behaviors, such as rape and child sexual abuse. The view that men are "naturally" promiscuous and women are "naturally" sexually conservative relies on the belief that male and female traits are "hard-wired," unchangeable and unaffected by context.

Although the sexed bodies approach has not generally been used to explain the relationship between the body and crime, the theoretical premise of the approach illustrates that it is necessary to understand the meanings associated with different bodies—male, female, Black, White—in order to understand crime as a social practice and the response of legal institutions to crime (Cossins 2003). The body matters, and what the body does matters. In this statement there are encapsulated two concepts: the social meanings that individuals ascribe to their female or male bodies (the sexed body) and the social meanings ascribed to what these specifically sexed bodies do (gender). Individuals and institutions construct "types" of men and "types" of women in social discourse so that bodies matter to those who commit crime (for example, male-on-male violence, men's sexual assault of women), to those who fear crime (the fear of crime is a fear of the sexed male body or a particular "raced" and sexed male body), and to those who seek to impose a rigid law-and-order agenda (for example, overpolicing of the adolescent, Black, male body).

When it comes to the construction of male sexualities, the body matters in understanding the cultural differentiation that is made between heterosexual and gay men and the fact that gay bashings are a particular criminal phenomenon. This differentiation must mean that different cultural meanings are ascribed to same-sexed bodies because of the expectations associated with the sexed male body. Similarly, it can be said that the body matters in attempting to understand the meanings attached to the body of the child sex offender, such as "monster," "predator," "pervert," and "deviant," since it is implicit in such descriptions that the body is male. But what is the relationship between how men's bodies are sexed and their engagement in particular sexual practices such as the sexual abuse of children? In particular, how do we *become* sexed and gendered subjects?

In considering these questions, it is obvious that masculine "identities" are not fixed and unchanging, given the different characteristics of the male body from childhood to adolescence to middle age and finally old age and the cultural values associated with differently aged men. This means that individuals and institutions *produce more than one type* of sexed male subject: hooligan, stud, father, worker, sports hero, boss, gayboy are different masculine identities with specific cultural meanings that are as much about the male body as they are about what the sexed male body does. What then is the relationship between sex and gender? If "[m]asculinity and femininity as forms of sex-appropriate behaviors are manifestations of a historically based, culturally shared [f]antasy about male and female biologies, [then] sex and gender are not arbitrarily connected. . . . [Indeed,] masculine and feminine forms of behavior are not arbitrary inscriptions on an indifferent consciousness which is joined to an indifferent body" (Gatens 1996, 13–14).

In other words, whereas the sexed bodies approach recognizes the cultural significance of the way the body is constructed in social discourse and how that construction (sexed male or female) affects the formation of individual consciousness, this individual consciousness informs the active social practices in which *differently* sexed bodies engage. But what informs the different social practices of *same*-sexed bodies, particularly sexual practices?

Masculinities are specific social practices that are within themselves highly variable, although, as I have argued, they are not arbitrarily related to sex. The different cultural meanings that are ascribed to the sexed male body will, therefore, depend on the social practices of the man in question, which are influenced by other factors such as race, class, and ethnicity. This suggests that a conceptual distinction can be made between the cultural significance of sex and the cultural significance of the social practices that sexed bodies engage in. Such a distinction warrants the continued use of the term *gender* as a way of describing the lived experiences of same-sexed bodies in response to a variety of cultural and structural constraints.

The sexed bodies approach reveals that the male body is associated with very particular cultural meanings: strength, reliability, courage, aggression, and toughness, in fact, everything the sexed female body is *not*. However, different categories of men are constructed by reference to the male body's social practices—crying versus stoicism, fighting versus fleeing—creating "real" men and sissies. In fact, ideals of manhood are very much premised on the heterosexual/homophobic divide, with the conditions of potency and prowess being tied to the male body that practices heterosexuality. The concept of gender tells us that the different cultural meanings ascribed to same-sexed bodies are contingent not only on sex but also on the specific sexual and social practices of the sexed male body. *Gender* is a term that describes the relationships of power that exist between men on the basis of these distinctions; for example, although it is implicit in the construction of the "stud" that his body is sexed male, the gendered dimension of the construct is dependent on particular sexual and social practices. Thus, in the construction of male subjectivities, men engage in both sexing and gendering processes to create oppositional relationships between each other and to create relationships of power with their objects of desire. In this way, the concepts of sex and gender are simultaneous processes, leading to different social experiences for different men.

So why is *child* sexual abuse a particular social and sexual practice for some men? Cultural values associated with different sexual practices are central to the social construction of masculinities and relationships of power between men. More particularly, "Although personal conceptions of masculine identity . . . vary according to race, class, age and other social variables . . . , there remains a stable common core . . . called 'heterosexual masculinity'" (Herek 1987, 72). Homophobia is a social practice that creates relationships of power between men—a man becomes a "faggot" or a "poofter" in the eyes of other men by reference not to his sexual characteristics but to his social practices. A man does not actually have to have sex with other men to be the recipient of gay jibes since heterosexual men regularly differentiate between each other based on a range of social practices that the male body does or fails to do. Across cultures, men engage in homophobic practices to differentiate between themselves and construct relations of power, so that homophobia can be a particular social practice for the accrual of power for any man irrespective of his class or racial background: "The taunt *'What are you, a fag?'* is used in many ways to encourage certain types of male behavior and to define the limits of 'acceptable' masculinity" (Lehne 1995, 332; emphasis in original).

The body is intrinsic to this differentiation between gay and straight men because of the dominance of the specific cultural values ascribed to the male body. For some men, gay bashings and other types of homophobia reaffirm their allegiance to a particular conception of the male body. Through homophobic practices, a man can prove or exaggerate his masculinity by constructing another man as a legitimate target for reaffirming his heterosexual status. The dominant forms of both homosexual and heterosexual masculinities are heterosexist in the sense that many men seek to define themselves as everything the female body is not. Thus, homophobia is a sexual practice that constructs relations of power between men, but it is always referable to a particular conception of the male body. In the practice of homophobia, the body matters.

This analysis raises the question of whether child sex offending is a particular social/sexual practice that involves the construction of relations of power and allows some men to express a type of sexuality characterized by dominance and control. In Western societies, the construction of masculine sexualities (as opposed to the ability to be sexual) involves the attribution of particular cultural values to the male body: virile, potent, penetrating, initiating, aggressive, conquering, focused, piercing, incisive, strong, purposeful, erect, unemotional, tough, hard-hitting, as well as impotence, such that the male body is a site for both success and failure. Men's sexual practices involve not only actual sexual acts but also a variety of ways in which this masculine sexual ideal is affirmed or at least the illusion of potency is created. Sexist jokes, sexual innuendo, sexual gestures toward women, sexual put-downs, and masturbatory gestures are examples of sexual practices that may create relations of power between men, as well as between women and men. At the heart of these sexual practices, a particular conception of the sexed male body is paramount since it is from the body that some men clearly believe their power is derived. Adherence to the masculine ideal (the sexed male body) is likely to lead to experiences of social inadequacy since most men will fail to live up to the ideal given its idealised and illusory nature. The masculine sexual ideal, as a cultural construct, is not a biological reality but rather an ideology (Kaufman 2007) that is always contested by other men and has to be proved and reaffirmed, thus creating experiences of success and failure, of both power and powerlessness. For those men who compete for status with other men through sexual practices, the stakes are extremely high since they know that sexual performance goes to the core of their self-worth as a man (their "manliness") and influences their social power with other men. This, then, raises the question of whether the same analysis can be made of child sex offending so that for some men, the struggle for experiences of power and the association of the male body with potency and prowess takes place through sexual behavior with children.

The foregoing discussion has shown that sexuality (as opposed to the ability to be sexual) is socially constructed through the attachment of particular cultural values both to the sexed male body and to the way that body behaves. Sexual practices occur in a relational context, and different men will create different masculine sexualities as a function of their dynamic positions within the structural divisions created by class, ethnicity, and race (Connell 1995a). For some men, it can be argued that sexual practices with children allow them to experience power since correspondence with the masculine ideal and experiences of potency are more likely with those who are perceived to have less social power than the individual man in question.

As a sexual practice, child sex offending is similar to those normative sexual practices that conform to the masculine sexual ideal, given the fact that the relationship of adult to child is a relationship of power par excellence, if it is accepted that up until a certain age, children do not have the developmental and cognitive abilities to consent to sexual relations. Indeed, offenders' self-report studies (Cossins 2000) have shown that they typically choose a child who is emotionally vulnerable, suggesting that the choice of a relatively passive, non-threatening, or vulnerable sexual partner (or image) is remarkably consonant with the masculine sexual ideal. A child has an inferior social status and represents no threat to an offender's sexual performance since a child's lack of adult sexual needs and sexual experience allows an offender to ignore any inadequacies he may have about his sexuality. Child sex offending also takes place in a cultural environment where the bodies of girls (who constitute the majority of victims) are inscribed with cultural meanings of desire in literature, the media, advertisements, film, and pornography. It is, therefore, arguable that child sex offending is consonant with normative masculine sexual practices in a cultural environment in which men's lives are characterized by a combination of experiences of powerlessness and power as a result of their complex relationships with other men.

What is meant by power and powerlessness? The power that men derive through interactions with other men is "inherently unstable" compared to power that men assert over women. Although men derive power from acting in concert together and from existing structures of power (Archer 1994; Connell 1995a), on an individual level, men's interpersonal power can be fragile, dynamic, and changing. Men's power is a competitive enterprise and involves contradictory experiences of power and powerlessness in a context of dynamic and changing gender relations between men, since "[s]ocial structures originate, are reproduced, and change through social practice" (Messerschmidt 1993, 62).

This chapter has shown that heterosexism, that is, the meanings given to the male body, is central to the reproduction of power through sexual practices. One of the ways that men can accrue experiences of power is through particular sexual practices with women, other men, or children. The sexual abuse of children can be seen as both an expression of an offender's public power (in the sense of being able to gain access to a child, gaining the trust of parents, and "grooming" a child) and an expression of his lack of personal power as a result of his relationships with other men. For some men, child sexual abuse may be a key experience through which power is derived, and chronic experiences of powerlessness may explain chronic practices of sex offending against children (Cossins 2000). Arguably, men engage in exploitative sexual practices in circumstances in which their power is in jeopardy and they have limited material and/or social resources for competing for status with other men. The choice of a child may be related to the lack of congruence with, or inability to conform to, some aspects of the masculine sexual ideal, so that engagement in "pedosexuality" may give an offender the illusion of achieving the standard prescribed by that ideal.

This hypothesis can explain the range of different men who engage in sex with children—from those with considerable public power (White, middle class) to those with little public power (Black, unemployed)—since the degree of public power a man has does not necessarily equate with his experiences of power at a personal level. This means that some men may experience "powerlessness within power," a concept that recognizes "that men's personal inadequacies and self-brutalization are the flip side to their mastery of the public sphere in capitalist patriarchy" (Liddle 1993, 116). As Kimmel (1994) has recognized, there is not necessarily a symmetry between the *public* power that men as a group may have, particularly White, middle-class men, and the *private* experience of power with partners, male peers, and authority figures.

This analysis does not, however, allow us to predict when a man will engage in child sexual abuse as a way of experiencing power. Even though different social variables, such as race, class, ethnicity, religion, and disability, produce particular structures of power among men and different experiences of power/powerlessness, not all men sexually abuse children. Is child sex offending, therefore, an indication of the *degree* of powerlessness experienced by offenders? Such a proposition would predict that the *least* socially powerful men engage in exploitative sexual practices to experience power (however illusory) and that, in particular, men from lower socioeconomic groups would commit more rape and child sexual abuse than other groups of men. However, victim-report studies show that child sexual abuse does not have socioeconomic, ethnic, or racial boundaries (Cossins 2000), so that it is not confined to the most socially disenfranchised men. It is also too simplistic to argue that child sexual abuse is a "resource for 'doing gender'" and accomplishing masculinity (Messerschmidt 1993, 84), since if everything a man does accomplishes masculinity, then gender collapses into sex and we are faced with deterministic explanations as to why men commit this crime.

As discussed earlier, "there are different forms of structural power and powerlessness among men" (Kaufman 1994, 152), with that power always being relative and contested, even for the most privileged men in a given society. Men "on top" compete with other men on top or those who aspire to be on top; they rarely compete directly with men from lower socioeconomic groups unless they are involved, for example, in violence in a public place. Heterosexist sexual practices are, arguably, practised by those men who adhere or aspire to the masculine sexual ideal, irrespective of their racial, ethnic, or socioeconomic background, and these practices reinforce the fact that the sexed male body is associated with cultural values that are illusory and ultimately impossible to achieve.

It is hypothesised that a man's particular attachment to the masculine sexual ideal and the link he makes between sexual prowess and experiences of power will be a key indicator that determines how he does sex and whom he chooses as a sexual partner. Paradoxically, even though it is considered to be pathological behavior, sex with children affirms all the aspects of the masculine sexual ideal and the cultural values ascribed to the sexed male body. It enables a man to be dominant, predatory, phallocentric, sexually successful, detached, self-focused, in control, and to minimise sexual inadequacy. However, a man may choose adult sexual partners with whom to derive similar sexual experiences, so that factors such as access, opportunity, risk of being caught, or religious beliefs may all contribute to the choice to sexually abuse a child.

The argument that derivation of power through sexual practices is central to understanding child sex offending has specific practical and intellectual consequences. This analysis applies to both homosexual and heterosexual offenders because of the centrality of heterosexism (the masculine sexual ideal), the sexed male body, sexuality, and power to the reproduction of both homosexual and heterosexual masculinities. Children are likely to be "emotionally congruent objects for sexual desire" (Finkelhor 1984, 39) for those men whose lives are characterized by chronic experiences of powerlessness as a result of their relationships with other men and who seek to alleviate that powerlessness through sexual practices, both homosexual and heterosexual. Although such a view challenges the discourse of deviance evident in other disciplines, it is consonant with historical evidence that shows that sexual practices with children were socially and legally tolerated and, even when criminalized, difficult to prosecute (Cossins 2000).

This analysis means that preventive measures need to take account of the cultural environment in which child sex offenders live, work, and socialize. Not only could this knowledge assist in attempting to illuminate an offender's original motivations for targeting children as objects of desire, but it may also be crucial to an offender's choices post conviction. This would mean that preventive programs would need to focus on those aspects of an offender's life that lead to experiences of powerlessness and the sexual behaviours by which the offender seeks to alleviate those experiences.

NOTE

1 For example, Fleming (1997) studied a random community sample of 710 Australian women and found that 33 percent had experienced noncontact or contact abuse before the age of sixteen, and 20 percent had experienced contact before the age of sixteen. In 2000, Dunne et al. (2003) conducted a survey of 1,784 Australian women and men aged eighteen to fifty-nine and found that 33.6 percent of women and 15.9 percent of men reported "nonpenetrative" sexual abuse before the age of sixteen, and 12.5 percent of women and 4 percent of men had experienced unwanted penetration or attempted penetration before the age of sixteen. Similar prevalence rates had previously been reported by Finkelhor, Hotaling, Lewis, and Smith (1990) and Anderson et al. (1993).

21

Locating a Secret Problem

Sexual Violence in Elementary and Secondary Schools

NAN D. STEIN

This is a story of a hunch and a hunt that began after many decades of studying peer-to-peer sexual harassment in schools (Stein 1981, 1992, 1995, 1999, 2005a, 2005b). Garden-variety sexual harassment seemed to have become more aggressive and violent, transforming itself into illegal sexual assault—by peers, during the school day, on school grounds, and occurring at younger and younger ages, no longer restricted to high school students. My hunch began when more lawyers than usual in a short period of time during the spring and summer of 2002 asked me to serve as an expert witness in Title IX lawsuits against school districts where sexual assaults by peers against their clients (usually girls but, in a few cases, some very young boys) had occurred on school grounds, during the school day.

To see if there was any foundation to my hunch, I turned to three sources of information: (1) a LexisNexis search of the fifty-three largest newspapers in the US to locate news reports of sexual assault by peers in schools; (2) a search for lawsuits or administrative complaints to state or federal agencies initiated by students against the school district in state or federal civil courts; and (3) a review of federally sponsored surveys of (a) school administrators about crime at their school or (b) students inquiring about their victimization (Stein, 2005b).

This chapter posits that over the course of the past few decades, incidents of sexual harassment in K–12 schools have been occurring at younger and younger ages and have become noticeably more sexually violent. I document the paucity of survey data from elementary and middle-school students and the general difficulty of acquiring data on sexual violence in schools using ethnographic data, narratives acquired from lawsuits and complaints, media reports, and federal survey data.

Sexual violence in schools, which often gets named as something else in an effort to cast it as benign (e.g., the use of the term "bullying"), frequently is not reported to law-enforcement or school officials; when it is surveyed, it is not disaggregated from incidents of physical violence, so these incidents of sexual violence are often classified as "physical violence." Moreover, the well-documented rise of teen dating violence (sometimes called "intimate partner violence"), as revealed though the Youth Risk Behavior Survey, may also lend evidence to an overall increase in teen violence, whether it is restricted to dating partners or not (Brown, Chesney-Lind, and Stein 2004; Stein 2005b).

In the midst of my quest, the survey questions for school administrators that the federal government had asked from 1998 to 2002 to determine sexual violence in schools changed in a way that rendered the problem of sexual violence invisible. All the questions related to gender/sexual violence in schools had been removed and merged with questions that asked about generic physical violence (see the postscript at the end of this chapter). Thus, the secret problem of sexual violence in schools had become even harder to locate than when I first initiated the review.

Despite the documented rise of sexual harassment and sexual violence in schools, the popular and more palatable term "bullying" is often used instead to describe these sexually violent incidents. Whether used innocently or as shorthand, when school officials call these sexual violent events "bullying," the violent and illegal (either under civil or criminal law) nature of these incidents is obscured and the school's responsibility and potential liability is deflected (Stein 2003; Brown, Chesney-Lind, and Stein 2004).

The final sections of this chapter cover possible reasons for the increase of sexual harassment and sexual violence in schools. My hypothesis is that the convergence of several developments has led to the erosion of attention to sexual harassment in schools. Finally, I conclude with a series of suggested measures to reduce sexual violence among youth in schools.

National Newspaper Reports of Sexual Assaults in Schools

Daily newspapers often include articles about incidents of sexual assaults that occur at schools during the course of the school day. My LexisNexis search for the years 2000–2004 produced eighty-four articles about incidents of sexual violence in middle schools and twenty-seven articles about incidents in elementary schools. The search was restricted to incidents that had happened during the school day, on the school grounds, and among children who were classmates. Two additional articles reported on three incidents among middle-school students that occurred on a school bus (Frazier 2001, 2003). In the vast majority of cases, the victims of these attacks were girls and the assailants were their male classmates. There were only a few instances where boys were the targets, and in those cases, other boys were their attackers and the sexual attacks often took place in the bathroom (*Katz v. St. John the Baptist Parish School*; Chanen and Padilla 2001; Pesznecker 2005). As we will see when we review the results from juvenile crime surveys, the picture that emerges from the incidents covered in newspapers (a nonscientific sample) comport with crime surveys—girls are much more likely than boys to be the victims of sexual assaults. Of all juvenile sex offenses, girls are victims in 82 percent of the cases, whereas boys are victims in 18 percent of the cases (Finkelhor and Ormrod 2000, 2–3).

Some national newspapers have conducted in-depth reporting on sexual assaults in their area schools. For example, over a two-year period in 2002–2004, eleven sexual batteries, 113 sexual offenses, and sixty-seven cases of sexual harassment were reported in Broward County public elementary schools. Many more incidents occurred at higher grade levels, for a total of forty sexual batteries (Malernee 2004). On the other side of the country in the San Francisco School District, twenty-five sexual-assault incidents occurred in the first five months of the 2003–2004 school year. Two took place at elementary schools, seventeen at middle schools, and six at high schools (Knight 2004). During the comparative period in the 2002–2003 school year, six incidents occurred across the district (2004).

Although the preponderance of victims in sexual assaults are girls (in fact, three-fourths of victims of juvenile sexual assault are female), young boys are also targeted (McCurley and Snyder 2004). In Louisiana, a lawsuit resulted from an attack on a five-year-old boy who went to the bathroom in the company of three other male kindergarten students (*Katz v. St. John the Baptist Parish School Board*). While in the restroom, the three boys sexually assaulted the one child by pulling down his pants, attempting anal intercourse with him, and forcing him to perform sexually explicit oral behavior with them. In another bathroom episode that occurred in the Minneapolis, Minnesota, public schools, a six-year-old boy was allegedly sexually assaulted by three boys between the ages of ten and twelve years old (Chanen and Padilla 2001). In November 2004, in Anchorage, Alaska, a six-year-old boy was sexually assaulted by another six-year-old classmate while the two boys were left unattended in a school bathroom (Pesznecker 2005). Clearly, bathrooms have emerged as dangerous places, even at age six (Brown, Chesney-Lind, and Stein 2004, 14).

Limited Survey Information about Sexual Violence in Schools

Survey data on the prevalence of sexual violence in elementary and middle schools (children younger than twelve years old) is difficult to obtain and has not been consistently collected, disaggregated, or reported. Researchers lack a complete picture of the violence that children experience, including whether that violence is experienced at home, in the streets, in public spaces, or at school. The paucity and the inconsistency of the information collected on students in this age group is largely due to resistance from parents who forbid researchers from gathering data from children about childhood (sexual) victimization (Brown, Chesney-Lind, and Stein 2004; Stein 2005b).

Only recently has self-reported data from children younger than twelve years old been collected. Since its origin in 1929, neither the FBI's Uniform Crime

Reporting (UCR) Program nor the Bureau of Justice Statistics' National Crime Victimization Survey (NCVS) collected information about crimes committed against persons younger than twelve years old and, therefore, could not provide a comprehensive picture of juvenile crime victimization (Finkelhor and Ormrod 2000). The new National Incident-Based Reporting System (NIBRS), which was designed to replace the UCR as the national database for crimes reported to law enforcement, now includes data about juvenile victims. However, participation by states and local jurisdictions is incremental and voluntary; at the current time, criminal incidents in large urban areas are particularly underrepresented (Finkelhor and Ormrod 2000).

In the 2004 analysis containing data from seventeen states, family members constitute 27 percent, acquaintances constitute 66 percent, and strangers constitute 3 percent of the offenders (McCurley and Snyder 2004). That such a large percentage of crimes are committed by acquaintances may indicate that some, or even a majority, of these incidents may be occurring at school. Unfortunately, information about the location of the crimes is not available from this report. Once again, yet another survey provides only partial, albeit new, information, in the quest to know the prevalence of sexual assaults that occur at school, during the school day, by students. The frustrating search to compose a full and accurate picture continues (Brown, Chesney-Lind, and Stein 2004, 13).

Additional information on sexual violence can be found in a report of school crime and safety based on 2000 data (Miller and Chandler 2003). These data were derived from a nationally representative sample of 2,270 public school principals who reported information about violent deaths, crime and violence frequency, school policies, disciplinary problems, and other information related to school crime. In a category titled "serious violent incidents," which includes rape, sexual battery, physical attack or fight with a weapon, threat of physical attack with a weapon, and robbery with or without a weapon, the authors reported that 20 percent of all schools experienced one or more serious violent incidents, with 14 percent of elementary schools, 29 percent of middle schools, and 29 percent of high schools reporting "serious violent incidents." The results for the category of "rape or attempted rape" revealed a total of 143 incidents in 126 middle schools, representing 1 percent of all schools. There were no reported rapes or attempted rapes in elementary schools. A total of 650 incidents of "sexual battery other than rape" occurred in 520 elementary schools, representing 1 percent of all schools. A total of 582 middle schools reported 1,141 incidents of "sexual battery other than rape," representing 4 percent of all schools (Miller and Chandler 2003).

Clearly, a self-reporting mechanism by school principals has limitations. Principals can only provide information that has come to their attention; therefore, undercounting is an inevitable problem. In addition, the survey may ask for information that principals did not retain (Miller and Chandler 2003). Moreover, some principals may withhold information from law enforcement for a variety of reasons, including preserving their school's reputation (Brown, Chesney-Lind, and Stein 2004; Stein 2005b).

Naming the Real Problem as Gendered or Sexual Violence

Interpersonal violence seems to be a normative feature in the lives of many youth. The existence of peer-to-peer sexual harassment in K–12 schools has been well documented for decades (AAUW 1993, 2001; Stein 1981, 1995, 1999; Stein, Marshall, and Tropp 1993; Strauss 1988). Sexual harassment is now accepted as an unfortunate fact of life. Nearly thirty years after the passage of Title IX, a 2000–2001 survey found rampant evidence of sexual harassment in schools (AAUW 1993, 2001). Students continue to report that school personnel behave in sexually harassing ways and/or that they do not intervene when sexual harassment occurs (Stein 1995, 1999).

In the most recent scientific survey about sexual harassment in schools, the American Association of University Women (AAUW), along with the Harris polling firm (2001), found that among 2,064 students in grades eight to eleven, sexual harassment was widespread in schools, with 83 percent of girls and 79 percent of boys indicating that they had been sexually harassed, and 30 percent of the girls and 24 percent of the boys reporting that they were sexually harassed "often." Nearly half of all students who experienced sexual harassment felt "very" or "somewhat upset" afterward, pointing to the negative impact that sexual harassment has on the emotional and educational lives of students (AAUW 2001). When compared to the 1993 AAUW survey on sexual harassment among eighth- to eleventh-graders, the results from 2001 show an increase in both awareness about, and incidents of, sexual harassment, yet students in 2001 had come to accept sexual harassment as a fact of life in schools (AAUW 2001). The greatest change in the eight-year period was in students' awareness of their schools' policies and materials to address sexual harassment (AAUW 2001).

Gay, lesbian, bisexual, and transgendered (GLBT) students report daily harassment, sometimes rising to the magnitude of criminal assault and/or grounds for federal civil rights lawsuits (Pogash 2004; Quinn 2002; Walsh 2003). In a variety of surveys, including a 2005 online survey of 3,450 students ages thirteen to eighteen and 1,011 secondary-school teachers (Harris Interactive and GLSEN 2005), as well as interviews of school staff and students and calls into hotlines (Human Rights Watch 2001), the overwhelming portrait is of a school climate that includes verbal and physical harassment because of perceived or actual appearance, gender, sexual orientation, gender expressions, race/ethnicity, disability, or religion (Harris Interactive and GLSEN 2005). One-third of teens report that students are harassed due to perceived or actual sexual orientation. Because of their sexual orientation, two-thirds of GLBT students have been verbally harassed, 16 percent have been physically harassed, and 8 percent have been physically assaulted (Harris Interactive and GLSEN 2005, 4). Results from educators show that 73 percent of them felt they had an obligation to create a safe, supportive learning environment for GLBT students, and 53 percent of them acknowledged that bullying and harassment of students was a serious problem at their schools (Harris Interactive and GLSEN 2005).

Educational personnel are also responsible for some of the sexual harassment, sometimes as perpetrators and other times as spectators. According to the 2001 AAUW survey, 38 percent of students report being sexually harassed by teachers and other school employees (AAUW 2001). Moreover, school personnel can turn away or ignore incidents of sexual harassment when they happen in front of them or when reports are brought to their attention (Stein 1995, 1999; Stein, Marshall, and Tropp 1993).

The federal courts, including the Supreme Court (*Davis v. Monroe County Board of Education*), have ruled that school districts have liability if they knew about peer-to-peer sexual harassment and did nothing to prevent it. After decades of battling for recognition of the problem, the Supreme Court's decision in the *Davis* case clarified the requirements and standards under Title IX and established that peer-to-peer sexual harassment exists among our youth and that adults are liable for damages.

The omission or denial of gender from the dominant construction of school safety and violence contributes to the disproportionate focus on the most extreme, rare forms of violence while the more insidious threats to safety are largely ignored (Lesko 2000; Stein 1995, 1999; Stein, Tolman, Porche, and Spencer 2002). An example of this failure to factor in the saliency of gender in school violence is reflected in the many reports and analyses of the spate of school shootings—the form of school violence that has attracted the most national attention and incited the most panic (Kimmel 2001). In general, the school shootings were widely reported in a gender-neutral way, when in fact, the majority of these tragedies were perpetrated by White middle-class boys who were upset about either a break-up or being rejected by a girl (e.g., Jonesboro, Arkansas; Pearl, Mississippi), or who did not meet traditional expectations and norms of masculinity (e.g., Columbine, Colorado), and were thus persecuted by their peers (Kimmel 2001; National Research Council and Institute of Medicine 2003; Perlstein 1998; Vossekuil et al. 2002).

This failure to consider the role of gender is also endemic to much of the bullying research. Researchers of bullying, for the most part, have unfortunately failed to consider the ways in which adolescent boys (and adult men) unmercifully police one another with rigid and conventional notions of masculinity and the imposition of compulsive heterosexuality. Not to factor in, or even recognize, these potent elements is to deny a central operating feature in boy culture, namely, the maniacally driven, tireless efforts to define oneself as "not gay." Although researchers such as J. Pleck (1981), Connell (1987, 1995a), Kimmel

(1987, 1996, 2001), Kimmel and Aronson (2000) and Messner (1990a) have written about this phenomenon and its consequences for several decades, most bullying researchers have failed to draw on their findings (Brown, Chesney-Lind, and Stein 2004; Stein 2005a).

Interestingly, the effectiveness of bullying training has been challenged by results from a study on sexual coercion in Australia (as part of a six-country study), which found that antibullying policies are not effective in reducing or eliminating sexual harassment (Ken Rigby personal correspondence September 4, 2004; Australian Broadcasting Online 2004). In a study of approximately two hundred fourteen-year-old students who attended four schools in Adelaide, South Australia, all of which had antibullying policies, a substantial minority said they would ignore sexual harassment if they saw it happening, and a smaller minority (boys) thought they would support the boy aggressor (Rigby and Johnson 2004). About 37 percent estimated that sexual harassment happened on a weekly basis at school with bystanders present, and somewhat higher estimates were obtained for some other countries that participated in the study (Rigby and Johnson 2004; Rigby personal correspondence). Among the Australian students, 14 percent indicated that they would report the harassment to a teacher (Rigby and Johnson 2004). In the absence of similar studies in the US, this sobering data from Australia points to the ineffectiveness of antibullying policies in changing or challenging the culture of sexual harassment in schools.

Mean Girls or Sexually Violent Hazing among Youth?

In the late spring through the early fall of 2003, a series of hazing episodes occurred among high school students. In Glenbrook, Illinois, the incident involved girl-on-girl violence as an initiation rite by the senior girls to younger girls; in both Mepham and Friendship, New York, boy-on-boy violence occurred within sports teams. These events offer some insight into the ways in which the problems are framed (and obscured) and point the way toward the need to understand these events as gendered and as violence (Stein 2005b). Interestingly, at the time these hazing episodes were being reported in the national media, girls as a whole were categorically being demonized as "mean," and this meanness was made equivalent to the perpetration of sexual violence (Brown, Chesney-Lind, and Stein 2004; Stein 2005b).

The hazing instances that involved boys on the football team at Mepham High School on Long Island, New York, and on the soccer team in Friendship, New York, resulted in criminal charges of sexual assault, sexual abuse, or sodomy—not merely criminal hazing or the overused term "bullying" (Healy 2003b, 2003c; Healy and Akhtar 2003; Kessler 2003; Schuster, Molinet, and Morris 2003; Staba 2003). The accusations against the older girls who hazed the younger girls in the Glenbrook, Illinois, incident did not include some of the horrific charges that appeared in the incidents at Mepham High School, where the younger boys were bound with duct tape, stripped naked against their will, and sexually assaulted and sodomized by the older boys on the football team. Indeed, the girls from Glenbrook were charged with assault as they mimicked violent masculinity in front of the boys who were videotaping their abuse of the young girls, showing the boys that they could both outgross and outperform them (Fuller 2003; Napolitano 2003; Stein 2005a).

Interestingly, the Mepham and Friendship cases did not produce a national outrage as did the incident with the girls from Glenbrook, Illinois (Paulson 2003; Roberts 2003). The Glenbrook incident generated a manufactured panic about the state of meanness among girls and the supposed rise in their violent conduct, yet there was never any mention of the increasing rates of rape and sexual assault of girls, particularly at the hands of boys and men they know (Stein 2005a, 2005b). However, the hazing behaviors of the boys from Mepham and Friendship did not generate discussions about the type of normative masculinity that includes perpetrating sexual violence coupled with colluding silence and lack of intervention from the other observing teammates (Brown, Chesney-Lind, and Stein 2004).

Some Hypotheses about the Increase in Sexual Violence in Schools

I propose that the convergence of several developments has led to the rise in sexual violence in schools and the erosion of attention to sexual harassment. Briefly, my hypotheses are the following: (1) new legal mandates that are largely symbolic attempt to elevate the "bullying" prevention framework over the civil rights framework of sexual harassment as discrimination and therefore create a distraction from the more pressing problems of sexual harassment and sexual violence; (2) zero tolerance, which is the hegemonic and conventional mantra of school and government officials, emphasizes suspensions and expulsions of alleged perpetrators instead of education, counseling, and reform; and (3) high-stakes standardized tests that all students must pass to be promoted take teachers' time and attention away from attending to the safety of their students. In total, the confluence of these three factors has produced schools that are leaner, meaner, and may have helped to create an atmosphere that has allowed sexual harassment and sexual violence to flourish (Stein 2005a, 2005b).

Action Steps

We need to acknowledge and confront the sexual violence problem in our country, whether it is enacted as sexual harassment, sexual assault, or sexually violent hazing. In addition, we need to implement immediate and vast corrective actions in order to curb and eliminate these injustices.

First, we must reconfigure the school violence prevention movement and discourse to acknowledge the presence of gendered violence in our schools among our youth. By using the momentum from the child-abuse scandal perpetrated by Catholic priests and hidden by the Church hierarchy, as well as sexual-assault scandals in the military and at other academic institutions, we need also to bring attention to the increasing incidence of sexual assault of girls that are occurring even among elementary and middle-school children, by their classmates, during the school day.

In addition, we need to add high-quality, age-appropriate, and successfully evaluated lessons about sexual violence, as it is experienced by both boys and girls, into the school curriculum, over the course of the whole year, throughout all grades. We can no longer rest on the original "stranger-danger" approach, which does not reflect the reality of sexual assault, rape, hazing, or child sexual abuse. Schools must adequately train staff to recognize these injustices and to intervene and teach about these troubling issues in the classroom—not just in the auditorium or the principal's office.

Furthermore, we need to equip witnesses and bystanders with strategies for intervention, ways to get help, and techniques to disrupt the assaults that are taking place in front of their eyes. The deleterious effects of being on the sidelines of these violent episodes or fearing that you might be next should not be minimized, though it cannot be compared to the terror experienced by those who have been sexually assaulted.

Equally important is to add quality mental-health services to our schools, including counseling groups for adolescents who find themselves in abusive relationships, either as abuser or victim. Professionally trained staff from sexual-assault and domestic-violence agencies, as well as a few gender-violence prevention groups composed of both men and women, are available to work in schools and lead counseling groups or classroom discussions in partnership with school staff. Finally, it is not enough to suspend the alleged perpetrators, ban them from graduation exercises or the prom, cancel the football or soccer season, or even to criminally charge the attackers. Rather, we must engage in deep and hard conversations both in school and in the larger community about the meanings of masculinity and the ways in which it is expressed: boys-on-boys, boys-on-girls, and even girls-on-girls, some of whom seem to yearn to be as tough as the guys.

At the national, state, and local levels, as a matter of policy, we must acquire data from elementary- and middle-school-aged children on their experiences, whether as witness/bystander, victim, or perpetrator of sexual harassment and sexual violence in schools. Gathering this data will take cooperation from parents and guardians to give researchers permission to ask questions of their young children about victimization, witnessing, and perpetration.

The problem of sexual violence among peers looms large in elementary and secondary schools. Sexual violence among youngsters is largely hidden—because of the ways the questions are asked and/or analyzed in federal surveys, because of the difficulty that researchers have in gaining access to children younger than twelve years old in order to learn about their experiences of victimization, witnessing, or perpetration, and finally because of the many other priorities (or one might also call them "distractions") that have put sexual violence and sexual harassment out of teachers' and administrators' minds, which are instead filled with national mandates for testing. However, we ignore sexual violence among youngsters at our peril; it will come back to haunt the whole society unless we work to expose it, teach about it, and eradicate it.

Postscript

In late January 2005, as I was reviewing a copy of the most recent school crime report, *Indicators of School Crime and Safety, 2004* (DeVoe, Peter, Kaufman, Miller et al. 2004), published by the US Departments of Education and Justice (NCES 2005–002/NCJ 205290), I was shocked to find out that it had omitted the information and the charts that disaggregated sexual-assault statistics.

The mapping of sexual violence in schools using information that had been available from 1998 through 2002 had become more difficult because data that had been available in prior reports had been removed. The Indicators of School Crime and Safety reports present a comprehensive measure of crimes occurring at the nation's schools using "indicators" considered significant (e.g., physical fights or threats with a weapon). From 1998 to 2002, one indicator that the report included was specific statistics on sexual battery and rape that happened in school and were reported to the police. But in the 2004 report, precise data on sexual violence had gone missing and was subsumed under broad categories of violence; all the sexual-violence data was aggregated under "serious violent" and "violent" crime. This new way of categorizing the sexual-violence statistics ensured that trends in sexual violence would be impossible to locate—sexual violence in schools had been rendered invisible to the public.

My Wellesley College research assistant, Hao Nguyen, and I began a correspondence in late February 2005 with the authors of the Indicators, a group of researchers employed at the Department of Justice, the Department of Education, and two of their subcontractors, the American Institutes for Research (AIR) and MPR Associates, informing them of our concerns about the difficulty of locating (or absence of) data on sexual violence in schools. Rape and sexual battery are inherently gendered crimes; the vast majority of the victims are females and the assailants are male. The gendered nature of these crimes sets them apart from the other crimes in the categories of "serious violent crime," "violent crime," and "theft." After a month of correspondence, we were delighted to learn that they accepted our arguments and agreed to report total incidence of rape and sexual assault. This significant change in the way data on sexual violence in schools is reported will help researchers and the public understand the context and role of this growing pandemic and will allow us to locate with more clarity this secret problem.

ACKNOWLEDGMENTS

The author thanks friend and Wellesley College colleague Sally Engle Merry for countless conversations, walks, and precision guidance with a title for this chapter. In addition, Wellesley College students Janet Megan Ditzer and Hao M. Nguyen provided valuable research assistance over several years.

Portions of this chapter have appeared in Lyn Mikel Brown, Meda Chesney-Lind, and Nan Stein, "Patriarchy Matters: Toward a Gendered Theory of Teen Violence and Victimization," Wellesley College Center for Research on Women, Working Paper No. 417, 2004; in Nan Stein, "Bullying and Harassment in a Post-Columbine World," in *Child Victimization*, ed. Kathy Kendall-Tackett and Sarah Giacomoni (Kingston, NJ: Civic Research Institute, 2005); and in Nan Stein, "A Rising Pandemic of Sexual Violence in Elementary and Secondary Schools: Locating a Secret Problem," *Duke Journal of Gender Law and Policy* 12 (spring 2005): 33–52.

22

Where Are the Children?

Theorizing the Missing Piece in Gendered Sexual Violence

NANCY WHITTIER

Feminists have been central to virtually every era of activism around child sexual abuse, from moral reformers in the 1800s and early 1900s to the 1980s' survivors' movement (Breines and Gordon 1983; Freedman 2013; Sacco 2009; Whittier 2009). Most recently, feminist analysis of child sexual abuse grew in the 1970s alongside that of rape, as participants in consciousness-raising groups discovered that many of them had been sexually assaulted as children, often by relatives. Feminist antirape activists included the rape of girls in their theory, activism, self-defense training, and crisis services. Rape, regardless of age, was understood as an act of power, violence, and male domination; girls were doubly vulnerable because of their relatively powerless position as minors, especially within families. Sexual abuse of boys was also attributed to patriarchal domination, which could be directed at other powerless groups besides women. Developed at the grassroots and through widely read books like Florence Rush's *The Best Kept Secret* (1980) and Sandra Butler's *Conspiracy of Silence* (1985), this view of child sexual abuse spread widely. But it did not persist. As the issue gained mainstream media attention and people from diverse political perspectives identified as survivors and joined self help and activist groups, feminist analyses moved from the center to the periphery. Relatively quickly, the idea of incest and child sexual abuse as essentially different from the rape of adult women gained dominance. I traced this chain of events in *The Politics of Child Sexual Abuse* (Whittier 2009).

At present, policy, mainstream culture, and most academic research treat sexual assault as having different causes, patterns, and consequences depending on the age of the victim, while feminist work on rape and sexual assault largely ignores minors. There is excellent and extensive research on the prevalence and patterns of child sexual abuse, much of it produced by David Finkelhor's Crimes Against Children Research Center, but little other recent feminist sociological work on child sexual abuse. In preparation for this chapter, I found that, in the past twenty years, only four articles on child sexual abuse or incest appeared in *Gender & Society*, two in *Signs*, eight in *Sex Roles*, none in *Feminist Studies*, and virtually none in the major generalist sociology journals.[1]

Given that a large proportion of survivors of rape and other forms of sexual violence are under eighteen, feminists should attend more to child sexual abuse as both part of and distinct from other forms of sexual violence. In this chapter, I outline a feminist sociological analysis of child sexual abuse. Drawing together scholarship on child sexual abuse and feminist theory, I sketch out how, as with rape, child sexual abuse is an important dimension of a system of inequality that has both structural and cultural dimensions. I center the intersectional dimensions of sexual violence (including age), complicated questions of adolescent sexual agency, and the role of the state in structuring definitions and responses to sexual violence.

Like the rape of adults, sexual assault against children is shaped by gender and power. The facts that sexual assault is more common against girls than against boys, and that male offenders are more common than female, indicate the importance of gendered power structures in shaping patterns (Nelson and Oliver 1998). Specifically, 17.4 percent of girls and 4.2 percent of boys ages fourteen to seventeen report ever having been sexually assaulted by adults or peers, and 3.6 percent of girls and 0.4 percent of boys report having been raped; more than 90 percent of perpetrators of sexual assault against girls and boys are male (Douglas and Finkelhor 2005; Finkelhor et al. 2013). (These figures exclude sexual harassment and other noncontact offenses.) Multiple forms of power come into play, including patriarchal power in the family, adults' power over children, and the different positions of girls and boys in educational settings and the public sphere. Institutions, including economics and "state agencies and public policy" also commit and permit violence against children differentially, according to race and class (Bray 2011; Richie 2012).

Gendered discourses also limit and structure how both adults and children understand sexual violence (Warner 2009; Whittier 2009). The meanings of child sexual abuse are constructed through discourses that reflect existing interests and power relations (Boyd 2009; Warner 2009; Whittier 2001). Nelson and Oliver (1998) show that gender shapes young adults' accounts of their childhood and adolescent experiences of sexual contact with adults; discourses of male sexuality as agentic makes men less likely to understand their childhood experiences as nonconsensual. Even the self-constructed narratives of survivors do not inevitably subvert gendered power. "Oppositional" discourse by adult survivors, Naples (2003a) argues, is potentially transformative, but it can be limited by the dominance of experts in its production (for example, in professional therapy) and by an individualized focus (Alcoff 2009). As survivor activists gained access to mainstream media, their narratives were refracted through medicalized frames of injury and powerlessness while offenders were cast as pedophiles and criminals, with little mention of gender or power (Whittier 2009).

Largely outside sociology, feminist literary theorists have drawn on feminist trauma theory, which builds on the work of Judith Herman (Herman 1997;

Herman [1981] 2000), and has been influential in feminist therapy and organizing by survivors of child sexual abuse (Champagne 1996; Courtois 1988; Doane and Hodges 2001). Linking subjectivity and social inequality, feminist trauma theory argues that childhood trauma both causes emotional difficulties for individuals and primes them to be compliant citizens. It suggests that assault and trauma flourish in the context of male domination, the patriarchal family structure, and larger societal patterns of war and the drive for dominance and control. Social theorists from diverse perspectives have critiqued a focus on the psychological consequences of sexual assault rather than on its social and structural aspects (Bumiller 2008; Mardorossian 2002). However, theorizing how gendered subjectivity, interpretations of experience, discourse, and structural inequality interact to shape child sexual abuse is consistent with feminist sociological theory that emphasizes how emotion, identity, and daily lives are shaped by gender as an institution (Lorber 1994). Analyzing how interiority and subjectivity are linked to power is thus important for understanding child sexual abuse in terms of gendered power (Whittier 2009).

These gendered processes are related but not identical to those shaping sexual violence against adults. In the remainder of this essay, I detail three key elements of a feminist sociological analysis of child sexual abuse. First, an analysis of child sexual abuse should be intersectional, especially given the long history of unequal adjudication based on race and class, and we need to include age as a central dimension of power and inequality (Collins 2000). Second, scholarship on adolescent girls' sexuality and their experiences of sexual assault raises important questions about agency and the discrepancies between law and lived experience. Third, the literatures on moral panic and on carceral feminism do implicitly engage with child sexual abuse. I draw out their implicit models of the issue to suggest that, although these perspectives contain important critiques of the state, neither helps understand child sexual abuse itself.

Race, Class, Age, and Intersectional Feminist Theory

Little existing scholarship on child sexual abuse and incest considers race or class, and assaults against children are only briefly mentioned in the major works on race and violence (an important exception is Wilson 1994). Considerable scholarship shows how race and class shape rape, however, including increased vulnerability to assault in economically precarious neighborhoods, Black women's historically widespread rape by White men, the use of rape charges to control Black men through lynching, and higher prosecution and conviction rates for Back assailants, especially with White victims (Freedman 2013; Collins 2000; McGuire 2010; Richie 2012). Many cases of rape of Black girls by White men that sparked activism and outrage historically were considered especially egregious because of the age of the victim, but not understood as a separate category of "child sexual assault" (Freedman 2013; McGuire 2010).

It is clear, however, that child sexual abuse plays out differently depending on the race and class of the assailant and victim. Activists and service providers note the challenges for communities of color, including reluctance to report assailants who may receive disproportionate sentences or to air dirty laundry in public, well-founded mistrust of police, and fear of deportation (Murphy 2002; Simmons 2006). Some communities of color experience disproportionate rates of child sexual assault; Native American activists, in particular, have documented widespread assaults by both Native and non-Native men, with virtual impunity (Deer 2006; Erdrich 2013). Low-income children, who may live with more unrelated adults and have less parental supervision, are also more vulnerable to assault (Richie 2012). Low-income and racial minority families also are under greater scrutiny by state agencies, such as child protective services, and thus more subject to intervention (Polsky 1991; Roberts 2006). For racially and class-privileged families, an image of respectability and social power can enable incest to go undetected (Sacco 2009). Further, prevailing discourse about the risks of girls' sexualization is shaded by ideas about race and class. This includes the idea that incest occurs mainly in marginalized families, and that it is mainly disreputable strangers who threaten children. Broad ideas of sexual innocence are raced and classed, including the ideas that White girls' innocence is especially threatened, and that girls of color are naturally hypersexual (Renold and Ringrose 2013). Meanwhile, discourses of male sexual agency are magnified for boys of color, who are feared as sexually aggressive but whose own sexual victimization is virtually invisible.

Corrigan (2006) documents that risk assessment scales for sex offenders disproportionately increase penalties for Black, Latino, and low-income offenders. At the same time, people incarcerated for child sexual abuse and rape are more White and middle-class than the general prison population (Douglas and Finkelhor 2005). Rather than indicating less racial and class bias in prosecution of sex crimes, this may reflect a lower priority on prosecuting sexual assault against children of color and low-income children. While critique of the race and class dimensions of the state is crucial, we also need much more research and theorizing on sexual assault against working class, poor, and racialized children.

Highly publicized cases of child sexual assault, such as the child rapes at Penn State or the clergy abuse cases in the Catholic Church, illustrate the power dynamics outside the family, with institutionally powerful assailants operating while their organizational supervisors and subordinates remained silent. While the fact that these assaults were committed by men against boys may explain part of the publicity they received, they clearly reflect age-related power as well as the ability of powerful institutions to protect themselves.

Age is thus a central intersectional dimension for understanding sexual violence. A large proportion of rapes reported to law enforcement are against minors; an estimated 51 percent of all female forcible rape victims are under the age of eighteen and an estimated 16 percent are under the age of twelve (Langan and Harlow 1994).[2] Children and adolescents are individuals whose legal rights and social, economic, and political power are limited. As a result, they are vulnerable to assault and exploitation by adults, who have more power on all these dimensions. They have less recourse to intervention and little influence over the relevant institutions (e.g., child protective services, foster care, criminal justice) (Armstrong 1994). Theorizing sexual violence intersectionally allows us to consider how gender, race, class, and age interact to shape experiences, interpretations, and responses, and points to the need for research guided by this approach.

Agency and Victimization in Adolescent Sexuality

If we want to understand sexual assault against children and teens, we need to engage with the extensive feminist scholarship on childhood and adolescence. In particular, the work on adolescence and sexuality points to a complex landscape for adolescent girls, who must navigate their own desires, sexual stigma, sexual harassment, coercion, and assault from age mates and older men (Pascoe 2011; Schalet 2011; Tolman 2012) in a legal context that defines much of girls' sexuality as child sexual abuse.

Consensual sexuality for adolescent girls is shaped by "the persistence of institutionalized heterosexuality . . . that continues to reproduce gender inequities in heterosexual romantic and sexual relationships" (Tolman 2012, 752). Adolescent girls are sexualized through body image, sexual harassment in schools, dress codes, and heteronormative discourses that elide the possibility of girls' sexual desire. Renold and Ringrose (2013), summarizing this work, emphasize the constant tension between pleasure and danger for girls, whose sexual agency is denied and for whom the risk of sexual harm is both ever-present and culturally overwrought. Adolescent girls' subjective feelings of sexual desire or empowerment are inextricably linked to media representations and expectations of pleasing their (male) partners (Lamb and Peterson 2012). Heterosexual experiences often reflect "intimate injustice," in which boys' pleasure and desire are prioritized over girls' (McClelland 2010, cited in Tolman 2012). These gender inequities connect girls' consensual and nonconsensual sexual experiences. Hlavka (2014) vividly documents how adolescent girls understand sexual assault by adults and older teens as the normal result of men's sexual natures and girls' failure to say no.

Scholars who study consensual sexual activity in the lives of adolescent girls rarely put their work in the context of child sexual abuse. But while children, young adolescents, and girls of seventeen are quite different, they are often conflated in the law, under which sexual contact before the age of consent is a crime (Lamb and Peterson 2012).[3] In some jurisdictions, consensual relationships between teenagers are illegal regardless of participants' ages; in others, they are considered child sexual assault if one teenager turns eighteen before the other. Enforcement is more likely in same-sex relationships and for youth of color, as in a case where an African American girl who turned eighteen was convicted of a felony for her relationship with another girl who was still underage (Tolman 2012). Teenagers also can be prosecuted under child pornography law in "sexting" cases (Walsh, Wolak, and Finkelhor 2013). Producing or distributing sexual images of people under the age of eighteen is illegal, even if the people involved are over the age of consent and the sexting is consensual. (Indeed, photographing oneself nude can and has been considered producing child pornography.)

These issues present obvious problems for bringing together feminist theories of adolescent sexuality and child sexual abuse, since the legal model embedded in child sexual abuse law is the statutory impossibility of consent, yet a central problematic in studies of adolescent sexuality is the tension between sexual desire and societal shaping and silencing of that desire. At the same time, statutory rape and child pornography laws based on age rather than consent have been supported by many feminists because they enable prosecution by eliminating the defense of consent (Freedman 2013). We are left with the conceptual and empirical problem of recognizing girls' sexuality and agency without ignoring their structural inequality or domination by adults. This is a complicated and controversial task. Feminist scholars may draw lines in different places, but we are not well served by ignoring the dilemma or by separating scholarship on adolescent sexuality from scholarship and law on child sexual abuse.

Moral Panics and Carceral Feminism

A final set of questions emerges from work by scholars who critique moral panics around child sexual abuse, and those who critique feminist campaigns to mobilize the state's punitive power against sexual violence, which Elizabeth Bernstein (2010, 2012) terms "carceral feminism." These are distinct approaches, but they share an implicit theory of child sexual abuse. Moral panic analyses deal primarily with culture and mass media and argue that fear-mongering representations of child sexual abuse promoted by "child savers" serve the interests of authorities who aim to expand social control. Carceral feminist critiques also treat the underlying problem as overblown and focus on the threat to women and children from the growing punitive state. Both approaches focus on constructions of and responses to the problem rather than the issue of child sexual abuse itself. What are the implications of these analyses for feminist theories of child sexual abuse?

Moral Panic and Child Sexual Abuse

Theories of moral panic have been very influential in analyses of child sexual abuse, including most writing by progressives (Best 1990; Davis 2005; Hacking 1991; Jenkins 1998; Lancaster 2011; Victor 1998). The general point is that public concern about child sexual abuse varies historically, with times of rising concern considered waves of irrational public fear, "wildly exaggerated and wrongly directed" (Victor 1998) out of proportion to the actual problem and produced by overzealous "child savers." There are a number of specific claims about what occurs in panics, including that extreme cases are used to stand in for routine cases (i.e., abduction/murders stand in for incest); media coverage and experts express exaggerated alarm with little dissent; and the scope of media coverage and concern are out of proportion to the actual problem (Victor 1998). As shown in previous research (Whittier 2009), none of these claims were empirically true for concern over child sexual abuse during the most recent alleged moral panic, from 1980–2005. Bray (2011) and Jenkins (2001) similarly show that the moral panic analysis of child pornography is empirically wrong. More recently, critics of sex offender registration and notification have argued that a moral panic has encouraged witch hunts against innocent people, who are falsely charged with child sexual assault and placed on sex offender lists (Lancaster 2011). There are some such cases, which are travesties, and sex offender legislation is indeed punitive and counterproductive (Corrigan 2006). But the assumption in this writing is that these cases are typical; in an ironic twist, they come to stand in for the more common and routine cases of child sexual abuse, in which charges and convictions are very rare (Cheit 2014). The underlying theory of child sexual abuse in moral panic writing is that it is uncommon and that existing social responses are not only sufficient but excessive. There is solid empirical evidence that neither assertion is true. It is striking that this model of child sexual abuse—which centers false accusations by children and by punitive mothers in custody disputes—has received so little feminist critique. This stands in stark contrast to feminist theories of sexual assault against adults. The difference is not simply the acceptance of victims' truth claims. Rape of adult women is accepted as common precisely because feminist theories understand how cultural, economic, and political power enable and produce it through cultural representations that normalize violence and eroticize female submission, women's economic dependence on abusive husbands, and political processes that allow institutions like the military or prisons to avoid addressing the issue. Child sexual abuse is similarly produced through cultural representations that eroticize childhood, children's economic dependence on adults, political processes that fail to provide alternatives or power to children in abusive situations, and so forth. If we theorize child sexual abuse in these terms, the inadequacy of understanding the issue through a moral panic lens becomes apparent.

Child Sexual Abuse in a Carceral State

We are living during a growing prison industrial complex, with rising incarceration rates and sentence lengths. Racist logics organize arrest, conviction, and sentencing, and adults and children of color experience violence at the hands of state actors and agencies (Alexander 2010; Richie 2012). Feminists' reliance on the carceral state for relief is clearly problematic. Elizabeth Bernstein's (2010; 2012) influential formulation of "carceral feminism" and her critique of antitrafficking feminists for their drive to criminalize prostitution and their collusion with the control of women internationally is persuasive and productive (see also Doezema 2010; Parrenas 2011). Critiques of carcerality have been widely accepted among progressive academics (e.g., Bumiller 2008). The challenge for feminists theorizing child sexual abuse is to discern its relationship to carceral feminism and to crime in general.

We ought to be cautious about generalizing the analysis of carceral feminism to child sexual abuse and perhaps to sexual violence more generally. Corrigan (2013) shows that critiques of feminist influence over criminal justice responses to rape overestimate the success of the women's movement; similarly, they overestimate feminist influence over responses to child sexual abuse. Unlike sex trafficking and some other forms of sexual violence, the state's response to child sexual abuse has not been driven by feminists, many of whom have opposed harsh sex offender policies (Whittier 2009). More important, feminist sociologists should not allow the important critiques of carcerality to substitute for feminist analysis of child sexual abuse itself.

Law and discourse about child sexual abuse are obviously severe. But prosecution and conviction rates are low and sentences relatively short. Severe postincarceration penalties, through the lifelong effects of sex offender registries, coexist with minimal prosecution (Cheit 2014). Prosecution rates for rape overall have decreased as prosecutors choose only the cases most likely to win (Corrigan 2013), and doubts about child witnesses have decreased prosecution in child sexual abuse cases even more (Cheit 2014). In fact, Corrigan (2006) suggests that sex offender registration actually has decreased prosecution and conviction. Prosecutors are reluctant to subject seemingly respectable defendants to lifelong penalties, and families are reluctant to bring charges against relatives. At the same time, as defendants refuse plea bargains that would classify them as sex offenders, more cases go to trial where conviction rates are low. Contrary to the idea that carceral feminism has shifted to focus on threats outside the family (Bernstein 2010), 70 percent of convictions nationally in 1992 for rape of children under the age of twelve were for incest and another 24 percent for assaults by acquaintances; for children over twelve years old, 36 percent of rape convictions were for incest and 45 percent for rapes committed by acquaintances (Langan and Harlow 1994).

Even feminists and progressives decry the cover-ups and downplaying that allow rapists and child abusers to go unprosecuted. In other words, child sexual abuse is a case for which a general critique of a carceral approach can be hard to sustain, because it is difficult to rule out state responses, although some advocates of restorative justice do so (Murphy 2002). Given children's structural powerlessness, what societal responses could effectively intervene in child sexual abuse without strengthening a racist and sexist criminal justice system? In general, despite the harsh rhetoric, carceral responses may strengthen state control but without having much actual effect on child sexual abuse.

Conclusions

Despite increasing public awareness and state intervention, child sexual abuse remains prevalent, follows existing inequalities, and societal responses are inadequate. State responses and the legal and cultural definitions of abuse are often punitive and counterproductive. As with rape, understanding processes of definition and response is crucial to understanding child sexual abuse and how to end it. But we also ought to continually raise the question of how cultural representations and state responses affect children in sexually abusive circumstances.

Overall, how should we theorize child sexual abuse? We should analyze incest and child sexual abuse as a gendered issue that is both similar to and distinct from other forms of sexual violence. A theory of rape that ignores sexual assault against minors is incomplete, particularly given the prevalence of rape against children and adolescents. Child sexual abuse is fundamentally shaped by intersectional inequalities of gender, race, and class, which structure individual-level experiences, prevalence, cultural representations, and state and institutional responses. An intersectional feminist approach to sexual violence should also foreground age, recognizing children and adolescents as a group that is structurally unequal and subject to control and domination by adults. Just as scholars who study and theorize violence against women could benefit from attending to sexual assault against children and adolescents, those who study child sexual abuse should engage with the literature on rape, and those who study adolescent sexuality should engage with the artificially separate literature on child sexual abuse. Such engagement has the potential to help us rethink the relationship between different forms of sexual violence and the tension between sexual agency and victimization. Scholars in these fields have much to learn from each other, and much to contribute to our understanding of child sexual abuse as an intersectionally shaped and gendered experience that is an important aspect of power and inequality.

NOTES

1 I searched by the subjects "incest" and "child sexual abuse." I excluded book reviews, articles on depictions in literature or film, and incidental mention. Of the eight articles in *Sex Roles*, most were social-psychological. *Social Problems* published one article, and *American Sociological Review (ASR)*, *American Journal of Sociology (AJS)*, *Social Forces*, and *Youth and Society* published none. Criminology journals published little, with one article in *Criminology* and three in *Deviant Behavior*, none with an analytical focus on gender. Even in journals focused on child abuse, virtually no articles focused on gender.

2 These figures exclude statutory rape and are based on reports to law enforcement in twelve states that collected data on the age of the victims.

3 In some states, there are separate statutes for sexual assault on a child over or under a certain age, e.g., age fourteen, but sexual contact is statutorily illegal in either case. Age of consent in the US ranges from sixteen to eighteen.

23

Rape Culture in Holy Spaces

Child Sexual Abuse by Clergy

ROSEMARY SULLIVAN

Beware of false prophets, which come to you in sheep's clothing, but inwardly they are ravening wolves.
—Matthew 7:15

The lower levels of hell are reserved for those who in times of moral crisis remain neutral.
—Dante Alighieri

When contacted by the *Boston Globe* in 2002 to comment on decades of allegations that he had raped and molested high school students, Rev. Robert Meffan freely answered the reporter's questions. He said, "I felt that by having this little bit of intimacy with them that this is what it would be like with Christ . . . I was trying to get them to love Christ even more intimately and even more closely . . . To me they were just wonderful, wonderful young people. It was a very beautiful, I thought, beautiful, spiritual relationship that was physical and sexual" (Pfeiffer 2002, 1). Robert Meffan continues to live freely in the community, having faced no arrest or prosecution for innumerable alleged sex crimes.

To understand the disastrous collapse of the Catholic Church in the US and Europe since the mid 1990s, one must understand rape culture. Sociologists define rape culture as a construct that "refers to a society that contains within it practices and ideologies that minimize the negative impacts of victimization, while condoning and perpetuating the perpetration of acts of sexual violence" (Kelner 2013, 9).

This chapter will explore the specific mechanisms of rape culture that contribute to the sexual violence perpetrated against boys and girls by Catholic priests. Distinct focus will be given to seminary training, clerical narcissism, and the perversion of the Sacrament of Penance and Reconciliation as well as key findings from several international inquiries. David Finkelhor's (1979) four preconditions model will be applied to these Catholic-specific factors to illustrate how rape culture manifests in particular behaviors. Testimony and personal narratives from victims and abusive priests will highlight the points described in the chapter.

For the purposes of this chapter, specific attention to the cultural aspect of sexual violence within the Catholic Church is crucially important. As with all religions, Catholicism uses rituals and ceremonies to connect to individuals on a cognitive, emotional, spiritual, and mystical level. For billions of believers, the Catholic faith structures everything about their lives, either consciously or unconsciously. As with other religions, no single definition can capture the totality of "culture," but a solid working definition comes from Ashford, LeCroy, and Lortie as "the entirety of knowledge, beliefs, experiences, meanings, hierarchies, notion of time, roles, special relations, concept of the universe, and material objects and possessions shared by a population and transmitted to future generations" (2006, 9).

Simply attending a Catholic Mass underscores Ashford et al.'s description of culture. Sitting in a church, one is struck by the physical environment: cathedral ceilings, soft light filtered through stunning stained glass, rich wooden pews polished to shiny smoothness, an altar elevated in the center draped by ornate coverings, a crucifix exalting a tortured yet serene Christ, the echoing stillness, the resonant sounds of prayers chanted in unison, plangent choirs, and a priest resplendent in satin robes. Identity binds the communicants and the clergy—we are not just anyone, we are *Catholics*. But what is a Catholic? According to Reverend Thomas Doyle:

> Catholicism is a spiritual force, a way of life, and a religious movement. It is also a complex socio-cultural reality and a worldwide political entity. It has the power to touch the spiritual, moral, emotional, psychic, and economic lives of members and non-members alike. It has had more impact on world history than any other religious body. (Doyle 2006, 189)

Doyle's quote suggests a religion that dominates life on an individual and global scale, yet in the past fifteen years in particular, the world has witnessed the spectacular implosion of the Roman Catholic Church in the US, South America, and Europe. The seemingly never-ending reports of child molestation and rape are rivaled only by the continuing hideousness of conspiracy and collusion by clergy leadership. This chapter will discuss how rape culture manifests in Catholicism through specific pathologies at the root of clerical abuse and the effect on its victims.

The Roman Catholic Church as a Gendered Organization

The Catholic Church is a medieval monarchy. The pope is the king, with bishops and cardinals as princes. The pope is also the sovereign of the Vatican State, with cardinals appointed as ambassadors, or papal nuncios. The Vatican uses ecclesiastical substructures to enforce compliance in cardinals, bishops, priests, nuns, and other religious entities. Historically (and many would say currently) the Catholic Church elevates their own legal structure (Canon Law) over the civil laws of the countries where they are located. This monarchal framework serves to consolidate power in the hands of a relatively small all-male group, the Roman Curia, that enforces doctrines and preserves the organization's commitment to orthodoxy. (Doyle 2003, 2006; Frawley-O'Dea 2004b; Shupe 2007). This structure and adherence to Canon Law is another explanation as to why sexually abusive priests are not reported to civil authorities. This centralization of power also illustrates why there is a split between what is termed "the institutional church" versus day-to-day existence in parishes around the world. While individual churches and pastors may span the continuum of conservative to progressive, all Catholic churches must retain obedience to the institutional Church. As would be expected, the Church, with its distinct theology, is highly controlling and involved in the training of priests.

Across the globe, the Catholic Church has wielded immense power and authority at multiple levels: individual, community, and political. While the incessant drumbeat of sexual abuse scandals has damaged its reputation and status, it remains an undeniable cultural influence. Max Weber's typology of organizational structures focused upon the distinctions between traditional forms of authority and bureaucratic strategies of exerting power, and types of control. In his later work, he transitioned to the study of religion and religious structures. As sociologist Julian Freund (1968) writes, "What is important for [Weber's] sociology of religion is man's religious activity, or conduct, in relation to supernatural forces" (187). For Weber, religion is a blend of magic, asceticism, and mysticism; power and authority is how individuals relate to and organize themselves within that structure. To describe this phenomenon, he defined power as "the probability that one actor in a social relationship will be in position to carry out his own will without resistance" (Freund 1968, 221). Weber also identified three types of authority: charismatic, traditional, and legal-rational. Charismatic authority is defined as the immense personal magnetism of a leader. Historically figures like Jesus, Gandhi, and Martin Luther King, Jr. are examples of charismatic visionaries. Traditional authority is exemplified by deference to a dominant personality and adherence to established traditions and order. Lastly, legal-rational authority is based on rules and a codification system; this type of authority is vested in office holders rather than individuals (Allen 2004). The Catholic Church, for reasons that will be illustrated throughout this chapter, is best understood as a traditional authority, although it is administered through a massive bureaucratic structure.

The intensely controlling nature of the institutional church is one manifestation of its oppressively gendered hierarchy. As Acker (1990) suggests, although highly structured organizations are purportedly rational and focused on instrumental goals, assumptions built into their construction of jobs and bodies are not gender-neutral. She writes, "To say that an organization . . . is gendered means that advantage and disadvantage, exploitation and control, action and emotion, meaning and identity, are patterned through and in terms of a distinction between male and female, masculine and feminine" (ibid., 146). According to Acker's theory, male-dominated organizations like the Catholic Church reproduce traditional gender relations through the gendered organization of work, gendered segregation that reinforces status inequality, and through knowledge systems that invent, disseminate, and reproduce cultural images of gender.

The Catholic Church, historically and currently, uses its cultural, economic, and spiritual power to reinforce an intensely gendered and oppressive organizational structure. In her 2018 address to the Voices of Faith Conference in Rome on National Women's Day, the former president of Ireland, Mary McAleese, advocated for the Catholic Church to include women in positions of authority long held by celibate men. As she dismantled the oppressive systems of the institutional Church she summarized need for change: "the Catholic Church has long since been a primary global carrier of the virus of misogyny. It has never sought a cure, though a cure is freely available. Its name is 'equality'" (2018).

Scope of Sexual Abuse within the Catholic Church

The John Jay College of Criminal Justice completed two studies (2004, 2011) that extensively examined the causes of clerical sexual abuse. Key findings included:

- Four to 6 percent of priests have abused children sexually.
- Homosexuality is not the reason why the majority of clerical abuse victims were boys (81 percent). The report determined that the overrepresentation of male victims was because of easier access to boys. As more girls became accepted in church roles (i.e., altar servers) those numbers increased as well.
- Celibacy was not a causative factor in the sexual abuse of children.
- Seminary training, especially the lack of attention paid to human development and the challenges of celibacy, were important factors.
- Recruitment of sexually, psychologically, and socially immature seminarians is a major component in the ongoing crisis.
- The majority of abusive priests were ephebophiles (sexual attraction to postpubertal children), not pedophiles (sexual attraction to prepubertal children). This is an important distinction in terms of psychological treatment.
- Child abuse reports have been declining since 2007. Critics allege that this is only a lull. As more recently abused children grow into adulthood, numbers could rise.

- Bishops mishandled the reports of sexual abuse by priests, exponentially increasing the problem.
- It is impossible to predict which seminarians/priests will become sex offenders.

Some scholars have criticized the reports' findings (Doyle 2006; Fox 2011; Frawley-O'Dea 2011; Shupe and Sipe 2011). They note that the majority of information analyzed by the John Jay researchers comes directly from diocesan files whose release must be authorized by bishops. This clearly represents a self-serving conflict of interest. In addition, the studies did not include any crimes reported to other agencies or non-Catholic sources, such as individual therapists. The John Jay College's reports also cannot ensure that the data received by bishops are honest and accurate. A damning incident with the then Governor of Oklahoma, James Keating, highlights this conflict of interest. Bishop Wilton Gregory appointed Gov. Keating as chair of the National Review Board (NRB). The NRB was created after the Charter for the Protection of Children and Young People, which every diocese adopted. Keating famously resigned from the National Review Board after he found it impossible to conduct investigations into reports of child abuse.

To the anger of many US bishops, Keating compared the Catholic Church to the Mafia. When asked to publicly apologize he responded, "My remarks, which some bishops found offensive, were deadly accurate. I make no apology. . . . To resist grand jury subpoenas, to suppress the names of offending clerics, to deny, to obfuscate, to explain away, that is the model of a criminal organization, not my church" (Webster 2003, n.p.).

A. W. Sipe (2011), a therapist for abusive priests and prolific author about clerical sex offenders, believes that the John Jay report grossly underestimated the number of abusive priests. Sipe's research (2007) estimates that 9 percent of priests have sexually offended. In the general population, based on statistics from the US Department of Justice (n.d.), approximately 10 percent of child sex offenders are nonfamily members. Sipe (2011) also criticized the lack of knowledge of the research team about issues related to clericalism and seminary training. Numerous international studies support Sipe's findings including four separate reports in Ireland, three reports covering all of the US dioceses by the John Jay College of Criminal Justice, and numerous published investigations in Australia, Germany, the Netherlands, England, Wales, Thailand, Mexico, and Chile.

Every investigation uncovers layers of corruption, enabling of sex offenders by clergy, and a trail of devastated victims and families. As always, any statistic should be critiqued as low, given that sexual violences are generally widely underreported crimes. All of the international reports illustrate that, in most cases, clerical perpetrators enjoy long careers as rapists and molesters. It cannot be stated enough that sexual abuse by Roman Catholic clergy is not an event of the past. The most recent large-scale investigation occurred in 2018 in Pennsylvania. In this landmark case, which prompted new investigations in every diocese around the US, a grand jury issued a report that found evidence of abuse of more than one thousand children by hundreds of priests (Holpuch 2018).

The Preconditions Model and Rape Culture

As a preeminent researcher of sexual offenders, David Finkelhor (1979) developed a model to describe specific conditions that must exist for a perpetrator to act upon his impulses to abuse children. Finkelhor's model has been widely cited and critiqued (Ward and Hudson 2001) but ultimately remains an important clinical framework for understanding, and ultimately interrupting, sexual offenders. Known as the Preconditions Model, it is the mechanism that alchemizes the academic concepts of rape culture with actual assaults. Finkelhor describes four conditions that must occur before an offender commits child sexual abuse. They are defined as: motivation to sexually abuse, overcoming internal inhibitors, overcoming external inhibitors, and overcoming resistance by the child. Specifically, motivation to sexually abuse is defined as a combination of factors: emotional congruence, sexual arousal, and blockage.

Emotional congruence is defined as an offender who looks to children to meet emotional needs. In addition, sexual congruence between adults and children is often correlated with low self-esteem in the offender, aggressive thoughts and behaviors, and the lack of emotionally intimate connection with age-appropriate peers. This is likely due to the arrested development of the perpetrator, and the often-mentioned offender characteristic of psychosexual immaturity. Second, sexual arousal is defined as paraphilia that is deviant sexual attraction to children. Finally, the term blockage is defined as a situation in which offenders use children for sexual gratification because they are blocked from having healthy, intimate relationships with other adults. An example would be an adult who has poor social skills and fears rejection. These emotional factors "block" them from pursuing appropriate adult relationships. When these three factors occur in concert, the precondition of motivation is met.

Overcoming internal inhibitors is defined by Finkelhor, Cuevas, and Drawbridge as the emotional process in which "an adult must overcome any internal inhibitions—guilt feelings, moral scruples, fear of punishment—that they have against sexual contact with children" (2016, 32). Finkelhor et al. highlight that overcoming this internal barrier requires a lack of empathy for the child. In addition, cognitive distortions that encourage abuse (rationalizing, justifying, minimizing) are also found to contribute to disinhibition.

Overcoming External Inhibition

External disinhibition relies heavily on the structures of the offender's social environment. A perpetrator actively seeks to separate children from protective adult supervision and carefully chooses the location of abuse to ensure privacy. Generally, through the process of deliberate planning, an offender sets the stage for an eventual sexual assault. Overcoming the external barriers that generally shield children from exploitation is crucial to the perpetrator's ultimate goal of abuse. As Finkelhor and colleagues note, "many of these offenders perpetrated these crimes when they perceived risks to be low" (2016, 34).

Overcoming the Child's Resistance

All children, in their own way, resist sexual assault. Some attempts at resistance are obvious: running away, fighting back, and disclosing their apprehension about a particular person or place. Other methods of resistance are opaque: dissociation, somatic complaints, indiscriminate fearfulness, sleep disturbances, numbing through substance abuse or self-harm, and generalized behavioral instability. According to Finkelhor's model, offenders must develop strategies to fight children's attempts to protect themselves. Child abusers accomplish this in the following ways: violence, threats, inducing crippling guilt and shame, convincing a child of his or her "specialness" or offering a destructive form of love to a desperately needy child. All of these methods have one goal: to remove barriers to rape and sexual abuse.

In the Catholic Church, these four preconditions exist in individual offending priests and in the larger structure of the Church. On an individual level, earlier sections in this chapter describe "psychosexual immaturity" as identical to Finkelhor's description of emotional congruence. Mandatory celibacy and Catholic moral teaching is strikingly similar to Finkelhor's description of blockage. At a larger level, Finkelhor's preconditions that require empathic bankruptcy and the removal of barriers to abuse occur not only at an individual level but also across the larger structures of the Catholic Church. The constant recycling of abusive priests across parishes by bishops has ensured an endless supply of children to victimize. The intense desire to protect the Church from scandal, rather than offering support and protection to children, is shockingly callous. The intimidating and hostile reaction (interpersonally and litigiously) to abused children and their families by Church hierarchy are as equally heinous as the pedophile priest who threatens a child. Rape culture creates the social context for abuse, and Finkelhor's theory explains the mechanism used to enact it.

The Rape Culture of Catholic Clergy

Clericalism

Despite the beauty of the opulent church scene depicted earlier in this chapter, clericalism is the seeding ground for a unique form of malignant narcissism found within the clergy. This deep pathology, is described by Sipe:

> The veneer of holiness and altruism that cloaks the institution of the Roman Catholic Church secretes a clerical culture infused by excessive narcissism. The institution is not what it appears in its public pronouncements, ritual manifestations, and glorious vesture. I have seen how its self-serving elements have had a pervasive destructive influence in propagating toxic spirituality that enables and fosters sexual assault on vulnerable children and minors and yet protects and projects an image of perfection and moral purity. (Sipe et al. 2013, 3)

Although not the only factor contributing to child sexual abuse by priests, clericalism plays a major role in creating the context in which sexual violence occurs. For hundreds of years Catholic teaching dictated that celibate men would lead the church and shape the spiritual lives of its members. As the human embodiment of Christ, priests live in a sphere above and beyond the laity. This exalted status exists because, theoretically, at a young age they have been called to a holy and divine vocation.

As they begin their formation and training, seminarians are instructed to view their sacrifice as divine and reject any sense of loss that may arise. Set apart from their peers, priests now must live in insular, all-male seminary environments, and reject any expression of sexuality or intimacy. Part of this process is to renounce most of the major psychosocial milestones expected of secular adults. As they begin their formation and training, they learn that membership in the celibate priesthood is proof of their ecclesiastical superiority. In reality, the process of Catholic seminary training and the adherence to its mandates creates stunted development in men. Their emotional and psychosexual identity development is deliberately shut down in adolescence, while the external environment tells them that they are divine and exceptional. For even the most stable man, this conflict is difficult. For others, whose pathology runs deeper, Catholic seminary life and education foments intense narcissism.

The behavioral manifestations of clerical narcissism may be masked by a kind face and a gentle voice but are also marked by entitlement, demands for gratification, a lack of empathy, false humility, the complete refusal to think about another's experience, and the drive to fulfill their desires, regardless of the consequences to someone else. Frawley-O'Dea (2007) writes, "Clericalism justifies rigidly hierarchical power arrangements by declaring that . . . the individual [priest] is entitled to the power he wields and the deference he demands. It is a phenomenon that divides people into categories, emphasizing status differences rather than the commonalities of the human condition" (152).

Shupe (2007) describes how children and adults were indoctrinated to accept without question the special status of priests: "Religious education is accompanied by a thoroughgoing indoctrination in the etiquette and demeanor required. . . . in the presence of priests and nuns . . . deference to their religious authority and the purported wisdom which goes with that authority, must be the norm to be followed at all times" (59).

Many scholars suggest that the clericalism of offending priests fuels abuse, but the clericalism of bishops, cardinals, and popes enables abusers. The need to protect the Church at all costs, the willingness to sacrifice countless children to voracious sexual predators, the insistent, blind refusal to heed warnings of professionals within and outside Catholicism, and the belief that their judgment is superior are crucial factors in this tragedy. Abuse victims and their parents have approached Catholic leaders expecting an apology and a pastoral response but were met with hostility, blame, chastisement, and scorn. Marie Collins, an outspoken and eloquent advocate for survivors of clergy sexual abuse in Ireland recalled the first time she disclosed that she had been raped as a child while bed-bound in Dublin's largest children's hospital:

> I was forty-seven before I spoke of my abuse for the first time; this was to a doctor who was treating me. He advised me to warn the Church about this priest. I arranged a meeting with a curate in my parish. I was very nervous. It would be only the second time I had spoken to anyone about what had happened to me. This priest refused to take the name of my abuser and said he saw no need to report the chaplain. He told me what had happened was probably my fault. This response shattered me. I did not turn against my religion, I turned against myself. (Collins 2012, n.p.)

The priest who raped Marie Collins was well known to the archdiocese, before and after her experience. In his position as chaplain at the children's hospital, Rev. Paul McGennis strategically picked the sickest children who tended not to have many visitors. He would rape and molest children and photograph his acts in an effort to create his own child pornography library. He was caught when he sent his film to be developed in England. English authorities turned his lewd photos over to Irish law enforcement. The Gardaí (Irish police) did not open an investigation, but arranged a meeting with the archbishop of Dublin, John Charles McQuaid. McGennis confessed his behavior to McQuaid, and the archbishop concluded that McGennis was "curious" about female anatomy. McQuaid arranged counseling sessions with a respected Catholic gynecologist to "educate" McGennis, and returned him to ministry. He continued to abuse children for another thirty-five years (Department of Justice and Equality 2009).

The ordeal Marie Collins suffered illustrates Doyle's ideas about the multilayered impact of clericalism in child sexual abuse cases: "There are three aspects of clerical abuse that seem directly related to clericalism: the seduction [grooming] of the victim, the lack of resistance to prolonged abuse and, the inability to report" (2006, 17). In this case, as a priest in an overwhelmingly Catholic country, working in a Catholic hospital and interacting with children and families of devout Catholic faith it was easy for McGennis to identify and groom victims. Collins recalls:

> I took my Catholic religion very seriously and had just made my confirmation. I was sick, anxious and away from home and family for the first time. I felt more secure when the Catholic chaplain of the hospital befriended me, visited me and read to me in the evenings. . . . My abusers' assertion that he was a priest and could do no wrong rang true with me; I had been taught that priests were above the normal man. (Collins 2012, n.p.)

When Doyle speaks of "lack of resistance to prolonged abuse" (2003, 17), he is referring not only to the dyad of victim-perpetrator, but of the dynamic between perpetrator and a social and ecclesiastical culture determined to live in denial, which allows for prolonged access to victims. The combination of a terrified child silenced by an abuser's social status and willful blindness by clergy and laypeople, make it nearly impossible for victims to report clerical sex crimes. Indeed, the official response to Collins when she did try to report her abuse clearly shows why so many boys and girls do not even try.

Although it may be comforting to view this case as "historical," similar reports of clerical abuse continue to this day. Marie Collins's rapist began abusing children in the 1950s. The sheer number of victims is not known. He did not face prosecution and imprisonment until 2011, at the age of eighty-one. In an effort to show the magnitude of this problem, the website BishopAccountability.org tracks prosecutions, convictions, and civil lawsuits throughout the world. It is updated frequently, with new reports each time. While specifics may differ from victim to victim, like Marie Collins's case, each case has at least one factor in common: perpetrators and Catholic leaders who adhere to clericalist belief systems at all costs.

Formation and Seminary Training

Formation refers to the specific process of education and training to become a Catholic priest or nun. There are various steps involved in the process to enter religious life. To begin, an individual goes through the process of "discernment." This is largely an internal spiritual experience where a man or woman begins to notice or acknowledge being "called by God" to become a priest or nun. During this time a person immerses himself or herself in Catholic life: attending Mass regularly, becoming involved in church functions and volunteerism, respecting Catholic sacraments, and meeting with religious mentors to continue exploring their religious direction. Historically, young men entered the seminary, a theological institute akin to a boarding school or college environment as early as thirteen years old (Schuth 2004, 2012; Doyle 2003, 2006; Sipe 2013; Sipe, Doyle, and Wall 2016; Frawley-O'Dea 2004a and b; Keenan 2012).

The requirements in the 1950s, '60s, and '70s were that young men feel "called" into the priesthood, and little else. In the mid 1980s, due to a severe shortage of priests, many seminaries closed. Those that remained required older applicants, usually after university training, and most included psychological testing before admission (Schuth 2004, 2012). Despite the increasingly tighter seminary admission standards, all applicants must enter training committed to Catholic moral teachings, as illustrated by the Catholic Diocese of Arlington (n.d.) advertisement on its website, below:

> Baptized, confirmed, and practicing Roman Catholic men with a desire to serve God and His people as a priest must possess the following general qualifications:
>
> - Good moral character
> - A high school diploma with favorable academic abilities
> - Emotional balance and maturity
> - Psychological readiness and capacity to pursue a sustaining, life-long commitment
> - Maturity to recognize and the willingness to respond to the needs of others
> - A developing spirit of detachment that helps him be in the world but not of the world
> - Be between the ages of seventeen and fifty-five (Rare exceptions are considered on a case-by-case basis.)
> - Does not have personal financial liability, i.e., car or personal loans, credit card(s), etc., versus personal assets that exceed $3,000; nor have total outstanding college student loan debt that exceeds $60,000
> - Not suffer from a disordered sexual orientation, i.e., not consider oneself to be homosexual

Currently, most seminaries require a four-year undergraduate degree before accepting an applicant. Four years of seminary followed by one year of internship with an ordained priest and a man can be ordained as a priest. The process from discernment to ordination takes approximately nine years.

Many researchers have cited seminary training as an important factor in understanding sexual abuse by priests. (Schuth 2004, 2012; Doyle 2003, 2006; Sipe, Doyle, and Wall 2016; Keenan 2012). Prospective priests, typically adolescents or young adults, attend seminary to become experts in Catholic theology and Catholic moral teaching. The Catholic faith only condones sexual activity within opposite sex marriages and only for the purposes of conceiving children. Therefore, any other kind of sexual activity is considered deviant. Use of contraception, even within an opposite sex marriage, is a grave sin, as it is seen as an affront to creating life. The two pillars of Catholic moral teachings are procreative heterosexual couples and celibate clergy. The former creates new Catholics and the latter sacrifice their bodies and their desires to attain a higher level of spirituality, or in the church's ideal, chaste perfection. Seminarians, who are often quite young, are expected to renounce their sexuality as part of the training process. Trainee priests are immersed in rigid orthodoxy, which is highly restrictive, judgmental, and separated from the "real-world" nature of human sexuality and its consequences, either positive or negative. Thomas Doyle describes the seminary experience as such:

> The seminarians were young boys whose meaningful emotional and sexual development was paused at a most crucial age. As they progressed to ordination some left the seminary, but those who remained were expected to have thoroughly internalized the theory of celibacy. Upon completion of their formation, these men were thrust into the world and expected to live a totally chaste life. Their maturation had been effectively stopped in their early teens. Many were, what one priest referred to as "the best educated 14 year olds in our society . . . young teenagers in the bodies of men." (2006, 10)

Marie Keenan (2012) offers this analysis:

> The process of entrance into seminary life meant saying goodbye to what one was accustomed to. In the new environment of seminary, compliance and deference, rather than autonomy and honesty, were valued. Often strategies of shame and fear were used to this end . . . [seminaries] set the tone for clerical life which included silence and denial, an atmosphere of deference and submission, and an environment where conflict and emotions were permitted to find expression only in covert ways. . . . [T]his way of living provided the structure for an environment where sexual abuse by clergy became possible. (51)

As a psychotherapist and a researcher, Keenan spent many years treating priests who had sexually abused children. In her book, she uses transcripts from therapy sessions to highlight the many factors that drive priests to assault children. Describing seminary life, one priest said:

> Sex was dirty and sinful and we needed to purify ourselves. Every week we had two lectures from a priest in the Diocese and I tell you that everything about sex was bad, bad, bad . . . I believe in the seminary we lived as though there was no other commandment . . . there was only one thing in morality and that was sex . . ." (135)

Entry into this intense and isolated world as teenagers left some seminarians vulnerable to victimization as well. In addition to allegedly sexually abusing young boys as a parish priest, the now laicized Cardinal Theodore McCarrick, allegedly sexually assaulted numerous seminarians and new priests throughout several dioceses. In 2018 the Vatican banished him to a life of prayer in a friary in Kansas. As with other cases of clerical abuse, McCarrick rose through the ranks of the clergy, promoted and protected by his superiors, despite frequent official complaints against him to the Vatican from 1993 to 2016 (Bruenig 2018; McElwee and Schlumpf 2018; Goodstein and Otterman 2018).

Many analysts (Schuth 2004, 2012; Doyle 2003, 2006; Sipe 2013; Sipe, Doyle, and Wall 2016; Frawley-O'Dea 2004a and b; Keenan 2012) support the conclusions that seminaries create a strong foundation for clericalism, combined with a sexually and emotionally repressive environment of young men cut off from outside support or influences. These findings are also supported by three studies from the John Jay College of Criminal Justice (2004, 2011) that criticized the structure and education in seminaries. These reports also showed that many priests that sexually abused children began doing so while in seminary.

Celibacy

Why does celibacy exist in Catholicism? Theologically speaking, celibacy is categorized as "mortification of the flesh" by those who practice it. Celibacy exists to achieve a higher spiritual plane than that of laypersons. James Martin, a popular and progressive Catholic priest, describes his relationship to celibacy in this way: "One of the many goals of celibacy is to love people as freely as possible and as profoundly as possible . . . besides its other roots, religious chastity was meant as another way to love others and serve the community. . . . There are many ways of loving, besides sex, through actions just as meaningful. Jesus was celibate. That doesn't mean he was a pedophile. Neither am I" (Martin 2017, n.p.).

Beyond the theological explanation of celibacy and chastity (which are interchangeable terms), religious scholars have identified other reasons to require clergy to remain unmarried and not sexually active. Over thousands of years celibacy and chastity have allowed the Catholic Church to concentrate their power socially and economically (Keenan 2012; Shupe 2008; Sipe 2003). Upon the death of an unmarried and childless priest, any family inheritance of money or land would be transferred to the Church. With no spouse or heirs, a priest would dedicate himself to serving with no emotional or financial entanglements, to the great social and economic benefit of the Church. This encapsulation of unmarried men and women in separate communities supported the gendered orthodoxy of Catholicism.

Media reports about clergy sexual abuse of children began increasing in the late 1990s, exploding in 2002 with the coverage of the Boston Archdiocese, continuing consistently since then. Initially, much speculation centered on the role that clergy celibacy played in explaining why priests would target children sexually. Numerous recent studies discount celibacy as a major causative factor but do recognize celibacy as another way in which Catholic orthodoxy about sexuality is intrinsically disordered (Fox 2011; Frawley-O'Dea 2004a, 2004b; Keenan 2012; Schuth 2004, 2012; Sipe 2003, 2005, 2007; Verhoeven 2015). The reasons for discounting celibacy as a major cause of rape and sexual assault of children are:

- While celibacy is required of all priests since the Middle Ages, only a relatively small proportion have abused children.
- Celibacy occurs outside of religious life and does not create sex offenders. There are certainly times when individuals are not sexually active. It is also common that people in committed relationships, for a variety of reasons, experience long spells of sexual inactivity.
- Female members of religious orders are also celibate, yet are very rarely sexual abusers.
- Heterosexually identified noncelibate men outside of religious life are the overwhelming majority of sex offenders.
- Sexual abuse of minors occurs in other religious groups that do not require celibacy.

Although celibacy may not be a causative factor in child sexual abuse, it can contribute to an overall attitude toward sexuality that leads to pathological rationalizations in priests with a predilection toward assaultive behavior. This was highlighted by D'Alton, Guilfoyle, and Randall (2013) in their qualitative study of priests who admitted sexually abusing children. The authors identified a trend they labeled "bidirectional foreclosure" in priests with inappropriate sexual impulses toward minors. In essence the priests were attracted to a celibate life as an answer to stifling the urges to sexually offend. Since the "chaste" environment of religious life supported eliminating any form of sexual expression, this dynamic served interests in both directions. One priest, who admitted to having multiple male victims explained: "I had decided at 14 or 15 I was going to become a priest and it [sexual behavior] wasn't going to be a part of my life . . . I kind of closed it down, I suppose" (D'Alton, Guilfoyle, and Randall 2013, 700).

For as long as celibacy has been required, the secret sex lives of clergy existed side by side. Researchers estimate that approximately 50 percent of priests are actually celibate, with the other half regularly engaged in age-appropriate heterosexual and homosexual relationships, sometimes lasting for decades (Sipe 2003, 2007, 2008; Frawley-O'Dea 2007, Anderson 2007, Sipe, Doyle, and Wall 2016; Keenan 2012; Verhoeven 2015). Obviously, in an organization that emphasizes chastity and sexual purity, this reality must be denied and disavowed. The sexual assault of minors became conflated with adult consensual sexual activities in this environment of desperate secrecy and scandal avoidance. In this context a major exception was ignored: consensual adult sexual relationships are not crimes, but raping and sexually assaulting children are heinous moral and legal offenses.

Structure of Confession

The act of confessing one's sins to a priest is a deeply sanctified Catholic sacrament. Technically termed the Sacrament of Penance and Reconciliation, a penitent reveals the thoughts, words, and deeds that illustrate the sin that they have committed. A priest grants absolution for the confessed sins, and the sinner is reconciled with God and the church. Most importantly, the "seal of confession" cannot be breached, meaning that whatever was said between priest and sinner must be kept in absolute secrecy. When a priest confesses his sexual offenses to another priest or superior, no reports to civil authorities can be made, according to Canon law. In May 2018 the National Board for Safeguarding Children in Europe continued to support the elevating of Canon Law over secular mandated reporting law. The board reiterated its stance to the London *Sunday Times* that abusers who confess to rape and other sexual assaults must not be reported to civil authorities claiming, "The sacramental seal is inviolable [and], therefore, it is absolutely forbidden for a confessor to betray in any way a penitent in words or in any manner and for any reason" (McCarthy 2018, n.p.).

Several researchers have identified how the structure of confession enabled the sexual abuse of children by priests, who themselves attended confession. In Keenan's (2012) qualitative study on sexually abusing priests the subject of perverting the confessional was frequent: "In a strange way the sacramental of confession let us off the hook rather lightly and perhaps allowed us to minimize what was happening. . . . The practice allowed us to feel that the disapproval and shame we experienced in telling was short-lived and never likely to be discussed anywhere except there . . ." (164).

Confession allowed slates (and souls) to be wiped clean; forgiveness was granted and a priest had another chance to beat the impulses to offend. When they failed to stop abusing (as most of them did), the Sacrament of Penance and Reconciliation was there to provide relief and absolution. For many sexually abusive priests, perverting this sacrament was integral to rapaciously pursuing children.

Effect on Victims

The devastating effect of child sexual abuse on survivors is extensive and well researched (Sipe, Doyle, and Wall 2016; Bowers 2010; Calkins, Fargo, Jeglic, and Terry 2015; Doyle 2003, 2006; Frawley-O'Dea 2004b, 2011; Freiburger 2011; Plante and McChesney 2011). Survivors of clerical sexual abuse experience additional, unique trauma. In the limited research that exists about this subpopulation, one term emerges repeatedly: soul murder (Sipe 2007; Doyle 2003, 2005; Frawley-O'Dea 2011). Soul murder is defined as the catastrophic consequence of sexual abuse by priests on an individual's mental health and spiritual health. Soul murder represents an intersubjective experience of sexual abuse by the clergy: the social rejection and alienation that occurs, the expected yet devastating psychological pathology that forms in response, and the spiritual and religious identity confusion.

Spiritual abuse, a necessary precursor to soul murder, is defined by Ward and Hudson (2011) and Dorr (2000) as "[a] misuse of power in a spiritual context whereby spiritual authority is distorted to the detriment of those under its leadership" (901). In Ward's study several themes were identified by victims who were abused in the context of their religious beliefs: seeing the religious leader as the highest form of spiritual authority, spiritual bullying, spiritual neglect, external/internal tension, and manifestation of internal states.

In Catholicism, these themes have distinct meaning. The previous discussion of clericalism reflects the themes of spiritual authority. Spiritual bullying occurs at many levels for survivors of clergy sexual violence: through direct and indirect threats by the offending priest himself and by the bishops who receive reports. Survivors of clergy abuse commonly report fears of being ostracized by the community, the fear of being retraumatized during legal battles, and fear of going to hell. Spiritual neglect occurs when a priest engages with a child to satisfy his deviant sexual urges rather than for spiritual development. Neglect also occurs when church leadership abandons children and their families when they attempt to report the abuse.

External and internal tensions for survivors of clerical sexual abuse refer to the existential crisis that often accompanies the experience: How can God let this happen? Is God punishing me? Is everything I believed just a lie? Finally, according to Ward, (2011) manifestation of internal states refers to the biopsychosocial damage suffered by victims. In social work practice, as in other "helping professions," treatment focuses on the psyche, soma, and societal level to bring a person back to whole health. Harm and strength are assessed in the physiological dimension (injuries, infections, neurological changes due to trauma), the psychological dimension (mental illness, addiction, emotional regulation), and the sociocultural level (changes to detrimental systems, advocacy, development of support networks). One of the unique challenges to victims trying to recover from clerical abuse is the way in which Catholicism inflicts pain and trauma at multiple levels (the individual parish, betrayal by regional archdioceses, and obfuscation by the papacy). Perhaps the most moving description of soul murder is captured by a poem written by an anonymous survivor of clerical sexual abuse:

> I was not allowed to scream in church
> I wanted to scream when you put your hands on me

I wanted to scream when I could feel your pulse flutter like
A moth's wings underneath your olive skin
I wanted to scream in the confessional
When you'd lie, and absolve, and sin
And gore your meat hooks through my mind
Telling me that you were god's punishment and fulfillment
A proxy

Conclusion

After decades of reports detailing the appalling crimes perpetrated by clergy upon children, the structures of the Catholic Church that perpetuate rape culture remain largely unchanged. While victims bravely lay bare their pain and anguish, missives from the Vatican continue to reinforce elements of Catholicism that allowed abuse to flourish unabated. While Pope Francis has excelled in public relations and image rehabilitation, very few substantive changes have occurred. Civil laws and the criminal justice system have improved in their efforts to punish offenders and enablers, but the Catholic Church remains ensconced in Canon Law, diplomatic immunity, and a culture of secrecy and miasma dating back centuries. Andrew Madden (2010) an articulate and outspoken victim and advocate described recent attempts at reform as "window dressing." Window dressing, for many victims, was on full display at the February 2019 Vatican summit on child sexual abuse. Long on rhetoric, short on specifics, many victims expressed their disappointment that nothing actionable resulted from the meeting. Colm O'Gorman, a survivor of childhood sexual abuse by a priest offered this analysis,

> [The Catholic Church] routinely rolled out such commitments, has occasionally rolled out new policies, guidelines and rules for over three decades and then has gone on to completely ignore them or refuse to implement them because they weren't mandated or required by canon law. . . . We need to see the Vatican open up its records and files to a proper independent investigation of exactly what it has done going back many decades by an appropriate authority, for instance the UN Committee on the Rights of the Child. . . . (McDonald 2019, n.p.)

And yet, as quickly as this chapter was written, more scandals unfolded, more communities initiated investigations, and more victims shared their experiences of soul murder. In a meeting with Pope Francis in 2018, Juan Carlos Cruz, James Hamilton, and José Andrés Murillo spoke for all victims of clerical abuse:

> For almost 10 years we have been treated as enemies because we fight against sexual abuse and cover-up in the church . . . We spoke in great detail and pain and it was very raw . . . Our only triumph is having said to the head of the church, the

pope, that there is a crisis, and that something concrete must be done. The church must return to being a champion of the abused, not a refuge for abusers. (Provoledo 2018)

Cruz appreciated the apparent heartfelt apology from Pope Francis, who had previously branded him a liar when he publicly accused Reverend Fernando Karadima of rape. Despite the pontiff's tears and regret, church leadership quickly retreated to the safe world created for them by rape culture. What was Karadima's punishment? A lifetime of prayer in Chile.

SECTION 5

Commodified Bodies

Agency or Violation?

Controversy seems to lie at the heart of gender issues. There is now both legal and public acknowledgment that sexual harassment, rape, intimate partner violence, and child abuse are social problems, although not immune to debate. Controversies around the commodification of bodies in sex work and pornography are emblematic of a much deeper definitional schism that anchors most of the contested areas of sex and gender relations in society. There are still deep theoretical—and ideological—divisions over what constitutes sexual oppression and sexual liberation, and moral debates abound. Seidman links these "boundary disputes" to contestation over meanings and competing understandings of marriage, family, work, intimacy, and private and public spheres (2002, 96). These complex moral and legal disputes have fractured families, communities, and societies internally and created tensions internationally.

Affirming complexities within the sex industry, Weitzer (2009, 2010) identifies two dominant paradigms that represent diametrically opposed interpretations involving the condemnation versus normalization of sex work (2010, 5). He insists, however, that these dominant paradigms are essentialist and one-sided, favoring instead what he calls the *polymorphous* paradigm that "holds there is a constellation of occupational arrangements, power relations, and worker experiences. . . . [P]olymorphism is sensitive to complexities and to the uneven distribution of agency, subordination, and workers' control" (2010, 6).

Complexity notwithstanding, a common critique of linking pornography and sex work with gender violence is the claim that such analyses are "sex-negative." According to Alcoff (2018, 87), so-called "sex-positive" approaches that value sex for its contributions to human well-being by decoupling it from reproduction or other justifications often blur the extent to which sex is often *not* a positive, enriching experience. She observes, "Creating the effective possibility of a sex-positive attitude will not come about by diminishing the attention we give to sexual violations, or by protecting the sphere of pleasure from political analysis and moral evaluation" (ibid.).

In this section, we present documented patterns that illuminate deleterious consequences of pornography, prostitution, and other sex work for some persons. We articulate the competing political frames of discourse about these issues, focusing on how gendered violence occurs and is experienced. We problematize the commodification of bodies, situating it within the domain of neoliberal economic exchange that, as we have seen throughout this volume, is exploitative, producing and reproducing inequality regimes (Acker 2006). Agency and victimization are not mutually exclusive, and the literature increasingly demonstrates that the escalation of neoliberalism and the expansion of contemporary sex industries are causes for public concern.

Pornography and Violence

Prior to the emergence of the "sexual revolution" of the 1960s, pornography was neither as mainstream nor as available as it is today and advocacy against it was primarily the preserve of a small contingent of religious conservatives. Second-wave feminism emerged simultaneously with the sexual revolution and some scholars suggest that the most revolutionary change was in the sexual attitudes and practices of women, not men (Ehrenreich, Hess, and Jacobs 1986). Some activists in the feminist movement embraced the use of pornography as a tool for the sexual liberation of women.

In the late 1970s, the dual threats of changing sexual mores and feminist politics were central themes in the crystallization of the New Religious Right in the US, which made pornography a central issue. Ironically, it is during the same period that pornography became the subject of radical feminist critique that argued the sexual-liberation movement, and particularly pornography, actually produced more mechanisms to oppress women than to liberate them (Kappeler 1986). Antipornography feminism encompassed wide-ranging concerns, however, including rape, incest, domestic violence, sexual harassment, child abuse, and forced prostitution. "In fact, antipornography feminists' objections to pornography were inextricably bound up with their belief that pornography (along with other sexist media) played a central role in sanctioning and perpetuating these other forms of gender-based violence and subordination" (Bracewell 2016, 25). Much of the liberal feminist mainstream, however, supported use of pornography in the "private sphere" as a matter of choice and to avoid the slippery slope of censorship.

The debate intensified throughout the 1980s and 1990s, featuring the passage of ordinances in Canada and several US cities that claimed violent pornography violated the civil rights of women. The trade-offs of focusing control only on pornography that met criteria defined as *violent* constituted a new "liberal antipornography feminism" that undermined the original wider-focused critique and contributed to the carceral turn in feminism (Bracewell 2016). Efforts in the 1990s to manage access to pornography under the rubric of hate speech/hate crimes also exemplify this turn.

The proliferation of pornographic materials and access to them on the internet is one of the major concerns among current critics, including a resurgent antipornography feminist movement in the United Kingdom (Long 2012). Still the debate in both scholarly and legal communities revolves around marshalling data to uncover empirical relationships of pornography to violence. There is still no definitive research that finds pornography to be a *direct cause* of gender violence, but increasingly sophisticated contemporary studies are reflective of the complex outcomes of the massive marketing of sexual images—many infused with violence.

Pornography and Harm

The production and use of pornography is a global phenomenon, a multibillion dollar business that among other venues comprises 12 percent of the "visible" internet (DeKeseredy and Corsianos 2016, 1) and a significant portion of the anonymous "dark web," where an estimated 80 percent of sites are linked to pedophilia, including child pornography and child abuse (Greenberg 2014). DeKeseredy and Corsianos report that more than 40 percent of internet users consume pornography, accounting for 20 percent of search engine requests every day; pornographic sites get more traffic than Google or Yahoo (2016, 1–2). Studies from a variety of countries, including Canada, Australia, Cambodia, Italy, Taiwan, and Scandinavian countries, suggest that a significant number of children, especially boys, are exposed to pornography (Flood 2009). Romito and Beltramini (2011) cite research from Northern Europe that shows almost all boys and between 60 and 80 percent of girls have watched pornography, especially that which is accessible online.

Both experimental and nonexperimental research in psychology converge in finding associations between pornography use and men's attitudes regarding violence against women (Hald, Malamuth, and Yuen 2010). Among men who manifest other risk factors for sexual aggression, pornography use intensifies the effect (APA 2007; Romito and Beltramini 2011); these data include consumption of nonviolent pornography (Hald, Malamuth, and Yuen 2010). Recent research on college men found that more than 75 percent consume pornography, with a significant minority (more than 45 percent) doing so weekly (Foubert et al. 2011). Fraternity members at a public university who consume both mainstream and violent pornography articulated stronger intent to rape and acceptance of rape myths, and less willingness to intervene as a bystander if they encountered a gender violence scenario; and the more violent the material consumed, the higher the likelihood of violent responses (ibid).

Women and children who have been sexually abused or are victims of intimate partner violence often report that their perpetrators used violent pornography to normalize humiliating and violent practices or that pornography use was otherwise involved in their victimization (Romito and Beltramini 2011, 1314). Similar findings emerged from recent qualitative research from the staunchly conservative US "heartland" (DeKeseredy and Hall-Sanchez 2017). Women in Long's (2012) study of twenty-first-century antipornography feminists in the UK were clear about how pornographic images affect their sense of self and provoke distress; they also recognize the potential harm to their younger siblings and children.

Data on the effects of pornography on children is particularly concerning. A significant number of children and young people use pornography to learn about sex (Romito and Beltramini 2011), a primer that is likely to shape perceptions of traditional gender roles, the objectification of women, and the normalization of violence. Research has shown that unwanted exposure to pornography is particularly shocking and distressing for children (Flood 2009). Children between the ages of eleven and seventeen who participated in an Australian study described feeling "sick," "shocked," "embarrassed," "repulsed" and "upset" by viewing offensive content on the internet (Aisbett 2001, 41, cited in Flood 2009).

Flood speculates that "young people's use of pornography may have further negative impacts on their sexual and intimate relationships, given that research among adults highlights such impacts as decreased sexual intimacy, perceived (and actual) infidelity and sexual 'addiction'" (2011, 393). Indeed, Harry Brod (2007) argues that pornography has a detrimental effect on male sexuality. He asserts that although patriarchy clearly operates to the advantage of men over women, one of its contradictions as an oppressive system is that it also disadvantages the group it privileges. Thus, the consumption of pornography can alienate men from their own sexuality by promoting both a consumer orientation toward sex and ideologies that promote, by example, violence against women.

Prostitution and Sex Trafficking as Gendered Violence

Prostitution, the sale of sex acts for money, is frequently touted as an ancient institution, and its persistence is used to justify its existence. Yet, the seemingly insatiable demand for commercial sex fueled by globalization and facilitated by the ease of consumption through the internet and corporate tourism packages has motivated strong critiques among scholars and activists. That a substantial amount of sex work may occur through trafficking in persons, contracted without the free consent of the women (and sometimes men) involved contributes to the problematic nature of the industry and the conflicted responses to it.

Unlike prostitution in the more historical understanding of the word, trafficking is considered a major social problem, particularly during the last several decades (Stewart 2014). Interest groups (some on the political right and some closely associated with radical feminism) have struggled to define it as such in order to prioritize political agendas, some of which may be more ideological than empirically grounded. Stewart warns that "this 'new' social problem has deep and conflicting roots in ideologies about impoverished countries, in the ethic of human rights and protection, in governmental interest in border control, in constructions of slavery, and in constructions of gender, particularly those about women's bodies" (2014, 19). As with other areas that we have explored, then, we must exercise caution in drawing conclusions about sex work, particularly that which is presented under the umbrella of trafficking. So much of the contemporary dialogue about it is filtered through agencies and agents that use imprecise and frequently confusing language and who may erroneously collapse trafficking and prostitution into the same category (Stewart 2014, 311). Scrutiny of methods and discourses in this area is critically important and intersectionality is an important analytic lens.

Prostitution and Harm

It is clear that demand for sexual services, although substantial, is not the only driver of the sex industry. Women in sex work are anchored to their local communities or are mobile in the global service economy—either by choice or by coercion and conscription. Denise Brennan's observation about sex workers in the Dominican Republic's tourism industry captures the complexity of the situation for many: they "are at once independent and dependent, resourceful and exploited. They are local agents caught in a web of global economic relations" (2002, 156). Women may migrate to sex work in the face of extreme poverty and growing economic disparities in their countries of origin (Corrin 2005; Kligman and Limoncelli 2005; Stewart 2014; Hudgins, this volume). Given women's responsibility for the well-being of their families, the migration market is "a highly gendered affair" (Outshoorn 2005, 143). These structural conditions, in and of themselves, constitute harm.

Women continue to constitute the majority of prostitutes and sex workers. Whatever the conditions of their work, street prostitutes or brothel workers, legal or illegal, they are frequently the victims of a wide range of violent abuse. Farley's (2004) research suggests clients sexually assault at least half, more likely three-quarters, of prostitutes and that prostitutes are more likely than other women to be assaulted with weapons. Race, ethnicity, and class are factors that make sex workers even more vulnerable, although legalization advocates do not often address this problem. Length of time in prostitution and extreme poverty are predictors of even greater violence (Farley 2004, 1095).

Sanders (2004) finds that female street prostitutes face both public and private risks. The public risks include harassment and violence from clients and other predatory men, police, and the general public. She also found that women were subject to harassment and violence from street protesters against prostitution in their neighborhoods. Punitive policing and zoning ordinances makes the conditions of their work all the more hazardous (Sanders 2004). Reviews of violence against prostitutes in areas where prostitution has been decriminalized or legalized suggests the risk of harm remains. This is true despite the fact that protecting sex workers and their clients from violence and disease is the primary rhetorical logic for legalization (Farley 2004; see also Raymond, this volume).

Male sex workers, although a minority, also experience violence and violation—especially those who are younger and more vulnerable. Similar to women, the type of sex work in which they engage is related to risks (e.g., street prostitution versus "inside" work with higher status clients). Male prostitutes, like their female counterparts, encounter rape and sexual assault, although the most common form of abuse for men appears to be homophobic and heterosexist verbal abuse (Scott et al. 2005); conversely, they also experience more power over their work and job satisfaction than female prostitutes do (Weitzer 2009), a situation that may be enhanced by their gender.

Weitzer (2009) and others insist that some forms of prostitution are safe and rewarding; perhaps this is so. Farley's conclusion in reviewing the substantial literature on prostitution, however, is that it is "multi-traumatic with extremely high rates of physical and sexual violence perpetrated against people who are vulnerable usually as a result of gender, poverty, previous history of sexual assault, marginalization because of race or ethnicity, or a combination of these factors" (2005, 951). Weitzer's own review of the literature on sex work found that transgender sex workers are situated at the bottom of the status hierarchy of sex workers, have higher HIV infection rates, have undesirable work locations wherein they make the least money, and are "more likely than males to be assaulted or raped while at work" (2009, 223).

Research on the lived experiences of many women involved in prostitution affirms the difficulty of simplistic analysis. As Peterson-Iyer observes, "Perhaps the most accurate judgment that can be made is the one reached by Jackie Mac-Millan: 'Women neither choose prostitution 'freely,' nor do they become prostitutes because they have absolutely no other choice. Women choose prostitution as a means of survival among their very limited options'" (1998, 37).

Sex Tourism and Trafficking

Perhaps the most attention, in both the political realm and the mass media over the past decade, has been focused on sex tourism and trafficking. It is estimated that the value of the market for trafficking of women and girls for sexual exploitation is more than $99 billion per year and that more than twenty million persons, including two million children, are bought and sold each year. More than 95 percent of victims are women and girls (Equality Now n.d.). According to the United Nations,

> [T]he concept of trafficking refers to recruitment, transportation, transfer, harboring or receipt of persons, by means of the threat or use of force or other forms

of coercion, of abduction, of fraud, of deception, of the abuse of power or of a position of vulnerability or of the giving or receiving of payments or benefits to achieve the consent of a person having control over another person, for the purpose of exploitation. Exploitation shall include, at a minimum, the exploitation of the prostitution of others or other forms of sexual exploitation, forced labour or services, slavery or practices similar to slavery, servitude or the removal of organs. (United Nations 2000)

Although many people consider trafficking in women to be a "subset of the broader category of prostitution" (Kligman and Limoncelli 2005, 120), it clearly involves other forms of forced labor and includes the abuse of men and boys. And like other gender violence phenomena, sex trafficking is deeply embedded in systems rooted in global inequalities between wealthy and impoverished countries (Stewart 2014, 312). For example, poverty, displacement by war and/or agricultural policies are among the factors that may drive some women into sex work in South and East Asia (ibid.).

Sex work, and indeed sex tourism, in many parts of the world was fueled and organized during the first wave of globalization in the late nineteenth and twentieth centuries (Kligman and Limoncelli 2005, 118), with a large demand-push from militarization (Stewart 2014). It has increased for the same structural reasons in the first years of the twenty-first century (Corrin 2005; Tambiah 2005). Initially, women were recruited and/or trafficked to service military men of their own ethnic and or national heritage; but proscriptions against interethnic sex have declined in recent years (Kligman and Limoncelli 2005). In fact, companies and governments marketing the lure of sex with "exotic" women court both military and nonmilitary men, especially from the West. The socialization of military personnel for violence also raises the risk of abuse and death for sex workers in militarized environments (Tambiah 2005).

Increasingly, the neoliberal sex industry markets sex tourism not just to men but to women, most notably wealthy White women from the West. Although there have been attempts to align women's decisions to engage in sex tourism with desire for romance rather than for exploitative sex, research has found more similarities than differences in men and women's motivations and consumption patterns (Phillips, 2008).

Since the collapse of the Soviet Union, the poorest Eastern European countries have become supplier states of sex workers for the wealthier European countries. Prior to 1989, these countries had comparatively little income inequality and high rates of government spending on the social well-being of citizens. Since these countries have reorganized as market economies, the economic disparities within already gendered systems have become comparable to those in wealthier countries and a devastating reality for women. The gap between the wealthy and poor there, as in the US, has only increased in times of economic growth (Corrin

2005; Kligman and Limoncelli 2005). Since data show that 50 percent of the world's extreme poor are women (Sanchez and Munoz-Boudet 2018), it is no surprise that so many migrate or find themselves deceptively trafficked into the violent world of street tricks and brothels with promises of marriage or legitimate work.

Trafficking does not always involve transport across borders or cross-cultural indentures. In Iraq, the ancient shari'a law providing for "temporary marriages" has recently been deployed by clerics to trap, groom, and prostitute young girls and teens for lucrative profits, sometimes for as little as a half hour, using legitimate "marriage offices" as a front (Al-Maghafi 2019). Loss of virginity is, of course, a family disgrace and a frequent trigger for honor killings. With the rise of Sharia law in postconflict Iraq, girls' and women's rights have suffered tremendously. According to Al-Maghafi, "the strength of the Shia religious establishment, backed by the intimidatory weight of armed Shia militias, appears to have given Shia clerics a sense of total impunity" (ibid., n.p.).

Throughout the research on trafficking, effects of the confluence of race, class, gender, and sexuality in the lives and experiences of vulnerable women, men, and children loom large. As White Stewart suggests, "women throughout the world are unequal to men, [but] when one intersects male privilege with white privilege, those women who are brown or Black are even more vulnerable than those who are White. Those 'like us' are less likely to be commodified than those who can be sexually and racially 'othered.'" (2014, 313). A recent meta-analysis of forty-one studies from around the world (including Asia, North America, Central and Western Europe, Central and South Africa, the Middle East, Latin America, and Russia) implicates gender inequality, policing practices, structural policy changes, social stigmatization of sex work, and drug use in "the high burden of violence against sex workers globally" (Deering et al. 2014, e42). These researchers observed that large gaps in epidemiological data demonstrate the need for research and structural interventions to respond to this growing public health crisis.

Perspectives on Commodification

By and large, the persistence of the legal definition of pornography as a form of speech, and the guarantee of free speech provided under the First Amendment to the US Constitution, has set the stage for a legal stalemate between abolitionists and their opponents in the pornography debate. It seems that few in the US, other than the most radical conservatives, are prepared to challenge the slippery slope of free-speech guarantees. That includes those who express a personal distaste for pornography. Concerning prostitution, the demands for legalization of sex work generally express the good intentions of providing legal protection and workers' rights to those involved in commercial sex trades.

The deep wedge that the pornography debate has driven into the feminist community may be a manifestation of distinctly different stances toward justice articulated in antipornography and libertarian perspectives (Levy 1993). We might also extend this analysis to the debate over whether prostitution is just another form of work that deserves legal protection or is a particularly exploitative situation, exacerbated by its links to overt physical and emotional violence. Using Gilligan's (1982) typology of adversarial and situational moralities, Levy suggests that the inability of feminists to reach consensus has less to do with attitudes toward censorship than with perceptions of justice. The liberal stance is consistent with the typically male moral-ethical system of determining justice through balancing the proposed regulation against the rights of individuals. In the case of pornography, the liberal opponents of pornography legislation see the issue as a "choice between absolute free speech and censorship" (Levy 1993, 17).

For abolitionist feminists, these issues are not either/or propositions but are embedded in complex situations in which the potential for harm should outweigh the preservation of a decidedly sexist legal system in which purportedly neutral justice is often skewed toward protecting the privilege of men. The theoretical logic of the abolitionist stance is thus more consistent with the typically female "ethic of care" that Gilligan delineates in her work: "While an ethic of justice proceeds from the premise of equality—that everyone should be treated the same, an ethic of care rests on the premise of nonviolence—that no one should be hurt" (1982, 174).

In any case, most feminists do agree that despite the many legal gains of the past sixty years, the status of women in political and economic systems across the world is precarious at best. As we have shown throughout this volume, women are still the majority of the world's poor, underrepresented demographically and substantively in legislative bodies and courts, and deprived of the rights to good health, literacy, and self-determination in many corners of the world. Eradicating the conditions within which the commodification of bodies occurs requires a transnational sea change in the political will of men and women and a recognition of the lucrative profits that sex work generates for entrepreneurs and corporate elites alike.

Stewart reminds us that the moral panic about trafficking, frequently defined as a critical global social problem, masks these deeper structural issues as it seems to have eclipsed concerns about violence against women more generally, "and more specifically child abuse, family violence, elder abuse, and marital rape" (2014, 320). If we situate the debates around pornography, prostitution, and trafficking within the global context that features the absence of substantive justice, connections to violence and violation become clear and the need to address gender violence in all of its forms takes on a new sense of urgency.

The chapters in this section reflect various characterizations and responses to pornography, prostitution, and trafficking—as well as the continuing debates that surround them. The authors explore the complexity of these issues in relation to race, gender, economic issues, and political ideologies in both historical and contemporary contexts.

SUGGESTIONS FOR FURTHER READING

Noel B. Busch-Armendariz, Maura B. Nsonwu, and Laurie C. Heffron, *Human Trafficking: Applying Research, Theory, and Case Studies*, 2017

Walter S. DeKeseredy and Marilyn Corsianos, *Violence Against Women in Pornography*, 2015

Julia Long, *Anti-Porn: The Resurgence of Anti-Pornography Feminism*, 2012

Ronald Weitzer, ed., *Sex for Sale: Prostitution, Pornography, and the Sex Industry*, 2nd ed., 2010

The Night Shift

technicolordust

They say you see
someone's soul
Through their eyes
I see their souls
In the money they
Slide into my jacket

I see his soul when
He takes me for a ride
As he drives deeper
Into the night
And I fake my pleasure

They also say that
I should be ashamed
For who I am as they
Spit and sneer parading
Ground they supposedly
Stand on so far above
Me
Sometimes I wonder
On the long walks I
Take at night
Hoping these won't be my
last steps what
They would say when
They need to feed
Their kids and
They have no where
Else to
go.

24

Pornography and Black Women's Bodies

PATRICIA HILL COLLINS

For centuries the black woman has served as the primary pornographic "outlet" for white men in Europe and America. We need only think of the black women used as breeders, raped for the pleasure and profit of their owners. We need only think of the license the "master" of the slave women enjoyed. But, most telling of all, we need only study the old slave societies of the South to note the sadistic treatment—at the hands of white "gentlemen"—of "beautiful young quadroons and octoroons" who became increasingly (and were deliberately bred to become) indistinguishable from white women, and were the more highly prized as slave mistresses because of this. (Walker 1981, 42)

Alice Walker's description of the rape of enslaved African women for the "pleasure and profit of their owners" encapsulates several elements of contemporary pornography. First, Black women were used as sex objects for the pleasure of White men. This objectification of African American women parallels the portrayal of women in pornography as sex objects whose sexuality is available for men (McNall 1983). Exploiting Black women as breeders objectified them as less than human because only animals can be bred against their will. In contemporary pornography women are objectified through being portrayed as pieces of meat, as sexual animals awaiting conquest. Second, African American women were raped, a form of sexual violence. Violence is typically an implicit or explicit theme in pornography. Moreover, the rape of Black women linked sexuality and violence, another characteristic feature of pornography (Eisenstein 1983). Third, rape and other forms of sexual violence act to strip victims of their will to resist and make them passive and submissive to the will of the rapist. Female passivity, the fact that women have things done to them, is a theme repeated over and over in contemporary pornography (McNall 1983). Fourth, the profitability of Black women's sexual exploitation for White "gentlemen" parallels pornography's financially lucrative benefits for pornographers (Eisenstein 1983). Finally, the actual breeding of "quadroons and octoroons" not only reinforces the themes of Black women's passivity, objectification, and malleability to male control but reveals pornography's grounding in racism and sexism. The fates of both Black and White women were intertwined in this breeding process. The ideal African American woman as a pornographic object was indistinguishable from White women and thus approximated the images of beauty, asexuality, and chastity forced on White women. But inside was a highly sexual whore, a "slave mistress" ready to cater to her owner's pleasure.[1]

Contemporary pornography consists of a series of icons or representations that focus the viewer's attention on the relationship between the portrayed individual and the general qualities ascribed to that class of individuals. Pornographic images are iconographic in that they represent realities in a manner determined by the historical position of the observers as well as their relationship to their own time and to the history of the conventions which they employ (Gilman 1985). The treatment of Black women's bodies in nineteenth-century Europe and the US may be the foundation upon which contemporary pornography as the representation of women's objectification, domination, and control is based. Icons about the sexuality of Black women's bodies emerged in these contexts. Moreover, as race/gender-specific representations, these icons have implications for the treatment of both African American and White women in contemporary pornography.

I suggest that African American women were not included in pornography as an afterthought, but instead, form a key pillar on which contemporary pornography itself rests. As Alice Walker points out, "the more ancient roots of modern pornography are to be found in the almost always pornographic treatment of Black women who, from the moment they entered slavery . . . were subjected to rape as the 'logical' convergence of sex and violence. Conquest, in short" (1981, 42).

One key feature about the treatment of Black women in the nineteenth century was how their bodies were objects of display. In the antebellum American South White men did not have to look at pornographic pictures of women because they could become voyeurs of Black women on the auction block. A chilling example of this objectification of the Black female body is provided by the exhibition, in early nineteenth-century Europe, of Sarah Bartmann, the so-called Hottentot Venus. Her display formed one of the original icons for Black female sexuality. An African woman, Sarah Bartmann was often exhibited at fashionable parties in Paris, generally wearing little clothing, to provide entertainment. To her audience she represented deviant sexuality. At the time European audiences thought that Africans had deviant sexual practices and searched for physiological differences, such as enlarged penises and malformed female genitalia, as indications of this deviant sexuality. Sarah Bartmann's exhibition stimulated these racist and sexist beliefs. After her death in 1815, she was dissected. Her genitalia and buttocks remain on display in Paris (Gilman 1985). [*Editor's note*: Sarah Bartmann's remains are no longer on display, having been repatriated to South Africa for burial in 2002 (Parkinson 2016).]

Sander Gilman explains the impact that Sarah Bartmann's exhibition had on Victorian audiences:

> It is important to note that Sarah Bartmann was exhibited not to show her genitalia—but rather to present another anomaly which the European audience . . . found riveting. This was the steatopygia, or protruding buttocks, the other physical characteristic of the Hottentot female which captured the eye of early European travelers. . . . The figure of Sarah Bartmann was reduced to her sexual parts. The audience which had paid to see her buttocks and had fantasized about the uniqueness of her genitalia when she was alive could, after death and dissection, examine both. (1985, 213)

In this passage Gilman unwittingly describes how Bartmann was used as a pornographic object similar to how women are represented in contemporary pornography. She was reduced to her sexual parts, and these parts came to represent a dominant icon applied to Black women throughout the nineteenth century. Moreover, the fact that Sarah Bartmann was both African and a woman underscores the importance of gender in maintaining notions of racial purity. In this case Bartmann symbolized Blacks as a "race." Thus the creation of the icon applied to Black women demonstrates that notions of gender, race, and sexuality were linked in overarching structures of political domination and economic exploitation.

The process illustrated by the pornographic treatment of the bodies of enslaved African women and of women like Sarah Bartmann has developed into a full-scale industry encompassing all women objectified differently by racial/ethnic category. Contemporary portrayals of Black women in pornography represent the continuation of the historical treatment of their actual bodies. African American women are usually depicted in a situation of bondage and slavery, typically in a submissive posture, and often with two White men. As Bell observes, "this setting reminds us of all the trappings of slavery: chains, whips, neck braces, wrist clasps" (1987, 59). White women and women of color have different pornographic images applied to them. The image of Black women in pornography is almost consistently one featuring them breaking from chains. The image of Asian women in pornography is almost consistently one of being tortured (Bell 1987, 161).

The pornographic treatment of Black women's bodies challenges the prevailing feminist assumption that since pornography primarily affects White women, racism has been grafted onto pornography. African American women's experiences suggest that Black women were not added into a preexisting pornography but rather that pornography itself must be reconceptualized as an example of the interlocking nature of race, gender, and class oppression. At the heart of both racism and sexism are notions of biological determinism claiming that people of African descent and women possess immutable biological characteristics marking their inferiority to elite White women (Fausto-Sterling 1989; Gould 1981; Halpin 1989). In pornography these racist and sexist beliefs are sexualized. Moreover, for African American women pornography has not been timeless and universal but was tied to Black women's experiences with the European colonization of Africa and with American slavery. Pornography emerged within a specific system of social class relationships.

This linking of views of the body, social constructions of race and gender, and conceptualizations of sexuality that inform Black women's treatment as pornographic objects promises to have significant implications for how we assess contemporary pornography. Moreover, examining how pornography has been central to the race, gender, and class oppression of African American women offers new routes for understanding the dynamics of power as domination.

Investigating racial patterns in pornography offers one route for such an analysis. Black women have often claimed that images of White women's sexuality were intertwined with the controlling image of the sexually denigrated Black woman: "In the United States, the fear and fascination of female sexuality was projected onto black women; the passionless lady arose in symbiosis with the primitively sexual slave" (Hall 1983, 333). Comparable linkages exist in pornography (Gardner 1980). Alice Walker provides a fictional account of a Black man's growing awareness of the different ways that African American and White women are objectified in pornography: "What he has refused to see—because to see it would reveal yet another area in which he is unable to protect or defend Black women—is that where White women are depicted in pornography as 'objects,' Black women are depicted as animals. Where White women are depicted as human bodies if not beings, Black women are depicted as shit" (Walker 1981, 52). Walker's distinction between "objects" and "animals" is crucial in untangling gender, race, and class dynamics in pornography. Within the mind/body, culture/nature, male/female oppositional dichotomies in Western social thought, objects occupy an uncertain interim position. As objects White women become creations of culture—in this case, the mind of White men—using the materials of nature—in this case, uncontrolled female sexuality. In contrast, as animals Black women receive no such redeeming dose of culture and remain open to the type of exploitation visited on nature overall. Race becomes the distinguishing feature in determining the type of objectification women will encounter. Whiteness as symbolic of both civilization and culture is used to separate objects from animals.

The alleged superiority of men to women is not the only hierarchical relationship that has been linked to the putative superiority of the mind to the body. Certain "races" of people have been defined as being more bodylike, more animallike, and less godlike than others (Spelman 1982, 52). Race and gender oppression may both revolve around the same axis of disdain for the body; both portray the sexuality of subordinate groups as animalistic and therefore deviant. Biological notions of race and gender prevalent in the early nineteenth century that fostered the animalistic icon of Black female sexuality were joined by the appearance of a racist biology incorporating the concept of degeneracy

(Foucault 1980). Africans and women were both perceived as embodied entities, and Blacks were seen as degenerate. Fear of and disdain for the body thus formed a key element in both sexist and racist thinking (Spelman 1982).

While the sexual and racial dimensions of being treated like an animal are important, the economic foundation underlying this treatment is critical. Animals can be economically exploited, worked, sold, killed, and consumed. As "mules," African American women become susceptible to such treatment. The political economy of pornography also merits careful attention. Pornography is pivotal in mediating contradictions in changing societies (McNall 1983). It is no accident that racist biology, religious justifications for slavery and women's subordination, and other explanations for nineteenth-century racism and sexism arose during a period of profound political and economic change. Symbolic means of domination become particularly important in mediating contradictions in changing political economies. The exhibition of Sarah Bartmann and Black women on the auction block were not benign intellectual exercises—these practices defended real material and political interests. Current transformations in international capitalism require similar ideological justifications. Where does pornography fit in these current transformations? This question awaits a comprehensive Afrocentric feminist analysis.

Publicly exhibiting Black women may have been central to objectifying Black women as animals and to creating the icon of Black women as animals. Yi-Fu Tuan (1984) offers an innovative argument about similarities in efforts to control nature—especially plant life—the domestication of animals, and the domination of certain groups of humans. Tuan suggests that displaying humans alongside animals implies that such humans are more like monkeys and bears than they are like "normal" people. This same juxtaposition leads spectators to view the captive animals in a special way. Animals require definitions of being like humans, only more openly carnal and sexual, an aspect of animals that forms a major source of attraction for visitors to modern zoos. In discussing the popularity of monkeys in zoos, Tuan notes: "Some visitors are especially attracted by the easy sexual behavior of the monkeys. Voyeurism is forbidden except when applied to subhumans" (1984, 82). Tuan's analysis suggests that the public display of Sarah Bartmann and of the countless enslaved African women on the auction blocks of the antebellum American South—especially in proximity to animals—fostered their image as animalistic.

This linking of Black women and animals is evident in nineteenth-century scientific literature. The equation of women, Blacks, and animals is revealed in the following description of an African woman published in an 1878 anthropology text:

She had a way of pouting her lips exactly like what we have observed in the orangutan. Her movements had something abrupt and fantastical about them, reminding one of those of the ape. Her ear was like that of many apes. . . . These are animal characters. I have never seen a human head more like an ape than that of this woman. (Halpin 1989, 287)

In a climate such as this, it is not surprising that one prominent European physician even stated that Black women's "animallike sexual appetite went so far as to lead black women to copulate with apes" (Gilman 1985, 212).

The treatment of all women in contemporary pornography has strong ties to the portrayal of Black women as animals. In pornography women become nonpeople and are often represented as the sum of their fragmented body parts. Scott McNall observes:

> This fragmentation of women relates to the predominance of rear-entry position photographs. . . . All of these kinds of photographs reduce the woman to her reproductive system, and, furthermore, make her open, willing, and available—not in control. . . . The other thing rear-entry position photographs tell us about women is that they are animals. They are animals because they are the same as dogs—bitches in heat who can't control themselves. (McNall 1983, 197–98)

This linking of animals and White women within pornography becomes feasible when grounded in the earlier denigration of Black women as animals.

Developing a comprehensive analysis of the race, gender, and class dynamics of pornography offers possibilities for change. Those Black feminist intellectuals investigating sexual politics imply that the situation is much more complicated than that advanced by some prominent White feminists (see, e.g., Dworkin 1981) in which "men oppress women" because they are men. Such approaches implicitly assume biologically deterministic views of sex, gender, and sexuality and offer few possibilities for change. In contrast, Afrocentric feminist analyses routinely provide for human agency and its corresponding empowerment and for the responsiveness of social structures to human action. In the short story "Coming Apart," Alice Walker describes one Black man's growing realization that his enjoyment of pornography, whether of White women as "objects" or Black women as "animals," degraded him:

> He begins to feel sick. For he realizes that he has bought some of the advertisements about women, black and white. And further, inevitably, he has bought the advertisements about himself. In pornography the black man is portrayed as being capable of fucking anything . . . even a piece of shit. He is defined solely by the size, readiness and unselectivity of his cock. (Walker 1981, 52)

Walker conceptualizes pornography as a race/gender system that entraps everyone. But by exploring an African American man's struggle for a self-defined standpoint on pornography, Walker suggests that a changed consciousness is essential to social change. If a Black man can understand how pornography affects him, then other groups enmeshed in the same system are equally capable of similar shifts in consciousness and action.

NOTE

1 Offering a similar argument about the relationship between race and masculinity, Paul Hoch (1979) suggests that the ideal White man is a hero who upholds honor. But inside lurks a "Black beast" of violence and sexuality, traits that the White hero deflects onto men of color.

25

Pornographic Values
Hierarchy and Hubris

ROBERT JENSEN

Political debates grow out of differing answers to one of our most fundamental questions: "What does it mean to be human?" This is especially true of the pornography debate. That question reminds us that all political positions are based on underlying moral claims. In this context, "moral" does not mean preachy judgments about conventional rules, especially for sexual behavior but rather how we might balance a yearning for self-realization with the need for stable, respectful communities that make it possible for individuals to fulfill their potential, as free as possible from the constraining effects of systems of domination. What do we owe ourselves and what obligations do we have to others? Answers not only vary among individuals within a culture and between different cultures but also change over time with new challenges, hence "What does it mean to be human at this particular moment in history?"

Despite the cliché "you can't legislate morality," there are moral claims at the core of all political proposals. Every position in the pornography debate is based on a sexual ethic, and the outcome of the political struggle will advance the underlying ethic.

I have been involved in that debate—within feminism and progressive politics as well as the wider culture—for a quarter century. More than ever, I believe the radical feminist critique of pornography provides the best framework for understanding the production and consumption of graphic sexually explicit material. In that quarter century, the trends—in the pornography industry, the material it produces, and the ways images are used (Dines 2010; Jensen 2011)—demonstrate the compelling nature of that analysis, even though in that same period this radical feminist critique has been eclipsed by postmodern and liberal positions (Taormino, Penley, Shimizu, and Miller-Young 2013) that either celebrate or capitulate to an increasingly pornographic culture.

To state it bluntly, over the past twenty-five years, the pornographers and their allies have won, and radical feminism has lost. There is more pornography, more easily available, and much of it more openly cruel and degrading to women and more overtly racist than ever. Pornographers and their allies have advanced their underlying libertarian sexual ethic, which focuses on individual choices in the moment and ignores or downplays the constraints and opportunities that structure choices.

How does a pornographic culture answer the question about "being human," in regard to our relationship to each other and to mediated images?

Pornography's answer about human relationships and the nature of power: The domination/subordination dynamic is inevitable, because it is the way humans are designed. So get used to the same old hierarchy.

Pornography's answer about images and the nature of technology: The more mediated our lives, the better, because it gives us a sense of control over our experience. So get used to a new level of hubris.

My response: Both these answers are wrong, with destructive consequences beyond pornography. This chapter explains the feminist critique of pornography, analyzes the corrosive nature of hierarchical power and technological hubris, and poses questions about a healthy sexual ethic.

Pornography: A Radical Feminist Critique

"Radical" is often used to dismiss people or ideas as "crazy" or "extreme," but here it describes an analysis that seeks to understand, address, and eventually eliminate the root causes of inequality. Radical feminism opposes patriarchy, the system of institutionalized male dominance, and understands gender as a category that established and reinforces inequality. The goal is the end of—not accommodation with—patriarchy's gender system and other domination/subordination dynamics.

Radical feminists understand men's efforts to control women's sexuality and reproduction as a key feature of patriarchy. As feminist philosopher Frye puts it, "For females to be subordinated and subjugated to males on a global scale . . . billions of female individuals, virtually all who see life on this planet, must be reduced to a more-or-less willing toleration of subordination and servitude to men," and "[t]he primary sites of this reduction are the sites of heterosexual relation and encounter" (1992, 130).

Beyond the sex/gender system, radical feminism's focus on the way in which patriarchy normalizes hierarchy leads not just to a critique of men's domination of women but also to a deeper understanding of systems of power more generally. While not sufficient by itself, the end of patriarchy is a necessary condition for liberation more generally.

Radical feminism addresses many issues, including men's violence and the sexual exploitation of women and children. Pornography, prostitution, and stripping are the major sexual-exploitation industries in the contemporary US, presenting objectified female bodies to men for sexual pleasure. Boys and vulnerable men are also used in the exploitation industries that cater to gay men, but the vast majority of people used are girls and women. In heterosexual pornography, the negative psychological and physical consequences for female performers are far more dramatic than for male performers (Whisnant and Stark 2004).

The critical feminist analysis demonstrates that pornography is not "just sex on film" but sex routinely presented within a domination/subordination dynamic. Pornography eroticizes men's domination of women, along with other forms of inequality, especially racism. This analysis, developed within the larger feminist project of challenging men's violence against women, was first articulated clearly by Andrea Dworkin (1979) who identified what we can call the elements of the pornographic:

1. Objectification: when "a human being, through social means, is made less than human, turned into a thing or commodity, bought, and sold"
2. Hierarchy: "a group on top (men) and a group on the bottom (women)"
3. Submission: when acts of obedience and compliance become necessary for survival, members of oppressed groups learn to anticipate the orders and desires of those who have power over them, and their compliance is then used by the dominant group to justify its dominance
4. Violence: "systematic, endemic enough to be unremarkable and normative, usually taken as an implicit right of the one committing the violence" (Dworkin 1988, 266–67)

This framework, developed further by Dworkin along with MacKinnon (1987), sparked organizing efforts for a civil rights approach to replace failed obscenity laws (MacKinnon & Dworkin 1997). Although the law didn't change, this analytic framework continues to be useful in understanding the pornography industry's expansion (Dines 2010). As pornography depicting relatively conventional sexual acts became commonplace, producers of "gonzo" pornography (industry terminology for movies with no pretense of plot, in which performers acknowledge the camera and speak directly to the audience) dominated the market and pushed the limits of social norms and women's bodies with the routine use of double penetrations (vaginal and anal penetration by two men at the same time), double vag (two men penetrating a woman vaginally), double anal (two men penetrating a woman anally), gagging (forcing the penis down a woman's throat so far that she gags), and ass-to-mouth (a man removing his penis from a woman's anus and placing it directly into her mouth or the mouth of another woman).

Although there is variation in the thousands of pornographic films produced commercially each year, the main themes have remained consistent: (1) all women always want sex from men, (2) women like all the sexual acts that men perform or demand, and (3) any woman who resists can be aroused by force, which is rarely necessary because most of the women in pornography are the "nymphomaniacs" of men's fantasies (Jensen 2007, 56–57). While both men and women are portrayed as hypersexual, men typically are the sexual subjects who control the action and dictate the terms of the sex. Women are the sexual objects that fulfill male desire.

The radical feminist critique highlights not only that much of pornography is pornographic, reflecting, and reinforcing patriarchy's domination/subordination dynamic, but that pop culture is increasingly pornified (Paul 2005). Pornography is a specific genre, but those elements of the pornographic also are present in other media.

Pornography's Hierarchy

It is common to distinguish between sex categories based on biological realities of reproduction (male and female) and gender categories based on culture (men and women). While we have limited understanding of how differences in male and female biology might influence intellectual, emotional, and moral differences between the sexes, there is no evidence those differences are relevant to political status: men and women have equal claim to citizenship.

The denial of equality to women is a product of patriarchy, typically rationalized with God or evolution. "Gender fundamentalists," whether conservatives rooted in theology or secular folk offering sociobiology/evolutionary psychology arguments for patriarchal practices (Buss 1994), assert that there are large differences between male and female humans that are largely immutable, despite considerable evidence to the contrary (Zell, Krizan, and Teeter 2015). The equality claim, which is accepted in the formal political sphere, is routinely ignored in other realms of contemporary life—people assert the need for, or inevitability of, inequality, most notably in sexual behavior, intimate relationships, and family life. Gender fundamentalists refuse to consider whether patriarchal ideology is consistent with decent answers to "What does it mean to be human?"

In the version of patriarchy dominant in the US, the sexual-exploitation industries are a routine part of contemporary culture. Some aspects are criminalized and other aspects regulated, but the vast majority of men have some experience with at least one of these industries that buy and sell women's bodies for sex.

Whatever one's view of the role of intimacy and sexuality in human society, it is difficult to imagine achieving gender equality when members of one group (women) can routinely be bought and sold by members of another group (men) for sexual pleasure. Supporters of the sexual-exploitation industries focus on women's right to choose to participate in these activities. While individual choice is a component of any free society, people choose within parameters set by larger cultural and economic forces. To define freedom as choice, abstracted from the reality of a society and its values/norms/practices, is simplistic. To contend that such a thin conception of freedom can produce gender equality is to obscure hierarchy. Under conditions of real equality, it is hard to imagine that such exploitation practices would exist.

Pornography's Hubris

Human beings are storytelling animals, and stories often deal with intimacy and sexual behavior. Humans also are tool-making animals, and we have invented increasingly complex tools for telling stories. What we might call "pornographic fundamentalists" believe it is a good thing for people to tell any sexual stories they find arousing, and "media fundamentalists" believe it is a good thing for people to use every media technology to tell all stories. Fundamentalists refuse to consider whether specific sexual stories told with specific media technologies are consistent with our best answers to "What does it mean to be human?" That pornographic/media fundamentalism does not just critique narrow-minded moralistic judgments but rejects the possibility of any deeper moral evaluation of these cultural practices.

Do the sexual stories of the pornography industry, which so routinely celebrate men's dominance, advance self-realization? Do those stories help build stable, respectful communities? Does the intensity of graphic sexually explicit images delivered through film/video enhance our capacity to achieve these goals? Exploring sexual themes in art can help people struggle with the power and mystery of desire, but what are the long-term effects of reducing sex to pleasure acquisition through a screen? Do those mediated experiences erode our ability to connect to each other sexually in person? Is it possible that sex and intimacy are realms of human experience that do not translate well to explicit representation in mass media?

My experience has led to clear choices for myself, but these are not questions that have single, definitive answers for all. Fearful of the conversation, pornographic/media fundamentalists tend to avoid these questions and try to marginalize anyone who wants to ask them. Better that we check our hubris—the assumption that our ability to do something means we have the wisdom to understand what we are doing and can control its effects—and proceed with caution.

A Sexual Ethic: What Is Sex for?

Radical feminism challenges us to ask an often-overlooked question: What is sex for? Of the ways people might understand sexuality in their lives, which are most consistent with self-realization and stable, respectful communities? At times, especially within certain religious traditions, rigid answers to the question have been imposed on people in ways that were routinely constraining and sometimes inhumane. But because some people have answered a question badly does not mean we should, or can, avoid the question (Jensen 2014).

Sex is central to reproduction but clearly plays a role in human life far beyond reproduction. The varied ways that different societies have made sense of these questions indicates that there likely is no single answer for all times and places. Even within an individual's life, sex can play a different role at different times. As young people, sex may be primarily about exploring ourselves and our limits as we mature, while as adults, the most important function of sex may be to foster intimacy within a primary relationship. In general, we can think of sex as a form of communication, a way we learn not only about others but about ourselves. We can collectively try to understand which conceptions of sex are most healthful without claiming definitive knowledge or the right to impose judgments on others.

An analogy to food is helpful. Just as we recognize that sex is more than the acquisition of pleasure, eating is more than just the acquisition of calories. US food companies tend to encourage what Berry (1990, 147) calls "industrial eating," just as pornography offers a kind of "industrial sex." Eating processed fast food is a different experience than eating food to which one has a more direct connection in production or preparation. Processed fast food creates distance between us and the living world, and the same is true of processed fast sex. In both cases, people's reflexive response often is, "But I like it." Fast food and fast sex both are efficient at producing a certain type of pleasure, but what is lost in normalizing those forms of pleasure?

Conclusion

What does it mean to be human at this particular moment in history? Our answer must be consistent with core progressive principles of dignity (all people have the same claim to being human), solidarity (human flourishing depends on loving connections to others), and equality (dignity and solidarity are impossible without social and economic justice).

A sexual ethic consistent with these widely held moral principles would reject the hierarchy of patriarchy and hierarchy more generally, recognizing that systems of domination and subordination are inherently abusive. When there is no common understanding of what roles sex plays in our lives, people are more likely to get hurt more often, not just psychologically but physically. In patriarchy, those injuries will be endured mostly by women and children. The conversation about a sexual ethic is not a restriction of anyone's freedom but a part of the quest for a more expansive freedom for all.

A sexual ethic consistent with just, sustainable communities would question the technologizing of all human activity. That does not mean that mediated storytelling with sexual themes is inherently negative, only that we need to consider not only the pleasures of sex through technology but the deeper implications. We need not romanticize a mythical golden age to recognize that what we call progress does not always enhance the quality of our lives.

Radical feminist critics of pornography are often accused of being prudes, or the more academically fashionable pejorative "sex negative," but critiquing the negative aspects of patriarchal sex is not prudish. It is not antisex to critique a pornographic culture that accepts overtly misogynistic and racist images designed to produce sexual stimulation, which are easily accessible not only to adults but to children at the beginning stages of their sexual development.

A friend, who does not share the radical feminist position, once suggested I was "overwrought" about the subject. Would it be better to be underwrought? Or to not be wrought at all? My level of "wroughtness" is based on research and critical thinking, along with my experience and the experiences of hundreds of people I have talked to in the course of this work—men who have told me they feel trapped by their habitual use of pornography, which was undermining their ability to be truly intimate with a partner; women whose partners lost interest in intimacy and sex once the men started using pornography habitually; and other women whose partners started demanding degrading and/or painful sexual acts they had seen in pornography. Are those people overwrought in their struggles?

Our pornified and pornographic culture leaves us with challenging questions: Why do so many people need films of other people having sex to feel sexual, and why do so many people want pictures of sex that eroticize domination/ subordination? Why are most of those people men? Are we afraid that we can't transcend patriarchal ideas that are deeply woven into the fabric of contemporary society and that we cannot turn away from the screens that proliferate in our lives? Are we afraid that we have not only become consumers of goods but consumers of the most basic human experiences?

Those questions have nothing to do with a fear of sex but rather identify reasonable fears of who, or what, we have become in a hypermediated patriarchal society. If we were to look to pornography for answers to this most basic question—"What does it mean to be human at this particular moment in history?"—it is difficult to imagine a just, sustainable human future. Our task is to face those fears and imagine the future differently.

26

Making Sense of Sex Work, Prostitution, and Trafficking—in the Classroom and Beyond

CHRYSANTHI S. LEON AND COREY SHDAIMAH

Controversial topics require that we explore how we can help ourselves and others communicate across ideological divides. Our opinions and actions should be informed by the full range of relevant information. While we and many of our readers may encounter difficulties with such divides in a classroom setting, this exploration is of broader significance. Indeed, the 2016 election cycle raised concerns that too many people engage in dialogue in what have been referred to as "echo chambers," where discussion with like-minded others simply reinforces our own previously held opinions.

As this volume and our own work demonstrate, our beliefs have an effect on the decisions we make. Many people are involved in creating or implementing programs, including those in (or entering) the human services or criminal justice professions, advocates, policymakers, and citizens who vote. They allocate resources in ways that affect people's current and future health, safety, well-being, employment, and relationships. Low-income and otherwise marginalized populations who are overly represented in (often-intertwined) systems of surveillance and assistance (Gilliom 2001; Gustafson 2013; Tiger 2013) are particularly vulnerable to these decisions. Sex workers, especially those who are engaged in street-based work, who are people of color, or are transgender, are among these vulnerable populations. It is important that we make sure to acknowledge ideological divides and recognize our own internal biases in order to "get it right" when we create policy to address sex work, trafficking, and prostitution.

Feminist Perspectives: Inclusive, Reflective, and Critical

In this chapter we examine the intersection of feminism with sex work, prostitution, and trafficking. Although feminism is a broad category that includes contested perspectives, a number of shared characteristics unite feminist stances "[t]hese characteristics include addressing issues of power, emotion, notions of objectivity/subjectivity, researcher reflexivity, and power and authority in re/presentation" (Harrison, MacGibbon and Morton 2001, 326). In addressing these issues, feminism uses the category of gender as a way to understand social structure, norms, and interactions.

The lens of gender directs us to examine policies that disproportionately affect women and gender minorities (Hawkesworth 2006). As feminist scholars, teachers, and activists we prioritize those who are primarily affected by policies in order to critically analyze such policies from their perspective (Harding 2004, 7).[1] To this end, we also engage in a series of practices that promote reflection on how our biases and assumptions influence our actions. These practices include engagement with potential biases to avoid relying only on viewpoints that confirm our preexisting beliefs, as we discuss below. Such rigorous critical approaches may also mitigate reductionist and incomplete scholarship. These practices may also address the concerns of criminal justice scholars and community groups who seek to create more effective policies that are grounded in real-world experiences (Leon 2011; Shdaimah 2010; Wolf 2001).

Sex work, trafficking, and prostitution are subjects that involve contested ideas about gender and sexuality and, therefore, have been the subject of feminist analysis. In contrast to the ideal notions of feminist inquiry and dialogue that we have just explained, sex work, trafficking, and prostitution debates are far too often characterized by approaches that deny a range of voices and question the agency of those arguably most affected by policy and programs. Many feminist perspectives are polarized, such as the early "abolitionist" and "pro-sex" camps. Abolitionist feminism focuses on what it considers to be inherent harms of sexual exploitation, including pornography, as well as all forms of sex work (MacKinnon 2004). Pro-sex feminism emphasizes the pleasures of sexuality free from coercion and its economic potential when it is treated as legitimate work or a business enterprise (Vance 1984). While many feminist researchers challenge polarized perspectives that run counter to the feminist principles we outline here, they persist in current policy and advocacy debates around prostitution, trafficking, and sex work.

Language both reflects and shapes our beliefs, thus demanding careful attention to the way we talk about people and how people talk about themselves. Sex work is a broad term that includes a wide variety of sexual or sexualized acts that can include (legal or illegal) phone sex, pole dancing, and prostitution. The term was coined by Carol Leigh in order to encompass this broad range of activities and to emphasize its labor aspects, both to destigmatize it and as part of a strategy to advocate for labor protections (Leigh 1997). Not all people who might fall under this definition embrace the term. For example, some in our studies do not identify with the labor aspects of their work, nor do they see "sex worker" as an identity in the way that the term might imply; rather it is just something they do. Others, such as abolitionist feminists, reject the term because they believe the exchange of sexual services for money or goods is inherently exploitative. They may also believe that the existence of such exchanges is harmful in itself, regardless of whether they harm individual women and children.

Prostitution is a subcategory of sex work that involves the exchange of sex for money or goods. It is often used in popular discourse to refer to types of sex work that are legally regulated or criminalized. Sex trafficking is a relatively new term. The US Victims of Trafficking and Violence Protection Act (P.L. 106–386—OCT. 28, 2000) considers all sexual acts with minors for money or goods to be trafficking, regardless of whether the minor consented and/or whether a third party was involved. Trafficking is defined for adults as involving any form of coercion including physical harm or threats to an individual or their family. Some consider all exchanges of sex for money as trafficking, rejecting the idea that the exchange of sex for money or goods can ever be free of coercion. In the next section, we examine why contested definitions of sex work, trafficking, and prostitution persist.

Why Is It Difficult to Keep an Open Mind about Sex Work, Prostitution, and Trafficking?

We often come to our chosen vocation as advocates, organizers, teachers, students, or healers with a sense of purpose. When this sense of purpose is a driving force in our career choice, it can be accompanied by passionate and deeply held convictions. These convictions are sometimes a result of personal and professional experience; at other times we may be deeply affected by what we read in the news, or by learning of the plight of others. They may also come from personal, professional, or religious ethics and values.[2] Passion is a powerful motivator, and is valuable in spurring us to learn and take action. It may also provide a useful framework with which to critically interrogate concepts, arguments, and policies. On the other hand, our passions and convictions may create biases (McDermott and Varenne 1995), becoming an obstacle to meaningful discourse and reflection. Even critical analytic lenses, when applied only to certain groups or in certain ways, may become circular feedback loops that reinforce what we think we know and block discrepant input. In our experience as researchers and activists, these concerns are present in the area of sex work and human trafficking, which evoke strong emotions and convictions. Sex work therefore is a useful example to explore both the difficulty and the necessity of communication across ideological divides.

The act of selecting and privileging particular information that is compatible with our own views is referred to in the psychological literature as "confirmation bias," which "connotes the seeking or interpreting of evidence in ways that are partial to existing beliefs, expectations, or a hypothesis in hand . . . the inappropriate bolstering of hypotheses or beliefs whose truth is in question" (Nickerson 1998, 175). Confirmation (or confirmatory) bias is an unintentional and common aspect of the cognitive processes that help people make sense of the world (Haselton, Nettle, and Murray 2015). Psychological research shows that firmly held beliefs are hard to change (Adame 2016). It is therefore not a value judgment to recognize that human beings may ignore evidence contrary to their beliefs. Instead it is a warning that reminds us that the process of being open to new information, particularly when it challenges our world view, requires effort and practice.

Hurdles to Understanding

We each have more than ten years of experience as teachers and scholars in our disciplines. In addition to our roles as teachers, we have many other professional experiences outside of academia. For both of us, teaching and research inform each other: what we investigate outside the classroom informs what we communicate to our students, and what our students talk about informs how we focus our research and explain our findings. Our commitments as feminist scholars often center on challenging preexisting notions, equipping our students to be more reasoned, careful, and effective advocates and future professionals. Specific to sex work, we have encountered common but inaccurate assumptions in our teaching, research, and community involvement.

A growing body of empirical research, including our own, challenges these assumptions and shades them with more nuance than typically expressed. In other work we have described this as a "misfit" between our data and conventional wisdom (Shdaimah and Leon 2018). In this section we will describe three of the most salient hurdles to broader understanding, followed by our examination of the ideological divide that can undermine good conversations.

Help and Rescue versus Harm and Unintended Consequences

Concern for people affected by poverty, coercion, and abuse is often translated into a belief that people, particularly sex workers, need our help. Despite scholarly criticism that document the unintended harms caused by this prevalent "rescue" narrative when it is used to create policies (Kinney 2014; Hill 2014), this narrative persists in the public imagination. Students come to our classes with messages from popular culture that motivate them to become involved and, in some cases, ignite a passion that turns into a career path (Leon, Shdaimah, and Baboolal 2017). As teachers, we often share our students' passion and commitment to social justice. Such passions and concerns are not exclusive to the classroom but also arise in our discussions with policy-makers, as described in the case study below. These passions, while important motivating forces, often shape our convictions into deeply ingrained personal biases.

The tendency to view problems through our own perspective is evident in the way individual interventions through criminal justice, rather than social welfare, make sense to professionals who are grounded in justice systems and state-sponsored social services. Even when professionals recognize that societal factors (such as poverty, the dearth of affordable housing and living wage jobs and global inequality) shape when and how people engage in sex work, helping people through new criminal laws or the use of police and courts may seem like a useful response (Leon and Shdaimah 2012; O'Brien 2013). However, such responses often leave marginalized groups subject to more abuse (see also Hill 2014). For example, writing about the implementation of antitrafficking policies in Thailand and the US, Edith Kinney (2017) documents the way police raids to ostensibly rescue sex workers actually undermine the safety and stability of poor people (see Hudgins, this volume). Such oversights and unintended harm are usually not the result of bad intent but bureaucratic requirements and misunderstanding of economic and structural impediments.

Professionals may find themselves pulled in conflicting directions or between competing conceptions of how to address clients, an experience described as "justice dissonance" (Whittle 2017). Professionals and well-intentioned advocates may also fail to recognize how criminalization often harms the most vulnerable. This may be because they are so overburdened as frontline workers that they may not have time to reflect on the larger structures and downstream consequences (Lipsky 1980; Emerson 1983). They also may see themselves as prohibited from or incapable of addressing anything other than individual behaviors, especially when they sense a pressing need for change (Whittle 2017).

The impulse to rescue and its conflict with person-centered responses was at the forefront of one of Leon's most painful moments as a scholar advocate. As we discuss, both of us have learned lessons worth sharing from community collaborations, including the incident below that Leon often shares with students who want their work to have an effect beyond the academy.

"Rape Doesn't Mean the Same Thing to Them"

As a scholar not long out of graduate school, Leon was invited to collect data for a new effort to address prostitution.[3] This effort was spearheaded by a local judicial officer and a community services organization in partnership with stakeholders from each step in the criminal justice process and from social service agencies. Tasked with laying the groundwork for a new intervention, Leon conducted a study that included interviews, observations, and focus groups with a broad cross-section of people either involved with sex work or with professional or personal experience with prostitution in the community.

Before beginning the research, Leon and her team of students completed training in the protection of human subjects in research and received approval for the research from the university's Institutional Review Board (IRB). During a focus group with street-based sex workers in which they were asked to share what kinds of services or programs would be welcome, several participants disclosed that they had been raped by people in positions of authority (in fact the same two men had raped two of them). Following the ethical guidelines of sociology and the requirements of the IRB, Leon provided them with contact information for counseling and discussed a range of possible actions they could take, with or without her help. She also checked in with the group again a week later. All research participants were adamant on both occasions that they did not want to report the crimes because of their fears that they would be beaten in reprisal.

This was an emotionally difficult revelation but not uncommon for professors who teach and research in areas related to trauma and abuse. While wishing to "help" as actively as she could, the ethical situation was clear: unless specific harm was imminent or harm to someone under eighteen had occurred, the clearly stated preferences of the people involved had to take precedence, *and they did not want to report*. One of the reform group stakeholders who attended the focus group explained away the disclosure by stating, "rape doesn't mean the same thing to them." This was also awful to hear, but Leon understood it in the context of the service provider trying to justify the decision not to pursue legal action. Regardless of the source of this dismissal or its intention, it magnified how professionals become inured to the shared humanity of their clients and may take paternalistic views that reinforce stigma and justify harm.

Leon shared the general description of this incident with the stakeholder group as part of a periodic progress report. The group was horrified to hear about the sexual assaults; one stakeholder was also horrified that Leon had not called the police. Leon carefully explained the ethical obligation to allow study participants to determine how they wanted to handle something so painful, rather than stepping in to handle it as we saw fit. The judicial officer was unswayed, and instead told Leon that she must not care about the rape victims. She threatened to have the prosecutor subpoena Leon's records in order to force participation in a criminal investigation. However, Leon had taken the precaution to de-identify the data and had the support of her university for refusal to cooperate. Although she was indeed contacted by a prosecutor, no further action was taken.

While we will return to this experience below for what it teaches us about communication, it is instructive here because it illustrates that good people can disagree about the right actions to help others, and that such disagreement is shaped by professional experiences, personal biases and expectations. For feminist scholars, one of the takeaways is that even when we are spurred to action, we must never lose sight of the fact that people can be further harmed by our interventions. This emphasizes the importance of including the perspectives of affected populations. Had the vulnerable people who shared their experiences been exposed to law enforcement, it is possible that they would have faced the physical reprisals they feared, as well as the disempowering experience of being forced to discuss their victimization and participate in a criminal process against their will.[4]

Victimization and Limited Choice versus Agency as Capability

A good guideline for situations when people disagree about the right course of action is to ask what the affected people themselves want.[5] This approach recognizes the agency of each human being. Unfortunately, we have noticed that sex workers—like other marginalized groups—are commonly assumed to be an exception, unable to make good choices or articulate their needs (Baylson 2017; Steele 2017). The belief that sex workers are passive victims underlies the misguided rescue impulse described above. Insights based on empirical studies reveal a continuum of vulnerability and harm among those who are involved in exchanging sex for money or goods. Studies commonly find that reduced power makes sex workers vulnerable to harm and exploitation: when laws target individual sex workers through criminalization, they lose autonomy and leverage, increasing health and safety risks (Brewis and Linstead 2000; International Union of Sex Workers 2010; Lutnick and Cohan 2009; Sanders 2005; Scoular 2010). Sources of coercion that increase vulnerability can be intended or unintended; they can come from pimps, traffickers, clients, communities, law enforcement and service providers (e.g., Baylson 2017; Steele 2017).

Ample empirical research demonstrates that the most vulnerable sex workers are capable of rational and ethical decision making, even within a limited universe of options. Interviews with people engaged in street-based sex work reveal that some explicitly choose sex work because it offers freedom that contrasts with the state-based control they experience in other areas of their lives (Boitin 2013). Among those who may not have freely chosen entry into sex work, people retain the capacity to make decisions for themselves and to act in their best interests (Shdaimah and Leon 2015; Showden 2011; Wiechelt and Shdaimah 2015). More complex portrayals of sex workers emphasize their resilience and strength, even in the face of inequalities and victimizations that circumscribe their choices (Showden and Majic 2014).

Research that asks sex workers about their experiences from a perspective that allows for their agency describes how sex workers use protective strategies against violence (Oselin and Cobbina 2017; Hail-Jares 2016). Our own research emphasizes the component of agency that involves moral calculations, often missing from prevailing views of sex workers. Along with considerations of the costs and benefits of engaging in street-based sex work, women we talked to explained that decisions to prostitute were made in reference to other possible forms of survival, including theft and other actions that would harm others. Others appreciated the flexibility of sex work that allowed them to maintain their responsibilities as caregivers, which they viewed as part of their moral and familial obligations (Shdaimah and Leon 2016).

Many of those who choose sex work, particularly women and transgender people, do so due to their social and economic vulnerability in a capitalist, patriarchal society with a limited range of safe and sufficient opportunities to meet their own and their families' needs (O'Connell Davidson 1998). The recognition of limited options as a form of coercion has paved the way for rehabilitative approaches to sex work, even where it may also be criminalized (Baylson 2017). However, most rehabilitative approaches retain a paternalistic orientation and use punitive measures, such as in the case of prostitution courts that use a "carrot and stick" approach to coerce compliance with the goal of rescuing sex workers to reduce crime (Shdaimah 2020).

The oversimplification of victimization that confuses limited choice with the inability to make rational and ethical decisions often leads to further victimization by reinforcing a loss of control and agency (Lamb 1996; Showden 2011). The prevalence of trauma among sex workers, particularly the most vulnerable lower-echelon workers (Sallman 2010), should make this phenomenon even more concerning to those who wish to help through services and rehabilitation. One of the hallmarks of trauma is loss of control: even well-intended interventions may cause further loss of control and retraumatize trauma victims and thus be at cross-purposes with stated educational, policy, and programmatic goals (Center for Substance Abuse Treatment, Substance Abuse and Mental Health Services Administration 2014).

Agency and self-advocacy are possible even within the constraints of top-down regimes inspired by the false narrative of rescue and passive victimization. For example, Hua Boonyapisompparn has described her experience working with a US-funded HIV/AIDS prevention program called Sisters that provides services to transgender women living in Pattaya Thailand (Boonyapisomparn 2017). Though the program had to function within the overarching concerns of a foreign government, the community was able to use the Sisters drop-in center to create a safe trans space that enabled agency and self-advocacy.

Demanding Sole Control versus Collaboration

Our students and colleagues often share a negative view of collaboration, whether as students who resist participating in a group project or as scholars who engage in research with community partners without relinquishing control over the data or the decision-making. Some students resent the logistical burden of having to find time to work together outside class, or worry that they will do the bulk of the work and carry "freeloaders." Agencies and policymakers may shy away from including stakeholders with conflicting or controversial opinions due to practical difficulties. Those who complain that shared work is unnecessary or inefficient often miss the value inherent in struggling through the perceived obstacles.

Calls for community-engaged research have been praised by many academics and policymakers as a means to better policy and programming (Simonds et al. 2013). However, *in practice*, participatory methods are often used as a means to bring community members into fuller participation in research studies and compliance with policy rather than as an invitation to equally share the crafting of research, policy, and programming (Shdaimah, Stahl, and Schram 2011). Real participation and consultation is often messier, more unpredictable, and more time-consuming than most researchers, policy makers, or students are willing and able to undertake.

A panel discussion with students, community activists, and scholars about research with sex workers and other stigmatized populations that we held in October 2017 highlighted a number of such difficulties.[6] Service providers, policymakers and their respective constituents may have conflicting agendas, with the former focused more on meeting urgent needs while the latter may be more focused on advancing knowledge for its own sake. Sex worker activists and community organizations may have their own goals and timelines that may not be compatible with the goals of researchers, leading to aggravation for both groups. Researchers' findings may prove antagonistic or irrelevant to the agendas of service providers. Such is the concern, for example, when we reported the limited long-term value of court-affiliated prostitution diversion programs (Leon and Shdaimah 2012). While we cautioned that these findings should be taken in a context of limited resources and lack of systemic change, there is the danger that findings may be used to fault program participants and criminal justice personnel for failures that are beyond their control. Researchers' ethical obligations may differ from the ethical obligations of other stakeholders and conflict with their professional roles, as was evident in the case study described above with the divergent responses to sexual assault disclosures.

Discussion and Recommendations

As educators, we have seen how powerful it can be for students to build upon the passion stimulated by antitrafficking discourse and unpack more nuanced empirical realities. This works best when it is not top-down instruction but a participatory teaching and learning experience. Pedagogical approaches that center students as experts (Davis and Roswell 2013; Aronson 1978) not only empower students but can also defuse resistance and defensiveness. For example, in a recent seminar, Leon offered a very vocal antitrafficking student activist in the class the option to fulfill a required assignment by reading several viewpoints, including those of a probation officer, a law enforcement officer, and self-identified sex workers, and presenting these to the class. The student rose to the occasion and gave a sensitive account that not only moved the class discussion forward but seemed to expand her own worldview, as reflected in the language she used in later discussions which included an emphasis on women's autonomy and an awareness of structural conditions.

For those who have the power to shape policy, it is not enough to become educated consumers of information on prostitution, trafficking, and sex work. A body of evidence already documents policies, as implemented, that have harmed vulnerable populations by inaccurate definitions of the problem and their analogous solutions. Jo Phoenix describes an understanding of "trafficking" that is simultaneously under- and overinclusive. On the one hand, an overly narrow focus on sexual activity excludes other forms of trafficking, such as agricultural or domestic labor (Phoenix 2009). Such exclusion means that exploitive practices may continue unaddressed, and also prevents us from seeing trafficking as fundamentally a problem of capitalist economies and exploitation, rather than an issue of sex (O'Brien 2013). On the other hand, definitions of trafficking that include *all* forms of commercial sexual activity undermine the rational and ethical dimensions of sex worker decision making, which, in turn, undermine analyses of the structural conditions that shape women's choices.

We must avoid taking shortcuts and commit to thinking through ethical implications of policies and interventions. One way to expose inaccuracies is by closely following how policies are to be implemented in order to assess their (un)intended consequences as they play out on the ground. An important way to gauge the existing or potential consequences of a policy is to speak with those who are charged with their implementation or are its targets who best know how, *in practice*, they will work. For example, Arizona's Project ROSE (Reaching Out to the Sexually Exploited) was based on an inaccurate understanding of sex work as universally exploitative and therefore worked from a rescue perspective that failed to investigate the consequences of the program. Project Rose coerced participation through a sting operation that arrested people suspected of prostitution for the purposes of then "offering" a therapeutic program as an alternative to arrest "for their own good" (Wahab and Panichelli 2013, 347). However, not all individuals arrested were eligible for the program (Strangio 2017) nor did all eligible individuals elect to participate. These individuals therefore were charged with criminal offenses, making them *more* vulnerable and *more* likely to engage in illegal sex work by *in*creasing the difficulty of seeking legal employment and fraying any existing cooperation between sex workers and community providers.

Borrowing from the language of addiction recovery, we urge policymakers and others to "play the tape to the end": thinking through all the potential consequences that people in sex work have told us can arise from criminal justice system involvement. Coerced program participation is problematic in itself, but especially so if the stakes can include direct and painful outcomes related to incarceration like losing child custody, housing, and other aspects of stable family life.

While we contend that the consequences of policies as implemented must be in consultation with those who implement and are affected by them, we recognize that these groups are diverse. There is no singular voice or particular story of sex work. Feminist inquiry calls for a diversity of voices and experiences. This may be particularly difficult in the area of sex work, prostitution, and trafficking because people involved in it are so often stigmatized and criminalized. Those charged with policy implementation also face hurdles to sharing their perspectives in policy debates due to professional or agency restrictions, or their lack of access to or familiarity with media and policy arenas. Therefore stakeholders may not be willing and able to share their stories.

Kate D'Adamo (2017) suggests reading outside of accepted scholarly and mainstream media sources and seeking out alternative sources and self-published accounts such as the Tits and Sass blog or the Red Umbrella Project. Participatory research methods, such as photovoice (Cheng 2013) or everyday world policy analysis (Naples 2003b) produce knowledge based on the perspectives of those affected by policy. As researchers, we can create these; as voters, service providers, or policymakers, we can seek out such research as a basis for decision making or intervention. Advocates, policymakers, organizers, and researchers can also work together to combine their knowledge and skills. Collaborative work conducted by the Baltimore nonprofit Power Inside, Baltimore City Department of Justice, and researchers from Johns Hopkins University on a study of women released from prison in Baltimore revealed a series of longtime practices that presented serious hurdles for reintegration that were overlooked and, in some cases, easily remedied (McLean, Robarge, and Sherman 2006; Power Inside n.d.). The Red Umbrella Project worked with nonprofit advocacy and research organizations Mama Cash and the Open Society Institute to compile resources for sex worker organizations and best practices for funders who seek to contribute to the well-being of sex workers (Red Umbrella Fund 2014).

Similarly, as consumers of media, voters, and financial supporters, we have an obligation to seek out media, candidates, and charities that center the active involvement of vulnerable groups. This can include seeking those that forefront voices of people with first-hand experience or valuing programming that builds on the skills and resilience of sex workers, such as peer mentoring. We should also avoid the easy out of allowing our purchases to do our ethical work. For example, consider what to do after watching a testimonial documentary like *Very Young Girls*, which provides a curated set of perspectives from a peer mentoring program under the leadership of sexual exploitation survivor Rachel Lloyd (Leon, Shdaimah, and Baboolal 2017). We *can* choose to respond to the appeal to text our financial support as the credits roll. But, we must *also* attend to the voices excluded from GEMS, a program that only accepts cisgender women

(Strangio 2017). Similarly, when Facebook offers us the opportunity to buy pajamas made by "rescued sex slaves" (Miller 2015), as ethical consumers and contributors we need to know more. This could include checking whether sites like Charity Navigator provide evidence of good financial management and whether person-first groups like Sex Workers Outreach Project (SWOP) have an assessment but can also trigger deeper questions such as how our financial choices may mask our complicity.

Erin O'Brien (2013) suggests that one of the reasons for an underinclusive definition of trafficking, which focuses only on sexual exploitation, is that a more complete definition would implicate nearly all consumers of goods produced by cheap labor. Confronting such implications with integrity would require that a much broader swath of individuals ask at whose expense we live our comfortable lives and require a broader change of practice. An "end demand" campaign for agricultural trafficking, for example, might include that we all stop purchasing cheap chocolate (Human Trafficking Project 2009).

A pragmatic recommendation for all those involved in research, direct service work, or in shaping policy emerges from our own community collaboration experience and from insights given by community activists about their frustrations when working with academics[7]: make expectations clear. Both of us have learned lessons from our experiences in court and community group collaboration that the case study Leon described above crystallizes. In that example, court personnel and researchers brought very different assumptions about ethics to the shared work. It is unfortunate that these divergences were not made explicit until a critical juncture when sexual assaults were revealed. To avoid misunderstandings, conflict, and resentment collaborations should establish clear and regular communications (Sullivan, McPartland and Fisher 2013). Collaborators should discuss their respective timelines and how the data will be collected, analyzed, and presented including questions of authorship and ownership. Research into effective partnerships also suggests engaging in mutual learning and cross-training (Sullivan, McPartland and Fisher 2013, 12; Shdaimah, Stahl and Schram 2011), which can also help address the confirmation bias problems we have described.[8] Without mutual respect and clear communication up front and ongoing, community groups can feel badly used by researchers or other program administrators who may seem to be promoting their own agendas.

Policymakers, researchers, and practitioners who are interested in challenging their understanding as contexts change and new information emerges can take several steps to cultivate their ability to reflect. Sex work, prostitution, and trafficking come attached to ideological assumptions that may prevent us from taking in evidence, such as the distinctions between individual and structural coercion (Phoenix 2009). The research and our own experiences show the difficulty of being open to ideas that do not comport with preexisting beliefs, especially when they are firmly held. We urge students, educators, and policymakers to cultivate mechanisms to sustain awareness of confirmatory bias, challenge our own stances, and take in new information and diverse opinions to understand and evaluate these practices.

ACKNOWLEDGMENTS

We thank Jonas Rosen for his outstanding research assistance. Our thinking on this work has evolved through conversations with our colleagues, most especially Katie Hail-Jares. In addition, we refine our methods and interpretations each time we present or teach on this work, so we thank all students and colleagues who have engaged in dialogue with us about sex work.

NOTES

1 For a more in-depth discussion of our feminist methodology as it relates to work with vulnerable populations, see Shdaimah and Leon, 2018.

2 This is often the case for the students we teach in criminal justice (Courtright and Mackey 2004; Walters and Kremser 2016) and social work (Miller, Deck, Grise-Owens, and Borders 2015).

3 This was the term used by the professionals, and some of the community members.

4 Survivors of sexual assault differ in their opinions about and experiences with the criminal justice system, but it is a deeply held tenet of most survivor-led organizations that the survivor should have as much choice and control as possible. (See for example, Generation Five and KYIX.)

5 See Hail-Jares, Shdaimah, and Leon 2017, which puts the voices of sex workers and frontline criminal justice personnel at the forefront.

6 Panel discussion, "Moving Away from Damage-Centered Research," St. Francis University October 30, 2017. www.crimcast.tv.

7 In various contexts, we have heard this kind of frustration from community-based sex worker advocates. Federally funded research into community/researcher collaborations (not restricted to sex work) indicates that these are widespread:

> For researchers, especially those in academic settings, publishing study findings in peer-reviewed journals and obtaining grants are crucial, as these are means to maintaining employment and being promoted. RPPS participants reported that, at times, these needs are inconsistent with practitioners' needs. Practitioners need products that are translatable and written in lay language, which can be challenging and time consuming for researchers. Practitioners need results to inform and improve practice and policy and to demonstrate the effectiveness of their programs. It is important for collaborators to be aware of these needs and to discuss them at the start of the collaboration. Study participants stated that being explicit and identifying expectations at the beginning of the process and presenting what one hopes to gain from the collaboration is one way to ensure all collaborators get what they need. (Sullivan, McPartland, and Fisher 2013, 17)

8 There is some evidence indicating that presentation of recommendations that are inconsistent with loosely held prior beliefs can reduce confirmation bias (Schwind et al. 2012).

27

Intimate States

Policies and Their Effects on Sex Workers

ANASTASIA HUDGINS

In the weeks and months following the 2008 Cambodian law change that further criminalized sex work, the sex worker union and local sex worker activists fielded calls from sex workers. They complained of physical abuse and humiliation by police, confinement in nongovernmental organizations' (NGO) shelters and government detention centers without due process, arbitrary arrest for possessing condoms, and other actions. In an example of participatory democracy, some of the five thousand mostly female members of the sex worker union held a march, issued a personal appeal to the prime minister that they published in the newspaper, and staged a cabaret/fashion show where they made their complaints public to an audience of representatives from the Cambodian government, NGOs, and multilateral organizations. The chief complaints were that due to a new law their work had been criminalized and further stigmatized, police were harassing them and denying them due process. Rather than being criminalized, they asserted, sex work should be recognized as work, as it was the means of support for many women and their families. They made a point to say that they were not unconcerned with sex trafficking but felt that sex trafficking had been broadly defined and wrongly included them, making them an inappropriate target for "rescue" by the police.

In this chapter I argue that policies such as Cambodia's Law on Suppression of Human Trafficking and Sexual Exploitation (TIPSE) and the United States Trafficking Victims Protection Act (TVPA), along with its annually required Trafficking in Persons (TIP) Report, are couched as humanitarian laws and policies but that their on-the-ground applications frequently fail the very people they are intended to help[1]. I build on the work of multiple scholars and activists who call for trafficking itself to be more thoroughly problematized, if not outright rejected, as a framework for understanding and acting on people who sell sex in many forms (Agustín 2007; Saunders 2000; Lerum et al. 2012; Hoefinger 2016).

The TVPA discursively constructs the US as having authority to regulate other countries—exerting a legal framework over the world that reflects earlier imperial relationships. In so doing, it obligates countries to conform with its framing of trafficking problems and solutions under threat of economic sanctions. The

TIP Report relies on overly broad definitions of trafficking which result in the conflation of voluntary and involuntary sex work, and frames "trafficking" solely as demand for victims, a problem to be solved through police action and judicial intervention. Embedded in TVPA and the TIP Report are the presumption that interpretations of proper policing are the same around the world, and the assumption that sex workers are victims who should be protected through police and NGO "rescues" and housing in shelters. Indeed, the TVPA requires this. The actions Cambodia undertakes to conform with the TVPA are damaging for women whose precarity leads them to take up work in the commercial sex industry, as this chapter details. It is abhorrent that the sex workers' low social status positions them to absorb the pressures that Cambodia's limited and compromised criminal and judicial systems face in meeting the requirements of these laws.

In 2008 I returned to Cambodia to learn more about Cambodia's TIPSE law and how it would affect sex workers. Why had the new law been enacted? How was it being received, especially by sex workers, and how was it being executed? What would happen to the estimated twenty-eight thousand women working in the sex industry in Cambodia (Steinfatt and Baker 2011) who, with the passage of the law, had effectively become criminals? How would it affect Cambodia's ranking in the ever-important TIP Report, which has the power to affect the country's economic future?

TVPA

The US Victims of Trafficking and Violence Protection Act of 2000 (TVPA) and its reauthorizations address trafficking in persons worldwide by allowing for the prosecution of US citizens who engage in sex with minors abroad, by providing foreign countries with assistance to combat trafficking of their citizens or within their borders, and through legislation that allows for a panoply of laws related to trafficking in persons both in the US and abroad. It defines a criminal justice approach as the correct way to address trafficking and sets rewards and punishments for countries that do or do not implement the appropriate measures.

TIP REPORT

Under the TVPA, the Trafficking in Persons (TIP) Report must be published annually by the US Department of State in June. It ranks the countries of the world, according to the standards laid out in the TVPA, into four categories: Tiers 1, 2, 3, and the Tier 2 Watch List. A low ranking threatens a country's aid packages from the US, the International Monetary Fund, and from Development Banks. As of 2010, the US includes itself in the ranking.

TIPSE LAW

Cambodia's Law on Suppression of Human Trafficking and Sexual Exploitation 2008 (TIPSE) defines illegal actions including trafficking, prostitution, child prostitution and pornography and describes the penalties. Article 24 of the TIPSE Law was of critical importance to many sex workers because it further criminalized their labor.

I was also curious to learn what the impact of the TVPA and the TIPSE Law (Ministry of Justice 2008) had been on a brothel village outside Phnom Penh where I'd first conducted research in 2000–2001 with debt-bonded young women who had migrated illegally from Vietnam to work in Svay Pak, the brothel village. There had been twenty-five brothels housing some 320 women in 2001, but in 2008 that had all changed. Walking through the village, the difference was striking. Where the economy of the village had been centered on the commercial sex industry, now it revolved around recycling and textiles with parts of the village transformed into a trash dump for plastics recycling. The store fronts where the brothel-based sex workers used to beckon clients—businessmen from Asia, local men, and a few European and North American men—were now filled with towering piles of pants pockets bound for one of the many nearby garment factories, with a few people crouched over fabric cutting out pockets with scissors. A Christian organization had transformed several brothels into a kindergarten. The drop-in center for sex workers remained, but it was only open a few hours a week.

A friend who lived in the village related the events of the past several years. He said that after the commando-style raid in 2003 that had been conducted by a Christian NGO based in Virginia with minimal input from the Cambodian police,[2] the police had set up a gate to block the road into the village for about six months. After they left, brothels were still open—"closed in the front, open in the back"—but with continued police pressure the brothel owners finally sold their properties and left Svay Pak.

The absence of open-air brothels could have been taken to mean that the policy had worked: the brothels closed. But in fact, my friend and others said that sex workers had simply moved around the city and to other provinces, and brothel owners bought property in other areas. The shift in the village economy as well as the political activity by unionized sex workers in Phnom Penh and the complaints the activity was based on alerted me to the effect of these policies on sex workers in Cambodia. Public health experts told me that sex workers who had been brothel-based had been easy to approach for harm-reduction efforts to protect their health and well-being and that of their clients.

With the increased scrutiny of sex workers and brothels, women instead had turned to work as "entertainment workers" in hotels, beer gardens, karaoke bars—still selling sex but removed from the public eye and away from the protection of harm-reduction policies. Although the health of many sex workers was likely negatively affected by these policies (Decker et al. 2015), the remainder of this chapter focuses on the political implications of the policies on the body politic of sex workers, as well as their physical bodies, and how, in its framing of the problem of trafficking, the TIP Report sets up an ends-oriented approach that ignores how the goals of the policy are achieved as well as the fact that the execution of the policy further harms women who work in the commercial sex industry.

The TIPSE law that had many in an uproar was a sixteen-page document written by a UNICEF consultant, and approved by Cambodian lawmakers in February 2008 (Ministry of Justice 2008). With a vagueness likely due to its brevity, the law covers definitions and descriptions of illegal actions and their penalties, including trafficking, prostitution, child prostitution, and pornography. For the protesting sex workers, the most important part of the law was Article 24, that states: "A person who willingly solicits another in public for the purpose of prostituting himself or herself shall be punished with imprisonment from 1 to 6 days and a fine from 3,000 to 10,000 riels."[3] This law denied the women the right to earn an income in a way that they had determined was appropriate for them. Among those who were arrested for solicitation and then taken to a shelter for trafficked women—despite not having been trafficked—were some women who described how their rights were violated through a special arrangement by police and NGOs, as I describe below.

The Victims of Trafficking and Violence Protection Act was established in 2000 to address a rising concern about trafficking. It requires the US Department of State to issue an annual Trafficking in Persons Report in which the US ranks the world's countries (including itself, as of 2010) into three tiers and a "watch list" based on how much human trafficking takes place within or across their borders, what steps they take to reduce it, and how effective they are in reducing it. Those countries deemed to make egregiously insufficient efforts are placed in the third tier. Countries' placement into these different tiers can greatly affect them, as movement to the third tier can come with financial penalties and sanctions levied against them by the US, the International Monetary Fund, and multilateral development banks. Over the years, the report has evolved to include the recommendation that countries also implement the means to rehabilitate sex trafficking victims so they can reduce women's vulnerability and reenter society safely, for example by supporting NGO and government shelters for trafficked women (see Shih 2015 for a critique of this practice).

Staff of the US Department of State make the rankings, and the Secretary of State finalizes countries' positions, but the US president has the final say and may choose to enforce or waive any sanctions (US Department of State 2017). Critics of the ranking process point out that data collection methods and sources are not transparent (Agustín 2007; Chen 2011), and that these rankings may be based on political calculations (Hudgins 2007). For example, it was noted in a bipartisan Congressional Research Service evaluation of the TIP Report that "observers alleged" that Malaysia was moved from the third tier to the Watch List as a response to its support for the Trans-Pacific Partnership (which the US supported at the time), despite its lack of progress in combating human trafficking (Rosen 2017, 26). Similar instances of politicization as well as the ability to both rank particular countries and to apply financial penalties via supra-state financial institutions smack of imperialism on the part of the US and reveal the bald political-economic power embedded in the legislation, leading one to question whether the victims in the TVPA are doubly victimized.

The TIP Report describes the phenomenon of trafficking as one that can be analyzed and solved by employing analogies of supply and demand, meaning the supply of women and the demand for them. A focus on demand, not supply, requires an emphasis on criminal justice techniques for stemming the demand. And although TIP Reports acknowledge that trafficking is caused by socioeconomic problems, only "law-and-order" type approaches positively influence a country's ranking. According to this rationale, there is a high occurrence of sex trafficking because greedy or lustful people take advantage of women's "inherent" vulnerability and power differential. However, a focus on demand denies the prevalence of voluntary sex work, thereby denying its relevance as an economic strategy that the sex workers and their families deploy. Consequently, policy makers do not consider structural issues as key to resolving the sex work problem and, in fact, deny that addressing poverty and gender equity is a solution that can effectively limit commercial sex work. In my 2001 research, I found that the contemporary economic policies in Vietnam that liberalized the economy (Tep and Ek 2000; Tep, Ek, and Maas 2000; Tran Thi Van An 1999; Vu Tuan Anh et al. 2000) were a driving factor in the women's migration for work in the Cambodian sex industry (Hudgins 2006).

Cambodia has been ranked in the third tier twice, in the second tier eight times, and in the Watch List six times. Indeed, prior to 2008 Cambodia had occupied the Tier 2 Watch List, and faced the possibility of being moved to Tier 3 (due to rules that limit the number of years a country can be on the Watch List). But with the 2008 law, the country's status was elevated to Tier 2. Inquiries to government officials and members of UN agencies revealed several possibilities. Some felt that the prime minister's wife was offended by prostitution and that she influenced the creation of the law. Others pointed to the law as an election-year gesture. A subset of officials said that the law didn't offer material change from previous laws but was being enforced more robustly. Yet many of the Cambodian and international activists I worked with felt that the law came about as a result of pressure from the US in the form of the TIP Report. Some activists, however, said that asserting that the US was responsible reified the law's power and increased its hegemony, and their chief concern was to contest police abuse and the stigma against sex workers.

Regardless of the cause of the law change, Cambodia was rewarded in the 2008 TIP Report. Its Cambodia country narrative states: "In February 2008,

Cambodia's new Law on the Suppression of Human Trafficking and Commercial Sexual Exploitation was promulgated and went into effect immediately. This legislation provides law enforcement authorities the power to investigate all forms of trafficking and is a powerful tool in efforts to prosecute and convict traffickers and have them face stringent punishments" (US Department of State 2008, 83). The implications are important, as I describe below.

On its face, the US Victims of Trafficking and Violence Protection Act encourages governments to address their country's trafficking problems, as Cambodia did with the passage of the TIPSE Law. But the TVPA's neoliberal framework and emphasis on police action rewards the capture, enumeration, and containment of women's bodies as evidence that the law is "working." Not only does this wrongly overascribe the category of "trafficked" to many women, it renders them passive in the law, invisible except as victims.

By failing to recognize and support women's agency, the TVPA facilitates a scenario where Cambodia relies on sex workers' low social position and denial of their agency to bolster the credibility of state efforts to reduce trafficking. This "law-and-order" approach stipulates a narrow set of interventions which fail to result in qualitative or measurable improvements in many women's lives. In the case of Cambodia, the TVPA makes it more likely that vulnerable women's needs and voices are subsumed by the state's need to comply with the TVPA's requirements for arrests and rescues. That, combined with competition among NGOs for funding to continue their work with trafficked women, effectively disempowers the very people the law is intended to help, as the following stories illustrate.

While I was in Cambodia sharing dinner with an activist friend one night, I learned of a particular story of overreach by police and a shelter that seemed to point toward the conflation between trafficking victim and voluntary sex worker that the union members complained about in their protests, as well as collusion between the police and shelter. Over the past few days my friend, "Sokhun" had been fielding increasingly frantic phone calls from the husband of a sex worker who had been arrested under Article 24, along with her manager and four coworkers after a raid by twenty heavily armed police. Her husband met her at the police station, but some hours later he didn't know where she had been taken, and he asked Sokhun to intercede. Sokhun had searched for her at a well-known, well-funded shelter for trafficked women where women are commonly taken by police, one that, in her experience, paid the police to release the women to the NGO so it could increase its tally of "rescued" trafficking victims under its care.

While we were having dinner, the husband called again, crying that his wife had indeed been taken to that shelter, and the shelter was pressuring him to require her to stay so she could learn to sew. He said neither of them wanted her to have to do this work but that as a trash collector he didn't earn enough to support them. They couldn't do without the income her work brought in—much more than sewing would provide if she were even able to get a job in one of the many garment factories that had sprung up. The shelter would not allow him to speak with his wife, and they would not say when they would release her. My friend raised an eyebrow, explaining, "I can say it is kidnapping. But they don't call it that. It's funny [NGO's name] can claim it this way. The staff told the husband, 'You know the police arrested your wife and we went to the police to pay compensation to get your wife and we are helping your wife.' It's lying—paying compensation to the police to help his wife! This is cooperation between the police and [the NGO]!"

Another interview revealed an even more disturbing instance of collusion between an NGO and the police. One woman had gone to a sex worker health clinic that was operated by an NGO that also housed rescued sex workers. This clinic was open for walk-in visits by independent sex workers not housed at the shelter. Like other clinics for sex workers, those with the ability to pay are required to make a small payment for the services they receive while those who are very poor can have the fees waived. The interviewee pointed out that this meant that the shelter knew which patients had money and which didn't. After police raided a brothel or arrested independent sex workers in the area, the police and shelter staff worked together to separate those women who were known to have money from those who did not. Those who did have money were arrested and asked to pay a police bribe to be quickly released, and those who did not have money were arrested and taken to the shelter where the NGO would keep them as long as possible so as to show a higher rate of occupancy, according to the informant.

Similar complaints are made in a Human Rights Watch World Report (2010), and the 2009 TIP Report country narrative about Cambodia criticizes the way the TIPSE Law was interpreted and applied.

> Because the new law covers a wide range of offenses, not all government officials have appeared to distinguish between the law's articles on trafficking offenses and non-trafficking crimes such as prostitution, pornography, and child sex abuse. As a result, law enforcement has focused on prostitution-related crimes, and many police, courts, and other government officials appear to believe that enforcing all prostitution articles of the law contributes to efforts to combat trafficking. Following the passage of the law, Cambodian police conducted numerous raids on brothels, and detained a large number of women in prostitution, while failing to arrest, investigate or charge any large number of persons for human trafficking offenses. (US Department of State 2009, 96)

But the US may be giving mixed messages. One longtime NGO worker described a meeting she had attended at the US Embassy a few years prior to this 2008 interview, along with thirty to forty other NGOs working in Cambodia in the field of trafficking. She said that the US Embassy had been instructed to communicate to the Cambodian government the number of arrests and rescues they would need to make to improve their ranking in the TIP Report. There "were very specific conditions [that had to happen to keep Cambodia off the Tier 3 list], like 100 women had to be rescued—this is the US government saying this. And of course, 100 women were rescued. Not 99, not 101, but 100. It was hysterical. [They also said] how many people must be convicted. . . . The police will take anybody."

I assert that this collusion between police and NGO shelters was a result of the TVPA's carrot and stick approach, which rewards countries for criminal-justice type interventions and punishes them through economic sanctions should they only address structural problems through interventions focused on literacy, health, gender equality, and poverty eradication. The collusion was also linked to the failure to clearly differentiate between voluntary and involuntary sex work by too broadly defining trafficking victims in the TIP Report.

The TIP Report defines trafficking as when "a commercial sex act is induced by force, fraud, or coercion, or in which the person induced to perform such an act has not attained 18 years of age" (US Department of State 2017, 3). Yet the report also offers a catch-all statement that renders the definition of trafficking as overly broad. That statement reads: "Sex trafficking also may occur through a specific form of coercion whereby individuals are compelled to continue in prostitution through the use of unlawful 'debt,' purportedly incurred through their transportation, recruitment, or even their 'sale'—which exploiters insist they must pay off before they can be free. Even if an adult initially consents to participate in prostitution it is irrelevant: if an adult, after consenting, is subsequently held in service through psychological manipulation or physical force, he or she is a trafficking victim and should receive benefits. . . ." (US Department of State 2017, 17).

This statement overlooks the fact that many sex workers are debt-bonded because they have received an advance on their earnings, or because they took out a loan from a brothel owner under an agreement to work in the brothel, selling sex to pay off the loan. Agustín's work reveals that many who are debt-bonded willingly enter into such bondage because they cannot otherwise afford to travel and that debt-bondage is a means to an end for them (2003, 2007). Derks et al. states: "Statements about 'debt-bonded' or 'indentured' women, or women who are 'sold,' may appear straightforward at first but in fact leave unanswered many questions regarding the practices, contracts, people and implications involved" (Derks, Henke, and Ly 2006, 16). Steinfatt and Baker (2011) ask us to consider voluntary and involuntary labor more broadly:

> If sex workers are to be labeled as trafficked purely on the basis that they would not choose voluntarily to enter prostitution if they perceived another possible

choice to be economically viable, then any person laboring at any job consisting of perceived drudgery would also be considered trafficked, and the entire meaning for the term is changed. The heart of concern with human trafficking is the use of force, fraud, or coercion to produce labor, and the victimization of children. (Steinfatt and Baker 2011, 3)

A view of the women as victims predetermines the response to the sex-work/trafficking problem. Such a perspective implies that women are brought into the sex industry, not that they choose the sex industry. This assumption shapes the questions that are asked and the solutions that are pursued. In defining the problem as caused by demand, policy makers fail to see other significant factors at play, factors subsumed under the "supply" category. Looking at the problem from a "supply" perspective, one can see how the women and their families might profit from the commercial sex industry, however bleakly.

Most of the brothel-based women in my 2000–2001 study come from impoverished situations, and sex work provides a source of income that is better paid, with fewer hurdles to leap (such as literacy, job skills, social networks) than work in the formal economy. In this realistic scenario, women's choices are shaped both by individual agency and structural conditions. An examination of supply would have to address these structural conditions. Women would have to be seen as rational actors, not simply victims of someone else's profit motive. Incorporating these factors would require a much more comprehensive response than simply arresting the brothel owners, clients, pimps, and traffickers, and rescuing women.

The women in my 2001 study spoke of solving their family's problems and of being negatively affected by poverty. For them, sex work was the best of many bad choices. Many of the women I spoke with in Cambodia expressed a desire to earn money for their family members as a rationale for coming to the brothel village. Here I excerpt their words.

My mother has no money. People told me about this place, recruited me. But it is my decision to come. When I'm sad, it's when I worry about my mother. That I have not made enough money for her, to help her.
—Twenty-eight-year-old woman in Cambodia for three years

I don't have a mother or father. My life is very poor and difficult. I don't have any money. My sister is ill. Life is very difficult. We don't have enough food and water to survive on. I had to look for a way to make money to help my sister. I came here with a friend. She told me about the life here, but I decided to come here to help make money for my sister. I only have my older sister. I grew up without parents.
—Twenty-four-year-old woman in Cambodia for one year

My family is very poor. If they were doing well, I would not be here. My parents are very old and I have to work to take care of the family.
—Twenty-five-year-old woman in Cambodia for two to three years

My aunt brought me here. My mother doesn't even know about this. I came because we have a large family and I need to work.
—Twenty-two-year-old woman in Cambodia for one year

I had a job outside [of the brothel village], but my boss returned to Vietnam. My mother didn't have any money and we had to pay off debts, so I came here to borrow money from the brothel owner to give to my mother to pay back the debts. Because of our situation, I had to come here to borrow money.
—Twenty-five-year-old woman in Cambodia seven to eight months

I have a friend who has helped me, who told me that if I make enough money she'd help me get back home. But I don't want to go home. I want to stay here with my brothel owner.
—Eighteen-year-old woman in Cambodia for five months

Another woman, Diep, said that she wants to work in the brothel village and earn a lot of money for her future, when she gets old and sick. "But I cannot earn a lot of money because I'm not pretty, and I'm older than others in the brothel. It's depressing and sad." Instead, using the English she has learned, she works helping the brothel owner deal with the clients. She said:

At the moment my mother is sick, and the house is ramshackle and has a leaky roof. I'm thinking that if I go back to Vietnam, I need to have money to build my house and repair it, and pay off the debts she owes to people in Vietnam. I also need some funds to start a business when I go back home. But in this type of situation—I'm not pretty, I don't have many clients, how can I make money to go back home? That is why I had to stay longer, to earn more money.
—Diep, twenty-six-year-old debt-bonded sex worker

In the interviews I conducted with sex workers, all but one of the women said they wanted to leave. But in the same breath of saying they wanted to leave, they also said they needed the job because they wanted to earn money to help their families—building a house, financially supporting their family, or sending a sibling to school, for example. Policy makers have no concept of these factors yet push their agendas forward on the simplistic construction of commercial sex workers as victims, with no input from the women themselves. As Carol Vance asks: "Are criminal law and police action the best remedy for these and other situations?" (Vance 2012, 212). The proposed solution is premised on a moralistic understanding of womanhood and childhood (Hecht 1998), and the moralizing gets in the way of solving real problems. The physical and mental violence women experience through prostitution is reinforced by the structural violence of the policies that fail to recognize the structural problems that led women to sex work in the first place.

The policies discussed in this chapter are meant to be humanitarian policies. While policies have weaknesses and blind spots, the "law-and-order" approach to sex work in the TVPA and its TIP Report relies on a superficial understanding of sex work, of sex workers, and of the context in which the commercial sex industry takes place. In the expression of this superficial understanding, the sex workers are cast as victims of fraud and force, victimized at the hands of evil perpetrators, not as people making rational and difficult decisions. The reports must be examined with a critical eye because they seek not only to represent the experiences of vulnerable populations worldwide but also to guide interventions on their behalf. The US paradigm for intervention sets up women as soft targets for police and for NGOs that specialize in trafficking victims, both of which rely on the capture of "trafficked" women to bolster their credibility and their social and economic capital at the expense of the women's rights.

Rather than have actors in these policies limited to those of victims, perpetrators, or rescuers—a framework that closes the door to other interpretations and solutions and makes the existing approach seem commonsensical—opportunities for real humanitarianism should be opened. An improvement would be to support broad-based initiatives that work to decrease the supply of ready participants in the informal economy of commercial sex work. Addressing health concerns through harm-reduction, gender equality in education and pay, migration policies that decrease immigrants' vulnerability, decriminalizing sex work, and decreasing income inequality would address the underlying causes of the attraction of the commercial sex industry as the best among many bad options for work. Bringing sex work organizations to the table when creating policies meant to regulate them would make strides toward allowing room for the voices of the so-called victims to be included in defining the problem, determining responses, or preventing the problem from happening in the first place.

A focus on supply instead of demand, would have to acknowledge the structural problems affecting women and their families, and the reality that many in the commercial sex industry are not forced into prostitution but enter it deliberately for any number of reasons. It is ironic that the very causes of a purported increase in the number of sex trafficking cases (see page 34 of 2017 TIP Report for statistics [US Department of State 2017])—a decreased social safety net—are not addressed in the TIP Report.

Neoliberal structural adjustment programs implemented worldwide increase social vulnerability. They cut spending on education, health, and welfare, they shrink the role of government in the provision of services, and they eliminate environmental and workers' protections. These policies function to create the precariat (Standing 2011), which Butler defines as "the politically induced condition in which certain populations suffer from failing social and economic networks of support and become differentially exposed to injury, violence, and death" (Butler 2009, ii). Under neoliberalism, the precariat, which includes the women in my study, is subjected to increased policing and surveillance, an approach that causes "enticements to social justice and rights [to] remain unattended by sexual humanitarian interventions" (Hoefinger 2016, n.p.).

During an interview with a nun whose life's work focused on minimizing the social vulnerability of poor women and girls, she discussed how a food program at Cambodian schools helped provide girls with an education. The project worked to provide at least one meal a day to school children, which meant that it cost families less to send their children to school than it did to have them stay home, thus ensuring that girls obtained a basic education. She pointed out that the 2008 global financial crisis resulted in severe cuts to food programs, and that schools had stopped providing a meal to students. She expected enrollment of girls in school to decrease, which in her judgment would increase the numbers of girls who would turn to sex work to support themselves and their families. This simple and effective type of intervention is not discussed in the TIP Report because the report is not concerned with causes for an increasing supply of women and girls into the commercial sex industry. This should change.

NOTES

1 While the report includes labor, sex, and organ trafficking, debt-bondage, and child soldiers, I focus solely on women who were working in the commercial sex industry, many of whom may be defined as "trafficked" by the report, even though they would not so describe themselves.

2 This raid was aired on television in the US, and the secretary of state, Colin Powell, lauded the NGO and awarded it a $1 million grant (NBC 2003).

3 Equivalent to $0.75 to $2.50.

PART III

Toward Nonviolence and Gender Justice

The last part of this book focuses on a very important aspect of contemporary discourse on gender violence—creating social change. We present a variety of perspectives on what can be done to bring about positive social change and to ultimately achieve justice and equity in gender relations. We offer a roundtable of chapters that explore routes toward nonviolence in gender relations from the perspectives of law, philosophy, linguistics, political science, theological studies, sociology, social work, and women and gender studies contributors.

Thinking about Change

In a small village in Kenya where taboos about talking about rape are strong, a family whose daughter was assaulted decides to "show their neighbors that it is the *rapist* who should be ashamed, and that they are proud of standing up for justice for their daughter" (Power 2009, n.p.). From such individual acts of courage and conviction to the larger efforts of the global #MeToo movement, change is underway.

In previous sections, we have explored the routes and contexts of gender violence as it occurs throughout the world. In this closing section, we address the potential for change and suggest ways to create nonviolence in social relations, with a particular focus on gendered violence and its potential remedies.

Moving from Violence to Nonviolence

What will it take to diminish or end gender violence? The history of gender violence, and how it relates to political and social structures can provide guidance. Knowledge of how gendered social structures of inequality contribute to gendered expectations and social scripts, which in turn contain the blueprint for violence, may inspire alternative choices. First, scholars, activists, and people of all political persuasions must work to make the invisible visible. As long as gender exists as a system of "omnipresent yet partly hidden plans" (Griffin 1992), which supports abuses and reproduces inequities, many of us will remain ignorant of its dangers.

What seems clear is that change takes place, and sometimes rapidly. Where for centuries women in Niger have had very little recourse to end a marriage that might be violent or simply not loving, in one generation their options have opened up and divorce is now within comparatively easy reach with support of the government and religious figures (Searcey 2019). Similarly, in Ireland, a historically Catholic theocracy, abortion rights were granted to women in 2018 effectively overcoming religiously based conservatism (de Freytas-Tamura 2018). How such social mores undergo rapid change is worth considering as instructive models.

We must inspect how masculinities and femininities are constructed and parse out the results of building rigidly defined systems of identity, taking into account the extent to which our lives are organized through inequality regimes (Acker, 2006) and the ubiquitous influence of neoliberalism as it undermines equity in the twenty-first century. The rituals that shape manhood from boyhood should come under scrutiny; the voices of men who have resisted or been excluded could serve as possible guides. Though we have pointed to the culture of technology and the internet as sites of tremendous hostility toward women, they also contain locations of reexamination where what it means to be men is analyzed with a goal to create healthier masculinities, decentering violence. Women's voices, many of which articulate the experience of patriarchy from the vantage point of its margins, must also be included in the dialogue. How do we understand the varying responses to patriarchy and feminism that these voices express?

The binary construction of gendered identity potentially places people in opposition to self and other. Discourses and practices of male/female disparity, complicated by the omnipresence of race, class, and sexuality often makes us unknowable, strange, and other as gendered beings, and this otherness contributes to violence. At the same time, we must continue to explore the specificity of maleness and femaleness cross-culturally, to understand how privilege is bestowed and difference is practiced in the lives of men and women. Without knowing, we cannot hope to move beyond conceptions of otherness fraught with hostility and fear in our own communities, countries of origin, and beyond.

As we begin to understand the coerced nature of dichotomous gender systems, their effect on the individual's propensity for aggression and/or passivity will become clearer. Although it is imperative that we work to restructure systems that uphold and maintain gender violence, global solutions cannot take place without the action of individuals; and no individual can take responsibility for altering our entire system. As Connell points out, "gender customs came into existence at specific moments in time and can always be transformed by social action" (2011, 22) which can begin with our own choices. Starting from the parameters of our lives, we must identify the small changes that we can make that will contribute to the broader solutions.

Each of us must acknowledge our relationship to violence as members of social systems. In the US cultural context, violence is advocated as "the normal, appropriate and necessary behavior of power and control" (Ewing 1982, 7). As the contributors to this volume show, the practice of violence across the globe is gendered. Through the threat of violence, citizens come to accept fear and anxiety as inevitable features of social life. Increasing militarization adds to the problem. Through the advocacy of violence as an effective form of behavior, men are permitted to abuse women, other men, and children. This privilege is real whether specific men take advantage of that option or not.

Because changes in gender relations will take many forms and be precipitated by many factors, each of us must become familiar with how the interpersonal and the institutional connect. While we are no doubt endowed with human agency, we are at the same time influenced in our desires and our choices by the traditions of the past, the shape of contemporary institutions such as religion, education, and family, and the expectations attendant on our "doing gender" in culturally appropriate ways (West and Zimmerman 1987). Although change can develop in each of these areas, the most far-reaching and effective changes will combine both the personal and the institutional.

Signs of Change

It is heartening that politically influential organizations have issued official statements acknowledging that corporal punishment has negative consequences for children (American Academy of Pediatrics n.d.) and that sexual assault and domestic violence and discrimination and abuse toward LGBTQ+ citizens imperil the physical and emotional well-being of Americans (American Medical Association 2019). Indeed, using a public-health framework to conceptualize and respond to gendered violence has emerged as a promising approach to addressing this widespread, multifaceted problem (Novello et al. 1992). Even a bastion of traditional masculinity, *Men's Health*, recently focused on the ways in which men's incapacity to talk about their own vulnerability is linked to escalating suicide rates for men in the US. Evans posits that "not talking about mental health is literally killing men" (2018, n.p.).

We have also seen progress in the legal arena. In 2013, for example, Congress reauthorized the Violence Against Women Act (VAWA), which was originally passed in 1994. As the first US federal law to address gender-based crimes by providing funding for police, prosecution, and services for adult victims, the VAWA is significant for its recognition that violence against women is a gender-bias crime; it acknowledges that acts of violence against women discriminate against women as a social category. In what has been called "a giant step forward," Congress "extended the act's protections to teenage victims" when it reauthorized the VAWA in 2000 (Barnett, Miller-Perrin, and Perrin 2005, 246). In January 2019, however, VAWA was allowed to expire. Though it was eventually reauthorized the future of this critical legislation is not clear.

International dialogue among women has become an important factor in forcing governments to pay attention to problems to which they have, both overtly and covertly, contributed. In 1993, the United Nations (UN) announced the Declaration on the Elimination of Violence Against Women (United Nations 1994). This document continues to form the framework for international efforts to reduce gender violence. Gender violence occupied a significant position on the agenda at the 1995 Fourth World Conference on Women in Beijing, where topics ranging from control of reproductive capacity to domestic violence to rape and sexual abuse within the context of war were addressed as urgent issues concerning women from every country. The conference resolutions compelled governments around the world to acknowledge and reform policies and practices that support gender violence. Following the conference, the UN Development Fund for Women (UNIFEM) launched an international campaign urging governments to devise national plans of action to eradicate violence against women.

The International Violence Against Women Act of 2018 was introduced in the US Congress as an effort to make gender equality and the prevention of global gender-based violence central to US foreign policy. Sadly, it is unlikely that the bill will move forward during the Trump administration. However, it is essential to take the long view to address issues of such long standing.

Two developments in international law represent tremendous progress regarding rape in armed conflict. In 1996 the International Criminal Court in The Hague announced several indictments for rape during the Bosnian War. In 1998 the tribunal passed judgement relating to the conflict in Rwanda in which, for the first time, rape was considered as a form of genocide (Wood 2004). Organized rape in times of war is now understood to be a crime against humanity (Simons 1996). Ongoing efforts by groups such as the Global Fund for Women recognize that in order to reach equality and create peace "cultures of violence both in the home and in conflict situations" must be transformed (Grossman and Smith 2004, inside front cover).

Unarmed civilian protection offers a potential alternative to militarized responses to conflict, thereby producing more lasting security and peace. This methodology trains civilians—both international and local—to reduce conflict by offering "accompaniment, presence, rumor control, community security meetings, securing safe passage, and monitoring" (Julian and Schweitzer 2015, 2). Currently employed in South Sudan, where peacekeeping teams comprised of women who hold influence in their communities have been established for the first time (Draper 2015), this strategy shows promise as a bulwark against gender-based violence (Coomariswamy 2015). Initial data suggests significant reduction in rapes and assaults against women. Intervention without arms offers a transformational approach that holds potential for peace and security through building connections across ethnic, tribal, and regional differences while simultaneously engaging women in leadership (see Draper 2015; Dziewanski 2015; Coomaraswamy 2015; Koopman 2012).

As we write, the #MeToo and Time's Up movements represent high-profile efforts to address sexual assault and gender equity respectively. While endeavors to address these problems have been underway for decades, the speed with which these two crusades have moved to successfully draw attention to issues and jump-start conversations around the world has been astounding. In the US, the largest number of women ever elected to Congress took office in January of 2019. Many ran as a direct result of these and other resistance movements formed to respond to political backlash against gender and racial equity progress made earlier in the new century. There is a palpable sense that global consciousness is being raised.

The capacity for change is real. Sweden serves as inspiration for equality for women, embodying the multifaceted changes that could lead to a reduction in gender violence. The Women in Work Index 2019 ranks it among the top three countries for women's economic empowerment. Through policies aimed at rebalancing equality between men and women such as the most generous parental leave in the world, curricula that aim to restructure gender roles starting in preschool, adoption of gender-neutral pronouns that have become common usage, one of the highest proportions of women lawmakers, and a law that specifies that explicit consent must be given for sex acts to be considered voluntary, Sweden is leading the world in enacting changes that are referenced throughout this volume as necessary to reduce incidence of gender violence (Salam 2019).

Like any book, this one has been limited by space constraints to what we see is the most virulent and established forms of gender violence. We would like to encourage readers to use it as a starting point to understand not only the phenomenon of gender violence but also to expand an understanding of conceptual and theoretical frameworks that seek to explain it. If we are to work toward ending gender violence, it is not enough simply to inform ourselves about the facts and occurrences of gender violence, or about the historical, philosophical, cultural, and interpersonal conditions that encourage and permit it. We must go on to learn about—and to create—the conditions that make gender violence *impossible*.

The chapters that follow comprise a few of the many voices that have offered visions and plans for a more peaceful future. The suggestions presented by the authors range from policy and program initiatives to altered forms of language and new patterns of consciousness. Some of these ideas and practices have emerged as a result of sustained scholarly research on gender violence issues, others out of the social activism of countless women and male allies; many represent the praxis inherent in value-rational and/or community action research. We envision strands of a web that connect the disparate views, which, when woven together, provide a greater understanding of how we can eradicate gender violence and reconstitute social structures to facilitate justice rather than oppression.

These voices contribute to the search for an answer to the riddle of gender violence. It is likely that there are many answers, or at least many parts to the answer. Indeed, it is the thesis of this book that we must understand the works of many people, across many disciplines, in order to comprehend the nature and scope of gender violence, as well as its resolutions. It is our hope that this book will open up more possibilities for change.

SUGGESTIONS FOR FURTHER READING

Chimamanda Ngozi Adichie, *We Should All Be Feminists*, 2014
Patricia Hill Collins and Sirma Bilge, *Intersectionality*, 2016
Raewyn W. Connell, *Confronting Equality: Gender, Knowledge and Global Change*, 2011
Michael Kaufman, *The Time Has Come: Why Men Must Join the Gender Equality Revolution*, 2019
Michael A. Messner, Max A. Greenberg, and Tal Peretz, *Some Men: Feminist Allies and the Movement to End Violence Against Women*, 2015

From Reimagining History

Marcus Amaker and Marjory Wentworth

This year, we've done laps around despair;
and we've grown tired of running in circles
so we stepped off the track and began to walk.
As the earth shifted beneath our feet,
we moved forward together. Our hearts
unhinged, guide us toward a city
remade by love, into a future
that our past could never have imagined,
beginning today.

28

Educating for Social Change

Feminist Curriculum and Community Partnerships for Advocacy Training

JENNIFER NACCARELLI AND SUSAN L. MILLER

Advocacy training programs offer a strategy to deploy undergraduate education and fieldwork as mechanisms for social change. Embedded in a Women and Gender Studies curriculum, they train future professionals to address the consequences of intimate partner violence (IPV)[1] and contribute to prevention techniques by generating informed college graduates who actively confront and challenge gender norms. A feminist training orientation fosters intergenerational relationships between experienced and new advocates; doing so highlights and revives the feminist orientations of the early battered women's movement. Ideally, students acquire an experiential understanding of intersectional identities and the systems and institutions that shape them.

Merging feminist practices with the principles of trauma-informed care integrates a deeper understanding of trauma into activism and service agencies. The potential for social change, however, relies on integrating the lessons learned from the past forty years of advocacy on behalf of victims/survivors of IPV. For example, feminist critiques point to an imbalance in power dynamics when service is framed as an exchange between "haves" and "have nots" (see Balliet and Heffernan 2000; Naples and Bojar 2002; Costa and Lejong 2012), lacking a real commitment to social change. Given the varied backgrounds among professionals in the field, a systematic plan to generate new advocates who understand their work as part of a larger movement for social change is essential. Feminist academic programs focused on gender-based violence are particularly suited for transformational learning and practice by training students to address both individual and structural consequences of oppression.

Numerous options are available to gain professional experiences while pursuing an undergraduate degree. Internship experiences are common practice for undergraduate students across academic disciplines. Through internships, students are exposed to various professions, learning about where they would like to position themselves professionally after graduation. Such opportunities may or may not be credit bearing and do not necessarily contribute to the local community or engage in social change. Service learning projects in undergraduate institutions differ from traditional internships. They are based upon the concept of community engagement where university students provide their labor and utilize their talents to remedy an unmet need or confront a social problem.

Service learning opportunities expanded significantly during the 1990s when organizations such as Campus Compact cultivated students as both "active learners" and "responsible citizens" through a network of community-engaged learning opportunities (Balliet and Heffernan 2000). At their best they are embedded within a robust curriculum in which academic knowledge supports and informs student engagement and where productive collaborations among the institution and community agencies evolve. At their worst, service learning projects can fall into a trap of elite volunteerism and approach community engagement as remedying perceived deficits. A Women and Gender Studies curriculum, combined with a focus on gender-based violence, can avoid this pitfall because of the reflexive practice it cultivates in students while training them to confront structural inequality and gender norms. However, feminist critiques of service learning and the current state of IPV service provision must be addressed to demonstrate how feminist-based advocacy training programs serve as a catalyst for social change.

Shared Commitments and Community Partnerships: A Case Study

It is possible to craft productive university relationships with community partners in a way that fosters social change (see Sheridan and Jacobi 2013). Costa and Leong conclude their review essay on feminist service learning by arguing that "[b]y paying closer attention to the relationships of power that structure civic engagement projects and by making those a focus of both course analysis and practice, and epistemological reflection, faculty and students together with community partners can perhaps begin to unravel the knots of inequality that have so long tied them to one another" (2012, 279).

The Domestic Violence Prevention and Services (DVPS) program at the University of Delaware provides this type of experience and prepares undergraduate students for careers dedicated to social change. Housed within the Department of Women and Gender Studies, the DVPS program provides experiential exposure to the range of careers in IPV prevention and survivor advocacy while focusing on the needs of local IPV survivors and learning from the community organizations that serve them. This program is the only IPV advocacy training program currently available to undergraduates in the US.

The DVPS program offers a competitive major-based concentration with a funded field experience component. It is interdisciplinary in nature and draws its seven core faculty from Women and Gender Studies, Criminal Justice, Sociology, Human Development and Family Sciences, and Communications. While the contributing faculty all represent their disciplinary orientations, only Women and Gender Studies majors are eligible to apply to the concentration. Embedding advocacy coursework along with foundational courses in the Women and Gender studies curriculum ensures that the examination of gender-based violence and interventions is structured by feminist praxis and analysis.

Community partnerships are the foundation of the DVPS program. The program was developed and implemented through a collaboration between the Delaware Coalition Against Domestic Violence (DCADV) and Women and Gender Studies at the University of Delaware in 2011. Based on shared commitments to sustain the feminist origins of the movement, it cultivates continued growth and engagement with more inclusive and evolving feminist principles. Central among our shared values is the advocate/academic collaboration. This is evidenced through mutual commitments that include connecting direct service and advocacy work with scholarship on violence against women, serving survivors of IPV, supporting a knowledgeable and highly skilled community of advocates, fostering collaboration between the university and domestic violence (DV) agencies, and providing students with field experiences to complement coursework (Naccarelli and Post 2014). These shared commitments have epistemological value, balancing different types of knowledge evolving from practitioners, academics, and students.

From the program's conception, the extensive knowledge and skills of advocates and the experiences of survivors informed the curriculum. The course content and curriculum were developed and are revised in coordination with the DCADV's training criteria for becoming a certified Domestic Violence Specialist in the state of Delaware. The specific training areas required by the DCADV Domestic Violence Specialist designation are distributed across the required courses in the concentration. Students graduate with all of the topical requirements satisfied and are therefore advanced in their progression toward state certification. Course content also relies upon the expertise of the contributing faculty. Core faculty in the program periodically meet with representatives from the DCADV to discuss content revisions and the requirements of the program demonstrating the value of their mutually transformative relationship. This ensures integration of best practices for advocates and their organizations, attention to the needs of survivors, and inclusion of current academic research.

One technique to formalize and make visible the value of this collaboration to university constituents is to annually offer a required course taught by the Executive Director of the DCADV. This entails an institutional commitment on the parts of both the department and the coalition. The department financially supports the course and generates enrollment beyond the scope of DVPS program students, concurrently bringing new students into the program through exposure to courses. The DCADV designs the content and provides instruction and mentoring to university students.

Student feedback indicates the pedagogical power of community professionals as instructors, inspiring students through first-hand stories of advocacy. In this course they are motivated to distinguish themselves as young professionals building their public identity. Students take advantage of guest speakers organized by the DCADV to identify agencies with which they would like to work. The community advocates who address the class gain an entry point to serve as future mentors to students pursuing their required practicum experiences and certification. Ideally, this course comes before students' field experiences and facilitates their entry into the state's DV services.

Another central feature sustaining and formalizing relationships between the university and community partners is the paid three-hundred-hour direct service practicum available to students accepted into the concentration. With the practicum, students extend their exposure to state advocates beyond the DCADV and begin a minimum six-month relationship with a service provider. This experience begins the summer prior to graduation once students have significantly progressed through both their Women and Gender Studies curriculum and the DVPS program coursework.

Students report that the coursework/practicum combination validates the benefits of both. A student completing the practicum reports, "this placement really puts into perspective everything that is taught in our Women and Gender Studies courses on campus. I got to take what I learned in class and apply it to what I experienced everyday [sic] while working with the victims. I realized that the materials covered in class provide accurate information about the . . . victims." Curricular preparation also exposes students to the range of skills they will utilize in advocacy settings. Another student reflected on the practicum explaining, "Everyday [sic] was a different way to involve myself in firsthand learning experiences . . . students who will take this placement after me will truly apply all the things they have learned from our DV classes."

The DVPS program partners annually with six to ten agencies throughout the state. Qualifying partner agencies grant students the opportunity to directly assist survivors, perpetrators, children, and other family members with matters specifically related to their IPV experience as the first step toward careers in IPV advocacy. This decision requires exposure to the actual work. A graduate shares that direct service practice enables students to "truly get down and dirty and . . . [be] able to work with clients and do a lot of what the supervisors do."

After this experience students are able to make informed decisions about the aspects of IPV services and systems that interest them for job searches and graduate education. More importantly they can evaluate if they have the capacity to commit to a career that continually exposes them to the trauma of others. Often this solidifies students' decisions to enter this work. One student explained, "I think the best part about my practicum experience was definitely getting hands on experience in this field. I truly felt like I made a difference for many of these victims, and helping them really affirmed that this is what I want to do with my life." In this way the program may generate stability in an industry struggling with high turnover and advocate burnout. It also supports agencies by providing staff with specialized training who can better respond to survivor/victims' needs. On average, by the time of their graduation, each concentration student works for five hundred hours with survivors and their families. Annually, DVPS program students deliver more than thirty-two hundred hours of work to survivors and agencies across the state. It is important to note the university and the department financially support the practicum through grants, endowments, and the annual budget. This is a critical step to ensure that students from all socio-economic levels can afford to pursue this work as undergraduates. A funded program can generate a diverse future workforce in the field. Student funding also addresses feminist critiques of service learning projects and institution building that use unpaid labor (see Bojar 2000).

Compensation for labor also generates both accountability and self-efficacy among student participants. On completing the practicum experience, one student summarized with pride, "After my initial training I almost felt like this was an actual job, having my own clients and caseload, etc. This internship gives an opportunity to see what doing this work is really like." Another student confirms this source of motivation, "The best parts of my practicum are when clients tell me they had no idea I was an intern . . ." Students are not volunteers operating from a position of benevolent abundance but are professional advocates in training.

Students in the program also provide a crucial connection to sustain and develop advocate/academic partnerships. They often function as the best liaisons to strengthen and deepen relationships with community partners and ensure that the scholarship and training acquired in coursework matches the real needs of advocates and survivors. Students enter the field equipped with theories and knowledge of best practices, informed by their mentors, their classwork, and their fieldwork. Students are thus uniquely situated to recognize why the ideal often is quite distant from actual practice. One student reflected upon that dissonance, "[t]his placement requires students to interact with victims one-on-one and learn the best ways to discuss difficult topics with them. It's one thing to learn these methods in a classroom, but it is completely different when you are thrown into a real-life situation."

Returning to a classroom with ample space for reflection and processing, students share their experiences with one another and the faculty. Using this model, similar programs can be replicated at other institutions interested in fostering undergraduate education that facilitates social justice, transformation, and community collaboration.

Feminism in the Field

Another central shared commitment between the DCADV and Women and Gender Studies is a focus on sustaining and cultivating the feminist origins and new priorities of the movement against IPV. Students are eager to apply new strategies for client care, self-care, and a feminist orientation particularly in tune with a power analysis of institutions and a deep understanding of intersectionality, to the advocacy agencies that employ them.

During the summer of 2016, under the leadership of the DCADV, a student conducted ten in-depth interviews with DVPS program graduates as part of the DCADV's DELTA FOCUS project that sought to understand the students' experiences transitioning into the workforce.[2] The ten students interviewed were asked about their academic background and interests, motivations for joining the program, experiences within the program, professional experiences post-graduation, and understanding of the state of the field in Delaware. In these interviews and through the practicum exit evaluations many report that their undergraduate training provided them with unique skills and preparation compared with other new professionals in the workforce.

The concepts of gender norms, structural inequality, and intersectionality are carried from the classroom to the field. Students explain that they approached their work "grounded in a feminist framework" and that they understood how "gender inequality and norms play into DV."[3] Furthermore they recognize how their academic understanding of intersectionality prepared them for navigating the complexities of the field. Graduates felt prepared "to incorporate that [intersectional] understanding to recognize/validate how various identities shape victims' experiences."[4] They also understand how their own identities shape their interactions with clients, agencies, and systems.

Although students in the social sciences are exposed to the concept of intersectionality in their coursework, they often lack the personal experience to recognize how it shapes the realities of their own lives and the lives of others. The exposure to academic concepts combined with the lived experience of the practicum generate a deep understanding of how experiences of trauma are exacerbated by social locations such as race, class, ability, sexuality, and gender identity. A student explains, "The best part was that I worked with a diverse population and was able to develop my abilities with various populations." Students witness how social locations determine access to resources and treatment within criminal justice and social service systems.

Many graduates of the program communicate their desire to seek employment with agencies that are structured by feminist values and analysis. They note mixed feelings about leaving "the feminist bubble of the concentration."[5] Students recognize that some organizations are informed by feminist principles while many others are not. Upon graduation they actively seek ways to sustain the feminist community that surrounded them during their undergraduate experiences, even if their current agency is not informed by feminist practices.

The value of reflexivity in the context of a supportive community is a commonly expressed theme among both participants and graduates. In the words of one graduate, "I think there can never be enough opportunities to reflect, and I liked having friends in the practicum to talk with as well. These discussions helped me to relate to other victim service interns and voice our often shared concerns about the system in which we were working." Graduates from the program recommend sustained relationships with fellow concentration students after graduation to retain a feminist community of colleagues[6] Practicum supervisors understand their guidance as a means to generate social change and honor their personal commitments to feminism. Through intergenerational mentoring they pass on not only institutional memory and advocacy techniques, but also workplace navigation skills. One mentor teaches students to pay close attention to power differentials: "as a supervisor, it is essential to hear from all levels of staff and to design discussions and decision making . . . inclusive of all perspectives. Being aware of one's own power is essential to doing so."[7] Another mentor writes of the importance of young professionals observing women in leadership positions: "Feminism is evident in my leadership style by being an example of a strong female with many different roles within the organization— including mentoring younger staff and interns."[8] This supervisor clarifies that this is especially important within male-dominated systems such as criminal justice institutions.

Students value mentors who provide models for their developing professional identities. One student articulates how her relationship with her supervisor was critically important, "[e]specially as someone who worked in such a hypermasculine system, it was really important for me to have a space to discuss everything. I think for me, what helped the most though was being able to sit down and talk to my supervisor. Being able to . . . discuss how I am feeling about what I am doing with someone who has worked in the field for years was so valuable."

Although sometimes discouraged by the state of the systems within which they work, students ultimately leave their practicum feeling that they are agents of social change. Their experiences and training are powerful sources of motivation and self-efficacy. One writes, "It was disheartening to see the system fail so many victims, but it also made me realize that I want to help change that in the future." Another student supports these sentiments explaining, "I feel like I am [a] stronger advocate for victims and systems. I have a deeper understanding about policy changes that need to be made to improve the criminal justice system."

When coupled with intensive experience in a supportive environment, with space for reflection and articulation, the inspiration to act becomes real. Students need academic study of theory and concepts, exposure to diverse models for change, real-life engagement with individuals and communities touched by violence, and the formalized spaces (within the community and the classroom) to engage in self-reflection and articulate experiences. This balance of priorities cultivates graduates who engage in this work, "with a level head but not with a cold heart." Advocacy training within a Women and Gender Studies curriculum structures the journey from inspiration to action and trains a new generation of graduates committed to the work of social change.

ACKNOWLEDGMENTS

We remain grateful for the expertise, feedback, and collaborative spirit of the Delaware Coalition Against Domestic Violence and all of our community partners. We would also like to thank the Department of Women and Gender Studies and the College of Arts and Sciences for their ongoing encouragement and institutional support. The launch of this program and its growth is made possible by financial support from the Verizon Foundation.

NOTES

1   We use both DV and IPV interchangeability in this chapter to reflect historical linguistic choices as well as contemporary ones (e.g., courts and most state coalitions tend to use DV while many practitioners and academics tend to use IPV).

2   DELTA FOCUS, Domestic Violence Prevention Enhancements and Leadership Through Alliances, Focusing on Outcomes for Communities United with States is a program funded by the CDC emphasizing the primary prevention of IPV.

3   DCADV, Summary, 2.

4   Ibid.

5   DCADV, Summary, 3.

6   Delaware Coalition Against Domestic Violence, DVPS Graduate Interviews: Theme Coding Worksheet, Summer 2016, 4.

7   Supervisor Survey, 2017, #1.

8   Supervisor Survey, 2017, #2.

29

Preventing Gender Violence, Transforming Human Relations

A Case for Coeducation

IRENE COMINS MINGOL

The gender perspective is a decisive force in contemporary approaches to peace studies.[1] The incorporation of the gender perspective into this field in the 1980s was a clear milestone in the development of peace studies (Martínez Guzmán 2001, 67), since then it has become one of the discipline's fundamental, integral, and transversal components. There are two broad lines of inquiry within the gender approach in peace studies (Comins Mingol 2009, 457). On the one hand, the *critical perspective* sheds light on the types of direct, structural, and cultural violence women are subjected to, and analyzes and challenges their situation of subordination and the denial of their rights. On the other hand, the *constructive perspective* seeks to recognize women's legacy as peacebuilders and proposes new, more flexible and peaceful ways of being female and male.

Both these lines of inquiry are not only fundamental but also interdependent and interact to develop mutually. If we restrict ourselves to the critical perspective, we risk falling into a victimizing and reductionist view of women's experience that not only conceals the important role women play as peacebuilders but also helps to normalize the notion of women as victims. Through these two processes—the first critical and the second constructive—gender becomes an essential factor in defining a culture for peace in which we can rebuild new, more flexible and less violent ways of being female and male.

This chapter focuses on the constructive perspective, on analyzing women's legacy in peace building, and on how we might incorporate this legacy into education. This will be done not only as a historical record recognizing women's contributions but particularly to integrate the values of peace that have been assigned and developed exclusively by women, to become, through coeducation, human values and not merely gender values.

Women and Peace: Reasons for the Connection

Although not all women are peaceful nor all men violent, it is nonetheless true that there are important gender differences in their use of violence. Indeed, it is striking that most violent acts—those involving direct violence—are perpetrated by men, and that men are also more sensitive than women to those environmental factors that have an important influence on antisocial behavior (Fisas 1998, 8). Several reasons have been put forward to explain the link between women and peace, which I now summarize in four broad categories, listed from the lowest level of explanatory capacity and consensus to the highest.

(1) For some authors, biological differences between the sexes are the main reason why men are more aggressive and women more peaceful. These contentions have been strongly criticized by feminist authors, who refute such biological determinism. They defend their arguments with numerous historical data on women's direct or indirect participation in armed organizations and violent acts, or in men's participation in the peace movement and other social movements for peace. It can therefore be clearly stated that women are *naturally* no more peaceful than men, nor are men *naturally* no more peaceful than women. Only the women and men who want to be peaceful and behave accordingly can be described as such.

(2) The second line of reasoning is based on women's exclusion from power and the military in particular. Women's historical exclusion from the armed forces has allowed them to accumulate and nurture feelings, experiences, and social skills that differ from those acquired through military training. Moreover, because women have been considered as *outsiders* to military operations and wars, in many countries they have more opportunities and freedom to engage in endeavors to promote peace, encourage dialogue and peaceful coexistence between women from communities in conflict, and propose innovative solutions to armed hostilities.

(3) The third explanation contends that the link between women and peace has to do with women's experience of subordination and oppression. The institutionalized dependence of women on men for protection against male aggression, and for employment, promotion, and validation, has given women a motive to seek male approval. According to Claudia Card, the reason why women are more relational and have a greater capacity for empathy and peace can be found in their subordinate situation. Card argues that women tend to establish a network of relationships as a buffer against violence in intimate relations, and that men do not build these networks because they have no need to do so (Card 1995, 81–83).

(4) The fourth argument is grounded in the historical socialization of women in caring and life-sustaining tasks. The practice of caring implicitly entails the development of certain capabilities and skills such as empathy, responsibility, patience, tenderness, and commitment, all of which are fundamental elements in a culture of peace. Thus, we are formed by what we do, and this historical caring role attributed to women in both the private (caring for children, older people, the sick, looking after the home, etc.) and the public spheres (as nurses, teachers, etc.) has developed certain skills for peace in women that we could share with all human beings if such caring tasks were shared with men.

In this chapter I focus on this latter perspective, since it has the most solid grounding and support in the relevant literature. The analysis of women's roles in peacebuilding does not revolve around essentialist principles but rather is based on the recognition of the influences that women's historical socialization as carers have had on the development of certain moral concerns and abilities. As Elise Boulding states (2000, 109), women's knowledge and their worlds of experience has equipped them to function creatively as workers for peace in ways that men's knowledge and experience have not prepared them for. Needless to say, this can change. If men and women shared their worlds of experience more with one another, human development would take a major step forward.

Care Ethics: Context and Antecedents

In her work *In a Different Voice*, published in 1982, Carol Gilligan first spelled out the different moral capacity women have developed through their socialization and the practice of caring. Until then, the theory of moral development had adhered unwaveringly to the theory put forward by Gilligan's teacher and mentor, Lawrence Kohlberg. Gilligan attempted to expand Kohlberg's moral theory to include an analysis of women's moral experiences, as Kohlberg's theory was based on a study of eighty-four boys over a period of more than twenty years (Gilligan 1982, 40).

Among the anomalies Gilligan detected in Kohlberg's moral development scale was the persistently low score women obtained compared to their male peers (Benhabib 1990, 120). This anomaly was due to the fact that although moral development theory was based only on the study of male experience, its universality was assumed when applied to both women and men. In her analysis of women, Gilligan detected a different, more relational moral voice, which prioritized the preservation of interpersonal relationships, in contrast to the *justice ethics* of Kohlberg's moral development theory, in which obeying universal moral standards was most highly valued (Lynch 2016, 10). This difference in women's moral perspective is due to the sexual division of labor and the sharp divide between the public and the private spheres. Hence, men and women develop two different moral perspectives that align with this unequal allocation of responsibilities: *care ethics* versus *justice ethics*.

How Care Ethics Contributes to Peace

The thinking behind caring and its practice involves the development of moral values, skills and competences such as empathy, patience, perseverance, responsibility, commitment, mentoring, listening, and tenderness. All these values are important in building a culture of peace. As Betty Reardon points out, "for above all a culture of peace would be a culture of caring" (2001, 85). As well as these moral values, the practice of caring helps to develop three groups of skills that are crucial in constructing a culture for peace: skills for developing and sustaining lives; skills for the peaceful transformation of conflicts; and civic and social commitment skills.

Skills for developing and sustaining lives. Care and attention tasks are necessary to meet every individual's basic needs; they are essential for survival and well-being. Human development is nourished not only by higher incomes and a clean environment but also by care. The tasks of caring and attending to others are the way we maximize the resources available to satisfy our basic needs, and in themselves they supply the need for affection and emotional support that all human beings have.

Skills for the peaceful transformation of conflicts. In her work *Maternal Thinking: Towards a Politics of Peace* (1989), Sara Ruddick explains how caring for children develops women's techniques for the peaceful transformation of conflicts. Above and beyond caring for children, or *maternal thinking*, socialization in the value of caring generally develops peaceful techniques for transforming conflict, of which three contributions are worthy of mention (Comins Mingol 2014).

First, in response to conflict, the thinking behind care ethics is that no one should emerge as the loser; rather all parties should emerge satisfied in one way or another, in such a way that interpersonal relationships are not broken. Second, it is also important to listen to as many voices as possible. Sensitivity to others' needs and taking responsibility for their care is what enables women to listen to different voices than their own and include different points of view in their judgments. Thus, Carol Gilligan's work shows how the apparent diffusion and confusion of women's judgment is an example of women's strength and moral responsibility (Gilligan 1982, 38). Finally, in situations of conflict, satisfying needs takes precedence over meting out punishment (Gay 2016). By contrast, although justice ethics theorists take satisfaction of needs into account and recognize its importance, their focus lies in punishing and regulating aggression.

Civic and social commitment skills. In turn, socialization and the practice of caring develop women's commitment to the welfare of society as a whole, not just that of their immediate families. This explains their higher presence in social and volunteer movements, and their participation in informal politics in its many forms. Specifically, in the 1990s and the first years of this century, women's movements and initiatives for peace have proliferated in response to the escalation of horrific wars during that period; women have been closely involved in peace processes and postwar reconstruction programs, both in countries immersed in armed conflicts and in those that, in recent decades, have not directly been through wars (Magallón Portolés 2006). Of particular note are the women's movements for peace in the Middle East (Women in Black in Israel, Women against Occupation, and Bat Shalom Jerusalem Women's Action Center, etc.), and women's actions in the countries of the former Yugoslavia (women's groups against the wars in Croatia, Slovenia, Kosovo, and Bosnia and Herzegovina; Women in Black in Belgrade), and in Latin America (Colombian Women's Peaceful Route, Women in Black Movement, and the Mothers and Grandmothers of the Plaza de Mayo in Argentina, etc.).

For all these reasons, caring can be understood as a fundamental source of the values of peace, which we must nourish and sustain among all human beings. It is our duty to reconstruct this universal heritage of a culture of peace in a nongendered way.

A Feminist Care Ethics

In light of the contributions of the practice of care to peace building, we can vindicate the importance of first reconstructing, and then generalizing, this value as a human value and not simply a gender value. I now explore two facets of the reconstruction of the value of care.

First, the value of care has fallen into disuse among younger generations. Globalization, our model of development, and the logic of competitiveness prevailing in our neoliberal societies constrain solid caring relationships among people. What Leonardo Boff refers to as the "dictatorship of the way-of-being through work" (2008, 66) has led to the instrumentalization of human relationships and nature. In response to the logic of domination and economic accumulation, there is a need to promote the alternative logic of the sustainability of life, a logic that is constructed on the relational foundations of caring. We must leave behind a culture of domination and enter a culture of care.

Second, I refer to *reconstructing* the value of care because not everything about the practice of care is positive. We must find a point where care ethics and justice ethics can cooperate (Held 2006), since the decisions about who cares and for what, how much, and how also involve criteria of justice. It is therefore important to clarify that care ethics is a feminist ethics. Care ethics has sometimes been labeled as conservative by those who think, for example, that it reinforces the traditional roles of women as carers. However, the view that care ethics legitimizes the traditional subordination of women is seriously mistaken (Richards 2013). What could be more revolutionary than dismantling the patriarchal gender hierarchy to reveal the most basic ways of how we think we should live and what we should do? Care ethics appeals to the transformation of society, politics, laws, economic activity, the family and personal relationships beyond patriarchal assumptions. According to Gilligan, "Our exploration has led us to see the ethic of care, grounded in voice and relationship, as an ethic of resistance both to injustice and to self-silencing. It is a human ethic, integral to the practice of democracy and to the functioning of a global society. More controversially, it is a feminist ethic, an ethic that guides the historic struggle to free democracy from patriarchy" (2013, 175).

It is because of the existing social structures that caring work, in homes and institutions, is largely done by women and is unrecognized, and either unpaid or badly paid. Giving care work its due value would subvert this hierarchy that ensures caring remains in a marginal and exploited position (Mahon and Robinson 2011).

The feminist revolution will be domestic or it will not be. In today's society, the veil of formal equality hides what is still an anachronistic reality. Although considerable formal and legal progress has been made in the public sphere, no parallel advancement has taken place in the private sphere, at the heart of which sexist gender relationships continue to predominate alongside the unequal distribution of care work. We must escape from the perverse accommodations in which the patriarchal system has socialized us, both as woman-carer-submissives who take on other people's tasks, and as man-dependent-dominators who leave their life-maintenance tasks to other people (women). Unlearning this sexist model would broaden the horizons of self-realization, freedom, and equity that we have as people, and would help us to design a fairer, more peaceful and rewarding future.

We cannot refer to gender violence without speaking about the unequal distribution of care tasks. Patriarchal men frequently feel their masculinity is under threat when women subvert these roles, and may react violently. "Violence erupts especially when power is threatened or in danger of losing its hold" (Held 2010, 120). Violence thus becomes an instrument of power and is a strategy to ensure domestic work continues to be done by women.

Therefore, "primary transformation must come in the lifestyle of men" (Hathaway and Boff 2014, 117). To radically transform this misogynist culture, men must do more than merely "not harass." The opposite of a male culture of violence is a male culture of care. We must appeal for masculinities to include care for oneself and others, and recognize that the needs for attachment are healthy and normal and not "feminine." Degendering care and generalizing it as a human value will liberate all of us, men and women. As Bourdieu tells us,

> Male privilege is also a trap, and it has its negative side in the permanent tension and contention, sometimes verging on the absurd, imposed on every man by the duty to assert his manliness in all circumstances. [. . .] *Manliness*, understood as sexual or social reproductive capacity, but also as the capacity to fight and exercise violence (especially in acts of revenge), is first and foremost a *duty*. (2001, 50–51)

Coeducation in Care

It is therefore a pressing matter to reconstruct and recognize the true value of care for two fundamental reasons. First, because the unequal distribution of care as a value and occupation defined by gender causes injustices and unhappiness and demands the reconstruction of nongendered care. And second, because care is a source of values of peace. Coeducation refers to the importance of educating to eradicate the gender hierarchy between men and women, and to prevent the reproduction of sexist gender roles that continue to do so much harm to individual and social well-being.[2] The coeducational approach is relatively recent and aims to take a further step in educational reform for equality of opportunities between men and women.

What can we do to help universalize the value of care as a human value? Several approaches can be taken, through the mass media, education, or public policies, for example. In this chapter, we look at education because in order to learn to care we must *depatriarchalize* education; care must be included in the educational curriculum. "For all to learn to care, caring needs to be included in education, and certainly must be a major practice in education for a culture of peace in a gender perspective" (Reardon 2001, 85).

Feminism has helped to renew the educational agenda by taking into account the social construction of gender roles and the importance of coeducation as one of the mainstays of all education for peace (Moolakkattu 2006). Education must bring about a change in the gender role patterns instilled in boys and girls (Burguieres 1990). Masculine aggression is the result of specific types of socialization. In most societies boys are raised and educated to be aggressively competitive; they are given toy weapons and soldiers to play with, and are initiated into competitive games. In contrast, the majority of societies raise girls to be compassionate, obedient, and cooperative, and girls are expected to play with dolls or noncompetitive games. However, from infancy people should be raised and learn to care, share, and relate to other people and nature on an equal footing. These qualities, to a certain point, are found in girls because of the socialization they receive, but this should also be extended to boys.

Coeducation is important in creating a more peaceful, less violent culture. Several anthropological studies have shown that societies that have more equal gender roles are also more peaceful (Mead 2001). According to some authors, domestic violence against women is a means used by abusers to reproduce a dichotomous gender model, according to which aggression and violent action is a symbol of masculine identity (Anderson and Umberson 2001, 358–80). Coeducation would be the last step in the evolution from explicit education in a sexual role in the segregated school, to what appears to be equal education for all, but still implicitly reproduces the traditional sexual roles in the mixed school, and finally to the coeducational proposal that is explicitly and implicitly committed to eliminating gender hierarchies.

The foundations of the educational system in the West as we know it today were laid in Europe at the beginning of the eighteenth century (Subirats Martori 1994, 50). According to the predominant educational principles of that time, God created men and women to take on different social responsibilities, and their education should therefore reflect this difference accordingly. On this basis, the *segregated school* emerged and was the general norm for more than two hundred years.

Segregated schools had three notable characteristics: (1) the physical separation of boys and girls, (2) a different curriculum for girl and boy pupils, and (3) higher education accessible only to men. Through a differentiated curriculum, what girls learned at school was what society had typified as a culture belonging to women, and the same happened with boys' and men's culture. Girls learned skills related to the domestic environment and private life, while boys learned the skills necessary to perform successfully in the public sphere (Comins Mingol 2009, 463).

For many years segregated schools were deeply rooted in educational systems. At the end of the nineteenth century the first voices were heard advocating that women should receive a more robust school education, equivalent to that of men (Subirats Martori 1994, 62). Women's rights to midlevel and higher education were promoted, together with the desirability of educating girls and boys in the same institutions. However, the outcomes of these proposals varied from one country to another. In the US and some Protestant countries in the north of Europe such as Norway, Sweden, and Finland, mixed schooling had already been introduced in the nineteenth century. By contrast, in most Catholic European countries like Spain, Italy, France, or Portugal, there was a fierce opposition to introducing mixed schools and as a result they were only brought in on a very limited scale (Subirats Martori 1994, 52). In Spain, for example, mixed schools were recognized under the General Education Law of 1970; however, it was not until 1984 that single-sex education was explicitly forbidden (Cabaleiro Manzanedo 2005, 21).

With the generalization of mixed schools, it seemed that equality of opportunities had been achieved in the educational context. Several years would go by before this presumed neutrality and equality of the mixed school education system was called into question. Gradually it became clear that sexism had not disappeared with the introduction of the mixed school; rather, while sexism in segregated schools was explicit, in mixed schools it had taken on subtler, less obvious forms that were therefore more difficult to detect and eradicate. Other covert forms of discrimination persist under the veneer of formal equality, as several studies have brought into light. Sexism is transmitted through what has come to be known as the *hidden curriculum*, which is most obvious in textbooks and the differences in classroom interactions between teachers, and their boy and girl pupils.

By bringing together girls and boys in the same class, mixed schools did not consider the need to also combine traditionally masculine knowledge and experience, and traditionally feminine knowledge and experience so that the best of the two could be learned in conjunction with each other. Instead, traditionally masculine knowledge and experience was institutionalized as the only knowledge. The mixed school interpreted equality of opportunities as the predominance of one single way of seeing the world by attempting to eliminate differences through the suppression of female culture. In the best cases, equality means equality of access for women to traditionally male activities, although this is only a one-way process: men are not given access to traditionally female tasks (Ballarín Domingo 2001, 152). The prevailing model in schools is a masculine model that excludes everything that might be considered women's cultural heritage.

Thus, for example, caring is not included as a human value in the official curriculum, although it is transmitted through the hidden curriculum as a gender trait. The hidden curriculum may be defined as an unintentional but real way of transmitting gender stereotypes in the school. The manipulation of images in school textbooks is one of the most powerful ways in which this hidden, biased education in care is manifested. This also takes place, of course, through the written word. Phrases like *Mum looks after me*, *Mum cooks*, *the girl sets the table*, *Dad works*, or *Dad reads the newspaper* are just a few examples.

In recent years considerable effort has gone into revising and correcting textbooks to prevent such biased transmission, but much still remains to be done. School interaction is another way the hidden curriculum is revealed. School interaction consists of various aspects, including teachers' expectations of the way boys and girls should act. The expectation that girls will be more helpful and demonstrate more prosocial behaviors reinforces this attitude in them. This expectation, however, is grounded on social prejudice, since both boys and girls are capable of caring attitudes and showing responsibility for others. In addition, these expectations deny boys and young men the opportunity to express their caring side, since caring is considered to be a value that threatens their masculinity. The coeducational project sets out to create spaces where boys and young men can express and practice caring with complete freedom.

Human beings are born with pregendered capabilities for empathy, emotions and caring, which begs the crucial question, according to Carol Gilligan: How do we lose the capacity to care? What inhibits our ability to empathize with others?

In a study on masculinity and the school, Blye Frank held interviews with boys and young men in which they talked about the process of how men are formed. Their responses revealed how the construction of the masculine mystique entailed eliminating values of affection and caring for others. One example is that of a young man who said he did not tell his friends about his hobby of looking after plants, his interest in cooking, and his wish to be a nurse (Frank 1996). These are revealing illustrations of the cultural violence against boys and men caused by disassociating them from the sphere of care. Gilligan refers to this phenomenon as *moral injury*, which occurs with a "shattering of trust that compromises our ability to love" (Gilligan 2014, 90).

In adolescence identity construction is reinforced in two ways, in the manner in which intimacy and vulnerability have a feminine gender, while manliness implies emotional stoicism and independence (Gilligan 2014, 94). In *When Boys Become Boys* Judy Chu identifies this process at even younger ages, in the way boys, who at the age of four and five were attentive, authentic, and direct in their relationships with one another, enter a process of separation and inauthenticity. According to Chu, the boys had not lost their relational capabilities, but their socialization toward the cultural construction of masculinity, defined as the opposite of femininity, appears to force a division between what they know and what they show (Chu 2014). In the voices of adolescents, we hear signs of *moral injury*, at the time when they are forced, by virtue of the masculine mystique, to betray what until that moment they considered the right way to be—intimate, expressing affection, and sensitive; a betrayal that is sanctioned as appropriate in the eyes of the world.

In the history of Western thought, we find symbolic, and extreme, stories of this betrayal of affection and intimacy, such as Agamemnon sacrificing his daughter Iphigenia, or Abraham preparing to sacrifice Isaac, among many others. These are actions in which the intimate bond of filial trust is betrayed in the name of a superior ideal, actions that are culturally lauded and rewarded with honor. As a life-centered ethics, care ethics can help us to resignify the concept of the human being, beyond any binary or dichotomous view between genders, and to break violent identity constructions.

Care needs to be included in the school curriculum, not as a gender trait but as a human value. Care must form part of the knowledge included in the curriculum. In general, the knowledge transmitted through the education system is clearly androcentric. This system only includes the knowledge traditionally attributed to men, while ignoring the contributions from experiences traditionally attributed to women. These absences are a grave mutilation of the history of humanity and a serious lacuna in scientific discourse. We must include care as an explicit part of the curriculum both for boys and girls as a means of recovering a human competence for peace.

As well as leaving out many of women's experiences and their contributions to culture, the knowledge hierarchy in the school curriculum is also androcentric. Subjects such as mathematics, physics, and chemistry are judged important and crucial for adult life, whereas learning to care for a newborn baby, prepare a meal, or attend to daily needs are not regarded as essential; indeed, the reasoning goes, these tasks do not require knowledge the school should be responsible for, because they are not considered as fundamental knowledge. The standardization of curricula for boys and girls has led to the loss of learning about knowledge and activities that, because they were previously exclusive to girls' education, have been devalued to the point that they are now completely absent from the mixed school curriculum.

Eliminating sexism from education and constructing the coeducational school therefore requires that boys and girls be given equal attention and treatment; in addition, however, it also requires the reconstruction of the system of values and attitudes transmitted, and a rethinking of educational content. In sum, it requires rebuilding culture, reincorporating guidelines and viewpoints traditionally created by women, and making them available to boys and girls, without distinction (Comins Mingol 2009). "What should be taught in the new college? [. . .] Not the arts of dominating other people; not the arts of ruling, of killing, of acquiring land and capital. [. . .] It should teach the arts of human intercourse" (Woolf 1999, 61).

Nel Noddings (2002) was one of the first authors to propose reorganizing the school curriculum to include the full scope of caring: caring for oneself, caring for those closest to us, caring for the community, caring for foreigners, caring for humanity, and caring for nature. The scant importance the curriculum gives to the diversity and wealth of knowledge humanity has accumulated in the private sphere mutilates the body of social and historically created knowledge. We must bring into the curriculum the value of caring, which although socially and historically attributed to women, can and must, be turned into a human value in which all of us should be educated. As Betty Reardon tells us, "Equality between men and women is an essential condition of a culture of peace. Thus, education for gender equality is an essential component of education for a culture of peace." (Reardon 2001, 21).

Conclusions

The objectives and advantages of egalitarian coeducation in care can be classified in five groups; these objectives synergistically interlink the *critical* and *constructive perspectives* in gender and peace studies described at the beginning of this chapter:

1. The first objective is that care tasks be shared between men and women, thereby achieving fairer levels of distribution of work and time, and ending phenomena such as the double workload and glass ceiling for women. Both instrumental care tasks (domestic, such as washing up, cooking, cleaning, or shopping) and caring for others (looking after children, people who are ill, old or dependent) must be shared.

2. Second, men must be able to enjoy and be enriched by a world of emotions, by intimate and private life, an aspect also being demanded by the new masculinity movements. This would allow men to be free of the burden of manliness, of this *moral injury* that prevents them from recognizing and attending to their needs for attachment. It is important that we are aware of the way in which men are also victims of the patriarchal system.

3. Third, coeducation in care would give men more personal autonomy, training them in the self-care skills that women develop throughout their lives and that better prepare them to cope with separation or loneliness. The feeling of dependence the man-dependent-dominator experiences with regard to the care tasks done by women is one of the seeds of domestic violence, a violence that is strategic in ensuring that domestic work continues to be done by women.

4. Fourth, the socialization and practice of care implies educating in values of peace as an alternative to socialization in aggression, thus shattering the masculine mystique. The practice of care develops skills such as tenderness, empathy, patience, commitment, and the peaceful transformation of conflict.

5. Finally, such changes could have consequences for saving our planet. We need a new ethic that encourages us to venerate life, to take care of it, and to respect it (Comins Mingol 2016). As the international declaration of the Earth Charter states, "The choice is ours: form a global partnership to care for Earth and one another, or risk the destruction of ourselves and the diversity of life." We must promote that all human beings participate in a meaningful way in activities that promote the support and care of life. That change will heal the Earth and us with it.

In sum, the way forward is to construct new ways of being female and male that are fairer and freer, more rewarding and peaceful for everyone—to educate for peace through coeducation in the values of care.

NOTES

1 This research was supported by the Spanish Ministry of Economy and Competitiveness [grant number FEM2015–65834-C2–2-P "La resignificación de la mujer-víctima en la cultura popular: implicaciones para la innovación representacional en la construcción de la vulnerabilidad y la resistencia"], and the University Jaume I [grant number P1·1B2015–21 "Testimonio ético y comunicación para el cambio: análisis de modos de re-significación de la figura de la víctima y de re-situación de los agentes sociales"].

2 The term is used differently in Europe and the US. In the US, mixed-gender education and coeducation are synonymous, both referring to the education of males and females in the same school. In Europe, mixed-gender education and coeducation have different meanings. While mixed-gender education refers to space, and the need to mix boys and girls in the same classrooms, coeducation refers also to contents, and the need to mix and share in the curricula contents traditionally attributed to each gender without distinction. Coeducation, in this sense, will mean a step forward toward the elimination of gender hierarchy.

30

Queer Organizing, Racial Justice, and the Reframing of Intimate Partner Violence

ELIZABETH B. ERBAUGH

Decades of queer and trans[1] activism and research have made clear that intimate partner violence cuts across gender and sexual identities, communities, and relationship types. A gradual willingness to acknowledge queerness and gender fluidity, and to ask the right questions about the connections among identities, experiences, and behaviors, yields mounting evidence that lesbian, gay, bisexual, queer, and trans (LGBTQ+)[2] youth and adults suffer multiple forms of violence at rates as high or higher than those among straight and cisgender people (Brown and Herman 2015; Kann et al. 2016; National Coalition of Anti-Violence Programs 2017a, 2018). Simultaneously, scholars and activists of color have recognized gains of the feminist antiviolence movement while naming its shortcomings with respect to intersections of gender with race, ethnicity, class, and sexuality. Several exemplary interventions such as these appear within the present volume.

LGBTQ+ and racial justice organizing have borne fruit in new social movements, national and transnational dialogues, and legislative and legal debates. These developments highlight the centrality of race, class, gender, and sexuality to dynamics of power and violence in society, including intimate relationships. It is no coincidence that the founders of #BlackLivesMatter brought years of organizing experience in queer, feminist, antiracist, and anticlassist movements to that historic and transformational social intervention (Garza 2017; Khan-Cullors 2018; Tometi 2018). LGBTQ+ communities and communities of color have called for broad reimaginings of the underlying social forces that manifest in multiple forms of violence. Emergent understandings acknowledge the ways that institutional, structural, cultural, and physical violence especially target people of color—both cis and transgender.

Queer, trans, and racial justice organizing highlight structural patterns in the causes and consequences of violence against queer and trans people, people of color, and immigrant people that demand intersectional interpretation. Recent political events and collective actions across the US make visible the deep racism, imperialism, classism, sexism, homophobia, and transphobia shaping the foundations of the dominant culture and its institutions. In this context, intersectional organizing and analysis provide unmatched insights and resources for interrupting interpersonal and institutional cycles of violence.

As overlapping communities of scholars and activists who are queer, trans, and people of color grow weary from ceaseless efforts to turn the battleship of the feminist antiviolence movement away from neoliberal "law-and-order" and "tough-on-crime" approaches toward intersectional analysis and transformative action, responses from the movement and from the wider society have been mixed (Whittier, this volume). The #MeToo (Burke 2018) and "Time's Up" phenomena of 2017 and 2018 suggest that US-based antiviolence feminism remains focused mainly on men's violence against women in elite, mostly white contexts, while demonstrating some willingness to financially support antiviolence efforts led by women of color and working-class women, "not to mention . . . lesbian, bisexual and transgender women" (timesupnow.com). The feminist antiviolence movement has belatedly begun to acknowledge that it has some catching up to do.

Study of intimate partner violence (IPV) in LGBTQ+ communities has illuminated pitfalls in dominant theoretical and practical approaches to domestic violence. A body of studies, edited volumes, and other written accounts began to emerge three decades ago in public recognition that violence occurs in lesbian and gay relationships (Lobel 1986; Island and Letellier 1991; Renzetti 1992; Renzetti and Miley 1996; Leventhal and Lundy 1999; Kaschak 2001; Ristock 2002; Ristock 2011), that IPV affects trans and intersex people[3] (Courvant 1997; Courvant and Cook-Daniels 1998), and that IPV in LGBTQ+ relationships occurs at rates roughly on par with those in straight relationships (Brown and Herman 2015).

Responses to LGBTQ+ IPV originate both from within queer and trans communities themselves and from organizations in the mainstream feminist antiviolence movement. These responses provide models of expansive approaches to IPV violence as it affects all communities. Drawing upon research and activism addressing LGBQ and trans[2] experiences of IPV, this chapter examines attempts to improve access of LGBTQ+ communities to interventions and services for interrupting and recovering from IPV. This examination reveals the potential of queer, trans, and antiracist community organizing and scholarship to center intersectionality, to expand conceptual frameworks of violence, and to improve practical responses to include a broad range of identities and communities.

Structural Roots of Intimate Partner Violence

Two sets of assumptions underlie dominant approaches to domestic violence with specific consequences for LGBQ and trans communities: first, the structural factors thought to contribute to IPV, and second, the gendered and racialized construction of the categories of "victim" (or "survivor") and "perpetrator."

Feminist movements against domestic violence and sexual assault succeeded in making men's violence against women visible to the research, social service, and criminal justice sectors as a serious social problem with structural and cultural roots. Theories based in the feminist "violence against women" framework (as opposed to the "family violence" framework) focused mainly on the rootedness of gender violence in patriarchal social systems and gender socialization (Kurz 1997).

The feminist framework targeted patriarchal heterosexual gender dynamics with results that were positive in the shorter term but ultimately constraining and potentially counterproductive for the antiviolence movement in the longer term. While it helps to explain some individual men's violence against women, particularly in white, middle-class, and heterosexual contexts[4], the mainstream heteronormative feminist framework does not adequately explain women's violence against women, men's violence against men, or violence involving people whose lives and identities do not neatly fit the gender binary or "the presumed neutrality of whiteness" (Puzan 2003).

Beth Richie (2012, 2015) has explained that the feminist antiviolence movement—including women of color and lesbian and queer women and men—initially adopted an "everywoman" approach. Emphasizing that most domestic violence is committed by men against women, antiviolence feminists historically focused on gender as the main structural arrangement via which abusers exercise power and control over their partners. This analysis marginalized other dimensions of power, domination, privilege, and oppression that contribute to intimate violence (see Collins 2000; Crenshaw 1991).

The "everywoman" approach distilled the numerous and complex structural origins of IPV into a simpler explanation that revolves around gender for reasons that Richie describes as strategic. On the whole, it was not the aim of domestic violence scholars and activists to prevent anyone experiencing violence from accessing resources and support. Rather, the urgent need to cultivate a widespread public commitment to reversing the social crises of male violence and female victimization led to the development of educational campaigns, social services, and criminal justice interventions that were built upon dichotomous conceptualizations of gender and sexuality (Renzetti and Miley 1996).

These campaigns and interventions heightened the visibility of men's violence against women and expanded resources for addressing the problem—at least in its most extreme, end-stage, physical forms. But these resources were directed primarily toward a limited segment of the population whose identities and experiences corresponded to their heteronormative, white orientation (VanNatta 2005). Problematically, the interventions also relied heavily upon criminal justice responses that disproportionately affect communities of color. The neoliberal focus on criminalization has limited the movement's ability to protect people of color and LGBTQ+ communities (Mogul, Ritchie, and Whitlock 2011; Whittier, this volume; Murch 2016).

LGBQ and trans people constitute a diverse range of communities whose members are marginalized based on a number of social factors but who share in common the experience of marginalization based on hierarchies of gender and sexuality. Since this marginalization was replicated in the feminist domestic violence framework, reincorporating queer and trans experiences of violence into the framework would require, at a minimum, revamping its core strategic assumptions.

Structural dynamics beyond patriarchy contribute significantly to IPV across all communities, and identities beyond gender are central to individuals' perspectives and experiences of violence. Intersectional feminisms and critical race theories reintegrated race, ethnicity, and imperialism into the center of analysis. Heterosexism, homophobia, and the gender binary, too, are building blocks in the construction of social hierarchies and are fundamental to LGBTQ+ experiences of cultural and interpersonal violence, both within intimate relationships and in larger social contexts (Butler 2004; Sedgwick 2008). Just as sexism and misogyny are now elemental to common understandings of domestic violence, homophobia and heterosexism must be fully incorporated into these understandings, as must racism, classism, xenophobia, and other systems of domination.

One step in developing a more complete analysis of the structural factors underlying IPV entails understanding the implications of homophobia, heterosexism, and heteronormativity *for both LGBTQ+ and straight relationships*. Homophobia refers to outright antigay hostility; heterosexism and heteronormativity refer to the more insidious, yet potentially more socially potent, centering of heterosexual identities and experiences to the exclusion (or at least the marginalization) of nonheterosexual ones.

Homophobia is likely a factor in heterosexual IPV but certainly plays an important and specific social role in IPV involving LGBTQ+ people. IPV can be conceptualized as occurring within three concentric circles: the intimate relationship, its immediate social circle, and the larger society (Centers for Disease Control and Prevention 2018). For LGBTQ+ people, the immediate social environment generally includes some family members, acquaintances, and coworkers who express homophobic attitudes or who can be expected to respond negatively to the revelation of a nonheterosexual orientation or nonbinary gender identity. A homophobic or transphobic social environment, particularly in one's extended family or work environment, can limit access to social and economic support systems that might otherwise lessen the likelihood of IPV, or offer support when such violence occurs or is threatened (Balsam 2001).

In the larger society, everyday homophobia and racism, including the constant threat and widespread social tolerance of homophobic, transphobic, and racist violence, constitute an ever-present backdrop for queer and trans experiences of IPV. LGBTQ+ life is characterized by frequent encounters with homophobia and threatened or actual violence. Antigay or transphobic violence may be more socially accepted than other forms of violence (Lyons 2006). As a *Will and Grace* reboot kicked off in fall 2017, it was notable that the plotline of an especially campy episode a decade earlier, "Von Trapped," had taken homophobic violence as inevitable. As Megan Mulally's character Karen put it, "you hit a queer with a bottle, they're like, 'Eh—all in a day.'" Later in the episode, when flying objects hit both Sean Hayes and Taye Diggs in the head, each of their characters commented, "Eh—all in a day" (Burrows 2006). This sanitized fictional account reflected social awareness of anti-LGBTQ+ violence as daily reality—one that has changed little in the intervening decade.

Social tolerance of everyday violence shapes the attitudes of individuals—both LGBTQ+ and straight—who staff social service organizations, health care institutions, and criminal justice systems. Antigay, transphobic, and racialized violence have historically been practiced by police and otherwise officially sanctioned (Whitlock 2005). Racial justice activists called upon police forces to mandate that officers wear body cameras, but evidence from randomized trials indicates that body-worn cameras may have limited effect on police use of force (Yokum, Ravishankar, and Coppock n.d.). Accountability has little meaning in the absence of negative social and institutional consequence.

Homophobia, transphobia, and related threats of violence exacerbate isolation, power, and control in violent LGBTQ+ relationships; moreover, homophobia can be strategically deployed by abusers in either LGBTQ+ or straight relationships (Allen and Leventhal 1999). Within the social-ecological framework of the relationship, its surrounding community, and society (CDC 2018), we need to improve our collective understanding of how cycles of violence develop in LGBTQ+ relationships, how homophobic, transphobic, and racist attitudes and stereotypes are exploited by abusers in both LGBTQ+ and heterosexual relationships, and how homophobia, transphobia, and racism prevent survivors from seeking or accessing competent services. Further, in order to avoid retraumatizing victims, antiviolence organizations must examine how heterosexism, heteronormativity, and white supremacy shape their agendas and the attitudes and practices of their personnel.

Gender, Sexuality, Race, and the Victim-Perpetrator Binary

Like the gender binary, the victim-perpetrator binary is pervasive in dominant approaches to domestic violence. Antiviolence professionals serving both straight and LGBTQ+ communities regularly channel clients toward services and criminal justice systems based on their assessment of which of the two roles the client most closely fits. Based on the dominant explanatory framework in which patriarchy is viewed as the core structural cause of domestic violence, the victim and perpetrator roles have traditionally been implemented in a gendered fashion. The victim or survivor role is generally associated with women and femininity, and the perpetrator role with men and masculinity. Angela Davis (1983), like Ida B. Wells (1892), cautions that these gendered constructions are simultaneously, dangerously racialized.

Gendered and racialized constructions of identity permeate both commonly held stereotypes and professional approaches to IPV. As with the patriarchal structural analysis of domestic violence, gendered assignment of the victim and perpetrator roles may be functional for most cases in which abuse occurs between a man and a woman, both of whom are exclusively heterosexual, and neither of whom has a history of gender transition—but not in all of them.

When the gender and/or racial-ethnic identities of the individuals in a violent, intimate relationship assume some nonnormative configuration, the standard white patriarchal analysis of victim and perpetrator roles does not apply. Nor does it apply in every heterosexual relationship, nor in every relationship in which both partners are White. However, outside observers—whether encountering a violent relationship socially or professionally—may assume that the partner they read as more "masculine" and/or "non-White" is the perpetrator, and the partner they read as more "feminine" and/or "White" is the victim or survivor.

These assessments are often wildly inaccurate—victims and perpetrators are not so easily recognized as we might suspect, whether or not the individuals undergoing assessment fit binary gender categories (Marrujo and Kreger 1996). It is impossible to know on sight, or based on how a voice sounds over the telephone, how an individual or their partner identifies with regard to gender. The gender identities of the participants in a given relationship may counter normative gender stereotypes, and first impressions based on racialized, gender-normative assumptions are unreliable indicators of which partner has the upper hand in an abusive dynamic.

Acknowledging and responding to IPV as a serious problem in LGBTQ+ communities requires detachment of the victim and perpetrator categories from preconceived gender and racialized constructions of identity. The domestic violence movement as a whole embodies the belief, borne out by empirical findings (Avakame 1998), that IPV has special characteristics, and is especially dangerous, precisely because it occurs between intimates. If, however, only gender-normative, heterosexual man-woman pairings are seen as having potential for intimate violence, the intimate nature of violence in queer intimate partnerships is rendered "culturally unintelligible" (Butler 1990).

Based on the heteronormative domestic violence framework, outsiders to a violent nonheterosexual relationship might acknowledge the violence but deny that it is taking place between intimates, and thereby downplay its seriousness. So a neighbor hearing a "fight" between women, or between men, through the adjoining wall may not make the call. Law enforcement and social service personnel may exacerbate these misperceptions. For example, police officers might dismiss IPV between two men as a "fight between roommates," or as otherwise less serious than violence between a man and his woman partner (Leff 2008).

LGBTQ+ people themselves might not take seriously their own experiences of IPV, because they are unable to mentally project themselves into the gendered, racialized stereotypes commonly associated with the victim and perpetrator roles (Muñoz 1999). Abusers may take advantage of this internalized disidentification, and of similar confusion on the part of fellow community members and domestic violence professionals (Goddard and Hardy 1999; Allen and Leventhal 1999). On the other hand, challenging the heteronormative, gendered and racialized assumptions associated with the victim and perpetrator roles increases the likelihood that IPV among LGBTQ+ people will be recognized as both truly intimate and truly violent.

The victim/survivor and perpetrator categories are far from useless. On the contrary, the theoretical formulation and practical implementation of these categories in legal and social service structures has enabled widespread dissemination of an analysis of power and control in relationships. These dual categories constitute a clear conceptual framework based upon which many survivors of violence can access the support of service agencies and criminal justice systems. Experienced advocates serving LGBTQ+ communities are among those who support continued use of these categories and the provision of separate services for clients who are determined to be either survivors or perpetrators (Goddard and Hardy 1999; Grant 1999).

The ways these roles are conceptually connected to gender and racialized identities, and the exclusion of nonnormative gender identities and other categories of identity from consideration in assessing individuals' roles in violence, merit serious review, however. Relying upon gendered binaries in isolation from other dimensions of identity restricts complete understanding of the contexts, causes and correlates of IPV in both LGBTQ+ and heterosexual relationships. Moreover, oversimplified gendered application of the victim-perpetrator binary reinforces the notion that patriarchy is the main contributing factor to domestic violence, while minimizing the other hierarchical structural arrangements that contribute to violence.

The heteronormativity (centering of normative gender identities and heterosexual relationships) of dominant understandings of domestic violence reinscribes the othering that fuels homophobic, transphobic, and racist violence against LGBTQ+ people and people of color. It further eclipses perspectives and experiences of LGBTQ+ people to define the universe of domestic violence so that they and their intimate relationships cannot intelligibly be located within it. Power and control must be conceptualized both apart from gender stereotypes, and in ways that incorporate intersecting sources of personal identity beyond gender. More sophisticated intersectional understandings of individuals' identities and roles in intimate relationships are crucial in assessing cases of IPV, and in providing appropriate services to individuals with a wide range of gender, sexual, racial-ethnic, and class identities.

Queering Responses to Intimate Partner Violence

Experienced antiviolence advocates working with both straight and LGBTQ+ communities know that several criteria must be met in order to effectively interrupt IPV. First, the survivor must acknowledge the violence and its destructive potential, hopefully with the aid of others in near social proximity. Then the survivor requires somewhere to go for help where the violence will readily be acknowledged as legitimate and dangerous by those in a position to offer helpful resources. The services offered there must be competent and well informed, both at the level of institutional policies as well as in the attitudes and behaviors of individual staff members and volunteers. Ideally these services must be based on a solid understanding of the social, cultural, and economic context of the survivor's relationship and of what is at stake in considering whether to leave it.

Feminist domestic violence activists have worked tirelessly to establish public awareness and competent social services so that women survivors of men's violence are able to see their situations as legitimately dangerous, to seek appropriate services, and to reestablish safety and security for themselves and their children. The movement has recognized the need not to revictimize heterosexual women survivors of violence once they enter criminal justice, medical, and social service systems seeking support and has made leaps forward in this regard. Commensurate changes on behalf of LGBTQ+ survivors remain necessary. As the domestic violence movement has confronted patriarchy, so, too, must it confront heteronormativity and white supremacy.

LGBTQ+ survivors face the risk of revictimization by other community members, criminal justice systems, and social service agencies due to the same heterosexist and homophobic attitudes that lead to antigay violence and, when internalized, IPV in their relationships. In particular, victims who are read as masculine, or whose abusive partners are read as feminine, may face disbelief or dismissal of their fears or suffering, either in their communities or in service institutions. They may be told that violence against men or violence committed by women does not constitute domestic violence, that there are no services available for someone in their situation, or even that "a real man" or "a real butch" could "take it" (Allen and Leventhal 1999).

Men or masculine people who report sexual violence face particular risk of having their claims minimized or even ridiculed (Pelka 1997). Gender stereotypes may be exploited to humiliate men or masculine people who are victimized, or to demonize women or feminine people who use violence (Russo 2001).

On the other hand, internalized stereotypes about masculinity and femininity may reinforce the social acceptability of violence committed against the more feminine partner as part and parcel of the more masculine partner's gender role.

If, in the face of prevailing gender stereotypes, an LGBTQ+ person comes to view their own situation as a legitimate case of IPV, they must be able to access competent professional resources where risks of revictimization are minimized. Provided that a domestic violence agency exists in the area where they live, and that they are "out" enough about their gender and sexual identity to feel comfortable contacting that agency in a crisis, an LGBTQ+ client must be able to trust that the services will be suitable, respectful, and based upon accurate information about their identity and specific needs.

In addition to redefining the structural contexts and personal identities associated with IPV, antiviolence organizations are developing responses and interventions that are sensitive to these expanded definitions. Responses to IPV in LGBTQ+ communities emerge primarily from two distinguishable but overlapping sources. LGBTQ+ communities create new organizations tailored from the ground up to their own experiences and needs, and institutions previously established within the heterosexual battered women's movement alter their approaches to accommodate LGBTQ+ communities. LGBTQ+-specific organizations may either use approaches based on the traditional heteronormative service model, or they may diverge from it and use LGBTQ+ community-driven models. Perhaps the best antiviolence programs blend what has been learned from heteronormative domestic violence practice with what has been excluded from it.

Queer communities began establishing their own organizations to address violence in the late 1970s. Some LGBT+ organizations focus on both antigay hate violence and IPV. Like the feminist battered women's movement, the LGBTQ+ antiviolence movement got its start in community organizing and has become increasingly institutionalized. As a rule, LGBTQ+ antiviolence organizations combine services to address domestic violence, based at least in part on the "traditional" model, with community organizing approaches, which may or may not evolve into a more service-oriented approach. LGBTQ+ community organizing against violence continues to take place both within and outside established nonprofit organizations (Ristock 2011).

Institutionalized organizations within the LGBTQ+ antiviolence movement more than doubled in number between 2006 and 2017—there are now more than fifty such organizations in the US alone—and continue to develop impressive levels of expertise in serving LGBTQ+ communities (National Coalition of Anti-Violence Programs 2017b). While the movement has decentralized somewhat, the majority of these organizations are still located in urban centers of the US and Canada with large queer populations, including Boston, Los Angeles, New York, San Francisco, and Seattle (tnlr.org; lalgbtcenter.org; avp.org; sfcenter.org;

nwnetwork.org). Some LGBTQ+ IPV programs are linked to, or incorporated within, local LGBTQ+ community centers. To varying degrees, they draw upon service approaches originally developed by the battered women's movement, adapting them as necessary for LGBTQ+ clients.

The success of any antiviolence institution's attempt to address the local LGBTQ+ community's needs depends upon a number of factors. These include the representation of LGBTQ+ people among the agency's staff and volunteers; the existence of meaningful partnerships with local LGBTQ+ communities and organizations; effective means of addressing homophobia, transphobia, and heterosexism within the organization and its institutional network; the applicability of intake forms, procedures, counseling, and other services to the full range of human gender and sexual identities; and the ability to objectively and continually evaluate the existing service model and adapt it where necessary. Grassroots LGBTQ+ groups and established LGBTQ+ antiviolence agencies constitute deep founts of expertise in these and other areas.

If a service agency initially based in the heteronormative framework can demonstrate to the local queer community that it has become knowledgeable and not merely "open and affirming," but truly welcoming and responsive to LGBTQ+ identities and needs, including those of LGBTQ+ people of color, the local queer and trans community may well come to trust the agency and to access its services (Gentlewarrior 2009). If the agency partners effectively with existing LGBTQ+ communities and organizations, hires openly LGBTQ+ staff and volunteers of diverse backgrounds, and consistently tailors its programming, forms, and procedures in accordance with a strong antiheterosexist and antiracist agenda, it will likely become known as a safe and helpful place for queer and trans people to go for support when intimate partner violence occurs or is threatened.

Responding to LGBTQ+ intimate partner violence requires the staff and volunteers of an antiviolence agency to develop the awareness, skills and appropriate tools to meet the needs of LGBTQ+ clients from all of the racial-ethnic and class backgrounds represented in their local community. Some of these needs resemble those of heterosexual and gender-normative clients, while others differ in important ways. For example, a crisis counselor should understand that for a transsexual man or woman seeking shelter, retrieving specific clothing items, hormone supplements, shaving equipment or makeup from home may be a matter of daily survival, or at least of preservation of one's sense of security and well-being. It is the responsibility of antiviolence agencies and their personnel to educate themselves (with the input of qualified, and *compensated*, LGBTQ+ advisors) about daily realities of LGBTQ+ life relevant to intimate partner violence, personal safety, and dignity.

At a more fundamental level, the organization and its personnel must acknowledge and address heterosexism, transphobia, and white supremacy within the organization on an ongoing basis. Heterosexism, homophobia, transphobia, and racism not only contribute to intimate partner violence, but also shape institutional agendas and personal attitudes (PCHR 2017; Giwa and Greensmith 2012). In order to serve individuals and communities beyond the heteronormative framework, antiviolence organizations must confront manifestations of heterosexism and other social hierarchies within domestic violence service provision itself, as well as within intimate relationships.

The feminist domestic violence movement has successfully articulated and disseminated an analysis of patriarchy as a root structural cause of gender violence generally, and of intimate partner violence specifically. Queering dominant approaches to intimate partner violence requires centering the perspectives and experiences of queer-identified people, intersex people, transgender and transsexual people, bisexual people, lesbians, and gay men. These populations include people of color, immigrants (documented and undocumented), working-class people, young people, elders, people with disabilities, HIV-positive people, and members of drag, leather, poly, and other subcultural and marginalized communities.

In order to effectively interrupt and transform cycles of violence that harm multiple communities, antiviolence movements must expand their analyses to confront the forms of violence associated with intersecting social hierarchies beyond patriarchy. As many others in this volume argue, confronting heteronormativity and white supremacy in our institutions, our communities, and ourselves is urgently necessary in order to prevent and respond effectively to intimate partner violence in all of our communities.

NOTES

1 My use of the term "trans" encompasses transgender and trans(s)exual identities.

2 "LGBTQ+ is an acronym for Lesbian, Gay, Bisexual, Trans, Queer/Questioning, and others. It refers to a population of people united by having gender identities or sexual orientations that differ from the heterosexual and cisgender majority" (UCF SJA 2018). I also use "LGBQ and trans" where appropriate in this chapter to acknowledge transgender identities and communities as distinct from lesbian, gay, bisexual and queer identities and communities.

3 See Accord Alliance (n.d.), Chase (2002), Fausto-Sterling (2000), and ISNA (2006) for discussions of intersex and DSD.

4 Ristock's indispensable edited volume (2011) provides helpful examinations of intersections of gender, sexuality, race, class, and culture as the overarching context for violence and for attempted interventions in LGBTQ+ intimate partner violence. The volume edited by Sokoloff, with Pratt (2005), offers discussions of domestic violence in marginalized communities, and directly addresses race, ethnicity, class, migration, and sexuality as factors in domestic violence.

31

Revisiting the Impact of the Sex Industry and Prostitution in Europe

JANICE G. RAYMOND

One of the most visible developments in the sex industry during the last forty years has been its rapid expansion and massive diversification. Globalization of the economy means globalization of the sex industry, whether one is confronted with sex trafficking, prostitution, mail-order bride marketers, lap dancing and other sex clubs, sex tourism, and/or pornography. There are few countries in which the sex industry is shrinking.

The sex industry thrives on renaming its sexual exploitation as "sex." Pornography is called *erotica* or *adult videos*; prostitution is renamed as *sex work* or *sexual services*; pimps are now called *third-party business managers* or *erotic entrepreneurs*; and lap dancing or sex clubs are called *gentlemen's entertainment*.

The internet has greatly enhanced the reach of the sex industry. The *World Sex Guide*, an internet-based trove of information, caters to men who are routine or prospective prostitution users. It informs them of any kind of sexual predilection they might seek, including child sexual abuse, specific brothels in specific countries, and even evaluations of particular women in these venues.

In March of 2018, however, the US Senate passed H.R. 1865 known as FOSTA-SESTA, legislation that takes aim at websites that facilitate and profit from prostitution and sex trafficking—in other words, online pimping. In a rare historic bipartisan vote (97–2), the *Fight Online Sex Trafficking Act* removes impunity from more than 130 websites that were formerly shielded from legal liability for their ads promoting and enabling prostitution and sex trafficking. Immediately after the legislation was passed, many websites such as craigslist, Reddit, the Erotic Review, and Cityvibe moved fast to close down their prostitution ads. The website of Backpage.com, the largest purveyor of online sexual exploitation, was seized by the FBI on April 6, 2018, in an action that confiscated everything and shuttered the website.[1]

One of the biggest moneymakers in the pornography industry is material called *gonzo* that depicts "hard-core, body-punishing sex in which women are demeaned and debased."[2] Pornography's industrial scope has gone from VCRs and DVDs to cable TV, video-on-demand, streaming, and cell-phone tailored films. Internet search engines list top father-daughter incest movies. And there are online video blurbs for "sexy dead girls."

What is most disturbing about all this information is that not only is the sex industry big business but that the selling of *its products*—pornography, prostitution, sex tourism, mail-order brides—all depend on the commodification of mainly women and children and has become much more acceptable, more normal, and even fashionable and cool. And those who raise criticisms of the industry and its spinning of sexual exploitation into hot sex, are labeled out of touch, moralistic, and repressed. Ultimately, the sex industry has made sexual exploitation not only normal but also respectable. As one woman explained: "It's like a joke among my close male friends . . . I'll ask, 'What did you do last night?' and they say, 'I was up till five in the morning jerking off to the Internet.'"[3] And numerous women have commented that many men seem incapable of having sexual relationships or, for that matter, genuine emotional relationships with women who don't act like women depicted in pornography.

For many men, however, pornography is not enough. They want to enact the fantasies, the transgressions and ultimately the degradation and violence of pornography with a class of women set aside to fulfill their fantasies in prostitution. The sex industry expands to accommodate all tastes and all demands. For example, men buying women in prostitution don't just want the local women—they want women from other countries who will fulfill their fantasies who, according to their racial preferences, are stereotyped as more exotic, pliable, willing, or sexy. Especially in European countries that have legalized prostitution, most of the women in the sex industry have been trafficked from other countries.

Legalization of Prostitution Regimes in European Countries

The normalization of sexual exploitation has been greatly enhanced by the legalization and/or decriminalization of the sex industry in various countries in Europe. People often don't understand that legalization of prostitution means not only legalization of the women exploited in prostitution, but also legalization of the sex industry and its pimps, sex buyers, and brothels, removing criminal status from each of these groups.

Some pro-sex work advocates prefer the term *decriminalization of prostitution*, meaning that the prostitution industry should not be subject to any kind of state regulation. In their opinion, prostitution is simply *sex work*. But legalization and decriminalization of the system of prostitution have the same outcome in that they make the sex industry legal, i.e., by not making it illegal.

Legalization has been a gift to traffickers and pimps who, overnight, become legitimate businessmen. Prostitution becomes a public offering and governments derive enormous revenues from its legal legitimation. Legalization, or what I call state-sponsored prostitution, has become so normalized in some countries that brothels in New Zealand and elsewhere gain acceptance by, for example, raising money for charity by throwing open their doors to the public for on site tours to display their *merchandise*.[4]

The impact of the sex industry's expansion doesn't stop with legitimation of prostitution through state approval. The state is also called upon to fund the "sexual rights" of people with disabilities to ensure that disabled (mainly) men have access to sexual services. In the State of Victoria, Australia, state-employed caretakers (who are mostly women) are expected to take these men to specialty brothels that advertise facilities for the disabled and literally facilitate their physical positions if the men are not able to engage in sexual activities without assistance. "It is the 'rights' of men that are being catered to here. Disabled women are not mentioned."[5]

When I first published an earlier version of this chapter, which in its original rendering was my testimony before the European Parliament in 2004, countries that had legalized prostitution dominated the debate over prostitution policy in Europe. At the turn of the twenty-first century, a handful of countries had chosen to legalize prostitution including the Netherlands, Germany, Austria, and Switzerland.

For purposes of this essay, the Netherlands will serve as a case study to illustrate the failure of legalized prostitution policy during the last seventeen years in Europe. Two official reports—the Daalder Report of 2007 and the National Police Service Report of 2008, are especially instructive. These reports, in combination with other sources, present evidence of the crumbling Dutch prostitution legislation enacted in the year 2000. Both reports have high value because they come from, or are commissioned by, official bodies that have an established interest in representing the success of the legislation, yet actually they present evidence of its lack of success. These reports are also representative of the failure of legalized prostitution in other countries such as Germany, where official reports document there is "hardly any measurable positive impact [that] has been observed in practice . . . No short-term improvements that could benefit the prostitutes themselves are to be expected."[6]

In the years immediately following passage of the legislation in the Netherlands, official opinion claimed that the new law *lifting the general ban on brothels* had been successful. The 2004 Dutch governmental National Action Plan on Trafficking in Human Beings alleged, "The licensed and monitored sectors of the sex industry have now been cleaned up considerably."[7] In 2008 an annual police publication stated that half the police forces reported the licensed prostitution industry "was (as good as) free of any abuses."[8] Official optimism, however, was short-lived.

Public policies should be tested by how they fulfill their goals. The failure of the legalization legislation in the Netherlands can be illustrated by the breakdown of its following objectives.

Legalization of Prostitution Would Better Protect Prostituted Women and Promote Their Well-Being

The 2007 Daalder Report commissioned by the Dutch Ministry of Justice found that "[t]he prostitutes' emotional well-being is now lower than in 2001 on all measured aspects, and the use of sedatives has increased."[9] It acknowledged that prostituted women "suffer high levels of distress."

The 2008 National Police Service Report entitled *Beneath the Surface (Schone Schijn)* was commissioned by the National Prosecutors' Office. It chronicled the results of an inquiry begun in 2006 that tracked gangs of traffickers in the prostitution districts of three cities in the Netherlands. Criminal gangs working as pimps and bodyguards were found to have violently victimized dozens of women in prostitution over many years within the *licensed sector.* "The prostitutes were totally in the power of the gang. They were never left alone or left unobserved. They were beaten and terrorized. They had to work long hours and to hand over all of their earnings, and some were forced to abort . . . or to have their breasts surgically enlarged."[10] Pimps even specified the women's bra cup size to the doctors.[11]

Legalization Would Free Women from Pimp Control and Make Them Independent Agents

The 2007 Daalder Report found that the "great majority" of women in legal window prostitution have pimps or so-called boyfriends.[12] "Pimps are still a very common phenomenon . . . the fact that the number of prostitutes with pimps does not seem to have decreased is a cause for concern."[13] Brothel owners as well exert control over the women's performance and take-home pay. In visiting the window brothels, the researchers noted that many of the prostituted women "involuntarily" handed over their earnings to their pimps.[14] Some women interviewed stated that they had to change their "workplace" at the behest of their pimps—for example, when the pimps thought they did not make enough money at a particular brothel. Other women indicated that they themselves changed their location to escape from their pimps.[15]

The National Police Service Report also specified the ways in which prostituted women were subject to pimp control in the licensed window brothels of Amsterdam, Alkmaar, and Utrecht. The women were "snatched" from their original pimps, "induced to 'switch' voluntarily," and threatened if they dared to lodge reports of intimidation. Victims' statements also exposed the mix of seduction, force, and violence used to get them to acquiesce to their pimps' bidding. Others were told that their freedom could only be gained if they paid a sum varying from €30,000 to €240,000 to their pimps. Foreign-born women's passports were confiscated, and some women feared being murdered if they escaped.[16]

Since the 2000 law legalized pimping, the pervasiveness of pimping is significant. So-called third-party business managers turned out to be just regular abusive pimps after all. Given the fact that pimps commonly exploit women in both the Dutch legal and nonlegal sex industries, it appears not to matter much whether women are in either quarter, since both are pimp-controlled.

Legalization of Prostitution Would Reduce Trafficking

Before passage of the proposed legalization law in 1998, members of a police policy and advice group on trafficking in human beings had expressed concern that the law would attract foreign traffickers.[17] That concern has been substantiated. At a 2004 criminology conference, one of the Netherlands's top organized crime specialists, Cyrille Fijnaut, told the conference that the legalization of prostitution in the Netherlands had "greatly increased trafficking."[18] Louise Shelley, who attended the conference, said that Russian and Ukrainian attendees who went on one of the famous tours of the red-light district stated, "All they saw there were women from their own countries."[19]

Because of criminal infiltration of the legalized prostitution tolerance zones that were set up in major Dutch cities such as Amsterdam and Rotterdam, municipalities began large-scale closures of these zones from 2003 onward, only three years after the law went into force. Billed as restricted areas where men could buy women legally and, allegedly, where women could sell sex safely, these zones quickly became unsafe and sordid places for women.[20]

During 2007–2008, Amsterdam shut down one-third of its licensed window brothels. Europol confirmed that local Dutch pimps and brothel owners had formed online links with foreign pimps and traffickers who brought women into the country and treated them as "a piece of garbage," often resorting to violence and murder.[21]

In brothel investigations, officials looked for women without legal entry or residence papers. Legal papers, however, do not mean that those who possess them are not trafficked. Because a number of foreign-born women in prostitution have legal entry documents or come from Eastern European countries within the European Union (EU), authorities often assume these women are not trafficked and exploited. With legal papers, pimps and traffickers can easily move women into the country. Searching for evidence of trafficking mainly based on women without legal documents is an outdated strategy in a Europe that increasingly is without national borders.

Legalization of Prostitution Would Remove Organized Crime from the Prostitution Sector

In acknowledging that the sex industry continues to be dominated by organized crime, former mayor of Amsterdam Job Cohen has stated, "We have seen that in the last years that trafficking in women is becoming more, so in this respect the legalizing of prostitution didn't work out."[22]

How can the removal, or even the reduction, of organized crime be achieved when the criminals are baptized as newborn legal entrepreneurs? The Daalder Report interviewed forty-nine prostitution venue owners, many of whom in a former life had been illegal operators in the sex industry, i.e., former criminals whose status had been transformed into legitimate businessmen overnight by the lifting of the ban on brothels. In understated language, the report confirmed that because "A large part of the current owners has already been working as a business owner in that illegal sector, it seems plausible that owners are less inclined to conform to government authority than most other Dutch people."[23] Less inclined indeed!

Several past and present Amsterdam city councilors, in addition to the mayor and deputy mayor, have criticized the hold of organized crime on the prostitution sector. Roel van Duijn, an Amsterdam city councilor from the Green Party, spent several years investigating the trafficking in women in the illegal prostitution sector and stated, "The illegal circuit is rife with sex slavery." His criticisms are not limited to the illegal sector. He also wants to abolish legal prostitution because "prostitution has always been an illegal area" with women in the sex industry who "continue to suffer from traumatic experiences."[24]

In 2007, Frank de Wolf, a Labour Party city councilor and an HIV-AIDS researcher, told the *Washington Post*: "In the past, we looked at legal prostitution as a women's liberation issue; now it's looked at as exploitation of women and should be stopped." He added, "Amsterdam's police force is overwhelmed and ill-equipped to fight the sophisticated foreign organized crime networks operating in the city. Laws designed to regulate prostitution and brothel operators have instead opened the trade to criminal gangs."[25]

Legalization Will Improve the Situation of Women in the Sex Industry

All proposals to legalize prostitution and decriminalize the sex industry claim with full confidence that normalizing prostitution will radically improve the health and well-being of women. Despite its temperate tone, the Daalder Report reached damning conclusions about the welfare of women in the Dutch sex industry when it stated, "The prostitutes' emotional well-being is now lower than in 2001 on all measured aspects."

In responding to regime failures, however, the recommendations of the Daalder Report minimize the exploitation of women in the sex industry by using the language of *labor relations* to tone down abuse. The report recommends authorities should better clarify the "right form of labor relations" within the prostitution sector and should enhance the power of the brothel owners. "The more instructions are given by the business owner, and the greater his say in all kinds of matters, the sooner the existence of an employer-employee relation will be established."[26] This is an astoundingly awful conclusion.

When a country establishes prostitution as work, it is almost impossible for an officially commissioned report to frame its conclusions outside the labor paradigm. Thus the abuse, the distress, the lack of autonomy, and the low levels of emotional well-being of women chronicled in the reports mentioned are minimized as occupational hazards to be remedied by better work conditions and reduction of harm.

An aim of the prostitution legislation was to regularize the status of women as workers and to provide them with benefits. The majority of women, however, do not want to be regular salaried employees for several reasons. Many do not want to pay taxes, arguing that they earn very little. More importantly, the majority of women want to retain their anonymity because they fear the exposure of providing contact information by registering with relevant authorities.

All paeans to legalized prostitution regimes promote the myth that women can become regular employees with access to social security, disability, and pension benefits. However, when prostituted women in the licensed prostitution sector were asked whether these benefits or others were most important to them, most stated they were not as important as anonymity.[27] Women wanted no record created of their time in prostitution, given the stigma attached to women in prostitution. Although they were aware that failing to register would have negative consequences for their future social security entitlements, they chose not to institutionalize their *labor status* and receive the economic benefits of registration.

Few municipalities have initiated any strategies that assist women to leave prostitution in spite of earlier parliamentary encouragement that urged the cities and towns to launch exit programs. In 2004, the government also sent a brochure to all municipalities offering assistance in developing exit policies and programs. Only 6 percent of municipalities responded.[28] As the National Police Service Report clearly stated, "There appears to be an emerging national consensus that the law of 2000 has been a failure."[29]

What's the Alternative?

Rather than harm minimization, abolitionist prostitution policy aims to *eliminate* the harm that women experience in prostitution. The immediate cause of harm to the prostituted woman is the sex buyer, mainly the men who purchase women for commercial sexual exploitation.

As human trafficking became an increasing global problem in the 1990s, Sweden took an intensive look at its prostitution policy. It concluded that a country couldn't resolve its sex trafficking problem without targeting the demand for prostitution. In 1999, Sweden passed landmark legislation that made it illegal to buy "sexual services." The legislation was built on a public consensus that the system of prostitution promotes violence against women by normalizing sexual exploitation. Thus, in a society that aspires to advance women's equality, it is unacceptable for men to purchase women for sexual exploitation, whether rationalized as a sexual choice or as *sex work*.

Sweden's innovative approach stands out as an exemplary model of lawmaking that reduces prostitution, penalizes men, and protects women. The Swedish law clearly articulates that prostitution is *men's violence* against women and, as such, it prohibits the purchase of "sexual services" within the larger framework of a Violence Against Women Bill that addresses other forms of violence against women. The law does not penalize the prostituted women who are acknowledged as victims and provides generous victim assistance.[30]

Sweden does not penalize persons in prostitution who are the victims but makes resources available to them. Instead it targets and exposes the anonymous men—the historically invisible buyers who purchase mainly women and children for the sex of prostitution—and the pimps and other perpetrators of commercial sexual exploitation. The key to the law's effectiveness lies not so much in penalizing the sex buyers (punishments are modest) but in removing the invisibility of the buyers and making their crimes public. Men now fear being outed as prostitution users.

Sweden's law is both legislative and normative. It makes prostitution users legally accountable for their actions while at the same time sends the message that there are societies that do not accept the buying of women for sexual exploitation as normal "work." By recognizing that prostitution is violence against women, the law establishes that prostitution is a human rights violation and a crime. The legislation educates other countries, as well as individuals and organizations, about how to combat male sexual exploitation and violence.

In 2010, the government of Sweden published an evaluation of the first ten years of the law. While acknowledging that much remains to be done, the report's findings are overwhelmingly positive:

- Street prostitution has been cut in half, "a direct result of the criminalization of sex purchases."
- There is no evidence that the decrease in street prostitution has led to an increase in prostitution elsewhere, whether indoors or on the internet.
- Extensive services exist in the larger cities to assist those exploited by prostitution.

- Fewer men state that they purchase sexual services.
- More than 70 percent of the Swedish public supports the law.[31]

Initially critical, police now confirm the law works well and has had a deterrent effect on pimps and traffickers, who find in Sweden an intolerant environment in which to sell women and children for sex. Based on national criminal police reports over the last decade, it appears that Sweden is the only country in Europe where prostitution and sex trafficking have not increased. The Swedish model became the Nordic model when it was passed in both Norway and Iceland.

Norway criminalized sex buying in 2009, and in 2014 the government commissioned an evaluation of the law. It found that in combination with laws against trafficking and pimping, the law has reduced the market for prostitution in Norway with the most profound changes occurring in Oslo. Here street prostitution has decreased by 35 to 60 percent, and there has been a reduction of indoor prostitution of 10 to 20 percent.[32] Like Sweden, it is more difficult to buy sex because the buyer is afraid of being caught, and the law has made Norway a less attractive place for pimps and traffickers to set up shop. Nor has the Norwegian law increased violence against women in prostitution as some pro-sex work advocates have claimed.

It is no accident that the Nordic countries have been the first to challenge legalization of prostitution and, instead, take legal action against the sex buyers. Studies confirm these countries lead the world on most indicators of gender equality.[33] Gender equality experts and advocates have long pointed out that in economics, politics, and social services, the Nordic countries top the charts. A less noticed equality indicator is that Nordic countries outpace others in legal action to stem the sex trade by addressing its heretofore-anonymous perpetrators, the sex buyers.

Other countries in Europe that have followed the Nordic model are Northern Ireland (2015), France (2016), and the Republic of Ireland (2017). Legislation against sex buying in each of these countries passed by overwhelming majorities. Countries outside of Europe that have also passed Nordic model legislation are Canada, and the Republic of Korea. In spite of the fact that foundations such as George Soros's Open Society Foundation have poured money into supporting legal campaigns for total decriminalization and legalization of prostitution and the sex industry,[34] these countries chose instead to create legislation that decriminalizes the women and criminalizes sex buyers, pimps, and brothels. It is clear that abolitionist policy, which helped generate the Nordic model, has achieved significant legal success, not only in the Scandinavian context but in other countries as well.

What could be called a sea change is taking place in Europe as countries turn away from legalization of prostitution and decriminalization of the sex industry and put the focus on the men who purchase women's bodies for sexual exploitation. Rather than sanctioning prostitution, these countries are decriminalizing the women and confronting the demand by penalizing the men who buy women for the sex of prostitution.

There have been a number of strategic European reports and resolutions, which have found that countries with legalized prostitution regimes have higher inflows of human trafficking. In 2005, the European Parliament commissioned a report of eleven countries in Europe entitled "National Legislation on Prostitution and the Trafficking in Women and Children." Undertaken by Transcrime, a joint research center from two universities in Italy, the study included an examination of the way a country's legislation influenced the number of trafficking victims. The report found, "the model that seems to produce less victims [of trafficking] is prohibitionism." In this report, Sweden falls under their typology of prohibitionism.[35]

In 2012, researchers associated with the German Institute for Economic Research analyzed 116 countries and reviewed case studies of legalized regimes in Denmark, Germany, and Switzerland, with variations in the different countries accounted for. For example, it is irrelevant if third parties—pimps—facilitate the prostitution businesses. The authors found that it was not the type of legalization that mattered but rather whether prostitution was legal or not.[36]

In 2014, the European Parliament adopted a nonbinding resolution, calling on EU member states to reduce the demand for prostitution by criminalizing the act of purchasing commercial sexual exploitation. Referred to as the Honeyball resolution—named for Minister of the European Parliament (MEP) Mary Honeyball who launched it—the resolution emphasized that prostitution violates human dignity and human rights whether it is forced or voluntary. The resolution also calls for exit strategies and income generating alternatives for women who want to leave prostitution.[37] Many pro-sex work advocates protested the resolution, but many abolitionists contested this protest. Especially noteworthy was the support for the Honeyball resolution that came from survivors of prostitution and trafficking. Although nonbinding, it is hoped that the resolution will pressure countries to reexamine their prostitution policies.

Also in 2014, the Parliamentary Assembly of the Council of Europe (PACE) issued a report on prostitution, trafficking, and modern slavery in Europe. The report stated, "In 1999, Sweden was the first country to criminalise the purchase of sexual services, with proven positive results in terms of reducing the demand for trafficking. Since then, other countries have followed the same path or have taken steps in this direction."

Regarding policies on prostitution, the first five sections of final resolution number 1983 calls upon countries to:

- Consider criminalising the purchase of sexual services, based on the Swedish model, as the most effective tool for preventing and combating trafficking in human beings;

- Ban the advertising of sexual services, including forms of disguised advertising;
- Criminalise pimping, if they have not already done so;
- Establish counselling centres providing prostitutes with legal and health assistance, irrespective of their legal or migrant status;
- Set up "exit programmes" for those who wish to give up prostitution, aimed at rehabilitation and based on a holistic approach including mental health and health care services, housing support, education, and training and employment services.[38]

The recent PACE report and resolution signal an encouraging turnaround from PACE's 2007 report urging member states instead to make policy distinctions between voluntary and forced prostitution and follow empowerment strategies for women based on a regulatory model common in legalized prostitution countries. Although the 2014 report and other parts of the resolution address recommendations for countries that have a legal regulated system of prostitution, the resolution clearly states that the Swedish model criminalizing the "purchase of sexual services is the most effective tool for preventing and combating trafficking in human beings."[39]

Conclusion

Legalization of prostitution was promoted with the argument that legitimation of prostitution would control and curb the expansion of the sex industry and restrict the number of brothels, sex clubs, and entrepreneurs that could operate. But instead of restricting its expansion, legalization has increased the reach of the sex industry, promoted sex trafficking, created the conditions for organized crime to infiltrate the sex trade, legal and illegal, and made no measurable improvements in the well-being of prostituted women.

The goal of any industry, legitimate or not, is to expand. Advocates of legalization invoke a peculiar argument when they rationalize that legalization will bring the sex industry under control, restricting its reach and abuse. The expansion of the legal and illegal sex industry is not restricted to countries with legalized prostitution regimes only in Europe. Legalization of prostitution in the State of Victoria, Australia, also resulted in massive expansion of the sex industry.

When women in prostitution are redefined as *sex workers*, the whole industry is also presented as *work*. Men who buy women for the sex of prostitution are redefined as ordinary *customers*, and pimps as *third-party business managers*.

Legalization or decriminalization of the sex industry doesn't address its primary consequence—that women in prostitution are *segregated* as a legal class whose occupation is to provide sexual services to men and to satisfy their sexual gratifications. We need to ask: Is prostitution a career to which we want young girls to aspire?

The least discussed part of the prostitution and trafficking chain has been the men who buy women for sexual exploitation in prostitution, pornography, sex tourism, and mail-order bride marketing. As the #MeToo revelations of male sexual assaults and harassment have demonstrated, it is not acceptable to shrug one's shoulders and say "men are like this," "boys will be boys," or "prostitution is inevitable."

Sweden's law against the buying of "sexual services" has been a model that should be emulated elsewhere. There is an urgent need for governments to put male buyers of women and children in prostitution on the policy and legislative agenda, taking seriously that the problem of global sex trafficking will not be dented unless those who create the demand for prostitution are addressed and punished. Sweden and the other countries that have passed laws against sex buying have clearly chosen to resist the legalization/decriminalization of prostitution and instead to address prostitution as a form of violence against women.

Antitrafficking policies and programs must address organized prostitution and domestic trafficking. Most trafficking is *for* prostitution, and operates within the context of domestic sex industries. International women are trafficked into domestic sex industries, and both international and local women are trafficked within countries. In the face of a transnational sex industry that traffics women and children into all parts of the globe and that draws them into the industry at home and abroad, antitrafficking and antiprostitution legislation must be made more powerful than the sex industry it aims to eradicate.

NOTES

1 Cecilia Kang and Sheryl Gay Stolberg, "Sex Trafficking Bill Heads to Trump, Over Silicon Valley Concerns," *The New York Times*, March 21, 2018. www.nytimes.com.

2 Gail Dines, *Pornland: How Porn Has Hijacked Our Sexuality* (Boston: Beacon Press, 2010).

3 David Amsdem, "Not Tonight Honey. I'm Logging On," *New York Magazine*, October 20, 2003. http://nymag.com.

4 Lynley Bilby, "Brothel's fundraiser for kids charity slammed," *New Zealand Herald*, February 17, 2016. www.nzherald.co.nz.

5 Mary Sullivan and Sheila Jeffreys, *Legalising Prostitution Is Not the Answer: The Example of Victoria, Australia* (Coalition Against Trafficking in Women, Australia and USA, 2001). www.catwinternational.org.

6 Federal Ministry for Family Affairs, Senior Citizens, Women and Youth, *Report by the Federal Government on the Impact of the Act Regulating the Legal Situation of Prostitutes (Prostitution Act)*, 2007, 79–80. www.bmfsfj.de.

7 National Police Service, Criminal Investigations Department (KLPD), "Beneath the Surface (Schone Schijn): The Identification of Human Trafficking in the Licensed Prostitution Sector," English summary, translated by Lotte Constance Van de Pol, June 5. 2009.

8 National Police Service, "Beneath the Surface," 12.

9 A. L. Daalder, "Prostitution in the Netherlands Since the Lifting of the Brothel Ban" (Amsterdam: WODC, Ministry of Justice, 2007), 47.

10 Lotte Constance Van de Pol, *Supplementary Affidavit*, Bedford et al. v. Attorney General of Canada, Ontario, Canada Superior Court of Justice (07-CV-329807PD1), (June 5, 2009), 6.

11 National Police Service, "Beneath the Surface," 20.

12 The Red Light District of Amsterdam is famous for its prostitution windows—street-level rooms with windows—where women in prostitution are posed in scantily clad alluring postures to attract buyers. Hordes of mostly male tourists each year are attracted to the windows because they can choose women from these displays. Often men ogle, spit and yell profanities as they gaze at the women in the windows.

13 Daalder, "Prostitution in the Netherlands," 13.

14 Ibid., 79.

15 Ibid., 69.

16 National Police Service, "Beneath the Surface," 18.

17 Bureau NRM, "Trafficking in Human Beings," First Report of the Dutch National Rapporteur (The Hague: 2002), 84.

18 Louise Shelley, "The Price of Sex," *St. Petersburg Times*, October 20, 2004. www.freerepublic.com.

19 Ibid.

20 Janice G. Raymond, *Not a Choice, Not a Job: Exposing the Myths about Prostitution and the Global Sex Trade* (Dulles, Virginia: Potomac Books/University of Nebraska Press, 2013), 88–89. See also Chapter 3, "Prostitution Nation: The State of Prostitution in the Netherlands," for a full examination of the Dutch prostitution regime.

21 Andrew Balcombe, "Human Trafficking in Holland: Experts Talk About Sex Slavery," *Hague/Amsterdam Times*, December 1, 2009.

22 Victor Malarek, *The Johns: Sex for Sale and the Men Who Buy It* (New York: Arcade Publishing, 2009), 220.

23 Daalder, "Prostitution in the Netherlands," 53.

24 Margaret Strijbosch, "Legalised Prostitution: A Dying Trade," *Radio Netherlands Worldwide*, October 31, 2009. www.rnw.nl.

25 Molly Moore, "Changing Patterns in Social Fabric Test Netherlands' Liberal Identity," *Washington Post*, June 23, 2007. www.washingtonpost.com.

26 Daalder, "Prostitution in the Netherlands," 61, 63.

27 Ibid., 67.

28 Ibid., 70.

29 National Police Service, "Beneath the Surface," 20.

30 Ministry of Industry, Employment and Communications, Government of Sweden, "Fact Sheet on Prostitution and Trafficking in Women," April, 2003. www.sweden.gov.se.

    For further information on the Swedish law and the government's policy on trafficking, see Government Offices of Sweden, Against Prostitution and Trafficking, 2009. www.sweden.gov.se.

    See also Gunilla Ekberg, "The Swedish Law that Prohibits the Purchase of Sexual Services," *Violence Against Women* 10, 10 (October 2004): 1187–218.

31 (SOU) Statens Offentliga Utredningar, "Prohibition of the Purchase of a Sexual Service: an Evaluation 1999–2008," English Summary (2010) 29–44. www.nj.se.

    See also Max Waltman, "Sweden's Prohibition of Purchase of Sex: The Law's Reasons, Impact and Potential," *Women's Studies International Forum* 34, (2011), 449–474.

32 Ingeborg Rasmussen et al., "Evaluation of the Ban on the Purchase of Sexual Services," Report No. 2014/30 (Ministry of Justice and Emergency Department, 2014). http://todaango.org.il.

    See also "Evaluation of Norwegian Legislation Criminalising the Buying of Sexual Services (Summary)," 2014. https://rm.coe.int.

33 UNDP (United Nations Development Programme), "UN Development Report," 2016. http://hdr.undp.org. The *UN Development Report* includes a Gender Development Index (Table 4). Several of the Nordic countries are listed in the Group 1 of this index with Norway ranking #1, which is the highest rank. Two European countries that have legalized prostitution, Germany and the Netherlands, are respectively ranked lower in Groups 2 and 3 on the gender development scale.

A more dynamic look at the current closing of the gender gap in countries around the world is the annual World Economic Forum, "Global Gender Gap Report," 2016. http://reports.weforum.org. This report rates countries on success in closing their social and economic gender gaps. The report ranks Iceland, Norway, and Sweden respectively as #1, #3, and #4 that have closed over 80 percent of their gender gaps.

34 Jody Raphael, "Decriminalization of Prostitution: The Soros Effect," *Dignity: A Journal on Sexual Exploitation and Violence* 3, no. 1 (2017), Digital Commons. http://digitalcommons.uri.edu.

35 Transcrime for the European Parliament, "National Legislation on Prostitution and the Trafficking in Women and Children," Contract IP/C/FEMM/ST/2004–05 (September, 2005). www.europarl.europa.eu.

36 Seo-Young Cho, Axel Dreyer, and Eric Neumayer, "Does Legalized Prostitution Increase Human Trafficking?" World Development 41, 1 (2012), 67–82. https://ec.europa.eu.

37 European Parliament, "Sexual Exploitation and Prostitution and Its Impact on Gender Equality" (Resolution accepted February 26, 2014). www.europarl.europa.eu.

38 Parliamentary Assembly, "Council of Europe Report on Prostitution, Trafficking, and Modern Slavery in Europe," Rapporteur Jose Mendes Bota (Doc. 13446/Final Report and Resolution, Approved April 8, 2014). http://assembly.coe.int.

39 Ibid.

32

Advances and Limitations of Policing and Human Security for Women

Nicaragua in Comparative Perspective

SHANNON DRYSDALE WALSH

Recent scholarship has called for the gendering of security to specifically include women in the assessment of what constitutes insecurity. Women's police stations are significant for advancing security for women in several ways: they are specialized for women, staffed entirely by women, much more approachable than nonspecialized police units, and visible to victims and survivors as security resources. They also help to increase gender consciousness, and their institutional form transforms incentives so that women's security does not "compete" with other types of security. However, there are multiple limitations to using the state and the police—which have often been the perpetrators of or accomplices to violence—in order to address violence against women. These limitations include having an incomplete toolkit for addressing broader forms of marginalization that put women at risk for violence. Also, women's police stations tend to be institutionally marginalized and underfunded. In order to provide a type of security that fully embodies the principles of human security, women's policing must be part of broader programs addressing underlying issues that make women more vulnerable to becoming victims of violence in the first place—such as inequality, structural violence, poverty, and lack of access to education and healthcare.

A Survivor's Story

Managua, Nicaragua, has more the feel of a small town than a large city. People are generally easygoing and love to chat. I found the early morning hours were a temporary respite from the blistering heat and humidity that usually strike with the late-morning sun. Despite the mild weather, it was not the beginning of a relaxing day. Security alarms were ringing everywhere and people were briskly passing by as I waited on a large rock outside the entrance to one of the women's police stations. The officers told me that there was something wrong with the alarm system and that the station would open up once they got it fixed.

Rosa (a pseudonym) walked up and took a seat beside me as others started to gather and wait for the station to open. We struck up a friendly conversation and she told me she had come for another visit to the women's police station to have them help process her domestic violence case. With a tone of resignation, she noted that her husband had beaten her repeatedly, a replay of the victimization she and her mother had endured earlier in life. Rosa, who was on her way to work, and trying to support her children now as a single mother, was anxious for the station to open. She was glad that she had been assigned a pro bono lawyer. However, she doubted it would help very much because her husband had money and could afford to hire three different private lawyers.

I asked if the police had been helpful. She replied that she was glad they were there but that it was difficult to wait for service when you have children and work, and that the police station was always very busy. Rosa decided to leave about five minutes before they fixed the alarm system. The station opened about an hour late. Although this was not a typical day, with the broken alarms and the station opening much later than usual, Rosa was experiencing some of the many typical frustrations with the police and the justice system. The police were always very busy. In part, this was a perverse outcome of their good public relations encouraging women to contact them for services. In my multiple trips to police stations in and around Managua, the small waiting areas were almost always standing room only with lots of children there missing out on the chance to play or learn. Women generally had to make multiple trips in order to process their cases.

This process can be revictimizing because women are inevitably asked to visit the women's police stations multiple times and repeatedly tell the story of their victimization to different people. Though the state is supposed to be empowering women through this process, it is, in fact, disempowering them by requiring them to use the precious few resources they have (time and money) when they are already in an extraordinarily vulnerable position, forcing them to seek help in the first place. Even though free legal assistance is made available through most women's police stations, women have had to pay for it with their sheer effort under difficult circumstances.[1]

The first women's police station was established in Nicaragua in 1993, and now there are more than 135 stations throughout the country. Women's police stations are staffed entirely by women, and established with this specialized structure in part to create a place where women feel safe reporting violence. Prior to the establishment of women's police stations, police often dissuaded women from pressing charges, ignoring them or even making them feel guilty about the violence perpetrated against them (Jubb et al. 2008, 30). Police officers had also been known to turn victims away and tell them to behave themselves in order to avoid violence.

In response to this widespread discrimination, women's and feminist movements demanded institutional reforms, the provision of comprehensive services for victims, and state provision of access to justice and a commitment to prevent, punish, and eliminate violence against women (Jubb et al. 2008, 22–25). While pressure from women's movement actors was a catalyst for the creation of women's police stations, there was resistance from within the state and the police themselves that required a long period of negotiations and seed funding from international donors before they took root.[2] Women's police stations offer a wide range of prevention and direct services, including receiving complaints, providing psychological services, investigating cases, making arrests, and conducting community outreach and training (Jubb et al. 2010, 247–48).

While there is a need and demand for services to help women victims and survivors of violence, there are multifaceted issues with trying to address violence against women within the security apparatus of the state. Women in general report that they feel more comfortable going to the women's police stations and that this is a big improvement over the old system where there were not specialized officers and women were treated with dismissive attitudes toward victims of domestic violence. However, even though the women's police stations have teams of officers, psychologists, and legal advisers, police have an incomplete toolkit and can only help women in limited ways to live a life free of violent victimization.

Women's police stations can provide a gateway to access the justice system, but they cannot address the broader systemic structural violence that women experience. Paul Farmer describes the concept of structural violence as violence that is "exerted systematically—that is, indirectly—by everyone who belongs to a certain social order" (2004, 307). In Nicaragua, the social and economic structures that disproportionately marginalize women and make them dependent upon their male partners make women particularly vulnerable to sustained violence. This is a worldwide pattern (True 2012). Finally, despite the fact that Nicaragua has the only network of women's police stations in Central America, many do not view violence against women as a security priority, and the stations tend to be underfunded, understaffed, and barely able to meet the demand for their services.

Women's police stations and women's policing units have become more common throughout the world (Pruitt 2013). There has been some research on how women's police stations provide security for women (for example, Hautzinger 2002; Jubb and Izumino 2002; Jubb et al. 2010; Santos 2004) but none that explicitly examine their advances and limitations for providing *human* security. In this chapter, I focus on women's police stations in Nicaragua. Even though they are an improvement over traditional policing, I demonstrate how providing human security for women in the robust sense requires broad institutional and cultural transformation beyond what can be provided for by women's policing.

Women's Police Stations and Human Security

Over the past two decades, scholars have adopted the concept of "human security" to focus on security within borders. This is an appropriate and useful theoretical lens through which to understand the limits and advances of state-based attempts to gender security since women can lack security even in a country that is secure in the more traditional sense of lacking external or internal threats to national security (Ballaeva 2007; United Nations Development Program 1994). Several scholars have also called for the gendering of security to specifically include women in the assessment of what constitutes insecurity (Blanchard 2003; Chenoy 2005; Hoogensen and Stuvøy 2006; Hudson 2005; Hudson 2009; Hudson et al. 2009; Shepherd 2010; Sjoberg and Martin 2010; Tickner 1992, 1995, 2004; Wibben 2011). Women's police stations have become increasingly popular worldwide as an attempt to meet states' obligations to respond to the security threats that are disproportionately faced by women (such as sexual violence and intimate partner violence). Nicaragua has one of the more extensive systems of women's police stations in Latin America, which are operated by women for women and children.

The early 1990s marked a transition from thinking of security almost exclusively in terms of "state security" or "national security" focused on securing national borders to a "human security" framework, as widely disseminated in the 1994 Human Development Report (UNDP 1994). This report argued that a "secure state" with secure borders could still be inhabited by "insecure people." There has been extensive academic debate among those who favor a narrower versus wider definition of security.[3] However, considering the shockingly high rates of violence against women in Central America, it is evident that women in the region are insecure by even a more narrow definition of human security.

In a 2006–2007 survey, 48 percent of Nicaraguan women who had once had a partner (married or unmarried) reported that they had been a victim of verbal or psychological abuse. In addition, 27 percent reported that they had been subjected to physical abuse, and 13 percent reported sexual abuse by their partner or ex-partner (ENDESA 2006–2007, 29). Other surveys in Nicaragua report even higher levels of violence against women. An older study of domestic violence against women in Nicaragua found that 52 percent of ever-married women reported having experienced physical partner abuse at some point in their lives, with a median duration of abuse lasting five years. Twenty-one percent of ever married women reported physical, sexual, *and* emotional abuse, and the likelihood of abuse increased while women were pregnant (Ellsberg et al. 2000). In addition, women are at risk of violent victimization for a broad range of reasons, suggesting that the human security approach that focuses on multidimensional ways to address security problems is necessary.

What is human security? The 2000 UN Millennium Summit agreed on the importance of both "freedom from want" and "freedom from fear" as security concerns (Commission on Human Security 2003). In 2003, the UN's Commission on Human Security rearticulated the importance of shifting to a new paradigm of security that centers on people, not states. It conceptualizes human security broadly: enhancement of human freedoms and human fulfillment; protection from threats; and, the creation of systems that provide people with the building blocks of survival, livelihood, and dignity, offering individuals opportunities and choices to fulfill their own potential (Commission on Human Security 2003). The Commission on Human Security argued that human security complements, but is distinct from, state security in four respects. In terms of human security, (1) the concern is the individual and the community rather than the state; (2) menaces to security include threats and conditions that have not always been classified as threats to state security; (3) the range of actors is expanded beyond just the state; and (4) achieving human security includes empowering people to fend for themselves, and not simply protecting people.

Women's police stations are examples of institutional forms that embody these principles of human security. They are concerned with the individual and community; rather than the state, by focusing on victimization of women and children within state borders. Perpetrators of violence against women and children are recognized as security threats and criminals by women's police stations.[4] Women's police stations, situated within the state, coordinate with nonstate actors in order to improve women's security. Women's police stations can and do empower women in significant ways, though the tools for doing so are relatively limited, and local or uneven institutional implementation often deviates from institutional design.

The kinds of security risks that women face in their daily lives are different from those of men. For example, women are at higher risk for being victimized within the home, and are at higher risk than men for sexualized violence. Since the security risks for women are specialized, a justice system that ignores gender specific differences will inevitably fail to protect women from crimes to which they are disproportionately vulnerable. Although women's movements have at times resisted engaging the state out of legitimate concerns about co-optation, feminist political scientists increasingly recognize that it is necessary for women's movements to intervene, monitor, provide training, and have an increased presence within state bureaucracies in order to appropriately address women's issues (Franceschet 2010; Medie 2013; Staudt 1998, 56; Weldon 2002). In part, women's police stations were constructed in order to improve human security for women. In the following section, I briefly discuss the advantages of this specialized form of policing as well as some key limitations.

Advances and Precarious Positioning of Women's Police Stations

The state is in a precarious position to provide security for women, given that states have at times been a source of threat to their own people. Before the 1979 Sandinista Revolution in Nicaragua, the police (then, the National Guard) worked for the Somoza dictatorship to "maintain order" through violent and coercive means and committed massive human rights violations against real and perceived revolutionaries. Despite the fact that the police were restructured after the Revolution, which dismantled the National Guard, the population at large remained wary of police as a provider of public security. Even after undergoing police reforms and bringing more women into the force, the police as a whole were not providing adequate security for abused women. Specialized women's policing was proposed by women across different sectors in the state and civil society as necessary for improving security and police responsiveness for women victims of violence (Jubb et al. 2008). Women's police stations are precariously situated as a part of the police, which functions as the coercive and repressive arm of the state.

At the same time, specialized institutions that focus on mitigating violence against women help to improve responsiveness to victims in significant ways. Specialization on the structural level helps to reshape institutional incentives such that attending to women victims is an explicit aim of officers within the women's police stations. S. Laurel Weldon (2002) notes that these institutions can help to transform unequal relations of power between men and women and correct for existing gender biases. For example, while far from ideal, women's police stations in Brazil have resulted in a vast improvement in police responsiveness to violence against women (Santos 2005). While these institutions are no guarantee of improving women's security, the lack of them is a virtual guarantee that improvements will not be made and an indicator that the state is failing to secure one of the most basic rights for its women citizens: the right to live a life free of violence. As one interviewee in Nicaragua states: "Violence [against women] is worldwide. There should be women's police stations throughout Central America, because people come and people go and the attention [to victims] should be specialized for women. It is very important that women do not feel alone in the moment that they encounter aggression and violence. If they feel 'if you hit me, I am going to report you to the police,' that already earns them a little respect."[5]

Some of the scenarios that compelled women to advocate for women's police stations include a historical lack of services for women, widespread lack of gender consciousness within the police, and incidents of women being turned away when seeking police protection. Gender consciousness emerged in part through practices of consciousness-raising efforts by Latin American feminists (Jubb and Izumino 2002). As is most relevant to the work of the police, having gender consciousness, at a minimum, would mean viewing violence against women as an expression of male domination or patriarchy (Santos 2005, 49). One interviewee recounts the stark differences between regular police stations and the women's police stations in the late 1990s:[6]

> [In a regular police station] . . . there were times that you would go and spend the entire day waiting. And they would prioritize robbery or something else that was a priority . . . the usual reaction was that "she deserves it" . . . The women's police stations, just getting inside the buildings, was a friendlier environment. . . . It was a place that was nice and clean, where people donated some toys so that children could stay entertained. And there was also some coordination so that someone could look after the children at the time that the mother was with the officer. This was another point: there was privacy. There was an office. You could go inside and close the door and talk with the officer or psychologist or social worker.

Human Security and the Limitations of Women's Police Stations

Although women's police stations advance human security in significant ways, they have several limitations for advancing security within the human security framework. Women's police stations and officers treat violence against women within a narrow justice system framework of response to security threats. They are limited by this role and their institutionally limited toolkit so that they cannot address broader structural forms of violence that make women vulnerable to physical and emotional violence. In addition, women's policing is still not taken as seriously as other forms of policing and goes under resourced. There are also several other limitations regarding the culture, practice, and relationships between the police and civil society. In order to provide a type of security that fulfills broader principles of human security, women's policing must be a part of more comprehensive (state and nonstate) programs that address underlying and interconnected issues of structural violence, women's inequality, poverty, lack of access to education, lack of access to healthcare, and other risks for women's security that make them more vulnerable to becoming victims of violence in the first place. Women's police stations are designed to be a gateway to the justice system. The readily available tools for police officers are to facilitate obtaining restraining orders and facilitating the advancement of legal cases against aggressors through the court system. However, few victims of violence follow through with cases. They often want and need something different that women's police stations can only provide indirectly. It is not practical for most women to simply leave their aggressors because they (and their children) are economically dependent upon them and they have no safe place to go or they are in love with them (which can be a result of traumatic bonding similar to the Stockholm syndrome). In response, women often express a desire to have police help "fix" their relationships. If they were not so physically and economically vulnerable, women might be empowered to effectively demand that their abusers leave or negotiate community intervention. However, the institutional design of women's police stations fails to meet the complex needs of women victims.

Scholarship on women's police stations is rooted in feminism and spans sociology, anthropology, and political science. Critiques of women's police stations focus in part on their failure to implement the feminist goals that were a catalyst for their creation (Hautzinger 2002; Jubb and Izumino 2002; Jubb et al. 2010; Santos 2005). Scholarship on Brazil notes that a lack of gender consciousness among male and female police officers is a serious limitation (Hautzinger 2002; Santos 2005). The reality in Nicaragua is different from that in Brazil: Nicaraguan female police in general demonstrate a higher degree of gender consciousness than is apparent in the accounts of Brazilian female officers. I agree with these scholars that a lack of gender consciousness is an obstacle to empowering women and engendering justice. However, I interpret the instances of lack of sensitivity toward victims in Nicaragua primarily as an outcome of fatigue and frustration from having to apply a limited toolkit for the provision of justice. Women victims of violence need far more comprehensive services and resources than the justice system can provide, such as a way to take care of their children if they are to even consider transitioning away from living in a situation of violence. While victims may request reconciliation, it is not always or even usually because women really want to stay in their relationships. They just want the abuse to stop. However, the police and justice system provide them with no viable alternative that other institutions (such as child protection services) might be able to provide if resources were available.

Focusing on the ways in which women's police stations do and do not implement human security ideals (in addition to feminist ones) highlights the problems that are rooted in an institutionally limited toolkit. It also suggests some avenues for improvement. Women's human security cannot be delivered holistically by the police but rather must be delivered by the police working in close coordination with nonstate actors who are not limited by the institutional structure of the police. Close coordination between the police and nonstate actors has enabled the women's police stations in Nicaragua to make many more advances than would have otherwise been possible. This coordination helps to explain the improved performance of the women's police force, despite having relatively little funding.

For example, the women's movement, with the financial support of several international donors, constructed several women's clinics, including the Ixchen Women's Center, the Association for the Assistance of the New Family in Nicaragua (ANFAM, Asociación para el Apoyo de la Nueva Familia en Nicaragua), and the Si Mujer Foundation. These clinics have coordinated with

women's police stations to provide additional services for victims seeking policing services. For many years, ANFAM performed forensic medical evaluations
for women victims of violence and had the only forensic medicine specialist
on staff that was recognized by the state.[7] Since 1998, the state has had forensic
medicine specialists. These specialists and many others within the state (such
as psychologists, lawyers, and judges) who now provide services to victims of
violence began their work at the women's health centers. Although coordination
between the state and women's movement organizations has been necessary in
order to compensate for a lack of state services, the coordination itself made
it possible to improve them. However, advances are no guarantee of sustained
success. As the political and economic climate changes, so does the capacity of
the state to coordinate with civil society, as do the resources that donors have
available to sustain state institutions. The current president in 2016 is Daniel
Ortega, himself accused of violence against women and protected from potential charges through political immunity. Thus, Nicaragua faces at least two serious challenges for the capacity of state institutions to address violence against
women: the global economic downturn and opposition from powerful state
actors that include the president.[8]

Conclusion

Women's police stations in Nicaragua have improved security in significant
ways. However, they have neither the mandate nor the institutional capacity to
improve security for women in the most substantial ways by providing pathways
to other forms of security. Women's police stations have limited resources and
incentives to implement a broader human security agenda. In order to provide
a sense of security that fulfills the principles of human security in the robust
sense, they must become part of more comprehensive (state and nonstate)
programs that address underlying and interrelated risks to women's security,
including structural violence, women's inequality, and poverty, as well as lack
of access to education and healthcare. Addressing these broader issues would
contribute to preventing abuse since these are factors that make women more
vulnerable to becoming victims of violence. The institutional design of women's
police stations seems premised on the idea that violence against women is the
most significant security risk for women seeking services. However, there are
significant security risks to following through with filing and following up on
a police complaint and eventually leaving an aggressor. These include falling
deeper into poverty and hunger or angering an aggressor who may violently
retaliate.

Women's police stations are an advance in many ways but also have many
drawbacks. They are much better than nonspecialized police forces, which
traditionally have not addressed violence against women as a crime and have

generally refused to implement the law even after domestic violence was criminalized. Having state institutions that address violence against women through a justice system that is not integrated with broader development institutions is problematic for improving women's security. Because women are disproportionately poor and economically dependent upon abusive partners, women's policing alone will be unlikely to provide them with a viable pathway out of a violent household. It is imperative that international donors focus on gendered forms of development such as education and job training programs for women, access to affordable healthcare, state subsidies for child care, enforceable regulations for child support, and temporary or permanent housing for women. Small, local NGOs are often the most capable institutions to implement these programs and can help to both strengthen and monitor the state. Broad-based development programs are not as popular in the modern era of international donor agendas. However, these programs are necessary for providing human security for women who need viable pathways to economic and other forms of security *in order* to achieve bodily security.

ACKNOWLEDGMENTS

I give my heartfelt thanks to the many women in Nicaragua who shared their time and knowledge. I am grateful for comments and suggestions from the book editors [from which this chapter is reprinted] and from Christina Ewig, Terry MacDonald, Lesley Pruitt, Joseph Staats, Aili Mari Tripp, Jaqui True, and Jeremy Youde. This research was funded by the Fulbright-Hays Foundation, Mellon/American Council of Learned Societies, American Political Science Association Fund for the Study of Women and Politics, and the National Endowment for the Humanities.

NOTES

1 See Dána-Ain Davis's discussion of institutional time, "Knowledge in the Service of a Vision: Politically Engaged Anthropology," in *Engaged Observer: Anthropology, Advocacy and Activism*, eds. Victoria Sanford and Asale Angel-Ajani (New Jersey: Rutgers University Press, 2006), 228–38.

2 Anonymous interview from Managua, Nicaragua conducted by the author on February 29, 2008.

3 See reviews of these debates in Bellamy and McDonald 2002; Hoogensen and Stuvøy 2006; King and Murray 2001; Thomas and Tow 2002.

4 This undermines recent and still-prevalent norms that violence against women is a private family matter rather than a public security issue.

5 Anonymous interview from Managua, Nicaragua. Interview conducted by the author on July 24, 2006.

6 Anonymous interview from Managua, Nicaragua. Interview conducted by the author on October 29, 2013.

7 Anonymous interview from Managua, Nicaragua. Interview conducted by the author on February 26, 2008.

8 International donors supporting women's police stations have been withdrawing from Central America. There is evidence that Daniel Ortega continually sexually abused his stepdaughter Zoilamérica Narváez, who revealed this in 1998 (Ojito 1998). Ortega has maintained political immunity from his crimes. Even though he was a leftist leader of the revolution, he has since posed obstacles for coordination between the state and women's organizations in Nicaragua, reportedly fearing that women's organizations were helping Zoilamérica Narváez (Meléndez 2013; Narváez 2002).

33

Forks in the Road of Men's Gender Politics

Men's Rights versus Feminist Allies

MICHAEL A. MESSNER

For more than a century, men have responded to feminist movements in the US and in other Western jurisdictions in varying ways, ranging from outright hostility, to sarcastic ridicule, to indifference, to grudging sympathy, to enthusiastic support (Kimmel 1987; Messner 1997). This chapter argues that large-scale social changes—those shaped by social movements, changing cultural beliefs, and shifts in political economy—create moments of historical gender formation that in turn shape, constrain, and enable certain forms of men's gender politics. In particular, I trace the two most politically engaged tails of a continuum of gender politics—anti-feminist men's rights groups and pro-feminist men allies— with an eye to understanding how moments of historical gender formation shape men's gender politics. First, I draw from an earlier study that outlined the context that gave rise to opposing US men's movements in the 1970s and 1980s (Messner 1997), reiterating parts of that analysis that are relevant to thinking about the concurrent and mutually antagonistic rise of men's anti-feminism and men's pro-feminism. Second, I draw from a recent study of men anti-rape and anti–domestic violence activists in the US, to illuminate men's current engagements with feminism and gender politics (Messner, Greenberg and Peretz 2015).

The 1970s and the present moment generated possibilities for men's gender politics: forks in the road, as it were. The image of historical forks in the road implies choices for men's responses to feminism but not an unlimited range of "free" choices. Rather, feminist challenges and shifts in the gender order confront men with a limited field of structured options: stop dead in your tracks, befuddled; attempt a U-turn and retreat toward an idealized past of male entitlement; turn right and join a backlash against feminism; or bend left and actively support feminism. Adapted from Omi and Winant's (1986) theory of racial formation, I introduce *historical gender formation*, a concept that provides a more nuanced view of the dynamics of gender politics than the dualistic image of a fork in the road. Central to the theory of racial formation is the idea that the grassroots racial justice movements of the 1950s through the 1970s wrested concessions from the state, altered the ways in which racial categories were defined, and created new foundations upon which subsequent racial tensions and politics arose. Similarly, the women's movements of the 1960s and 1970s wrested concessions from the state, challenged and partially transformed cultural values about sex and gender, and succeeded in bringing about substantial reforms in various social institutions. Thus, men's engagements with gender politics today take place in a very different context—one partly transformed by feminism—than they did in the 1970s. I will demonstrate that the 1970s and the present are two moments of gender formation that create different limits and possibilities for men's engagements, both for and against feminism.

1970s Gender Formation: The Women's Movement and Men's Liberation

By the early 1970s, following several years of organizing, the women's liberation movement had exploded on to the social scene. In the US, the most visible feminist activism took place "in the streets": small local consciousness-raising groups, grassroots groups linked by word-of-mouth and hand-printed newsletters, a sprouting of local rape-crisis centers and women's shelters run by volunteers in private homes or low-rent storefronts, all punctuated by mass public demonstrations for women's rights (Allen 1970; Stansell 2010). In other words, in relation to male-dominated institutions like the state, the economy, military, religion, or medicine, feminism in the US was mostly on the outside looking in (with academia, where feminists gained an earlier foothold, a partial exception). The 1970s, then, was a time of deeply entrenched gender inequality across all institutions, against which a grassroots women's movement was organizing on many fronts, characteristically in alliance with gay rights and other social justice movements.

By the early 1970s a few US men—many of them veterans of the new left, antiwar and student movements—responded to the reemergence of feminism in the 1960s by organizing men's consciousness-raising groups and networks, and asking a potentially subversive question: what does feminism have to do with us (Men's Consciousness-Raising Group 1971)? Some leaders promoted the idea of a "men's liberation movement" that would work symmetrically with the women's liberation movement to bring about progressive personal and social change (Farrell 1974; Nichols 1975). They reasoned that a men's liberation program that emphasized potential gains *for men* might draw more interest than one that positioned men as oppressors whose only morally correct action was guilty self-flagellation. The language of sex roles, emerging at that time as the dominant discourse of liberal feminism—just one of multiple feminist positions that emerged in the wake of the 1960s rebirth of feminism—was an ideal means through which to package feminism for men in a way that lessened the guilt and maximized the potential gain that men might expect from "liberation" (Messner 1998). The "female sex role" had clearly oppressed women, men's liberationists argued, and "the male sex role" also harmed men.

Leaders posited men's liberation as the logical flipside of women's liberation but they walked a tightrope from the start. They acknowledged that sexism had oppressed women and privileged men; it was pretty hard to ignore that 59 percent wage gap, the obvious lack of women in political and corporate leadership positions, or the ubiquitous violence against women. But they sought to attract men to feminism by stressing how the "male sex role" was "impoverished," "unhealthy," even "lethal" for men's health, emotional lives, and relationships (Jourard 1974). Thus, from the outset, there was tension in men's liberation's attempt to focus simultaneously on men's institutional power over women *and* on the "costs of masculinity" to men. Savvy men's liberation leaders sought to connect these seemingly contradictory positions by demonstrating that it was in fact men's attempts to secure access to the institutional privileges of masculinity that enforced boys' and men's emotional stoicism, lack of empathy for self and others, physical risk-taking, and unhealthy daily practices like smoking and drinking. Progressive men's liberationists drew from the works of psychologist Joseph Pleck (1977) who argued that while women were *oppressed* by the female sex role, men were *privileged and simultaneously dehumanized* by the male sex role. The social change corollary to this was the assertion that, when men committed themselves to bringing about full equality for women, this would create the conditions for the full humanization of men, including healthier and longer lives and more satisfying relationships with intimate partners, friends, and children.

It did not take long before serious slippage began to occur with men's liberationists' attempts to navigate the tension between emphasizing men's privileges and the costs of masculinity. Less politically progressive leaders began to assert a false symmetry, viewing men and women as differently but equally oppressed by sex roles (Farrell 1974; Goldberg 1976). This assertion generated critical distrust from politically radical women, and vigorous debate from more politically radical men in the movement. By the mid to late 1970s, men's liberation had split directly along this fissure. On the one hand, men's rights organizations stressed the costs of narrow conceptions of masculinity to men, and either downplayed or angrily disputed feminist claims that patriarchy benefited men at women's expense. On the other hand, a profeminist (sometimes called "antisexist") men's movement emphasized the primary importance of joining with women to do away with men's institutionalized privileges. Patriarchy may *dehumanize* men, profeminists continued to insist, but the costs that men pay for adherence to narrow conceptions of masculinity are linked to the promise of patriarchal power and privilege.

In short, men's liberation had premised itself upon a liberal language of symmetrical sex roles, which contributed both to its promise as a movement and to its eventual demise. Following the fissuring of men's liberation, the men's rights movement continued to deploy a narrowly conservative language of sex roles.

Now severed from its progressive roots, a more reactionary tendency within the men's rights movement unleashed overtly antifeminist and sometimes outright misogynist discourse and actions (Baumli 1985). Meanwhile, the emergent profeminist men's movement largely rejected the language of sex roles, adopting instead a radical language of gender relations that facilitated an activist focus on ending men's institutional privileges and men's violence against women (Messner 1997, 1998).

By the mid-1970s the women's movement had altered the political context in ways that made a men's rights movement possible, if not inevitable. The men's rights movement was not simply a kneejerk backlash against feminism; it was a movement that co-opted the liberal feminist language of symmetrical sex roles and then turned this language back on itself. Men's Liberationist turned men's rights advocate Warren Farrell (1974), for instance, borrowed Betty Friedan's (1963) idea that a "feminine mystique" oppressed women, arguing that men were trapped in a "masculine mystique" that narrowly positioned them as breadwinners and protectors. In response to feminist criticisms of the effects on women of being constructed as "sex objects," Farrell posited an equally negative effect on men in being constructed as "success objects." Herb Goldberg's 1976 book *Hazards of Being Male* asserted that male privilege is a "myth." Men actually have it worse than women, Goldberg argued, due to the fact that the male role is far more rigid than the female role, and because women have created a movement through which they can now transcend the limits of culturally imposed femininity. Men's rights organizations broke from the men's liberation movement's gender symmetry and began to articulate a distinct discourse of overt and angry antifeminist backlash. By the late 1970s and early 1980s, men's rights advocates were claiming that men are the true victims of prostitution, pornography, dating rituals, sexist media conventions, divorce settlements, false rape accusations, sexual harassment, and domestic violence (Baumli 1985). And in subsequent decades, the beating heart of the men's rights movement has been organizations that focus—largely through the internet—on fighting for fathers' rights, especially in legal cases involving divorce and child custody (Dragiewicz 2008; Menzies 2007).

Shifting Gender Formations

In the 1980s and into the 1990s the radical power of feminism fractured under a broadside of antifeminist backlash (Faludi 1991), and fragmented internally from corrosive disputes among feminists around issues of race and class inequalities, and divisive schisms that centered on sex work and pornography (Echols 2002). Some key political efforts by US feminists such as the Equal Rights Amendment (ERA) had failed, and feminism was less visible as a mass movement. However, in 1989 sociologist Verta Taylor argued that the US feminist movement had not disappeared; rather, this was a time of "movement abeyance," when activists in submerged networks continued to fight for equality, sustaining below-the-radar efforts that created the possibility for future political mobilizations. At the same time, in Canada, Australia, and other jurisdictions where women's policy machineries were established, feminist networking and activism went "mainstream," as did states' commitment to gender mainstreaming globally (see Bacchi and Eveline 2003; Franzway, Court, and Connell 1989).

But there was something more happening in the 1980s and 1990s US gender politics than "movement abeyance." Feminist momentum from the 1970s and networks of feminist activists combined with three substantial and interrelated social changes: the institutionalization and professionalization of feminism; the emergence of a widespread postfeminist cultural sensibility; and shifts in the political economy, including deindustrialization and the rise of a neoliberal state that slashes taxes for corporations and the rich, cuts public welfare and education, and celebrates individualism and the primacy of the market. These three changes created the current moment of gender formation that makes possible a range of men's engagements with gender politics, including men's rights organizing and profeminist men's activism that take substantially different forms than they did in the 1970s.

Professionally Institutionalized Feminism

The mass feminist movement was in decline in the 1980s and 1990s US, but this was also a time of successful and highly visible feminist institutional reform, including the building of large feminist advocacy organizations like the National Organization for Women (NOW) and the National Abortion Rights Action League (NARAL), the institutionalization of women's and gender studies in universities, and the stabilization of myriad community and campus-based rape crisis and domestic violence centers (Martin 1990). Thus, as was occurring in Canada, Australia, and elsewhere, feminists reformed police practices and legal responses to rape and domestic violence; workplaces incorporated sexual harassment trainings; and schools revised sexist curricula and expanded opportunities for girls' sports. These reforms were accompanied by the creation and expansion of professional sub-fields and occupational niches that focused on women's issues in social work, law and psychology.

The institutionalization of feminism created new challenges for feminists, not the least of which was what Markowitz and Tice (2002) called "the paradoxes of professionalization." On the one hand, professionalization created the conditions for sustaining feminist reform efforts on many fronts, including the creation of career paths for feminists in law, academia, medicine, social work, and other professions (Staggenborg 1988). But on the other hand, it led to a diversion of activist energies away from radical social change efforts toward finding sustainable funding sources for service provision, and also ushered in different organizational processes, with bureaucratic hierarchies displacing earlier feminist commitments to democratic decision-making processes.

US feminists also managed to wrest significant concessions from the state, including the 1974 passage of Title IX (federal law related to gender equity in schools), and the 1994 Violence Against Women Act, which altered the landscape for feminist work against gender-based violence. Even given the fact that state support for women's issues in the US remained minimal, Kristen Bumiller (2013) argues that such "feminist collaboration with the state" threatens to water down, or even sever, the language and grassroots politics of feminism. Moreover, with the continuing decline of the welfare state and the concomitant expansion of neoliberalism, what Ruth Gilmore (2007) calls "the nonprofit industrial complex" emerged as a sort of "shadow state" (Wolch 1990), funded by an exploding number of foundations, and advancing professionalized public health-oriented approaches to issues like violence against women.

The rise of professionally institutionalized feminism, in short, broadened and stabilized the field of feminist action, while simultaneously thinning its political depth, threatening even to make feminist language and analysis disappear altogether: university women's studies programs become "gender studies programs"; "violence against women" morphs to "gender-based violence"; and feminist organizations created by and for women become mixed-gender organizations whose historical roots are easily forgotten in the crush of day-to-day struggles to measure and document the effectiveness of service provisions, needed to win continued funding from foundations or the state (Messner, Greenberg, and Peretz 2015). Professionally institutionalized feminism was also accompanied by a widespread shift in cultural values about gender: namely, the emergence of a postfeminist sensibility.

Postfeminism

As movement feminism receded from public view in the 1990s, a new and controversial "postfeminist" discourse emerged. Feminist scholars have explored and debated the claim that a whole generation of younger people express a postfeminist worldview. On the one side, drawing from public opinion data, sociologists Hall and Rodriguez (2003) found little support for claims of widespread adherence to postfeminism, which they defined as including antifeminist beliefs. But on the other side most scholars have drawn a distinction between postfeminism and opposition to feminism. Postfeminist narratives normally include an appreciation for feminist accomplishments, coupled with a belief that the work of feminism is in the past, and thus that feminist collective action is no longer necessary (Butler 2013). Sociologist Jo Reger (2012) argues that younger women and men for the most part agree with feminist positions on equal opportunities for women and men but tend to experience feminism as both "everywhere and nowhere." The "everywhere" refers both to feminism's professional institutionalization and to the ways that liberal feminist values have permeated popular culture in much the same way that fluoride invisibly permeates public drinking water (in fact, Reger [2012]) refers to today's youth as "generation fluoride"). However, feminism today is also experienced as "nowhere": young people do not see an in-the-streets mass feminist movement, nor do they see any reason for one. The continuing work of professional feminism is, to most young people, as invisible as the cavity-prevention work of fluoride in our public waters.

As with any widely shared generational sensibility, postfeminism contains its own contradictions and limits. Most of the younger women in the supposedly "postfeminist" generation studied by Aronson (2003) appreciated the accomplishments of the feminist movement and many recognized the existence of continued gender inequalities. However, Aronson described roughly half of them as "fence-sitters," passive supporters of feminist goals, thus leaving open the question of how, or under what conditions, postfeminist consciousness might convert to feminist identification and political action. Pomerantz and her colleagues (2013) show that postfeminist discourse makes it hard for schoolgirls to name sexism when it happens, yet they argue that postfeminist narratives have a built-in instability, especially when they run up against the lived reality of continuing sexist constraints on girls. For instance, girls and young women (often supported by their fathers and mothers) can become instant gender equity activists when they discover that they are not being given equal athletic opportunities in schools or colleges, or when college women survivors of sexual assault learn that their own institutions are neither supporting them nor holding perpetrators accountable. In other words, when groups of girls and women bump up against sexist institutional constraints, it is possible for an individualist postfeminist sensibility to convert to collective feminist actions. And when it does, such feminist action is often given form and facilitated by existing institutionalized professional feminism—for instance, campus rape crisis centers or women's law centers.

This feminist optimism, however, faces an uphill struggle against the regressive tendencies built into a postfeminist sensibility that is coterminous with a larger political shift to neoliberal celebrations of individual market consumption choices as drivers for progress. And postfeminism is perfectly consistent with—indeed is shaped by and helps to naturalize—the eclipse of feminist language and politics within the professionalized nonprofit industrial complex. Postfeminism also works in tandem with shifts in the political economy, including the nearly four-decade-long trend of deindustrialization that accompanied the ascendance of neoliberalism and that has disproportionately rendered poor and blue-collar young men redundant, a shift eventually referred to by some as "the decline of men."

Deindustrialization and "The Decline of Men"

The early 1980s recession accelerated a continuing deindustrialization of the American labor force that resulted in the elimination of millions of unionized jobs, rising levels of structural unemployment, and the growth of low-paid nonunionized service sector jobs (Wilson 1989). As in the UK under Margaret Thatcher, in Australia under John Howard, and in Canada under Stephen Harper, the policies of Reaganomics facilitated this economic restructuring by tugging the nation away from a New Deal/Great Society welfare state toward a state based on neoliberal ideas that celebrated individualism and the primacy of the market, while slashing taxes on rich individuals and corporations and cutting support for welfare and education. These shifts continued in subsequent decades, resulting in the dramatic growth of a super-rich class of people, a shrinking middle class and a growing proportion of working poor in the population. The economic restructuring that accelerated from the 1980s and 1990s had multiple and devastating effects; however, for my purposes here, I want to focus on how the neoliberalization of the economy was especially devastating for families headed by blue-collar male wage earners. As women flowed into the labor market by the millions—as much out of necessity as for reasons sparked by ideals of feminist empowerment—the more educated ones poured into a growing field of professional occupations, while the greater mass of women filled an expanding array of low-paid pink collar and service sector jobs (Charles and Grusky 2004). While professional class men continued to fare reasonably well in this economic restructuring, blue-collar and poor men—disproportionately men of color—faced an increasingly bleak field of economic opportunity (Wilson 1996).

As the 1990s came to a close, Connell (1995a) documented how the crumbling structural foundation for the male breadwinner role had escalated the gender insecurities of young working-class men. Deteriorating public schools, declining hope for decent jobs in inner cities, and the expansion of prisons combined to create—for younger generations of Black and Brown boys and young men—contexts conducive to skyrocketing school dropout rates, neighborhood gang activity, illegal commerce in the informal economy, and high levels of domestic abuse and other forms of violence against women (DeKeseredy, Shahid, and Schwartz 2003; Flores and Hondagneu-Sotelo 2013; Rios 2011). And right at the time, when the broader culture is trumpeting the arrival of "involved fatherhood," the constraints on young poor and working-class men make the achievement of the middle-class ideal of an involved breadwinning father increasingly unreachable.

Men and Gender Politics Today

The three trends I have outlined—professionally institutionalized feminism, the emergent culture of postfeminism, and a post-industrial political economy characterized by deindustrialization and neoliberal state policies—together help to constitute the present moment of gender formation. Next, I will sketch how these three trends together make possible particular forms of men's antifeminist and profeminist actions.

Possibilities for Antifeminist Men's Rights Activism

By the 2000s, shifts in the political economy, combined with the increased visibility of women in higher education, popular culture and politics, and the growing public awareness of the institutionalization of women's rights, sparked journalistic and political hand-wringing about a supposed "war against boys" in public schools and a widespread "decline of males" in the public sphere (Sommers 2001; Tiger 2000). These escalating public concerns about boys and men created fertile ground for a resurgent men's rights movement.

But it is unlikely that we will see a widely popular or even marginally successful frontal attack on feminism from men's rights groups. This is in part because the same postfeminist sensibility that views feminism as a movement of the past is likely also to view aggressively anti-feminist men's rights activism as atavistically misogynistic. As values favoring public equality for women are increasingly institutionalized and defined not in a language of politicized feminism but more in a common-sense language of equity and fairness, this shift also contracts the possibilities for antifeminism. In a sense, I am suggesting that the institutional deck is stacked against overt antifeminist backlash, be it frontal attacks on Title IX in schools, or men's rights groups' challenges to the state's (still minimal) support for women's shelters. While this outcome can and should be seen as feminist success, I am not arguing that it is time for a celebratory feminist victory lap. History, to be sure, has not ended. Dragiewicz's (2008; 2011) research on US men's rights groups' attempts to stop state funding of women's shelters shows how this moment of gender formation still includes openings for antifeminist backlash, as does Girard's (2009) and Mann's (2012) research on similar efforts in Canada. However, the story at the heart of this research also illustrates the legal limits of such backlash; after all, professional feminist legal activists defeated the antifeminist actions analyzed by Dragiewicz, Girard, and Mann. Today, contingent on the specifics of national political developments, institutionalized feminism continues to influence legal and other decision making, albeit in a context that is often marked by deep controversy (Brodie 2008). Arguably, institutionalized feminism in the US now occupies a legal high ground, notwithstanding one that is still sometimes contested.

Rather than overt antifeminist backlash, I argue that what is more likely to gain traction today in the US is a "kinder, gentler" form of men's rights discourse and organizing, such as that now characterized by Warren Farrell, often considered the "godfather" of the men's rights movement. Farrell's analysis in the 1980s and early 1990s drifted from the liberal feminist symmetry of men's liberation to asserting in his book *The Myth of Male Power* (1993) that there are many ways in which men are victimized by women's less visible forms of power. For instance, in response to women's attempts to stop sexual harassment in workplaces, Farrell claimed that in fact it was male employers who were disempowered and victimized by their secretaries' "miniskirt power, cleavage power, and flirtation power." In his more recent public speeches, however, Farrell appears to have returned to a less combative language of gender symmetry, reminiscent of his mid-1970s perspective (Farrell 2014). While it may seem on the surface that men are privileged with higher status and higher paying jobs, Farrell asserts, men pay a huge price for accepting the increased responsibilities that come with these jobs. Women just don't choose to enter higher paying careers, he claims, and they are smart to reject the stress; their lives are better for it. Farrell's insistence that gender divisions of labor result not from institutional discrimination against women but rather from the accumulated individual "choices" of women and men is consistent with current neoliberal cheerleading for individual women to "lean in" to compete with men as professionals or corporate leaders. But Farrell's twist is that women's refusals to lean in and compete are actually healthy and smart choices; men are the chumps for working so hard for public success.

Farrell's strategy is to raise sympathies for men, not to engage in antifeminist polemics. In a postfeminist context, this more moderate men's rights discourse is likely to ring true as reasonable, as common sense. In this worldview, the women's movement succeeded in improving women's lives, and the logical flip-side is this: in the absence of a symmetrical men's movement to improve men's lives, men suffer harm. While antifeminist vitriol continues to mark men's rights discourse on the internet (Dragiewicz 2008, 2011), the emergent "moderate" voice of the men's rights movement does not directly attack feminism or disparage women. Rather, it maneuvers in the postfeminist interstices between the "everywhere" and the "nowhere" of feminism. The means to improve men's lives are articulated to the general public in a depoliticized and individualized "equality language" (Behre 2015) that resonates in a postfeminist and neoliberal context where present-day feminism seems to be "nowhere." Meanwhile, leaders such as Farrell (2014) are apparently coming to realize that they need not rant to a men's rights audience that feminism is "everywhere," privileging women and holding men down. This is what these men already know; it is the fluoride in their ideological waters.

As a result, men's rights rhetoric that contains an *implicit antifeminism* is likely to resonate with men who feel insecure or embattled. And I would speculate that moderate men's rights leaders' focus on individual choice and their implicit antifeminism resonates best with educated middle-class White men who do not want to appear to be backward misogynists. A central aspect of privileged men's gender strategies in recent years, after all, is to present one's self as an educated modern man who is supportive of gender equality. And this is achieved partly by projecting atavistic sexism on to less educated men, poor men, immigrant men and men of color (Dekeseredy, Shahid and Schwartz 2003; Hondagneu-Sotelo and Messner 1994).

In this context, is there a potential for less educated poor and working class men to constitute a sort of lumpen anti-feminist army for men's rights? After all, declining economic opportunities for working class men to achieve a traditional conception of the male breadwinner role, combined with the perception that the law favors mothers over fathers in divorce and custody settlements might seem to create a perfect storm for the creation of an army of angry working class fathers ready to join men's rights organizations (Kimmel 2013). Thus far, this has hardly been the case. Most leaders of the men's rights movement are not poor and working class men; rather, they are men with the educational and financial resources needed to form organizations, create websites or hire attorneys. But just as the multibillionaire Koch brothers' well-financed right-wing antistatism appeals to many lower-middle-class Whites, the men's rights movement's anti-feminist backlash rhetoric could possibly appeal to men with less education and fewer resources, men who may have a powerful father hunger but feel that their "rights" have been denied them by controlling mothers, and especially by the state.

Indeed, in their study of poor working-class fathers in Philadelphia and Camden, sociologists Edin and Nelson (2014) found that the men they studied frequently express "a profound, abiding mistrust of women"; they think "the system" that enforces child support automatically and unfairly favors mothers, who themselves are gatekeepers who keep the men away from their own children. These men feel as though they have few rights, while both mothers and "the system" treat them as though they are "just a paycheck" (when many of these fathers have no regular paycheck). In fact, this discourse is precisely what is commonly disseminated on men's rights internet sites (Dragiewicz 2008, 2011; Mann 2005; Menzies 2007). The common feminist retort to fathers' rights claims have in the past been something like this: "When you share fully in the *responsibilities* of birth control, and then also share equally the *responsibilities* of child support and childcare *before* divorce, *then* you can share parental rights afterwards." But the stories of poor fathers reported by Edin and Nelson (2014) illustrate the inadequacy of this rejoinder. These are men who desire deeply to be foundational and present in their children's lives but who face seemingly insurmountable institutional barriers to achieving and sustaining this parental ideal. To date, there is very little evidence that masses of poor fathers are joining as foot soldiers in antifeminist collective action. But if current industrial nations continue to lack the will to address the many ways in which a huge strata of young men are being treated as dispensable by the economy and the criminal justice system, it is possible that some of these men will find resonance with internet-based antifeminist men's rights discourse that blames women and the liberal state for men's woes.

Possibilities for Men's Profeminist Activism

The recent institutionalization and professionalization of feminism has included a modest expansion of opportunities for men professionals to work on gender issues in social work, academia, law, and other fields. This expanding base of men's professional action in gender fields carries both promise and risk. Especially given the recent explosions of public awareness of sexual assault and domestic violence in academia, the military, and men's sports, this moment of opportunity and risk is nowhere more apparent than within the array of professional fields that confront violence against women. In 2014, even the president of the US—not usually a platform for feminist calls for action—called on men to take an active role in ending violence against women.

Feminist women toiled for the past half-century to transform public awareness about violence against women, and to create and sustain rape crisis centers and domestic violence shelters. For the most part, feminist women welcome male allies who step up to prevent future acts of sexual and domestic violence. But some feminists in the antirape and anti–domestic violence community are also cautious about the ways in which male allies still benefit from male privilege that works to the detriment of women professional colleagues (Messner, Greenberg, and Peretz 2015). And in a context of postfeminism, long-time feminist activists fear that, just as the field of gender-based violence prevention has expanded to include more men, the politics underlying antiviolence actions have thinned, severing action from feminist historical and political roots (Greenberg and Messner 2014).

In short, I suggest that while feminists continue to strategize vigilantly against eruptions of misogynist antifeminist backlash, a less obvious but perhaps greater challenge springs from the ways in which the very conditions of historical gender formation that facilitate men's movement into professionalized "gender work" also threaten to eclipse feminism altogether. In particular, widespread ideologies of postfeminism, coupled with depoliticized and marketized antiviolence initiatives, threaten to further erase feminist women's organizational leadership as well as the feminist analysis that underlies antiviolence work. Today's antiviolence workers commonly refer to "the movement" not as an eruption of mass activism, but as a network of likeminded antiviolence professionals, and they talk of "politics" not in terms of activism aimed to bring about structural transformations but as strategies designed to keep their organizations funded (Messner, Greenberg, and Peretz 2015). Much of the violence prevention curricula deployed in schools and communities today has jettisoned the feminist idea that violence against women springs from men's overconformity with dominant conceptions of masculinity instead deploying a pragmatic (and more individualistic) strategy of teaching boys and men to make "healthy choices"—a discourse that, not incidentally, is shaped so that it can be subjected to "metrics" that document program effectiveness in support of continuing requests for state or foundation funds.

What are the forces that potentially counter the depoliticization of antirape and anti–domestic violence work? One—though this is likely to be temporary—is the continued presence of older feminist women in the field, who mentor younger cohorts of professional women and men in ways that keep feminist analysis and goals at the center of the work. A second source of change, potentially more transformative, lies in the recent growth of diversity among men in the antiviolence field. As the field has expanded in the US, the opportunities for men to work in internships and paid jobs in rape and domestic violence prevention, state and foundation funders have increasingly targeted violence prevention efforts to communities of boys and men considered to be "at risk" due to poverty, crumbling schools, and high rates of gang violence and drug use. There is a widely held perception in the field today that boys of color from poor communities will be more open to learning from young men from their own communities, who look and talk more like they do. This in turn has created a demand for a more racially diverse influx of young men into violence prevention work.

The growing number of young African American and Latino men entering antiviolence work is infusing a much-needed intersectional perspective into professional antiviolence work. Intersectionality—the perspective that takes the simultaneity of gender, race, class, and other forms of "intersecting" inequalities as its conceptual core—has long been central in academic feminism (Collins 1990; Crenshaw 1991). Indeed, it could be argued that, within academic feminism, intersectionality has for some years been a paradigmatic theoretical perspective and research approach (McCall 2005). But the radical insights of feminist intersectionality risk being diluted or even lost in professionally institutionalized violence prevention efforts.

Men of color's movement into professionalized antiviolence work brings to the field not so much a background in academic intersectionality but rather an experience-based *organic intersectionality*, different in two ways from the experiences of most White middle-class men in the field. First, young men of color frequently begin with a commitment to addressing boys' vulnerabilities to various forms of violence—in the home, in the street, and from police. These young men often began working with boys around gang and substance abuse issues, in college internships and then paid jobs in non-profit organizations. In that work, they discovered the links between young men's vulnerabilities to multiple forms of violence with their experiences with rape and domestic violence. In short, it was through doing "race and class" work with young men that many of these antiviolence workers "discovered" gender. This in turn created the possibility for an analysis of violence that does not always start with gender as necessarily being foundational (as it so often does with White middle-class men who enter the antiviolence field), instead developing into an intersectional understanding of violence, grounded organically in the everyday experiences of race, class, and gender as interlocking processes (Messner, Greenberg, and Peretz 2015).

This organically intersectional analysis underlies a second difference between young men of color and White middle-class men in the antiviolence field. Young men of color tend to view the now-standard curricula deployed in school- and community-based violence prevention efforts as flat, one-dimensional, and thus inadequate. Instead, these young men are innovating and even departing from the standard curricula, developing approaches that draw, for instance, from "theatre of the oppressed" radical community education pedagogies that plumb the everyday life experiences of boys in order to "make it real." Men of color's emergent organically intersectional pedagogies frequently also circle back to academic feminist intersectionality, discovering there a ready resource for understanding connections between violence against women with other forms of "gender-based violence"—like sexual abuse and homophobic bullying of boys and transgender youth—as well as with forms of violence that may not be so obviously (or at least primarily) *about* gender—such as gang violence or police violence. The progressive potential of the rise of organic intersectionality in the antiviolence field is twofold. First, it has direct appeal to young boys in poor communities because they can see their stake in working for change in their schools and communities. Second, it can reinfuse a powerful dose of radical social justice–oriented politics back into a professionalized antiviolence field that in recent years has seen a severe thinning of its politics, and a near evaporation of its ability to address connections between gender-based violence with broader social justice issues like poverty, warfare, and cuts in public support for schools and families.

Conclusion

In this chapter I have argued that large-scale changes created by social movements and shifts in political economy generate moments of *historical gender formation* that in turn shape, constrain, and enable certain forms of men's gender politics. The gender formation of the 1970s, constituted by a mass feminist movement operating for the most part outside of male-dominated institutions, created a context for the rise of an internally contradictory men's liberation movement that soon split into an antifeminist men's rights movement and supportive pro-feminist men's organizations.

For feminism, and for men's activism around gender issues, the current moment of gender formation is constituted in part by three large shifts that accelerated in the 1980s and 1990s: the professional institutionalization of feminism, the rise of postfeminism, and neoliberal transformations in the political economy. In the US and across western jurisdictions, the radical possibilities of feminism were largely eclipsed behind the rise of nonprofit and state-driven initiatives that confront issues like gender-based violence through a professionalized and marketized public health model. While this context has not closed off the possibilities for men's antifeminist backlash—including vitriolic internet-based misogyny and efforts to oppose state funding for "women's issues"—I have pointed to two formations that might prove to be of greater concern than overt antifeminism. First, postfeminism and neoliberalism create a context conducive to a "kinder-gentler" moderate men's rights strategy that skirts analysis of structural inequalities in favor of a common-sense celebration of individual choice for women and men. This approach, if successful, will further erode feminist gains in public life, while affording already-privileged men a language through which they can position themselves not as atavistic backlashers but as modern "new" men who are supportive of equal choices for women and men, unfettered by state policies.

Second, I have argued that the current moment of gender formation has expanded the possibilities for men's participation as allies with women in anti-violence work. While this is a welcome development for most feminists, on the one hand, the current professionalization of gender work in a context of post-feminism risks eclipsing the language and progressive possibilities of feminism, right at a time when men are moving into the field. On the other hand, the linkages of institutionalized antiviolence work with a growing public concern with "at-risk" boys and young men in poor schools and communities has drawn more young men of color into the field. In other words, the very social forces—neoliberalization of the economy, criminalization of poor young men of color—that some fear might form the basis for an army of angry antifeminist men's rights activists, have also created the conditions for a movement of young men of color into the gender-based violence prevention field.

This influx of men of color into the antiviolence field has introduced a perhaps unexpected progressive counterforce against the ways in which professionalized antiviolence efforts under neoliberalism approach sexual assault or domestic violence as discrete, public health issues. Men of color's organically intersectional understandings of violence, coupled with resources from feminist social justice research, have led to the development of innovative strategies in the field that offer a progressive challenge to the depoliticizing drift of conventional professionalized and marketized antiviolence work. For the most part, this challenge emerges not in the language of a narrowly professionalized liberal feminism but packaged instead in a broadened "social justice" framework within which feminist ideas about men's violence against women are a central thread in a broad intersectional framework that also addresses the institutionalized violences of racism, poverty, unemployment, declining schools, and the criminal justice system.

Does feminism risk being lost in the social justice configuration now emerging in the professionalized antiviolence field? Do women's concerns with sexual assault and domestic violence risk being subordinated once again to men's concerns about class and race issues? Yes. But the intersectional social justice framework also holds the promise of broadening feminism beyond the limits of the individualistic white professional class feminism so often criticized by feminist women of color. And here is where the continued importance and power of feminist professionals and institutions come into play: veteran feminists can keep alive the flame of a feminism that burns brightly precisely because its politics remain ignited by deep and multilevel commitments to justice efforts.

34

Linguistic Nonviolence and Human Equality

WILLIAM GAY

Linguistic violence, whether intentional or unintentional, is, at the least, disrespectful to the persons to whom it is addressed. Moreover, linguistic violence typically precedes and sustains physical violence. People find disrespecting and even killing individuals and groups easier to do when linguistic terms used to describe others reduce them to an inferior or even subhuman status. By contrast, linguistic nonviolence at least removes words of disrespect and can reduce physical violence against persons. Linguistic nonviolence, by changing our language, can change our thought and can contribute to attitudes and behaviors that foster human equality and support the quest for social justice (Gay 1998a).

This chapter seeks to support the claims outlined above. The first section of this chapter will review the concept of linguistic violence and will illustrate some of its manifestations. Gender violence, racist violence, heterosexist violence, and many other forms of violence depend on demeaning language. The realities of linguistic violence stretch from the extremes of totalitarian and genocidal language all the way down to very subtle forms, such as the language found in children's jokes that convey mean attitudes toward others.

The second section of this chapter will present the concept of linguistic nonviolence and will address its role in reducing not only linguistic violence but also physical violence. Alternative terms and modes of speaking and writing are possible. The terms of discourse can be placed on a continuum from the most negative through the more neutral to the most positive. Among the terms of discourse, choice is possible. Even if positive terms and modes of expression are not present they can be developed, because linguistic creativity is also possible. Positive self-description by members of oppressed groups is an important step toward self-affirmation and toward social acceptance and respect.

In the third and final section, the practice of linguistic nonviolence will be related to the quest for comprehensive justice and equality for all persons. This quest needs to be global and is closely connected with nonviolent strategies for social and political protest and change. While ending linguistic violence against women or any other group is not sufficient for ending gender violence or any other type of violence, the advancement of linguistic nonviolence in any of these areas is a significant achievement.

The Concept of Linguistic Violence

Numerous writers have applied the concept of violence to more than direct bodily injury. Within philosophy, Newton Garver, for example, has developed a typology of violence that includes overt (physical) and covert (psychological) forms, as well as personal and institutional forms (1968). In Garver's terms, what I call linguistic violence can occur as covert institutional violence or as covert personal violence, since the harm is more psychological than the types of physical violence found in overt forms. The covert harm is institutional when it is a consequence of the established lexicon and grammar of a language (*la langue*) that legitimates unequal social and political roles and opportunities. The covert harm is personal when it results from an individual intentionally or unintentionally employing in speaking or writing (*la parole*) a negative term against another person or group when some of the alternative terms available are more neutral or even positive.

Of course, some writers oppose the extension of "violence" to language. Thomas Platt, for example, rejects this extension, pointing out that as the application of a term becomes broader, its specificity decreases even to the point that it can refer to almost anything (1992). I have responded to this objection elsewhere in defending the reality of linguistic violence (1999). Moreover, by now, the concept of linguistic violence is broadly used in academic and even more popular sources (Friedrich 2007). So, what is the scope of linguistic violence and how, precisely, can language be violent?

Throughout history, linguistic violence has occurred alongside physical violence, often preceding, facilitating, and rationalizing physical violence. Cross-culturally linguistic violence against women, against racial, ethnic, and religious groups, and against LGBTQ+ people is especially common. But, how does language do violence? How can language hurt or harm us? Stephanie Ross contends, "Words can hurt, and one way they do is by conveying denigrating or demeaning attitudes" (1981). To support her view, Ross utilizes Joel Feinberg's contention that hurt is a species of harm and that victims are necessarily aware of hurts. (For example, while assault is an incidence of hurt, undetected burglary is a case of harm.) Ross presents the distinction between offense and oppression as parallel to Feinberg's distinction between hurt and harm. As she puts it, "One can be oppressed unknowingly but offense requires (logically or conceptually) the awareness and acknowledgment of its victim" (1981, 97). Thus, we are conscious of the hurt inflicted by offensive language, though we may not be aware of the harm perpetuated by oppressive language.

Ross does not argue that some language is oppressive, but I do. I contend that oppressive language, like offensive language, involves linguistic violence, though its victims more frequently are not conscious of how it harms them. This type of linguistic violence is commonly viewed as part of what Johan Galtung terms cultural violence or the ways social systems use their various institutions, including language, to promote the legitimacy of their forms of social hierarchy or social discrimination (1990). While I support this view, I do not go so far as some writers. Ellen Gorsevski, for example, asserts that linguistic violence is a form of physical violence (1998). While linguistic violence, at least in its forms that are offensive and hurtful, can have measurable physical consequences, I do not emphasize these consequences. The psychological consequences of linguistic violence are often paramount and can more readily be traced to linguistic causes than can physical consequences.

So, if linguistic violence is real and includes both offensive and oppressive types that are parts of language as a system (*la langue*) and in its use (*la parole*), can anything be done to reduce the scope of linguistic violence and its deleterious consequences? The issue is whether linguistic violence is an unavoidable consequence of the institution of language and the speech acts of individuals or whether through conscious effort it can be eliminated or at least reduced. I argue here that linguistic violence can be reduced and, thereby, can advance human equality and social justice. I will focus on efforts to identify and at least reduce the many forms of linguistic violence (Gay 1998a). This continuum contains numerous abusive forms, such as racist, sexist, and heterosexist discourse. David Burgest, for example, notes how racist language serves to justify and rationalize the formation of groups for purposes of isolation (1973). Luce Irigaray observes that sexist language, along with racist language, pervades the history of discourse (1989). Jean Bethke Elshtain stresses the violence of sexist language (1982). Deborah Cameron goes further, stating, "Sexist language teaches us what those who use it and disseminate it think women's place ought to be: second-class citizens, neither seen nor heard, eternal sex-objects and personifications of evil" (1985, 91). These attitudes make clear several of the ways in which sexist language is violent. Cameron says such attitudes and terminology refer "to violent speaking and writing and to violent-centric language" (1985, 4). Sexist language comprises a large component of this violent language.

Another arena in which abusive language abounds is in the derogatory terminology used to describe LGBTQ+ people (McConnell-Ginet 2001). In relation to working with homeless LGBTQ+ youth who enter the Ali Forney Center in New York City, the largest agency in the world serving homeless LGBTQ+ youth, Heather Gay comments, "they experienced increased levels of verbal abuse in their homes due to their LGBTQ identities, which often then escalated to physical violence. This is often the cause of [their] becoming homeless—either because they are fleeing verbal (linguistic) and physical violence in their homes, or because their parents have told them they can no longer live there due to their LGBTQ identity" (personal communication 2017). Put in context, while about half (51 percent) of hate crime incidents are motivated by race-based bias, sexual orientation is the third-highest motivator of hate crime incidents (17 percent) (HRC 2017).

In brief, race, gender, and sexual orientation are indicators of the most likely victims of linguistic and physical violence. Within the LGBTQ+ community, people of color and transgender and gender nonconforming individuals are especially prone to be victims of gender violence and hate crimes. As Heather Gay observes, "Many of our trans female youth describe intense gender violence that happens every day simply walking down the street. They receive an incredibly heightened level of verbal and physical abuse as compared to their LGB peers. They are "cat-called," spoken to in a derogatory manner by strangers, and physically attacked just for walking down the street. We see this particularly with our trans female clients, though our TGNC [transgender/gender nonconforming] clients experience higher levels of verbal and physical violence overall" (personal communication 2017). A report by the National Coalition of Anti-Violence Programs that focuses on LGBTQ+ survivors of violence states, "the most common types of hate violence reported were verbal harassment (20 percent), threats or intimidation (17 percent), and physical violence (11 percent)" (National Coalition of Anti-Violence Programs 2017, 12). While these statistics do not establish that reducing linguistic violence would reduce physical violence, they do support the view that linguistic violence and physical violence are closely connected. These statistics are also consistent with what occurs across the spectrum of violence from subtle forms through programs of genocide in relation to how linguistic violence precedes and sustains physical violence (Gay 2007). So, measures to reduce the various forms of violence are crucial. For example, for over four decades the Center for Anti-Violence Education (CAE) has been providing violence prevention programs, including free preteen through adult programs in self-defense and online resources such as safety tips for at-risk persons for when they are on the streets, in transportation, at home, and with friends (Center for Anti-Violence Education n.d.).

The Concept of Linguistic Nonviolence

Language does not so much determine thought as, for practical purposes, it makes some rows much easier to hoe and makes others require arduous and often unappreciated labor. However, such difficult linguistic labor is a key component in resistance by the oppressed. The aim is not to socialize any disenfranchised groups into the linguistic practices of the power elite. Instead, the aim is the transformation of language and the social relations on which it rests (Gay 2018). For this task, feminism provides several models for those wishing to supplant linguistic violence against women and other linguistically abused groups in society. These models include both methods for empirical research and recommendations for political action. A response to sexist language, however, should be distinguished from the general struggle against oppression, as Lisa Heldke and Peg O'Connor show in presenting the interconnections among racism, sexism, and heterosexism (2004). Nevertheless, a response to sexist language is an important part of this much broader struggle. In this regard care ethics has provided feminism with an important orientation for moving beyond linguistic and physical violence.

Care ethics stresses the way in which persons are entangled in a web of dynamic relationships that they may wish to maintain or repair. Care ethics also replaces the punitive orientations of retribution found in corporal punishment, capital punishment, and international war. Carol Gilligan's seminal work *In a Different Voice* distinguishes "Justice Ethics" and "Care Ethics" (1982). "Justice Ethics" represents the abstract and retributive approach traditionally favored in philosophy and by men. Alternatively, "Care Ethics" is a relational approach to morality that avoids generalization in favor of particularity and connection. Gilligan notes, "While an ethic of justice proceeds from the premise of equality—that everyone should be treated the same—an ethic of care rests on the premise of nonviolence—that no one should be hurt" (1982, 174). Her perspective has been appropriated in many fields. Nel Noddings proceeded to argue that duty itself emerges out of care and that certain intimate situations of caring, such as the one between a mother and her child, are natural (1984). Sara Ruddick, Virginia Held, and Betty Reardon also made important contributions. A further point that is stressed increasingly is that care need not remain solely in the female realm and that an ethics of care applies to all human beings (Hamington 2004; see also Comins Mingol, this volume).

We can choose various ways to practice linguistic nonviolence (Gay 1998b). Whether we are conscious of their effects, altered terminology and changed descriptions can comfort and even advantage us. For example, language comforts us when used to affirm diversity and achieve recognition. Lucius Outlaw argues linguistic transformations designed to raise consciousness and alter behavior were central features in the struggle for civil rights by African Americans (1974; 2005). An example from the historical period to which he refers is the expression "Black is beautiful." Particular terms, with their respective histories, are being used in new ways. Many feminists have written extensively along lines similar to Outlaw. The effort to shift from the use of "Miss" or "Mrs." to use of "Ms." is one example. Just as "Mr." does not convey the marital status of a man, even so "Ms." does not convey the marital status of a woman. Use of "Mr." or "Ms." is neutral on marital status and even sexual orientation, though the binary designation of gender remains. In relation to the LGBTQ+ community, Heather Gay adds, "Continuing to normalize people's identities in our culture at large (in schools, families, churches, etc.) is one of the best ways to try to reduce and combat the linguistic and physical violence against LGBTQ youth" (personal communication, 2017). In relation to pronoun use, the contemporary way transgender people are referring to pronouns is by saying "Personal Gender Pronouns" (or PGPs). Someone's personal gender pronoun indicates who they "are" and not just a preference. So, using someone's Personal Gender Pronoun is affirming and reduces linguistic violence against TGNC people.

The absence of negative terms in the public sphere, however, can mask the continuation of negative attitudes and terminology in the private sphere. It can be more like negative peace and can do little or nothing to reduce injustice. For example, broadcasters in local and national news media may avoid using terms such as "dyke" or "fag" or even "homosexual," but they may continue to hold discriminatory views and even use such derogatory terms when they think their remarks are not being broadcast or recorded. In the same way, a government may cease referring to a particular nation as "a rogue state," yet may continue to foster prejudice toward this nation and its inhabitants. Regardless, even if terminated, negative terms that have been spoken or written continue to have negative effects, as happened following the remarks by Donald Trump that protested protecting immigrants from Haiti, El Salvador, and several African nations that he termed "shithole countries" and, in this case, the terms were not retracted and no apology was issued (Dawsey 2018).

When prejudices remain unspoken, at least in public forums, their detection and eradication are difficult. Persons who bite their tongues to comply with the demands of political correctness may have changed their way of speaking in public but not their way of thinking, speaking, and behaving when outside public scrutiny. Efforts to establish a practice of linguistic nonviolence that is analogous to positive peace are part of a larger struggle to reduce cultural violence (Gay 2018). Linguist Patricia Friedrich describes empirically how language can foster violence or nonviolence and argues that we should use nonviolent language to foster nonviolent society (2007). For moving toward her version of a practice of linguistic nonviolence, she stresses efforts to advance communicative peace, linguistic choice, and languages of wider communication. Communicative peace would be part of the practice of linguistic nonviolence. Linguistic choice is part of the development of alternative cultural production. The fault is not with language, but the responsibility is with us in how we speak and act.

The Quest for Justice and Equality for All

Three strategies are especially important for supplanting linguistic violence against women and other oppressed groups and for developing practices of linguistic nonviolence and greater human equality.

Breaking the Violence of Silence without Resorting to Violence

The silence surrounding child abuse, partner abuse, and social discrimination—domestic to international injustice—is all too pervasive. Often in the face of linguistic violence and even physical violence, we remain silent. In many cases silence itself is violence. To remain silent before the injustices around us is to be complicit with their perpetuation. However, in breaking the silence, our aim should be to avoid violence in either its physical or verbal forms. Étienne Balibar has argued convincingly against the thesis of the "convertibility" of violence (2015). "Counter violence" and "revolutionary violence," like state violence, are all forms of violence, and those who wish to advance human equality need to be vigilant if they are to avoid lapses into violence—whether they seek to establish or to maintain what their group presently views as "law-and-order" or justice.

Nevertheless, in breaking the silence, several levels of nonviolent discourse and action are open to us. At the level of speech, we can use diplomacy to address injustice and engage progressively in discussion, negotiation, and arbitration. In our actions, we can also progress from intervention to disruption (Gürsözlü 2014). All of these forms of speaking and acting can remain nonviolent. Genuine peace making and efforts to advance social justice and human equality need to occur between silence and violence (Gay 1994).

An interesting example of a nonviolent response to the violence of silence can be found in women's sports. Darcy Plymire and Pamela Forman review how women in sports are often assumed to be lesbians and, as a consequence, athletes, coaches, and administrators in women's sports avoid giving any appearance of or voice to lesbianism in sports (2000). Since the common prejudice is that fans and sponsors would abandon women's sports if lesbian athletes were to be visible and vocal as lesbians, the "code of silence" that has resulted has given these athletes few options for breaking the silence—until the internet. Plymire and Forman document how the internet offers fans a chance to challenge the "code of silence" and contribute to discussions among those who are supportive of lesbians in sport. More broadly, they conclude that the embracing of "out" lesbian athletes as role models in these internet sites could serve as a positive step for all women athletes.

Using and Transforming the Oppressor's Language

In an analysis of derogatory terms Lynne Tirrell shows why individual speakers cannot easily escape the socially established meaning of their utterances. She reviews the "Absolutist" position on derogatory terms, noting, "the Absolutist takes the assertional commitments of the derogatory term. . . . to be *nondetachable*" (1999, 52). Then, she considers the opposing position of "Reclamation" that connects retaining labels with regaining power. She notes that even if members of an in-group use a term like "dyke" as a "badge of pride," the negative meaning is likely to serve as the default when clear markers are absent (1999, 56). So, what is to be done? bell hooks addresses the need to use the oppressor's language even though it is the "language of conquest and domination" and retains "the sound of slaughter and conquest" (1994, 169). In relation to resistance, "Learning to speak

English, learning to speak the alien tongue, was one way enslaved Africans began to reclaim their personal power within a context of domination" (1994, 170). Despite the tensions and even the contradictions, the oppressor's language can be used by the oppressed to resist and to forge an alternative cultural production that can counter the hegemonic worldview that has been imposed on them.

The practice of forging such linguistic alternatives encounters formidable resistance from established prejudices, as has become evident in antiheterosexism training sessions in which some heterosexuals suggest that reverse discrimination occurs against heterosexuals or that nonheterosexuality is a deficit (Peel 2001). Research on how educational institutions respond to people with disabilities provides a further demonstration of how deeply these prejudices are entrenched. This research confirms what we might expect, namely, the situation is even more difficult for lesbian, gay, bisexual, and transgender students with disabilities. While colleges generally accommodate these students in relation to their disabilities, LGBT students with disabilities—multiple cultural minorities— are nevertheless simultaneously also marginalized because of their sexual orientation (Harley et al. 2002). So, whether the struggle is against heterosexism, sexism, racism, or any other oppression, the effort must go beyond transforming language to transforming the prejudices and biases at the cultural base.

Pursuing Cultural Transformation

As children, we learn language. Most of us learn only one language. If we are lucky, this language, our native tongue, coincides with the language that currently provides the most linguistic capital in the society in which we live (Bourdieu 1982). Regardless, whether we know the official language or a dialect relegated to low social esteem, whether we know only one or many languages, in whatever language we speak and write, we are faced with its lexicon and grammatical structure which have embedded within them a wide range of terms that express not only arbitrary designations of particularity but also actual relations of power.

Within virtually every community, specific social groups are arbitrarily but systematically denied possibilities open to other, more privileged social groups. We have clear examples of such discrimination in practices of colonialism, racism, sexism, and heterosexism. In part, liberation movements try to break the ideology that members of the oppressed group are dysfunctional and incapable in relation to the areas of opportunity denied to them. They are arguing that discrimination against them, opportunities denied to them, are unjustified because the differences between them and the dominant group are not functionally significant. Changing language is crucial, but this effort faces numerous cultural barriers.

Spanish peace researcher Francisco Muñoz coined the term "violentology perspective" (*perspectiva violentológica*) to refer to the problem that research focused on violence, even when undertaken by advocates of nonviolence, makes violence appear to be more pervasive than it is (2001, para. 10). Persons who seek to eliminate or reduce gender violence and other forms of unjust violence can fall victim to the cognitive dissonance that Muñoz describes. In their cases, while they desire nonviolence and human equality, they often give more attention to conceptualizing and criticizing the large-scale violence of war and the widespread occurrence of violence against women and other marginalized and oppressed groups. While the violentology perspective is descriptive of how we take for granted the practicality of and the justification for violence, it also calls for greater emphasis on the diverse and extensive occurrences of nonviolence and for their expansion. Even advocates of nonviolence need to move to the next level. Prescriptively, while we need to expose the various types of physical and linguistic violence and the structural and cultural forms that support them, we also need to develop not only alternative discourses but also practices that advance nonviolence.

Irene Comins Mingol and Sonia París Albert, Spanish collaborators with Francisco Muñoz, have extended to gender studies and peace studies the nonkilling perspective (2009). As initially developed by political scientist Glen Paige, the nonkilling perspective maintains that human beings can live in societies in which they do not kill other human beings and perhaps also neither kill members of many other species nor cause serious harm to the environment (2009). If we cannot advance nonkilling, we will have difficulty in trying to reduce lesser forms of violence. Based on their use of Gilligan and Ruddick, Comins Mingol and París Albert contend the nonkilling paradigm fosters the needed traits of empathy, responsibility, and patience (Comins Mingol and París Albert 2009, 279). In particular, they stress that we generally have alternative nonviolent responses available during and after conflict and that we should train for and make use of these alternatives.

Traditional academic approaches of conflict resolution and conflict management are negative because they aim to either eliminate or administer conflict. Resolution or elimination of conflict is not feasible to the extent that conflict is built into how diverse individuals and cultures approach differences. Management or administration of conflict also has limits to the extent that it operates as an external authority in relation to conflict. Conflict transformation aims to operate within conflict, rather than being imposed upon conflict. Conflict transformation accepts conflict and places in the hands of those involved the responsibility for seeking to implement nonviolent practices. To facilitate conflict transformation, Comins Mingol and París Albert propose that we "*disaccustom* ourselves to violence" and instead cultivate the practice and then the habit of what they term "conflict transformation" (2009, 275). In place of efforts to eliminate or administer conflict, conflict transformation prepares the persons involved in conflict to seek "peaceful alternatives that avoid the use of violence" (ibid.). In this regard, they stress that human beings have capacities for "harmonious coexistence, for reciprocal care and the peaceful transformation of conflicts" (ibid.).

París Albert and Comins Mingol have also responded to those in neuroscience who dismiss notions of freedom in human action and, instead, seek explanations of human behavior in terms of neurons (2013). In contrast, and in line with care ethics, they stress the relational and intersubjective character of science and other human enterprises and regard such activities as value laden in ways that are more realistic than ones found in supposedly objective and value neutral approaches. Significantly, they do not claim that human beings are nonviolent by nature. They readily affirm that human beings are "conflictive beings." However, in relation to the conflicts that we regularly face, they assert our responses "may be either violent or peaceful" (2013, 76). They stress that the alternatives open to individuals in conflicts include not only whatever may be in our genes but also and significantly the influences of our social environment (2013, 80). Hence, efforts by individuals and groups working for social justice and human equality can advance their goals by stressing the development of individual and social behaviors that promote nonviolence. These efforts can contribute to making nonviolent response even more widely available, appealing, and practical. Such efforts need to occur at all levels—from our homes, to our educational and criminal justice systems, and all the way up through national and international relations.

Paulo Freire talks about "untested feasibility" (1972). We will not know whether we can succeed if we do not try. Moreover, only making an effort when success seems assured sells us short. Our personal failure at achieving social justice and human equality or, at best, our limited partial success is not the measure. The goal is not individual success in one's own efforts. Many of the women suffragists who worked so hard to win for women the right to vote did not live to see its reality. The prospect that we will not see human equality and social justice in our lifetime points to the importance of our keeping alive the passion and action that are needed in this multigenerational quest. As Bourdieu says, we can change the social world by "changing the representation of this world" (1991, 128). Basically, speakers and writers can shape a new and a more just understanding of reality by articulating alternative descriptions of the world. However, in order to challenge the cultural base of a society and to forge alternatives, we need oppositional concepts. Since sexist language is an instance of linguistic violence, nonsexist language needs linguistic nonviolence as an oppositional concept or it will be in danger of only eliminating the violence of sexist language and not eliminating other forms of linguistic violence. Just as we distinguish negative peace (the mere absence of war) from positive peace (the presence of justice), we can distinguish a discourse that is merely politically correct (the mere absence of ethnocentric, racist, sexist, heterosexist, and classist discourse in the public sphere) from a discourse that arises from a culturally transformed base (the presence in society and language of the primacy of our common humanity and shared interests as members of the same species) (Gay 1997).

Linguistic violence against women and other social groups—and even physical violence against human beings—can be overcome. We have a moral duty to seek to supplant these forms of violence. Reducing or even ending linguistic violence against women or any other group will not be sufficient for ending gender violence and other types of violence, but advancement of linguistic nonviolence in any of these areas is a significant achievement in itself and as a means toward further reductions in violence in all its human manifestations. Through the practice of linguistic nonviolence and restriction to nonviolent social interventions, we can expand human equality and social justice not only in our individual language and actions but also within our communities and progressively throughout the entire world.

COPYRIGHT ACKNOWLEDGMENTS

BIBLIOGRAPHY

Aborisade, Richard A. 2014. "Barriers to Rape Reporting for Nigerian Women: The Case of Female University Students." *International Journal of Criminology and Sociological Theory*, 7 (2): 1–14.

Abrahamsen, D. 1960. *The Psychology of Crime*. New York: Columbia University Press.

Abrams, Jamie R. 2016. "Debunking the Myth of Universal Male Privilege." *University of Michigan Journal of Law Reform* 49 (2):303–34.

Accord Alliance. n.d. Accessed April 16, 2018. www.accordalliance.org.

Acevedo, Martina J. 2000. "Battered Immigrant Mexican Women's Perspectives Regarding Abuse and Help-Seeking." *Journal of Multicultural Social Work* 8 (3–4): 243–82.

Acker, Joan. 1990. "Hierarchies, Jobs, Bodies: A Theory of Gendered Organizations." *Gender & Society* 4 (2): 139–58.

———. 2006. "Inequality Regimes: Gender, Class, and Race in Organizations." *Gender & Society* 20 (4): 441–64.

Adair, Phillipe, and Oksana Nezhyvenko. 2017. "Assessing How Large is the Market for Prostitution in the European Union." *Ethics and Economics* 14 (2): 116–36.

Adame, Bradley J. 2016. "Training in the Mitigation of Anchoring Bias: A Test of the Consider-the-Opposite Strategy." *Learning and Motivation* 53 (February): 36–48.

Adams, David. 1989. "The Seville Statement on Violence: A Progress Report." *Journal of Peace Research* 26 (2): 113–21.

———, S. A. Barnett, N. P. Bechtereva, Bonnie F. Carter, Jose M. Rodriguez Delgado, Jose Luis Diaz, et al. 1990. "The Seville Statement on Violence." *American Psychologist* 45 (10): 1167–68.

Advocates for Youth. 2008. "The Facts: Gender Inequality and Violence Against Women and Girls Around the World." http://www.advocatesforyouth.org.

———. 2012. https://advocatesforyouth.org/resources/newsletters/november-2012-iyan -newsletter/

Agustín, Laura M. 2003. "Forget Victimization: Granting Agency to Migrants." *Development* 46 (3): 30–36.

———. 2007. *Sex at the Margins: Migration, Labour Markets and the Rescue Industry*. Zed Books: London.

Aisbett K. 2001. *Internet at Home: A Report on Internet Use in the Home*. Australian Broadcasting Authority: Sydney.

Ajzen, I. 1991. "The Theory of Planned Behavior." *Organizational Behavior and Human Decision Processes* 50: 179–211.

Al-Maghafi, Nawal. 2019. "In Iraq, Religious 'Pleasure Marriages' Are a Front for Child Prostitution." *Guardian*. www.theguardian.com.

Alcoff, Linda Martín. 2009. "Discourses of Sexual Violence in a Global Framework." *Philosophical Topics* 3 (2): 123–39.

———. 2018. *Rape and Resistance: Understanding the Complexities of Sexual Violation*. Medford, MA: Polity Press.

Alexander, Leigh. 2014. "But WHAT CAN BE DONE: Dos and Don'ts to Combat Online Sexism." http://leighalexander.net.

Alexander, Michelle. 2010. *The New Jim Crow*. New York: New Press.

Alfrey, Lauren, and France Widdance Twine. 2017. "Gender-Fluid Geek Girls: Negotiating Inequality Regimes in the Tech Industry." *Gender & Society* 3 (1): 28–50.

Ali, Kecia. "Slavery and Sexual Ethics in Islam." 2010. In *Beyond Slavery: Overcoming Its Religious and Sexual Legacies*, edited by Bernadette J. Brooten, 107–22. New York: Palgrave Macmillan.

Allen, Charlene, and Beth Leventhal. 1999. "History, Culture, and Identity: What Makes GLBT Battering Different." In *Same-Sex Domestic Violence: Strategies for Change*, edited by B. Leventhal and S. E. Lundy. Thousand Oaks, CA: Sage.

Allen, K. 2004. *Max Weber: A Critical Introduction*. London: Pluto Press.

Allen, P. 1970. *Free Space: A Perspective on the Small Group in Women's Liberation*. New York: Times Change Press.

Allen, S. M., and Ciambrone, D. 2003. "Community Care for People with Disability: Blurring Boundaries between Formal and Informal Caregivers." *Qualitative Health Research* 13: 207–26.

Alsdurf, J. M., and P. Alsdurf. "A Pastoral Response." 1988. In *Abuse and Religion: When Praying Isn't Enough*, edited by A. L. Horton and J. A. Williamson, 165–71. Boston: Lexington Books.

Alvaredo, Facundo, Lucas Chancel, Thomas Piketty, Emmanuel Saez, and Gabriel Zucman. 2018. "World Inequality Report Executive Summary 2018." https://wir2018.wid.world/executive-summary.html

Alvy, Lisa. 2004/2005. "Violence Against Women of Darfur, A Devastating Weapon of War and Terror." *National NOW Times* (Winter): 13.

Ambrose. 2000. *On Abraham*. Translated by Theodosia Tomkinson. Etna, CA: Center for Traditionalist Orthodox Studies.

American Academy of Pediatrics. n.d. "AAP Says Spanking Harms Children." Accessed February 22, 2019. www.aap.org.

American Association of University Women Foundation. 1993. *Hostile Hallways: The AAUW Survey on Sexual Harassment in America's Schools*. Washington, DC: AAUW.

American Association of University Women Foundation and Harris Interactive. 2001. *Hostile Hallways II: Bullying, Teasing and Sexual Harassment in School*. Washington, DC: Harris Interactive.

American Medical Association. 2019. "Improving Screening and Treatment Guidelines for Intimate Partner Violence (IPV) Against Lesbian, Gay, Bisexual, Transgender, Queer/Questioning, and Other Individuals." https://policysearch.ama-assn.org.

American Psychological Association. 2007. "Report of the APA Task Force on the Sexualization of Girls." www.apa.org.

Ames, Kenneth M. 2001. "Slaves, Chiefs and Labour on the Northern Northwest Coast." *World Archaeology* 33 (1): 1–17.

Amir, Menachem. 1971. *Patterns in Forcible Rape*. Chicago: University of Chicago Press.

Ammar, Nawal H. 2000. "In the Shadows of the Pyramids: Domestic Violence in Egypt." *International Review of Victimology* 7 (1–3): 29–46.

Amsden, David. 2003. "Not Tonight Honey. I'm Logging On." *New York Magazine*. October 20, 2003.

Anderson-Nathe, Ben, and Kiaras Gharabaghi. 2017. "Trending rightward: Nationalism, Xenophobia, and the 2016 Politics of Fear." *Child & Youth Services* 38 (1): 1–3.

Anderson, Christina. 2018. "Swedish Law Says Sex Minus Consent Is Rape." *New York Times*, May 24, 2018.

Anderson, J., J. Martin, P. Mullen, S. Romans, and P. Herbison. 1993. "Prevalence of Childhood Sexual Abuse Experiences in a Community Sample of Women." *Journal of American Academy of Child and Adolescent Psychiatry* 32: 911–19.

Anderson, Jane. 2007. "The Contest of Moralities: Negotiating Compulsory Celibacy and Sexual Intimacy in the Roman Catholic Priesthood." *Australian Journal of Anthropology* 18 (1): 1–17.

Anderson, Kristin L., and Debra Umberson. 2001. "Gendering Violence: Masculinity and Power in Men's Accounts of Domestic Violence." *Gender & Society* 15 (3): 358–80.

Anderson, Laurie Halse. 2019. "I've Talked With Teenage Boys About Sexual Assault for 20 Years. This Is What They Still Don't Know." *Time*, January 15, 2019.

Andrees, Beate and Patrick Belser. 2009. *Forced Labor: Coercion and Exploitation in the Private Economy*. Boulder, CO: Reinner and International Labour Organization.

Appiah, Kwame Anthony. 2018. "Should I Go to a Gender-Reveal Party?" *New York Times*, September 30, 2018.

Archer, John. 1994. "Power and Male Violence." In *Male Violence: The Territorial Imperative*, edited by J. Archer. London: Routledge.

———. 2000. "Sex Differences in Aggression between Heterosexual Partners: A Meta-Analytic Review." *Psychological Bulletin* 126 (5): 651–80.

Ardrey, Robert. 1961. *African Genesis: A Personal Investigation into the Animal Origins and Nature of Man*. New York: Atheneum.

———. 1966. *The Territorial Imperative: A Personal Inquiry into the Animal Origins of Property and Nations*. New York: Dell.

Arendt, Hannah. 2006. *Eichmann in Jerusalem: A Report on the Banality of Evil*. New York: Penguin.

Armstrong, Louise. 1994. *Rocking the Cradle of Sexual Politics*. Reading, MA: Addison-Wesley.

———. 2007. "Who Stole Incest?" In *Gender Violence: Interdisciplinary Perspectives*, 2nd edition, edited by Laura L. O'Toole, Jessica R. Schiffman, and Margie L. Kiter Edwards, 360–64. New York: New York University Press.

Aronson, Elliot. 1978. *The Jigsaw Classroom*. Thousand Oaks: Sage.

Aronson, J., and S. M. Neysmith, 1996. "'You're not just in there to do the work': Depersonalizing Policies and the Exploitation of Home Care Workers." *Gender & Society* 10: 59–77.

Ashford, Jose, Craig Winston LeCroy and Kathy Lortie. 2006. *Human Behavior in the Social Environment*. Belmont, CA: Wadsworth.

Association of American Colleges. 1978. *The Problem of Rape on Campus*. Washington, DC: Project on the Status and Education of Women.

Associated Press. 2007. "Authorities Rule Texas Mom's Death Suicide, Three Hanged Kids' Deaths Murder." *Fox News*, May 30, 2007.

Austen, Ian. 2012. "Report Cites Bias by Police in Killings in Canada." *New York Times*, December 17, 2012.

Australian Broadcasting Online, 2004. "Anti-Bullying Policies Failing to Cut School Harassment." June 18, 2004. www.abc.net.au.

Avakame, Edem F. 1998. "How Different Is Violence in the Home? An Examination of Some Correlates of Stranger and Intimate Homicide." *Criminology* 36 (3): 601–32.

Ayón, Cecilia, and David Becerra. 2013. "Mexican Immigrant Families Under Siege: The Impact of Anti-immigrant Policies, Discrimination, and the Economic Crisis." *Advances in Social Work* 14 (1): 206–28.

Baaz, Maria Eriksson, and Maria Stern. 2013. *Sexual Violence as a Weapon of War?: Perceptions, Prescriptions, Problems in the Congo and Beyond*. London: Zed Books Ltd.

Bacchi, C., and J. Eveline. 2003. "Mainstreaming and Neoliberalism: A Contested Relationship." *Policy and Society: Journal of Public, Foreign and Global Policy* 22 (2): 98–118.

Bachman, Ronet. 1992. *Death and Violence on the Reservation*. New York: Auburn House.

Baidawi, Adam. 2018. "Australian Prime Minister to Apologize to Child Sexual Abuse Survivors." *New York Times*, June 13, 2018.

Bailey, Moya. 2010. "They Aren't Talking about Me." March 14, 2010. www.crunkfeministcolle ctive.com.

Baker, Katharine K. 1997. "Once a Rapist? Motivational Evidence and Relevancy in Rape Law." *Harvard Law Review* 110 (January): 563–624.

Balibar, Étienne. 2015. *Violence and Civility: On the Limits of Political Philosophy*. Translated by G. M. Goshgarian. New York: Columbia University Press.

Ballaeva, E. A. 2007. "Gender-Related Aspects of Security." *Anthropology and Archeology of Eurasia* 45 (4): 56–66.

Ballarín Domingo, Pilar. 2001. *La educación de las mujeres en la España contemporánea (siglos XIX–XX)*. Madrid: Síntesis.

Balliet, Barbara J., and Kerrissa Heffernan, eds. 2000. *The Practice of Change: Concepts and Models for Service-Learning in Women's Studies*. Washington, D.C.: American Association of Higher Education.

Balo, Andy. 2014. "72 Hours of #Gamergate." *Medium*, October 27, 2014. https://medium.com.

Balsam, Kimberly F. 2001. "Nowhere to Hide: Lesbian Battering, Homophobia, and Minority Stress." In *Intimate Betrayal: Domestic Violence in Lesbian Relationships*, edited by E. Kaschak. New York: Haworth Press, Inc.

Bancroft, Lundy. 2002. *Why Does He Do That: Inside the Minds of Angry and Controlling Men*. New York: G. P. Putnam's Sons.

———, and Jay G. Silverman. 2002. "Assessing Risk to Children from Batterers." VAWnet.org. www.vawnet.org.

Barak, Gregg. 2003. *Violence and Nonviolence: Pathways to Understanding*. Thousand Oaks, CA: Sage.

Barling, J., A. Rogers, and E. Kelloway. 2001. "Behind Closed Doors: In-home Workers' Experience of Sexual Harassment and Workplace Violence." *Journal of Occupational Health Psychology* 6: 255–69.

Barnett, Ola, Cindy L. Miller-Perrin, and Robin D. Perrin. 2005. *Family Violence across the Lifespan: An Introduction*. Thousand Oaks, CA: Sage.

Barr, Juliana. 2005. "From Captives to Slaves: Commodifying Indian Women in the Borderlands." *Journal of American History* 92 (1): 19–46.

Barrett, Autumn R., and Michael L. Blakey. 2011. "Life Histories of Enslaved Africans in Colonial New York." In *Social Bioarchaeology*, edited by Sabrina C. Agarwal and Bonnie A. Glencross, 212–51. Malden: Wiley-Blackwell.

Barry, Ellen M. 2010. "From Plantations to Prisons: African American Women Prisoners in the United States." In *Beyond Slavery: Overcoming Its Religious and Sexual* Legacies, edited by Bernadette J. Brooten, 75–88. New York: Palgrave Macmillan.

Bartkowski, J. P. 1997. "Debating Patriarchy: Discursive Disputes over Spousal Authority among Evangelical Family Commentators." *Journal for the Scientific Study of Religion* 36 (3): 393–410.

———. 1995. "Spare the Rod . . . or Spare the Child? Divergent Perspectives on Conservative Protestant Child Discipline" *Review of Religious Research* 37 (2): 97–116.

———, and J. G. Read. 2003. "Veiled Submission: Gender, Power, and Identity Among Evangelical and Muslim Women in the United States." *Qualitative Sociology* 26 (1): 71–92.

Bates, Stephen. 2006. "Church Apologises for Benefiting from Slave Trade." *Guardian*, February 9, 2006.

Bauer, Heidi M., Michael A. Rodriguez, Seline S. Quiroga, and Yvette G. Flores-Ortiz. 2000. "Barriers to Health Care for Abused Latina and Asian Immigrant Women." *Journal of Health Care for the Poor and Underserved* 11 (1): 33–44.

Bauer, Irmgard L. 2014. "Romance Tourism or Female Sex Tourism?" *Travel Medicine and Infectious Disease* 12 (1): 20–28.

Bauer, M., and M. Ramírez. 2010. "Injustice on Our Plates: Immigrant Women in the US Food Industry." Montgomery, AL: Southern Poverty Law Center.

Baum, Katrina, and Patsy Klaus. 2005. "Violent Victimization of College Students, 1995–2002." US Department of Justice, www.bjs.gov.

Baumli F., ed. 1985. *Men Freeing Men: Exploding the Myth of the Traditional Male.* Jersey City: New Atlantis Press.

Bay, Mia. 2010. "Love, Sex, Slavery, and Sally Hemings." In *Beyond Slavery: Overcoming Its Religious and Sexual Legacies*, edited by Bernadette J. Brooten, 191–212. New York: Palgrave Macmillan.

Baylson, Mira. 2017. "Victim or Criminal? Street-Level Prostitutes and the Criminal Justice System." In *Challenging Perspectives on Street-Based Sex Work*, edited by Katie Hail-Jares, Corey S. Shdaimah, and Chrysanthi S. Leon, 136–52. Philadelphia, PA: Temple University Press.

Baynard, Victoria L., Linda M. Williams, Jane A. Siegel, and Carolyn M. West. 2002. "Childhood Sexual Abuse in the Lives of Black Women: Risk and Resilience in a Longitudinal Study." In *Violence in the Lives of Black Women: Battered, Black, and Blue*, edited by Carolyn M. West. New York: Hayworth.

BBC. 2007. "US Soldier Admits Murdering Girl." *BBC News.* February 22, 2007. http://news.bbc.co.uk/2hi/americas/6384781.stm.

Beal, Frances M. 1969. "Double Jeopardy: To Be Black and Female." In *Sisterhood is Powerful*, edited by Robin Morgan. New York: Vintage.

Beckhusen, Julia. 2016. "Occupations in Information Technology." American Community Survey Reports, ACS-35, Washington, DC: US Census Bureau.

Behre K. A. 2015. "Digging Beneath the Equality Language: The Influence of the Fathers' Rights Movement on Intimate Partner Violence Public Policy Debates and Family Law Reform." *William & Mary Journal of Women and the Law* 21 (3): 525–602.

Bell, C. C., and J. Mattis. 2000. "The Importance of Cultural Competence in Ministering to African American Victims of Domestic Violence." *Violence Against Women* 6 (5): 515–32.

Bell, Laurie, ed. 1987. *Good Girls/Bad Girls: Feminists and Sex Trade Workers Face to Face.* Toronto: Seal.

Bellamy, Alex J., and Matt McDonald. 2002. "'The Utility of Human Security': Which Humans? What Security? A Reply to Thomas & Tow." *Security Dialogue* 33 (3): 373–77.

Benedict, Helen. 2008a. "The Scandal of Military Rape." *Ms.* (Fall): 41–45.

———. 1992. *Virgin or Vamp: How the Press Covers Sex Crimes.* New York: Oxford University Press.

———. 2008b. "Why Soldiers Rape." *In These Times.* August 13, 2008.

Benhabib, Seyla. 1990. "El otro generalizado y el otro concreto: la controversia Kohlberg-Gilligan y la teoría feminista." In Seyla Benhabib and Drucilla Cornell, *Teoría Feminista y Teoría Crítica.* Valencia: Edicions Alfons el Magnànim.

Bent-Goodley, T. 2010. "Domestic Violence in the African-American Community." In *The War Against Domestic Violence*, edited by L. E. Ross. Boca Raton, FL: CRC Press.

——— and Fowler, D. N. 2006. "Spiritual and Religious Abuse." *Affilia: Journal of Women & Social Work* 21 (3): 282–95.

Berdahl, J. L., and Moore, C. 2006. "Workplace Harassment: Double Jeopardy for Minority Women." *Journal of Applied Psychology* 91: 426–36.

Bergman, M. E., R. Langhout, P. A. Palmieri, L. M. Cortina, and L. Fitzgerald. 2002. "The (Un)reasonableness of Reporting: Antecedents and Consequences of Reporting Sexual Harassment." *Journal of Applied Psychology* 87: 230–42.

Berk, Mark L., and Claudia L. Schur. 2001. "The Effect of Fear on Access to Care Among Undoc-umented Latino Immigrants." *Journal of Immigrant Health* 3 (3): 151–56.

Bernard, Cheryl, and Edit Schlaffer. 1989. "The Man in the Street: Why He Harasses." In *Feminist Frontiers II: Rethinking Sex, Gender, and Society*, edited by Laurel Richardson and Verta Tay-lor, 384–87. New York: Random House.

Bernstein, Elizabeth. 2012. "Carceral Politics as Gender Justice?" *Theory and Society* 41: 233–59.

———. 2010. "Militarized Humanitarianism Meets Carceral Feminism." *Signs* 36: 45–71.

Berry, D. B. 1995. *The Domestic Violence Sourcebook: Everything You Need to Know*. Los Angeles: Lowell House.

Berry, W. 1990. *What Are People For?* San Francisco, CA: North Point Press.

Best, Joel. 1990. *Threatened Children*. Chicago: University of Chicago Press.

Biber, J. K., D. Doverspike, D. Baznik, A. Cober, and B. A. Ritter. 2002. "Sexual Harassment in Online Communications: Effects of Gender and Discourse Medium." *CyberPsychology & Behavior* 5: 33–42.

Birch, Kean. 2017. "What Exactly Is Neoliberalism?" *Conversation*. https://theconversation.com.

Black, Michelle C., Kathleen C. Basile, Matthew J. Breiding, Sharon G. Smith, Mike L. Walters, Melissa T. Merrick, Jieru Chen, and Mark S. Stevens. 2011. "The National Intimate Partner and Sexual Violence Survey (NISVS): 2010 Summary Report." Atlanta, GA: National Center for Injury Prevention and Control, Centers for Disease Control and Prevention.

Black Women's Blueprint. 2016. "An Open Letter from Black Women to the Slutwalk." *Gender & Society* 30 (1): 9–13.

Blackman, Jerome, and Kathleen Dring. 2016. *Sexual Aggression against Children: Pedophiles and Abusers' Development, Dynamics, Treatability, and the Law*. New York: Taylor and Francis.

Blackmon, Douglas A. 2008. *Slavery by Another Name: The Re-Enslavement of Black Americans from the Civil War to World War II*. New York: Doubleday.

Blanchard, Eric M. 2003. "Gender, International Relations, and the Development of Feminist Security Theory." *Signs: Journal of Women in Culture and Society* 23 (4): 1289–312.

Blanguernon, C. 1955. *Le Hogger (The Hogger)*. Translated from the French for the Human Rela-tions Area Files by Thomas Turner. Paris: B. Arthaud.

Blickenstaff, Jacob Clark. 2005. "Women in Science Careers: Leaky Pipeline or Gender Filter?" *Gender and Education* 17 (4): 369–86.

Blight, Jake. 2000. *Transgender Inmates: Trends and Issues in Crime and Criminal Justice*. Canberra: Australian Institute of Criminology.

Blitz, John H. 1988. "Adoption of the Bow in Prehistoric North America." *North American Archaeologist* 9 (2): 123–45.

Bloch, Francis, and Vijayendra Rao. 2002. "Terror as a Bargaining Instrument: A Case Study of Dowry Violence in Rural India." *American Economic Review* 29 (4): 1029–43.

Block, Sharon. 2006. *Rape and Sexual Power in Early America*. Chapel Hill: University of North Carolina Press.

Blumenthal, Debra. 2010. "'As If She Were His Wife': Slavery and Sexual Ethics in Late Medieval Spain." In *Beyond Slavery: Overcoming Its Religious and Sexual Legacies*, edited by Bernadette J. Brooten, 179–89. New York: Palgrave Macmillan.

Bo, Dianna L. 2013. "Estimating the Organizational Cost of Sexual Assault in the US Military." Masters thesis, Naval Postgraduate School. https://calhoun.nps.edu.

Boadt, L. 1984. *Reading the Old Testament: An Introduction*. Mahwah, NJ: Paulist Press.

Boas, Franz. 1967. *Kwakiutl Ethnography*. Edited and abridged with an introduction by Helen Codere. Chicago: University of Chicago Press.

Bodley, John H. 2015. *Victims of Progress*, 6th ed. Lanham, MD: Rowman and Littlefield.

Boesch, Christophe, Catherine Crockford, Ilka Herbinger, Roman Wittig, Yasmin Moebius, and Emmanuelle Normand. 2008. "Intergroup Conflicts among Chimpanzees in Taï National Park: Lethal Violence and the Female Perspective." *American Journal of Primatology* 70: 519–32.

Boesten, Jelke. 2006. "Pushing Back the Boundaries: Social Policy, Domestic Violence, and Women's Organizations in Peru." *Journal of Latin American Studies* 38 (2): 355–78.

———. 2014. *Sexual Violence During War and Peace: Gender, Power, and Post-Conflict Justice in Peru.* New York: Palgrave Macmillan.

Boff, Leonardo. 2008. *Essential Care: An Ethics of Human Nature.* Waco: Baylor University Press.

Bograd, Michele. 2005. "Strengthening Domestic Violence Theories: Intersections of Race, Class, Sexual Orientation, and Gender." In *Domestic Violence at the Margins: Readings in Race, Class, Gender and Culture,* edited by Natalie J. Sokoloff, 25–38. New Brunswick, NJ: Rutgers University Press.

Bohmer, C., and A. Parrot. 1993. *Sexual Assault on Campus: The Problem and the Solution.* New York: Lexington Books.

Boitin, Margaret L. 2013. "New Perspectives from the Oldest Profession: Abuse and the Legal Consciousness of Sex Workers in China." *Law & Society Review* 47: 245–77.

Bojar, Karen. 2000. "Service-Learning and Women's Studies: A Community College Perspective." In *The Practice of Change: Concepts and Models for Service-Learning in Women's Studies,* edited by Heffernan, Kerrissa, et al., 57–67. American Association for Higher Education.

Bonilla-Silva, Eduardo. 2017. *Racism without Racists: Color-Blind Racism and the Persistence of Racial Inequality in America.* Lanham, MD: Rowman and Littlefield.

———. 2001. *White Supremacy and Racism in the Post-Civil Rights Era.* Boulder, CO: Lynne Rienner Publishers.

Bonta, J., and D. Andrews. 2010. "Viewing Offender Assessment and Rehabilitation through the Lens of the Risk-Needs-Responsivity Model." In *Offender Supervision: New Directions in Theory, Research, and Practice,* edited by F. McNeil, P. Rayner, and C. Trotter, 19–40. New York: Willan Publishing.

Boonyapisomparn, Nachale. 2017. "'HIV Is Not a Major Concern': Trans Identity, Public-Health Funding, and Sex Work." In *Challenging Perspectives on Street-Based Sex Work,* edited by Katie Hail-Jares, Corey S. Shdaimah, and Chrysanthi S. Leon, 101–13. Philadelphia: Temple University Press.

Botham, Fay. 2010. "The 'Purity of the White Woman, Not the Purity of the Negro Woman': The Contemporary Legacies of Historical Laws Against Interracial Marriage." In *Beyond Slavery: Overcoming Its Religious and Sexual Legacies,* edited by Bernadette J. Brooten, 249–64. New York: Palgrave Macmillan.

Boulding, Elise. 2000. *Cultures of Peace. The Hidden Side of History.* Syracuse: Syracuse University Press.

Bourdieu, Pierre. 1982. *Ce que parler veut dire: l'économie des échanges linguistiques.* Paris: Librairie Arthème Fayard.

———. 1991. *Language and Symbolic Power.* Edited by John B. Thompson. Translated by Gino Raymond and Matthew Adamson. Cambridge, MA: Harvard University Press.

———. *Masculine Domination.* 2001. Palo Alto: Stanford University Press. Bourque, Linda Brookover. 1989. *Defining Rape.* Durham, NC: Duke University Press.

Bowers, Robert. 2010. "A Pathway to Wholeness: Facing Faith Trauma in Boston and Ireland." *Studies: An Irish Quarterly Review* 99 (395): 277–87.

Bowles, Nellie. 2018. "Manosphere In a Panic: Are Your Swimmers In Peril?," *New York Times,* July 26, 2018.

Bowling, N. A., and T. A. Beehr. 2006. "Workplace Harassment from the Victim's Perspective: A Theoretical Model and Meta Analysis." *Journal of Applied Psychology* 91: 998–1012.

Boyd, Melanie. 2009. "Of Shards, Subjectivities, and the Refusal to 'Heal.'" In *Theorizing Sexual Violence*, edited by Renee Heberle and Victoria Grace. New York: Routledge.

Boxberger, Daniel. 1997. "Amerindian Slavery, Pacific Northwest." In *The Historical Encyclopedia of World Slavery, Vol. 1*, edited by Junius Rodriguez, 36. Santa Barbara: ABC-CLIO, Inc.

Brabeck, Kalina. M., and Michele R. Guzmán. 2009. "Exploring Mexican-Origin Intimate Partner Abuse Survivors Help-Seeking Within Their Sociocultural Contexts." *Violence and Victims* 24 (6): 817–32.

Bracewell, Lorna Norman. 2016. "Beyond Barnard: Liberalism, Antipornography Feminism, and the Sex Wars." *Signs: Journal of Women in Culture and Society* 42 (1): 23–41.

Bradley, Christine. 1994 [1990]. "Why Male Violence against Women Is a Development Issue: Reflections from Papua, New Guinea." UNIFEM Occasional Paper. New York: United Nations Fund for Women. Reprinted in *Women and Violence*, edited by M. Davies. London: Zed Books.

Braverman, Beth. 2013. "The High Cost of Sexual Harassment." *Fiscal Times*, August 22, 2013. www.thefiscaltimes.com.

Bray, Abigail. 2011. "Merciless Doctrines: Child Pornography, Censorship, and Late Capitalism." *Signs* 37: 133–58.

Breeden, Aurelien. 2019. "France Enacts Slate of Laws To Tackle Domestic Violence." *New York Times*, November 26, 2019.

Breiding, Matthew J., Jieru Chen, and Michele C. Black. 2014. *Intimate Partner Violence in the United States—2010*. Atlanta, GA: National Center for Injury Prevention and Control, Center for Disease Control and Prevention.

Breiding, Matthew J., Sharon G. Smith, Kathleen C. Basile, Mikel L. Walters, Jieru Chen, and Melissa T. Merrick. 2014. "Prevalence and Characteristics of Sexual Violence, Stalking, and Intimate Partner Violence Victimization—National Intimate Partner and Sexual Violence Survey, United States, 2011," 63 SS08 (September 5, 2014): 1–18. www.cdc.gov.

Breines, Wini, and Linda Gordon. 1983. "The New Scholarship on Family Violence." *Signs* 8: 490–53.

Brennan, Denise. 2002. "Globalization, Women's Labor and Men's Pleasure: Sex Tourism in Sosúa, the Dominican Republic." In *Urban Life: Readings in Urban Anthropology*, edited by George Gmelch and Walter P. Zenner. Prospect Heights, IL: Waveland Press.

Brewis, Joanna, and Stephen Linstead. 2000. "'The Worst Thing Is the Screwing' (1): Consumption and the Management of Identity in Sex Work." *Gender, Work & Organization* 7 (2): 84–97.

Briggs, Sheila. 2010. "Gender, Slavery, and Technology: The Shaping of the Early Christian Moral Imagination." In *Beyond Slavery: Overcoming Its Religious and Sexual Legacies*, edited by Bernadette J. Brooten, 159–76. New York: Palgrave Macmillan.

Brink, Ole. 2009. "When Violence Strikes the Head, Neck, and Face." *Journal of Trauma* 67 (1): 147–51.

Brinkerhoff, Merlin. B., Elaine Grandin, and Eugen Lupri. 1992. "Religious Involvement and Spousal Violence: The Canadian Case." *Journal for the Scientific Study of Religion* 31 (1): 15–31.

Brinkman, Britney G., Kelley Garcia, and Kathryn M. Rickard. 2011. "'What I wanted to do was . . .' Discrepancies Between College Women's Desired and Reported Responses to Gender Prejudice." *Sex Roles* 65: 344–55.

Britton, Dana. 2003. *At Work in the Iron Cage: The Prison as a Gendered Organization*. New York: New York University Press.

Brod, Harry. 2007. "Pornography and the Alienation of Male Sexuality." In *Gender Violence: Interdisciplinary Perspectives*, 2nd edition. Edited by Laura L. O'Toole, Jessica R. Schiffman, and Margie L. Kiter Edwards, 395–408. New York: New York University Press.

Brodie, Janine. 2008. "We are all equal now: Contemporary gender politics in Canada." *Feminist Theory* 9 (2): 145–64.

Brody, J. J. 1983. "Mimbres Painting." In *Mimbres Pottery: Ancient Art of the American Southwest*, edited by J. J. Brody, Catherine J. Scott and Steven A. LeBlanc, 69–127. New York: Hudson Hills Press in association with The American Federation of Arts.

Brooks, James F. 2002. *Captives and Cousins: Slavery, Kinship, and Community in the Southwest Borderlands*. Chapel Hill: University of North Carolina Press, Published for the Omohundro Institute of Early American History and Culture.

Broude, G. J., and S. J. Green. 1976. "Cross-Cultural Codes on Twenty Sexual Practices." *Ethnology* 15: 409–29.

Brown, George R., and Everett McDuffie. 2009. "Health Care Policies Addressing Transgender Inmates in Prison Systems in the United States." *Journal of Correctional Health Care* 15: 280–91.

Brown, Lyn Mikel, Meda Chesney-Lind, and Nan Stein. 2004. "Patriarchy Matters: Toward a Gendered Theory of Teen Violence and Victimization." Working paper no. 417. Wellesley, MA: Wellesley College Center for Research on Women.

Brown, Sarah. 2017. "Candice Jackson on Campus Sex Assault: 'We're Not Asking Schools to Step in as Courts of Law.'" *Chronicle of Higher Education*, October 26, 2017.

Brown, Taylor N. T., and Jody L. Herman. 2015. *Intimate Partner Violence and Sexual Abuse among LGBT People: A Review of Existing Research*. University of California School of Law, The Williams Institute.

Brown, Wendy. 2015. *Undoing the Demos: Neoliberalism's Stealth Revolution*. New York: Zone Books.

Brownmiller, Susan. 1975. *Against Our Will: Men, Women, and Rape*. New York: Fawcett Book/Ballentine Publishing Group.

Bruenig, Elizabeth. 2018. "He Wanted to Be a Priest. He Says Archbishop McCarrick Used That to Abuse Him." *Washington Post*, September 12, 2018.

Brunner, Laura K., and Maryanne Dever. 2014. "Work, Bodies and Boundaries: Talking Sexual Harassment in the New Economy." *Gender, Work and Organization* 21, no. 5 (September): 459–71.

Brush, Lisa D. 1990. "Violent Acts and Injurious Outcomes in Married Couples: Methodological Issues in the National Survey of Families and Households." *Gender & Society* 4: 56–67.

———. 2013. "Work and Love in the Gendered US Insecurity State." In *Gender, Violence, and Human Security: Critical Feminist Perspectives*, 109–31, edited by Aili Mari Tripp, Myra Marx Feree, and Christine Ewig. New York: New York University Press.

Bryant, Kimberly. 2014. "About Our Founder." Black Girls Code. www.blackgirlscode.com.

Bucha, Sanna. 2005. "Twice Damned." *Newsline*. http://newslinemagazine.com.

Buchanan, N. T., and Fitzgerald, L. F. 2008. "Effects of Racial and Sexual Harassment on Work and the Psychological Well-Being of African American Women." *Journal of Occupational Health Psychology* 13: 137–51.

Buchanan, N., and A. Ormerod. 2002. "Racialized Sexual Harassment in the Lives of African American Women." *Women and Therapy* 25 (3–4): 105–21.

Buchowska, Natalia. 2016. "Violated or Protected: Women's Rights in Armed Conflicts after the Second World War." *International Comparative Jurisprudence* 2 (2): 72–80.

Bui, Hoan N. 2003. "Help-Seeking Behavior among Abused Immigrant Women: A Case of Vietnamese American Women." *Violence Against Women* 9 (2): 207–39.

Bumiller, Kristin. 2008. *In an Abusive State: How Neoliberalism Appropriated the Feminist Movement Against Sexual Violence*. Durham, NC: Duke University Press.

Burbank, Victoria Katherine. 1994. *Fighting Women: Anger and Aggression in Aboriginal Australia*. Berkeley: University of California Press.

Bureau of Justice Statistics. 2005. "IPV in the United States: Victim characteristics." www.bjs.gov.

Burgess, Ann Wolbert, and Lynda L. Holmstrom. 1974. "The Rape Trauma Syndrome." *American Journal of Psychiatry* 131: 981–86.

Burgest, David R. 1973. "The Racist Use of the English Language." *Black Scholar* (September): 37–45.

Burguieres, Mary. 1990. "Feminist Approaches to Peace: Another Step for Peace Studies." *Millennium* 19 (1): 1–18.

Burke, Tarana. 2018. Me Too (website). https://metoomvmt.org.

Burt, Jo-Marie. 2013. "Historic Genocide Trial Nears End; Rios Montt Addresses the Court, Declares Innocence." *International Justice Monitor*. Open Society Justice Initiative, May 10, 2013. www.ijmonitor.org.

———. 2016. "Six Witnesses Recount Atrocities at Sepur Zarco on Day Two of Landmark Trial." *International Justice Monitor*. Open Society Justice Initiative, February 8, 2016. www.ijmonitor.org.

Burrows, James. 2006. "Von Trapped." In *Will and Grace*. USA: KoMut Entertainment with Three Sisters Entertainment and NBC Studios.

Buss, D. M. 1994. *The Evolution of Desire: Strategies of Human Mating*. New York: Basic.

Butler, Judith. 1990. *Gender Trouble: Feminism and the Subversion of Identity*. New York: Routledge.

———. 1993. *Bodies That Matter: On the Discursive Limits of Sex*. New York: Routledge.

———. 1997. *Excitable Speech: A Politics of the Performative*. New York: Routledge.

———. 2004. *Undoing Gender*. New York: Routledge.

———. 2006. *Precarious Lives: The Powers of Mourning and Violence*. New York: Verso.

———. 2009. "Performativity, Precarity and Sexual Politics." *Revista de Antropología Iberoamericana* 4(3): i–xiii. www.aibr.org.

———. 2013. "For White Girls Only? Postfeminism and the Politics of Inclusion." *Feminist Formations* 25 (1):35–58.

Butler, Sandra. 1985. *Conspiracy of Silence*. San Francisco: New Glide.

Buzawa, Eve S. and Carl G. Buzawa. 2003. *Domestic Violence: The Criminal Justice Response*. Thousand Oaks, CA: Sage.

———, and Evan D. Stark. 2011. *Responding to Domestic Violence: Integration of Criminal Justice and Human Services*. Thousand Oaks, CA: Sage.

Byerly, Carolyn. 2012. "Reformulation Theory: Gauging Feminist Impact on News of Violence Against Women." *Journal of Research on Women and Gender* 5: 1–20.

Cabaleiro Manzanedo, Julia. 2005. *Educació, dones i història. Una aproximació didáctica*. Barcelona: Icaria.

Cahill, Ann J. 2001. *Rethinking Rape*. Ithaca, NY: Cornell University Press.

Calkins, Cynthia, Jamison Fargo, Elizabeth Jeglic, and Karen Terry. 2015. "Blessed Be the Children: A Case-Controlled Study of Sexual Abusers in the Catholic Church." *Behavioral Sciences and the Law* 33: 580–94.

Call, V. and Heaton, T. 1997. "Religious Influence on Marital Stability." *Journal for the Scientific Study of Religion* 36 (3): 382–92.

Camerino, D., M. Estryn-Behar, P. Conway, B. van Der Heijden, and H. Hasselhorn. 2008. "Work-Related Factors and Violence among Nursing Staff in the European NEXT Study: A Longitudinal Cohort Study." *International Journal of Nursing Studies* 45: 35–50.

Cameron, Catherine M., ed. 2008. *Invisible Citizens: Captives and Their Consequences*. Salt Lake City: The University of Utah Press.

———. 2011. "Captives and Culture Change: Implications for Archaeology." *Current Anthropology* 52 (2): 169–209.

———. 2015. "The Effects of Warfare and Captive-Taking on Indigenous Mortality in Post-Contact North America." In *Beyond Germs: The Impact of Colonialism on Indigenous Health in America*, edited by Alan C. Swedlund, Catherine M. Cameron and Paul T. Kelton. Dragoon: Amerind Foundation.

Cameron, Deborah. 1985. *Feminism and Linguistic Theory*. New York: St. Martin's Press.

Campbell, Anne. 1999. "Staying Alive: Evolution, Culture, and Women's Intrasexual Aggression." *Behavioral and Brain Sciences* 22: 203–52.

Campbell, Catherine, and J. Mannell. 2016. "Conceptualising the Agency of Highly Marginalised Women: Intimate Partner Violence in Extreme Settings." *Global Public Health* 11 (1–2): 1–16.

Campbell, Erika. 2016. "Racializing Intimate Partner Violence among Black, Native American, Asian American and Latina Women." *International Journal of Progressive Education* 12 (2): 64–77.

Cannon, Clare, Katie Lauve-Moon, and Fred Buttell. 2015. "Re-Theorizing Intimate Partner Violence through Post-Structural Feminism, Queer Theory, and the Sociology of Gender." *Social Sciences* 4: 668–687.

Caputi, Jane, and Diana E. H. Russell. 1990. "Femicide: Speaking the Unspeakable," *Ms.* 1(2): 34–37.

Card, Claudia. 1995. "Gender and Moral Luck." In *Justice and Care, Essential Readings in Feminist Ethics*, edited by Virginia Held. Colorado: Westview Press.

Cardyn, Lisa. 2002. "Sexualized Racism/Gendered Violence: Outraging the Body Politic in the Reconstruction South." Michigan Law Review, 100 (4): 675–867.

Carillo, Roxanna. 1992. *Battered Dreams: Violence against Women as an Obstacle to Development*. New York: UNIFEM.

Carocci, Max, and Stephanie Pratt, eds. 2012. *Native American Adoption, Captivity, and Slavery in Changing Contexts*. New York: Palgrave MacMillan.

Castle, J. 2002. Domestic Violence and the Church. *The Herald of Hope*. www.heraldofhope.org.au.

Castro, Joy. 2018. "Gender, Race, and Credibility in the Age of Trump." *Women's Review of Books* 35 (1): 8–10.

Catalano, S. M. 2012. "Intimate Partner Violence, 1993–2010." Bureau of Justice Statistics. www.bjs.gov.

Catholic Diocese of Arlington. n.d. "How to Become a Priest," Accessed February 27, 2020. https://www.arlingtondiocese.org/vocations/for-men/how-to-become-a-priest/.

CEH (Commission for Historical Clarification). 1999. *Guatemala: Memoria del Silencio, Informe de La Comision para el Esclarecimiento Historico*. Guatemala: CEH.

Centano, Miguel A. and Joseph N. Cohen. 2012. "The Arc of Neoliberalism." *Annual Review of Sociology* 38: 317–40.

Center for Anti-Violence Education (CAE). n.d. Accessed 31 January 2017. https://caeny.org.

Center for Substance Abuse Treatment, Substance Abuse and Mental Health Services Administration, U.S. Department of Health and Human Services. 2014. *Trauma-Informed Care in Behavioral Health Services*. HHS Pub. No. (SMA) 13-4801, Treatment Improvement Protocol (TIP) Series No. 57.

Centers for Disease Control (CDC). 2012. "Bullying Surveillance Among Youths: Uniform Definitions for Public Health and Recommended Data Elements." https://www.cdc.gov/violenceprevention/pdf/bullying-definitions-final-a.pdf.

Centers for Disease Control and Prevention. 2013. "CDC Releases Data on Interpersonal and Sexual Violence by Sexual Orientation." www.cdc.gov.

———. n.d. Preventing Intimate Partner Violence. Accessed 2017. www.cdc.gov.

———. 2015. "Sexual Identity, Sex of Sexual Contacts, and Health-Related Behaviors among Students in Grades 9–12—United States and Selected Sites, 2015." www.cdc.gov.

———2018. The Social-Ecological Model: A Framework for Prevention. Accessed 2018. www.cdc.gov.

Cernovich, Mike. 2014. Twitter post. August 28, 2014, 2:57 p.m. https://twitter.com/Cernovich/status/505066536873521152.

Chalabi, Mona. 2016. "Sexual Harassment at Work: More than Half of Claims in US Result in No Charge." *Guardian*, July 22, 2016.

Chamallas, Martha. 1988. "Consent, Equality, and the Legal Control of Sexual Conduct." *Southern California Law Review* 61(May): 777–862.

Champagne, Rosaria. 1996. *The Politics of Survivorship*. New York: New York University Press.

Chan, D., C. Lam, S. Chow, and S. Cheung. 2008. "Examining the Job-Related, Psychological, and Physical Outcomes of Workplace Sexual Harassment: A Meta-Analytic Review." *Psychology of Women Quarterly* 32: 362–76.

Chan, Sewell. 2017. "Recy Taylor, Who Fought for Justice after a 1944 Rape, Dies at 97." *New York Times*, December 29, 2017.

Chancer, Lynn. 2005. *High Profile Crimes: When Legal Cases Become Social Causes*. Chicago: University of Chicago Press.

Chanen, David, and Howie Padilla. 2001. "School Was Scene of Earlier Assaults: New Reports Surface at Banneker." *Minneapolis Star Tribune*, December 19, 2001.

Chang, Emily. 2018. *Brotopia: Breaking Up the Boy's Club of Silicon Valley*. New York: Portfolio.

Charles, M. and D. B. Grusky. 2004. *Occupational Ghettos: The Worldwide Segregation of Women and Men*. Stanford: Stanford University Press.

Chase, Cheryl. 2002. "What Is the Agenda of the Intersex Patient Advocacy Movement?" Paper presented at First World Congress: Hormonal and Genetic Basis of Sexual Differentiation Disorders. Tempe, AZ, May 17–18, 2002.

Chavez, Leo R. 2008. *The Latino Threat: Constructing Immigrants, Citizens, and the Nation*. Palo Alto, CA: Stanford University Press.

Check, James V. P., Barbara Elias, and Susan A. Barton. 1988. "Hostility toward Men in Female Victims of Male Sexual Aggression." In *Violence in Intimate Relationships*, edited by Gordon W. Russell, 149–62. New York: PMA Publishing.

Cheit, Ross. 2014. *The Witch-Hunt Narrative: Politics, Psychology, and the Sexual Abuse of Children*. New York: Oxford University Press.

Chen, Dakeo. 2011. "Should Cambodia Accept Its Ranking?" *Phnom Penh Post*, July 13, 2011.

Cheng, Sealing. 2013. "Private Lives of Public Women: Photos of Sex Workers (Minus the Sex) in South Korea." *Sexualities* 16: 30–42.

Chenoy, Anuradha M. 2005. "A Plea for Engendering Human Security." *International Studies* 42 (2): 167–79.

Cho, Seo-Young, Axel Dreyer, and Eric Neumayer. 2012. "Does Legalized Prostitution Increase Human Trafficking?" *World Development* 41 (1): 67–82.

Choi, N., J. Burr, J. Mutchler, and F. Caro. 2007. "Formal and Informal Volunteer Activity and Spousal Caregiving among Older Adults." *Research on Aging* 29: 99–124.

Christiano, K. J. 2000. "Religion and the Family in Modern American Culture." In *Family, Religion, and Social Change in Diverse Societies*, edited by S. K. Houseknecht and J. G. Pankhurst. Oxford, England: Oxford University Press.

Chu, Judy. 2014. *When Boys Become Boys: Development, Relationships, and Masculinity*. New York: New York University Press.

Citron, Danielle Keats. 2009a. "Cyber Civil Rights." *Boston University Law Review* 89: 61–125.

———. 2009b. "Law's Expressive Value in Combating Cyber Gender Harassment." *Michigan Law Review*, 108 (3): 373–415.

———. 2014. *Hate Crimes in Cyberspace*. Cambridge, MA: Harvard University Press.

Clinton, Catherine. 2010. "Breaking the Silence: Sexual Hypocrisies from Thomas Jefferson to Strom Thurmond." In *Beyond Slavery: Overcoming Its Religious and Sexual Legacies*, edited by Bernadette J. Brooten, 213–28. New York: Palgrave Macmillan.

Coker, Ann L., Paige Hall Smith, Robert E. McKeown, and Melissa J. King. 2000. "Frequency and Correlates of Intimate Partner Violence by Type: Physical, Sexual, and Psychological Battering." *American Journal of Public Health* 90 (4): 553–59.

Collier, Richard. 1998. *Masculinities, Crime and Criminology: Men Heterosexuality and the Criminal(ised) Other*. London: Sage.

Collins, Marie. 2012. "Marie Collins Testifies to Abuse in Rome," Catholic Exchange. https://catholicexchange.com/marie-collins-testifies-to-abuse-in-rome/2.

Collins, Patricia Hill. 1986. "Learning from the Outsider Within: The Sociological Significance of Black Feminist Thought." *Social Problems* 33 (6): S14–S32.

———. 1990. *Black Feminist Thought: Knowledge, Consciousness, and the Politics of Empowerment*. Boston: Unwin Hyman.

———. 1991. *Black Feminist Thought: Knowledge, Consciousness, and the Politics of Empowerment*. New York: Routledge.

———. 2000. *Black Feminist Thought: Knowledge, Consciousness and the Politics of Empowerment, 2nd ed.* New York: Routledge.

———. 2004. *Black Sexual Politics: African Americans, Gender, and the New Racism*. New York: Routledge.

———, and Sirma Bilge. 2016. *Intersectionality*. Malden, MA: Polity.

Comins Mingol, Irene. 2009. "Coeducation: Teaching Peace from a Gender Perspective." *Peace and Change* 34 (4): 456–70.

———. 2014. "Rethinking Politics and Conflict Transformation from a Gender Perspective." *Philosophy. Bulgarian Journal of Philosophical Education*, 23 (3) :324–36.

———. 2016. "The Philosophy of Caring for Earth as Ecosophy" *Daimon* 67: 133–48.

———, and Sonia París Albert. 2009. "Nonkilling Philosophy." In *Toward a Nonkilling Paradigm*, edited by Joám Evans Pim, 283–84. Honolulu: Center for Global Nonkilling.

Commission on Human Security. 2003. "Human Security Now." New York: Commission on Human Security/United Nations Office for Project Services.

Conaway, Matthew. n.d. "Relative Deprivation of Masculinities: A Theory for Gender Violence?" *Academia*. Accessed March 7, 2019. www.academia.edu.

Connell, Raewyn. 2011. *Confronting Equality: Gender, Knowledge, and Global Change*. Malden, MA: Polity.

———. 2012. "Transsexual Women and Feminist Thought." *Signs* 37: 857–81.

Connell, R. W. 1987. *Gender and Power*. Palo Alto, CA: Stanford University Press.

———. 1991. "Live Fast and Die Young: The Construction of Masculinity among Young Working-Class Men on the Margin of the Labor Market." *Australian and New Zealand Journal of Sociology* 27 (2): 141–71.

———. 1995a. *Masculinities*. Berkeley: University of California Press.

———. 1995b. "Masculinity, Violence, and War." In *Men's Lives*, edited by Michael S. Kimmel and Michael A. Messner, 125–30. New York: Allyn and Bacon.

———, and J. Messerschmidt. 2005. "Hegemonic Masculinity: Rethinking the Concept." *Gender & Society* 19: 829–59.

Consorcio de Actoras de Cambio. 2006. Rompiendo el Silencio: Justicia para las mujeres victimas de la violencia sexual durante el conjlicto armado en Guatemala. Guatemala City: F & G Editores and Equipo Comunitaria de Ayuda Psicosocial.

Coomaraswamy, Radhika. 2015. "Preventing Conflict Transforming Justice Securing the Peace." A Global Study on the Implementation of United Nations Security Council resolution 1325. PeaceWomen. www.peacewomen.org.

Coontz, Stephanie. 2017. "Do Millennial Men Want Stay-at-Home Wives?" *New York Times,* March 31, 2017.

Cooper, Brittney C. 2017. "Disrespectability Politics: On Jay-Z's Bitch, Beyoncé's 'Fly' Ass, and Black Girl Blue." In *The Crunk Feminist Collection,* edited by Brittney C. Cooper, Susana Morris, and Robin M. Boylorn. New York: Feminist Press.

Cooper, H. M. 1984. *The Integrative Research Review: A Systematic Approach.* Beverly Hills: Sage.

———. 1998. *Synthesizing Research: A Guide for Literature Reviews,* 3rd ed. Thousand Oaks: Sage.

Corrigan, Rose. 2006. "Making Meaning of Megan's Law." *Law & Social Inquiry* 31: 267–312.

———. 2013. *Up against a Wall: Rape Reform and the Failure of Success.* New York: New York University Press.

Corrin, Chris. 2005. "Transitional Road for Traffic: Analysing Trafficking in Women from and Through Central and Eastern Europe." *Europe-East Asia Studies* 57 (4): 543–60.

Cortina, L. M., and Wasti, S. 2005. "Profiles in Coping: Responses to Sexual Harassment across Persons, Organizations, and Cultures." *Journal of Applied Psychology* 90: 182–92.

Cosgrove, Serena. 2016. "The Absent State." In *Gender Violence in Peace and War: States of Complicity,* edited by Victoria Sanford, Katerina Stefatos, and Cecilia M. Salvi, 158–70. New Brunswick: Rutgers University Press.

Cossins, Anne. 2000. *Masculinities, Sexualities and Child Sexual Abuse.* The Hague: Kluwer Law International.

———. 2003. "Saints, Sluts and Sexual Assault: Rethinking the Relationship between Sex, Race and Gender." *Social and Legal Studies* 12: 77–103.

Costa, Leeray M., and Karen J. Leong. 2012. "Critical and Feminist Civic Engagements: A Review." *Feminist Teacher* 22(3): 266–276.

Council on Foreign Relations. 2018. Global Conflict Tracker. www.cfr.org.

Courtright, Kevin E., and David A. Mackey. 2004. "Job Desirability among Criminal Justice Majors: Exploring Relationships between Personal Characteristics and Occupational Attractiveness." *Journal of Criminal Justice Education* 2: 311.

Courtois, Christine. 1988. *Healing the Incest Wound.* New York: Norton.

Courvant, Diana. 1997. "Domestic Violence and the Sex-or Gender-Variant Survivor." Portland, OR: The Survivor Project.

Courvant, Diana, and Loree Cook-Daniels. 2003. "Trans and Intersex Survivors of Domestic Violence: Defining Terms, Barriers, and Responsibilities." https://mnadv.org/

———, and Loree Cook-Daniels. 2005. *Trans and Intersex Survivors of Domestic Violence: Defining Terms, Barriers, and Responsibilities.* www.survivorproject.org.

Cox, J. 1989. "Karma and Redemption: A Religious Approach to Family Violence." *Journal of Religion and Health* 28 (1): 16–25.

Cox, John Woodrow., Steven Rich, Allyson Chiu, John Muyskens, and Monica Ulmanu. 2018. "More than 221,000 Students Have Experienced Gun Violence at School Since Columbine." *Washington Post,* April 20, 2018.

Crenshaw, Kimberlé. 1989. "Demarginalizing the Intersection of Race and Sex: A Black Feminist Critique of Antidiscrimination Doctrine, Feminist Theory and Antiracist Politics," *University of Chicago Legal Forum* 140: 139–67.

————. 1991. "Mapping the Margins: Intersectionality, Identity Politics, and Violence against Women of Color." *Stanford Law Review* 43 (6): 1241–99.

————. 2008. "Mapping the Margins: Intersectionality, Identity Politics, and Violence against Women of Color." In *The Feminist Philosophy Reader*, edited by Allison Bailey and Chris J. Cuomo, 265–78. Boston: McGraw-Hill.

Crofoot, Margaret C., and Richard W. Wrangham. 2009. "Intergroup Aggression in Primates and Humans: The Case for a Unified Theory." In *Mind the Gap: Tracing the Origins of Human Universals*, edited by Peter M. Kappeler and Joan B. Silk, 171–96. Heidelberg: Springer.

Croft, R., and P. Cash. 2012. "Deconstructing Contributing Factors to Bullying and Lateral Violence in Nursing Using a Postcolonial Feminist Lens." *Contemporary Nurse: A Journal for the Australian Nursing Profession* 4 (2): 226–42.

Cuevas, Carlos A., Chiara Sabina, and Emilie H. Picard. 2010. "Interpersonal Victimization Patterns and Psychopathology Among Latino Women: Results from the SALAS Study." *Psychological Trauma: Theory, Research, Practice, and Policy* 2 (4): 296–306.

Culp-Ressler, Tara. 2014 "The First College to Use Affirmative Action Was a Laughingstock: Now the Tide Is Turning." *ThinkProgress*. https://thinkprogress.org/the-first-college-to-use-affirma tive-consent-was-a-laughingstock-now-the-tide-is-turning-a912c34401d9/.

Curry, T. J. 1991. "Fraternal Bonding in the Locker Room: A Profeminist Analysis of Talk about Competition and Women." *Sociology of Sport Journal* 8: 119–35.

Dada, Carlos. 2014. "Guatemala Se Enjuicia:" *El Faro*. www.elfaro.net.

D'Adamo, Kate. 2017. "Sex (Work) in the Classroom: How Academia Can Support the Sex Workers' Rights Movement." In *Challenging perspectives on street-based sex work*, edited by Katie Hail-Jares, Corey S. Shdaimah, and Chrysanthi S. Leon, 195–217. Philadelphia, PA: Temple University Press.

Daily Beast. 2017. "Here Is the Powerful Statement a Wife Read Aloud to the Court and Her Abusive Husband." https://www.thedailybeast.com/here-is-the-powerful-statement-a-wife -read-aloud-to-the-court-and-her-abusive-husband.

D'Alton, Paul, Michael Guilfoyle, and Patrick Randall. 2013. "Roman Catholic Clergy Who Have Sexually Abused Children: Their Perceptions of Their Developmental Experience." *Child Abuse and Neglect* 37: 698–702.

Dames. 2015. "About." https://dmg.to/about.

Daniels, Jessie. 2009. *Cyber Racism: White Supremacy Online and the New Attack on Civil Rights.* Lanham MD: Rowman & Littlefield.

Dargis, Manohla. 2019. "Dear Diary: We're Still Refugees." *New York Times*, September 18, 2019.

Dart, Raymond A. 1953. "The Predatory Transition from Ape to Man." *International Anthropological and Linguistic Review* 1 (4): 201–18.

Dasgupta, Shamita D. 2005. "Women's Realities: Defining Violence Against Women by Immigration, Race and Class." In *Domestic Violence at the Margins: Readings in Race, Class, Gender and Culture*, edited by Natalie J. Sokoloff, 56–70. New Brunswick, NJ: Rutgers University Press.

Dastagir, Alia E. 2018. "Men Pay a Steep Price When It Comes to Masculinity." *USA Today*, April 26, 2018.

Davidson, T. 1978. *Conjugal Crime: Understanding and Changing the Wifebeating Pattern.* New York: Hawthorn.

Davies, Margaret. 1997. "Taking the Inside Out: Sex and Gender in the Legal Subject." In *Sexing the Subject of Law*, edited by N. Naffine and R. J. Owens. London: Sweet and Maxwell.

Davies, Miranda. 1994. "Understanding the Problem." United Nations' Resource Manual, *Strategies for Confronting Domestic Violence*. Reprinted in *Women and Violence*, edited by M. Davies. London: Zed Books.

Davis, Adrienne D. 1999. "The Private Law of Race and Sex: An Antebellum Perspective," *Stanford Law Review* 51: 221–88.

Davis, Angela. 1983. *Women, Race and Class*. New York: Random House.

Davis, Deirdre. 1994. "The Harm That Has No Name: Street Harassment, Embodiment, and African American Women." *UCLA Women's Law Journal* 4 (2): 133–78.

Davis, Joseph. 2005. *Accounts of Innocence*. Chicago: University of Chicago Press.

Davis, Simone, and Barbara Roswell, eds. 2013. *Turning Teaching Inside Out: A Pedagogy of Transformation for Community-Based Education*. New York: Springer.

Dawsey, Josh. 2018. "Trump Derides Protections for Immigrants from 'Shithole' Countries." *Washington Post*, January 12, 2018.

Deb, Sopan. 2018. "In Speech, Clinton Directs Barbs at Trump, Not Comey." *New York Times*, April 22, 2018.

Decker, Michelle R., Anna-Louise Crago, Sandra K. H. Chu, Susan G. Sherman, Meena S. Seshu, Kholi Buthelezi, Mandeep Dhaliwal, and Chris Beyrer. 2015. "Human Rights Violations against Sex Workers: Burden and Effect on HIV." *Lancet* 385 (9963): 186–99.

Deer, Sarah. 2006. "Federal Indian Law and Violent Crime." In *Color of Violence*, edited by INCITE! Women of Color Against Violence. Cambridge, MA: South End Press.

Deering, Kathleen N., Avni Amin, Jean Shoveller, Ariel Nesbitt, Claudia Garcia-Moreno, Puto Duff, Elena Argento, and Kate Shannon. 2014. "A Systematic Review of the Correlates of Violence against Sex Workers" *American Journal of Public Health*. 104, no. 5 (May): e42–e54.

de Freytas-Tamura, Kimiko. 2018. "Ireland Votes to End Abortion Ban, in Rebuke to Catholic Conservatism." *New York Times*, May 26, 2018.

De Genova, Nicholas P. 2002. "Migrant 'Illegality' and Deportability in Everyday Life." *Annual Review of Anthropology* 31: 419–67.

Dehue, F., C. Bolman, T. Völlink, and M. Pouwelse, M. 2012. Coping with Bullying at Work and Health Related Problems. *International Journal of Stress Management* 19: 175–97.

DeKeseredy, Walter S. and Marilyn Corsianos. 2016. *Violence Against Women in Pornography*. New York: Routledge.

DeKeseredy, Walter S. and Amanda Hall-Sanchez. 2017. "Adult Pornography and Violence Against Women in the Heartland: Results from Rural Southeast Ohio Study." *Violence Against Women* 23 (7): 830–49.

DeKeseredy W., A. Shahid, and M. D. Schwartz. 2003. *Under Siege: Poverty and Crime in a Public Housing Community*. Lanham, Maryland: Lexington Books.

de la Luz Lima, Maria. 1992. "Reforms in the Criminal Justice System." In *Violence against Women: Addressing a Global Problem*. Transcript of the Ford Foundation Women's Program Forum. New York: Ford Foundation.

Delgado, Richard. 1993. "Words That Wound: A Tort Action for Racial Insults, Epithets, and Name Calling." In *Words That Wound: Critical Race Theory, Assaultive Speech, and the First Amendment*, edited by J. M. Matsuda, C. R. Lawrence, R. Delgado, and K. Williams Crenshaw. Boulder: Westview Press.

Denham, Amy C., Pamela Y. Frasier, Elizabeth G. Hooten, Leigh Belton, Warren Newton, Pamela Gonzalez, Munni Begum, and Marci K. Campbell. 2007. "Intimate Partner Violence Among Latinas in Eastern North Carolina." *Violence Against Women* 13 (2): 123–40.

Dentan, R. C. 1991. "The Proverbs." In *The Interpreter's One-Volume Commentary on the Bible*, edited by C. M. Laymon, 324–8. Nashville, TN: Abingdon Press.

Department of Justice and Equality. 2009. "Report by Commission of Investigation into Catholic Archdiocese of Dublin." Dublin: Department of Justice and Equality. http://www.justice.ie/en/JELR/Pages/PB09000504

Derks, A., R. Henke, and V. Ly. 2006. *Review of a Decade of Research on Trafficking in Persons, Cambodia*. The Asia Foundation, and the Center for Advanced Study Cambodia. https://asiafoundation.org.

DeSouza, E. R., and Cerqueira, E. 2009. "From the Kitchen to the Bedroom: Frequency Rates and Consequences of Sexual Harassment among Female Domestic Workers in Brazil." *Journal of Interpersonal Violence* 24: 1264–84.

——, J. Solberg, and C. Elder, 2007. "A Cross-Cultural Perspective on Judgments of Woman-to-Woman Sexual Harassment: Does Sexual Orientation Matter?" *Sex Roles* 56: 457–71.

Devlin, Claire and Robert Elgie. 2008. "The Effect of Increased Women's Representation in Parliament: The Case of Rwanda." *Parliamentary Affairs* 61 (April): 237–54.

DeVoe, Jill, Katharin Peter, Phillip Kaufman, Amanda Miller, Margaret Noonan, Thomas Snyder, and Katrina Baum. 2004. *Indicators of School Crime and Safety: 2004*. NCES 2005–002/NCJ 205290. US Departments of Education and Justice. Washington, DC: US Government Printing Office.

Dewan, Shaila. 2005. "After 24 Years in Prison, Man Has a Reason to Smile." *New York Times*, December 8, 2005.

di Leonardo, Micaela. 1981. "The Political Economy of Street Harassment." *Aegis*: 51–57.

Dill, Kathleen. 2004. "Mediated Pasts, Negotiated Futures: Human Rights and Social Reconstruction in a Maya Community." PhD diss., University of California, Davis.

Dines, G. 2010. *Pornland: How Porn Hijacked Our Sexuality*. Boston, MA: Beacon.

——. 2015. *Today's Pornography and the Crisis of Violence Against Women and Children*. National Center on Sexual Exploitation, July 14, 2015. https://endsexualexploitation.org.

Dionisi, A. M., J. Barling, and K. E. Dupré, 2012. "Revisiting the Comparative Outcomes of Workplace Aggression and Sexual Harassment." *Journal of Occupational Health Psychology* 17: 398–408.

Doane, Janice, and Devon Hodges. 2001. *Telling Incest*. Ann Arbor: University of Michigan Press.

Dobash, R. Emerson, and Russell P. Dobash. 1979. *Violence against Wives: A Case against the Patriarchy*. New York: Free Press.

——. 1987. "The Response of the British and American Women's Movements to Violence against Women." In *Women, Violence and Social Control* edited by Jalna Hanmer and Mary Maynard. Atlantic Highlands, NJ: Humanities Press.

——. 1992. *Women, Violence and Social Change*. London: Routledge.

Doezema, Jo. 2010. *Sex Slaves and Discourse Masters*. New York: Zed.

Dolezal, Theresa, David McCollum, and Michael Callahan. 2009. *Hidden Costs in Health Care: The Economic Impact of Violence and Abuse*. Eden Prairie: Academy on Violence and Abuse.

Donald, Leland. 1997. *Aboriginal Slavery on the Northwest Coast of North America*. Berkeley: University of California Press.

Donaldson, Stephen. 1993. "A Million Jockers, Punks, and Queens." Just Detention International. www.justdetention.org.

Donohoe, William. 2003. "The Problem with Clericalism." *Society* 40 (3): 41–42. https://doi.org/ DOI https://doi.org/10.1007/s12115-003-1036-6.

Dorr, Donal. 2000. "Sexual Abuse and Spiritual Abuse." *Furrow* 51 (10): 523–31.

Dorsey, J. O. 1884. *Omaha Sociology*. Smithsonian Institution, Bureau of Ethnology, Third Annual Report, 1881–82: 205–370. Washington, DC: US Government Printing Office.

Douglas, Emily, and David Finkelhor. 2005. "Child Sexual Abuse Fact Sheet." University of New Hampshire: Crimes against Children Research Center. www.unh.edu.

Douglass, F. 1845. *Narrative of the Life of Frederick Douglass: An American Slave*, Boston: Published at the Anti-Slavery Office.

Doyle, Thomas. 2003. "Roman Catholic Clericalism, Religious Duress, and Clergy Sexual Abuse." *Pastoral Psychology* 51 (3): 189–231.

———. 2006. "Clericalism: Enabler of Sexual Abuse." *Pastoral Psychology* 54 (3): 189–213. https://doi.org/10.1007/S11089-006-6323-X.

Dragiewicz, M. 2008. "Patriarchy Reasserted: Fathers' Rights and Anti-VAWA Activism." *Feminist Criminology* 3(2): 121–44.

———. 2011. *Equality with a Vengeance: Men's Rights Groups, Battered Women, and Antifeminist Backlash*. Boston: Northeastern University Press.

Draper, Lucy. 2015. "Meet the All-Women Peacekeeping Force of South Sudan." Nonviolent Peaceforce, December 23, 2015. www.nonviolentpeaceforce.org.

Dreßing, Harald, Josef Bailer, Anne Anders, Henriette Wagner, and Christine Gallas. 2014. "Cyberstalking in a Large Sample of Social Network Users: Prevalence, Characteristics, and Impact upon Victims." *Cyberpsychology, Behavior, and Social Networking* 17 (2): 61–67.

Duggan, Maeve. 2014. "Online Harassment." Pew Research Center: Internet, Science & Tech, October 22, 2014. www.pewinternet.org.

Duggar, Celia W. 2011. "Senegal Curbs a Bloody Rite for Girls and Women." *New York Times*. October 15, 2011.

Dunne, Michael P., David M. Purdie, Michelle D. Cook, Frances M. Boyle, and Jake M. Najman. 2003. "Is Child Sexual Abuse Declining? Evidence from a Population-Based Survey of Men and Women in Australia." *Child Abuse and Neglect* 27: 141–52.

Dutton, Mary Ann., Leslye E. Orloff, and Giselle Aguilar Hass. 2000. "Characteristics of Help-Seeking Behaviors, Resources, and Service Needs of Battered Immigrant Latinas: Legal and Policy Implications." *Georgetown Journal of Poverty, Law, and Policy* 7 (2): 245–305.

Dworkin, Andrea. 1979. *Pornography: Men Possessing Women*. New York, NY: Perigee. Reprint, New York: Dutton, 1989.

———. 1981. *Pornography: Men Possessing Women*. London: Women's Press.

———. 1988. *Letters From a War Zone*. London: Secker and Warburg. Reprint, New York: Dutton.

———. 1992. "Women in the Public Domain: Sexual Harassment and Date Rape." In *Sexual Harassment: Women Speak Out*, edited by Amber Coverdale and Dena Taylor, 1–17. Freedom: The Crossing Press.

———. 1993. "Take Back the Day: I Want a Twenty-Four-Hour Truce During Which There Is No Rape." In *Letters from a War Zone*, edited by Andrea Dworkin, 162–71. Brooklyn, NY: Lawrence Hill Books.

Dziewanski, Dariusz. 2015. "The Unarmed Civilians Bringing Peace to South Sudan." *Guardian*, October 30, 2015.

Echols, Alice. 1984 [2002]. "The Taming of the Id: Feminist Sexual Politics, 1968–1983." In *Shaky Ground: The Sixties and Its Aftershocks*, edited by Alice Echols, 108–28. New York: Columbia University Press.

Eddy, Melissa, and Jessica Bennett. 2017. "Germany Is Told to Add 3rd Category On Gender." *New York Times*, November 9, 2017.

Edelson, Meredyth G., Audrey Hokoda, and Luciana Ramos-Lira. 2007. "Differences in Effects of Domestic Violence Between Latina and Non-Latina Women." *Journal of Family Violence* 22 (1): 1–10.

Edin, K. and T. J. Nelson. 2013. *Doing the Best I Can: Fatherhood in the Inner City*. Berkeley: University of California Press.

Edleson, Jeffrey L. 1999. "Children's Witnessing of Adult Domestic Violence." *Journal of Interpersonal Violence* 14 (8): 839–70.

Edwards, Alison. n.d. "Rape, Racism, and the White Women's Movement: An Answer to Susan Brownmiller." Chicago: Sojourner Truth Organization.

Edwards, Susan. 1987. "'Provoking Her Own Demise': From Common Assault to Homicide."
In *Women, Violence and Social Control* edited by Jalna Hanmer and Mary Maynard. Atlantic
Highlands, NJ: Humanities Press.

EEOC (Equal Employment Opportunity Commission). 2018. www.eeoc.gov.

Ehrenreich, Barbara, E. Hess, and G. Jacobs. 1986. *Re-Making Love: The Feminization of Sex.* New
York: Doubleday.

Eibl-Eibesfeldt, Irenäus. 1979. *The Biology of Peace and War: Men, Animals, and Aggression.* New
York: Viking Press.

Eisenstein, Hester. 1983. *Contemporary Feminist Thought.* Boston: G. K. Hall.

Ejército de Guatemala. 1965. *Manual de Guerra Contrasubversiva (resumen).* Guatemala City:
Ejército de Guatemala.

———. 1982. *Plan Victoria 82.* Guatemala City: Ejército de Guatemala.

Eldridge, Larry D. 1997. "Nothing New under the Sun: Spouse Abuse in Colonial America."
In *Gender Violence, Interdisciplinary Perspectives*, 1st ed., edited by L. L. O'Toole and
J. Schiffman, 254–65. New York: NYU Press.

Ellison, Christopher G., John P. Bartkowski, and Kristin L. Anderson. 1999. "Are There Religious
Variations in Domestic Violence?" *Journal of Family Issues* 20: 87–113.

———, Kristin L. Anderson. 2002. "Religious Involvement and Domestic Violence among US
Couples." *Journal for the Scientific Study of Religion* 40, no. 2 (June): 269–86.

Ellsberg, Mary, Rodolfo Pena, Andres Herrera, Jerker Liljestrand, and Anna Winkvist. 2000.
"Candies in Hell: Women's Experiences of Violence in Nicaragua." *Social Science and Medicine*
51: 1595–610.

Elshtain, Jean Bethke. 1982. "Feminist Discourse and Its Discontents: Language, Power, and
Meaning." *Signs: Journal of Women in Culture and Society* 7 (3): 603–21.

Elwér, S., L. Aléx, and A. Hammarström. 2010. "Health against the Odds: Experiences of Employees in Elder Care from a Gender Perspective." *Qualitative Health Research* 20: 1202–12.

Elwin, V. 1947. *The Muria and Their Ghotul.* Bombay: Oxford University Press.

Emerson, Robert M. 1983. "Holistic Effects in Social Control Decision-Making." *Law & Society
Review* 3: 425–55.

ENDESA (Encuesta Nicaragüense de Demografia y Salud). 2006–2007. *Informe Preliminar:
Encuesta Nicaraguense de Demografía y Salud ENDESA 2006/07.* Managua: Instituto Nacional
de Informacion de Desarrollo and Ministerio de Salud.

Engels, Friedrich. 2007 [1884]. *The Origin of the Family, Private Property, and the State, in Gender
Violence: Interdisciplinary Perspectives*, 2d ed., edited by Laura L. O'Toole, Jessica R. Schiffman, and Margie L. Kiter Edwards. New York: NYU Press.

Enloe, Cynthia. 1990. *Bananas Beaches and Bases: Making Feminist Sense of International Politics.*
Berkeley: University of California Press.

———. 2000. *Maneuvers: The International Politics of Militarizing Women's Lives.* Berkeley:
University of California Press.

———. 2013. *Seriously! Investigating Crashes and Crises as if Women Mattered.* Berkeley: University of California Press.

Epstein, Debbie. 1997. "Keeping Them in Their Place: Hetero/sexist Harassment, Gender and the
Enforcement of Heterosexuality" in *Sexual Harassment: Contemporary Feminist Perspectives*,
edited by Alison M. Thomas and Celia Kitzinger, 154–71. Philadelphia: Open University Press.

Equality Now. n.d. "Sex Trafficking Fact Sheet." Accessed January 18, 2019. www.equalitynow.org.

Erdland, P. A. 1914. *Die Marshall-insulaner (The Marshall Islanders).* Translated by Richard Neuse
for Human Relations Area Files. Münster: Anthropos Bibliothek Ethnological Monographs,
2 (1).

Erdrich, Louise. 2013. "Rape on the Reservation." *New York Times*, February 26, 2013.

Erez, Edna, and Kathy Laster. 2000. "Introduction." In *Domestic Violence: Global Responses,* edited by E. Erez and K. Laster. Bicester, UK: A B Academic.

Ertürk, Yakin. 2009. "15 Years of the United Nations Special Rapporteur on Violence Against Women, Its Causes and Consequences (1994–2009)—a Critical Review." UN Human Rights Council Report of the Special Rapporteur on Violence Against Women. https://www .refworld.org.docid/4a3f5fc62.html.

Espelage, Dorothy L., Jun Son Hong, Gabriel J. Merrin, and Jordan P. Davis. 2018. "A Longitudinal Examination of Homophobic Name-Calling in Middle School: Bullying, Traditional Masculinity, and Sexual Harassment." *Psychology of Violence* 8 (1): 57–66.

———, Kathleen C. Basile, Lisa De La Rue, and Merle E. Hamburger. 2015. "Longitudinal Associations Among Bullying, Homophobic Teasing, and Sexual Violence among Middle School Students." *Journal of Interpersonal Violence* 30 (14): 2541–61.

Essed, Philomena. 1991. *Understanding Everyday Racism: An Interdisciplinary Theory.* Thousand Oaks, CA: Sage.

Estrich, Susan. 1987. *Real Rape.* Cambridge, MA: Harvard University Press.

Evans, Sean. 2018. "Not talking about Mental Health is Literally Killing Men." *Men's Health,* May 2, 2018.

Evans-Pritchard, E. E. 1971. *The Azande.* Oxford: Oxford University Press.

Ewing, Wayne. 1982. "The Civic Advocacy of Violence." *M* (Spring): 5–7, 22.

Fackler, Martin. 2015. "U. S. Textbook Skews History, Prime Minister of Japan Says," *New York Times,* January 29, 2015.

Falk, Dean, and Charles Hildebolt. 2017. "Annual War Deaths in Small-Scale versus State Societies Scale with Population Size Rather than Violence." *Current Anthropology* 58 (6): 805–13.

Faludi, Susan. 1991. *Backlash: The Undeclared War against American Women.* New York: Crown.

Fantuzzo, John, and Rachel Fusco. 2007. "Children's Direct Exposure to Types of Domestic Violence Crime: A Population-based Investigation." *Journal of Family Violence* 22(7): 543–552.

Farley, Lin. 1978. *Sexual Shakedown: The Sexual Harassment of Women on the Job.* New York: McGraw-Hill.

———. 2017. "Reclaiming 'Sexual Harassment.'" *New York Times,* October 18, 2017.

Farley, Melissa. 2004. "'Bad for the Body, Bad for the Heart': Prostitution Harms Women Even If Legalized or Decriminalized." *Violence against Women* 10 (10): 1087–125.

———. 2005. "Prostitution Harms Women Even if Indoors" *Violence against Women* 11, no. 7 (July): 950–64.

Farmer, Paul. 2004. "An Anthropology of Structural Violence." *Current Anthropology* 45 (3): 305–25.

Farrell, W. 1974. *Liberated Man.* New York: Random House.

———. 1993. *The Myth of Male Power: Why Men are the Disposable Sex.* New York: Simon and Schuster.

———. 2014. *International Conference on Men's Issues—Day 2 Excerpt—Warren Farrell.* https://www.youtube.com/watch?v=V5PMS6VkJkY.

Fausto-Sterling, Anne. 1989. "Life in the XO Coral." *Women's Studies International Forum* 12(3): 319–31.

———. 2000. *Sexing the Body: Gender Politics and the Construction of Sexuality.* New York: Basic Books.

FBI (Federal Bureau of Investigation). 2013. "The Crime of 'Swatting.'" www.fbi.gov.

Feagin, Joe R. 1991. "The Continuing Significance of Race: Anti-Black Discrimination in Public Places." *American Sociological Review* 56, no. 1 (February): 101–16.

Feitlowitz, Marguerite. 1999. *A Lexicon of Terror: Argentina and the Legacies of Torture.* New York: Oxford University Press.

Felson, Richard. 2002. *Violence and Gender Reexamined.* Washington, DC: American Psychological Association.

Fenstermaker, Sarah, and Nikki Jones, 2011. eds. *Sociologists Backstage.* New York: Routledge.

Ferguson, R. Brian. 2013. "Pinker's List: Exaggerating Prehistoric War Mortality." In *War, Peace, and Human Nature: The Convergence of Evolutionary and Cultural Views,* edited by Douglas P. Fry, 112–31. Oxford: Oxford University Press.

Fergusson, David M., L. John Horwood, and Elizabeth M. Ridder. 2005. "Partner Violence and Mental Health Outcomes in a New Zealand Birth Cohort." *Journal of Marriage and Family* 67 (5): 1103–19.

Ferree, Myra Marx. 1990. "Beyond Separate Spheres: Feminism and Family Research." *Journal of Marriage and the Family* 52 (4): 866–84.

——, Judith Lorber, and Beth B. Hess. 2000. "Introduction." In *Revisioning Gender,* edited by M. M. Ferree, J. Lorber, and B. B. Hess. Walnut Creek, CA: Altamira.

Fielden, S., M. Davidson, H. Woolnough, and C. Hunt. 2010. "A Model of Racialized Sexual Harassment of Women in the UK Workplace." *Sex Roles* 62: 20–34.

Fineran, S., and J. E. Gruber. 2009. "Youth at Work: Adolescent Employment and Sexual Harassment." *Child Abuse and Neglect: The International Journal* 33: 550–59.

Finkelhor, David. 1979. *Sexually Victimized Children.* New York: The Free Press.

——, ed. 1984. *Child Sexual Abuse: New Theory and Research.* New York: Free Press.

Finkelhor, David, G. Hotaling, I. A. Lewis, and C. Smith. 1990. "Sexual Abuse in a National Survey of Adult Men and Women: Prevalence, Characteristics, and Risk Factors." *Child Abuse and Neglect* 14(1): 19–28.

Finkelhor, David, and Richard Ormrod. 2000. "Characteristics of Crimes against Juveniles." *Juvenile Justice Bulletin,* June. US Department of Justice, Office of Justice Programs, Washington, DC.

——, Heather Turner, Anne Shattuck, and Sherry Hamby. 2013. "Violence, Crime, and Abuse Exposure in a National Sample of Children and Youth." *JAMA Pediatrics* 167 (7): 614–21.

——, Carlos Cuevas, and Drawbridge, Dara. 2016. "The Four Preconditions Model: An Assessment." In *The Wiley Handbook on the Theories, Assessment, and Treatment of Sexual Offending,* edited by Beech, Anthony and Ward, Tony. Vol. 1. New Jersey: John Wiley & Sons, Ltd.

——. Heather A. Turner, Anne Shattuck, and Sherry L. Hamby. 2015. "Prevalence of Childhood Exposure to Violence, Crime, and Abuse: Results from the National Survey of Children's Exposure to Violence." *JAMA Pediatrics* 169 (August): 746–54.

Fisas, Vicenç. 1998. *El sexo de la violencia, Género y cultura de la violencia.* Barcelona: Icaria.

Fisher, Bonnie S., Francis T. Cullen, and Michael G. Turner. 2000. "The Sexual Victimization of College Women." *National Institute of Justice and Bureau of Justice Statistics,* Washington, DC. www.ncjrs.gov.

Fitzgerald, L. F., F. Drasgow, C. L. Hulin, M. J. Gelfand, and V. J. Magley. 1997. "Antecedents and Consequences of Sexual Harassment in Organizations: A Test of an Integrated Model." *Journal of Applied Psychology* 82: 578–89.

——, M. Gelfand, and F. Drasgow. 1995. "Measuring Sexual Harassment: Theoretical and Psychometric Advances." *Basic and Applied Social Psychology* 17: 425–45.

Fleming, Jillian M. 1997. "Prevalence of Childhood Sexual Abuse in a Community Sample of Australian Women." *Medical Journal of Australia* 166: 65–8.

Flood, Michael. 2009. "The Harms of Pornography Exposure among Children and Young People." *Child Abuse Review* 18: 384–400.

Flores, E. O. and P. Hondagneu-Sotelo. 2013 "Chicano Gang Members in Recovery: The Public Talk of Negotiating Chicano Masculinities." *Social Problems* 60 (4): 1–15.

Follis, A. B. 1981. *"I'm not a women's libber, but . . ." and Other Confessions of a Christian Feminist.* Nashville: Abingdon.

Foster, Frances Smith. 2010. "Mammy's Daughters; Or, the DNA of a Feminist Sexual Ethics." In *Beyond Slavery: Overcoming Its Religious and Sexual Legacies*, edited by Bernadette J. Brooten, 267–84. New York: Palgrave Macmillan.

Foubert, John D., Matthew W. Brosi, and R. Shawn Bannon. 2011. "Pornography Viewing among Fraternity Men: Effects on Bystander Intervention, Rape Myth Acceptance and Behavioral Intent to Commit Sexual Assault." *Sexual Addiction & Compulsivity: The Journal of Treatment & Prevention* 18 (4): 213–31.

Foucault, Michel. 1977. *Discipline and Punish: The Birth of the Prison.* Translated from the French by Alan Sheridan. New York: Vintage Books.

———. 1980. *Power/Knowledge: Selected Interviews and Other Writings, 1972—1977*, edited by Colin Gordon. New York: Pantheon.

Fortune, M. M., and C. G. Enger. 2005. "Violence against Women and the Role of Religion." Harrisburg, PA: National Online Resource Center on Violence Against Women.

Foster, Malcolm. 2013. "Japanese Mayor: Wartime Sex Slaves Were Necessary." *Seattle Times*, May 14, 2013.

Fox, Thomas. 2011. "Richard Sipe on the John Jay Report." *National Catholic Reporter Online*, May 19, 2011. www.ncronline.org.

Franceschet, Susan. 2010. "Explaining Domestic Violence Policy Outcomes in Chile and Argentina." *Latin American Politics and Society* 51 (3): 1–29.

Franco, Jean. 2007. "Rape: A Weapon of War." *Social Text* 25 (2): 23–37.

Frank, Blye W. 1996. "Masculinities and Schooling: The Making of Men." In *Systemic Violence: How Schools Hurt Children* edited by Juanita Ross Epp and Ailsa M. Watkinson. London: Falmer.

Franklin, Cortney A., Leana Allen Bouffard, and Travis C. Pratt. 2012. "Sexual Assault on the College Campus: Fraternity Affiliation, Male Peer Support, and Low Self-Control." *Criminal Justice and Behavior*, 39(11): 1457–1480.

Franks, Mary Anne. 2012. "Sexual Harassment 2.0." *Maryland Law Review* 71 (3): 655–904.

Franzway S., D. Court, and R. W. Connell. 1989. *Staking a Claim: Feminism, Bureaucracy and the State.* Sydney: Allyn and Unwin.

Fraser, Nancy. 2013. "How Feminism Became Capitalism's Handmaiden—and How to Reclaim It." *Guardian*, October 14, 2013.

Frawley-O'Dea, Mary Gail. 2004a. "Psychosocial Anatomy of the Catholic Sexual Abuse Scandal." *Studies in Gender and Sexuality* 5 (2): 121–37.

———. 2004b. "The History and Consequences of the Sexual Abuse Crisis in the Catholic Church." *Studies in Gender and Sexuality* 5 (1): 11–30.

———. 2007. *Perversion of Power: Sexual Abuse in the Catholic Church.* Nashville: Vanderbilt University Press.

———. 2011. "Soul Murder: The Spiritual Sequelae of Clergy Sexual Abuse with Focus on Roman Catholicism and Orthodox Judaism." www.samaritaninstitute.org.

Freedman, Estelle. 2013. *Redefining Rape.* Cambridge, MA: Harvard University Press.

Freiburger, James. 2011. *Clergy Pedophiles: A Study of Sexually Abusive Clergy and Their Victims.* Indiana: Author House.

Freire, Paulo. 1972. *Pedagogy of the Oppressed.* Translated by Myra Bergman Ramos. New York: Herder and Herder.

Freund, Julian. 1968. "The Sociology of Religion." In *The Sociology of Max Weber*, 176–218. New York: Random House.

Friedan, Betty. 1963. *The Feminine Mystique*. New York: Norton.

Friedman, Uri. 2016. "Why It's So Hard for a Woman to Become President of the United States." *Atlantic*, November 12, 2016.

Friedrich, Patricia. 2007. *Language, Negotiation and Peace: The Use of English in Conflict Resolution*. London: Continuum.

Frishtik, M. 1990. "Alimut Klapei Nashim Beyahadut" [wife abuse in Judaism]. *Hevra Urevaha* 11 (6): 26–44.

Frye, M. 1992. *Willful Virgin*. Freedom, CA: Crossing Press.

Fugate, Michelle, Leslie Landis, Kim Riordan, Sara Naureckas, and Barbara Engel. 2005. "Barriers to Domestic Violence Help Seeking: Implications for Intervention." *Violence Against Women* 11 (3): 290–310.

Fuller, Janet. 2003. "Teen Guilty of Taking Two Kegs to Hazing." *Chicago Sun Times*, July 16, 2003.

Fulton, A. 2017. "In Texas And Beyond, Mass Shootings Have Roots in Domestic Violence." *NPR*. www.npr.org.

Galloway, Alison. 1999. *Broken Bones: Anthropological Analysis of Blunt Force Trauma*. Springfield: Charles C. Thomas.

Galtung, Johan. 1990. "Cultural Violence." *Journal of Peace Research* 27, no. 3 (August): 291–30.

Garcia, Lorena, Eric L. Hurwitz, and Jess F. Kraus. 2005. "Acculturation and Reported Intimate Partner Violence Among Latinas in Los Angeles." *Journal of Interpersonal Violence* 20 (5): 569–90.

Garcia, Sandra. 2017. "The Woman Who Created #MeToo Long Before Hashtags." *New York Times*, October 20, 2017.

García-Moreno, Claudia, Cathy Zimmerman, Alison Morris-Gehring, Lori Heise, Avni Amin, Naeemah Abrahams, Oswaldo Montoya, Padma Bhate-Deosthali, Nduku Kilonzo, and Charlotte Watts. 2015. "Addressing Violence Against Women: A Call to Action." *Lancet* 385 (9978): 1685–95.

———, H. Jansen, M. Ellsberg, L. Heise, and C. Watts. 2005. "WHO Multi-country Study on Women's Health and Domestic Violence against Women: Initial Results on Prevalence, Health Outcomes and Women's Responses." Geneva: World Health Organization.

———, Lori Heise, Henrica A. F. M. Jansen, Mary Ellsberg, and Charlotte Watts. 2005. "Violence Against Women." *Science* 310 (5752): 1282–83.

Gardner, Carol Brooks. 1995. *Passing By: Gender and Public Harassment*. Berkeley, CA: University of California Press.

Gardner, T. A. 1980. "Racism in Pornography and the Women's Movement." In *Take Back the Night: Women and Pornography*, edited by L. Lederer. New York: Morrow.

Garfinkel, Harold. 1967. *Studies in Ethnomethodology*. Englewood Cliffs, NJ: Prentice Hall.

Garland, David. 2001. *The Culture of Control: Crime and Social Order in Contemporary Society*. Chicago: University of Chicago Press.

Garver, Newton. 1968. "What Violence Is." *Nation* 209 (June 24): 817–22.

Garza, Alicia. 2017. "A HerStory of the #BlackLivesMatter Movement." www.blacklivesmatter.com.

Gatens, Moira. 1996. *Imaginary Bodies: Ethics, Power and Corporeality*. London: Routledge.

Gauthier, Jeffrey 1999. "Consent, Coercion and Sexual Autonomy." In *A Most Detestable Crime: New Philosophical Essays on Rape*, edited by Keith Burgess-Jackson, 71–89. New York: Oxford University Press.

Gavey, N. 2005. *Just Sex? The Cultural Scaffolding of Rape*. New York: Routledge.

Gay, Roxane. 2017. *Hunger: A Memoir of (My) Body*. New York: Harper.

Gay, William. 1994. "The Prospect for a Nonviolent Model of National Security." In *On the Eve of the 21st Century: Perspectives of Russian and American Philosophers*, edited by William Gay and T. A. Alekseeva, 119–34. Lanham, MD: Rowman & Littlefield.

———. 1997. "Nonsexist Public Discourse and Negative Peace: The Injustice of Merely Formal Transformation." *Acorn: Journal of the Gandhi-King Society* 9, no. 1 (Spring): 45–53.

———. 1998a. "Exposing and Overcoming Linguistic Alienation and Linguistic Violence." *Philosophy and Social Criticism* 24:2/3: 137–56.

———. 1998b. "The Practice of Linguistic Nonviolence." *Peace Review* 10:4: 545–57.

———. 2007. "Language, War, and Peace." *Handbook of Language and Communication: Diversity and Change*, edited by Marlis Hellinger and Anne Pauwels, 493–521. Berlin: Bouton de Gruyter.

———. 2016. "Restorative Justice and Care Ethics: An Integrated Approach to Forgiveness and Reconciliation." In *The Philosophy of Forgiveness—Volume I: Explorations of Forgiveness: Personal, Relational, and Religious*, edited by Court D. Lewis, 31–58. Wilmington, DE: Vernon Press.

———. 2018. "The Role of Language in Justifying and Reducing Cultural Violence." In *Peace, Culture, and Violence*, edited by Fuat Gursozlu, 31–63. Leiden, Boston: Brill.

Gehl, Robert W. 2016. "Power/Freedom on the Dark Web: A Digital Ethnography of the Dark Web Social Network." *New Media & Society* 18 (7): 1219–35.

Geiger, Abigail, and Lauren Kent. 2017. "Number of Women Leaders around the World has Grown, but They're Still a Small Group." www.pewresearch.org.

Gelles, Richard J. 1974. *The Violent Home*. Beverly Hills, CA: Sage Publications.

Generation Five. n.d. "Resources." Accessed March 4, 2020. www.generationfive.org.

Gentlewarrior, S. 2009. "Culturally Competent Service Provision to Lesbian, Gay, Bisexual and Transgender Survivors of Sexual Violence." September. Harrisburg, PA: VAWnet. www.vawnet.org

Geto Boys. 1992. "Mind of a Lunatic." *UnCut Dope*, audio disc.

Gettman, Hilary J., and Michele J. Gelfand. 2007. "When the Customer Shouldn't be King: Antecedents and Consequences of Sexual Harassment by Clients and Customers." *Journal of Applied Psychology* 92: 757–70.

Gibbons-Neff, Thomas. 2018. "Reports of Sexual Assault in the Military Rise by 10 Percent, Pentagon Finds." *New York Times*, April 30, 2018.

Gibson, Candace. 2013. "For Immigrant Women, Health Care Remains Out of Reach." *Women's Health Activist* (November/December): 7, 10.

Giesbrecht, Norman, and Irene Sevcik. 2000. "The Process of Recovery and Rebuilding Among Abused Women in the Conservative Evangelical Subculture." *Journal of Family Violence* 15, no. 3 (September): 229–48.

Gill, Aisha K. 2014. "'Honour' and 'Honour'-Based Violence: Challenging Common Assumptions." In *"Honour" Killing and Violence: Theory, Policy and Practice*, edited by Aisha K. Gill, Carolyn Strange, and Karl Roberts, 1–23. London: Palgrave Macmillan.

Gilligan, Carol. 1982. *In a Different Voice: Psychological Theory and Women's Development*. Cambridge, MA: Harvard University Press.

———. 2013. *Joining the Resistance*. Cambridge: Polity Press.

———. 2014. "Moral Injury and the Ethic of Care: Reframing the Conversation about Differences" *Journal of Social Philosophy* 45, no. 1 (Spring): 89–106.

Gilligan, Leilah, and Tom Talbot. 2000. "Community Supervision of the Sex Offender: An Overview of Current and Promising Practices." Center for Sex Offender Management. www.ncjrs.gov.

Gilliom, John. 2001. *Overseers of the Poor: Surveillance, Resistance, and the Limits of Privacy*. Chicago: University of Chicago Press.

Gilman, Sander L. 1985. "Black Bodies, White Bodies: Toward an Iconography of Female Sexuality in Late Nineteenth-Century Art, Medicine, and Literature." *Critical Inquiry* 12(1): 205–43.

Gilmore, Ruth Wilson. 2007. "In the Shadow of the Shadow State." In *The Revolution Will Not be Funded: Beyond the Non-Profit Industrial Complex*, 41–52, edited by INCITE! Women of Color Against Violence. Cambridge, MA: South End Press.

Ging, Debbie. 2017. "Alphas, Betas, and Incels: Theorizing the Masculinities of the Manosphere." *Men and Masculinities*: 1–20. https://doi.org/10.1177/1097184X17706401

Ginorio, Angela B., Lorraine Gutiérrez, Ana Mari Cauce, and Mimi Acosta. 1995. "Psychological Issues for Latinas." In *Bringing Cultural Diversity to Feminist Psychology: Theory, Research, and Practice*, edited by Hope Landrine, 241–63. Washington, DC: American Psychological Association.

Girard, A. L. 2009. "Backlash or Equality? The Influence of Men's and Women's Rights Discourses on Domestic Violence Legislation in Ontario." *Violence against Women* 15 (1): 5–23.

Gismondi, Melissa J. 2018. "Why are 'Incels' so Angry? The History of the Little-Known Ideology behind the Toronto Attack." *Washington Post*, April 27, 2018.

Giuffre, Patti, Kirsten Dellinger, and Christine L. Williams. 2008. "No Retribution for Being Gay?: Inequality in Gay-friendly Workplaces." *Sociological Spectrum* 28 (3): 254–77.

Giwa, Sulaimon, and Cameron Greensmith. 2012. "Race Relations and Racism in the LGBTQ Community of Toronto: Perceptions of Gay and Queer Social Service Providers of Color." *Journal of Homosexuality* 59 (2): 149–85.

Glancy, Jennifer A. 2010. "Early Christianity, Slavery, and Women's Bodies." In *Beyond Slavery: Overcoming Its Religious and Sexual Legacies*, edited by Bernadette J. Brooten, 143–58. New York: Palgrave Macmillan.

Glaser, Barney G., and Anselm L. Strauss. 1967. *The Discovery of Grounded Theory: Strategies for Qualitative Research*. New York, NY: Aldine De Gruyter.

Gluck, B. 1988. Jewish Men and Violence in the Home: Unlikely Companions? In *A Mensch among Men: Explorations in Jewish Masculinity*, edited by Harry Brod, 162–17. Freedom, CA: Crossing Press.

Goddard, Alma Banda, and Tara Hardy. 1999. "Assessing the Lesbian Victim." In *Same-Sex Domestic Violence: Strategies for Change*, edited by B. Leventhal and S. E. Lundy. Thousand Oaks, CA: Sage.

Goldberg H. 1976. *The Hazards of Being Male: Surviving the Myth of Masculine Privilege*. New York: Signet.

Goldberg-Ambrose, Carole. 1992. "Unfinished Business in Rape Law Reform." *Journal of Social Issues* 48 (1): 173–85.

Gondolf, Edward W., and Ellen R. Fisher. 1988. *Battered Women as Survivors*. Lexington, MA: Lexington Books.

Goodall, Jane. 1979. "Life and Death at Gombe." *National Geographic Magazine* 155: 592–621.
———. 1986. *The Chimpanzees of Gombe: Patterns of Behavior*. Cambridge: Harvard University Press.

Goodman, Alan H., and T. L. Leatherman, eds. 1998. *Building a New Biocultural Synthesis: Political-Economic Perspectives on Human Biology*. Ann Arbor: The University of Michigan Press.

Goodman, Lisa, Mary Ann Dutton, Kevin Weinfurt, and Sarah Cook. 2003. "The Intimate Partner Violence Strategies Index: Development and Application." *Violence Against Women* 9 (2): 163–86.

Goodstein, Laurie, and Sharon Otterman. 2018. "Ousted US Cardinal Left A Trail of Abused Recruits." *New York Times*. July 16, 2018.

Gordon, Margaret T., and Stephanie Riger. 1989. *The Female Fear*. New York: The Free Press.

Gorsevski, Ellen W. 1998. "The Physical Side of Linguistic Violence." *Peace Review* 10 (4): 513–16.

Gould, Stephen Jay. 1981. *The Mismeasure of Man*. New York: Norton.

Gracie, Carrie. 2015. "China to End One Child Policy and Allow Two." *BBC*, October 29, 2015.

Graham-Kevan, Nicola, and John Archer. 2003a. "Intimate Terrorism and Common Couple Violence: A Test of Johnson's Predictions in Four British Samples." *Journal of Interpersonal Violence* 18 (11): 1247–70.

———. 2003b. "Physical Aggression and Control in Heterosexual Relationships: The Effect of Sampling." *Violence and Victims* 18 (2): 181–96.

Grant, Jamie M., Lisa Mottet, Justin Edward Tanis, Jack Harrison, Jody Herman, and Mara Keisling. 2011. *Injustice at Every Turn: A Report of the National Transgender Discrimination Survey*. Washington, DC: National Center for Transgender Equality.

Grant, Jennifer. 1999. "An Argument for Separate Services." In *Same-Sex Domestic Violence: Strategies for Change*. London: Sage Publishers.

Greenberg, Andy. 2014. "Over 80 Percent of Dark-Web Visits Relate to Pedophilia, Study Finds." *Wired*, December 30, 2014.

Greenberg, Max A., and Michael A. Messner. 2014. "Before Prevention: The Trajectory and Tensions of Feminist Anti-Violence." In *Gendered Perspectives on Conflict and Violence (Part B)*, edited by Marcia Texler Segal and Vasilikie Demos, 225–50. Bingley, UK: Emerald Group Publishing.

Gregory, J., and S. Lees. 1999. *Policing Sexual Assault*. London: Routledge.

Greitemeyer, T., and N. McLatchie. 2011. "Denying Humanness to Others: A Newly Discovered Mechanism by Which Violent Video Games Increase Aggressive Behavior." *Psychological Science* 22 (5): 659–65.

Griffin, Susan. 1992. *A Chorus of Stones: The Private Life of War*. New York: Doubleday.

Grimes, William. 2001 [1825]. *Life of William Grimes, the Runaway Slave: Written by Himself*. Chapel Hill: University of North Carolina (electronic version). https://docsouth.unc.edu.

Griner, Stacey B., Cheryl A. Vamos, Erika L. Thompson, Rachel Logan, Coralia Vasquez-Otero, and Ellen M. Daley. 2017. "The Intersection of Gender Identity and Violence: Victimization Experienced by Transgender College Students." *Journal of Interpersonal Violence* (August). https://doi.org/10.1177/0886260517723743.

Groden, Claire. 2014. "Why Is It So Hard to Determine Exactly How Many Women Are Raped Each Year?" *New Republic*, September 8, 2014.

Grossman, Leanne A., and Sande Smith. 2004. "Women Daring to Lead." The Global Fund for Women Report 2003–2004, San Francisco.

Grosz, Elizabeth. 1990. "A Note on Essentialism and Difference." In *Feminist Knowledge, Critique and Construct*, edited by S. Unew, 332–44. London: Routledge.

———. 1994. *Volatile Bodies: Toward a Corporeal Feminism*. Sydney: Allen and Unwin.

———, and Elspeth Probyn. 1995. *Sexy Bodies: Strange Carnalities of Feminism*. London: Routledge.

Gruber, James, and Susan Fineran. 2008. "Comparing the Impact of Bullying and Sexual Harassment Victimization on the Mental and Physical Health of Adolescents." *Sex Roles* 59: 1–13.

Gunn Allen, Paula. 1986. "Violence and the American Indian Women." In *The Speaking Profits Us: Violence in the Lives of Women of Color* edited by Maryviolet Burns. Seattle: Center for the Prevention of Sexual and Domestic Violence.

Gunnarsdottir, H., H. Sveinsdottir, J. Bernburg, H. Fridriksdottir, and K. Tomasson. 2006. "Lifestyle, Harassment at Work and Self-assessed Health of Female Flight Attendants, Nurses and Teachers." *Work* 27: 165–72.

Gürsözlü, Fuat. 2014. "Pluralism, Identity, and Violence." In *Peace Philosophy and Public Life: Commitments, Crises, and Concepts for Engaged Thinking*, edited by Greg Moses and Gail Presbey, 93–108, 171–72. Amsterdam, New York: Rodopi.

Gustafson, Kaaryn. 2013. "Degradation Ceremonies and the Criminalization of Low-Income Women." *UC Irvine Law Review* 3: 297–358.

Gutek, Barbara A. 1985. *Sex and the Workplace: Impact of Sexual Behavior and Harassment on Women, Men, and Organizations*. San Francisco: Jossey-Bass.

———, and Bruce Morasch. 1982. "Sex Ratios, Sex-Role Spillover, and Sexual Harassment of Women at Work." *Journal of Social Issues* 38 (4): 55–74.

Gutiérrez, Ramón A. 1991. *When Jesus Came, the Corn Mothers Went Away: Marriage, Sexuality, and Power in New Mexico, 1500–1846*. Stanford: Stanford University Press.

Habila, Helon. 2016. *The Chibok Girls, the Boko Haram Kidnappings and Islamist Militancy in Nigeria*. New York: Columbia Global Reports.

Hacker, Frederick F. 1976. *Crusaders, Criminals and Crazies: Terrorism in Our Time*. New York: W. W. Norton and Co.

Hacking, Ian. 1991. "The Making and Molding of Child Abuse." *Critical Inquiry* 17 (Winter): 253–88.

Hail-Jares, Katie. 2016. "Bad Dates: How Prostitution Strolls Impact Client-Initiated Violence." *Studies in Law, Politics, and Society* 71: 115–37.

Hajjar, L. 2004. "Religion, State Power, and Domestic Violence in Muslim Societies: A Framework for Comparative Analysis." *Law and Social Inquiry* 29 (1): 1–38.

Hald, Gert Martin, Neil M. Malamuth, and Carlin Yuen. 2010. "Pornography and Attitudes Supporting Violence against Women: Revisiting the Relationship in Nonexperimental Studies." *Aggressive Behavior* 36: 14–20.

Halevi, G., A. Djalovski, A. Vengrober, and R. Feldman. 2016. "Risk and Resilience Trajectories in War-Exposed Children Across the First Decade of Life." *Journal of Child Psychology and Psychiatry*, 57(10): 1183–193.

Hall, J. D. 1983. "The Mind That Burns in Each Body: Women, Rape, and Racial Violence." In *Powers of Desire: The Politics of Sexuality*, edited by A. Snitow, C. Stansell, and S. Thompson. New York: Monthly Review Press.

Hall, Ruth. 1985. *Ask Any Woman: A London Inquiry into Rape and Sexual Assault*. Bristol, UK: Falling Wall Press.

Hallowell, A. I. 1955. *Culture and Experience*. Philadelphia: University of Pennsylvania Press.

Halpin, Zuleyma Tang. 1989. "Scientific Objectivity and the Concept of 'the Other.'" *Women's Studies International Forum* 12(3): 285–94.

Hamberger, L. Kevin, and Clare E. Guse. 2002. "Men's and Women's Use of Intimate Partner Violence in Clinical Samples." *Violence against Women* 8 (11): 1301–31.

Hamington, Michael. 2004. *Embodied Ethics: Jane Addams, Maurice Merleau-Ponty, and Feminist Ethics*. Chicago: University of Illinois Press.

Hammer, Rhonda. 2002. *Antifeminism and Family Terrorism: A Critical Feminist Perspective*. Lanham: Rowman & Littlefield Publishers, Inc.

Harding, Kate. 2015. *Asking for It: The Alarming Rise of Rape Culture and What We Can Do About It*. Philadelphia: Da Capo Press.

Harding, Sandra. 2004. "Introduction: Standpoint Theory as a Site of Political, Philosophic, and Scientific Debate." In *The Feminist Standpoint Theory Reader: Intellectual and Political Controversies*. New York and London: Psychology Press.

Harkins, Leigh, and Louise Dixon. 2010. "Sexual Offending in Groups: An Evaluation." *Aggression and Violent Behavior* 15 (2): 87–99.

Harley, Debra A., Theresa M. Nowak, Linda J. Gassaway, and Todd A. Savage. 2002. "Lesbian, Gay, Bisexual, and Transgender College Students with Disabilities: A Look at Multiple Cultural Minorities." *Psychology in the Schools* 39 (5): 425–538.

Harris Interactive and GLSEN. 2005. *From Teasing to Torment: School Climate in America: A Survey of Students and Teachers.* New York: GLSEN.

Harris, M. 1977. *Cannibals and Kings.* New York: Vintage/Random House.

Harris, Richard J., Juanita M. Firestone, and William A. Vega. 2005. "The Interaction of Country of Origin, Acculturation, and Gender Role Ideology on Wife Abuse." *Social Science Quarterly* 86 (2): 463–83.

Harrison, Jane, Lesley MacGibbon, and Missy Morton. 2001. "Regimes of Trustworthiness in Qualitative Research: The Rigors of Reciprocity." *Qualitative Inquiry* 7 (3): 323–45.

Harris-Perry, Melissa. 2012. *Sister Citizen: Shame, Stereotypes, and Black Women in America.* New Haven, CT: Yale University Press.

Harrod, Ryan P., Pierre Liénard, and Debra L. Martin. 2012. "Deciphering Violence: The Potential of Modern Ethnography to Aid in the Interpretation of Archaeological Populations." In *The Bioarchaeology of Violence,* edited by Debra L. Martin, Ryan P. Harrod, and Ventura R. Pérez, 63–80. Gainesville: University of Florida Press.

———, and Debra L. Martin. 2014. "Signatures of Captivity and Subordination on Skeletonized Human Remains: A Bioarchaeological Case Study from the Ancient Southwest." In *Bioarchaeological and Forensic Perspectives on Violence: How Violent Death Is Interpreted from Skeletal Remains,* edited by Debra L. Martin and Cheryl P. Anderson, 103–19. Cambridge: Cambridge University Press.

Hart, B. 1992. *State Codes on Domestic Violence: Analysis, Commentary, and Recommendations.* Reno, NV: National.

Hartman, Saidiya. 2007. *Lose Your Mother: A Journey Along the Atlantic Slave Route.* New York: Farrar, Straus, and Giroux.

Haselton, M. G., D. Nettle, and D. R. Murray, 2015. "The Evolution of Cognitive Bias. The Handbook of Evolutionary Psychology." VII (41): 1–20. Wiley Online Library, https://onlinelibrary .wiley.com.

Hass, Giselle A., Mary Ann Dutton, and Leslye E. Orloff. 2000. "Lifetime Prevalence of Violence against Latina Immigrants: Legal and Policy Implications." In *Domestic Violence: Global Responses,* edited by E. Erez and K. Laster. Bicester, UK: A B Academic.

Hathaway, Mark, and Leonardo Boff. 2014. *El Tao de la Liberación. Una ecología de la transformación.* Madrid: Trotta.

Hautzinger, Sarah. 2002. "Criminalising Male Violence in Brazil's Women's Police Stations: From Flawed Essentialism to Imagined Communities." *Journal of Gender Studies* 11 (3): 243–51.

Hawkesworth, Mary. 2006. *Feminist Inquiry: From Political Conviction to Methodological Innovation.* New Brunswick: Rutgers University Press.

Hawks, Laura, Steffie Woolhandler, David U. Himmelstein, David H. Bor, Adam Gaffney, and Danny McCormick. 2019. "Association Between Forced Sexual Initiation and Health Outcomes Among US Women." *JAMA International Medicine.* https://jamanetwork.com.

Hayek, Friedrich. 1944. *The Road to Serfdom.* Chicago: University of Chicago Press.

Hazen, Andrea L., and Fernando I. Soriano. 2007. "Experiences with Intimate Partner Violence Among Latina Women." *Violence Against Women* 13, no. 6 (June): 562–82.

Healy, Patrick. 2003a. "Coach on L.I. Says He Knew of No Hazing." *New York Times,* October 1, 2003.

———. 2003b. "L.I. District Is Criticized in Hazing Case." *New York Times,* September 23, 2003.

———. 2003c. "School District in Hazing Case Draws Anger from Parents." *New York Times,* September 19, 2003.

———, and Faiza Akhtar. 2003. "Football Players on L.I. Face Abuse Accusations in Hazing." *New York Times*, September 12, 2003.

Hearn, Jeff. 1998. *The Violences of Men: How Men Talk about and How Agencies Respond to Men's Violence to Women*. Thousand Oaks: SAGE Publications Inc.

———. 2001. *Gender, Sexuality, and Violence in Organizations*. London: Sage.

———, and Wendy Parkin. 1987. *Sex at Work*. New York: St. Martin's Press.

Heberle, Renee. 1996. "Deconstructive Strategies and the Movement against Sexual Violence." *Hypatia* 11 (November): 63–77.

Hecht, Tobias. 1998. *At Home in the Streets: Street Children of Northeast Brazil*. Cambridge, England: Cambridge University Press.

Hegney, D., R. Eley, A. Plank, E. Buikstra, and V. Parker. 2006. "Workplace Violence in Queensland, Australia: The Results of a Comparative Study." *International Journal of Nursing Practice* 12: 220–31.

Held, Virginia. 2006. *The Ethics of Care: Personal, Political and Global*. Oxford: Oxford University Press.

———. 2010. "Can the Ethics of Care Handle Violence?" *Ethics and Social Welfare* 4 (2): 115–29.

Heldke, Lisa, and Peg O'Connor, eds. 2004. *Oppression, Privilege, and Resistance: Theoretical Perspectives on Racism, Sexism, and Heterosexism*. New York: McGraw-Hill.

Helliwell, Christine. 2000. "'It's Only a Penis': Rape, Feminism, and Difference." *Signs* 25, no. 3 (Spring): 789–816.

Hendrickson, R. 2000. "The Facts on File Dictionary of American Regionalisms." New York: Facts on File.

Herek, Gregory M. 1987. "On Heterosexual Masculinity: Some Psychical Consequences of the Social Construction of Gender and Sexuality." In *Changing Men: New Directions in Research on Men and Masculinity* edited by Michael S. Kimmel. Newbury Park, CA: Sage.

Herman, Judith. 2000 [1981]. *Father-Daughter Incest*. Cambridge, MA: Harvard University Press.

———. 2015 [1997]. *Trauma and Recovery: The Aftermath of Violence—From Domestic Abuse to Political Terror*. New York: Basic Books.

Herring, Susan. 2002. "The Rhetorical Dynamics of Gender Harassment On-Line." *Information Society* 15 (3): 151–67.

Hertzog, J. L., D. Wright, and D. Beat. 2008. "There's a Policy for That: A Comparison of the Organizational Culture of Workplaces Reporting Incidents of Sexual Harassment." *Behavior and Social Issues* 17: 169–81.

Hess, Amanda 2014. "Why Women Aren't Welcome on the Internet." *Pacific Standard*, January 6, 2014. https://psmag.com.

Higginbotham, B. J., S. A. Ketring, J. Hibbert, D. W. Wright, and A. Guarino. 2007. "Relationship Religiosity, Adult Attachment Style, and Courtship Violence Experienced by Females." *Journal of Family Violence* 22: 55–62.

Higginbotham, Evelyn Brooks. 1993. *Righteous Discontent: The Women's Movement in the Black Baptist Church, 1880–1920*. Cambridge, MA: Harvard University Press.

Hill, Annie. 2014. "Demanding Victims: The Sympathetic Shift in British Prostitution Policy." In *Negotiating Sex Work: Unintended Consequences of Policy and Activism*, edited by Carisa R. Showden and Samantha Majic, 77–98. Minneapolis: University of Minnesota Press.

Hill, C., and E. Silva. 2005. "Drawing the Line: Sexual Harassment on Campus." Washington, DC: AAUW Educational Foundation.

Hill, Robert J. 2009. "Incorporating Queers: Blowback, Backlash, and Other Forms of Resistance to Workplace Diversity Initiatives That Support Sexual Minorities." *Advances in Developing Human Resources* 11 (1): 37–53.

Hiraiwa-Hasegawa, Mariko. 1988. "Adaptive Significance of Infanticide in Primates." *Trends in Ecology and Evolution* 3 (5): 102–5.

Hlavka, Heather A. 2014. "Normalizing Sexual Violence: Young Women Account for Harassment and Abuse." *Gender & Society* 28 (3): 337–58.

Hobbes, Thomas. 2003 [1651]. *The Leviathan*. Bristol: Thoemmes Continuum.

Hoch, Paul. 1979. *White Hero, Black Beast: Racism, Sexism, and the Mask of Masculinity*. London: Pluto.

Hoebel, E. A. 1960. *The Cheyennes*. New York: Holt, Rinehart and Winston.

Hoefinger, Heidi. 2016. "Neoliberal Sexual Humanitarianism and Story-Telling: The case of Somaly Mam." *Anti-Trafficking Review* 7: 56–78.

Hoff Sommers, C. 1994. *Who Stole Feminism?* New York, NY: Simon and Schuster.

Hoffman, Jan. 2018. "Sex and Drugs Decline Among Teens, but Depression and Suicidal Thoughts Grow." *New York Times*, June 14, 2018.

Holland, Jack. 2006. *Misogyny: The World's Oldest Prejudice*. New York: Carroll and Graf Publishers.

Holloway, Karla F. C. 2011. *Private Bodies, Public Texts: Race, Gender, and a Cultural Bioethics*. Durham, NC: Duke University Press.

Holpuch, Amanda. 2012. "Daniel Tosh Apologizes for Rape Joke as Fellow Comedians Defend Topic." *Guardian*, July 11, 2012.

Holtzworth-Munroe, Amy, Jeffrey C. Meehan, Katherine Herron, Uzma Rehman, and Gregory L. Stuart. 2000. "Testing the Holtzworth-Munroe and Stuart (1994) Batterer Typology." *Journal of Consulting and Clinical Psychology* 68: 1000–1019.

Honan, Mat. 2014. "What Is Doxing?" *Wired*, March 6, 2014. wired.com/2014/03/doxing/

Honda, Mike. 2015. "Time for Abe to Apologize, Properly." CNN, April 29, 2015. www.cnn.com.

Hondagneu-Sotelo, Pierrette. 1994. *Gendered Transitions: Mexican Experiences of Immigration*. Berkeley, CA: University of California Press.

———, and M. A. Messner. 1994. "Gender Displays and Men's Power: The 'New Man' and the Mexican Immigrant Man." *Theorizing Masculinities*, edited by H. Brod and M. Kaufman: 200–18. Newbury Park, CA: Sage Publications.

Hood-Williams, John. 1996. "Goodbye to Sex and Gender." *Sociological Review* 44: 1–16.

———. 2001. "Gender, Masculinities and Crime: From Structures to Psyches." *Theoretical Criminology* 5: 37–60.

Hoogensen, Gunhild, and Kirsti Stuvøy. 2006. "Gender, Resistance, and Human Security." *Security Dialogue* 37 (2): 207–28.

hooks, bell. 1984. *Feminist Theory: From Margin to Center*. Boston, MA: South End Press.

———. 1994. *Teaching to Transgress: Education as the Practice of Freedom*. New York: Routledge.

———. 2003. *Rock My Soul: Black People and Self-esteem*. New York, NY: Atria.

Hope Rising. n.d. "Domestic Violence Statistics." Accessed August 30, 2017. http://hoperisingtx.org.

Hopkins, Dwight N. 2010. "Enslaved Black Women: A Theology of Justice and Reparations." In *Beyond Slavery: Overcoming Its Religious and Sexual Legacies*, edited by Bernadette J. Brooten, 287–303. New York: Palgrave Macmillan.

Horton, Anne L., and Barry L. Johnson. 1993. "Profile and Strategies of Women Who Have Ended Abuse." *Families in Society: Journal of Contemporary Human Services* 74: 481–92.

Houppert, Karen. 2008. "KBR's Rape Problem." *Nation*, May 5, 2008. www.thenation.com.

House, Carol C., William D. Kalsbeek, and Candace Kruttschnitt. 2014. National Research Council. *Estimating the Incidence of Rape and Sexual Assault*. Washington, DC: The National Academies Press. eBook. https://doi.org/10.17226/18605.

Houston, Shannon M. 2015. "Respectability Will Not Save Us: Black Lives Matter Is Right to Reject the 'Dignity and Decorum' Mandate Handed Down to Us from Slavery." *Salon*. www.salon.com.

HRC (Human Rights Campaign). 2017. http://hrc.org.

Htun, Mala, and S. Laurel Weldon. 2012. "The Civic Origins of Progressive Policy Change: Combating Violence against Women in Global Perspective, 1975–2005." *American Political Science Review* 106 (3): 548–69.

Hudgins, Anastasia. 2006. "Policies and Competing Understandings of Risk: Nongovernmental Organizations' Discourses on Vietnamese Commercial Sex Workers in Cambodia." Ph.D. diss., Temple University, Department of Anthropology.

———. 2007. "Problematizing the Discourse: Sex Trafficking Policy and Ethnography." In *Gender Violence: Interdisciplinary Perspectives*, 2nd edition, edited by Laura. L. O'Toole, Jessica R. Schiffman, and Margie L. Kiter Edwards, 409–14. New York: New York University Press.

Hudson, Heidi. 2005. "'Doing Security as though Humans Matter: A Feminist Perspective on Gender and the Politics of Human Security." *Security Dialogue* 36 (2): 155–74.

Hudson, Natalie Florea. 2009. *Gender, Human Security, and the United Nations: Security Language as a Political Framework for Women*. London: Routledge.

Hudson, Valerie M., Mary Caprioli, Bonnie Ballif-Spanvill, Rose McDermott, and Chad F. Emmett. 2009. "The Heart of the Matter: The Security of Women and the Security of States." *International Security* 33 (3): 7–45.

Huerta, M., L. M. Cortina, J. S. Pang, C. M. Torges, and V. J. Magley. 2006. "Sex and Power in the Academy: Modeling Sexual Harassment in the Lives of College Women." *Personality and Social Psychology Bulletin* 32: 616–28.

Human Rights Watch. 2001. "Hatred in the Hallways: Violence and Discrimination against Lesbian, Gay, Bisexual, and Transgender Students in US Schools." New York: Human Rights Watch.

———. 2010. "Off the Streets: Arbitrary Detention and Other Abuses against Sex Workers in Cambodia," *Human Rights Watch*. New York. ISBN: 1-56432-661 6. https://www.hrw .org/report/2010/07/19/streets/arbitrary-detention-and-other-abuses-against-sex-workers -cambodia

Human Trafficking Project. 2009. "Slavery and the Products We Buy." www.traffickingproject .org.

Humphrey, Stephen E., and Arnold S. Kahn. 2000. "Fraternities, Athletic Teams, and Rape: Importance of Identification with a Risky Group." *Journal of Interpersonal Violence* 15 (12): 1313–22.

Hutchinson, S., and B. Wexler. 2007. "Is 'Raging' Good for Health? Older Women's Participation in the Raging Grannies." *Health Care for Women International* 2: 88–118.

Hynes, Patricia. 2004. "On the Battlefield of Women's Bodies: An Overview of the Harm of War to Women." *Women's Studies International Forum* 27 (November–December): 431–45.

Ilies, R., N. Hauserman, S. Schwochau, and J. Stibal. 2003. "Reported Incidence Rates of Work-related Sexual Harassment in the United States: Using Meta-analysis to Explain Reported Rate Disparities." *Personnel Psychology* 56: 607–31.

Institute of Medicine Committee. 2011. "The Health of Lesbian, Gay, Bisexual, and Transgender People: Building a Foundation for Better Understanding." 63: 191–220.

International Union of Sex Workers. 2010. *IUSW Calls for Decriminalisation of Sex Work to Increase Worker Safety*. www.iusw.org.

Inter-Parliamentary Union. 2018. "Women in National Parliaments, Situation as of 1st December 2018." http://archive.ipu.org.

IPEU (Irish Presidency of the European Union), FGS Consulting, and McGolgan, A. 2004. "Report on Sexual Harassment in the Workplace in EU Member States." Government of Ireland.

Irigaray, Luce. 1989. "The Language of Man." Translated by Erin G. Carlston. *Cultural Critique* 13 (Fall): 191–202.

Irish Presidency of the European Union, FGS Consulting, and Aileen McGolgan. 2004. "Report on Sexual Harassment in the Workplace in EU Member States." www.unece.org.

Isaac, Mike. 2016. "Twitter Bars Milo Yiannopoulos in Wake of Leslie Jones's Reports of Abuse." *New York Times*, July 20, 2016.

Island, David, and Patrick Letellier. 1991. *Men Who Beat the Men Who Love Them: Battered Gay Men and Domestic Violence.* New York: Haworth Press.

ISNA. 2006. Intersex Society of North America. www.isna.org.

Jackson, D., Clare, J., and Mannix, J. 2002. "Who would want to be a nurse? Violence in the workplace—a factor in recruitment and retention." *Journal of Nursing Management* 10: 13–20.

Jacobs, Harriet A. 2001. *Incidents in the Life of a Slave Girl: Written by Herself: Contexts, Criticism*, edited by Nellie Y. McKay and Frances Smith Foster. New York: Norton.

Jankowiak, William, Monika Sudakov, and Benjamin C. Wilreker. 2005. "Co-Wife Conflict and Co-Operation." *Ethnology* 44 (1): 81–98.

Jäppinen, Maija, and Janet Elise Johnson. 2016. "The State to the Rescue? The Contested Terrain of Domestic Violence in Postcommunist Russia." In *Gender Violence in Peace and War: States of Complicity*, 146–57, edited by Victoria Sanford, Katerina Stefatos, and Cecilia M. Salvi. New Brunswick: Rutgers University Press.

Jefferson, Thomas. 1953. *Thomas Jefferson's Farm Book with Comments and Relevant Extracts from Other Writings.* Edited by Edwin Morris Betts. Princeton: Princeton University Press.

———. 1989. *The Jefferson Bible: The Life and Morals of Jesus of Nazareth.* Boston: Beacon.

———. 2002. *Notes on the State of Virginia*, edited by David Waldstreicher. Boston: Bedford/St. Martin's.

Jeffords, C. R. 1984. "The Impact of Sex-role and Religious Attitudes upon Forced Marital Intercourse Norms." *Sex Roles* 11: 543–52.

Jeltsen, Melissa. 2017. "Former Apple Engineer Describes Domestic Abuse in Chilling Courtroom Statement." *Huffington Post*, April 18, 2017. www.huffingtonpost.com.

Jenkins, Philip. 1998. *Moral Panic: Changing Concepts of the Child Molester in Modern America.* New Haven, CT: Yale University Press.

———. 2001. *Beyond Tolerance: Child Pornography on the Internet.* New York: New York University Press.

Jenness, Valerie. 2010. "From Policy to Prisoners to People." *Journal of Contemporary Ethnography* 39: 517–53.

———. 2015. "The Feminization of Transgender Women in Prisons for Men: How an Alpha Male Total Institution Shapes Gender." Paper presented at Annual Meeting, American Sociological Association, Chicago.

———, and Sarah Fenstermaker. 2014. "Agnes Goes to Prison: Gender Authenticity, Transgender Inmates in Prisons for Men, and the Pursuit of 'The Real Deal.'" *Gender & Society* 28: 5–31.

———, Cheryl L. Maxson, Kristy N. Matsuda, and Jennifer Macy Sumner. 2007. "Violence in California Correctional Facilities: An Empirical Examination of Sexual Assault." Report to the California Department of Corrections and Rehabilitation, State of California. Sacramento.

———, Cheryl L. Maxson, Jennifer Macy Sumner, and Kristy N. Matsuda. 2010. "Accomplishing the Difficult, but Not Impossible." *Criminal Justice Policy Review* 21: 3–30.

———, Lori Sexton, and Jennifer Sumner. 2011. "Transgender Inmates in California Prisons." Report to the California Department of Corrections and Rehabilitation, University of California, Irvine.

———, and Michael Smyth. 2011. "The Passage and Implementation of the Prison Rape Elimination Act: Legal Endogeneity and the Uncertain Road from Symbolic Law to Instrumental Effects." *Stanford Law & Policy Review* 22: 489–528.

Jensen, R. 2007. *Getting off: Pornography and the End of Masculinity*. Cambridge, MA: South End Press.

———. 2011. "Pornography as Propaganda." In *The Propaganda Society: Promotional Culture and Politics in Global Context*, edited by G. Sussman, 159–74. New York: Peter Lang.

———. 2014. "Pornographic and Pornified: Feminist and Ecological Understandings of Sexually Explicit Media." In *The Philosophy of Pornography: Contemporary Perspectives*, edited by J. Held and L. Coleman, 53–70. Lanham, MD: Rowman & Littlefield/Scarecrow Press.

Jeong, Sarah. 2015. *The Internet of Garbage*. New York: Forbes Media.

Jewish-American History Foundation. n.d. a "David Einhorn's Response to Rabbi Morris Raphall's 'A Biblical View of Slavery.'" "Jews in the Civil War." Accessed April 12, 2008. www.jewish-history.com.

———. n.d. b "Bible Views of Slavery." In *Fast Day Sermons: or, The Pulpit on the State of the Country*. New York: Rudd and Carleton, Under "Jews in the Civil War." Accessed November 6, 2009. www.jewish-history-com.

Jewkes, R., R. Morrell, Y. Sikweyiya, K. Dunkle, and L. Penn-Kekana. 2012. "Men, Prostitution and the Provider Role: Understanding the Intersections of Economic Exchange, Sex, Crime and Violence in South Africa." *PLoS ONE* 7 (7), e40821.

Jewkes, Rachel, Emma Fulu, Tim Roselli, and Claudia Garcia-Moreno. 2013. "Prevalence of and Factors Associated with Non-Partner Rape Perpetration: Findings from the UN Multi-country Cross-sectional Study on Men and Violence in Asia and the Pacific." *Lancet Global Health* 1: 208–18.

Jhally, Sut. 1997. "Advertising and the End of the World." Northampton, MA: Media Education Foundation. DVD.

Jobvite Resources. 2015. "2015 Hiring Trends: An Infographic Snapshot." www.jobvite.com.

John Jay College of Criminal Justice. 2004. "The Nature and Scope of Sexual Abuse of Minors By Catholic Priests and Deacons in the United States 1950-2002." United States Conference of Catholic Bishops: Washington, DC.

———. 2011. "The Causes and Context of Sexual Abuse of Minors by Catholic Priests in the United States 1950-2010." New York: United States Conference of Catholic Bishops: Washington: DC.

Johnson, Chalmers. 1978. "Perspectives on Terrorism." In *The Terrorism Reader*, edited by Walter Laqueur, 269–70. Philadelphia: Temple University Press.

Johnson, Michael P. 1995. "Patriarchal Terrorism and Common Couple Violence: Two Forms of Violence against Women." *Journal of Marriage and the Family* 57 (2): 283–94.

———. 1999. "Two Types of Violence against Women in the American Family: Identifying Patriarchal Terrorism and Common Couple Violence." Paper presented at the National Council on Family Relations annual meeting, November, Irvine, CA.

———. 2001. "Conflict and Control: Symmetry and Asymmetry in Domestic Violence." In *Couples in Conflict*, edited by A. Booth, A. C. Crouter, and M. Clements, 95–104. Mahwah, NJ: Erlbaum.

———. 2005. "Domestic Violence: It's Not about Gender—Or Is It?" *Journal of Marriage and Family* 67 (5): 1126–30.

———. 2006. "Gendered Communication and Intimate Partner Violence." In *The Sage Handbook of Gender and Communication*, edited by B. J. Dow and J. T. Wood, 71–88. Thousand Oaks, CA: Sage.

———. 2008. *A Typology of Domestic Violence: Intimate Terrorism, Violent Resistance, and Situational Couple Violence.* Boston, MA: Northeastern University Press.

Johnson, Sylvester. 2010. "The Bible, Slavery, and the Problem of Authority." In *Beyond Slavery: Overcoming Its Religious and Sexual Legacies,* edited by Bernadette J. Brooten, 231–48. New York: Palgrave Macmillan.

Johnston, Barbara Rose. 2010. "Chixoy Dam Legacies: The Struggle to Secure Reparation and the Right to Remedy in Guatemala." *Water Alternatives* 3 (2): 341–61.

Jones, Nikki. 2008. *Between Good and Ghetto: African-American Girls and Inner-City Violence.* New Brunswick, NJ: Rutgers University Press.

Jordan, Jan. 2004. *The Word of a Woman? Police, Rape and Belief.* New York: Palgrave Macmillan.

Jourard, S. M. 1974. "Some Lethal Aspects of the Male Role." In *Men and Masculinity,* edited by J. H. Pleck and J. Sawyer, 21–29. Englewood Cliffs, NJ: Prentice-Hall.

Jubb, Nadine, and Wânia Pasinato lzumino. 2002. "Women and Policing in Latin America: A Revised Background Paper." www.yorku.ca.

———, Gloria Camacho, Almachiara D'Angelo, Bina Yáñez de la Borda, Kattya Hernández, Ivonne Macassi León, Cecilia MacDowell Santos, Yamileth Molina, and Wânia Pasinato. 2008. *Regional Mapping Study of Women's Police Stations in Latin America.* Quito, Ecuador: Centre for Planning and Social Studies.

———, Gloria Camacho, Almachiara D'Angelo, Kattya Hernández, Ivonne Macassi, Liz Melendez, Yamileth Molina, Wânia Pasinato, Veronica Redroban, Claudia Rosas, et al. 2010. *Women's Police Stations in Latin America: An Entry Point for Stopping Violence and Gaining Access to Justice.* Quito, Ecuador: Centre for Planning and Social Studies.

Judd, Margaret A. 2002. "Ancient Injury Recidivism: An Example from the Kerma Period of Ancient Nubia." *International Journal of Osteoarchaeology* 12: 89–106.

Julian, Rachel, and Christine Schweitzer. 2015. "The Origins and Development of Unarmed Civilian Peacekeeping." *Peace Review: A Journal of Social Justice,* 27: 1–8.

Jung, Min-kyung. 2017. "Park Administration Kept Parts of 'Comfort Women' Agreement Secret." *Korea Herald,* December 27, 2017.

Judt, Tony. 2010. *Ill Fares the Land.* New York: The Penguin Press.

Kaminer, Ariel. 2013. "Yale Tries to Clarify What Sexual Misconduct Is in a New Guide" *New York Times,* September 14, 2013.

Kang, Cecilia, and Sheryl Gay Stolberg. 2018. "Sex Trafficking Bill Heads to Trump, over Silicon Valley Concerns," *New York Times,* March 21, 2018.

Kanin, Eugene J. 1969. "Diadic Aspects of Male Aggression." *Journal of Sex Research* 5: 12–28.

Kann, Laura, Emily O'Malley Olsen, Tim McManus, William A. Harris, Shari L. Shanklin, Katherine H. Flint, Barbara Queen, Richard Lowry, David Chyen, Lisa Whittle, et al. 2016. "Sexual Identity, Sex of Sexual Contacts, and Health-Related Behaviors Among Students in Grades 9–12—United States and Selected Sites, 2015." *Centers for Disease Control and Prevention, Morbidity and Mortality Weekly Report* 65 (9).

Kanter, Rosabeth Moss. 1977. *Men and Women of the Corporation.* New York: Basic Books.

Kantor, Glenda Kaufman, Jana L. Jasinski, and Etiony Aldarondo. 1994. "Sociocultural Status and Incidence of Marital Violence in Hispanic Families." *Violence and Victims* 9 (3): 207–22.

Kappeler, Susanne. 1986. *The Pornography of Representation.* Minneapolis: University of Minnesota Press.

KARAMAH: Muslim Women Lawyers for Human Rights. n.d. "*Zina*, Rape, and Islamic Law: An Islamic Legal Analysis of the Rape Laws in Pakistan." Accessed February 18, 2019. http://karamah.org.

Kaschak, Ellyn, ed. 2001. *Intimate Betrayal: Domestic Violence in Lesbian Relationships.* New York: Haworth Press.

Katz, Jackson. 2012. "Violence Against Women—It's a Men's Issue." Filmed November 2012 at TEDxFiDiWomen, San Francisco. Video, 17:40. www.ted.com.

Kaufman, Michael. 1994. "Men, Feminism, and Men's Contradictory Experiences of Power." In *Theorizing Masculinities*, edited by Harry Brod and Michael Kaufman. Thousand Oaks, CA: Sage.

———. 2007. "The Construction of Masculinity and the Triad of Men's Violence." In *Gender Violence: Interdisciplinary Perspectives*, 2nd edition, edited by Laura L. O'Toole, Jessica R. Schiffman, and Margie L. Kiter Edwards, 33–55. New York: New York University Press.

Kearl, Holly. 2014. Stop Street Harassment. www.stopstreetharassment.org.

Keenan, Marie. 2012. *Child Sexual Abuse & the Catholic Church: Gender, Power and Organizational Culture*. New York: Oxford University Press.

Keller, Michael H., and Gabriel J. X. Dance. 2019. "Child Sex Abusers Elude Flimsy Digital Safeguards." *New York Times*. November 10, 2019.

Kelly, Annie. 2018. "The Housewives of White Supremacy," *New York Times*, June 1, 2018.

Kelly, Jocelyn, and Alejandra Azuero Quijanol. 2012. "A Tale of Two Conflicts." *Understanding and Proving International Sex Crimes*. Harvard Humanitarian Initiative. https://hhi.harvard.edu.

Kelly, Liz. 1988. *Surviving Sexual Violence*. Minneapolis: University of Minnesota Press.

Kelly, Ursula. 2006. "'What Will Happen If I Tell You?' Battered Latina Women's Experiences of Health Care." *Canadian Journal of Nursing Research* 38 (4): 78–95.

Kelner, Alexandra. 2013. "The United States of Rape: A Theory of Rape Culture in American Public Policy." Masters thesis, California State University, 2013.

Kennedy, Elizabeth. 2003. "Victim Race and Rape." *Feminist Sexual Ethics Project*. Brandeis University website. www.brandeis.edu.

Kent, Tara E. 2007. "The Confluence of Race and Gender in Women's Sexual Harassment Experiences." In *Gender Violence: Interdisciplinary Perspectives*, 2nd edition, edited by Laura L. O'Toole, Jessica R. Schiffman, and Margie L. Kiter Edwards, 172–80. New York: New York University Press.

Kessler, Robert. 2003. "Two Teens Attacked Three Separate Times at Camp." *Newsday*, September 16, 2003.

Keynes, John Maynard. 1925. "Am I a Liberal?" *Nation and Athenaeum*, Part I (August 8 1925): 563–64 and Part II (August 15 1925): 587–88.

Khan, Shaan. 2016. "What's Really Behind India's Rape Crisis." *Daily Beast*, March 25, 2016. www.thedailybeast.com.

Khan-Cullors, Patrisse with Asha Bandele. 2018. *When They Call You a Terrorist: A Black Lives Matter Memoir*. New York: St. Martin's Press.

Kimmel, Michael. 1987. "Men's Responses to Feminism at the Turn of the Century." *Gender & Society* 1, no. 3 (September): 261–83.

———. ed. 1990. *Men Confront Pornography*. New York: Crown.

———. 1994. "Masculinity as Homophobia: Fear, Shame, and Silence in the Construction of Gender Identity." In *Theorizing masculinities* edited by Harry Brod and Michael Kaufman. Thousand Oaks, CA: Sage.

———. 1996. *Manhood in America: A Cultural History*. New York: Free Press.

———. 2001. "Snips and Snails . . . and Violent Urges." *Newsday*, March 8, 2001.

———. 2005. "Vatican's New Plan to Curb Abuse Is Based on Flawed Understanding of Human Sexuality." *Chronicle of Higher Education*, October 14, 2005.

———. 2009. *Guyland: The Perilous World Where Boys Become Men*. New York: Harper Perennial.

———. 2013. *Angry White Men: American Masculinity at the End of an Era*. New York: Nation Books.

———, and Amy Aronson. 2000. *The Gendered Society Reader*. New York: Oxford University Press.

King, Anna. 2009. "Islam, Women and Violence." *Feminist Theology: The Journal of the Britain & Ireland School of Feminist Theology* 17 (3): 292–328.

King, Gary, and Christopher J. L. Murray. 2001. "Rethinking Human Security." *Political Science Quarterly* 116 (4): 585–610.

Kinney, Edith. 2014. "Raids, Rescues, and Resistance: Women's Rights and Thailand's Response to Human Trafficking." In *Negotiating Sex Work: Unintended Consequences of Policy and Activism*, edited by Carisa R. Showden and Samantha Majic, 171–94. Minneapolis: University of Minnesota Press.

———. 2017. "Policing, Protectionism, and Prevention: Prostitution, Sexual Delinquency, and the Politics of Victimhood in Thai and American Antitrafficking Campaigns." In *Challenging Perspectives on Street-Based Sex Work*, edited by Katie Hail-Jares, Corey S. Shdaimah, and Chrysanthi S. Leon, 152–82. Philadelphia: Temple University Press.

Kipnis, Laura. 2017. *Unwanted Advances: Sexual Paranoia Comes to Campus*. New York: HarperCollins.

Kirkwood, Catherine. 1993. *Leaving Abusive Partners: From the Scars of Survival to the Wisdom for Change*. Newbury Park, CA: Sage.

Kirsch, Adam. 2018. "French Novelist Imagined Sexual Dystopia. Now It's Arrived," *New York Times*, July 12, 2018.

Klein, Renate C. A., and Robert M. Milardo. 2000. "The Social Context of Couple Conflict: Support and Criticism from Informal Third Parties." *Journal of Social and Personal Relationships* 17(4–5): 618–37.

Klevens, J. 2007. "An Overview of Intimate Partner Violence among Latinos." *Violence against Women*. 13, no. 2 (February): 111–22.

Kligman, Gail, and Stephanie Limoncelli. 2005. "Trafficking Women after Socialism: To, Through, and From Eastern Europe." *Social Politics* 12 (1): 118–40.

Knadler, Stephen. 2004. "Domestic Violence in the Harlem Renaissance: Remaking the Record in Nella Larsen's *Passing* and Toni Morrison's *Jazz*." *African American Review* 38: 99–118.

Knickmeyer, N., H. M. Levitt, S. G. Horne, and G. Bayer. 2003. "Responding to Mixed Messages and Double Binds: Religious Oriented Coping Strategies of Christian Battered Women." *Journal of Religion and Abuse* 5: 29–53.

Knight, Heather. 2004. "Schools Report More Sexual Assaults." *San Francisco Chronicle*, April 2, 2004.

Know Your IX (KYIX). n.d. "About." www.knowyourix.org.

Kohn, Sally. 2016. "What the Stanford Case Tells Us About the Rape Crisis We Face Today." *Refinery* 29, June 9, 2016. www.refinery29.com.

Koopman, Sara. 2012. "Making Space for Peace: International Accompaniment in Columbia (2007–2009)." PhD diss., The University of British Columbia.

Kotese, M. 2017. "China Now Has 33,5 Million More Men Than Women." What's on Weibo: Reporting Social Trends in China. www.whatsonweibo.com.

Kowaleski-Wallace, Elizabeth. 1997. *Consuming Subjects: Women, Shopping, and Business in the Eighteenth Century*. New York: Columbia University Press.

Krenkel, Scheila, Carmen Leontina Ojeda Moré, and Cibele Cunha Lima da Motta. 2015. "The Significant Social Networks of Women Who Have Resided in Shelters / Las Redes Sociales Significativas de Mujeres Encaminadas Para Casa de Acogida / As Redes Sociais Significativas de Mulheres Acolhidas em Casa-Abrigo." *Paidéia (Ribeirão Preto)* 25 (60): 125–33.

Krieger, N., J. Chen, P. Waterman, C. Hartman, A. Stoddard, M. Quinn, and E. Barbeau. 2008. "The Inverse Hazard Law: Blood Pressure, Sexual Harassment, Racial Discrimination, Workplace Abuse and Occupational Exposures in US Low-income Black, White and Latino Workers." *Social Science and Medicine* 67: 1970–81.

Kristof, Nicholas. 2005. "The Rosa Parks for the 21st Century." *New York Times*, November 8, 2005
———. 2008. "The Weapon of Rape." *New York Times*, June 15, 2008.
———. 2017. "11 Years Old, a Mom, and Pushed to Marry Her Rapist in Florida." *New York Times*, May 26, 2017.

Krogstad, Jens Manuel. 2016. "Key Facts about How the US Hispanic Population Is Changing." *Pew Research Center*. www.pewresearch.org.

Krug, E. G., L. Dahlberg, J. Mercy, A. Zwi, and R. Lozano. 2000. "World Report on Violence and Health." Geneva: World Health Organization.

Kullgren, Jeffrey T. 2003. "Restrictions on Undocumented Immigrants' Access to Health Services: The Public Health Implications of Welfare Reform." *American Journal of Public Health* 93 (10): 1630–33.

Kuo, Feng-Yang, Chih-Yi Tsend, Fan-Chaun Tseng, and Cathy S. Lin. 2013. "Study of Social Information Control Affordances and Gender Difference in Facebook Self-Presentation." *Cyberpsychology, Behavior, and Social Networking* 16 (9): 635–44.

Labovitz, Gail. 2010. "The Purchase of His Money: Slavery and the Ethics of Jewish Marriage." In *Beyond Slavery: Overcoming Its Religious and Sexual Legacies*, edited by Bernadette J. Brooten, 91–105. New York: Palgrave Macmillan.

Lacey, Marc. 2004. "In Congo War, Even Peacekeepers Add to Horror." *New York Times*, December 18, 2004.

Lagae, C. R. 1926. *Les Azande ou Niam-Niam*. Bibleothéque-Congo 18. Brussels: Vromant. English translation published by Human Relations Area Files, New Haven, CT, 1999.

Lahr, M. Mirazón, F. Rivera, R. K. Power, A. Mounier, B. Copsey, F. Crivellaro, J. E. Edung, J. M. Maillo Fernandez, C. Kiarie, J. Lawrence, et al. 2016. "Inter-Group Violence among Early Holocene Hunter-Gatherers of West Turkana, Kenya." *Nature* 529 (7586): 394–98.

Lai, Tracy A. 1986. "Asian Women: Resisting the Violence." In *The Speaking Profits Us: Violence in the Lives of Women of Color*, edited by Maryviolet Burns. Seattle: Center for the Prevention of Sexual and Domestic Violence, 1986.

Lamb, Sharon. 1996. *The Trouble with Blame: Victims, Perpetrators, and Responsibility*. Boston: Harvard University Press.

———, and Zoë Peterson. 2012. "Adolescent Girls' Sexual Empowerment." *Sex Roles* 66: 703–12.

Lambert, H. E. 1956. *Kikuyu Social and Political Institutions*. London: Oxford University Press.

Lambert, Patricia M. 1997. "Patterns of Violence in Prehistoric Hunter-Gatherer Societies of Coastal Southern California." In *Troubled Times: Violence and Warfare in the Past*, edited by Debra L. Martin, 77–109. Amsterdam: Gordon and Breach.

Lancaster, Roger. 2011. *Sex Panic and the Punitive State*. Berkeley: University of California Press.

Landsbaum, Claire. 2016. "Father of Stanford Swimmer Who Raped Unconscious Woman Won't Say His Son Committed a Crime." *Cut*, June 6, 2016 www.thecut.com.

Lane, T. 2003. "In Bangladesh, Women's Risk of Domestic Violence Is Linked to Their Status." *International Family Planning Perspectives* 29 (3): 147.

Langan, Patrick, and Caroline Harlow. 1994. *Child Rape Victims, 1992: Crime Data Brief*. Washington, DC: US Department of Justice. www.bjs.gov.

Larsen, Clark Spencer, ed. 2001. *Bioarchaeology of Spanish Florida: The Impact of Colonialism*. Gainesville: University Press of Florida.

Latina Feminist Group. 2001. *Telling to Live: Latina Feminist Testimonios*. Durham, NC: Duke University Press.

Lawrence, Bonita. 2013. *Voix Feministes/Feminist Voices*. Ottawa: CRIAW/ICREF.

Laws, Charlotte. 2013. "I've Been Called the 'Erin Brockovich' of Revenge Porn, and for the First Time Ever, Here Is My Entire Uncensored Story of Death Threats, Anonymous and the FBI." *xoJane*, November 21, 2013.

LeBlanc, M. M., and E. K. Kelloway. 2002. "Predictors and Outcomes of Workplace Violence and Aggression." *Journal of Applied Psychology* 87: 444–53.

Lee, John Y. 2001. "Placing Japanese War Criminals on the U. S. Justice Department's 'Watch List' of 3 December 1996." In *Legacies of the Comfort Women of World War II*, edited by Margaret Stetz and Bonnie B. C. Oh, 152–67. Armonk, NY: M. E. Sharpe.

Lee, Roberta K., Vetta L. Sanders Thompson, and Mindy B. Mechanic. 2002. "Intimate Partner Violence and Women of Color: A Call for Innovations." *American Journal of Public Health* 92, no. 4 (April): 530–34.

Leff, Lisa. 2008. States Addressing Gay Domestic Violence. *Washington Post*, August 28, 2008.

Lehne, Gregory K. 1995. "Homophobia among Men: Supporting and Defining the Male Role." In *Men's Lives* edited by Michael S. Kimmel and Michael A. Messner, 325–36. Boston: Allyn and Bacon.

Leiby, Michele L. 2009. "Wartime Sexual Violence in Guatemala and Peru." *International Studies Quarterly* 53 (2): 445–68.

Leigh, Carol. 1997. "Inventing Sex Work." In *Whores and Other Feminists*, edited by Jill Nagel, 226–31. New York: Routledge.

LeMaire, Kelly L., Debra L. Oswald, and Brenda L. Russell. 2016. "Labeling Sexual Victimization Experiences: The Role of Sexism, Rape Myth Acceptance, and Tolerance for Sexual Harassment." *Violence and Victims* 31 (2): 332–46.

Lemieux, Patrice, Stuart J. McKelvie, and Dale Stout "Self-reported Hostile Aggression in Contact Athletes, No Contact Athletes and Non-athletes." 2002. *Athletic Insight: The Online Journal of Sport Psychology* 4, no. 3 (December).

Leo, Jana. 2010. *Rape New York*. New York: The Feminist Press.

Leon, Chrysanthi S. 2011. *Sex Fiends, Perverts, and Pedophiles: Understanding Sex Crime Policy in America*. New York: New York University Press.

Leon, Chrysanthi, and Corey S. Shdaimah. 2012. "JUSTifying scrutiny: State Power in Prostitution Diversion Programs." *Journal of Poverty*, 16: 250–273.

Leon, Chrysanthi, Corey S. Shdaimah, and Aneesa A. Baboolal. 2017. "The Portrayal of Street-Based Sex Work in Very Young Girls: How People Get There and Why They Stay." In *Challenging Perspectives on Street-based Sex Work*, edited by Katie Hail-Jares, Corey S. Shdaimah, and Chrysanthi S. Leon, 113–36. Philadelphia, PA: Temple University Press, 2017.

Leon, Chrysanthi, David L. Burton, and Dana Alvare. 2011. "Net-widening in Delaware: The Overuse of Registration and Residential Treatment for Youth Who Commit Sex Offenses." *Widener Law Review* 17 (1): 127–58.

Lerner, Gerda. 1986. *The Creation of Patriarchy*. New York: Oxford University Press.

Lerum, Kari, Kiesha McCurtis, Penelope Saunders, Stéphanie Wahab. 2012. "Using Human Rights to Hold the US Accountable for its Anti-Sex Trafficking Agenda: The Universal Period Review and New Directions for US Policy." *Anti-Trafficking Review* 1.

Lesko, Nancy. 2000. *Masculinities at School*. Thousand Oaks, CA: Sage.

Leung, Shirley, "In 2018, There Is No Excuse for Topless Dancers at a Corporate Event." *Boston Globe*, June 14, 2018.

Leventhal, Beth, and Sandra E. Lundy eds. 1999. *Same-Sex Domestic Violence: Strategies for Change*. Thousand Oaks, CA: Sage.

LeVine, R. A. 1959. "Gusii Sex Offenses: A Study in Social Control." *American Anthropologist* 61: 965–90.

Levi-Strauss, Claude. 1969. *The Elementary Structures of Kinship*. Boston: Beacon.

Levitt, Heidi M., and Kimberly Ware. 2006. "'Anything with Two Heads Is a Monster': Religious Leaders' Perspectives on Marital Equality and Domestic Violence." *Violence Against Women* 12: 1169–90.

Levy, Ellen. 1993. "She Just Doesn't Understand: The Feminist Face-Off on Pornography Legislation." *On the Issues* (Fall): 17–20.

Lewis, Ruth, Susan Marine, and Kathryn Kenney. 2016. "'I get together with my friends and try to change it'. Young Feminist Students Resist 'Laddism', 'Rape Culture' and 'Everyday Sexism.'" *Journal of Gender Studies* 27 (1). https://doi.org/10.1080/09589236.2016.1175925.

Leyaro, Vincent, Pablo Selaya, and Neda Trifkovic. 2017. "Fishermen's Wives: On the Cultural Origins of Violence against Women." Helsinki: WIDER Working Paper Series, No. 205, World Institute for Development Economic Research (UNU-WIDER).

Lhooq, Michelle. 2015. "What the 'Eat Sleep Rape Repeat' Shirt at Coachella Says About Rape Culture at Music Festivals." *Thump*, April 13, 2015. https://thump.vice.com.

Li, Man Yu, Irene Frieze, Catherine So-kum Tang. 2010. "Understanding Adolescent Peer Sexual Harassment and Abuse: Using the Theory of Planned Behavior." *Sexual Abuse: Journal of Research and Treatment* 22: 157–71.

Liang, Belle, Lisa Goodman, Pratyusha Tummala-Narra, and Sarah Weintraub. 2005. "A Theoretical Framework for Understanding Help-Seeking Processes among Survivors of Intimate Partner Violence." *American Journal of Community Psychology* 36, no. 1–2 (September): 71–84.

Liddle, A. M. 1993. "Gender, Desire and Child Sexual Abuse: Accounting for the Male Majority." *Theory, Culture and Society* 10: 103–26.

Liddle, James R., Todd K. Shackelford, and Viviana A. Weekes-Shackelford. 2012. "Evolutionary Perspectives on Violence, Homicide, and War." In *The Oxford Handbook of Evolutionary Perspectives on Violence, Homicide, and War*, edited by Todd K. Shackelford and Vivian A. Weekes-Shackelford, 3–22. Oxford: Oxford University Press.

Lim, Sandy, and Lilia M. Cortina. 2005. "Interpersonal Mistreatment in the Workplace: The Interface and Impact of General Incivility and Sexual Harassment." *Journal of Applied Psychology* 90 (3): 483–96.

Lin, Yu-Hua, and Hsueh-Erh Liu. 2005. "The Impact of Workplace Violence on Nurses in South Taiwan." *International Journal of Nursing Studies* 42, no. 7 (September): 773–78.

Lipsky, Michael. 1980. *Street-level Bureaucracy: Dilemmas of the Individual in Public Services*. New York: Russell Sage Foundation.

Lipsky, Sherry, Raul Caetano, Craig A. Field, and Gregory L. Larkin. 2006. "The Role of Intimate Partner Violence, Race, and Ethnicity in Help-Seeking Behaviors." *Ethnicity and Health* 11 (1): 81–100.

Lobel, Kerry. 1986. *Naming the Violence: Speaking Out about Lesbian Battering*. Seattle: Seal Press.

Lockhart, P. R. 2018. "Students from Parkland and Chicago Unite to Expand the Gun Control Conversation." *Vox*. www.vox.com.

Londoño, Ernesto. 2017. "In the Americas, Chile's Leader Is the Last Woman Standing." *New York Times*, June 24, 2017.

Long, Julia. 2012. *Anti-Porn: The Resurgence of Anti-Pornography Feminism*. London: Zed Books.

Lonsway, Kimberly A., and Joanne Archambault. 2012. "The 'Justice Gap' for Sexual Assault Cases." *Violence Against Women* 18 (February): 145–68.

Lopez, G. 2018. "2018 Was by Far the Worst Year on Record for Gun Violence in Schools." *Vox*. www.vox.com.

Lopiano, D., G. Gurney, B. Porto, D. B. Ridpath, A. Sack, M. Willingham, and A. Zimbalist. 2016. *The Drake Group Position Statement: Institutional Integrity Issues Related to Athlete Sexual Assault and Other Forms of Serious Misconduct*. The Drake Group. http://thedrakegroup.org.

Lorber, Judith. 1994. *Paradoxes of Gender*. New Haven, CT: Yale University Press.

Lorde, Audre. 2017. *Your Silence Will Not Protect You: Essays and Poems*. London: Silver Press.

Lorenz, Konrad Zacharias. 1966. *On Aggression*. London: Methuen.

Lottes, Ilsa L. 2011. "Rape Supportive Attitude Scale." In *Handbook of Sexuality-Related Measures*, 3rd edition, edited by Terri D. Fisher, Clive M. Davis, William L. Yarber, and Sandra L. Davis, 515–16. New York: Routledge.

Lutnick, Alexandra, and Deborah Cohan. 2009. "Criminalization, Legalization or Decriminalization of Sex Work: What Female Sex Workers Say in San Francisco, USA." *Reproductive Health Matters* 17 (34): 38–46.

Lux, Kimberly. 2009. "Work, Violence, or Both? Framing the Sex Trade and Setting an Agenda for Justice" *Advocates' Forum*. 1–13.

Lynch, Colum. 2004. "U. N. Says Its Workers Abuse Women in Congo." *Washington Post*, November 27, 2004.

Lynch, Roxanna Jesse. 2016. *Care: An Analysis*. Leuven: Peeters.

Lynch, Teresa, Jessica Tompkins, Irene Driel, and Niki Fritz. 2016. "Sexy, Strong, and Secondary: A Content Analysis of Female Characters in Video Games across 31 Years." *Journal of Communication* 6 (4): 564–84.

Lyons, Christopher J. 2006. "Stigma or Sympathy: Attributions of Fault to Victims and Offenders of Bias Crime." *Social Psychology Quarterly* 69 (1): 39–59.

MacKinnon, Catharine A. 1979. *Sexual Harassment of Working Women: A Case of Discrimination*. New Haven, CT: Yale University Press.

———. 1987. *Feminism Unmodified: Discourses on Life and Law*. Cambridge, MA: Harvard University Press.

———. 2004. "Pornography as Trafficking." *Michigan Journal of International Law* 26:993–1012.

———. 2006. "Are Women Human?" *Guardian*, April 12, 2006. www.guardian.co.uk/world/2006/apr/12/gender.politicsphilosophyandsociety.

———, and Andrea Dworkin. 1997. *In Harm's Way: The Pornography Civil Rights Hearings*. Cambridge, MA: Harvard University Press.

MacLean, Nancy. 2017. *Democracy in Chains: The Deep History of the Radical Right's Stealth Plan for America*. New York: Viking.

Madden, Andrew. 2010. "Apostolic Visitation is Self-Serving, Window-Dressing Nonsense." http://jrnl.ie/33205.

Magallón Portolés, Carmen. 2006. *Mujeres en pie de paz, pensamiento y prácticas*. Madrid: Siglo XXI.

Mahon, Rianne, and Fiona Robinson. 2011. *Feminist Ethics and Social Policy: Towards a New Global Political Economy of Care*. Vancouver: University of British Columbia Press.

Maiskii, I. 1921. *Sovremennaia Mongolia*, translated for Human Relations Area Files by Mrs. Dayton and J. Kunitz. Irkutsk: Gosudarstvennoe Izdatel'stvo, Irkutskoe Otedelenie.

Malamuth, Neil M. 1989. "Sexually Violent Media, Thought Patterns, and Anti-Social Behavior." *Public Communication and Behavior* 2: 159–204.

Malarek, Victor. 2009. *The Johns: Sex for Sale and the Men Who Buy It*. New York: Arcade Publishing.

Malernee, Jamie. 2004. "Harassment Programs Scrutinized: School Must Do Better Job, Experts Say." *South Florida Sun-Sentinel*, February 8, 2004.

Malinowski, B. 1929. *The Sexual Life of Savages in North-Western Melanesia*. London: G. Routledge and Sons.

Malkin, Victoria. 2007. "Reproduction of Gender Relations in the Mexican Migrant Community of New Rochelle, New York." In *Women and Migration in the US-Mexico Borderlands: A Reader*, edited by Denise A. Segura and Patricia Zavella, 415–37. Durham, NC: Duke University Press.

Mann, Ruth M. 2005. "Fathers' Rights, Feminism, and Canadian Divorce Law Reform, 1998–2003." *Studies in Law Politics and Society* 35: 31–68.

———. 2012 "Invisibilizing Violence against Women." In *Power and Resistance*, 5th edition, edited by W. Antony and L. Samuelson, 48–71. Halifax, Nova Scotia: Fernwood.

Manosphere Glossary. n.d. RationalWiki website. Accessed June 15, 2018. https://rationalwiki.org.

Mansfield, P. K., P. B. Koch, J. Henderson, J. R. Vicary, M. Cohn, and E. W. Young. 1991. "The Job Climate for Women in Traditionally Male Blue Collar Occupations." *Sex Roles* 25: 63–79.

Mardorossian, Carine M. 2002. "Toward a New Feminist Theory of Rape." *Signs* 27 (3): 743–75.

Markowitz, Lisa, and Karen W. Tice. 2002. "Paradoxes of Professionalization: Parallel Dilemmas in Women's Organizations in the Americas." *Gender & Society* 16, no. 6 (December): 941–58.

Marks, Jonathan. 2015. *Tales of the Ex-Apes: How We Think about Human Evolution*. Oakland: University of California Press.

Marrujo, Becky, and Mary Kreger. 1996. "Definition of Roles in Abusive Lesbian Relationships." In *Violence in Gay and Lesbian Domestic Partnerships*, edited by C. M. Renzetti and C. H. Miley. New York: Harrington Park Press.

Marsh, Jaimee, Sonya Patel, Bizu Gelaye, Miruts Goshu, Alemayehu Worku, Michelle Williams, and Yemane Berhane. 2009. "Prevalence of Workplace Abuse and Sexual Harassment among Female Faculty and Staff." *Journal of Occupational Health* 51: 314–22.

Marshall, Lydia W., ed. 2015. *The Archaeology of Slavery: A Comparative Approach to Captivity and Coercion*. Occasional Paper No. 41. Carbondale: Southern Illinois University, Center for Archaeological Investigations.

Martin, Debra L. 1997. "Violence against Women in the La Plata River Valley (AD 1000–1300)." In *Troubled Times: Violence and Warfare in the Past*, edited by Debra L. Martin and David W. Frayer, 45–75. Amsterdam: Gordon and Breach.

———, and David W. Frayer. 1997. *Troubled Times: Violence and Warfare in the Past*. Amsterdam: Gordon and Breach.

———, and Ryan P. Harrod. 2015. "Bioarchaeological Contributions to the Study of Violence." *Yearbook of Physical Anthropology* 156 (S59): 116–45.

———, Ryan P. Harrod, and Misty Fields. 2010. "Beaten Down and Worked to the Bone: Bioarchaeological Investigations of Women and Violence in the Ancient Southwest." *Landscapes of Violence* 1 (1): Article 3.

———, and Caryn E. Tegtmeyer, eds. 2017. *Broken Bones, Broken Bodies: Bioarchaeological and Forensic Approaches to Accumulative Trauma and Violence*. Lanham: Lexington Books.

Martin, Genevieve, and Monique Tardif. 2014. "What We Do and Don't Know about Sex Offenders' Intimacy Dispositions." *Aggression and Violent Behavior* 19: 372–82.

Martin, James. 2017. "It's Not About Celibacy: Blaming the Wrong Thing for Sexual Abuse in the Church." https://www.americamagazine.org/politics-society/2017/12/15/its-not-about-celibacy -blaming-wrong-thing-sexual-abuse-church.

Martin, Nick. 2016. "Former Stanford Swimmer Gets Six Months in Jail for Sexual Assault of Unconscious Woman." *Washington Post*, June 3, 2016.

Martin, Patricia Yancey. 1990. "Rethinking Feminist Organizations." *Gender & Society* 4 (2): 182–206.

———. 2016. "The Rape Prone Culture of Academic Contexts: Fraternities and Athletics." *Gender & Society* 30, no. 1 (February): 30–43.

Martin, Patricia Yancey, and Robert A. Hummer. 1989. "Fraternities and Rape on Campus." *Gender & Society* 3: 457–73.

Martin, Susan E., and Nancy Jurik. 2007. *Doing Justice/Doing Gender: Women in Legal and Criminal Justice Occupations*. Thousand Oaks, CA: Sage.

Martínez Guzmán, Vicent. 2001. *Filosofía para hacer las paces*. Barcelona: Icaria.

Martino, Wayne 2000. "Policing Masculinities: Investigating the Role of Homophobia and Heteronormativity in the Lives of Adolescent School Boys." *Journal of Men's Studies* 8(2): 213–236.

Marx, Karl. 1978. "The German Ideology: Part I." In *The Marx-Engels Reader*, edited by Robert C. Tucker. New York: Norton.

Masood, Salman. 2017. "Pakistani Village Council Arrested After Ordering Girl's Rape." *New York Times*, July 28, 2017.

Massey, Douglas S., Jorge Durand, and Nolan J. Malone. 2002. *Beyond Smoke and Mirrors: Mexican Immigration in an Era of Economic Integration*. New York, NY: Russell Sage Foundation.

Matamonasa-Bennett, Arieahn. 2015. "'A Disease of the Outside People': Native American Men's Perceptions of Intimate Partner Violence." *Psychology of Women Quarterly* 39(1): 20–36.

Matchen, J., and DeSouza, E. 2000. "The Sexual Harassment of Faculty Members by Students." *Sex Roles* 42: 295–306.

Matias, J. Nathan, Amy Johnson, Whitney Erin Boesel, Brian Keegan, Jaclyn Friedman, and Charlie DeTar. 2015. "Reporting, Reviewing, and Responding to Harassment on Twitter." *Women, Action, & the Media*. https://arxiv.org.

Matsuda, Mari. 1993. *Words That Wound: Critical Race Theory, Assaultive Speech, and the First Amendment*. New York: Routledge.

Maxwell, John Francis. 1975. *Slavery and the Catholic Church: The History of Catholic Teaching Concerning the Moral Legitimacy of the Institution of Slavery*. Chichester, UK: Barry Rose, in association with the Anti-Slavery Society for the Protection of Human Rights.

Maybury-Lewis, D. 1967. *Akwẽ-Shavante Society*. Oxford, UK: Clarendon Press.

McAleese, Mary. 2018. "The Time Is Now for Change in the Catholic Church." www.women sordination.org.

McCall, Leslie. 2005. "The Complexity of Intersectionality" *Signs* 30 (3): 1771–800.

McCarthy, Justine. 2018. "Priests told not to report confessions of child abuse by National Board for Safeguarding Children in the Catholic Church." *Times*, May 13, 2018. www.thetimes.co.uk.

McClelland, Sara I. 2010. "Intimate Justice: A Critical Analysis of Sexual Satisfaction." *Social and Personality Psychology Compass* 4: 663–80.

McConnell-Ginet, Sally. 2001. "'Queering' Semantics: Definitional Struggles." In *Language and Sexuality: Contesting Meaning in Theory and Practice*, edited by Kathryn Campbell-Kibler, Robert J. Podesva, Sara J. Roberts, and Andrew Wong, 137–60. Stanford: CSLI Publications.

McCurley, Carl, and Howard Snyder. 2004. "Victims of Violent Juvenile Crime." *Juvenile Justice Bulletin*, July. Washington, DC: US Department of Justice, Office of Justice Programs.

McDermott, Ray, and Hervé Varenne. 1995. "Culture as Disability." *Anthropology & Education Quarterly* 26 (3): 324–48.

McDonald, Paula. 2012. "Workplace Sexual Harassment 30 Years On: A Review of the Literature." *International Journal of Management Reviews* 14: 1–17.

McDonald, Sarah. 2019. "'Tools of Satan': Pope Denounces Paedophile Priests as He Demands Battle Against Abusers." *Irish Independent*, February 25, 2019. www.independent.ie.

McDonald, Soraya Nadia. 2014. "'Gamergate': Feminist Video Game Critic Anita Sarkeesian Cancels Utah Lecture after Threat." *Washington Post*, October 15, 2014.

———. 2017. "'The Rape of Recy Taylor' Explores the Little-known Terror Campaign Against Black women." *The Undefeated*. https://theundefeated.com.

McElwee, Joshua, and Heidi Schlumpf. 2018. "McCarrick Renounces Place in College of Cardinals After Revelations of Abuse." https://www.ncronline.org/news/accountability/mccar rick-renounces-place-college-cardinals-after-revelations-abuse

McFarlane, Judith, and Ann Malecha. 2005. "Sexual Assault among Intimates: Frequency, Consequences and Treatments." http://www.ncjrs.gov.

McGuire, Danielle. 2010. *At the Dark End of the Street: Black Women, Rape, and Resistance—A New History of the Civil Rights Movement from Rosa Parks to the Rise of Black Power*. New York: Knopf.

McLaughlin, Heather, Christopher Uggen, and Amy Blackstone. 2012. "Sexual Harassment, Workplace Authority, and the Paradox of Power." *American Sociological Review* 77 (4): 625–47.

McLean, Gladys, and Sarah Gonzalez Bocinski. 2017. *The Economic Cost of Intimate Partner Violence, Sexual Assault, and Stalking.* Washington, DC: Institute for Women's Policy Research.

McLean, Rachel L., Jacqueline Robarge, and Susan G. Sherman. 2006. "Release from Jail: Moment of Crisis or Window of Opportunity for Female Detainees?" *Journal of Urban Health: Bulletin of the New York Academy of Medicine* 83 (3): 382–93.

McNall, Scott G. 1983. "Pornography: The Structure of Domination and the Mode of Reproduction." In *Current Perspectives in Social Theory*, edited by Scott McNall, Vol. 4 Greenwich, CT: JAI Press.

McNeal, Cosandra, and Paul R. Amato. 1998. "Parents' Marital Violence: Long-Term Consequences for Children." *Journal of Family Issues* 19 (2): 123–39.

Mead, Margaret. 1932. *The Changing Culture of an Indian Tribe.* New York: Columbia University Press.

———. 1935. *Sex and Temperament in Three Primitive Societies.* New York: Morrow.

———. 2001. *Sex and Temperament in Three Primitive Societies.* New York: Perennial.

Medie, Peace A. 2013. "Fighting Gender-Based Violence: The Women's Movement and the Enforcement of Rape Law in Liberia." *African Affairs* 112 (448): 377–97.

Mehdi, Rubya. 1997. "The Offense of Rape in the Islamic Law of Pakistan." In *Women Living Under Muslim Laws, Dossier 18*, edited by Marie-Aimée Hélie-Lucas and Harsh Kapoor, Boite Postale 23, 34790 Grabels, France. www.wluml.org.

Meléndez, José. 2013. "Daniel Ortega es un Abusador Sexual; Insiste su Hijstra." *CRHoy: Noticias 24/7. Costa Rica*, August 15, 2014. www.crhoy.com.

Menjivar, Cecilia. 2000. *Fragmented Ties: Salvadoran Immigrant Networks in America.* Berkeley, CA: University of California Press.

———, and Olivia Salcido. 2002. "Immigrant Women and Domestic Violence: Common Experiences in Different Countries." *Gender & Society* 16 (6): 898–920.

Men's Consciousness-Raising Group. 1971. *Unbecoming Men.* Washington, New Jersey: Times Change Press.

Menzies, R. 2007. "Virtual Backlash: Representations of Men's 'Rights' and Feminist 'Wrongs'" in Cyberspace. In *Reaction and Resistance: Feminism, Law, and Social Change*, edited by D. E. Chunn, S. B. Boyd, and H. Lessard, 65–97. Vancouver: UBC Press.

Merry, Sally Engle. 2009. *Gender Violence: A Cultural Perspective.* Hoboken, NJ: Wiley Blackwell.

Messerschmidt, James. 1993. *Masculinities and Crime: Critique and Reconceptualization of Theory.* Lanham, MD: Rowman and Littlefield.

———. 1997. "Varieties of 'Real Men.'" In *Gender Violence: Interdisciplinary Perspectives*, 1st edition, edited by L. L. O'Toole and J. R. Schiffman. New York: NYU Press.

Messias, Deanne K. Hilfinger, M. DeJong, and K. McLoughlin. 2005. "Expanding the Concept of Women's Work: Volunteer Work in the Context of Poverty." *Journal of Poverty* 9: 25–47. https://doi.org/10.1300/J134v09n03_02.

———, Eun-Ok Im, Aroha Page, Hanna Regev, Judit Spiers, Laurie Yoder, and Afaf Ibrahim Meleis. 1997. "Defining and Redefining Work: Implications for Women's Health." *Gender & Society* 11(3):296–323.

Messing, Karen, and Piroska Östlin. 2006. "Gender Equality, Work and Health: A Review of the Evidence." Geneva: World Health Organization.

Messner, Michael A. 1990a. "Boyhood, Organized Sports and the Construction of Masculinities." *Journal of Contemporary Ethnography* 18 (4): 416–44.

———. 1990b. "When Bodies are Weapons: Masculinity and Violence in Sport." *International Review for the Sociology of Sport* 25 (3): 203–20.

———. 1997. *Politics of Masculinities: Men in Movements*. Lanham, Maryland: Altamira Press.

———. 1998. "The Limits of 'the Male Sex Role': An Analysis of the Men's Liberation and Men's Rights Movements' Discourse." *Gender & Society* 12 (3): 255–76.

———. 2016. "Bad Men, Good Men, Bystanders: Who Is the Rapist?" *Gender & Society* 30, no. 1 (February): 57–66.

———, Max A. Greenberg, and Tal Peretz. 2015. *Some Men: Feminist Allies and the Movement to End Violence against Women*. New York: Oxford University Press.

Metcalf, Stephen. 2017. "Neoliberalism: The Idea That Swallowed the World." *Guardian*. www.theguardian.com.

Meyer, Mary K. 2003. "Ulster's Red Hand: Gender, Identity, and Sectarian Conflict in Northern Ireland." *In Women, States and Nationalism: At Home in the Nation?*, edited by Sita Ranchod-Nilsson and Mary Ann Tetreault New York: Routledge.

Meyer, Robert, and Michel Cukier. 2006. "Assessing the Attack Threat due to IRC Channels." *International Conference on Dependable Systems and Networks (DSN)*: 467–72. https://doi .org/10.1109/DSN.2006.12.

Meyers, Marian. 1997. *News Coverage of Violence Against Women: Engendering Blame*. Newbury Park, CA: Sage Publications.

Miles, A. 2000. *Domestic Violence: What Every Pastor Needs to Know*. Minneapolis, MN: Augsburg Fortress Press.

Mill, John Stuart. 1988 [1869]. "The Subjection of Women." In *The Domestic Assault of Women: Psychological and Criminal Justice Perspectives*, edited by Donald Dutton. Newton, MA: Allyn and Bacon.

Miller, Amanda, and Kathryn Chandler. 2003. *Violence in US Public Schools: 2000: School Survey on Crime and Safety. Statistical Analysis Report*. Washington, DC: US Department of Education, National Center for Education Statistics, NCES 2004–314, October 2003.

Miller, J. Jay, Stacy M. Deck, Erlene Grise-Owens, and Kevin Borders. 2015. "Undergraduate Student Perceptions of Social Work Licensure: An Exploratory Study." *Journal of Baccalaureate Social Work* 20 (1): 43–61.

Miller, Peggy, and Nancy Biele. 1993. "Twenty Years Later: The Unfinished Revolution." In *Transforming a Rape Culture*, edited by Emilie Buchwald and Pamela Fletcher, 47–54. Minneapolis: Milkweed Editions.

Miller, Sarah. 2015. "Buy These Pajamas & Rescue a Prostitute: Or, Why Rescue Brands Are Dumb." *Jezebel*, March 2, 2015. https://jezebel.com.

Miller, Susan L. 1993. "Arrest Policies for Domestic Violence and Their Implications for Battered Women." In *It's a Crime: Women and Justice*, edited by Roslyn Muraskin and Ted Alleman. Englewood Cliffs, NJ: Prentice Hall.

Miller, Susan, and LeeAnn Iovanni. 2007. "Domestic Violence Policy in the United States: Contemporary Issues." In *Gender Violence: Interdisciplinary Perspectives*, 2nd edition, edited by Laura L. O'Toole, Jessica R. Schiffman, and Margie L. Kiter Edwards, 287–96. New York: New York University Press.

Minder, Raphael. 2019. "Women's Day Is Dampened by Spain's Vox." *New York Times*, November 26, 2019.

Miner-Rubino, Kathi, and Lilia M. Cortina. 2007. "Beyond Targets: Consequences of Vicarious Exposure to Misogyny at Work." *Journal of Applied Psychology* 92: 1254–69.

Ministry of Justice. 2008. "Law on Suppression of Human Trafficking and Sexual Exploitation, 2008." Cambodia Internal Legislation. https://ihl-databases.icrc.org.

Moe, Angela M. 2007. "Silenced Voices and Structured Survival: Battered Women's Help Seeking." *Violence Against Women* 13 (7): 676–99.

———, and Myrtle P. Bell. 2004. "Abject Economics: The Effects of Battering and Violence on Women's Work and Employability." *Violence Against Women* 10 (1): 29–55.

Mogul, Joey, Andrea J. Ritchie, and Kay Whitlock. 2011. *Queer (In)Justice: The Criminalization of LGBT People in the United States.* Boston, MA: Beacon Press.

Mohammed, E., E. Shapiro, L. Wainright, and A. Carter. 2015. "Impacts of Family and Community Violence Exposure on Child Coping and Mental Health." *Journal of Abnormal Child Psychology* 43(2): 203–215.

Moolakkattu, John. 2006. "Feminism and Peace Studies: Taking Stock of a Quarter Century of Efforts." *Indian Journal of Gender Studies* 12 (2).

Moore, Molly. 2007. "Changing Patterns in Social Fabric Test Netherlands' Liberal Identity," *Washington Post*, June 23, 2007.

Moradi, Fazil. 2016. "The Force of Writing in Genocide: On Sexual Violence in the al-Anfâl Operations and Beyond." In *Gender Violence in Peace and War*, edited by Victoria Sanford, Katerina Stefatos, and Cecelia M. Salvi, 102–15. New Brunswick, NJ: Rutgers University Press.

Moran, Rachel. 2013. *Paid For: My Journey Through Prostitution.* Dublin, Ireland: Gill & Macmillan.

Morgan, Karen, and Suruchi Thapar Björkert. 2006. "'I'd rather you'd lay me on the floor and start kicking me': Understanding Symbolic Violence in Everyday Life." *Women's Studies International Forum* 29: 441–52.

Morgan, Rachel E., and Grace Kena. 2018. "Criminal Victimization, 2016: Revised." *US Department of Justice Office of Justice Programs Bureau of Justice Statistics Bulletin*, October 2018.

Morse, Barbara J. 1995. "Beyond the Conflict Tactics Scale: Assessing Gender Differences in Partner Violence." *Violence and Victims* 10 (4): 251–72.

Muller, Martin N. 2007. "Chimpanzee Violence: Femmes fatales." *Current Biology* 17 (10): 365–56.

Mulvey, Laura. 1975. "Visual Pleasure and Narrative Cinema." *Screen* 16: 6–18.

Muñoz, Francisco A. 2001. *La Paz Imperfecta.* Granada: Universidad de Granada.

Muñoz, José. 1999. *Disidentifications: Queers of Color and the Performance of Politics.* University of Minnesota Press.

Murch, Donna. 2016. "The Clintons' War on Drugs: When Black Lives Didn't Matter." *New Republic*, February 9, 2016.

Murdaugh, Carolyn, Salena Hunt, Richard Sowell, and Irma Santana. 2004. "Domestic Violence in Hispanics in the Southeastern United States: A Survey and Needs Analysis." *Journal of Family Violence* 19 (2): 107–15.

Murdock, George. P., and Douglas. R. White. 1969. "Standard Cross-Cultural Sample." *Ethnology* 8: 329–69.

Murphy, Gillian. 2002. *Beyond Surviving.* New York: Ms. Foundation for Women.

Murphy, Heather. 2017, "New Scrutiny for Men Who Rape." *New York Times.* October 31, 2017.

Murphy, Yolanda, and Robert Murphy. 1974. *Women of the Forest.* New York: Columbia University Press.

Naccarelli, Jennifer, and Carol Post. 2014. "Domestic Violence Prevention and Training Program: An Innovative Academic Activist Partnership." Paper presented at Innovative Partnerships to Reduce Gender-Based Violence Conference & Law Enforcement Training, Newark, Delaware.

Namie, Gary. 2012. "2017 WBI US Workplace Bullying Survey." San Francisco, CA: Workplace Bullying Institute. www.workplacebullying.org.

Naples, Nancy A. 2003a. "Deconstructing and Locating Survivor Discourse: Dynamics of Narrative, Empowerment, and Resistance for Survivors of Childhood Sexual Abuse." *Signs: Journal of Women in Culture and Society* 28, no. 4 (Summer): 1151–85.

———. 2003b. *Feminism and Method: Ethnography, Discourse Analysis, and Activist Research.* New York: Routledge.

Naples, Nancy A., and Karen Bojar, eds. 2002. *Teaching Feminist Activism: Strategies from the Field.* New York: Taylor & Francis.

Napolitano, Jo. 2003. "Girls' Game Turns Violent." *New York Times*, May 8, 2003.

Narváez, Zoilamérica. 2002. "Case 12,230: Zoilamérica Narváez vs. the Nicaraguan State." *Envio: Política, Sociedad, Cultura, Economía.* www.envio.org.ni.

Nash, Jennifer C. 2009. "Black Women and Rape: A Review, of the Literature." Waltham, MA: Feminist Sexual Ethics Project, Brandeis University. www.brandeis.edu.

Nash, Shondrah Tarrezz. 2005. "Through Black Eyes: African American Women's Construction of Their Experiences with Intimate Male Partner Violence." *Violence Against Women* (11): 1420–40.

Nason-Clark, N. 1997. *The Battered Wife: How Christians Confront Family Violence.* Louisville, Kentucky: Westminster John Knox Press.

Nason-Clark, N., and C. Clark Kroeger. 2004. *Refuge from Abuse: Healing and Hope for Abused Christian Women.* Downers Grove: Il: InterVarsity Press.

National Center for Injury Prevention and Control. 2003. "Costs of Intimate Partner Violence Against Women in the United States." Atlanta: Centers for Disease Control and Prevention.

National Coalition Against Domestic Violence. 2019. "National Statistics Domestic Violence Fact Sheet." https://ncadv.org/statistics.

National Coalition Against Domestic Violence (NCADV). 2015. *Domestic Violence National Statistics.* www.ncadv.org.

National Coalition of Anti-Violence Programs. 2015. "Lesbian, Gay, Bisexual, Transgender, Queer, and HIV-Affected Hate Violence in 2015." www.avp.org.

———. 2017a. *Lesbian, Gay, Bisexual, Transgender, Queer, and HIV-Affected Intimate Partner Violence in 2016.* New York, NY: Emily Waters.

———. 2017b. https://ncavp.org.

———. 2018. *A Crisis of Hate: A Report on LGBTQ Hate Homicides in 2017.* www.avp.org.

National Network to End Domestic Violence (NNEDV). 2006. *Domestic and Sexual Violence Fact Sheet.* NNEDV website. https://nnedv.org.

National Research Council and Institute of Medicine. 2003. *Deadly Lessons: Understanding Lethal School Violence.* Washington. DC: National Academy Press.

National Sexual Violence Resource Center (NSVRC). n.d. Statistics About Sexual Violence. NSVRC. Accessed July 29, 2017. www.nsvrc.org.

Nazario, Sonia. 2019. "Someone Is Always Trying to Kill You." *New York Times*, April 17, 2019.

NBC. 2003. "Children for Sale" *Dateline. NBC News.* January 23, 2003. www.msnbc.msn.com.

———. 2017. "Sexual Assault Reports in US Military Reach Record High: Pentagon." *NBC News*, May 1, 2017.

Nelson, Andrea, and Pamela Oliver. 1998. "Gender and the Construction of Consent in Child-Adult Sexual Contact." *Gender & Society* 12: 554–77.

Newman, Andy. 2018. "'Male'? 'Female'? Or 'X'? Drive for a Third Choice on Government Forms." *New York Times*, September 28, 2018.

New York Times. 1963. "Truman Opposes Biracial Marriage." *New York Times*, September 12, 1963.

"News. Iraq: U. S. Soldiers Accused of Sex Assaults." 2005. *Off Our Backs*, May-June: 7–8.

Ngai, Mae M. 2004. *Impossible Subjects: Illegal Aliens and the Making of Modern America.* Princeton, New Jersey: Princeton University Press.

Nichols, Jack. 1975. *Men's Liberation: A New Definition of Masculinity.* New York: Penguin.

Nickerson, Raymond S. 1998. "Confirmation Bias: A Ubiquitous Phenomenon in Many Guises." *Review of General Psychology* 2 (2): 175–220.

Nielsen, M., B. Bjørkelo, G. Notelaers, and S. Einarsen. 2010. "Sexual Harassment: Prevalence, Outcomes, and Gender Differences Assessed by Three Different Estimation Methods." *Journal of Aggression, Maltreatment and Trauma* 19: 252–74.

Nishida, T. 1989. "Social Conflicts between Resident and Immigrant Females." In *Understanding Chimpanzees*, edited by P. G. Heltne and L. A. Marquardt, 68–89. Cambridge: Harvard University Press.

Nishida, Toshisada, Mariko Hiraiwa-Hasegawa, Toshikazu Hasegawa, and Yukio Takahata. 1985. "Group Extinction and Female Transfer in Wild Chimpanzees in the Mahale National Park, Tanzania." *Zeitschrift für Tierpsychologie* 67 (1): 284–301.

Noddings, Nel. 1984. *Caring: A Feminine Approach to Ethics and Moral Education.* Berkeley: University of California Press.

———. 2002. *Educating Moral People: A Caring Alternative to Character Education.* New York: Teachers College Press.

Nolen, Stephanie. 2005. "Not Women Anymore . . ." *Ms.* (Spring): 56–58.

Noll, Mark A. 2006. *The Civil War as a Theological Crisis.* Chapel Hill: University of North Carolina Press.

Noor, Azman Modh. 2010. "Rape: A Problem of Crime Classification in Islamic Law." *Arab Law Quarterly* 24: 417–38.

Norcross, John C., and Bruce E. Wampold. 2011. "What Works for Whom: Tailoring Psychotherapy to the Person." *Journal of Clinical Psychology* 67: 127–32.

Nordland, Rod. 2017. "Welcome to Dubai. Now, Please, Stop Holding Hands." *New York Times*, November 12, 2017.

North, Anna. 2018. "#HimToo, the Online Movement Spreading Myths about False Rape Allegations, Explained: The Hashtag Could Hurt Male Survivors." *Vox*, October 10, 2018. www.vox.com.

Novak, Shannon A. 2006. "Beneath the Façade: A Skeletal Model of Domestic Violence." In *The Social Archaeology of Funerary Remains*, edited by Rebecca Gowland and Christopher J. Knüsel, 238–252. Oxford: Oxbow Books.

Novello, Antonia C., Marek Rosenberg, Linda Saltzman, and John Shosky. 1992. "A Medical Response to Domestic Violence." *JAMA* 267 (23): 3132.

NPR. 2006. Gloria Steinem Interview by Tom Ashbrook. *On Point*, WBUR Boston. www.onpointradio.org.

O'Brien, Erin. 2013. "Ideal Victims in Human Trafficking Awareness Campaigns." In *Crime, Justice and Social Democracy: International Perspectives*, edited by K. Carrington, M. Ball, E. O'Brien, and J. M. Tauri, 315–26. Basingstoke, UK: Palgrave Macmillan.

O'Brien, Robert M. 1987. "The Interracial Nature of Violent Crimes: A Reexamination," *American Journal of Sociology* 92, no. 4 (January): 817–35.

Ó Ciardha, Caoilte, Theresa Gannon, and Tony Ward. 2016. "The Cognitive Distortions of Child Sexual Abusers." In *The Wiley Handbook of Theories, Assessments, and Treatment of Sexual Offending*, edited by Anthony Beech and Tony Ward. Vol. 1. New Jersey: John Wiley & Sons, Ltd.

O'Connell Davidson, Julia. 1998. *Prostitution, Power and Freedom*, 146–59. Cambridge, UK: Polity Press.

O'Connor, T. P., and Duncan, J. B. 2011. "The Sociology of Humanist, Spiritual, and Religious Practice in Prison: Supporting Responsivity and Desistance from Crime." *Religions* 2: 590–610.

O'Donnell, Sue, Judith MacIntosh, and Judith Wuest. 2010. "A Theoretical Understanding of Sickness Absence among Women Who have Experienced Workplace Bullying." *Qualitative Health Research* 20: 439–52.

Offen, Karen. 2000. *European Feminisms, 1700—1950*. Stanford, CA: Stanford University Press.

Oh, Bonnie B. C. 2001. "The Japanese Imperial System and the Korean 'Comfort Women' of World War II." In *Legacies of the Comfort Women of World War II*, edited by Margaret Stetz and Bonnie B. C. Oh, 3–25. Armonk, NY: M. E. Sharpe.

Ojito, Mitra. 1998. "Conversations/Zoilamerica Narvaez: A Victim of Sexual Abuse in a Prison of Political Ideals." *New York Times*, March 29, 1998.

Okin, Susan Moller. 1999. *Is Multiculturalism Bad for Women?* Princeton, NJ: Princeton University Press.

Oliver, Brian E. 2007. "Preventing Female-Perpetrated Sexual Abuse." *Trauma, Violence, & Abuse* 8, no. 1 (January): 19–32.

Olsen, K., L. Durwood, M. DeMeules, and K. McLaughlin. 2016. "Mental Health of Transgender Children Who Are Supported in Their Identities." *Pediatrics* 137 (3).

Omi, Michael, and Howard Winant. 1986. *Racial Formation in the United States: From the 1960s to the 1980s*. New York: Routledge and Kegan Paul Inc.

O'Neill, Patrick Howell. 2014. "8chan, the Central Hive of Gamergate, Is Also an Active Pedophile Network." *Daily Dot*, November 17, 2014. www.dailydot.com.

Oparah, Julia C. 2012. "Feminism and the (Trans)Gender Entrapment of Gender Nonconforming Prisoners." *UCLA Women's Law Journal* 18: 238–71.

Oppenheim, Maya. 2019. "Trump Administration 'Rolling Back Women's Rights by 50 Years' by Changing Definitions of Domestic Violence and Sexual Assault." *Independent*, January 24, 2019.

Oselin, Sharon S., and Jennifer E. Cobbina. 2017. "Holding Their Own: Female Sex Workers' Perceptions of Safety Strategies." In *Challenging Perspectives on Street-Based Sex Work*, edited by Katie Hail-Jares, Corey S. Shdaimah, and Chrysanthi S. Leon, 78–101. Philadelphia, PA: Temple University Press.

Osofsky, Joy, and Howard J. Osofsky. 2018. "Challenges in Building Child and Family Resilience after Disasters." *Journal of Family Social Work* 21(2): 115–128.

O'Toole, Laura. 2007. "Subcultural Theory of Rape Revisited." In *Gender Violence: Interdisciplinary Perspectives*, 2nd edition, edited by Laura L. O'Toole, Jessica R. Schiffman, and Margie L. Kiter Edwards, 214–22. New York: New York University Press.

———, Jessica R. Schiffman, and Margie L. Kiter Edwards, eds. 2007. *Gender Violence: Interdisciplinary Perspectives*, 2nd edition. New York: New York University Press.

Outlaw, Lucius. 1974. "Language and Consciousness: Toward a Hermeneutic of Black Culture," *Cultural Hermeneutics* 1, no. 4 (February): 403–13.

———. 2005. *In Search of Critical Social Theory in the Interests of Black Folk*. Lanham, MD: Rowman & Littlefield.

Outshoorn, Joyce (ed). 2005. "The Political Debates on Prostitution and Trafficking of Women." *Social Politics* 12 (1): 141–51.

Paige, Glen D. 2009. *Nonkilling Global Political Science*. Honolulu: Center for Global Nonviolence.

Pappas, Nick, T., Patrick T. McHenry, and Beth Skilken Catlett, 2004. "Athlete Aggression on the Rink and off the Ice: Athlete Violence and Aggression in Hockey and Interpersonal Relationships." *Men and Masculinities*, 6(3): 291–312.

París Albert, Sonia and Irene Comins Mingol. 2013. "Epistemological and Anthropological Thoughts on Neurophilosophy: An Initial Framework." *Recerca* 13: 63–83.

Parkinson, Justin. 2016. "The Significance of Sarah Baartman." *BBC News Magazine*, January 7, 2016. https://www.bbc.com/news/magazine-35240987

Parreñas, Rhacel. 2011. *Illicit flirtations*. Palo Alto, CA: Stanford University Press.

Pascoe, C. J. 2011. *Dude, You're a Fag*. Berkeley: University of California Press.

——— and Jocelyn A. Hollander. 2016. "Good Guys Don't Rape: Gender, Domination, and Mobilizing Rape." *Gender & Society* 30 (1): 67–79.

Passel, Jeffrey S., and D'Vera Cohn. 2012. *US Foreign-Born Population: How Much Change From 2009 to 2010?* Washington DC: Pew Research Center.

Passero, Nina. 2015. "Effects of Participation in Sports on Men's Aggressive and Violent Behaviors." Online Publication of Undergraduate Studies. https://steinhardt.nyu.edu.

Pateman, Carole. 1980. "Women and Consent." *Political Theory* 8: 149–68.

Patrick, D. L., Bell, J. F., Huang, J. Y., Lazarakis, N. C., & Edwards, T. C. 2013. "Bullying and Quality of Life in Youths Perceived as Gay, Lesbian, or Bisexual in Washington State, 2010." *American Journal of Public Health*, 103, e1–e7.

Patterson, Orlando. 1982. *Slavery and Social Death: A Comparative Study*. Cambridge MA: Harvard University Press.

Paul, P. 2005. *Pornified: How Pornography is Transforming Our Lives, Our Relationships, and Our Families*. New York, NY: Times Books.

Paulson, Amanda. 2003. "Female Aggression: Brutal Hazing Ritual Renews Nation's Interest in Female Anger." *Christian Science Monitor*. (May 13): 4.

Payne, Diana L., Kimberly A. Lonsway, and Louise F. Fitzgerald. 1999. "Rape Myth Acceptance: Exploration of Its Structure and Its Measurement Using the Illinois Rape Myth Acceptance Scale." *Journal of Research in Personality* 33 (March): 27–68.

PCHR (Philadelphia Commission on Human Relations). 2017. "Report on Racism and Discrimination in Philadelphia's LGBTQ Community." PCHR website. Accessed April 16, 2018. https://pchrlgbt.org.

Peel, Elizabeth. 2001. "Mundane Heterosexism: Understanding Incidents of the Everyday," *Women's Studies International Forum* 24 (5): 541–54.

Pelka, Fred. 1997. "Raped: A Male Survivor Breaks His Silence." In *Gender Violence: Interdisciplinary Perspectives*, edited by Laura. L. O'Toole and Jessica R. Schiffman, 209–14. New York: New York University Press.

Pence, Ellen L., and Michael Paymar. 1993. *Education Groups for Men Who Batter*: The Duluth Model. New York: Springer.

Perilla, Julia L. 1999. "Domestic Violence as a Human Rights Issue: The Case of Immigrant Latinos." *Hispanic Journal of Behavioral Sciences* 21 (2): 107–33.

Perlstein, Daniel. 1998. "Saying the Unsaid: Girl Killing and the Curriculum." *Journal of Curriculum and Supervision* 14 (1): 88–104.

Pesznecker, Katie. 2005. "Parents Go after District for Rape." *Anchorage Daily News*, March 5, 2005.

Petersilia, Joan. 2008. "California's Correctional Paradox of Excess and Deprivation." In *Crime and Justice* 37: 207–78.

Peterson, Cora, Sarah DeGue, Curtis Florence, and Colby N. Lokey. 2017. "Lifetime Economic Burden of Rape Among US Adults." *American Journal of Preventive Medicine* 52 (January): 691–701.

Peterson-Iyer, Karen. 1998. "Prostitution: A Feminist Ethical Analysis." *Journal of Feminist Studies in Religion* 14 (2): 19–44.

Petrosky, E., Janet M. Blair, Carter J. Betz, Katherine A. Fowler, Shane P. D. Jack, and Bridget H. Lyons. 2017. "Racial and Ethnic Differences in Homicides of Adult Women and the Role of Intimate Partner Violence—United States, 2003–2014." *Morbidity and Mortality Weekly Report* 66, no. 28 (July): 741–46.

Pevey, C., C. Williams, and C. Ellison. 1996. Male God Imagery and Female Submission: Lessons from a Southern Baptist Ladies' Bible Class. *Qualitative Sociology*. 19 (2): 173.

Pfeiffer, Sacha. 2002. "He Invoked Religion for Sexual Acts." *Boston Globe*, December 4, 2002, sec. Special Report. www.bostonglobe.com.

Phillips, Dave. 2017. "Inquiry Opens into How a Network of Marines Shared Illicit Images of Female Peers." *New York Times*. March 6, 2017.

Phillips, Joan. 2008. "Female Sex Tourism in Barbados: A Postcolonial Perspective." *Brown Journal of World Affairs* 14 (2): 201–12.

Phillips, Lynn M. 2000. *Flirting with Danger: Young Women's Reflections on Sexuality and Domination*. New York: New York University Press.

Phillips, Nickie D. 2017. *Beyond Blurred Lines: Rape Culture in Popular Media*. Lanham: Rowman and Littlefield.

Phillips, Whitney. 2013. "Don't Feed the Trolls? It's Not That Simple." *Daily Dot*, June 10, 2013. www.dailydot.com.

Phoenix Jo. 2009. "Frameworks for Understanding." In *Regulating Sex for Sale: Prostitution, Policy Reform and the UK*, edited by J. Phoenix. Bristol, UK: The Policy Press, 2009.

Phrase Finder. n.d. "Rule of Thumb." Accessed August 27, 2011. www.phrases.org.uk.

Pina, A., and Gannon, T. A. 2012. "An Overview of the Literature on Antecedents, Perceptions and Behavioural Consequences of Sexual Harassment." *Journal of Sexual Aggression* 18 (2): 209–32.

Pineau, Lois 1996. "A Response to My Critic." In Date Rape: Feminism Philosophy and the Law, edited by L. Francis, 63–107. University Park: Pennsylvania State University Press.

Pinker, Steven. 2011. *The Better Angels of Our Nature: Why Violence Has Declined*. New York: Viking.

Plante, Thomas, and Kathleen McChesney. 2011. *Sexual Abuse in the Catholic Church: A Decade of Crisis, 2002–2012*. Santa Barbara, CA: Praeger.

Platt, Thomas. 1992. "The Concept of Violence as Descriptive and Polemic." *International Social Science Journal* 44 (2): 185–91.

Pleck, Elizabeth. 1987. *Domestic Tyranny*. New York: Oxford University Press.

———. 1989. "Criminal Approaches to Family Violence 1640–1980." In *Family Violence*, edited by Lloyd Ohlin and Michael Tonry. Chicago: University of Chicago Press.

———. 1990. "Rape and the Politics of Race, 1865–1910." Working paper no. 213. Wellesley, MA: Wellesley College Center for Research on Women.

———, and Joseph H. Pleck. 1980. *The American Male*. Englewood Cliffs, NJ: Prentice Hall.

Pleck, Joseph H. 1977. "Men's Power with Women, Other Men, and in Society: A Men's Movement Analysis." In *Women and Men: The Consequences of Power*, edited by A. L. Horton and J. A. Williamson, 417–33. Cincinnati, Ohio: Office of Women's Studies, University of Cincinnati.

———. 1980. "Men's Power with Women, Other Men, and Society: A Men's Movement Analysis." In *American Man*, edited by Elizabeth H. Pleck and Joseph H. Pleck. Englewood Cliffs, NJ: Prentice Hall.

———. 1981. *The Myth of Masculinity*. Cambridge, MA: MIT Press.

Plymire, Darcy C., and Pamela J. Forman. 2000. "Breaking the Silence: Lesbian Fans, the Internet, and the Sexual Politics of Women's Sport." *International Journal of Sexuality and Gender Studies* 5 (2): 141–53.

Pocar, Fausto. 2012. "Forward." In *Understanding and Proving International Sex Crimes*, edited by Morten Bergsmo, Alf Butenschøn Skre, and Elizabeth J. Wood. Beijing: Torkel Opsahl Academic E-Publisher.

Pogash, Carol. 2004. "California School District Settles Harassment Suit by Gay Students." *New York Times*, January 7, 2004.

Polsky, Andrew. 1991. *The Rise of the Therapeutic State*. Princeton, NJ: Princeton University Press.

Pomerantz S., R. Raby, and A. Stefanik. 2013. "Girls Run the World? Caught between Sexism and Postfeminism in School." *Gender & Society* 27 (2): 185–207.

Pope Nicholas V. 1455. *Romanus Pontifex*. January 8, 1455.

Porter, Roy. 1986. "Rape—Does It Have a Historical Meaning?" In *Rape*, edited by Sylvana Tomaselli and Roy Porter. New York: Blackwell.

Posadas, Jeremy. 2017. "Teaching the Cause of Rape Culture: Toxic Masculinity." *Journal of Feminist Studies in Religion* 33 (1): 177–79. https://doi.org/10.2979/jfemistudreli.33.1.23.

Potter, H. 2007. "Battered Black Women's Use of Religious Services and Spirituality for Assistance in Leaving Abusive Relationships." *Violence Against Women* 13 (3): 262–84.

Power, Samantha. 2009. "A Christian Lawyer's Global Crusade." *New Yorker*, January 19, 2009.

Power Inside. n.d. "Our Mission." Accessed March 12, 2019. http://powerinside.org.

"Prevention for Teens: What to Do If You Are a Cyber Bullying Victim." n.d. ETCB Organization website. Accessed March 12, 2019. www.endcyberbullying.org.

Price, Lisa S. 2005. *Feminist Frameworks: Building Theory on Violence Against Women*. Halifax, Canada: Fernwood Publishing.

Prieur, Jean-Marc, ed. 1989. *Acta Andrea*. Corpus Christianorum, Series Apocryphorum 5–6. Tournhout. Belgium: Brepols.

Prois, Jessica and Carolina Moreno. 2018. "The #MeToo Movement Looks Different for Women of Color. Here Are 10 Stories." *Huffington Post*. Accessed January 2, 2018. www.huffingtonpost.com.

Provoledo, Elisabetta. 2018. "Abuse Victims Meet with Pope Francis: 'We Need Concrete Actions.'" https://www.nytimes.com/2018/05/02/world/americas/chile-abuse-catholic-church.html

Pruitt, Lesley. 2013. "All-Female Police Contingents: Feminism and the Discourse of Armed Protection." *International Peacekeeping*. 20 (1): 67–79.

Ptacek, J. 1999. *Battered Women in the Courtroom: The Power of Judicial Responses*. Boston: Northeastern University Press.

Puzan, Elayne M. 2003. "The Unbearable Whiteness of Being (in Nursing)." *Nursing Inquiry* 10 (3): 193–200.

Quadagno, Jill. 1987. "Theories of the Welfare State." *Annual Review of Sociology* 13: 109–28.

Quinn, Andrew. 2002. "Nevada School District to Pay Student in Gay-Bashing Case." *Boston Globe*, August 29, 2002.

Quinn, Zoë. 2017. *Crash Override: How Gamergate (Nearly) Destroyed My Life, and How We Can Win the Fight Against Online Hate*. New York: Public Affairs.

Radford, Jill. 1987. "Policing Male Violence—Policing Women." In *Women, Violence and Social Control* edited by Jalna Hanmer and Mary Maynard. Atlantic Highlands, NJ: Humanities Press.

Rainie, Lee, Sara Kiesler, Ruogu Kang, and Mary Madden. 2013. *Anonymity, Privacy, and Security Online*. Pew Research Center: Internet, Science & Tech.

Rankine, Claudia. 2014. *Citizen: An American Lyric*. Minneapolis, Minnesota: Graywolf Press.

Rape Abuse and Incest National Network (RAINN). 2018. "Scope of the Problem: Statistics." RAINN website. Accessed March 9, 2020. www.rainn.org/statistics/scope-problem.

Raphael, Jody. 2013. *Rape Is Rape: How Denial, Distortion, and Victim Blaming Are Fueling A Hidden Acquaintance Rape Crisis*. Chicago: Lawrence Hill Books.

Rassam, Amal. 1980. "Women and Domestic Power in Morocco." *International Journal of Middle East Studies*. 12 (2): 171–79.

Rattray, R. S. 1923. *Ashanti*. Oxford, UK: Clarendon.

———. 1927. *Religion and Art in Ashanti*. Oxford, UK: Clarendon.

Reardon, Betty. 2001. *Education for a Culture of Peace in a Gender Perspective*. Paris: UNESCO.

Red Umbrella Fund. 2014. "Funding for Sex Workers Rights: Report." Red Umbrella Fund website. www.redumbrellafund.org.

Redfern, Rebecca C., Margaret A. Judd, and Sharon N. DeWitte. 2016. "Multiple Injury and Health in Past Societies: An Analysis of Concepts and Approaches, and Insights from a Multi-Period Study." *International Journal of Osteoarchaeology* 27 (3): 418–27.

Reger, J. 2012. *Everywhere and Nowhere: Contemporary Feminism in the United States*. New York and Oxford: Oxford University Press.

Reina, Angelica S., and Brenda J. Lohman. 2015. "Barriers Preventing Latina Immigrants from Seeking Advocacy Services for Domestic Violence Victims: A Qualitative Analysis." *Journal of Family Violence*. 30 (4): 479–88.

———, Brenda J. Lohman, and Marta María Maldonado. 2014. "'He Said They'd Deport Me': Factors Influencing Domestic Violence Help-Seeking Practices Among Latina Immigrants." *Journal of Interpersonal Violence*. 29 (4): 593–615.

Reinhartz, Adele. 2000. "Margins, Methods, and Metaphors: Reflections on a Feminist Companion to the Hebrew Bible." *Proof-texts*. 20 (1): 43–60.

Religion News Blog. 2007. "Experts: Black Church Can Better Address Domestic Violence." Religion News Blog. Accessed April 15, 2011. www.religionnewsblog.com.

REMHI (Recuperación de la Memoria Histórica). 1998. Guatemala: Nunca Mas, Informe de La Recuperacion de La Memoria Historica. Guatemala: Oficina de derechos humanos del Arzobispado de Guatemala.

Rennison, Callie Marie. 2003. *Intimate Partner Violence, 1993–2001*. Washington, DC: US Department of Justice, Bureau of Justice Statistics.

Renold, Emma, and Jessica Ringrose. 2013. "Feminisms Re-figuring 'Sexualisation,' Sexuality and 'The Girl.'" *Feminist Theory* 14 (3): 247–54.

Renzetti, Claire M. 1992. *Violent Betrayal: Partner Abuse in Lesbian Relationships*. Newbury Park, CA: Sage Publications, Inc.

———. 2009. "Economic Stress and Domestic Violence." *CRVAW Faculty Research Reports and Papers*. Paper 1. http://uknowledge.uky.edu/crvaw_reports/1.

———, Jeffrey L. Edleson, and Raquel Kennedy Bergen, eds. 2001. *Sourcebook on Violence against Women*. Thousand Oaks, CA: Sage.

———, and C. H. Miley. 1996. *Violence in Gay and Lesbian Domestic Partnerships*. New York: Harrington Park.

Rice-Oxley, M, and A. Nardelli. 2015. "Syrian Refugee Crisis: Why Has It Become So Bad?" *Guardian*, September 4, 2015.

Rich, Adrienne. 1980. *Compulsory Heterosexuality and Lesbian Existence*. New York: Only Women Press.

Rich, C., Schutten, J. K., and Rogers, R. A. 2012. "'Don't Drop the Soap': Organizing Sexualities in the Repeal of the US Military's 'Don't Ask, Don't Tell' Policy." *Communication Monographs*. 79 (3): 269–91.

Richards, David A. 2013. *Resisting Injustice and the Feminist Ethics of Care*. New York: Routledge.

Richardson, Laurel. 1993. "Writing: A Method of Inquiry." In *Handbook of Qualitative Research*. Edited by Norman Denzin and Yvonne Lincoln, 516–29. Thousand Oaks, CA: Sage.

———. 2001. "Getting Personal: Writing-Stories." *Qualitative Studies in Education* 14 (1): 33–38.

Richie, Beth E. 2005. "A Black Feminist Reflection on the Antiviolence Movement." In *Domestic Violence at the Margins*, edited by N. J. Sokoloff. New Brunswick, NJ: Rutgers University Press.

———. 2012. *Arrested Justice: Black Women, Violence and America's Prison Nation*. New York, NY: New York University Press.

———. 2015. "Reimagining the Movement to End Gender Violence: Anti-racism, Prison Abolition, Women of Color Feminisms, and Other Radical Visions of Justice." Keynote. *Miami Race and Social Justice Law Review* 5: 257–74.

Rigby, Ken, and Bruce Johnson. 2004. "Students as Bystanders to Sexual Coercion." *Youth Studies Australia* 23 (2): 11.

Ríos, Elsa A. 2007. *On the Road to Social Transformation: Utilizing Cultural and Community Strengths to End Domestic Violence: Publication of the National Latino Alliance for the Elimination of Domestic Violence*. New York: National Latino Alliance for the Elimination of Domestic Violence.

Rios, V. M. 2011. *Punished: Policing the Lives of Black and Latino Boys*. New York and London: New York University Press.

Risman, Barbara. 2004. "Gender as a Social Structure: Theory Wrestling with Activism." *Gender & Society* 18 (4): 429–50.

Ristock, Janice I. 2002. *No More Secrets: Violence in Lesbian Relationships*. New York: Routledge.

———. 2011. *Intimate Partner Violence in LGBTQ Lives*. New York, NY: Routledge.

Roberts, Dorothy. 1998. *Killing the Black Body: Race, Reproduction, and the Meaning of Liberty*. New York: Vintage.

———. 2006. "Feminism, Race, and Adoption Policy." In *Color of Violence*, edited by INCITE! Women of Color against Violence. Cambridge, MA: South End Press.

———. 2010. "The Paradox of Silence and Display: Sexual Violation of Enslaved Women and Contemporary Contradictions in Black Female Sexuality." In *Beyond Slavery: Overcoming Its Religious and Sexual Legacies*, edited by Bernadette J. Brooten, 41–60. New York: Palgrave Macmillan.

Roberts, Selena. 2003. "Code of Silence Corrupts the Young." *New York Times*, September 28, 2003.

Robertson, Adi. 2015. "'About 20' Police Officers Sent to Gamergate Critic's Former Home After Fake Hostage Threat." *Verge*, January 4, 2015. www.theverge.com.

Rocko, Rick Ross, and Future. 2013. "U.O.E.N.O." *Gift of Gab 2*. MP3 album.

Rogers, L. C. 1984. "Sexual Victimization: Social and Psychological Effects on College Women." PhD diss., Auburn University, Alabama.

Romero, Simon, and Taylor Barnes. 2013. "American Woman Gang-Raped and Beaten on Brazilian Tourist Van." *New York Times*, April 1, 2013.

Romero, Sylvia, and Melissa Romero Williams. 2013. "The Impact of Immigration Legislation on Latino Families: Implications for Social Work." *Advances in Social Work* 14 (1): 229–46.

Romito, Patrizia, and Lucia Beltramini. 2011. "Watching Pornography: Gender Differences, Violence and Victimization. An Exploratory Study in Italy." *Violence Against Women*. 17 (10): 1313–26.

Rosen, Liana W. 2017. "The State Department's Trafficking in Persons Report: Scope, Aid Restrictions, and Methodology." Congressional Research Service Report R44953. Washington, D.C.: Congressional Research Service. https://fas.org/sgp/crs/row/R44953.pdf.

Rospenda, K., J. Richman, J. Ehmke, and K. Zlatoper. 2005. "Is Workplace Harassment Hazardous to Your Health?" *Journal of Business and Psychology* (20): 95–110.

Ross, Stephanie. 1981. "How Words Hurt: Attitude, Metaphor, and Oppression." In *Sexist Language: A Modern Philosophical Analysis*, edited by Mary Vetterling-Braggin. New York: Littlefield, Adams and Co.

Rossi, H. n.d. "Sparing the Rod." Religious Tolerance. Accessed February 1, 2012. www.religioustolerance.org.

Rottenberg, Dan. 2011. "Male Sex Abuse and Female Naiveté: What Should Women Do?" Broad-StreetReview.com. www.broadstreetreview.com.

Rotundo, M., D. H. Nguyen, and P. R. Sackett. 2001. "A Meta-Analytic Review of Gender Differences in Sexual Harassment." *Journal of Applied Psychology* 86: 914–22.

Rousseau, Jean-Jacques. 2008 [1762]. *The Social Contract*. Translated by George D. H. Cole. New York: Cosimo, Inc.

Rubin, Alissa J., and Elian Peltier. 2018. "Does France Protect Minors? #MeToo Sets Off Legal Furor." *New York Times*, April 14, 2018.

Rubin, Gayle. 1976. "The Traffic in Women: Notes on the Political Economy of Sex." In *Toward an Anthropology of Women*, edited by Rayna Rapp Reiter. New York: Monthly Review Press.

Ruby, Robert H., and John A. Brown. 1993. *Indian Slavery in the Pacific Northwest*. Spokane: The Arthur H. Clark Company.

Ruddick, Sara. 1989. *Maternal Thinking: Towards a Politics of Peace*. New York: Women's Press.

Ruff O'Herne, Jan. 1994. *50 Years of Silence*. Sydney: Editions Tom Thompson.

Ruggles, David. 1971. "The Abrogation of the Seventh Commandment, by the American Churches [1835]." In *Early Negro Writing*, 1760–1837, edited by Dorothy Porter, 478–93. Boston: Beacon.

Ruiz, Ariel G., Jie Zong, and Jeanne Batalova. n.d. "Immigrant Women in the United States." Migration Policy Institute. Accessed March 20, 2015. www.migrationpolicy.org.

Rumney, Philip N. S. 2007. "In Defence of Gender Neutrality Within Rape." *Seattle Journal for Social Justice* 6 (1): 481–526.

Rush, Florence. 1980. *The Best Kept Secret: Sexual Abuse of Children*. New York: McGraw-Hill.

Russo, Ann. 2001. "Lesbians, Prostitutes, and Murder: Deconstructing Media Distortions." In *Taking Back Our Lives: A Call to Action for the Feminist Movement*, edited by A. Russo. New York: Routledge.

Ryan, Christopher, and Cacilda Jethá. 2010. Sex at Dawn: *The Prehistoric Origins of Modern Sexuality*. New York: HarperCollins.

Sacco, Lynn. 2009. *Unspeakable: Father-Daughter Incest in American History*. Baltimore, MD: Johns Hopkins University Press.

Safraoui, Samyra Rose. 2014. "Physical, Emotional, and Competitive Aggression Tendencies in Contact and Non-Contact Collegiate Athletes." Online Theses and Dissertations 220. https://encompass.eku.edu.

Saguy, Abigail C. 2003. *What Is Sexual Harassment? From Capitol Hill to the Sorbonne*. Berkeley: University of California Press.

Salam, Maya. 2019. "On International Women's Day, a Look at a Feminist Country." *New York Times*. March 8, 2019.

Sallmann, Jolanda. 2010. "Living with Stigma: Women's Experiences of Prostitution and Substance Use." *Affilia* 25 (2): 146–59.

Salter, Anastasia, and Bridget Blodgett. 2017. *Toxic Geek Masculinity in Media*. New York: Palgrave Macmillan.

Salter, Michael. 2012. "Invalidation: A Neglected Dimension of Gender-based Violence and Inequality." *International Journal of Crime and Justice*, 1 (1): 3–13.

———. 2017. "From Geek Masculinity to Gamergate: the Technological Rationality of Online Abuse." *Crime Media Culture* 3 (3): 1–18.

Sanchez, Sonia. 1981. "Memorial." In *Black Sister*, edited by Erlene Stetson. Bloomington: Indiana University Press.

Sánchez-Páramo, Carolina, and Ana Maria Munoz-Boudet. 2018. "No, 70% of the world's poor aren't women, but that doesn't mean poverty isn't sexist." *Let's Talk Development* (blog), *World Bank*. March 8, 2018. http://blogs.worldbank.org.

Sanday, Peggy Reeves. 1981. *Female Power and Male Dominance: On the Origins of Sexual Inequality*. New York: Cambridge University Press.

———. 1990. *Fraternity Gang Rape: Sex, Brotherhood, and Privilege on Campus*. New York: New York University Press.

———. 2000. *Fraternity Gang Rape: Sex, Brotherhood, and Privilege on Campus*. New York: New York University Press.

Sanders, Teela. 2004. *Sex Work: A Risky Business*. Portland: Willan.

Sanford, Victoria. 2003. *Buried Secrets: Truth and Human Rights in Guatemala*. New York: Palgrave Macmillan.

———. 2014. "Command Responsibility and the Guatemalan Genocide: Genocide as a Military Plan of the Guatemalan Army under the Dictatorships of Generals Lucas Garcia, Ríos Montt, and Meija Victores." *Genocide Studies International* 8 (1): 86–101.

———, Katerina Stefatos, and Cecilia M. Salvi, eds. 2016. *Gender Violence in Peace and War: States of Complicity*. New Brunswick, NJ: Rutgers University Press.

Santos, Cecília MacDowell. 2004. "En-Gendering the Police: Women's Police Stations and Feminism in São Paulo." *Latin American Research Review* 39 (3): 29–55.

———. 2005. *Women's Police Stations: Gender, Violence, and Justice in São Paolo, Brazil*. New York: Palgrave Macmillan.

Saul, Stephanie. 2017a. "'Victim Feminism' and Sexual Assault on Campus." *New York Times*, November 3, 2017.

———. 2017b. "When Rapists on Campus Attack Again," *New York Times*, December 24, 2017.

Saum, Christine A., Nicole L. Mott, and Erik F. Dietz. 2001. "Rohypnol, GHB, and Ketamine: New Trends in Date-Rape Drugs." In *The American Drug Scene: An Anthology*, edited by J. A. Inciardi and K. McElraths. Los Angeles, CA: The Roxbury Publishing Company.

Saunders, Penelope. 2000. "Working on the Inside: Migration, Sex Work, and Trafficking in Persons." *Legal Link* (Australia) 11 (2).

———, A. Huynh, and J. Goodman-Delahunty. 2007. "Defining Workplace Bullying Behaviour Professional Lay Definitions of Workplace Bullying." *International Journal of Law and Psychiatry* (30): 340–54.

Sawer, Marian. 2000. "Parliamentary Representation of Women: From Discourses of Justice to Strategies of Accountability." *International Political Science Review/Revue internationale de science politique, Women, Citizenship, and Representation/Femmes, citoyenneté et représentation* 21 (October): 361–80.

Scanzoni, L. D. 1988. "Contemporary Challenges for Religion and Family from a Protestant Woman's Point of View." In *The Religion & Family Connection: Social Science Perspectives*, edited by D. Thomas, 125–42. Provo, Utah: Brigham Young University Press.

———, and N. A. Hardesty. 1992. *All We're Meant to Be: Biblical Feminism for Today, 3rd Revised Edition*. Grand Rapids, MI: William B. Eerdmans Publishing Company.

Schaafsma, Polly. 2007. "Head Trophies and Scalping: Images in Southwest Rock Art." In *The Taking and Displaying of Human Body Parts as Trophies by Amerindians*, edited by Richard J. Chacon and David H. Dye, 90–123. New York: Springer.

Schafer, Judith K. 1994. *Slavery, the Civil Law, and the Supreme Court of Louisiana*. Baton Rouge: Louisiana State University Press.

Schalet, Amy. 2007. "The History of the Anti-Rape and Rape Crisis Center Movements." In *Encyclopedia of Violence Against Women* edited by Claire Renzetti. Thousand Oaks, CA: Sage.

———. 2011. *Not Under My Roof*. Chicago: University of Chicago Press.

Schniedewind, W. 2004. *How the Bible Became a Book: The Textualization of Ancient Israel*. United Kingdom: Cambridge University Press.

———, and Rendsburg, G. 2010. "The Siloam Tunnel Inscription: Historical and Linguistic Perspectives." *Israel Exploration Journal*, 60: 188–203.

Schussler, Fiorenza. 1985. "The Will to Choose to Reject: Continuing Our Critical Work." In *Feminist Interpretation of the Bible*, edited by L. Russell, 126–36. Philadelphia, PA: Fortress Press.

Schuster, Karla, Jason Molinet, and Keiko Morris. 2003. "Trouble for Team: Mepham Football Players Accused of Sex Abuse at PA Camp." *Newsday*, September 11, 2003.

Schuth, Katarina. 2004. "Seminaries and the Sexual Abuse Crisis: A Review and Critique of the National Review Board's Report." *America Magazine*, March 22, 2004: 16–18.

———. 2012. "A Change in Formation: How the Sexual Abuse Crisis Has Reshaped Priestly Training." *America Magazine*, no. 5125. www.americamagazine.org.

Schwartz, M. D., and W. S. DeKeseredy. 1997. *Sexual Assault on the College Campus: The Role of Male Peer Support*. Thousand Oaks, CA: Sage.

Schwind, Christina, Jürgen Buder, Ulrike Cress, and Friedrich W. Hesse. 2012. "Preference-Inconsistent Recommendations: An Effective Approach for Reducing Confirmation Bias and Stimulating Divergent Thinking?" *Computers & Education* 58: 787–96.

Scott, R. 2009. A Contextual Approach to Women's Rights in the Qur'an: Readings of 4:34. *Muslim World* 99 (1): 60–85.

Scott, J., V. Minchiello, R. Marino, G. P. Harvey, M. Jamieson, and J. Brown. 2005. "Understanding the New Context of the Male Sex Work Economy." *Journal of Interpersonal Violence* 20 (3): 320–42.

Scoular, Jane. 2010. "What's Law Got to Do with It? How and Why Law Matters in the Regulation of Sex Work." *Journal of Law and Society* 37 (1): 12–39.

Searcey, Dionne. 2019. "Divorces Show Women's Gains in West Africa." *New York Times*, January 7, 2019.

Sears, K., R. Intrieri, and D. Papini. 2011. "Sexual Harassment and Psychosocial Maturity Outcomes Among Young Adults Recalling Their First Adolescent Work Experiences." *Sex Roles* 64: 491–505.

Sedgwick, Eve Kosofsky. 2008. *Epistemology of the Closet*. Berkeley: UC Press.

Sedziafa, Alice Pearl, Eric Y. Tenkorang, and Adobea Y. Owusu. 2016. "Kinship and Intimate Partner Violence Against Married Women in Ghana: A Qualitative Exploration." *Journal of Interpersonal Violence* 33 (14): 2197–224.

Segura, Denise A., and Patricia Zavella. 2007. *Women and Migration in the US-Mexico Borderlands: A Reader*. Durham, NC: Duke University Press.

Seidman, Steven. 1992. *Embattled Eros: Sexual Politics and Ethics in Contemporary America*. New York: Routledge.

———. 2003. *The Social Construction of Sexuality*. New York: Norton.

Sen, Gita, and Caren Grown. 1987. *Development Crises and Alternative Visions: Third World Women's Perspectives*. New York: Monthly Review Press

Sentencia Condenatoria en contra de José Efraín Ríos Montt. 2013. Condenado par Genocidio. Guatemala City: F&G Editores.

Sexton, Lori, Valerie Jenness, and Jennifer Macy Sumner. 2010. "Where the Margins Meet." *Justice Quarterly* 27: 835–60.

Shalhoub-Kevorkian, Nadera. 2000. "The Efficacy of Israeli Law in Preventing Violence within Palestinian Families Living in Egypt." In *Domestic Violence: Global Responses*, edited by E. Erez and K. Laster. Bicester, UK: A B Academic.

Shaman, Christina. 2017. "From Constitution to Classroom: Can an ERA Prevent Sexual Assault in K–12 Schools?" *Women's eNews*, September 7, 2017.

Shannon-Lewy, C. and V. T. Dull. 2005. "The Response of Christian Clergy to Domestic Violence: Help or Hindrance?" *Aggression and Violent Behavior* 10 (6): 647–59.

Shdaimah, Corey S. 2010. "Taking a Stand in a Not-so-perfect World: What's a Critical Supporter to Do?" *University of Maryland Journal of Gender, Race, Class and Religion* 10 (1): 89–111.

——. 2020. "Prostitution Diversion Programs." In *Women and Crime Encyclopedia*, 3 volumes., edited by F. P. Bernat and K. Frailing. Hoboken, NY: John Wiley & Sons Inc.

——, and Chrysanthi S. Leon. 2015. "'First and Foremost They're Survivors': Selective Manipulation, Resilience, and Assertion Among Prostitute Women." *Feminist Criminology* 10 (4): 326–47.

——, and Chrysanthi Leon. 2016. "Counter-Narratives as Stigma Management: Relationships of Care and Caution Among Women Engaged in Street Level Prostitution." *Studies in Law, Politics, and Society* 71: 43–62.

——, and Chrysanthi Leon. 2018. "Whose Knowledges? Moving Beyond Damage-Centered Research in Studies of Women in Street-Based Sex Work." *Criminological Encounters*. 1 (1): 19–30.

——, Roland W. Stahl, and Sanford F. Schram. 2011. *Change Research: A Case Study on Collaborative Methods for Social Workers and Advocates*. New York: Columbia University Press.

Sheffield, Carole J. 1987. "Sexual Terrorism: The Social Control of Women." In *Analyzing Gender: A Handbook of Social Science Research*, edited by Beth Hess and Myra Marx Ferree, 171–89. Thousand Oaks: Sage Publications.

——. 2007. "Sexual Terrorism." In *Gender Violence: Interdisciplinary Perspectives, 2nd edition*, edited by Laura L. O'Toole, Jessica R. Schiffman, and Margie L. Kiter Edwards, 111–30. New York: New York University.

Shell-Duncan, Bettina, Katherine Wander, Ylva Hernlund, and Amadou Moreau. 2011. "Dynamics of Change in the Practice of Female Genital Cutting in Senegambia: Testing Predictions of Social Convention Theory." *Social Science & Medicine* 73 (October): 1275–83.

Shepard, Melanie F., and Ellen L. Pence. 1999. "An Introduction: Developing a Coordinated Community Response." In *Coordinating Community Responses to Domestic Violence: Lessons from Duluth and Beyond*, edited by M. F. Shepard and E. L. Pence. Thousand Oaks, CA: Sage.

Shepherd, Laura J. 2010. "Feminist Security Studies." In *The International Studies Encyclopedia*, edited by Robert A. Denemark. Malden, MA: Wiley Blackwell.

Sheridan, Mary P., and Tobi Jacobi. 2013. "Critical Feminist Practice and Campus-Community Partnerships: A Review Essay." *Feminist Teacher* 24(1-2): 138–150.

Shih, Elena. 2015 "The Anti-Trafficking Rehabilitation Complex." *Contexts*. 13(1).

Showden, Carisa R. 2011. *Choices Women Make: Agency in Domestic Violence, Assisted Reproduction, and Sex Work*. Minneapolis: University of Minnesota Press.

——, and Samantha Majic. 2014. *Negotiating Sex Work: Unintended Consequences of Policy and Activism*. Minneapolis: University of Minnesota Press.

Shupe, Anson. 2007. *Spoils of the Kingdom: Clergy Misconduct and Religious Community*. Chicago: University of Illinois Press.

——. 2008. *Rogue Clerics: The Social Problem of Clergy Deviance*. New Jersey: Transaction Publishers.

Shupe, Anson and Richard Sipe. 2011. "Report on Catholic Priest Pedophile Problem Misses the Mark." http://www.bishop-accountability.org/news2011/05_06/2011_05_20_Shupe_Reporton.htm

Siegle, Del. 2010. "Cyberbullying and Sexting: Technology Abuses of the 21st Century." *Gifted Child Today* 33, no. 2 (Spring): 14–65.

Silva, Daniella. 2019. "Nearly 400 Children Rescued and 348 Adults Arrested in Canadian Child Pornography Bust." *NBC News*. www.nbcnews.com. Accessed December 2, 2019.

Silvey, R. 2006. Consuming the Transnational Family: Indonesian Migrant Domestic Workers to Saudi Arabia. *Global Networks* 6: 23–40.

Simonds Vanessa W., Nina Wallerstein, Bonnie Duran, and Malia Villegas. 2013. "Community-Based Participatory Research: Its Role in Future Cancer Research and Public Health Practice." *Preventing Chronic Disease* 10.

Simons, Marlise. 1996. "U.N. Court, for First Time, Defines Rape as War Crime." *New York Times*, June 28, 1996.

———. 2018. "Rape Charges for Jihadist Police Chief." *New York Times*, April 15, 2018.

Simmons, Aisha. 2006. "The War Against Black Women, and the Making of NO!" In *Color of Violence*, edited by INCITE! Women of Color against Violence. Cambridge, MA: South End Press.

Sipe, A. W. Richard. 2011. "Catholic Seminaries: The Inside Story." http://www.awrsipe.com/reports/2011/2011-09-06-seminaryevaluation.htm.

———. 2003. *Celibacy in Crisis: A Secret World Revisited.* New York: Brunner-Routledge.

———. 2005. "The Celibate Myth: Priests Who Sexually Abuse and the System That Surrounds Them." www.awrsipe.com.

———. 2007. "Loss of Faith & Clergy Sexual Abuse." www.awrsipe.com.

———. 2008a. "Celibacy Today: Mystery, Myth, and Miasma." *Cross Currents* 57 (4): 545–62.

———. 2008b. "Preliminary Considerations for the Understanding of the Genealogy of Sexual Abuse by Catholic Clergy." www.awrsipe.com

———. n.d. "Unspeakable Damage: The Effects of Clergy Sexual Abuse." Accessed February 27, 2020. www.awrsipe.com.

———, Marianne Benkert, and Thomas Doyle. 2013. "Spirituality and the Culture of Narcissism." www.bishop-accountability.org.

Sipe, A. W. Richard, Thomas Doyle, and Patrick Wall. 2016. *Sex, Priests, and Secret Codes: The Catholic Church's 2000 Year Paper Trail of Sexual Abuse.* Lanham, US: Taylor Trade Publishing.

Sjoberg, Laura, and Jillian Martin. 2010. "Feminist Security Theorizing." In *The International Studies Encyclopedia*, edited by Robert A. Denemark. Malden, MA: Wiley Blackwell.

Slawsky, Richard. 2005. "Bank One Seeks to Make Amends for Past Ties to Slavery." *Louisiana Weekly*, February 14–20, 2005.

Sledge, Matt. 2017. "Court Watchers Demand New Orleans DA Stop Arresting Accusers in Rape Cases as Material Witnesses." *New Orleans Advocate*, April 11, 2017.

Smith, Andrea. 2005. *Sexual Violence and American Indian Genocide.* Cambridge, MA: South End Press.

Smith, Joanne, Meghan Huppuch, and Mandy ven Deven. 2011. *Hey Shorty! A Guide to Combating Sexual Harassment and Violence in Schools and on the Streets.* New York: The Feminist Press.

Sokoloff, Natalie J. 2008. "Expanding the Intersectional Paradigm to Better Understand Domestic Violence in Immigrant Communities." *Critical Criminology* 16 (4): 229–55.

———, and Christine Pratt, eds. 2005. *Domestic Violence at the Margins: Readings on Race, Class, Gender and Culture.* New Brunswick, NJ: Rutgers University Press.

Solnit, Rebecca. 2012. "Best of TomDispatch: Rebecca Solnit, The Archipelago of Arrogance." *TomDispatch* (blog). 2:31 p.m., August 19, 2012. www.tomdispatch.com.

Sommers, C. 2001. *The War Against Boys: How Misguided Feminism is Harming Our Young Men.* New York: Simon and Schuster.

Sontag, Deborah. 2015. "Transgender Woman Cites Attacks and Abuse in Men's Prisons." *New York Times*, April 5.

Southall, Ashley. 2015. "Penn State, Finding Harassment and Hazings, Suspends Recognition of a Fraternity." *New York Times*, May 27, 2015.

Spelman, Elizabeth V. 1982. "Theories of Race and Gender: The Erasure of Black Women." *Quest* 5(4): 36–62.

———. 2008. Gender and Race: "The Ampersand Problem in Feminist Thought." In *The Feminist Philosophy Reader*, edited by A. Bailey and C. Cuomo, 265–78. New York: McGraw-Hill.

Spencer, B., and F. J. Gillen. 1927. *The Arunta. 2 vols.* London: Macmillan.

Spencer, Susan D. 2012. "Detecting Violence in the Archaeological Record: Clarifying the Timing of Trauma and Manner of Death in Cases of Cranial Blunt Force Trauma Among Pre-Columbian Amerindians of West-Central Illinois." *International Journal of Paleopathology* 2 (2–3): 112–22.

Spraitz, Jason, and Kendra Bowen. 2016. "Techniques of Neutralization and Persistent Sexual Abuse by Clergy: A Content Analysis of Priest Personnel Files from the Archdiocese of Milwaukee." *Journal of Interpersonal Violence* 31 (15): 2515–38. https://doi.org/10.1177/0886260515579509.

Staba, David. 2003. "High School Player Is Charged in Sexual Abuse." *New York Times*, October 14, 2003.

Staggenborg, S. 1988. "The Consequences of Professionalization and Formalization in the Pro-Choice Movement." *American Sociological Review* 53 (4): 585–605.

Standing, Guy. 2011. *The Precariat: The New Dangerous Class.* London: Bloomsbury Academic.

Stansell, C. 2010. *Feminist Promise: 1792 to the Present.* New York: Random House.

Stark, S., O. S. Chernyshenko, A. R. Lancaster, F. Drasgow, and L. F. Fitzgerald. 2002. "Toward Standardized Measurement of Sexual Harassment: Shortening the SEQ-DoD Using Item Response Theory." *Military Psychology* 14: 49–72.

Starna, William A., and Ralph Watkins. 1991. "Northern Iroquoian Slavery." *Ethnohistory* 38 (1): 34–57.

Statt, Nick. 2017. "Swatting Over Call of Duty Game Results in Deadly Police Shooting of Kansas Man." *Verge.* December 29, 2017.

Staude-Müller, Britta Hansen, and Melanie Voss. 2012. "How Stressful Is Online Victimization? Effects of Victim's Personality and Properties of the Incident." *European Journal of Developmental Psychology* 9 (2): 260–74.

Staudt, Kathleen A. 1998. *Policy, Politics, and Gender: Women Gaining Ground.* West Hartford, CT: Kumarian Press.

Stearns, Carol, and Peter Stearns. 1986. *Anger: The Struggle for Emotional Control in America's History.* Chicago: University of Chicago Press.

Steele, Daniel J. 2017. "Listening to Voices of the Exploited: Law Enforcement and Sex Trafficking in the United States." In *Challenging Perspectives on Street-Based Sex Work*, edited by Katie Hail-Jares, Corey S. Shdaimah, and Chrysanthi S. Leon, 282–98. Philadelphia, PA: Temple University Press.

Stein, Nan. 1981. *Sexual Harassment of High School Students: Preliminary Research Results.* Unpublished manuscript. Boston: Massachusetts Department of Education.

———. 1992. *Secrets in Public: Sexual Harassment in Public (and Private) Schools.* Working paper no. 256. Wellesley, MA: Wellesley College Center for Research on Women.

———. 1995. "Sexual Harassment in K–12 Schools: The Public Performance of Gendered Violence." *Harvard Educational Review, Special Issue: Violence and Youth* 65 (2): 145–62.

———. 1999. *Classrooms and Courtrooms: Facing Sexual Harassment in K–12 Schools.* New York: Teacher's College Press.

———. 2003. "Bullying or Harassment? The Missing Discourse of Rights in an Era of Zero Tolerance." *Arizona Law Review* 45 (3): 783–99.

———. 2005a. "Bullying and Harassment in a Post-Columbine World." In *Child Victimization*, edited by Kathy Kendall Tackett and Sarah Giacomoni. Kingston, NJ: Civic Research Institute.

———. 2005b. "A Rising Pandemic of Sexual Violence in Elementary and Secondary Schools: Locating a Secret Problem." *Duke Journal of Gender Law and Policy* 12 (Spring): 33–52.

———, Nancy Marshall, and Linda Tropp. 1993. "Secrets in Public: Sexual Harassment in Our Schools; A Report on the Results of a Seventeen Magazine Survey." Unpublished manuscript. Wellesley, MA: Wellesley College Center for Research on Women.

———, Deborah Tolman, Michele Porche, and Renee Spencer. 2002. "Gender Safety: A New Concept for Safer and More Equitable Schools." *Journal of School Safety* 1 (2): 35–50.

Steinfatt, Thomas, and Simon Baker. 2011. "Measuring the Extent of Sex Trafficking in Cambodia: 2008 (UNIAP Trafficking Estimates Competition)." Bangkok: UNIAP. http://un-act.org.

Steinmetz, Simona; Haj-yahia, Muhammad M. 2006. "Definitions of and Beliefs About Wife Abuse Among Ultraorthodox Jewish Men From Israel" *Journal of Interpersonal Violence*, 21 (4): 525–54.

Steinmetz, Suzanne K. 1977–78. "The Battered Husband Syndrome." *Victimology* 2 (3 sup 4): 499–509.

Stephens, Dionne P., and Layli D. Phillips. 2003. "Freaks, Gold Diggers, Divas, and Dykes: The Sociohistorical Development of Adolescent African American Women's Sexual Scripts." in *Sexuality & Culture* 7 (1): 3–49.

Stephenson, W. 1953. *The Study of Behavior: Q-Technique and Its Methodology*. Chicago: University of Chicago Press.

Stern, Judith M. 2004. "Traumatic Brain Injury: An Effect and Cause of Domestic Violence and Child Abuse." *Current Neurology and Neuroscience Reports* 4: 179–81.

Stetz, Margaret D. 2001. "Wartime Sexual Violence against Women: A Feminist Response." In *Legacies of the Comfort Women of World War II*, edited by Margaret Stetz and Bonnie B. C. Oh, 91–100. Armonk, NY: Routledge.

———. 2002. "Representing 'Comfort Women:' Activism through Law and Art." *Iris* 45: 26–29, 83–84.

Stewart, Mary White. 2014. *Ordinary Violence: Everyday Assaults against Women Worldwide, 2nd edition*. Santa Barbara, CA: Praeger.

Stock, S. R., and F. Tissot. 2012. "Are There Health Effects of Harassment in the Workplace? A Gender-Sensitive Study of the Relationships between Work and Neck Pain." *Ergonomics* 55: 147–59.

Stohr, Mary K. 2015. "The Hundred Years' War: The Etiology and Status of Assaults on Transgender Women in Men's Prisons." *Women & Criminal Justice* 25: 120–29.

Stoller, R. J. 1979. *Sexual Excitement*. New York: Pantheon Books.

Stout, D. B. 1947. *San Blas Cura Acculturation*. New York: Viking Fund Publications in Anthropology.

Strangio, Chase. 2017. "Project ROSE: A Case Study on Diversion, Sex Work, and Constitutionality." In *Challenging Perspectives on Street-Based Sex Work*, edited by Katie Hail-Jares, Corey S. Shdaimah, and Chrysanthi S. Leon, 243–57. Philadelphia, PA: Temple University Press.

Straus, Murray A. 1991. "Children as Witness to Marital Violence: A Risk Factor for Life Long Problems among a Nationally Representative Sample of American Men and Women." Paper presented at the Ross Roundtable on Children and Violence, Washington, DC.

———, and Richard J. Gelles. 1990. *Physical Violence in American Families*. New Brunswick, NJ: Transaction.

Strauss, Ansel, and Juliet Corbin. 1998. *Basics of Qualitative Research: Techniques and Procedures for Developing Grounded Theory, 2nd. edition*. Thousand Oaks, CA: Sage.

Strauss, Susan. 1988. "Sexual Harassment in the School: Legal Implications for Principals." *Bulletin* 72 (506): 93–7. Reston, VA: National Association of Secondary School Principals.

Street, A. E., J. L. Gradus, J. Stafford, and K. Kelly. 2007. "Gender Differences in Experiences of Sexual Harassment: Data from a Male-Dominated Environment." *Journal of Consulting and Clinical Psychology*. 75: 464–74.

Stubbs, Julie. 2002. "Domestic Violence and Women's Safety: Feminist Challenges to Restorative Justice." In *Restorative Justice and Family Violence*, edited by Heather Strang and John Braithwaite. Cambridge: Cambridge University Press.

Subirats Martori, Marina. 1994. "Conquistar la igualdad: la coeducación hoy." *Revista Iberoamericana de Educación* 6.

Sudarkasa, N. 1996. The Strength of Our Mothers: *African and African American Women and Families: Essays and Speeches*. Trenton, NJ: Africa World Press.

Sue, D. W. 2010. *Microaggressions in Everyday Life: Race, Gender, and Sexual Orientation*. Hoboken: John Wiley & Sons.

Suetonius. 1997. *Lives of the Caesars: Vespasian 3: Suetonius, vol. 2*. Translated by J. C. Rolfe, Loeb Classical Library (rev. ed.). Cambridge, MA: Harvard University Press.

Sugarman, David B., and Susan L. Frankel. 1996. "Patriarchal Ideology and Wife-Assault: A Meta-Analytic Review." *Journal of Family Violence* 11 (1): 13–40.

Sullivan, Mary Lucille. 2007. *Making Sex Work: A Failed Experiment with Legalised Prostitution*. North Melbourne: Spinifex Press.

Sullivan, Mary, and Sheila Jeffreys. 2001. "Legalising Prostitution Is Not the Answer: the Example of Victoria, Australia." Coalition Against Trafficking in Women. www.catwinter national.org.

Sullivan, Rose, and Claes, Jacalyn. 2015. "A Different Kind of Fraternity: Psychological Change and Group Dynamics of Male Batterers." *Smith College Studies in Social Work*. 85 (1): 30–53.

Sullivan, Tami. P., Tara McPartland, and Bonnie S. Fisher. 2013. *Guidelines for Successful Researcher-Practitioner Partnerships in the Criminal Justice System: Findings from the Researcher-Practitioner Partnerships Study (RPPS)*. Washington, DC: US Department of Justice, National Institute of Justice.

Sumner, Jennifer, and Valerie Jenness. 2014. "Gender Integration in Sex-Segregated Prisons." In *The Handbook of LGBT Communities, Crime, and Justice*, edited by Dana Peterson and Vanessa R. Panfil. New York: Springer.

———, and Lori Sexton. 2015. "Same Difference: The 'Dilemma of Difference' and the Incarceration of Transgender Prisoners." *Law & Social Inquiry* 41 (3): 616–42.

Swan, Suzanne C., and David L. Snow. 2002. "A Typology of Women's Use of Violence in Intimate Relationships." *Violence against Women* 8 (3): 286–319.

Swim, Janet, Lauri L. Hyers, Laurie L. Cohen, and Melissa J. Ferguson. 2001. "Everyday Sexism: Evidence for Its Incidence, Nature, and Psychological Impact from Three Daily Diary Studies." *Journal of Social Issues* 57 (1): 31–53.

Sykes, Gresham. 1958. *The Society of Captives: A Study of a Maximum Security Prison*. Princeton, NJ: Princeton University Press.

Taibi, Catherine. 2013. "'Keep Calm and Rape' T-Shirt Maker Shutters after Harsh Backlash." *Huffington Post*, June 25, 2013. www.huffingtonpost.com.

Talentino, Jia. 2018. "The Rage of the Incels." *New Yorker*, May 15, 2018.

Tambiah, Yasmin. 2005. "Turncoat Bodies: Sexuality and Sex Work under Militarization in Sri Lanka." *Gender & Society* 19 (2): 243–61.

Tancred-Sheriff, Peta. 1989. "Gender, Sexuality and the Labour Process." In *The Sexuality of Organization*, edited by J. Hearn, D. L. Sheppard, P. Tancred-Sheriff, and G. Burrell. London: Sage.

Taormino, T., C. Penley, C. P. Shimizu, and M. Miller-Young, eds. 2013. *The Feminist Porn Book: The Politics of Producing Pleasure*. New York: Feminist Press.

Tasso, Anthony, Lona Whitmarsh, and Ann Ordway. 2016. "Intimate Partner Violence within Military Families: Intervention Guidelines for Relational Aggressors." *Family Journal: Counseling and Therapy for Couples and Families.* 24 (2): 114–21.

Tattum, Delwyn and David Lane. 1994. *Bullying in Schools.* Stoke-on-Trent. England: Trentham.

Taylor, Colin. 2001. *Native American Weapons.* Norman: University of Oklahoma Press.

Taylor, R. J., and L. M. Chatters. 1991. Religious life. In *Life in Black America*, edited by J. S. Jackson, 105–23. Newbury Park, CA: Sage.

Taylor, Sonya Renee. 2018. *The Body Is Not an Apology: The Power of Radical Self-Love.* Oakland, CA: Berrett-Koehler Publishers.

Taylor, V. 1989. "Social Movement Continuity: The Women's Movement in Abeyance." *American Sociological Review* 54 (5): 761–75.

Temkin, Jennifer. 1986. "Women, Rape and Law Reform." In *Rape*, edited by Sylvana Tomaselli and Roy Porter. Oxford, UK: Blackwell.

Tep, Mony, and Salan Ek. 2000. "Crossing Borders, Crossing Realities: Vietnamese Sex Workers in Cambodia." CARAM (Coordination of Action Research on AIDS and Mobility) Cambodia.

Tep, Mony, Salan Ek, and Marjolein Maas. 2001. "Different Mindsets, Different Risks: Looking at Risk Factors Identified by Vietnamese Sex Workers in Cambodia." *Research for Sex Work* 4: 4–6.

Theidon, Kimberly. 2009. "Reconstructing Masculinities: The Disarmament, Demobilization, and Reintegration of Former Combatants in Colombia." *Human Rights Quarterly* 31 (1): 1–34.

———. 2016. "A Greater Measure of Justice: Gender, Violence, and Reparations." In *Mapping Feminist Anthropology in the Twenty-First Century*, edited by Leni Silverstein and Ellen Lewin. New Brunswick, NJ: Rutgers University Press.

Thicke, Robin. 2013. "Blurred Lines." *Blurred Lines*, audio CD.

Thomas, Dorothy. 1994. "In Search of Solutions: Women's Police Stations in Brazil." In *Women and Violence*, edited by M. Davies. London: Zed Books.

Thomas, Nicholas, and William T. Tow. 2002. "The Utility of Human Security: Sovereignty and Humanitarian Intervention." *Security Dialogue* 33 (2): 177–92.

Thompson-Miller, Ruth, and Joe Feagin. 2014. *Jim Crow's Legacy: The Lasting Impact of Segregation.* New York: Rowman and Littlefield Publishers.

Tickner, Ann J. 1992. *Gender in International Relations: Feminist Perspectives on Achieving Global Security.* New York: Columbia University Press.

———. 1995. "Re-visioning Security." In *International Relations Theory Today*, edited by Ken Booth and Steve Smith. Cambridge: Polity Press.

———. 2004. "Feminist Responses to International Security Studies." *Peace Review* 16 (1): 43–48.

Tiger, L. 1969. *Men in Groups.* New York: Random House.

———. 2000. *The Decline of Males: The First Look at an Unexpected New World for Men and Women.* New York: St Martin's Press.

Tiger, Rebecca. 2013. *Judging Addicts: Drug Courts and Coercion in the Justice System.* New York: NYU Press.

Timberg, Craig. 2013. "How Violent Porn Sites Manage to Hide Information that Should Be Public." *Washington Post*, December 6, 2013.

Time's Up. 2018. "Open Letter from Time's Up." *New York Times.* www.nytimes.com.

Timmerman, G. 2003. "Sexual Harassment of Adolescents Perpetrated by Teachers and by Peers: An Exploration of the Dynamics of Power, Culture, and Gender in Secondary Schools." *Sex Roles* 48: 231–44.

Tjaden, Patricia, and Nancy Thoennes. 2000a. *Extent, Nature, and Consequences of Intimate Partner Violence: Findings from the National Violence Against Women Survey.* US Department of Justice, Office of Justice Programs. NCJ 181867.

———. 2000b. "Prevalence and Consequences of Male-to-Female and Female-to-Male Intimate Partner Violence as Measured by the National Violence Against Women Survey." *Violence Against Women* 6 (2):142–61.

———. 2006. *Extent, Nature, and Consequences of Rape Victimization: Findings from the National Violence Against Women Survey.* Washington, DC: US Government Printing Office.

Tkacz, C. B. 2006. "Are Old Testament Women Nameless, Silent, Passive Victims?" Catholic Answers. www.catholic.com.

Tolman, Deborah. 2012. "Female Adolescents, Sexual Empowerment and Desire." *Sex Roles* 66: 746–57.

Tomes, Nancy. 1978. "A 'Torrent of Abuse': Crimes of Violence between Working-Class Men and Women in London, 1840–1875." *Journal of Social History* 11: 328–45.

Tometi, Opal. 2019. "Fighting for Black Lives Worldwide." http://opaltometi.org

———. 2016. "Meet Opal Tometi." http://opaltometi.com.

Tønnessen, Liv. 2014. "When Rape Becomes Politics: Negotiating Islamic Law Reform in Sudan." *Women's Studies International Forum* 44 (May–June): 145–53.

Tooker, Elisabeth. 1991. *An Ethnography of the Huron Indians, 1615–1649.* Syracuse: Syracuse University Press.

Torraco, R. J. 2005. "Writing Integrative Literature Reviews: Guidelines and Examples." *Human Resource Development Review.* 4: 356–67.

Townes, Emilie M. 2010. "From Mammy to Welfare Queen: Images of Black Women in Public-Policy Formation." In *Beyond Slavery: Overcoming Its Religious and Sexual Legacies*, edited by Bernadette J. Brooten, 61–74. New York: Palgrave Macmillan.

Tracy, Carol E., Terry L. Fromson, Jennifer Gentile Long, and Charlene Whitman. 2013. "Rape and Sexual Assault in the Legal System." http://jpp.whs.mil.

Trafficking Victims Protection Act. 2001. "Implementation of the Trafficking Victims Protection Act." Hearing before the Committee on International Relations, House of Representatives, 107th Congress, 1st session, November 29. Serial No. 107–63.

Tran Thi Van Anh. 1999. "Women and Rural Land in Vietnam." In *Women's Rights to House and Land in China, Laos, and Vietnam*, edited by Irene Tinker and Gale Summerfield. Boulder: Lynne Rienner.

Transatlantic Slave Trade Database. n.d. Accessed May 28, 2010. www.slavevoyages.org.

Tripp, Aili Mari. 2015. *Women and Power in Postconflict Africa.* Cambridge, United Kingdom: Cambridge University Press.

True, Jacqui. 2012. *The Political Economy of Violence against Women.* Oxford: Oxford University Press.

Tuan, Yi-Fu. 1984. *Dominance and Affection: The Making of Pets.* New Haven, CT: Yale University Press.

Tung, Tiffany A. 2012. "Violence Against Women: Differential Treatment of Local and Foreign Females in the Heartland of the Wari Empire, Peru." In *The Bioarcheology of Violence*, edited by Debra L. Martin, Ryan P. Harrod, and V. Pérez, 180–98. Gainesville: University of Florida Press.

Turnbull, C. 1965. *Wayward Servants.* New York: Natural History Press.

Turshen, Meredeth. 2001. "The Political Economy of Rape: An Analysis of Systematic Rape and Sexual Abuse of Women during Armed Conflict in Africa." In *Victors, Perpetrators, or Actors: Gender, Armed Conflict, and Political Violence*, edited by Caroline O. N. Moser and Fiona C. Clark. London: Zed Books.

Tyson, Ann Scott. 2005. "Reported Cases of Sexual Assault in Military Increase." *Washington Post*. May 7, 2005.

UCF SJA. 2018. (Social Justice and Advocacy, University of Central Florida). "LGBTQ+ Terminology."

Underwood, Marion K. 2003. *Social Aggression among Girls*. New York: The Guilford Press.

United Nations (UN). 1994. "Declaration on the Elimination of Violence Against Women." http://www.un.org.

———. 2000. "Convention against Transnational Organized Crime, Supplemental Protocol to Prevent, Suppress and Punish Trafficking in Persons, Especially Women and Children." United Nations Office on Drugs and Crime. www.unodc.org.

United Nations Development Programme. 1994. "Human Development Report." Oxford: Oxford University Press.

———. 2016. "UN Development Report." UNDP. http://hdr.undp.org.

United Nations High Commissioner for Human Rights. 2019. "Children." www.unhcr.org.

United Nations Office on Drugs and Crime. 2014. "Global Study on Homicide 2013 Trends, Contexts, Data." UNODC. www.unodc.org.

United Nations Population Fund. n.d. "Gender-biased Sex Selection." Accessed February 23, 2019. www.unfpa.org.

———. 2014. "Women and Peace and Security." Security Council Report. www.securitycouncilreport.org.

———. 2016. "Report of the Secretary-General on Conflict-Related Sexual Violence." www.undocs.org.

United Nations Statistics Division. 2015. "The World's Women 2015: Trends and Statistics." https://unstats.un.org.

US Department of Health and Human Services (USDHHS). 2014. *Trauma-Informed Care in Behavioral Health Services*. Treatment Improvement Protocol (TIP) Series 57. HHS Pub No. (SMA) 13–4801. Rockville, MD: Substance Abuse and Mental Health Services Administration.

US Department of Justice. 2006. "Women of Color Network Facts and Stats Collection: Domestic Violence." www.doj.state.or.us.

———. n.d. "Raising Awareness of Sexual Abuse: Facts and Statistics." Accessed March 26, 2019. www.nsopw.gov

———. 2018. "Children Internet Safety." https://www.justice.gov/criminal-ceos/children-internet-safety

US Department of State. 2008. "Trafficking in Persons Report 2008." www.state.gov.

———. 2009. "Trafficking in Persons Report 2009." www.state.gov.

———. 2017. "Trafficking in Persons Report 2017." www.state.gov.

Valdovinos, Miriam G. 2016. "Cultivating Care: Understanding Intimate Partner Violence Experiences of Undocumented Latinas in Washington State." Doctoral Dissertation, University of Washington.

Vance, Carole S. 1984. *Pleasure and Danger: Exploring Female Sexuality*. Boston: Routledge and K. Paul.

———. 2012. "Innocence and Experience: Melodramatic Narratives of Sex Trafficking and Their Consequences for Law and Policy." *History of the Present* 2 (2): 200–18.

van der Toorn, K. 2007. *Scribal Culture and the Making of the Hebrew Bible*. Cambridge: Harvard University Press.

VanNatta, Michelle. 2005. "Constructing the Battered Woman." *Feminist Studies* 31 (2): 416–43.

Vargas, Edward D., and Maureen A. Pirog. 2016. "Mixed-Status Families and WIC Uptake: The Effects of Risk of Deportation on Program Use." *Social Science Quarterly* 97 (3): 555–72.

———, and Vickie D. Ybarra. 2017. "US Citizen Children of Undocumented Parents: The Link Between State Immigration Policy and the Health of Latino Children." *Journal of Immigrant Minority Health* 19 (4): 913–20

Vedantam, Shankar. 2018. "Why Now? The Psychological Forces Behind A Cultural Reckoning: Understanding #MeToo." *Hidden Brain*, July 27, 2018.

Verhoeven, Timothy. 2015. "Harmful or Benign? Transnational Medical Networks and the Celibacy of Priests." *Journal of Religious History* 39 (2): 244–60. https://doi.org/10.1111/1467-9809.12184.

Vessey, J., Demarco, R., and DiFazio, R. 2010. "Bullying, Harassment, and Horizontal Violence in the Nursing Workforce: The State of the Science." *Annual Review of Nursing Research*, 28: 133–57.

Victor, Daniel. 2016. "Texas Rape Victim Was Jailed for Fear She Would Not Testify, Lawsuit Says." *New York Times*, July 23, 2016.

———. 2018a. "Woman Who Was Raped as a Teenager Is Awarded $1 Billion in Damages." *New York Times*, May 23, 2018.

———. 2018b. "Florida Fraternity Sued Over Intimate Videos Shared on Facebook." *New York Times*, June 14, 2018.

Victor, Jeffrey S. 1998. "Moral Panics and the Social Construction of Deviant Behavior." *Sociological Perspectives* 41 (3): 541–65.

Vidales, Guadalupe T. 2010. "Arrested Justice: The Multifaceted Plight of Immigrant Latinas Who Faced Domestic Violence." *Journal of Family Violence* 25 (6): 533–44.

Vijayasiri, G. 2008. "Reporting Sexual Harassment: The Importance of Organizational Culture and Trust." *Gender Issues* 25: 43–61.

Villalón, Roberta. 2010. *Violence Against Latina Immigrants: Citizenship, Inequality, and Community*. New York, NY: New York University Press

Von Mises, Ludwig. 1949. *Human Action: A Treatise on Economics*. New Haven, CT: Yale University Press.

Vossekuil, Bryan, Robert Fein, Marisa Reddy, Randy Borum, and William Modzeleski. 2002. *Final Report and Findings of the Safe School Initiative: Implications for the Prevention of School Attacks in the United States*. U.S. Department of Education, Office of Elementary and Secondary Education, Safe and Drug-Free Schools Program, and U.S. Secret Service, National Threat Assessment Center, Washington, DC.

Vu Tuan Anh, Tran Thi Van Anh, and Terry G. McGee. 2000. "Household Economy under Impacts of Economic Reforms in Viet Nam." In *Socioeconomic Renovation in Viet Nam: The Origin, Evolution, and Impact of Doi Moi*, edited by Peter Boothroyd and Pham Xuan Nam. Ottawa: International Development Research Centre; Singapore: Institute of Southeast Asian Studies.

Wadud, Amina. 2006. *Inside the Gender Jihad: Women's Reform in Islam*. Oxford: Oneworld.

Wahab, Stephanie, and Meg Panichelli. 2013. "Ethical and Human Rights Issues in Coercive Interventions with Sex Workers." *Affilia* 28 (4): 344–49.

Wajcman, Judy. 2010. "Feminist Theories of Technology." *Cambridge Journal of Economics* 24 (1): 143–52.

Wakefield, J. 2015. "Children Spend Six Hours or More a Day on Screens." *BBC*. www.bbc.com.

Walby, Sylvia, Jude Towers, and Brian Francis. 2016. "Is Violent Crime Increasing or Decreasing? A New Methodology to Measure Repeat Attacks Making Visible the Significance of Gender and Domestic Relations." *British Journal of Criminology* 56 (6): 1203–34.

Walker, Alice. 1981. "Coming Apart." In *You Can't Keep a Good Woman Down*. New York: Harcourt Brace Jovanovich.

Walker, Lenore E. A. 1984. *The Battered Woman Syndrome*. New York: Springer Publishing.

———. 1989. *Terrifying Love*. New York: Harper and Row.

Walker, Phillip L. 1989. "Cranial Injuries as Evidence of Violence in Prehistoric Southern California." *American Journal of Physical Anthropology* 80 (3): 313–23.

Walsh, Mark. 2003. "Administrators Not Immune in Suit over Alleged Taunts." *Education Week* 22 (31): 4.

Walsh, Wendy, Janis Wolak, and David Finkelhor. 2013. *Sexting: When Are State Prosecutors Deciding to Prosecute? The Third National Juvenile Online Victimization Study (NJOV-3)*. Durham, NC: Crimes against Children Research Center.

Walters, Glenn D., and Jon Kremser. 2016. "Differences in Career Aspirations, Influences, and Motives as a Function of Class Standing: An Empirical Evaluation of Undergraduate Criminal Justice Majors." *Journal of Criminal Justice Education* 3: 312.

Wamser-Nanney, R., and K. Cherry. 2018. "Children's Trauma-Related Symptoms Following Complex Trauma Exposure: Evidence of Gender Differences." *Child Abuse and Neglect* 77: 188–97.

Wang, S., L. Hayes, and L. O'Brien-Pallas. 2008. *A Review and Evaluation of Workplace Violence Prevention Programs in the Health Sector: Final Report*. Toronto: Nursing Health Services Research Unit.

———, and Doris Chang. 2014. "Intimate Partner Violence Among Asian America and Pacific Islander Women." AAPA. https://aapaonline.org.

Ward, David. 2011. "The Lived Experience of Spiritual Abuse." *Mental Health, Religion & Culture* 14 (9): 899–915.

Ward, Tony, and Stephen Hudson. 2011. "Finkelhor's Precondition Model of Sexual Abuse: A Critique." *Psychology, Crime, & Law* 7: 291–307. https://doi.org/10.1080/10683160108401799.

Ware, K. N., H. M. Levitt, and G. Bayer. 2003. "May God Help You: Faith Leaders' Perspectives of Intimate Partner Violence Within Their Communities." *Journal of Religion and Abuse* 5: 55–81.

Warner, Sam. 2009. *Understanding the Effects of Child Sexual Abuse*. New York: Routledge.

Warshaw, Robin. 1988. *I Never Called It Rape: The MS Report on Recognizing, Fighting, and Surviving Date and Acquaintance Rape*. New York: Harper and Row.

Wasti, S., M. E. Bergman, T. M. Glob, and F. Drasgow. 2000. Test of the Cross-Cultural Generalizability of a Model of Sexual Harassment. *Journal of Applied Psychology* 85: 766–78.

Waters, H., A. Hyder, Y. Rajkotia, S. Basu, and A. Butchart. 2005. The Costs of Interpersonal Violence—An International Review. *Health Policy* 73 (3): 303–15.

Watson, Francis M. 1976. *Political Terrorism: The Threat and the Response*. USA: Robert B. Luce Publisher.

Watts, David P., Martin N. Muller, Sylvia J. Amsler, Godfrey Mbabazi, and John C. Mitani. 2006. "Lethal Intergroup Aggression by Chimpanzees in Kibale National Park, Uganda." *American Journal of Primatology* 68: 161–80.

Weber, L. 2010. *Understanding Race, Class, Gender, and Sexuality: A Conceptual Framework*. New York: Oxford University Press.

Websdale, N. 1998. *Rural Woman Battering and the Justice System: Ethnography*. Thousand Oaks, CA: Sage.

Webster, Edith. 2013. "One Year Later: The Catholic Abuse Scandal," BishopAccountability.org. http://www.bishop-accountability.org/news2003_01_06/2003_06_21_Webster_OneYear.htm.

Wei, H., and Chen, J. 2012. "Factors Associated with Peer Sexual Harassment Victimization Among Taiwanese Adolescents." *Sex Roles* 66: 66–78.

Weis, Kurt, and Sandra S. Borges. 1973. "Victimology and Rape: The Case of the Legitimate Victim." *Issues in Criminology* 8: 71–115.

Weiss, Sasha. 2014. "The Power of #YesAllWomen." *New Yorker*. Accessed May 26, 2018. www.newyorker.com.

Weitzer, Ronald. 2009. "Sociology of Sex Work." *Annual Review of Sociology* 35: 213–33.

———. 2010. *Sex for Sale: Prostitution, Pornography, and the Sex Industry*, 2nd Edition. New York: Routledge.

Weldon, S. Laurel. 2002. *Protest, Policy, and the Problem of Violence Against Women: A Cross National Comparison*. Pittsburgh, PA: University of Pittsburgh Press.

Wellesley Centers for Women. 2017. "Where are We Now: Justice and Gender-Based Violence Initiative." www.wcwonline.org.

Wells, Ida B. 1892. Southern Horrors: Lynch Law in All Its Phases. Pamphlet. *The New York Age Print*. www.gutenberg.org.

Wendorf, Fred. 1968. "Site 117: A Nubian Final Paleolithic Graveyard Near Jebel Sahaba, Sudan." In *The Prehistory of Nubia*, edited by Fred Wendorf, 954–95. Dallas: Southern Methodist University.

Wessler, Seth F. 2011. *Shattered Families: The Perilous Intersection of Immigration Enforcement and the Child Welfare System*. New York: Applied Research Center Report, November 2011.

West, Candace, and Don H. Zimmerman. 1987. "Doing Gender." *Gender & Society* 1: 125–51.

———, and Don H. Zimmerman. 1991. "Doing Gender." In *The Social Construction of Gender*, edited by Judith Lorber and Susan A. Farrell. Newbury Park, CA: Sage.

West, Carolyn M. 2005. "Domestic Violence in Ethnically and Racially Diverse Families: The 'Political Gag Order' Has Been Lifted." In *Domestic Violence at the Margins*, edited by N. J. Sokoloff. New Brunswick, NJ: Rutgers University Press.

———, Glenda Kaufman Kantor, and Jana L. Jasinski. 1998. "Sociodemographic Predictors and Cultural Barriers to Help-Seeking Behavior by Latina and Anglo American Battered Women." *Violence and Victims* 13 (4): 361–75.

West, Traci C. 2006. "An Antiracist Christian Ethical Approach to Violence Resistance." In *Women of Color Against Violence*, edited by INCITE!, 243–49. Brooklyn, NY: South End Press.

Wheeler, Skye. 2017. "'All My Body Was Pain:' Sexual Violence Against Rohingya Women and Girls in Burma." Human Rights Watch. www.hrw.org.

Whisnant, R., and C. Stark, eds. 2004. *Not for Sale: Feminists Resisting Prostitution and Pornography*. North Melbourne, Australia: Spinifex Press.

White, J. W., and M. P. Koss. 1993. "Adolescent Sexual Aggression within Heterosexual Relationships: Prevalence, Characteristics, and Causes." In *The Juvenile Sex Offender*, edited by H. E. Barbaree, W. L. Marshall, and S. M. Hudson, 182–202. New York: Guilford Press.

Whitlock, Kay. 2005. Corrupting Justice: *A Primer for LGBT Communities on Racism, Violence, Human Degradation and the Prison Industrial Complex*. Philadelphia: American Friends Service Committee.

Whittemore, Robin, and Kathleen Knafl. 2005. "The Integrative Review: Updated Methodology." *Journal of Advanced Nursing* 52(5): 546–53.

Whittier, Nancy. 2009. *The Politics of Child Sexual Abuse*. New York: Oxford University Press.

———. 2014. "Rethinking Coalitions Anti-Pornography Feminists, Conservatives, and Relationships between Collaborative Adversarial Movements" *Social Problems* 61 (2): 175–93.

———. 2001. Emotional Strategies. In *Passionate politics: Emotions and Social Movements*, edited by Jeff Goodwin, James Jasper, and Francesca Polletta. Chicago: University of Chicago Press.

Whittle, Tanya N. 2017. "Constructing Prisoner Reentry Service Providers' Roles and Perceptions of Law, Justice and Fairness." PhD diss., University of Delaware.

"Who We Are." n.d. Girls Who Code, Accessed July 7, 2015. http://girlswhocode.com.

Wibben, Annick T. R. 2011. *Feminist Security Studies: A Narrative Approach*. London: Routledge.

Wiechelt, Shelly A., and Corey S. Shdaimah. 2015. "Condoms and Cupcakes: Fostering Autonomy Through Relationships of Care With Women in Prostitution." *Journal of Progressive Human Services* 26 (2): 166–85.

Wilcox, David R. 1979. "The Warfare Implications of Dry-Laid Masonry Walls." *Kiva* 45: 15–38.

Wilding, Faith. 1998. "Where Is the Feminism in Cyberfeminism?" *N. Paradoxa* 2: 6–13.

Wilkinson, Paul. 1974. *Political Terrorism*. New York: John Wiley and Sons.

Wilkinson, Richard G. 1997. "Violence against Women: Raiding and Abduction in Prehistoric Michigan." In *Troubled Times: Violence and Warfare in the Past*, edited by Debra L. Martin and David W. Frayer, 21–44. Amsterdam: Gordon and Breach.

Williams, Christine L. 2007. "Sexual Harassment in Organizations: A Critique of Current Research and Policy." In *Gender Violence: Interdisciplinary Perspectives*, 2nd edition, edited by Laura L. O'Toole, Jessica R. Schiffman, and Margie L. Kiter Edwards, 157–17. New York: New York University Press.

Williams, Joyce E. 1984. "Secondary Victimization: Confronting Public Attitudes about Rape." *Victimology: An International Journal* 9: 66–81.

Williams, Linda. 2017. "Where Are We Now: Justice and Gender-Based Violence Initiative." Wellesley Centers for Women. www.wcwonline.org.

Williamson, Elizabeth, and Emily Steel. 2018. "Conspiracy Theories Made Alex Jones Very Rich. Now They May Bring Him Down," *New York Times*, September 7, 2018.

Willis, Paul. 2012. "Witnesses on the Periphery: Young Lesbian, Gay, Bisexual and Queer Employees Witnessing Homophobic Exchanges in Australian Workplaces." *Human Relations* 65 (12): 589–610.

Willness Chelsea R., Peirs Steel, and Kibeom Lee. 2007. "A Meta-analysis of the Antecedents and Consequences of Workplace Sexual Harassment." *Personnel Psychology* 60: 127–62.

Wilson, Deborah, Connie Kirkland, and Brandi Hephner LaBanc. 2014. "Addressing Sexual Assault and Interpersonal Violence: Athletics' Role in Support of Healthy and Safe Campuses." Indianapolis, IN: The National Collegiate Athletic Association (NCAA).

Wilson, Jason. n.d. "Hate Sinks." *New Inquiry*. Accessed on February 6, 2014. http://thenewinquiry.com.

Wilson, K. J. 2005. *When Violence Begins at Home: A Comprehensive Guide to Understanding and Ending Domestic Abuse*. Alameda, CA: Hunter House.

Wilson, Laura C., and Katherine E. Miller. 2016. "Meta-Analysis of the Prevalence of Unacknowledged Rape." *Trauma, Violence, & Abuse* 1 (2): 149–59.

Wilson, Margo, and Martin Daly. 1995. "An Evolutionary Psychological Perspective on Male Sexual Proprietariness and Violence Against Wives." *Violence and Victims* 8: 271–94.

Wilson, Melba. 1994. *Crossing the Boundary: Black Women Survive Incest*. Berkeley, CA: Seal Press.

Wilson, William Julius. 1989. *The Truly Disadvantaged*. Chicago, Illinois: University of Chicago Press.

———. 1996. *When Work Disappears: The World of the New Urban Poor*. New York: Knopf.

Wingfield, Adia Harvey. 2007. "The Modern Mammy and the Angry Black Man: African American Professionals' Experiences with Gendered Racism in the Workplace." *Race, Gender & Class* 14 (2): 196–212.

Withers, Bethany P. 2015. "Without Consequence: When Professional Athletes Are Violent Off the Field." *Journal of Sports & Entertainment Law*. http://harvardjsel.com.

Wolch J. 1990. *The Shadow State: The Government and the Voluntary Sector in Transition*. New York: The Foundation Center.

Wolf, Robert V. 2001. "Management Note: New Strategies for an Old Profession—A Court and a Community Combat the Streetwalking Epidemic." *Justice System Journal* 22 (3): 348–59.

Wolfgang, M. E., and F. Ferracuti. 1967. *The Subculture of Violence: Towards an Integrated Theory of Criminology*. London: Tavistock.

Women's Learning Partnership. 2012. "WLP Statement to the 57th Commission on the Status of Women." Women's Learning Partnership. www.learningpartnership.org.

Wood, Stephanie K. 2004. "A Woman Scorned for the 'Least Condemned' War Crime: Precedent and Problems Prosecuting Rape as a Serious War Crime in the International Tribunal for Rwanda." *Columbia Journal of Gender and Law* 13 (2): 274–327.

Woods, Ronald B. 2007. *Social Issues in Sport*, 2nd edition. Champaign, IL: Human Kinetics.

Woods, Krystle C, Nicole T. Buchanan, and Isis H. Settles. 2009. "Sexual Harassment across the Color Line: Experiences and Outcomes of Cross-Versus Intraracial Sexual Harassment Among Black Women." *Cultural Diversity and Ethnic Minority Psychology* 15 (1): 67–76.

Woolf, Virginia. 1999. *Tres Guineas*. Barcelona: Lumen.

World Bank. n.d. "Women, Business and the Law." Accessed May 4, 2018. http://wbl.worldbank.org.

World Health Organization. 2013. "Global and Regional Estimates of Violence Against Women: Prevalence and Health Effects of Intimate Partner Violence and Non-partner Sexual Violence." http://apps.who.int.

Wrangham, Richard W. 1999. "Evolution of Coalitionary Killing." *Yearbook of Physical Anthropology* 42: 1–30.

———, and Dale Peterson. 1996. *Demonic Males: Apes and the Origins of Human Violence*. Boston: Houghton Mifflin Company.

Wright, David P. 2010. "'She Shall Not Go Free as Male Slaves Do': Developing Views About Slavery and Gender in the Laws of the Hebrew Bible." In *Beyond Slavery: Overcoming Its Religious and Sexual Legacies*, edited by Bernadette J. Brooten, 125–142. New York: Palgrave Macmillan.

Yiannopoulos, Milo. 2014. "Feminist Bullies Tearing the Video Game Industry Apart." www.breitbart.com.

Ylló, K., and M. Bograd, eds. 1988. *Feminist Perspectives on Wife Abuse*. Newbury Park, CA: Sage.

Yoder, Janice D. 1991. "Rethinking Tokenism: Looking beyond Numbers." *Gender & Society* 5: 178–92.

Yokum, David, Anita Ravishankar, and Alexander Coppock. n.d. "Evaluating the Effects of Police Body-Worn Cameras: A Randomized Controlled Trial." The Lab @ DC. Accessed April 16, 2018. http://bwc.thelab.dc.gov.

Yoshimi, Yoshiaki. 2000. *Comfort Women: Sexual Slavery in the Japanese Military During World War II*. Trans. Suzanne O'Brien. New York: Columbia University Press.

Yoshioka, Marianne R., Louisa Gilbert, Nabila El-Bassel, and Malahat Baig-Amin. 2003. "Social Support and Disclosure of Abuse: Comparing South Asian, African-American and Hispanic Battered Women." *Journal of Family Violence* 18 (3): 171–80.

Young, Monte, dir. 2000. *Family Guy*. Season 2, episode 8, "I Am Peter, Hear Me Roar." Aired March 28, 2000, on FOX television.

Zacharek, Stephanie, Eliana Dockterman, and Haley Sweetland Edwards. 2017. "The Silence Breakers." *Time*. December 18, 2017.

Zanca, Kenneth J., ed. 1994. *American Catholics and Slavery: 1789–1866: An Anthology of Primary Documents*. Lanham, MD: University Press of America.

Zavella, Patricia. 2011. *I'm Neither Here nor There: Mexicans' Quotidian Struggles with Migration and Poverty*. Durham, NC: Duke University Press.

Zell, E., Krizan, Z., and Teeter, S. R. 2015. "Evaluating Gender Similarities and Differences Using Metasynthesis." *American Psychologist* 70 (1): 10–20.

Zimring, Franklin. 1989. "Toward a Jurisprudence of Family Violence." In *Family Violence* edited by Lloyd Ohlin and Michael Tonry. Chicago: University of Chicago Press.

Zippel, Katherine S. 2006. *The Politics of Sexual Harassment: A Comparative Study of the United States, the European Union, and Germany.* Cambridge, UK: Cambridge University Press.

Zirin, Dave. 2013. "How Jock Culture Supports Rape Culture, From Maryville to Steubenville." *Nation* October 25, 2013.

Zucchino, David, and Fatima Faizi. 2019a. "In One Afghan Province, Methodic Abuse of Boys." *New York Times*, November 26, 2019.

———. 2019b. "American Ambassador Says Afghans Coerced Retraction of Rape Allegations." *New York Times*, November 27, 2019.

CASES

Davis v. Monroe County Board of Education, 526 U.S. 629 (1999).

Katz v. St. John the Baptist Parish School Board, 860 /So, 2d 98 (La. App. 5 Cir. 2003).

Oncale v. Sundowner Offshore Services, Inc., 523 U.S. 75; 118 S. Ct. (1998).

ABOUT THE EDITORS

Laura L. O'Toole is Professor of Sociology in the Department of Cultural, Environmental, and Global Studies at Salve Regina University, where she previously served as Dean of Arts and Sciences. She also publishes about and promotes community-based learning and civic engagement for social change.

Jessica R. Schiffman was Assistant Professor and Associate Chair in the Department of Women and Gender Studies at the University of Delaware until her retirement in 2013. She is a co-editor of *Women's Studies in Transition: The Pursuit of Interdisciplinarity*.

Rosemary Sullivan is Professor of Social Work at Westfield State University. She is also a psychotherapist specializing in trauma and recovery and an advocate for the LGBTIA+ community.

ABOUT THE CONTRIBUTORS

Linda Martín Alcoff is Professor in the Department of Philosophy at Hunter College. Her interests include Feminist Epistemology, Feminist Theory, and Critical Race Theory. She is the author of *The Future of Whiteness* and *Visible Identities: Race, Gender, and the Self.*

Sofiá Duyos Álvarez-Arenas is a human rights activist and lawyer. She received her degrees in Spain, and since then has been working in the Human Rights Office of the Archbishop of Guatemala. She has conducted research on human rights, transitional justice, genocide prosecution, and violence against women.

Marcus Amaker, graphic designer, musician, and journalist, is the author of several books of poetry and is the poet laureate of Charleston, South Carolina.

Bernadette J. Brooten is the Kraft-Hiatt Professor of Christian Studies, of Women's and Gender Studies, of Classical Studies, and of Religious Studies at Brandeis University. Brooten heads a team of scholars, activists, artists, and policy analysts who are disentangling the nexus of slavery, religion, women, and sexuality.

Patricia Hill Collins is Distinguished University Professor Emerita at the University of Maryland. A sociologist of race, gender, and social class, Collins is perhaps best known for *Black Feminist Thought: Knowledge, Consciousness, and the Politics of Empowerment, Routledge,* published in 2000.

Irene Comins Mingol is Professor in the Department of Philosophy and Sociology at the University Jaume I of Castellón (Spain) and director of the Interuniversity Institute of Social Development and Peace. She wrote her PhD on *Care Ethics as Peace Education,* and has published about Philosophy for Peace, Peace Education, Anthropology for Peace, and Gender Issues.

Annie Cossins is Professor of Law and Criminology in the Faculty of Law, University of New South Wales, Australia. She is an expert on legal reform in the area of sexual assault and a scholar in theoretical criminology and the author of *Female Criminality: Infanticide, Moral Panics and the Female Body* and *Masculinities, Sexualities and Child Sexual Abuse.*

Kathleen Dill is a sociocultural anthropologist. In Guatemala she conducted research on local forms of transitional justice and social reconstruction. She facilitated the implementation of a satellite-based volcano monitoring system across Central America and conducted research on the politics of natural disasters and humanitarian aid.

Shannon Drysdale Walsh is Associate Professor of Political Science at the University of Minnesota, Duluth. Her primary focus is on the development and practices among police and courts that address violence against women in Latin America.

Elizabeth B. Erbaugh is Associate Professor of Sociology and Women's, Gender and Sexuality Studies at Stockton University. She conducts research and teaches courses on intersections of race, gender, and sexuality in social movements, public health, and public policy. Her publications often address health and violence in the LGBTQ+ population.

Sarah Fenstermaker is Professor Emeritus of Sociology in the Department of Feminist Studies at UC Santa Barbara. Her research focus is on work and gender, feminist inquiry, feminist theory, and research methods.

William Gay is Professor Emeritus of Philosophy at the University of North Carolina, Charlotte. His research focuses on linguistic violence and nonviolence and on peace and social justice. He has published seven books and more than one hundred book chapters and journal articles on these and related topics.

Ryan P. Harrod is Assistant Professor of Anthropology at the University of Alaska, Anchorage. He has authored, co-authored and co-edited four volumes on the topic of violence as well as journal articles. His area of specialization is identity, health and disease, conflict and violence, and social inequalities.

bell hooks has made significant contributions to intellectual life. As the author of numerous books on gender, race, class, and contemporary culture, her works include *Ain't I a Woman: Black Women and Feminism, Teaching to Transgress: Education as the Practice of Freedom, and Feminism is for Everybody: Passionate Politics.*

Anastasia Hudgins is a practicing sociocultural anthropologist, Adjunct Fellow at the Center for Public Health Initiatives at the University of Pennsylvania, and cofounder of Ethnologica, a research firm in Philadelphia. Hudgins draws on qualitative, participatory, and arts-based methods to reveal insights about health, community, and policy.

Valerie Jenness is Professor in the Departments of Criminology, Law and Society; Sociology; and Nursing at UCLA, Irvine. Her research is in the areas of deviance and social control, the politics of crime control, social movements and social change, and corrections and public policy.

Robert Jensen is Emeritus Professor in the School of Journalism at the University of Texas at Austin. His book, *The End of Patriarchy: Radical Feminism for Men*, offers a template for upending male dominance to create communities in concert with a more just world.

Michael P. Johnson is Emeritus Professor of Sociology, Women's Studies, and African and African American Studies at Penn State, where he taught sociology and women's studies for over thirty years and was designated an Alumni Teaching Fellow, Penn State's highest teaching award.

Chrysanthi S. Leon is Associate Professor of Sociology and Criminal Justice and Women and Gender Studies at the University of Delaware. She is an interdisciplinary scholar of penology and law and society and writes about sexual offending, sex work, and the impact of criminalization on vulnerable groups and their families. She is the author of *Sex Fiends, Perverts, and Pedophiles: Understanding Sex Crime Policy in America*.

Claudia Castro Luna is Washington State Poet Laureate. Born in El Salvador, she is the author of *Killing Marías* and *This City*.

Catharine A. MacKinnon is Elizabeth A. Long Professor of Law at the University of Michigan. She has served as Special Gender Advisor to the Prosecutor of the International Criminal Court. Her works include *Are Women Human?: And Other International Dialogues* and her casebook *Sex Equality*.

Debra L. Martin is Distinguished Professor of Anthropology at the University of Nevada, Las Vegas. She has co-edited and co-authored nine volumes on the topic of ancient violence as well as numerous journal articles. Her major focus is on the ways that violence becomes part of everyday life in various cultural settings, and how this places different groups, such as women and children, at risk.

Linda McCarriston, a citizen of both Ireland and the US, is Professor Emerita of Poetry, Creative Writing, and Literary Arts at the University of Alaska, Anchorage. She is the author of poetry collections including *Talking Soft Dutch*, *Eva-Mary*, which was shortlisted for the National Book Award, and *Little River: New & Selected Poems*.

DeAnne K. Hilfinger Messias has dedicated her career in international community health nursing, research, and education to improving the health and well-being of vulnerable women, their families, and communities. She has taught community health and women's health nursing at the undergraduate and graduate levels in Brazil and the US.

Michael A. Messner is Professor of Sociology and Gender Studies at the University of Southern California. His areas of research include sex and gender, gender and sport, and gender-based violence. Among his published works are *Gender Reckonings: New Social Theory and Research*, with James W. Messerschmidt, Patricia Yancey Martin, and Raewyn Connell.

Susan L. Miller is Professor in the Department of Sociology and Criminal Justice at the University of Delaware. Her research interests include gender-based violence, victimology, victims' rights, and criminal justice policy. Her book, *After the Crime: The Power of Restorative Justice Dialogues between Victims and Violent Offenders*, won the national 2012 Outstanding Book Award from the Academy of Criminal Justice Sciences.

Melinda Mills is Associate Professor of Women's and Gender Studies, Sociology, and Anthropology at Castleton University. Her research interests focus on race, class, and gender in popular culture representations, multiracial identity formation, interracial relationships, and street harassment. Her first book, *The Borders of Race*, examines the lived experiences of multiracial people.

Cherrie Moraga writes poetry, plays, essays, and memoirs. She was a co-editor of the influential feminist anthology, *This Bridge Called My Back: Writings by Radical Women of Color*, and is the author of *A Xicana Codex of Changing Consciousness: Loving in The War Years: Lo que nunca pasó por us labios*. She received the Rockefeller Fellowship for Literature and the Lambda Foundation "Pioneer" award.

Jennifer Naccarelli is Associate Chair and Associate Professor in the Department of Women and Gender Studies at the University of Delaware and the Director of the Domestic Violence Prevention and Services Program. She teaches in the fields of gender-based violence, women and religion, and feminist theory.

Bailey Poland is pursuing a PhD in the rhetoric and writing program at Bowling Green State University. She conducts archival research on women's rhetorical practices and studies digital rhetoric, especially as it pertains to gender. Poland is the author of *Haters: Harassment, Abuse, and Violence Online*.

Margaret Randall is a feminist poet, writer, photographer, and social activist with a commitment to humanistic values and combating a culture of violence. She sees art as a tool for change. She is the author of *Time's Language: Selected Poems 1959–2018* and *When Justice Felt at Home/Cuando La Justicia Se Sentía En Casa*.

Janice G. Raymond is the former codirector of the Coalition Against Trafficking in Women. She is the author of many books and articles, most recently *Not a Choice, Not a Job: Exposing the Myths about Prostitution and the Global Sex Industry*. Dr. Raymond is Professor Emerita of Women's Studies and Medical Ethics at the University of Massachusetts and the recipient in 2007 of the International Woman Award from the Zero Tolerance Trust in Scotland.

Peggy Reeves Sanday is Professor Emerita of Anthropology at the University of Pennsylvania and the author of five books and numerous articles with a primary focus on rape culture, violence against women, and the anthropology of gender.

Lee E. Ross is Associate Professor in the Department of Criminal Justice at the University of Central Florida. His interests include religion and social control theory and African American concerns in law enforcement. He is the author of *Domestic Violence and Criminal Justice*.

Natasha Sajé is Professor of English at Westminster College and a member of the poetry faculty at the Vermont College of Fine Arts. She has authored three books of poetry, including *Vivarium*, and is the recipient of multiple poetry awards.

Victoria Sanford is Professor and Chair of anthropology and founding director of the Center for Human Rights and Peace Studies at Lehman College. She is a member of the anthropology doctoral faculty at the Graduate Center, City University of New York.

Edwin M. Schur has widely published in the areas of legal sociology, criminology, and social deviance. His numerous books include *Labeling Women Deviant* and *The Americanization of Sex*. Before retirement he was Professor of Sociology at New York University.

Corey Shdaimah is Daniel Thursz Distinguished Professor of Social Justice and Academic Coordinator for the MSW/JD Dual Degree Program at the University of Maryland School of Social Work. Her research interests include street-based sex work, court-affiliated prostitution diversion programs, child care policy, and theory and practice knowledge. She has published extensively on criminal justice responses to sex work.

Carole J. Sheffield is Professor of Political Science and Women's and Gender Studies at the William Paterson University of New Jersey. She teaches and writes about violence against females, feminist theory, and social justice. She has received multiple honors for teaching including from the Carnegie Foundation for the Advancement of Teaching as the New Jersey Professor of the Year in 1997.

Warsan Shire is a poet and activist and the author of the poetry collections *Teaching My Mother How to Give Birth* and *Her Blue Body*. Born to Somali parents in Kenya and raised in London, her poetry appears in Beyoncé's *Lemonade*. Her poems often deal with the nexus of gender, sex, and displacement.

Sharon Smith is the author of *Women and Socialism: Class, Race and Capital, Revised and Updated Edition* and *Subterranean Fire (Updated Edition): A History of Working-Class Radicalism in the United States.*

Nan D. Stein is Senior Research Scientist at the Wellesley Centers for Women. Her research focus is on dating violence and the nexus of sexual harassment and gender violence in K–12 schools with a particular emphasis on policy development.

Margaret D. Stetz is Mae and Robert Carter Professor of Women's Studies and Professor of Humanities at the University of Delaware. She has published more than one hundred essays and more than three books on topics such as Victorian feminism, memoirs of women Holocaust survivors, the politics of animated films, British modernist literature, and neo-Victorian dress. In 2015, she was named by the magazine *Diverse: Issues in Higher Education* to its list of the twenty-five top women in US higher education.

technicolordust submitted "The Night Shift" to Power Poetry.

Miriam G. Valdovinos is Assistant Professor at the University of Denver School of Social Work. She teaches Qualitative Research Methods and Human Oppression. Her research is informed by her training in social welfare, psychology, public health, gender studies, and interdisciplinary studies.

Kristin M. Van De Griend is an independent consultant for health promotion programming and evaluations and an adjunct professor at Dordt College, the University of South Carolina, and Northwestern College.

Marjory Wentworth has published books of poems and a prizewinning children's story, *Shackles*. She is on the faculty of the Art Institute of Charleston and is the poet laureate of South Carolina.

Nancy Whittier is Sophia Smith Professor and Department Chair of Sociology at Smith College. She is the author of *The Politics of Child Sexual Abuse: Emotion, Social Movements, and the State* and *Frenemies: Feminists, Conservatives, and Sexual Violence.*

INDEX

CPSIA information can be obtained
at www.ICGtesting.com
Printed in the USA
LVHW100004160821
695370LV00008B/619